Developer's Workshop to COM and ATL 3.0

Andrew W. Troelsen

Wordware Publishing, Inc.

Library of Congress Cataloging-in-Publication Data

Troelsen, Andrew W.
    Developer's workshop to COM and ATL 3.0 / by Andrew W. Troelsen.
        p.   cm.
    ISBN 1-55622-704-3 (pb)
    1. Computer software--Development.   2. Object-oriented programming (Computer science).
    3. Active template library.   I. Title.

    QA76.76.D47 T76   2000
    005.26'8--dc21   00-025666
                                                                                   CIP

ISBN 1-55622-704-3
10 9 8 7 6 5 4 3 2 1
0003

Product names mentioned are used for identification purposes only and may be trademarks of their respective companies.

All inquiries for volume purchases of this book should be addressed to Wordware Publishing, Inc., at the above address. Telephone inquiries may be made by calling:

(972) 423-0090

Contents

Contents

Contents

Part 3: Core ATL

Chapter 6   An Introduction to the Active Template Library. 229

Contents

Part 4: COM Patterns

Contents

Part 5: Windowing

Contents

Dedication

To my wife, Amanda, who married me even though I was only on Chapter 7 at the time. Your love and support are amazing. You're my angel.

To Mary and Wally Troelsen (who also go by Mom and Dad), for not panicking too much when I was studying Sanskrit.

Finally, to Mrs. Heckman, who got this whole thing started.

Acknowledgments

Writing a book is by far the most complex undertaking I can remember. If it were not for the following people, I am certain I would have lost the last of my remaining hairs during its completion. Thanks to Jim Hill at Wordware Publishing, for presenting me with this unique opportunity to begin with. A big thanks to Beth Kohler (also at Wordware Publishing) for putting up with my numerous resubmissions and massaging the kinks in the original manuscript.

A very special thank you to Wade Coonrod, who took the time out of his extremely busy schedule to review this book somewhere between the hours of 2:00 a.m. and 6:00 a.m. Thanks as well to his wife, Darla, for not disowning him during this endeavor. Thanks to Gina McGhee and Tom Salonek for reviewing the early chapters of this text. As for any remaining typos, omissions, or illogic, the responsibility is mine alone.

Most importantly, thanks to my friends and family who put up with my absence while I hid away in the den for the last several months.

Introduction

Understanding COM takes time and energy. I can say with great confidence that there is always more to learn. However, as with most technologies, COM does provide a core body of knowledge that works as the backbone for just about everything else. For example, once you understand the building blocks of interfaces, coclasses, class factories, and COM binaries, the foundation is laid for numerous related aspects of COM, such as the ActiveX control, distributed COM, and connectable objects (just to name a few).

The relationship between COM and the numerous ActiveX technologies out there can be equated to an understanding of mathematics and the various applied sciences. If you don't understand how to work with basic algebraic equations, you can forget taking classes in physics, chemistry, and biology. The same holds true here: Without an understanding of the algebra of COM, forget the science of ActiveX. Moreover, without an understanding of COM, forget ATL.

Once an individual has come to understand the core building blocks of the COM architecture, the next logical step is to adopt a component framework to help lessen the burden of repetitive code. ATL is the C++ developer's COM framework of choice. With ATL by your side, you can successfully spend less time handing out interface pointers and more time concentrating on the domain-specific coding task at hand. However, an ATL developer who does not understand the architecture of COM is no better off than an MFC developer who has no understanding of the central Win32 APIs. This book offers a firm foundation in COM, as well as the ATL framework.

What You Need to Use This Book

Learning COM and ATL are not passive activities. A developer does not come to understand these complex systems because his current job demands it, because she owns a book on the topic, or because he or she flipped through the latest issue of *Microsoft Systems Journal*! You must dig in and make it happen. The philosophy of this book is that you gain an understanding of COM and ATL by <u>writing code yourself</u>. Lots of it.

To this end, every chapter in this book has a number of integrated lab assignments that give you numerous opportunities to build COM clients and servers both in raw C++ as well as ATL. To get the most out of this book (and the labs), you should have the following workstation configuration:

■ A full installation of Visual C++ 6.0 (which gives you a full installation of ATL).

■ A full installation of Visual Basic 6.0 (as we will build a number of VB test clients).

■ If you are interested in Java/COM integration, a full installation of Visual J++ 6.0.

■ A full installation of Visual Studio's online help (MSDN).

- Microsoft Internet Explorer 5 to test the various web-based clients.

As well, if you are interested in working though the distributed COM (DCOM) lab assignment, you will (of course) need two networked computers, ideally each running Windows NT to allow for the full range of DCOM options.

The source code (and screen shots) used in this book were built and tested on both Windows NT4 (SP5) and Win98 Second Edition. The source code was compiled using the Microsoft Visual Studio suite of tools, SP3.

Who Can Use this Book?

Anyone who is comfortable with the C++ language can successfully work though each and every lab in the book. Of course, the more you already know about C++ the better. However, Chapter 1 does offer a review of the key aspects of the language, such as the containment/delegation model, accessors and mutators, ad hoc polymorphism, the construction of object hierarchies, and template-based programming. On a related note, this text does <u>not</u> assume you have any current understanding of COM or ATL. Again, any knowledge you currently have will only add to your experience.

What Does This Book Cover?

Over the course of this book, you will be building more and more sophisticated COM objects, as each chapter introduces you to increasingly advanced techniques. The overall organization of this text is from the bottom up. We begin with a review of the key aspects of C++ and launch into interface-based programming from a "non-COM" perspective. After this point, we spend three chapters learning to create COM servers and COM clients "in the raw" using straight C++ and the Interface Definition Language (IDL).

Once you have the necessary background, the remainder of this book focuses on how ATL can help lessen your burden as a COM developer. Rather than simply pointing out which buttons to click in the integrated CASE tools, we will move deep within the ATL framework, and examine how ATL provides support for a number of advanced COM techniques such as COM exception handling, tear-off interfaces, and aggregation, as well as a web-enabled ActiveX control.

You will also find that many COM-related concepts are first presented in straight C++ and IDL, to help you really understand what ATL is doing on your behalf. Here is a walk-through of each chapter:

Part 1: Objects and Interfaces

Microsoft's Component Object Model is a language-neutral protocol; however, it is very C++ friendly. Part 1 begins with a painless refresher on the core foundations of object-oriented programming. More importantly, this section examines interface-based programming, the foundation of all things COM.

Chapter 1: A Review of Classic Object-Oriented Programming ATL not only demands a solid understanding of COM, but of C++ as well. This chapter begins by remembering our roots, and examines why structured programming is fading (has faded?)

into the background, overshadowed by the OO paradigm. The bulk of this chapter focuses on an understanding of the central pillars of C++ OOP: encapsulation, polymorphism (classical and ad hoc), and inheritance (the Is-A and Has-A relationships). We wrap up with a review of template-based programming, and see how this syntactical maneuver provides a generic form of source code reuse.

Chapter 2: Interface-Based Programming The central aspect of COM is the distinction between interface and implementation. While COM (and hence ATL) is hopelessly dependent on the interface, we can make use of the interface from a "non-COM" environment. In this chapter, you will come to see what an interface is and how to construct and implement such a creature in C++. You will see how the interface provides deeper encapsulation services, and learn how to implement interfaced-based polymorphism. As well, you will learn about the "interface contract" and how to safely extend a C++ class by versioning your interfaces.

Part 2: Core COM

ATL developers must know COM. COM developers must know C++ and IDL. Plain and simple. Part 2 walks you through the core aspects of COM from the ground up. You will have the chance to create a number of COM servers "wizard free." Here, you will build in-process and remote COM servers using nothing but C++, IDL, and a healthy dose of typing. This section breaks down into the following chapters:

Chapter 3: The Component Object Model The title says it all. Everything you know about objects and interfaces applies directly to COM development. In this chapter you will have the chance to build a COM-based DLL from the ground up, using the C++ programming language. This will expose you to IUnknown and the basic laws of COM identity, COM class factories, and component housing. As well, you will begin to learn about the system registry, the COM runtime, and the COM library. This will equip you to build C++ COM clients, which will wrap up this chapter.

Chapter 4: Type Information and Language Independence IDL is the official and correct way to describe your COM objects. One of the key reasons for doing so is to allow COM to make good on the promise of language independence. This chapter will get you up and running with the syntax of IDL, and pave the way for a number of advanced IDL constructs seen throughout the remainder of this book. Once you know how to write your interfaces, coclasses, and library statements in IDL, we wrap up this chapter by learning how to build COM clients in Visual Basic and Java (J++) which make use of the COM server you created in Chapter 3. We also examine the Visual C++ compiler extensions (smart pointers) that allow you to leverage type information when building C++ COM clients.

Chapter 5: Type Information and Location Transparency Another reason every COM project should begin with IDL is to achieve location transparency. This aspect of COM allows a COM client to access a COM server located anywhere around the world (literally) using the same block of code. This magic is provided (in part) by stubs and proxies, which are one byproduct of IDL. This chapter will dig into the architecture of DCOM, and introduce you to the inner workings of COM's marshaling layer. We will also come to understand how to configure declarative security using dcomcnfg.exe. By the end of this chapter, you will be able to remotely access the COM object you created in Chapter 3, using your language of choice. Once you have made it this far, you are completely prepared to make use of the Active Template Library.

Part 3: Core ATL

This section begins with what might be considered an ATL tutorial. Once you have become acquainted with the core CASE tools of the ATL framework, the remainder of this section examines a good deal of the raw source code while introducing you to a number of advanced COM and ATL topics.

Chapter 6: An Introduction to the Active Template Library This chapter is intended to get you up to speed with the ATL framework and the integrated CASE tools provided by ATL 3.0. We begin with the ATL COM AppWizard, and examine the details behind the choices you must make to allow this tool to assemble your component housing. You will then learn how to insert various COM objects into the AppWizard-generated server using the ATL Object Wizard. As well, you will learn about the numerous details of ATL programming such as adding/removing interfaces and coclasses, ATL debugging support, and the syntax of the registry scripting language.

Chapter 7: ATL COM Objects and COM Exceptions Once you are familiar with the ATL CASE tools, it is time to dig into the framework itself. We begin this chapter with a discussion of what multithreaded programming means to the COM developers of the world. You will come to understand the concept of an apartment as well as the various threading models provided by the Component Object Model and how ATL accounts for them. Next, we dig into the ATL source code and see how the framework provides support for core items such as IUnknown and come to understand the ATL COM map. We wrap up by learning how to throw COM exceptions in raw C++ as well as ATL and how to catch these error objects from Visual Basic and C++ clients.

Chapter 8: Object Identity and ATL COM provides a number of interesting (and somewhat strange) identity tricks. This chapter covers numerous advanced class composition techniques such as nested classes, tear-off interfaces, COM containment, and COM aggregation. You will learn how to resolve interface method name clashes in both C++ and ATL, as well as how to construct interface hierarchies. You will also come to learn a good deal more about the ATL COM map, and examine a number of additional macro entries that allow you to build sophisticated coclasses.

Chapter 9: Component Housing and ATL The innocent-looking object map structure found in every ATL project packs a wealth of information regarding your COM server. This chapter drills down into the object map and the underlying _ATL_OBJMAP_ENTRY structure. You will come to learn how ATL assembles your objects and class factories and how to override this behavior. This chapter will also illustrate how to customize the default ATL registration process, how to build COM object models, and how to assign COM categories to your coclasses.

Part 4: COM Patterns

IDispatch, IEnumXXXX, and IConnectionPoint are just some of the standard COM interfaces discussed in this section. The bulk of this section illustrates a number of "COM patterns" that enable your coclasses to function on the web and engage in bi-directional communications. As well, this section examines how one coclass can contain collections of other objects. We will be examining each of these topics in "raw C++" as well as "à la ATL."

Chapter 10: Scriptable Objects and ATL Not all COM-aware languages allow direct access to custom vTable interfaces. Some language mappings (such as VBScript) are only smart enough to communicate with COM objects supporting IDispatch. This chapter not only describes what this standard COM interface is doing under the hood, but also gives you a chance to build a number of IDispatch implementations yourself. As well, you will get to know the VARIANT data type and why we need it and how to use it. We will also learn how to construct arrays of VARIANT types (safe arrays) to help minimize round trips between the client and coclass. By the end of this chapter, you will understand how to access your ATL-savvy and raw C++ coclasses from a web-based client.

Chapter 11: COM Enumerators and COM Collections This chapter begins by examining a number of ways in which a COM object can return complex parameters to a COM client (arrays, interface pointers, structures, and so forth). With this background, the rest of the chapter discusses how a COM client can gain controlled access to sub-objects held in an object container, using COM enumerators and COM collections. You will then see how the ATL framework provides support for building each type of object container as well as examine what it would take in straight C++.

Chapter 12: Callback Interfaces and Connectable Objects COM's connectable object architecture allows clients and servers to engage in a two-way conversation. This chapter will begin by examining an ad hoc way to configure bi-directional communications using custom callback interfaces, and how VB and C++ clients may make use of it. Next, we examine the standardized architecture of "connectable objects." You will come to know the standard COM interfaces that enable this pattern (IConnectionPointContainer, IConnectionPoint, IEnumConnectionPoints, and IEnumConnections) and how ATL provides a default implementation of each.

Part 5: Windowing

Not all COM objects are invisible entities. Part 5 brings you up to snuff with ATL's support for building GUI-based coclasses. You will begin by examining how to build main windows and interactive dialogs in ATL, and wrap up by constructing an animated ActiveX control.

Chapter 13: Using ATL as a Windowing Framework Although you might not realize it, ATL does provide a set of templates to help build GUI-based Windows applications. Even though ATL does not provide all the bells and whistles of a full-blown application framework such as MFC, this chapter will show you how ATL provides just enough support to build stand-alone main windows and interactive dialog boxes. Even if you are not altogether interested in using ATL to build your next Windows application, the information presented here will provide the necessary background for the final subject of this book, ActiveX controls.

Chapter 14: Developing ActiveX Controls with ATL All of your hard work has brought you here, given that ActiveX controls require an understanding of each of the topics presented in the first 13 chapters of this book. Here you will come to understand the standard interfaces supported by an ActiveX control as well as how to build property pages for your ATL controls. Next, we will see how ATL provides framework support for your control projects, and wrap up by examining a number of advanced control topics such as "bindable" properties, property persistence, a licensed class factory, and basic Windows animation techniques.

Using the CD-ROM Lab Solutions

 The companion CD-ROM contains complete solutions for all of the lab work in this book. The solutions are indicated in the text with the icon at the left.

To install these files onto your hard drive, double-click on the Labs.exe self-extracting archive. This will move all files onto your hard drive under C:\COM ATL\Labs. Also note that each project will need to be recompiled before you can test the solutions!

Beginning with Chapter 3, every "raw C++" lab makes use of a custom *.reg file which must be merged into your system registry. If you forget to do so, the client solutions will not work! Be aware that the *.reg files make use of hard-coded path names, which more likely than not will not be the same as where you have chosen to install the sample code. Thus, you will need to edit the path to your specific path. For example, the CarInProcServer lab in Chapter 3 has the following *.reg file listing. Modify the section in **bold** to the correct path:

```
HKEY_CLASSES_ROOT\CLSID\{7AD2D539-EE35-11d2-B8DE-0020781238D4}\InprocServer32 = c:\My
Documents\ATL\Labs\Chapter 03\CarInProcServer\Debug\CarInProcServer.dll
```

Also realize that the ATL solutions must be registered on your machine before the clients can make use of them. ATL servers do not make use of *.reg files, but enter the correct information programmatically. To register the ATL sample solutions, rebuild the project. This will automatically register the COM server.

Into the Great IUnknown

So then, as you can see, we have quite the journey ahead of us. My suggestion is that you begin with Chapter 1 (even if you have a solid C++ background) and pound out the lab work. Many of the subsequent labs in this book revolve around the design notes (but not necessarily the code) of the labs presented in this first chapter.

Finally (and I cannot stress this enough), never be reluctant to access online help (MSDN) as you read this book. Learning COM is a complex, yet manageable, endeavor. As you work over the labs and read this material, realize that no one book can describe every detail of the Component Object Model. The Microsoft Developer Network (MSDN) is jam-packed with COM tutorials, sample code, documentation, and technical articles that extend and complement the information presented here. Remember, F1 is your friend.

Part 1

Objects and Interfaces

Chapter 1

A Review of Classic Object-Oriented Programming

Objectives:

- Contrast structured programming and object-based development.
- Review data encapsulation, accessors, and mutators.
- Know the roles of classical inheritance and the containment/delegation model.
- Understand classical and ad hoc polymorphism.
- Work with virtual and pure virtual functions.
- Review template-based programming.

Before you can rush off and create Component Object Model (COM) solutions, you really do need a solid grounding in object-oriented programming (OOP). Attempting to do so without such an understanding can muddle your overall impression of what COM is trying to achieve, leaving you frustrated and in the dark. To be sure, the more you understand OOP (especially C++-based OOP), the deeper your knowledge of the COM paradigm and the ATL framework.

Our goal for this initial chapter is to follow the migration from traditional structured programming in C to the object-oriented paradigm via C++. Along the way a number of C++ syntactical constraints will be reviewed, including how C++ measures up against the cornerstones of OOP: encapsulation, inheritance, and polymorphism. Finally, we wrap up with an overview of template-based programming, a cornerstone of ATL.

Life without Objects: Remembering Structured Programming in C

I'm quite sure that your daily programming tasks involve using objects at some level, and I'd bet you're happy about this. However, it is important to know exactly what problems object technology (and therefore COM and ATL) attempt to solve in the first place. In short, we need to "remember our roots" and see why procedural programming languages fall short in the current state of software engineering. To begin, let's journey back in time to a world without objects and tackle a simple development task using the structured programming (SP) language C.

Programmers using the C language (or any structured language for that matter) tend to work in the realm of global atoms. From a very high level, programs built using structured programming techniques operate something like this: A given application consists of some number of data points (e.g., variables), dwelling either in the program's global namespace (e.g., out of a function scope) or locally within some function scope.

Along with the program's internal data, SP applications are also composed of a number of global functions that operate on various portions of the application's data set. If you can't tell by now, the operative word in these last few paragraphs is "global." Structured languages such as C move data into and out of global functions to control the execution and flow of the program, as illustrated in Figure 1-1.

Figure 1-1:
Internal
organization of
an SP
application.

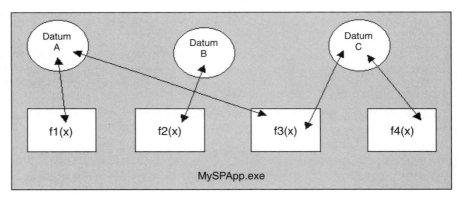

Here, MySPApp.exe consists of three pieces of global data, collectively operated on by four global functions. These data points may be any of C's intrinsic data types. For example:

```
/* A signed and unsigned data point. */
short gruntBonus;
unsigned long managerBonus;
/* A pointer to an intrinsic C data type (our friend the C-style string). */
char* pLastName;
/* Arrays of intrinsic types. */
int myLightBulbs[20];
char firstName[MAX_LENGTH];
```

While single data points are central to any programming language, it is always helpful to have the ability to assemble a collection of related data as a named entity, or user-defined types (UDTs). In C, this is achieved with the use of the **struct** keyword.

Programming with User-Defined Types (UDTs)

To illustrate the virtues of named custom types, imagine you are asked to develop a very simple C program modeling the creation, operation, and ultimate demise of a simulated automobile. After gathering the initial client requirements, you discover the program must support the following functionality:

1. Allow the end user to create a car, specifying a pet name and maximum speed.
2. Ensure the maximum speed is never greater than 500 MPH.
3. Display the max speed and pet name when necessary.
4. Accelerate the car in 10-mile increments.
5. Determine if the engine block cracks due to excessive speed (defined as the first 10-mile increment over the car's maximum speed).

Note: Throughout the course of this book, we will port the above requirements from C into C++, into an object supporting multiple interfaces, and finally into a "real DCOM" application. Furthermore, the automobile in question will be extended into the ATL framework to support COM error handling, aggregation, tear-off interfaces, connection points, and finally reincarnated into a full web-savvy ActiveX control. Just thought you'd like to know where we are heading.

Your first task as a C developer may be to determine the data types necessary for the project at hand, using a UDT to represent the concept of a car in the system. UDTs are very useful when creating program data types composed of a number of variables that seem to naturally work together as a whole. As you recall, the **struct** keyword allows us to refer to a collection of logically related data as a named type. Each member of the structure is called a *field*. Here is our simple CAR structure, which contains three fields:

```
/* The CAR structure. */
#define MAX_LENGTH      100
struct CAR
{
    char        petName[MAX_LENGTH];      /* Pet name */
    int         maxSpeed;                 /* Maximum speed */
    int         currSpeed;                /* Current speed */
};
```

Using this new UDT is straightforward. You may declare a CAR type just as you would declare any intrinsic C data type (recall that formal C syntax requires you to use the **struct** keyword when declaring UDT variables). To access the fields of this structure, you may use the dot operator (.) or arrow operator (->). Here is our CAR struct in action:

```
/* Creating a CAR variable. */
#include <string.h>
void main(void)
{
    struct CAR myCar;
    myCar.maxSpeed = 300;
    myCar.currSpeed = 60;
    strcpy(myCar.petName,"Fred");
}
```

Populating the Global Namespace

The next step in our simple C application is to identify the global functions that will manipulate CAR data types. Having thought about it for a moment, assume you write the following three global function prototypes. Notice how each function takes an existing CAR type variable (two by reference and one by value):

```
/* Global function prototypes. */
void DisplayCarStats(struct CAR c);      /* Pump CAR info to a Win32 console */
void CreateACar(struct CAR* c);          /* Prompt for user input */
void SpeedUp(struct CAR* c);             /* Add 10 to CAR currSpeed field */
```

When using UDTs, we can avoid more cumbersome (but logically equivalent) functions such as:

```
/* UDTs help avoid overbearing function signatures. */
void DisplayCarStats (char petName, int maxSpeed, int currSpeed);
void CreateACar(char* petName, int* maxSpeed, int* currSpeed);
void SpeedUp (char* petName, int* maxSpeed, int* currSpeed);
```

Hopefully you agree the proper use of UDTs lends itself to more robust and readable code. As we will see, object-oriented languages (such as C++) extend the notion of a simple UDT by providing a tight coupling between data and the functions that act on that data. So then, with the CAR structure and a set of global functions, you are free to flesh out the programmatic details of the application. To get the ball rolling, let's dust off our structured programming skills and put together a minimal and complete C program that meets the initial design requirements.

Lab 1-1: Structured Programming in C

It is likely that the information presented in this first lab will be nothing new to you—understood. However, we will be porting the ideas presented in this lab from SP to OOP, OOP to an interface-based solution, and finally to a DCOM server usable from C++, Java, and Visual Basic clients. Furthermore, the car in question will be reworked into various ATL-based solutions (including an animated ActiveX control) full of numerous bells and whistles. Therefore, at the very least completing this lab will pave the way to "real COM" development with ATL and refresh some C details which may have fallen to the wayside.

 The solution for this lab can be found on your CD-ROM under:
Labs\Chapter 01\CarInC

Step One: Prepare the Project Workspace

In this lab, we will create a simple automobile simulation written in the C programming language, appropriately called CarInC. Fire up Visual C++, select **File | New...** and create a Win32 Console Application project workspace (Figure 1-2). Select **OK** and from the resulting dialog select **empty project**.

Figure 1-2:
Creating a new
Win32 Console
Application.

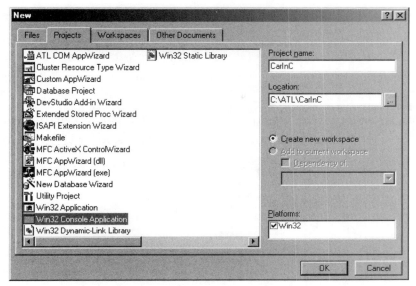

Next, insert a new empty text file (using the File | New... menu selection) named **main.c**, and define an empty main loop at the top of the file:

```c
/* main.c */
void main(void)
{
}
```

Step Two: Prototype the Global Functions and CAR Structure

We will be using the same CAR structure and function prototypes as defined earlier in this chapter. First, be sure to include the standard IO <stdio.h> and string manipulation <string.h> header files to your program, then add the following:

```c
/* main.c */
/* Defines and includes. */
#define MAX_LENGTH      100
#define MAX_SPEED       500
#include <stdio.h>                /* C input and output functions */
#include <string.h>              /* String manipulation functions */
/* The CAR structure. */
struct CAR
{
    char        petName[MAX_LENGTH];
    int         maxSpeed;
    int         currSpeed;
};
/* Global function prototypes. */
void DisplayCarStats(struct CAR c);
void CreateACar(struct CAR* c);
void SpeedUp(struct CAR* c);
/* Program entry point. */
void main(void)
```

```
{
}
```

Step Three: Implement the Global Car Functions

We now have three global functions to implement in our application. To keep things simple, implement each function within the same main.c file (somewhere below the main loop). The DisplayCarStats() function examines an incoming CAR variable and pumps the field data to a Win32 console using printf(). Notice we send in a copy of an existing CAR variable to ensure that this function cannot change the caller's original CAR data type:

```
/* Dump current stats about a given CAR. */
void DisplayCarStats(struct CAR c)
{
    printf("***********************************\n");
    printf("Your car is called: %s\n", c.petName);
    printf("It does up to %d\n", c.maxSpeed );
    printf("***********************************\n\n");
}
```

The CreateACar() function takes a pointer to an existing CAR variable and populates the fields based off user input. We could use scanf() in this function's implementation, however scanf() will misbehave if the buffer contains additional empty characters before the terminating NULL. Thus, if the pet name for the car is "My rusty clunker," we are out of luck. To rectify this, we will make use of the gets() function, which will read a string up until the first "\n" and append a NULL terminator. Here is the implementation of CreateACar()— without excessive error checking:

```
/* Fill the fields of a new CAR variable. */
void CreateACar(struct CAR* c)
{
    char  buffer[MAX_LENGTH];
    int   spd = 0;
    memset(c, 0, sizeof(struct CAR));
    /* Read in a string and set petName field. */
    printf("Please enter a pet-name for your car:");
    gets(buffer);
    /* Could check strlen() against MAX_LENGTH... */
    strcpy(c->petName, buffer);
    /* Be sure speed isn't beyond MAX_SPEED. */
    do
    {
        printf("Enter the max speed of this car:");
        scanf("%d", &spd);
    }while(spd > MAX_SPEED);
    /* Set remaining fields. */
    c->maxSpeed = spd;
    c->currSpeed=0;
}
```

The implementation of SpeedUp() is very simple. In keeping with our design notes, increase the current speed by 10 MPH and print to the console:

```
/* Increment the currSpeed field of a CAR by 10 and display new speed. */
void SpeedUp(struct CAR* c)
{
```

```
      if(c->currSpeed <= c->maxSpeed)
      {
            c->currSpeed = c->currSpeed + 10;
            printf("\tSpeed is: %d\n", c->currSpeed);
      }
}
```

Step Four: Implement the main() Loop

Here, we will create a CAR data variable, gather user input using CreateACar(), and display the new car information within a Win32 console. We will then accelerate the automobile until its engine block snaps into pieces, defined as 10 miles over the maximum:

```
/* Program entry point. */
void main(void)
{
      /* C syntax requires the struct keyword at declaration */
      struct CAR myCar;
      printf("***********************************\n");
      printf("The Amazing Car Application via C\n");
      printf("***********************************\n\n");
      CreateACar(&myCar);             /* Go create a car. */
      DisplayCarStats(myCar);         /* Display new car information */
      /* Speed up until engine block cracks */
      while(myCar.currSpeed <= myCar.maxSpeed)
            SpeedUp(&myCar);
      /* Final message... */
      printf("\n%s has blown up! Lead foot!\n", myCar.petName);
}     /* End of main */
```

There you have it—a simple structured programming example written in C. We have assembled a UDT with three fields and implemented a set of global functions to operate on variables of this type, all in keeping with our program specifications. Figure 1-3 shows some possible output of your structured programming application:

Figure 1-3:
The CarInC
application.

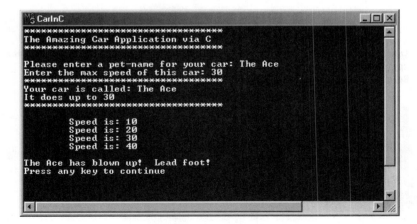

Problems with Structured Programming

The C program runs and meets all design specifications, so what is the problem with the application as it stands? To be honest, numerous full-blown applications have been written using the C language, so a partial answer is "nothing." However, imagine that this trivial application has been expanded beyond belief, and is now being used by a major vehicle manufacturer. To keep up with the new expanded design specifications, we may swell our application to define numerous UDTs and hundreds of global functions.

The first problem that creeps up using traditional structured programming is that the data and functions that are logically grouped together are not physically grouped together. Consider again the CAR structure. The first iteration of our program had three functions that seem to be related to the CAR data type based off the loose semantics of the function signatures. For example, we can gather that the DisplayCarStats() function operates on a CAR structure given its physical name and signature (a CAR variable type). However, what about a new function prototyped as the following:

```
/* The mystery parameter 'sp'. */
void ChangeSpeed(int sp);
```

This could be a function that operates on the maxSpeed field of a CAR type, or perhaps some other notion of "speed" in the revised program (speed of production, speed in a crash test, and so forth). Ambiguities of this nature show up often in traditional SP, as functions and the data they operate upon are only loosely bound together.

Another shortcoming of SP is that when you change your application's data, functions using that data must often change as well. Again, assume the CAR structure has undergone a redesign that changes the currSpeed field from an int to a float to allow for a finer grain of precision in the program:

```
/* Changing a field from an int to a float... */
struct CAR
{
     char       petName[MAX_LENGTH];
     float      maxSpeed;                    /* was an int */
     int        currSpeed;
};
```

In our current application, we have three functions that use the CAR structure directly. Upon recompiling, we are issued an explicit conversion warning (C4244 to be exact). Moreover, other run-time bugs show up as well, as seen in Figure 1-4:

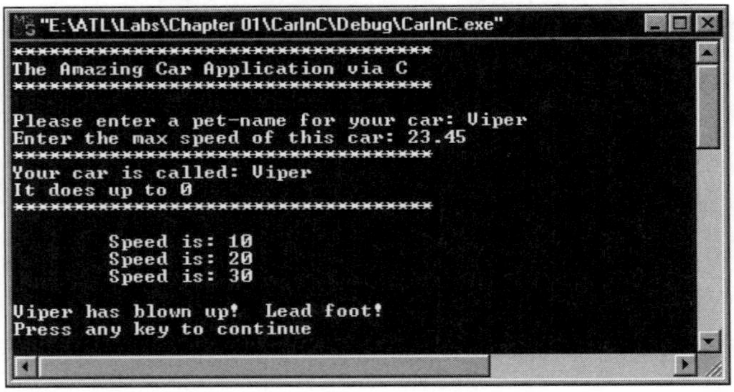

Figure 1-4:
Altering data
can result in
logical errors.

```
"E:\ATL\Labs\Chapter 01\CarInC\Debug\CarInC.exe"
**************************************
The Amazing Car Application via C
**************************************

Please enter a pet-name for your car: Viper
Enter the max speed of this car: 23.45
**************************************
Your car is called: Viper
It does up to 0
**************************************

          Speed is: 10
          Speed is: 20
          Speed is: 30

Viper has blown up! Lead foot!
Press any key to continue
```

As you can see, we have just broken the DisplayCarStats() method, as the printf() statement is looking for an incoming integer, but we just passed in a float:

```
/* Oops! maxSpeed is now a float. */
printf("It does up to %d\n", c.maxSpeed );
```

Obviously, we can easily modify this particular printf() statement to handle the change, but remember that the new iteration of our program may have hundreds of functions using this CAR structure. That sounds like hundreds of edits, endlessly searching source code for every function operating on the maxSpeed field of the CAR structure. That's no fun at all, even with a source code search utility!

A final headache with traditional SP is the almighty notion of code reuse. Recall that in SP, functions and the data they operate on are loosely coupled. If we wish to reuse a handful of our automobile functions in a new system, it is up to us to understand how discrete pieces interact. For example, assume you have a given function named Show() which operates internally on three pieces of global data:

```
/* This global function operates on three pieces of global data. */
void Show()
{
    gDatumA += 90;
    gDatumB = gDatumA + gSomeOtherGlobalDataPoint;
    printf("Data point B is currently %d\n", gDatumB);
}
```

Now, just for the sake of argument, if we wish to use the Show() function in a new program, we must also reuse the three pieces of global data that are referenced within the function's scope. If we don't grab the correct data definitions (and are unsure where to find them), we can't recompile—and thus can't reuse the code.

To sum up our quick remembrance of a world without objects, remember that structured programming works with (typically global) data and global functions. Because the two are only logically grouped together, not physically, we must have a keen understanding of our entire system to understand the impact of changing data types, editing functions, and reusing code.

Hopefully most of you out there do not have to work with traditional SP too much in your day-to-day programming tasks. However, it is important to remember what the C language has given us, as the next pit stop on the road to COM is that of classical object orientation using the C++ programming language.

Principles of Object-Oriented Languages

These days, numerous object-oriented languages (OOLs) exist. C++, Java, Visual Basic, and Object Pascal (Delphi) are but a tiny sampling of the popularity of object-oriented programming (OOP). Unlike C, object languages allow software engineers to physically group data and related functions into a single UDT called a *class*. When we bind together state (data) and behavior (functions) into a single named entity, we are able to model our software as entities we find in the real world.

Regardless of your language of choice, every OOL must be measured against three core principles of object technology, often termed the famed "pillars of OOP":

■ **Encapsulation:** How well does this language hide implementation details?

- **Inheritance:** How can I reuse my source code?
- **Polymorphism:** Can I treat related objects in a similar way?

Based on these traits, academics love to judge how worthy a given OO language is, not to mention the raging holy wars we developers tend to get into. To be honest, each language has pros and cons; however, and we will avoid such hostile conversations here. COM is Microsoft's binary object model, and being an object model, COM also contends with the issues of inheritance, encapsulation, and polymorphism. However, before we dive into the world of interfaces, coclasses, and class objects, we will examine the ins and outs of C++'s object standing. Later in Chapter 3, we will see how COM itself measures up against these same OO foundations.

From C Structures to C++ Classes

A class is a user-defined type, somewhat like the C structure we have already examined. However, recall that in traditional SP, the developer works with data and functions on a global level. We have seen how the C structure allows you to group related data together as one unit (the CAR structure) as opposed to a collection of separate variables. Here is another example of a C struct, this time modeling a simple employee:

Figure 1-5:
Merging related global data into a C structure.

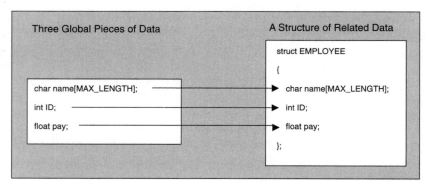

As before, we can now create variables of type EMPLOYEE and send them around to the set of global functions in our program:

```
/* Global functions operating on another C structure. */
void GiveBonus(struct EMPLOYEE *e, int amount);
void FireThisPerson(struct EMPLOYEE e);
```

Classes take the concept of grouping related items one step further, as we can define the set of data that represents the class (often called *attributes* or *properties*), as well as the set of functions which relate to this data (called *methods* in OO speak). Thus, a class is a description, or blueprint, for related functionality. An *object* is simply a variable of a given class, sometimes referred to as an *instance* of the class. Figure 1-6 illustrates a class named CEmployee, based off the previous EMPLOYEE struct and related global functions:

Figure 1-6:
Merging related
data and related
functionality
into a C++
class.

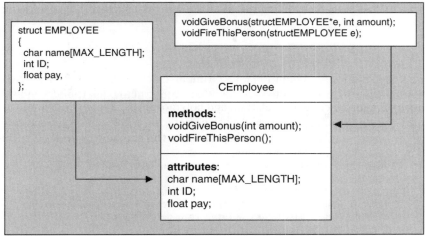

Note: By convention, class names typically begin with a "C-" prefix.

Creating and Destroying Objects: Constructors and Destructors

Classes developed in C++ are endowed with special methods allowing an object to be constructed and destroyed in an automatic and predictable manner. Rather than requiring users of your UDT to call class-specific creation and termination methods (e.g., Init(), Terminate(), Create(), KillThisObject(), and so on), C++ classes automatically receive a default constructor and a default destructor.

Constructors provide a simple way to initialize the state data of a new object as soon as the object user creates it. The default constructor of a class takes no arguments and hence sometimes goes by the name of the "no-arg" constructor. Constructors are called automatically whenever a new instance of the class is created, will always have the same name as the class itself, and do not provide a return value. In addition to the default constructor, a given class may have any number of custom constructors that do take arguments, allowing the object user to specify exactly how the internal data should be initialized. The ability for a class to define methods of the same name with different signatures is called *method overloading*.

Note: As soon as you add a custom constructor to a class definition, the default constructor is silently removed. You must specifically redefine the no-argument constructor in your class definition if you wish your class to support it.

A *destructor* allows the class designer to ensure any acquired resources (memory, data source connections, and whatnot) are automatically deallocated when the object is about to be destroyed. A destructor also takes the same name as the class, sporting a tilde (~) prefix, and returns nothing. Unlike constructors, destructors never take arguments and cannot be overloaded. Destructors are called automatically whenever an object is explicitly deallocated from memory using the **delete** keyword, or when the object naturally falls out of scope.

Building the Initial CEmployee Class

Here is an initial C++ definition for a CEmployee class that defines a single overloaded constructor with three arguments, the no-arg constructor, and the one and only destructor:

```
// Initial definition of the CEmployee class.
class CEmployee
{
public:
    // Must redefine no-argument constructor when overloading.
    CEmployee();
    CEmployee(int ID, char* name, float startingSalary);
    // Declare your destructors as virtual, to ensure proper clean-up
    // when casting a base class pointer to a derived class.
    virtual ~CEmployee();
};  // End class definitions with a semi-colon. Easily forgotten, hard to debug.
```

For the time being, assume we have written simple stub code for your constructors and destructor. With this assumption aside, an object user may now create various CEmployee objects using the following syntax:

```
// Create two instances of the CEmployee class.
void main(void)
{
    CEmployee Mary;                         // Calls default constructor.
    CEmployee Walter(15, "Walter", 99000);  // Overloaded constructor.
}   // Triggers destructor as objects fall out of scope.
```

Of course we may make pointers to objects as well. The **new** and **delete** keywords allow us to dynamically allocate and deallocate objects in C++:

```
// Dynamically create and destroy a CEmployee object.
void main(void)
{
    // Calls overloaded constructor.
    CEmployee *pZuZu = new CEmployee(50, "ZuZu", 500);
    // Calls destructor.
    delete pZuZu;
}
```

> **Note:** Never use the malloc() and free() functions of the C library to dynamically create or remove an object from memory, as these functions know nothing of C++ constructors and destructors!

Our simple CEmployee class is not too interesting at this point. It can be created in a handful of ways, and when it is no longer needed, the destructor will be called to perform any object cleanup. Classes become much more useful when we add internal data (which represents the state of a given object) and various public methods (to establish the behavior of the class), both of which require an understanding of encapsulation.

The Principle of Encapsulation

At the heart of any object language is the principle of encapsulation. This trait boils down to a language's ability to hide unnecessary implementation details from the object user. To borrow a classic example illustrating the reasoning behind encapsulation, consider your own real-world automobile. Every day you "send messages" to your car through the gas pedal, brakes, car radio, window wipers, and so forth. You rest assured that as you send these messages the car kindly responds (unless your warranty has just expired). You need not know or care exactly <u>how</u> the car accelerates, or <u>how</u> the radio plays the music. The details of these operations are encapsulated from view.

In object-oriented languages, a class also encapsulates the details of how it performs in response to the messages you send to it. For example, assume a co-worker has given you a brand new C++ class modeling a number of database-centric operations. As you examine the header file of this class (and the lavish comments your co-worker has included), you discover you can instantiate a new database object, create a file, and add columns using an overloaded constructor and a single method:

```
// Create a new CDataBaseObj object.
CDataBaseObj dbObj("CarsDataBase.txt");
dbObj.AddColumn("Pet Name");          // Send AddColumn message...
dbObj.AddColumn("Max Speed");         // Send another AddColumn message...
dbObj.AddColumn("Current Speed");     // Send yet another AddColumn message...
```

Ah, the beauty of encapsulation. As the object user, you have no need to worry about the numerous lines of code that create, open, and manipulate this new text file. You simply create an object and send it messages. Contrast this to traditional C, where we might have a DATABASE structure, and two global functions to create and add columns to the database. This demands that the developer understand not only the data involved, but the set of related functions as well.

Encapsulation allows us to have a tight coupling between data and related functionality. Typically, a class has instance data stored in the private sector. The values of the data held in the private sector constitute the current state of the object. Public member functions of the class (as well as any internal helper functions) operate on the state data internally behind the scenes whenever the object user sends messages. For example, Figure 1-7 illustrates three instances of the CDataBaseObj class, each maintaining a unique state:

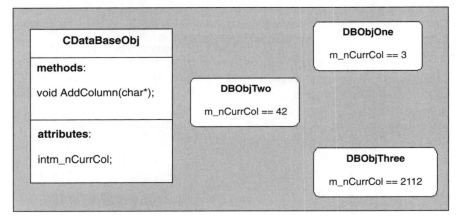

Figure 1-7: Each instance of a class typically maintains a unique state.

Specifying Encapsulation in C++

In C++, encapsulation is enforced at a syntactic level with the **public**, **private**, and **protected** keywords. Here is a breakdown of each level of visibility:

- **Public:** Any item listed under the public sector is directly accessible from the object itself, the object user, or any subclass.

- **Private:** Any data point or method listed in the private sector is usable only by the object itself. Neither object users nor any subclass can directly access these items.

- **Protected:** Methods and data points listed in the protected sector are accessible from the object itself as well as any descendents in the direct inheritance chain. The object user cannot access members in the protected sector.

In C++, the default visibility of a class is always private. Therefore, if you do not specify otherwise, each and every method or data point defined in your class will be inaccessible from an object instance:

```
// Visibility of a class is defaulted to private!
class CEmployee
{
    // Can't create this object (implicit private declaration).
    CEmployee();
    CEmployee(int ID, char* name, float startingSalary);
    virtual ~ CEmployee();
};
```

As a rule of thumb, data will reside in the private sector of a class. In this way, the state of the object is safe from invalid data assignments. The public sector typically provides any number of functions to retrieve and set this private data. Traditionally these methods are called accessors and mutators. Finally, when creating object hierarchies, a protected sector can be used to specify the set of inherited functionality (as we will see soon):

```
// Visibility levels for a typical class.
class CEmployee
{
public:
    // Visible methods.
private:
    // Hidden methods and data points.
protected:
    // Data and methods visible to this class and any sub-classes.
};
```

Accessors and Mutators: Safely Changing an Object's State Data

While constructors allow us to initialize an object to a default state, eventually some of the private state data defined by a class will need to be modified and retrieved by the object user over time. For example, assume the CDataBaseObj class maintains a private string data member that holds the current name of the data file. To keep the object's data safe from harm, we do not wish to define data directly in the public sector. Rather, we keep data private and provide public *accessors* (Get methods) and *mutators* (Set methods). In this way, we can safely return internal data to the object user and perform any data validations before we make assignments, as illustrated in Figure 1-8:

Figure 1-8:
Safe access to
the private
sector of a
class.

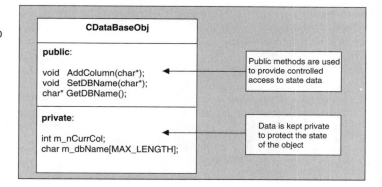

To preserve the encapsulation of the private data members, the class designer might create a class definition that looks something like the following:

```
// Definition of the CDataBaseObj class.
class CDataBaseObj
{
public:
      CDataBaseObj(char* dbName);
      CDataBaseObj();
      virtual ~ CDataBaseObj();
      // Accessor/mutator pair for internal string.
      void SetDBName(char* newName);
      char* GetDBName();
      void AddColumn(char* newCol);
private:
      // Instance data for the class.
      char m_dbName [MAX_LENGTH];
      int m_currCol;
};
```

As the object user can never directly access private members, the following code is illegal:

```
// Compiler error. Can't access private data.
CDataBaseObj myDB;
cout << myDB.m_dbName << endl;
```

Implementing Class Methods: The Scope Resolution Operator

Recall that when implementing class methods, you typically make use of the scope resolution operator (a double colon) to bind a given function implementation to a specific class. Here, we need to scope the SetDBName() and GetDBName() methods to the CDataBaseObj class. The implementation of the mutator method allows us to check the incoming data for a valid range, type, case, or whatnot, before changing the state of our object. The accessor method exists simply to return a copy of our private data to the object user:

```
// Mutator for a private data point.
// The SetDBName() method is bound to the CDataBaseObj class.
void CDataBaseObj::SetDBName(char* newName)
{
      // Here you may interrogate newName against any constraints before
      // assigning it to your data type. As well, this method may close down
      // the current data base, rename it, and open the new data file to accomplish
```

```
    // the task at hand.
    strcpy(m_dbName, newName)
}
// Accessor for a private data point.
char* CDataBaseObj::GetDBName()
{
    return m_dbName; // Safely return the buffer.
}
```

If you accidentally forget to bind a method implementation to a given class, you are bound to introduce a number of unresolved external errors. For example:

```
// This is not bound to the CDataBaseObj class...
// You just created a global function!
char* GetDBName()
{
    return m_dbName; // Compiler error. No global data point named m_dbName.
}
```

However, with the accessor and mutator methods correctly in place, the object user can now safely set and retrieve the object's instance data:

```
// Using an accessor and mutator set to safely work with a piece of private data.
void main(void)
{
    // Construct an object.
    CDataBaseObj myDB;
    // Set the name.
    myDB.SetDBName("MyNewDataBase.txt");
    // Get the name.
    cout << "The database is called:" << myDB.GetDBName();
}
```

Now that we have a solid understanding of encapsulation in C++, let's rework the previous CarInC program into an object-based solution.

Lab 1-2: A Well-Encapsulated Car

In this lab you will rework the functionality of the CarInC.exe application into an object-based solution using C++. Here you will create a class named (of course) CCar, blending together the global functions and CAR struct from the previous lab into a single cohesive unit. The key point of this lab is to illustrate the encapsulation of data and the use of accessors and mutators in your class design.

 The solution for this lab can be found on your CD-ROM under:
Labs\Chapter 01\CarInCPP

Step One: Prepare the Project Workspace and Insert the CCar Class

Start up Visual C++ and create a new empty Win32 Console Application named **CarInCPP.** Insert a new empty file named **main.cpp** into the project workspace. We will be making use of C++ IO streams, so include **<iostream.h>** before defining an empty main loop:

```
// Entry point for program.
#include <iostream.h>
```

```
void main(void)
{
}
```

Next, we must insert a new class into the program to represent our automobile. The simplest way to do this in the Visual C++ IDE is to right-click on the project node from ClassView and select **New Class...** from the context menu (see Figure 1-9).

From the resulting New Class Wizard utility, type in the name for this new class and click **OK**:

Figure 1-9: Accessing the New Class Wizard.

Figure 1-10: The Visual C++ New Class Wizard.

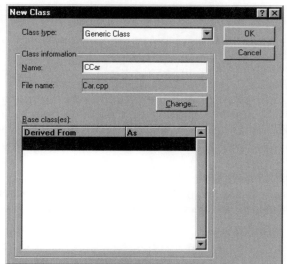

This tool will automatically define a default constructor and virtual destructor for the class as well as wrap the class definition with preprocessor calls to prevent multiple redefinition errors. As we will use the same program design notes as CarInC.exe, define some constant data for the speed upper limit and maximum pet name length. You can define these right inside the CCar header file (outside of the class scope), this time making use of the type safe C++ **const** keyword rather than C #define syntax:

```
// Program constants.
const
int MAX_LENGTH      = 100;
const int MAX_SPEED = 500;
```

Step Two: Define CCar's Public Interface

Next we must specify the public interface of our class. In other words, if some namespace in the application creates an instance of our CCar class, what methods are directly accessible to the object user? Define the CCar class to support the following public interface:

```
// Car.h
const int MAX_LENGTH   = 100;
const int MAX_SPEED    = 500;
#include <iostream.h>          // For C++ IO functions.
#include <stdio.h>             // For the gets() function.
#include <string.h>            // String stuff...
class CCar
{
public:
      // Public interface to the class.
      CCar();
      virtual ~CCar();
      void  DisplayCarStats();
      void  SpeedUp();
      // It is common to define access functions inline.
```

```
int   GetCurrSpeed()    { return m_currSpeed;}
int   GetMaxSpeed()     { return m_maxSpeed;}
char* GetPetName()      { return m_petName;}
// Generalized 'Set' function.
void  CreateACar();
private:
// Private instance data.
char      m_petName[MAX_LENGTH];
int       m_maxSpeed;
int       m_currSpeed;
};
```

Here, we have moved the global functions from the C example into our class's public sector. Notice how the signatures of these methods have cleaned up in the process: We have no need to send in any parameters to the DisplayCarStats() or SpeedUp() methods, as they internally operate on the object's private state data.

To finish up the class definition, you may wish to add some overloaded constructors that allow the object user to pass in data at the time of declaration. For this lab, the CreateACar() method is called by the object user as a secondary creation step to set all private in a single step (that is why we won't bother with individual Set functions for the data or overloaded constructors). Whatever additional modifications you may add to your CCar class, the point to remember here is that we have physically joined related data and functionality into a well-encapsulated unit.

Step Three: Implement the Methods of CCar

Implementing the methods of CCar is trivial. Add the following to your car.cpp file. The default constructor simply assigns the object's state data to safe empty values, with help from the member initialization list:

```
// CCar constructor.
CCar::CCar() : m_currSpeed(0), m_maxSpeed(0)
{
    // You could assign the above data to zero within the constructor block,
    // however savvy C++ folks prefer the more exotic member initialization list.
    strcpy(m_petName, "");
}
```

CreateACar() prompts for a pet name and maximum speed using gets(), cout, and cin:

```
// Create a new car based on user input.
void CCar::CreateACar()
{
    char  buffer[MAX_LENGTH];
    int   spd = 0;
    cout << "Please enter a pet-name for your car: " << flush;
    gets(buffer);            // Check against MAX if desired.
    strcpy(m_petName, buffer);
    do                       // Be sure speed isn't beyond reality...
    {
        cout << "Enter the max speed of this car: " << flush;
        cin >> spd;
        cout << endl;
    }while(spd > MAX_SPEED);
    m_maxSpeed = spd;
}
```

The only noticeable change to the DisplayCarStats() method is that we use the more elegant and OO-based cout as opposed to printf(). In addition, because this function operates on internal private state data, DisplayCarStats() needs no parameters.

```
// Implementation of DisplayCarStats.
void CCar::DisplayCarStats()
{
    cout << "**********************************" << endl;
    cout << "PetName is: " << m_petName << endl;
    cout << "Max Speed is: " << m_maxSpeed << endl;
    cout << "**********************************" << endl << endl;
}
```

And finally, SpeedUp() does just as you would expect: increases the current speed by 10 and prints the result using cout:

```
// Implementation of SpeedUp.
void CCar::SpeedUp()
{
    if(m_currSpeed <= m_maxSpeed)
    {
        m_currSpeed = m_currSpeed + 10;
        cout << "Speed is: " << m_currSpeed << endl;
    }
}
```

This completes the class definition and implementation of the CCar class. Go ahead and compile to ensure you have no typos. Now we need to take this class out for a test drive (pun intended).

Step Four: Implement the main() Loop

With our new OO version of the Car functionality complete, the client-side code in main() will clean up quite a bit from the original program in C. All we need to do is send messages to a new CCar instance:

```
// Program entry point.
#include "car.h"        // Don't forget this!
#include <iostream.h>
void main(void)
{
    cout << "**********************************" << endl;
    cout << "The Amazing Car Application via CPP"<< endl;
    cout << "**********************************"<< endl;
    CCar myCar;                      // Calls default constructor.
    myCar.CreateACar();             // Prompts user for input.
    myCar.DisplayCarStats();        // Show state.
    // Rev that engine!
    while(myCar.GetCurrSpeed() <= myCar.GetMaxSpeed())
         myCar.SpeedUp();
    // Explosion!
    cout << myCar.GetPetName() << " has blown up! Lead foot!" << endl;
}
```

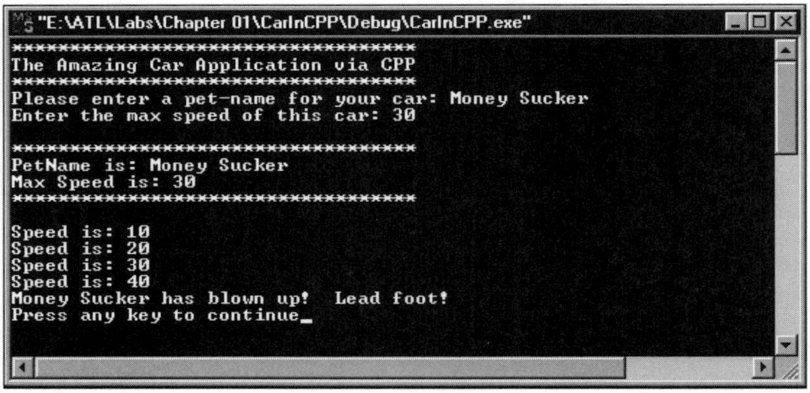

Figure 1-11:
The C++ car
application.

```
"E:\ATL\Labs\Chapter 01\CarInCPP\Debug\CarInCPP.exe"

*****************************************
The Amazing Car Application via CPP
*****************************************
Please enter a pet-name for your car: Money Sucker
Enter the max speed of this car: 30


*****************************************
PetName is: Money Sucker
Max Speed is: 30
*****************************************

Speed is: 10
Speed is: 20
Speed is: 30
Speed is: 40
Money Sucker has blown up!  Lead foot!
Press any key to continue_
```

At this point, we have moved a trivial C application into the world of objects in C++. The car example has served us well, and will continue to do so throughout this book. The next time we see our programmatic automobile will be in Chapter 3, where we develop a COM-based DLL to model our automobile logic.

So much for a lonely C++ class living in isolation. Robust OO systems usually involve numerous classes living together, often using one another in the process. In other words, classes can be defined by leveraging existing classes. This, of course, is the story of inheritance, which is the second pillar of OOP.

The Principle of Inheritance

Classes tend to work together both logically and physically. The principle of inheritance helps promote code reuse and allows you to group classes into a relational hierarchy. For example, we might all agree that CEmployee and CSalesEmployee are somehow logically related in a system. Using C++, we can model this relationship physically by establishing base and derived class relationships (you may know them as parent/child or super/subclass relationships). Classes may be related either by what is known as classical inheritance (Is-A) or the containment and delegation model (Has-A). In either light, inheritance always implies that one class is a specialized form of another.

The "Is-A" Relationship: Classical Inheritance

In classical inheritance, a subclass extends existing functionality from a superclass. Consider again our friend CEmployee. You have thoughtfully populated CEmployee's public interface with numerous methods, and preserved encapsulation with private data manipulated by public accessors and mutators. Now, imagine you wish to leverage CEmployee by deriving a new class called CSalesEmployee. CSalesEmployee is everything CEmployee is, plus a little bit more. You may wish to have the state of a CSalesEmployee object reflect the number of sales in a given week, a trait that a typical CEmployee object does not need to be concerned with. In effect, a CSalesEmployee "is a" type of CEmployee. The Is-A relationship can be diagrammed as so:

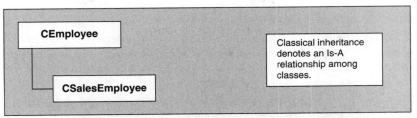

Figure 1-12: Classical inheritance suggests an Is-A relationship.

We will be building a complete Employee hierarchy at the end of this chapter, but for now let's just add the following methods to the public sector of the CEmployee class, and establish an Is-A relationship with CSalesEmployee:

```
// The CEmployee base class.
class CEmployee
{
public:
     CEmployee ();
     CEmployee (int ID, char* name, float startingSalary);
     virtual ~CEmployee();
     // These will be inherited by any sub class.
     void DisplayClassType() {cout << "I am a CEmployee object." << endl; }
     float GetPay() {return m_currPay/52;}
protected: // Grant access to sub classes, but not object user.
     float      m_currPay;
     int   m_ID;
     char  m_name[MAX_LENGTH];
};
```

Here, GetPay() is the accessor for the private m_currPay data point, which is computed on a (roughly) weekly basis.

A Brief Word on RTTI

The DisplayClassType() function prints out the class name and is a simple diagnostic run-time type information (RTTI) method at this point. RTTI is a facility of many OO languages, which provides a way to discover the functionality of an object at run time. This can be a very powerful trick.

Imagine, for example, that we have a collection object maintaining a large number of related (but not identical) objects. If we have some way to dynamically discover which sort of object we have just pulled from the collection, we can make a set of appropriate requests from the object. Many C++ frameworks (such as MFC) provide a set of RTTI functions to make use of. As well, most C++ compilers also offer the typeid() function to support basic RTTI. The problem is that RTTI tends to be a very compiler-specific protocol. Here we have simply rolled our own.

COM also provides a form of RTTI through a standard COM interface named IUnknown. One of the methods of IUnknown, QueryInterface(), also provides a way to discover the functionality of an object at run time. We will get to know interfaces in the next chapter, and IUnknown in Chapter 3. As for DisplayClassType(), we will see a real application for this method in our upcoming lab, so bear with me for now.

Subclassing in C++: Leveraging Base Class Functionality

Next, assume we wish to create a new class that leverages the behavior of CEmployee. Using classical inheritance, CSalesEmployee will inherit any public or protected member defined in CEmployee. Recall the distinction between the **public** and **protected** keywords: If an object user creates a CSalesEmployee object, all public methods of both CEmployee and CSalesEmployee are directly available, whereas the protected data is not. However, as you develop the functionality of CSalesEmployee, you may refer to the inherited protected members provided by your base class.

Our sales employee class needs to hold the current number of weekly sales and calculate its pay accordingly. Using C++ syntax, we may model the Is-A relationship between CEmployee and CSalesEmployee as the following:

```
// Using classical inheritance to model the Is-A relationship.
class CSalesEmployee: public CEmployee
{
public:
    CSalesEmployee(int ID, char* name, float startingPay, int sales);
    virtual ~ CSalesEmployee();
    // Methods unique to CSalesEmployee.
    int GetNumberOfSales() { return m_numberOfSales;}
    int SetNumberOfSales(int numb) { m_numberOfSales = numb;}
private:
    // Unique instance data to the sales employee class.
    int m_numberOfSales;
};
```

To set the state of the derived CSalesEmployee object we have two syntactical options available to us. The first option is to simply assign the inherited protected data from CEmployee in the body of our constructor as so:

```
// Call is automatically made to the default constructor of CEmployee.
CSalesEmployee::CSalesEmployee(int ID, char* name, float startingPay, int sales)
{
    m_ID = ID;                  // Inherited from CEmployee.
    strcpy(m_name, name);       // Inherited from CEmployee.
    m_currPay = startingPay;    // Inherited from CEmployee.
    m_numberOfSales = sales;    // Our custom data.
}
```

Doing so will trigger the default constructor of our base class (CEmployee) automatically. However, as our base class already has an overloaded constructor which knows how to assign the ID, name, and starting salary, we may use option two. Here we explicitly call a base class constructor and initialize the inherited data using the member initialization list:

```
// Explicitly call a base class constructor from the member initialization list.
CSalesEmployee::CSalesEmployee(int ID, char* name, float startingPay, int sales)
    : CEmployee(ID, name, startingPay)
{
    m_numberOfSales = sales;    // Now we can just worry about our unique data.
}
```

All things being equal, both approaches are more or less equivalent, so take your pick. Now with the Is-A relationship defined, we can make use of the inherited functionality of a CEmployee object from a CSalesEmployee instance:

```
// Using base and derived classes.
//
void main(void)
{
     // Create a base class and derived class.
     CEmployee joeBlow(20, "Joe", 45000);
     CSalesEmployee slickRyan(30, "Ryan", 20000, 500);
     // Ask each object to identify itself.
     joeBlow.DisplayClassType();         // Prints "I am a CEmployee object"
     slickRyan.DisplayClassType();       // Prints "I am a CEmployee object" (humm)
     // GetPay() has been inherited from CEmployee,
     // however it makes no use of the number of sales!
     cout << slickRyan.GetPay();
     // Returns m_numberOfSales
     cout << slickRyan.GetNumberOfSales();
}
```

We have indeed inherited base class functionality; however, our CSalesEmployee objects are not working quite as expected. Each object instance identifies itself as a CEmployee type. Ideally each object in the inheritance chain should respond to the DisplayClassType() message in its own unique way.

In addition, the GetPay() method which we inherited from CEmployee does not make use of the number of sales (which it should, to allow for commission). We will fix these problems when we examine polymorphism later in this chapter. For now, consider them "features" of the system.

Examining the "Has-A" Relationship: Containment and Delegation

So then, classical inheritance allows us to leverage code by creating a dependency on some class higher up the chain. The other sort of inheritance found in many OOLs (and the only form of inheritance supported by COM) is the Has-A relationship, also known as the containment/delegation model. Here, reuse is achieved when an outer class creates and uses inner classes to reuse code and extend its own functionality. If the outer class wishes to expose the inner class's functionality to the object user, it extends its <u>own</u> public interface with methods that simply make calls (or delegates) to the inner object. The Has-A relationship is diagrammed in Figure 1-13:

Figure 1-13:
Containment of objects.

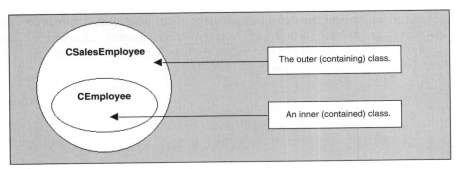

Note that users of outer objects (CSalesEmployee) typically have no knowledge that it maintains any inner objects (such as CEmployee) to help it get its work done. Why?

Encapsulation, of course! The outer class is in charge of creating and exposing the inner class's functionality through its own public sector. If we wish to reuse the CEmployee class as an inner object, we may define the CSalesEmployee class as the following:

```
// CSalesEmployee using containment to reuse existing functionality.
class CSalesEmployee
{
public:
    CSalesEmployee();
    CSalesEmployee(int ID, char* name, float startingPay, int sales);
    float GetPay();
    int GetNumberOfSales() { return m_numberOfSales;}
    int SetNumberOfSales(int numb) { m_numberOfSales = numb;}
    // We can now respond to this message our own way.
    void DisplayClassType() {cout << "I am a CSalesEmployee object." << endl; }
private:
    CEmployee m_Emp; // CSalesEmployee Has-A CEmployee .
    int m_numberOfSales;
};
```

The inner CEmployee object may be constructed using the member initialization list:

```
// The member initialization is a handy way to construct inner objects
CSalesEmployee::CSalesEmployee(int ID, char* name, float startingPay, int sales)
    : m_Emp(ID, name, startingPay)     // Inner objects created first.
{
    m_numberOfSales = sales;           // Assign sales data.
}
```

The GetPay() method of the salesperson is implemented with help from the inner object, m_Emp. Again, the act of extending the containing class's public interface to indirectly use inner objects is called *delegation*:

```
// The outer class makes use of the inner class to calculate the pay of a
// Sales employee.
float CSalesEmployee::GetPay ()
{
    // Delegate this call to the inner object to help get the real work done.
    return (m_numberOfSales * 5) + ( m_Emp.GetPay() );
}
```

As shown previously, DisplayClassType() is defined inline and prints out a unique string without any help from CEmployee at all. By using containment and delegation, both CEmployee and CSalesEmployee behave as unique entities, responding correctly to GetPay() and DisplayClassType():

```
// Working with contained and stand-alone objects.
void main(void)
{
    CEmployee joeBlow(20, "Joe", 45000);
    CSalesEmployee slickRyan(30, "Ryan", 20000, 500);
    // Ask each object to identify itself.
    joeBlow.DisplayClassType();        // "I am a CEmployee object"
    slickRyan.DisplayClassType();      // "I am a CSalesEmployee object"
    // GetPay() now returns a value based on commissions.
    cout << slickRyan.GetPay();
}
```

To see how to repair the previous Is-A relationship to behave the same as our Has-A relationship, we need to provide a way for a derived class to override methods declared in a base class. This is a call for polymorphism, which is the final pillar of object-oriented technology.

The Principle of Polymorphism

We clearly have some problems with our existing Is-A employee relationship. When we send the DisplayClassType() message to either a CEmployee or CSalesEmployee instance, we get back the same response. A similar problem exists with GetPay(). The principle of polymorphism allows related classes to respond uniquely to the same message. As with inheritance, we have two possible forms of polymorphism: classical and ad hoc.

Classical polymorphism is only supported by OOLs that also support classical (Is-A) inheritance. The two intimately rely on each other. If we have the luxury of classical inheritance in our OOL, we may allow each child class to interpret what a given message means to itself by overriding a default implementation defined in the base class. This allows class designers to access the default behavior supplied in a base class "as is" or to redefine how a subclass responds to the same message using "virtual" functions.

Defining Virtual Functions

In C++, we may specify which methods (also known as functions) can be overridden in a derived class using the **virtual** keyword. Let's begin to rectify the current problems with our employee hierarchy using virtual methods. As we will be making the DisplayClassType() and GetPay() methods virtual, any subclass of CEmployee can print out its own custom message and calculate pay its own way. Here is the reworked definition:

```
// CEmployee with virtual functions.
class CEmployee
{
public:
    ...
    // Although we define a default implementation for these functions, we also
    // allow sub classes to override these methods.
    virtual void DisplayClassType()
    {
        cout << "I am a CEmployee object." << endl;
    }
    virtual float GetPay();              // Implementation in CPP file.
protected:
    ...
};
```

CSalesEmployee may now override the base class version of DisplayClassType() and provide a more appropriate message:

```
// Overriding the inherited DisplayClassType() to work with a sales employee.
class CSalesEmployee : public CEmployee
{
public:
    // Let's redefine the inherited method.
    virtual void DisplayClassType()    // virtual keyword optional in subclass.
```

```
        {
                cout << "I am a CSalesEmployee object" << endl;
        }
        ...
        // Other functions and state data for sales employee.
};
```

This time, each object responds to the DisplayClassType() message in a much more intelligent manner through polymorphism:

```
// Create some objects and exercise the virtual functions.
CSalesEmployee slickRyan;
CEmployee ragingVirgil;
ragingVirgil.DisplayClassType();        // I am a CEmployee object.
slickRyan.DisplayClassType();           // I am a CSalesEmployee object.
```

We have also specified GetPay() as a virtual function of CEmployee. In this way, each object can determine how to calculate the correct pay. For example, CEmployee types get a fixed salary, and may thus implement GetPay() as the following:

```
// Pay each week for an employee.
float CEmployee::GetPay()
{
        return m_currPay/52;            // No taxes!
}
```

A CSalesEmployee needs to factor in commission based on number of sales. Rather than recoding the logic provided by the base class implementation of GetPay() in our subclass, we can explicitly call the base class version of this method (using the scope resolution operator) to help calculate the weekly pay:

```
// Pay each week for a sales employee.
float CSalesEmployee::GetPay()
{
        // Scope resolution operator calls base class implementation.
        return CEmployee::GetPay() + (m_numberOfSales * 5);     // 5 bucks a sale!
}
```

So then, classical polymorphism allows us to have classes related by inheritance rework how they respond to the same message. When we declare virtual base class functions, we give our subclasses a choice. The superclass says in effect, "I have a default implementation of this method for you. Use it if you wish, or redefine the behavior to suit your own needs" (we all should have such understanding parents). Keep in mind, however, that a subclass is never <u>required</u> to redefine a superclass behavior.

Enforcing Subclass Behavior with Pure Virtual Functions

Sometimes it is useful for a base class to define methods having no default implementation at all. In this case, we say the base class defines "pure virtual functions." Any class that specifies pure virtual functions is termed an *abstract base class*. Object users may never create object instances of abstract classes (as the object's implementation is not fully fleshed out) but <u>can</u> freely declare a pointer to one. The question is why would we bother to define methods that have no implementations?

Consider a simple class library that models a number of geometric shapes. We need to allow circles, triangles, and squares to render themselves to the screen based on a Draw()

method. Using classical polymorphism, we know that we could create a base class called CShape, and in that class we could simply declare a virtual Draw() method. Subclasses are free to override Draw() to render themselves appropriately when asked to do so, as suggested by Figure 1-14:

Figure 1-14: Shape class with a virtual Draw() method.

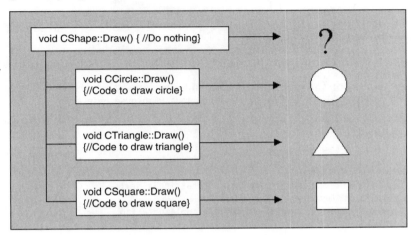

The trick to understanding the usefulness of pure virtual functions is to realize that you probably never intend an object user to make a CShape object directly. After all, how exactly would you draw a generic shape? This class exists simply to hold attributes and methods common to all descendents. Also recall that a subclass is <u>not required</u> to override a virtual member. It is completely possible that the CShape descendents (triangles, circles, and squares) could make use of the base class implementation—which is nothing. Clearly this is not a very useful shape library.

A better solution is to define the "form" of the Draw() method (meaning the parameters, return type, and method name) and declare it as pure virtual in CShape. In this way, each and every subclass <u>must</u> provide an implementation of Draw(), or else it will also be an abstract class as well. In C++, we declare pure virtual functions like so:

```
// To create a pure virtual function, use a 'virtual' prefix and '=0' suffix.
virtual void Draw () = 0;
```

Pure virtual functions allow a base class to enforce a desired form on subclasses. Here the parent class says, "If you want to live in my house, you must implement these methods yourself."

An Employee Hierarchy

To illustrate pure virtual functions, let's go back to the drawing board and rework CEmployee yet again into an abstract base class. This class exists simply to hold all data and functionality relative to any descendent, and cannot be directly created. Thus, we will also have to create another subclass to represent a standard full-time employee (we were using CEmployee for that purpose before, but as this new iteration contains pure virtual methods, we cannot create objects of this type). Our Employee hierarchy will have the following classes:

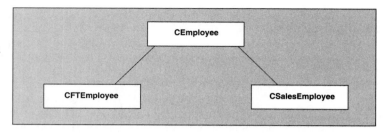

Figure 1-15:
The employee
class hierarchy.

Here is the class definition of the revitalized CEmployee abstract base class, this time supplying two pure virtual functions:

```
// An abstract base class, which holds attributes and methods for all descendents.
class CEmployee
{
public:
     CEmployee();
     CEmployee (int ID, char* name, float startingSalary);
     virtual ~CEmployee();
     // Pure virtual functions. No default implementation.
     virtual void DisplayClassType() = 0;
     virtual float GetPay() = 0;
protected:
     float m_currPay;
     int   m_ID;
     char  m_name[MAX_LENGTH];
};
```

As the current version of CSalesEmployee already implements what the pure virtual DisplayClassType() means to itself, we can leave this method unaltered. However, GetPay() is now declared as pure virtual, and must provide an implementation without any help from the base class implementation. As you can imagine, this method will return the weekly pay with commissions leveraging the inherited state data:

```
// This time we cannot leverage base class implementations...
float CSalesEmployee::GetPay()
{
     // The pay is a result of current pay + number of sales.
     return (m_currPay/52) + (m_numberOfSales * 5);
}
```

As for our new class, CFTEmployee can implement the pure virtual DisplayClassType() as so:

```
// Full time employee implementation of DisplayClassType.
void CFTEmployee::DisplayClassType ()
{
     cout << "Hello from CFTEmployee" << endl;
}
```

CFTEmployee's version of GetPay() is as you would expect. Simply return the weekly pay without commission:

```
// Full time employee implementation of GetPay.
float CFTEmployee::GetPay()
{
```

```
        // Calculate the pay.
        return m_currPay/52;
}
```

Polymorphism in Action: Using Base Class Pointers

We now have three classes in our employee hierarchy: CEmployee, the abstract base class used to hold all common employee information; CFTEmployee, the class representing a traditional full-time worker; and CSalesEmployee to model a worker paid with commissions. To see polymorphism in action, recall what was mentioned earlier: While you cannot make objects instances of an abstract base class, you can make pointers to them.

A base class pointer can be assigned to any subclass in the inheritance chain, and by casting the pointer to the object in question, we gain access to its public sector. Examine the following code, noting the special syntax used to deallocate each member in the base class pointer array:

```
// The base class pointer trick.
void main(void)
{
    CEmployee* theStaff[3];        // An array of base class pointers.

    theStaff[0] = new CFTEmployee(12, "Cindy", 50000);
    theStaff[1] = new CSalesEmployee(30, "Maxine", 9000, 40);
    theStaff[2] = new CFTEmployee(7, "Amanda", 90000);

    for(int i = 0; i < 3; i++)    // Late binding through polymorphism.
    {
        theStaff[i] -> DisplayClassType();
        theStaff[i] -> GetPay();
    }

    delete[] *theStaff;           // Insures all items in the array are destroyed.
}
```

I'm sure you can imagine what the output of this would look like (you'll see for yourself in the next lab). Using base class pointers, we achieve polymorphic behavior. It is at run time, not compile time, where the determined behavior is understood and the correct method is invoked. This allows OOLs to work with the *late binding* of the object, in order to determine which version of a virtual function to call by consulting the "virtual function table."

Understanding Virtual Function Tables

This bit of late binding magic is given automatically by the C++ compiler. Whenever you define a class containing virtual functions, the compiler silently adds a hidden member to your class, named the vPtr (virtual pointer). The vPtr in turn points to the class's vTable (virtual function table). This table is an array of addresses to function entry points. There is an entry in the vTable for each and every virtual function defined in the class. If the object user is sending messages to a CFTEmployee variable, the vTable is consulted, which points to the memory address of the implementation code (Figure 1-16):

Figure 1-16:
vPtr/vTable
relationship for
CFTEmployee.

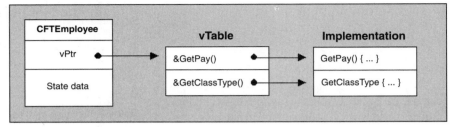

CSalesEmployee also has a vTable specifying the memory locations of its virtual function set. During run time, the class's **this** pointer is dereferenced to point to the correct vTable in the hierarchy, which in turn points to the correct implementation code. The usefulness of vPtrs and vTables is critical in COM development, and we will revisit this issue in Chapter 2. To whet your appetite, suffice it to say when a COM client calls interface methods on a COM object, it does so through the vPtr.

Understanding Ad Hoc Polymorphism

Before we finish our investigation of polymorphism, we need to consider ad hoc polymorphism. Some object-based languages do not support classical inheritance, and therefore we cannot establish base/derived class relationships. Ad hoc polymorphism allows objects not related by classical inheritance to respond uniquely to the same message. From the object user's perspective, if these methods have the same signature, we can send them the same messages. Figure 1-17 illustrates three class modules (CSquare, CCircle, and CTriangle) each supporting a Draw() method. Note that these classes have no common CShape base class to define a pure virtual (or even virtual) Draw() method. It is by slightly devious ways that these objects are related.

Figure 1-17:
Ad hoc
polymorphism.

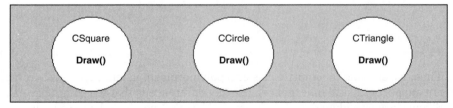

Visual Basic and Ad Hoc Polymorphism

Visual Basic is an OOL (object-oriented language) that only supports ad hoc polymorphism. Assume you have created a new Standard EXE project workspace in VB, and inserted three new *.cls files to define the CSquare, CCircle, and CTriangle classes (a *.cls file is used to define a class in VB; there is no "class" keyword).

Each class supports a method named Draw(), which in the real world might use VB graphic functions to render a shape, but for our purposes simply prints out some debug information. Here is the Draw() method for CSquare (the other drawing routines are similar—they just print out unique debug information):

```
' CSquare drawing routine. '
Public Sub Draw()
```

```
        Debug.Print "Drawing a square"
End Sub
```

If we place a single command button on the main
Form object (Figure 1-18) we may then add code to
the button's Click event.

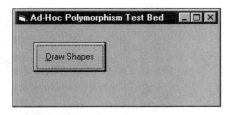

Figure 1-18: A VB form object serves as the main window.

By creating an array of Object data types, we
can set each index in the array to a new instance of
one of our classes (the intrinsic Object type provides late binding behavior in VB):

```
' Create an array of Object data types, setting each index to a custom class instance.'
Private Sub btnDraw_Click()
        ' Create an array of Object variables.
        Dim shapes(3) As Object
        ' Must use Set keyword when assigning values to objects!
        Set shapes(0) = New CCircle
        Set shapes(1) = New CSquare
        Set shapes(2) = New CTriangle
        Set shapes(3) = New CCircle
        Dim i As Integer
        For i = 0 To 3              ' Loop through each item in the object array.
                shapes(i).Draw
        Next i
End Sub
```

If you run this program, you will see the following pumped out to the Immediate window
(visible from the View | Immediate Window menu selection):

Figure 1-19:
VB program
output.

```
Immediate                                    ✕
┌──────────────────────────────────────────┐
│ Drawing a circle                        ▲ │
│ Drawing a square                          │
│ Drawing a triangle                        │
│ Drawing a circle                          │
│                                         ▼ │
└──────────────────────────────────────────┘
```

Thus, we are able to simulate classical polymorphism in languages such as VB, which do
not support classical inheritance. The key difference is that we do not have a common
Shape class providing default behaviors. Now that you have been refreshed with the basics
of encapsulation, inheritance, and polymorphism, the next lab will pull everything together
and allow you to construct the employee hierarchy we have been examining so far.

Lab 1-3: An Employee Hierarchy in C++

In this lab, you will create a small hierarchy of C++ objects. This will solidify (or refresh)
your understanding of the foundation of OO development: encapsulation, inheritance, and
polymorphism. As well, you will be designing an abstract base class that enforces a given
form on all descendents using pure virtual functions.

Most importantly, this lab will give you a chance to develop your own custom run-time
type information (RTTI) functionality which will provide a perfect stepping-stone to the
interface-based programming techniques introduced in the next chapter.

The solution for this lab can be found on your CD-ROM under:
Labs\Chapter 01\Employees

Step One: Create the Project Workspace and Initial Class Definitions

To begin this lab, create a new Win32 Console workspace (an empty project type will be fine) named **Employees**. As usual, insert a new text file named **main.cpp** and define an empty main loop. Now, using the New Class Wizard (Figure 1-20), insert the CEmployee base class and the following subclasses:

- **CFTEmployee**: Derive this class from CEmployee.
- **CSalesEmployee**: Also derive from CEmployee.

Figure 1-20:
Using the New Class Wizard to derive a new class.

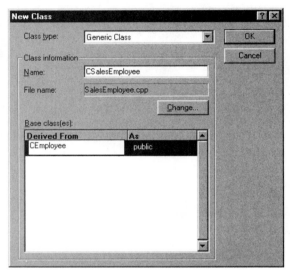

This will give you skeleton definitions for three new C++ classes. As you have seen in the reading, CEmployee will serve as an abstract base class for CFTEmployee and CSalesEmployee. Go ahead and compile to get a clean build.

Step Two: Implement the CEmployee Abstract Base Class

Define CEmployee to support the following protected data members and a custom constructor. Recall that any protected data will be visible to your subclasses, but not to the object user:

```cpp
// The abstract base class in the employee hierarchy.
class CEmployee
{
public:
    CEmployee();
    CEmployee(int ID, char* name, float startingPay);
    virtual ~CEmployee();
protected:
    float m_currPay;
    int   m_ID;
    char  m_name[MAX_LENGTH];    // Program defined const, set to 100.
};
```

Implement the overloaded constructor to set the internal state data:

```
// CEmployee's overloaded constructor.
CEmployee::CEmployee(int ID, char* name, float startingPay)
{
    m_ID = ID;
    strcpy(m_name, name);        // Don't forget to include <string.h>.
    m_currPay = startingPay;
}
```

Next, add the following methods to CEmployee's public interface:

```
// Custom RTTI method.
virtual char* DisplayClassType(EMP_TYPE* eType) = 0;       // enum defined below.
// Accessors (we don't need mutators for this lab, but feel free to add them)
virtual float GetPay() = 0;
char* GetName()    { return m_name;}
int GetID()        { return m_ID;}
```

Notice how our DisplayClassType() method has changed a bit from the last time we saw it. We will now return a string, which may be used to print out the class name and set the incoming EMP_TYPE enum to one of two values. This will be used in the calling logic to test which messages may be sent to a particular class. Define the EMP_TYPE enumeration in the header file of CEmployee (outside the class definition) as so:

```
// Full time (FT) or sales person (SP).
enum EMP_TYPE{FT = 0, SP = 1};
// The CEmployee base class.
class CEmployee
{
public:
    ...
protected:
    ...
};
```

Assuming all is well, let's begin to flesh out the CFTEmployee class next.

Step Three: Implement CFTEmployee

Define the following overloaded constructor for this class and set the inherited state data using the member initialization list:

```
// Use the member initialization list to set the inherited state data.
// (Don't forget to add this constructor to the class definition!)
CFTEmployee::CFTEmployee(int ID, char* name, float startingPay)
    : CEmployee(ID, name, startingPay)
{
}
```

CFTEmployee will not need to define any additional data, as it automatically receives the protected data defined in CEmployee.

As we are derived from an abstract base class, we now are under obligation to implement each pure virtual function defined in CEmployee. First, let's assume a full-time employee's weekly pay is just current salary/52 (hey, it's our model—who says we need taxes?):

```
// Don't forget to list the inherited functions in the class definition!
// be sure you remove the '=0' suffix, as this method is no longer pure virtual.
float CFTEmployee::GetPay()
{
    // Figure out the pay for a full time worker.
    return m_currPay/52;
}
```

A full-time employee will identify itself in the system using the GetClassType() method. Return a simple string such as "I am a full-time worker," and set the EMP_TYPE pointer to FT:

```
// We return a string specifying we are a full time worker.
char* CFTEmployee::DisplayClassType(EMP_TYPE* eType)
{
    *eType = FT;
    return "I am a Full-Time worker";
}
```

As we have implemented both pure virtual functions of CEmployee, this class is complete.

Step Four: Implement CSalesEmployee

Define the following overloaded constructor for this class. Next, add a private data member (of type int) named m_numberOfSales with an accessor and mutator. Set all state data in this constructor:

```
// Overloaded constructor for sales person.
CSalesEmployee::CSalesEmployee(int ID, char* name, float startingPay, int sales)
{
    // Could also use member initialization syntax.
    // Here we are making simple assignments.
    m_ID = ID;
    strcpy(m_name, name);
    m_currPay = startingPay;
    m_numberOfSales = sales;
}
// Prototypes of sales specific functions (inlined).
int GetNumberOfSales() { return m_numberOfSales;}
void SetNumberOfSales(int numb) { m_numberOfSales = numb;}
```

The GetPay() method will be calculated by taking the weekly pay plus five bucks for each sale made:

```
// Remember GetPay() is pure virtual...
float CSalesEmployee::GetPay()
{
    // Can't leverage base class functionality! There is none!
    return (m_currPay/52) + (m_numberOfSales * 5);
}
```

Finally, implement GetClassType() to return a unique string identifier, and set the EMP_TYPE pointer to SP:

```
// Our custom RTTI.
char* CSalesEmployee::DisplayClassType(EMP_TYPE* eType)
{
    *eType = SP;
```

```
        return "I am a Sales Person";
}
```

Compile your application (you should come through clean). Now we must add code to our main loop to create and manipulate these new object types, using our custom RTTI function and the "base class pointer trick" to exercise polymorphic activity.

Step Five: Polymorphism with Base Class Pointers

We will be creating an array of base class pointers for use in our main loop. For test purposes, create the array with an upper limit of 4, as defined by the MAX_EMPS constant. Set each index in the base class pointer array to a new instance of a given subclass:

```
// Using our hierarchy.
const int MAX_EMPS = 4;
void main(void)
{
        CEmployee* theStaff[MAX_EMPS];
        theStaff[0] = new CFTEmployee(30, "Fred", 30000);
        theStaff[1] = new CSalesEmployee(40, "Mary", 40000, 120);
        theStaff[2] = new CFTEmployee(15, "JoJo", 11000);
        theStaff[3] = new CSalesEmployee(1, "Jimmy Jones", 100000, 19);
...
}
```

To exercise the staff, implement a for loop to perform the following:

1. Loop through the CEmployee* array. Send in (by reference) an EMP_TYPE variable to DisplayClassType()and print out the returned string:

```
// Display the type of object we are working with.
EMP_TYPE e;
cout << theStaff[i]->DisplayClassType(&e) << endl;
```

2. Print out the name, ID, and pay for each member in the array:

```
// Get name.
cout << "Name is: " << theStaff[i]->GetName() << endl;
// Get ID.
cout << "ID is: " << theStaff[i]->GetID() << endl;
// Get pay.
cout << "Pay is: " << theStaff[i]->GetPay() << " a paycheck before taxes." << endl;
```

3. If the current member in the array is a salesperson (we determine this by examining the EMP_TYPE variable), print out the current number of sales. You will have to explicitly cast the array member to a CSalesEmployee pointer:

```
// Let's see if we have a salesperson.
if(e == SP)
{
        cout  << "–>My Sales are "
              << ((CSalesEmployee*)theStaff[i])->GetNumberOfSales()
              << endl << flush;
}
```

When the array has been iterated over completely, don't forget to delete the array of pointers! When you run the completed program, you will be able to interrogate each item (Figure 1-21):

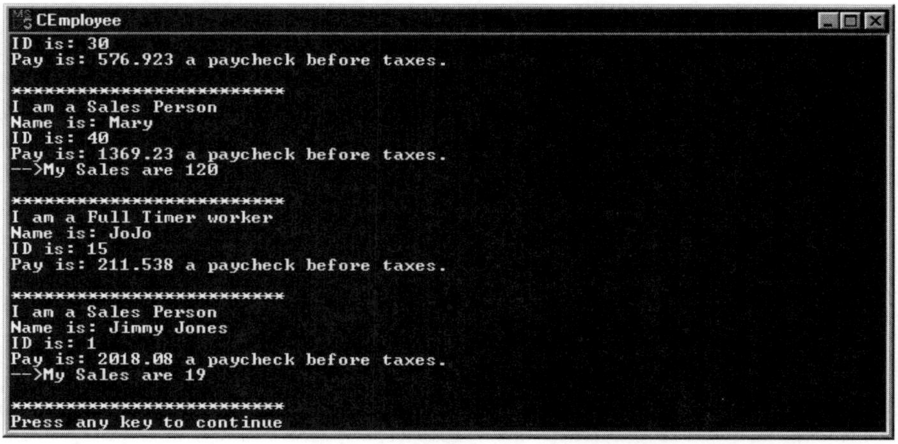

Figure 1-21:
The completed
employee
application.

```
MS CEmployee                                                    _□X
ID is: 30
Pay is: 576.923 a paycheck before taxes.

****************************
I am a Sales Person
Name is: Mary
ID is: 40
Pay is: 1369.23 a paycheck before taxes.
-->My Sales are 120

****************************
I am a Full Timer worker
Name is: JoJo
ID is: 15
Pay is: 211.538 a paycheck before taxes.

****************************
I am a Sales Person
Name is: Jimmy Jones
ID is: 1
Pay is: 2018.08 a paycheck before taxes.
-->My Sales are 19

****************************
Press any key to continue
```

Here is the complete code behind main():

```
// The main() loop.
const int MAX_EMPS = 4;
void main(void)
{
    // A cookie to see if we have a salesperson.
    EMP_TYPE e;
    // Make an array of Employee pointers.
    CEmployee* theStaff[MAX_EMPS];
    theStaff[0] = new CFTEmployee(30, "Fred", 30000);
    theStaff[1] = new CSalesEmployee(40, "Mary", 40000, 120);
    theStaff[2] = new CFTEmployee(15, "JoJo", 11000);
    theStaff[3] = new CSalesEmployee(1, "Jimmy Jones", 100000, 19);
    // Now go through each member in the array and
    // pull out the stats.
    for(int i = 0; i < MAX_EMPS; i++)
    {
        // Which class is here?
        cout << theStaff[i]->DisplayClassType(&e) << endl;
        // Get name.
        cout << "Name is: " << theStaff[i]->GetName() << endl;
        // Get ID.
        cout << "ID is: " << theStaff[i]->GetID() << endl;
        // Get pay.
        cout << "Pay is: " << theStaff[i]->GetPay()
                << " a paycheck before taxes." << endl;
        // Let's see if we have a salesperson (using our custom RTTI).
        if(e == SP)
        {
            cout << "-->My Sales are "
                    << ((CSalesEmployee*)theStaff[i])->GetNumberOfSales()
                    << endl << flush;
        }
        // Just to make it look nice.
        cout << endl;
        cout << "****************************" << endl;
    }
```

```
        // clean up.
        delete [] *theStaff;
}
```

Now that we have the core elements of C++ class construction firm in our mind, we will finish up this chapter by reviewing template-based programming. As I am sure you are aware, the Active Template Library makes substantial use of C++ templates in order to provide a number of core COM services. Our exploration of ATL begins in Chapter 6, but what would a C++ review be without a mention of generic template-based programming?

Reviewing Template-Based Programming

Inheritance is the classical way to reuse source code in OO-based languages. By creating base and derived class relationships, we are able to create hierarchies of classes. As we have seen, base classes tend to have a number of virtual and/or pure virtual functions that enforce a given behavior to each descendent. This is a good thing, of course, as the base class(es) can contain code which is easily reused (and possible reinterpreted) down the inheritance chain. However, there is another form of code reuse.

C++ templates allow you to create classes based off parameterized types. For example, imagine you were told to create a C++ class that can maintain a dynamic array of integers. You might begin by creating a C++ class that defines a private array of integers, which may be manipulated using a small set of public methods:

```
// The dynamic integer class.
class CIntArray
{
public:
    void Add(int newInt);       // Insert a new int into the array.
    void Remove(int index);     // Remove int at position 'index'.
    int Count();                // Get the current size of the array.
    int Item(int index);        // Retrieve item 'index' from the array.
private:
    int* m_arrayOfInts;         // Array of integers.
    int m_position;             // Current position in the array.
    int m_size;                 // Current size of the array.
};
```

As you can see, this C++ class allows the developer to add, remove, and reference a specific index in the array, as well as obtain the current count. Life appears well.

Now assume you wish to create another dynamic array class which operates on an underlying array of floats rather than integers. One option you have is to create another class, CFloatArray, which has the same member functions as CIntArray but manipulates a suitable array of floats:

```
// The dynamic float class.
class CFloatArray
{
public:
    void Add(float newFloat);   // Insert a new float into the array.
    void Remove(int index);     // Remove float at position 'index'.
    int Count();                // Get the current size of the array.
    float Item(int index);      // Grab out item 'index' from the array.
private:
```

```
    float* m_arrayOfFloats;    // Array of floats.
    int m_position;            // Current position in the array.
    int m_size;                // Current size of the array.
};
```

This approach leaves you with two C++ classes that essentially do the same thing. The situation could grow worse if you decide to create unique classes to represent shorts, longs, strings (char*), and so forth. Template-based programming allows you to create a generic C++ shell, which fills in the specifics by using a placeholder for various parts of the actual class definition. In many respects, template programming has a similar feel to C macros (#define). However, unlike magic macros, templates are type safe. To create a C++ template that abstracts away the differences between floats, integers, __int64s, shorts, doubles, and longs (among others), you could create the following:

```
// A C++ template which operates on 'some type'.
template <typename Type>
class CArray
{
public:
    void Add(Type newType);    // Insert a new Type into the array.
    void Remove(int index);    // Remove Type at position 'index'.
    int Count();               // Get the current size of the array.
    Type Item(int index);      // Grab out item 'index' from array.
private:
    Type * m_arrayOfTypes;     // An array of some type.
    int m_position;            // Position in the array.
    int m_size;                // Current size of the array.
};
```

Using a C++ template, we do not need to create a separate class to represent the minor code variations used to work with arrays of different types. The CArray class takes a single template parameter named Type, which is used as a placeholder throughout the class definition:

```
// Create some dynamic arrays using the CArray template.
void main()
{
    // Make an array of integers.
    CArray<int> intArray;
    intArray.Add(90);
    cout << "Int array has: " << intArray.Count() << "items inside." << endl;
    // Make an array of floats.
    CArray<float> floatArray;
    floatArray.Add(30.8);
    cout << "Float array has: " << floatArray.Count() << " items inside." << endl;
}
```

The beauty of this approach is that we can delay the specification of the type of data operated on until building the array template. In this example, the Type placeholder will "expand" to an integer, float, or what have you, based on the needs of the client.

Templates as Containers

We may also specify a C++ class as a template parameter. This approach allows us to create a generic "collection" object. For example, assume we have a number of C++ classes each representing a geometric shape. CHexagon, CSquare, and CCircle each have a class definition that looks like the following:

```
// Each of our shape classes defines a Draw() method.
class CHexagon
{
public:
    void Draw();             // Draw this shape.
    CHexagon();
    virtual ~CHexagon();
};
```

 The shapes template example is included on your CD-ROM under the Labs\Chapter 01\DrawTemplate subdirectory.

Now assume we wanted to create a template class which could take as a parameter any valid shape object, and invoke the correct Draw() method based on the placeholder class:

```
// CDrawTemplate renders any item defining a Draw() method.
template< typename TShape >
class CDrawTemplate
{
private:
    TShape theShape;
public:
    CDrawTemplate (){}
    virtual ~ CDrawTemplate (){}
    // Draw whichever shape we have.
    void DrawTheShape()
    {
        theShape.Draw();
    }
};
```

A C++ client could now send in any object containing a Draw() method as a template parameter to the CDrawTemplate class:

```
// Draw some objects with our C++ template.
int main(int argc, char* argv[])
{
    // Create a templatized hexagon.
    CDrawTemplate<CHexagon> h;
    h.DrawTheShape();
    // Create a templatized square.
    CDrawTemplate<CSquare> s;
    s.DrawTheShape();
    return 0;
}
```

If we assume each shape object implements Draw() using a simple cout statement, we could assume the output shown in Figure 1-22:

Figure 1-22:
Template
output.

When we begin our examination of the Active Template Library we will see just how help-ful templates can be to lighten the burden of creating boilerplate COM code. Until Chapter 6, just keep in mind that C++ templates can be used to create a generic class that is able to operate on "some type" specified by the template parameter set.

In these trivial examples, we examined templates specifying a single parameter. This is not a requirement of template-based programming. In fact, some ATL template classes take up to eight different parameters, each of which serves as a placeholder used through-out the class implementation.

That wraps up our rapid-fire C++ refresher. Chapter 2 will introduce you to another popular programming paradigm: interface-based development. The interface is an odd little creature living at the dead center of the COM universe, whose importance warrants a full discussion.

Chapter Summary

This first chapter was a whirlwind review of the cornerstones of classic object technology: encapsulation, inheritance, and polymorphism. Encapsulation allows us to scope the visi-bility of a class definition using the **public**, **private**, and **protected** keywords. Private data may be set and retrieved safely using public accessors and mutators, which enforce data safety.

Inheritance comes in two flavors: classical inheritance (Is-A) and the containment/del-egation model (Has-A). In either case, we are able to compose new classes based on existing ones. Closely related to inheritance is polymorphism. Polymorphism allows our objects to act as individuals in a system, responding in their own way to the same mes-sage. If an OOL supports classical inheritance, we may make use of either classical or ad hoc polymorphism. If the OOL in question does not support classical inheritance, we are stuck with ad hoc polymorphism, containment, and delegation.

Finally, we reviewed the use of C++ templates. Templates provide a way to create a generic shell operating on "some type." This approach to class design provides another form of source code reuse and allows developers to create classes that are not fully speci-fied until the object is created and specified by the calling syntax. As we will see beginning in Chapter 6, ATL makes substantial use of templates to help minimize redundant and boilerplate COM code.

Chapter 2

Interface•Based Programming

Objectives:

■ **Learn the philosophy of interface-based development.**

■ **Create and implement interfaces using C++.**

■ **Describe how interfaces provide encapsulation and polymorphism.**

■ **Understand "published" interfaces and how to version them safely.**

■ **Develop custom APIs to retrieve interface pointers.**

■ **Understand interface inheritance and interface hierarchies.**

The underlying backbone of COM is the concept of the *interface*. You simply cannot create COM solutions without them. Often, making the move from traditional OOP to the interface-based programming paradigm can be a bit jarring (just about as much so as the initial move from SP to OOP). Although COM is hopelessly dependent upon the use of interfaces, we can most certainly work with them in their own right.

To help you make the move into interface programming as gracefully as possible, this entire chapter examines the interface from a C++, and non-COM, perspective. By the end of this chapter you will be able to create and use C++ objects supporting multiple interfaces, and understand how the separation of interface from implementation is a modern refinement of classical OOP and the foundation of all things COM.

A Single Public Sector

In the previous chapter, you learned (or were reminded) that every C++ class defines a public sector (also known as the public interface of a class). In simplest terms, the *public sector* is the set of methods defined by a class that are accessible from an object instance. For example, the CCar class depicted in Figure 2-1 contains a public interface containing exactly three methods:

Figure 2-1:
A class with a
single public
interface.

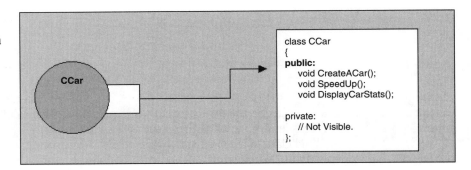

```
class CCar
{
public:
    void CreateACar();
    void SpeedUp();
    void DisplayCarStats();

private:
    // Not Visible.
};
```

So far we have created classes with a modest public interface, exposing only a handful of methods. Often C++ classes, especially those found in commercial class libraries, can define a huge number of methods in a class's single public interface. From a practical viewpoint, an extensive public sector can be intimidating to the object user, as a very large surface area is covered in a single class. From a design standpoint, a single large public sector can often be broken into logical individual "interfaces" providing a more manageable and scaleable object architecture.

Factoring a Single Public Interface into Discrete Interfaces

Let's examine a familiar class that has a mammoth public interface, and experiment with an alternative interface-based design. The CWnd class of MFC is the base class for all dialogs, graphical user interface (GUI) widgets, frames, and views in the library. This single class consists of over 100 methods the object user may call directly from an object instance. As you examine the full set of methods exposed by CWnd, you may realize that this mass of functions could be partitioned into smaller logical subsets. In fact, here is the online help listing from Microsoft Developer Network (MSDN) showing the various categories (e.g., logical subsets) of CWnd's functionality:

Figure 2-2:
A massive
public interface,
listed by related
functionality.

MSDN Library - July 1999
File Edit View Go Help

Show Locate Previous Next Back Forward Stop Refresh Home Print

CWnd Class Members

Initialization	Dialog-Box Item Functions	Initialization Message Handlers
Window State Functions	Data-Binding Functions	System Message Handlers
Window Size and Position	Menu Functions	General Message Handlers
Window Access Functions	Tool Tip Functions	Control Message Handlers
Update/Painting Functions	Timer Functions	Input Message Handlers
Coordinate Mapping Functions	Alert Functions	Nonclient-Area Message Handlers
Window Text Functions	Window Message Functions	MDI Message Handlers
Scrolling Functions	Clipboard Functions	Clipboard Message Handlers
Drag-Drop Functions	ActiveX Controls	Menu Loop Notification
Caret Functions	Overridables	

As mentioned, a large public interface can be intimidating to an object user. If you don't believe me, just create an instance of the CWnd class from within an MFC project, and apply the dot operator. The Visual C++ IntelliSense kicks in, displaying a drop-down list that scrolls for a <u>very</u> long time. While it is true that CWnd does contain methods that "belong together" (they are all window-related methods), it should be clear that this one class might be overburdened with a bit too much responsibility. Rather than exposing a single mammoth public interface to the object user, the class could expose a collection of interfaces, each with a well-defined set of semantically related functions.

Imagine that the CWnd class of MFC exposed a collection of interfaces such as IWindowText, IWindowMenu, IWindowInit, IWindowCoordinate, and so forth. Each of these interfaces would express a single set of related functions. Obviously, an interface named IWindowMenu would contain methods that manipulate a menu, IWindowInit may contain a number of creation-related methods, and so forth.

If this were the case (it isn't; the MFC library was not constructed using inter-face-based techniques), the object user could request access to a specific interface on the CWnd object and gain access to only the subset of functionality needed at that time. This would certainly scale down the burden of the object users, as they are working only with a specific aspect (e.g., behavior) of the class. When the user of the CWnd object desires another aspect supported by the class, he or she may obtain another interface from the object and access that set of related methods.

An Interface Expresses a Specific Behavior

Interface-based programming encourages the reuse of behavior. Once an interface has been designed, other classes could choose to implement it as well. For example, a status bar might like to support the functionality defined in IWindowText, a dialog class might support the IWindowInit interface to provide support for creating and initializing child controls, and so on. This approach can also help the object user, as he or she could begin to logically associate behaviors to classes supporting the same interface. One might say, "Hey, this class supports IWindowCoordinate, therefore I can call this set of methods." As we will see, interfaces inject polymorphic behavior into a system.

Before we get too far along, we need a working definition. For the time being, we will define an interface to be the following:

An *interface* is a collection of semantically related functions, which describe a single and unique behavior that may be supported by a class.

Note: By convention, interfaces begin with an "I-" prefix. Stick to this convention, as you will soon see that an interface is an abstract entity that is never directly creatable.

Diagramming Classes with Multiple Interfaces

A standard notation used to diagram a class that supports numerous interfaces is the "lolli-pop" or "jack" notation. Each interface supported by a class is represented by a separate jack (a.k.a. lollipop), representing a unique behavior the class provides. The rounded rect-angle in the diagram represents some implementation of the supported interfaces. Note that the implementation of the interfaces is irrelevant as far as the object user is concerned. All the user of the object is concerned with is which interfaces (a.k.a. behaviors) are supported. Our new mythical interface-based CWnd class is diagrammed in Figure 2-3:

Figure 2-3:
Factoring a
single interface
into discrete
interfaces.

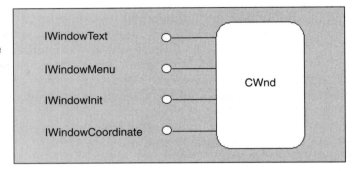

Figure 2-3:
Factoring a
single interface
into discrete
interfaces.

COM is an interface-based programming paradigm. Everything in COM revolves around the creation and implementation of interfaces, and you will see diagrams like this all throughout the COM literature. In many ways, an interface feels much like a public interface of a standard C++ class, with two important (and critical) exceptions: Interfaces <u>never</u> provide an implementation and <u>never</u> define state.

Defining an Interface Using C++

So then, an interface expresses a single, discrete functionality that a class may choose to support. This functionality is defined by a set of semantically related methods. It is the responsibility of the class, however, to decide exactly <u>how</u> the methods of a given interface will be implemented. The interface is used only to describe the "form" imposed on a class that is supporting it. If this sounds familiar, it should.

Recall that abstract base classes define pure virtual functions—methods that describe the general flavor of a functionality, but provide no implementation. The implementation details are determined by the derived subclass. Consider a C3DRect class inheriting a pure virtual method named Draw() defined in CShape:

```
// An abstract base class.
class CShape
{
public:
    virtual void Draw() = 0;
    // Other state data and member functions (public, private or protected).
};
// Simple sub class.
class C3DRect : public CShape
{
public:
    // Subclasses must implement pure virtual base class functions.
    virtual void Draw()
    {
        // Code to draw 3D rectangle
```

```
      }
};
```

Interfaces, from a syntactical level, are a collection of pure virtual functions (as you may have guessed). Interfaces do not define any state associated with the behavior; in other words, interfaces have no public, private, or protected data sector. However, a class supporting the interface may (and often will) define any number of data types to flesh out the implementation details of the interface methods. As you can see, an interface only describes <u>what</u> can be done. The supporting class defines <u>how</u> it is accomplished.

   Also note this: Supporting an interface is an all-or-nothing proposition. The implementing class cannot be selective when supporting interfaces—it is obligated to provide functionality for all defined methods. This should make sense. As an interface is a collection of pure virtual functions, the supporting class must define every member, or else it too will be an abstract class! We can define an interface in C++ quite easily:

```
// This interface describes generic drawing behavior.
interface IDraw
{
      virtual void Draw() = 0;
};
```

Truth be told, interfaces can be defined in C++ using the **class**, **struct**, or **interface** keywords. The benefit of using the **struct** or **interface** keyword is that the default visibility is public, where the default visibility of a class is private. The **interface** keyword is actually a typedef for **struct**, as defined in <objbase.h>. This is a core COM header file which we will make use of throughout the book, often indirectly by simply including <windows.h>. Here is the formal definition of interface:

```
// <objbase.h>
// The 'interface' keyword is not an inherit C++ keyword, but a redefinition of the
// C++ 'struct' keyword.
#define interface struct
```

Therefore, you may define the IDraw interface in the following syntax as well, both of which are logically equivalent to the **interface** keyword, and result in the same physical form (and implied behavior) imposed on the supporting class:

```
// Defining an interface with the class keyword.
// You must use the 'public' specifier when using the class keyword.
class IDraw
{
public:
      virtual void Draw() =0;
};
// Defining an interface with the struct keyword.
// Don't need to use the 'public' specifier, as a struct is automatically public.
struct IDraw
{
      virtual void Draw() = 0;
};
```

In keeping with the spirit of interface-based programming, we will stick with the **interface** keyword more often than not in this book (just be sure to #include <objbase.h> or <windows.h> in your project workspaces to grab the correct definition).

Supporting Interfaces in C++

When a class wishes to support a behavior specified by an interface, we make use of C++ public inheritance. Supporting a single interface looks like a simple case of subclassing using classical inheritance except this time we inherit no state and no implementation. We only inherit a set of pure virtual functions which we then may implement in a manner unique to our particular class.

As mentioned, a single class may expose any number of interfaces. C++ provides two mechanisms that allow a class to support numerous interfaces: multiple inheritance (MI) and/or a technique called *nested classes*. Either approach still yields the same result: an ordered layout in memory (vTables) supported by a given class. ATL uses MI to support multiple interfaces, whereas MFC uses the nested class technique. In Chapter 8 we will

see how nested classes can be used to resolve method name clashes (for example, what if your class supports two interfaces, each of which defines a method with the same name?). We will examine how to support multiple interfaces using MI, but for now here is the C3DRect class supporting the single IDraw interface, diagrammed in Figure 2-4.

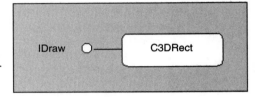

Figure 2-4: Our C3DRect class.

We may express this relationship in code as the following:

```
// C3DRect supports the IDraw interface.
class C3DRect : public IDraw
{
public:
    // No longer pure virtual.
    void Draw() { // Add your code here. }
private:
    // Any data points or private helper functions
    // the C3DRect class may need to draw itself.
};
```

Because the IDraw interface is completely abstract, C3DRect is now required to implement each method defined within it, which in this case happens to be exactly one. As you recall from Chapter 1, if we do not implement the methods of IDraw, we have a non-creatable abstract class.

> **Note:** This is worth repeating: What makes interface-based programming unique from traditional object-based development is the key point that interfaces never provide implementation, state data, or private helper functions. This is much unlike a traditional abstract base class which could provide all of the above, as well as a set of virtual functions.

Now that we can create and implement interfaces in C++, we need to take a look at what this new approach to class design gives us. In other words, "Why would I do this?" We have already seen how interface-based classes ease the burden of the object user. Next, let's examine how interfaces give us deeper encapsulation and a new approach to polymorphism.

Interfaces Provide Deeper Encapsulation

A core trait of interface-based programming is that object users can <u>only</u> access the object's functionality through the set of supported interfaces, not from the object instance itself. In COM development, clients never directly create object instances. Instead objects are created behind the curtains using functions of the COM library. These library functions return a requested interface to the client, leaving the user completely encapsulated from the details of the object's implementation, location, and activation.

As you recall from the previous chapter, when a class defines virtual functions, the C++ compiler silently inserts a hidden vPtr data member, which points to the vTable of the object. The vTable in turn points to the address of the function implementation. Every supported interface results in a new vPtr/vTable defined by the class. Interfaces, being a collection of pure virtual functions, enforce a physical layout on the object. To illustrate, let's create an additional interface for our graphical library named IShapeEdit:

```
// IShapeEdit provides behavior to modify an existing shape.
enum FILLTYPE { HATCH = 0, SOLID = 1, POLKADOT = 2 };
interface IShapeEdit
{
      virtual void Fill (FILLTYPE fType) = 0;  // Solid, hatch or polka dot enum.
      virtual void Inverse() = 0;
      virtual void Stretch(int factor) = 0;
};
```

This interface allows the object user to manipulate an existing shape in a number of ways. If we extend the functionality of C3DRect to support the IShapeEdit interface, we have now changed the physical layout of its vTables. Using standard multiple inheritance, we may modify the class definition to support IDraw and IShapeEdit as so:

```
// Added support for another interface using MI.
class C3DRect :public IDraw,
              public IShapeEdit
{
public:
      // IDraw interface methods.
      void Draw();
      // IShapeEdit interface methods.
      void Fill (FILLTYPE fType);
      void Inverse();
      void Stretch(int factor);
private:
      // State data used to give life to interface methods.
};
```

C3DRect now has a layout that looks like the following:

Figure 2-5: Internal layout of C3DRect supporting two interfaces.

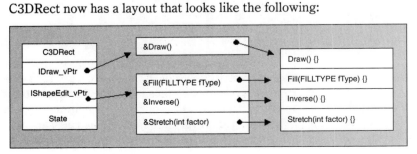

So what does all this have to do with encapsulation? Interface-based programming provides deeper encapsulation due to the simple fact that when an object user obtains an interface pointer from an object, that interface pointer is actually a pointer to the vPtr which points to the vTable! (Yes, the levels of indirection are staggering at first.) Given Figure 2-5, you can see that if a client has a pointer to IDraw, it may only access the members in the IDraw vTable. Clients holding IShapeEdit* variables have access to members in the IShapeEdit vTable.

If that isn't encapsulation, I am not sure what is. The client only holds a pointer to our class's vTable pointer, which contains no state and no implementation. Interface-based programming makes a clear distinction between the interface and the underlying implementation. In short, the interface is a first-class citizen in COM development. Of course we still have not addressed the issues of:

- How are these objects created?
- How does an object user obtain a given interface?
- How can an object user dispose of an object, if it did not directly create it?

We will be building our own limited interface-based API to address the questions above, mimicking the behavior found in the COM library, but first let's look at how the interface provides us with polymorphic behavior.

Interfaces Provide Polymorphic Behavior

Interfaces provide yet another way to bring polymorphic activity into our systems. Because interfaces provide only the "what" and not the "how" of a set of related methods, every class supporting the interface is allowed to implement the methods on its own terms. In Figure 2-6, we have three classes supporting the IDraw interface:

Figure 2-6:
Polymorphism
with IDraw.

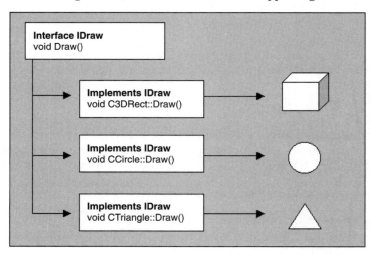

The implementation code used to render the images is of no importance to the interface user. In true COM development, this proposition becomes even more interesting as the objects supporting IDraw may be written in any number of languages, and may be located across the wire on a distant machine. From the user's perspective all that is known is the object supports a well-defined interface for drawing (IDraw) and if calls are made, the object responds.

Even though we have not yet looked at ways to obtain a given interface pointer, assume we have at our disposal some API functions that return IDraw pointers from various objects. An object user may create arrays of these interface pointers, and ask each shape to draw itself using interface-based polymorphism:

```
// Create an array of IDraw pointers.
IDraw* iFace[3];
// Get IDraw interface from some objects.
iFace[0] = GetIDrawFromCircle();
iFace[1] = GetIDrawFromSquare();
iFace[2] = GetIDrawFromTriangle();
// Now draw each one using the IDraw interface.
for (int i = 0; i < 3; i++)
    iFace[i]->Draw();
```

Interface pointers may work as parameters to functions as well, again providing polymorphism. For example, imagine that we have created an instance of each graphic object, and obtained access to the related IDraw interface. We might then write a function that takes a single IDraw pointer as the sole parameter. In this way, the function can operate with any object at all, as long as it supports the IDraw interface:

```
// This function can be sent any IDraw compatible object.
void RenderAShape(IDraw* pdrawObj)
{
    // Call the Draw method of the IDraw interface.
    pdrawObj->Draw();
}
```

Declaring Interface Variables

You should understand that we could never make an instance of an interface, just as we cannot make an instance of an abstract base class. In either case, however, we can make pointers to them. Therefore, you will never see code like this in the COM universe (in fact, you won't even compile):

```
// Can't make an instance of an interface!
IDraw theDrawer;        // Error!
```

To help your object users along, a common practice is to create a typedef for your interfaces that automatically accounts for the pointer's necessity. Many of the core COM interfaces (IUnknown, IDispatch, IClassFactory, and so on) include such a typedef, and you may wish to provide your own as well. Thus, given the existing IDraw interface definition, you may add the following typedef:

```
// MyInterfaces.h
typedef LPDRAW IDraw*;
```

The object user can then make use of this when working with your objects:

```
// Object user code.
#include "myinterfaces.h"
LPDRAW pDraw;
pDraw = GetIDrawFromTriangle();
pDraw->Draw();
```

Interfaces Define a Contract

If you have not noticed by now, interfaces add a level of indirection to the programming world. Object users drive around an object through a vTable pointer, and have the power to treat all objects supporting a given interface the same way using interface-based polymorphism. By using some API level support, we have isolated the object user from the activation details of the given object as well, providing a deeper level of encapsulation. In order for users to work with objects in this way, we need a set of rules to abide by.

As you read more and more about interface-based programming you are bound to run into the term *contract*. This sounds much more corporate than it really is. A contract in real-world terms involves at least two parties who make a solid and binding agreement. In interface-based programming, the contract revolves around the object user (henceforth referred to as the *client*) and the object itself (often called the *coclass* in COM speak).

The interface contract is very clear. The object itself agrees to the following:

"Once an object supports a given interface, the object in question must always continue to support the interface without modification (e.g., you can't go changing the names or parameter sets of the methods, you can't reorder the methods, and you certainly can't rename the interface itself)."

The client agrees to the following terms in the same contract:

"I, as a client, will abide by the calling conventions as set forth by the interfaces and methods contained within them."

By far, the most weight in this contract is placed on the object. First, an object needs to be quite certain the interface it is going to support will suit its needs, as once the interface is supported, there is no going back.

How to Keep Clients Happy: The Published Interface

Think about this contract in the terms of a C++ class library. Have you ever worked with a team using an in-house class library? What happens when some rogue programmer decides to check out some files from source code control and changes the method names, parameter arguments, or worse yet the name of the class? Of course, each and every line of code using that object instance is broken, and massive recompiles ensue. Interface-based programming explicitly states that once an interface is *published* (which may be defined as at least one object supports it and one client is using it), it becomes a fixed constant in the universe. If we did not enforce this rule, we will break clients, just like the rogue programmer.

The notion of the interface contract is extremely important in COM development, as the physical distance between a client and the object may span different processes or even different machines. If some programmer in sunny California changes an interface of some COM object you are using from frigid Minnesota, we have problems.

Of course, over time, interfaces will need to adapt. An interface such as IDraw may work for the time being, but what if you wish to extend the functionality of this interface to support drawing to an off-screen buffer or to render the image to a printer? In other words, how can we extend an object's functionality without breaking existing clients?

Versioning Published Interfaces

Once an interface is published, we cannot change it in any way. IDraw is a good start to a set of drawing related behaviors, but what if we wish to add in the support mentioned above? The standard way to extend an interface is to assemble a new interface deriving from an existing one. This technique is called *interface inheritance*. Realize that unlike classical inheritance, we do not inherit any state or implementation, rather we are simply augmenting an existing interface layout with our own.

The common naming convention used when extending an interface is to append numerical suffixes to the root name of the original interface (IDraw, IDraw2, IDraw3, ..., IDraw44). Here then is IDraw2, which derives from IDraw, and therefore inherits the pure virtual Draw() method:

```
// Interface inheritance
interface IDraw2 : public IDraw
{
      virtual void DrawToMemory() = 0;
      virtual void DrawToPrinter() = 0;
};
```

As seen in Figure 2-7, the layout for IDraw2 would be appended to that of IDraw:

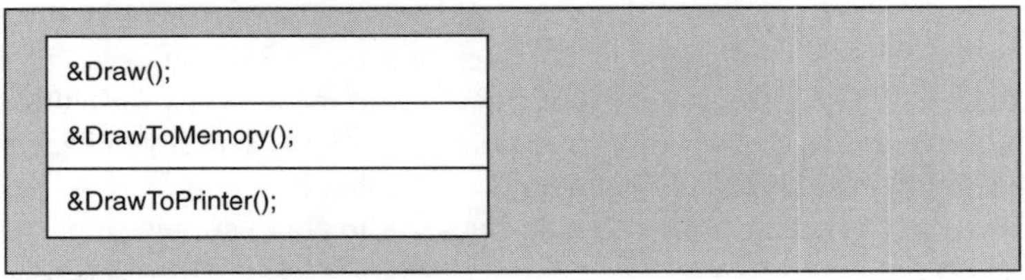

Figure 2-7:
Layout of
IDraw2.

Now assume that IDraw2 has become versioned as well. If we wish to safely extend IDraw2 to support the ability to draw to a metafile, we might write the following interface:

```
// Extending IDraw one level further...
interface IDraw3 : public IDraw2
{
      virtual void DrawToMetaFile() = 0;
};
```

This gives us the following layout for IDraw3:

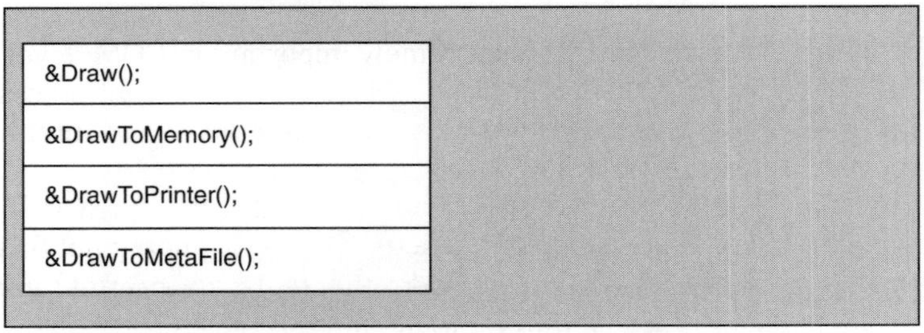

Figure 2-8:
Layout of
IDraw3.

Now, what if we wish to create a class that supports all drawing behaviors defined by each of the interfaces above? We simply write a class definition such as:

```
// Brings in the layout of IDraw, IDraw2 & IDraw3
class C3DRectEx : public IDraw3
{
public:
      // IDraw + IDraw2 + IDraw3
      virtual void Draw();
      virtual void DrawToMemory();
      virtual void DrawToPrinter();
      virtual void DrawToMetaFile();
};
```

Notice that our class derives only from the *n*th-most (most derived) interface in the inheritance chain which indirectly brings in the functionality up the inheritance chain. You might be tempted to set up the class definition to look like this:

```
// This will not work...
class CMegaDrawer : public IDraw, public IDraw2, public IDraw3
{
      // Humm...
};
```

However, you will not compile, as IDraw3 would hide the shared members of IDraw2, and IDraw2 would hide the members of IDraw (this is a C++-ism, not a restriction imposed by interface-based development). C++ does allow virtual inheritance to avoid this very situation; however, it is not as clean (or obvious) as simply directly deriving from the *n*th-most interface. This is the standard approach used in COM, so we'll stick to it.

So, to summarize the correct way to version interfaces: When versioning a published interface, create interface hierarchies using numerical suffixes to mark a logical and safe extension. The class implementing the members in the chain simply implements the most derived member.

The Wrong Way to Version Interfaces

One question that might come about is "Why not just tack on additional methods to an existing interface?" Why bother with IDraw, IDraw2, and IDraw3 as individuals if we could simply append additional methods to the original IDraw interface:

```
// A poorly versioned interface.
interface IDraw
{
      // Original IDraw: Developed 3/24/99
      virtual void Draw() = 0;
      // Extension 2: Modified 7/13/99
      virtual void DrawToMemory() = 0;
      virtual void DrawToPrinter() = 0;
      // Extension 3: Modified 9/2/99
      virtual void DrawToMetaFile() = 0;
};
```

This seems correct. You might assume that existing clients using the original iteration of IDraw (which contained Draw() only) would never call the second and third extensions, and therefore would never break. You're right! Technically, you could preserve existing client code when extending the original IDraw interface. These clients would be blissfully unaware of any method beyond Draw(), and their code base would reflect that fact. But how about the other way around?

Imagine a brand new client has activated an object supporting the latest and greatest version of IDraw (containing all four methods). This client naturally assumes that <u>all</u> objects supporting IDraw support the same layout. After all, the interface contract states that once a server supports an interface, it cannot modify the interface in any way.

Now the same client creates another object also supporting IDraw; however, this particular object only defines IDraw supporting an order of the <u>first extension</u>. If the client calls DrawToMetaFile(), it is making calls into sweet oblivion, and a crash is imminent. We have just broken polymorphism, as seen in Figure 2-9.

Figure 2-9: Non-standard versioning == loss of polymorphism.

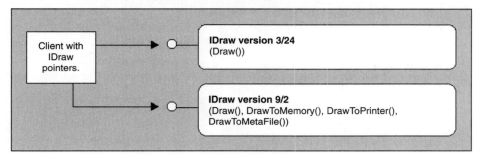

Of course, during the development cycle you will add and remove methods from the interfaces you are defining. Versioning an interface comes into play when you have published a given interface and wish to safely augment it, as specified by the contract.

Developing Interface Hierarchies

Hopefully you agree that we should always use standard interface versioning to safely extend a given interface. On a similar note, interface-based programming also gives you the ability to create hierarchies of interfaces to describe the relationships between related behaviors. This has the same flavor as building a traditional class library with the "no state, no implementation" provision.

Imagine you wanted to create a number of interfaces to represent different types of automobile behaviors. ICar may be a base interface that defines the standard behavior of any car, and may have pure virtual methods such as Go(), Stop(), WipeWindow(), and so forth. From ICar, you may derive other interfaces to model specific car types. I'll leave it to you to dream up the methods defined in each interface as you ponder Figure 2-10.

Figure 2-10: A hierarchy of related interfaces.

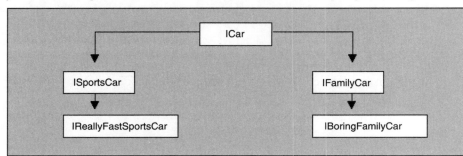

In C++, we can code the above interface hierarchy as such:

```
// The base interface: ICar.
interface ICar
{
    // All the ICar methods...
}
// ISportsCar.
interface ISportsCar : public ICar
{
    // ICar and ISportsCar methods...
}
// IReallyFastSportsCar.
interface IReallyFastSportsCar: public ISportsCar
{
    // ICar, ISportsCar and IReallyFastSportsCar methods...
}
// IFamilyCar.
interface IFamilyCar: public ICar
{
    // ICar and IFamilyCar methods...
}
// IBoringFamilyCar.
interface IBoringFamilyCar: public IFamilyCar
{
    // ICar, IFamilyCar and IBoringFamilyCar methods...
}
```

As before, a class wishing to support these behaviors would derive from the nth-most interface in the hierarchy, and acquire all functionality up the inheritance chain. For example, we may wish to model a standard sliding-door automobile as so:

```
// CMiniVan implements ICar, IFamilyCar and IBoringFamilyCar.
class CMiniVan : public IBoringFamilyCar
{
public:
    // ICar methods.
    // IFamilyCar methods.
    // IBoringFamilyCar methods.
};
```

We also may wish to develop a more exciting automobile by deriving from ISportsCar:

```
// This automobile implements ICar and ISportsCar
class CSportsSedan : public ISportsCar
{
public:
    // ICar methods.
    // ISportsCar methods.
};
```

When you are developing interface hierarchies, you are able to suggest an Is-A relationship within your objects. Without any offense intended: A minivan Is-A boring family car that Is-A family car which Is-A car.

Developing a Custom Interface-Based API: The Rect API

Let's shift gears now, and examine how we might provide functionality to work with classes supporting multiple interfaces. We will be developing our own custom API to create and extract interface pointers from the C3DRect object examined in this chapter. In "real COM" the API we use is collectively called the COM library, and our API will provide similar, but extremely limited, functionality. We will need to contend with the following:

- A client needs to be able to create a C3DRect object.
- A client must be able to ask for access to a given interface on the object.
- A client must be able to destroy the object when finished.

To keep things simple, our API will allow clients to work with a single global C3DRect pointer called ptheRect that may be created by the global CreateThe3DRect() function:

```
// Create the global 3D rectangle.
C3DRect* ptheRect = NULL;
void CreateThe3DRect()
{
    ptheRect = new C3DRect;
}
```

The DestroyThe3DRect() function simply deallocates the memory acquired from the CreateThe3DRect() call:

```
// Custom API to destroy a valid object
void DestroyThe3DRect()
{
    if(ptheRect)
      delete ptheRect;
}
```

No problems so far. A client can activate and deactivate the C3DRect object with these two functions of our 3DRect API. In the code block below, notice that the client does not directly create or destroy a C3DRect object:

```
// Clients create and destroy interface-based objects indirectly.
void main(void)
{
    // Activate the rect.
    CreateThe3DRect();
    // Terminate the rect.
    DestroyThe3DRect();
}
```

Identifying Interfaces

In order for a client to extract a specific interface from the object, we need to set up some further API level support. We will create a method that is able to return an interface pointer to a client. But first, we need a way to uniquely identify every possible interface used in our current application. One approach would be to assign a text literal to each interface and perform some sort of string comparisons to test which interface pointer to return.

A simpler approach (and the one taken by COM) is to use unique numerical values. Let's use numerical tags and define a custom enumeration called INTERFACEID:

```
// In our system, we assign a unique numerical value to each interface.
enum INTERFACEID
{
    IDRAW          = 0,      // ID for IDraw.
    ISHAPEEDIT     = 1,      // ID for IShapeEdit.
    IDRAW2         = 2,      // ID for IDraw2.
    IDRAW3         = 3       // ID for IDraw3.
};
```

Now that we have a way to refer to an interface by name in our code, we can create the final function in our API, GetInterfaceFrom3DRect(). This function will take two parameters: the requested interface identifier (from the INTERFACEID enum) and some place in memory to store the retrieved interface pointer. Furthermore, we will return a Boolean to indicate that the object did (or did not) support the requested interface. This will be handy for the client, as it can be used to test the success or failure of the function invocation (after all, who wants to call methods off a NULL pointer). Here is the prototype for the GetInterfaceFrom3DRect() function:

```
// Send in the number of the interface (INTERFACEID) and this method will return
// a valid interface pointer.
bool GetInterfaceFrom3DRect(INTERFACEID iid, void** iFacePtr);
```

Recall that an interface is really a pointer to a vPtr (which points to the vTable and to the implementation). We may generically represent any interface pointer as a void** parameter (an empty pointer to a pointer). Here is an implementation of the GetInterfaceFrom3DRect() API function:

```
// Dish out interface pointers to the client.
bool GetInterfaceFrom3DRect(INTERFACEID iid, void** iFacePtr)
{
    if(ptheRect == NULL){
        cout << "You forgot to create the 3DRect!" << endl;
        return false;
    }
    if(iid == IDRAW){        // They want access to IDraw.
        // Cast the client's pointer to the IDraw interface of ptheRect.
        *iFacePtr = (IDraw*) ptheRect;
        return true;
    }
    if(iid == ISHAPEEDIT) {// They want access to IShapeEdit.
        // Cast the client's pointer to the IShapeEdit interface of ptheRect.
        *iFacePtr = (IShapeEdit*) ptheRect;
        return true;
    }
    // I have no clue what you want.
    *iFacePtr = NULL;        // Just to be safe.
    cout << "C3DRect does not support interface ID: " << iid << endl;
    return false;
}
```

Hopefully, the inner workings of this function remind you of the custom RTTI example assembled in the previous chapter (remember the employee hierarchy?). What did we do when we wished to extract the essence of a salesperson from a generic CEmployee base class pointer? We performed an explicit cast:

```
// Do we have a sales employee?
if(e == SP)
{
    cout << "->My Sales are "
    << ((CSalesEmployee*)theStaff[i])->GetNumberOfSales()
    << endl;
}
```

We are doing the exact same operation here in the implementation of GetInterfaceFrom3DRect():

```
// Hand off pointer to IShapeEdit, and place it in the void** parameter (iFacePtr).
*iFacePtr = (IShapeEdit*) ptheRect;
```

When a client requests access to a given interface from the global C3DRect object, we first check if we support the required interface, and if so, we cast the empty void** to the given interface pointer by making an explicit cast. In effect, we are handing out the "IDraw-ness" or "IShapeEdit-ness" of the object. Don't let the slightly modified syntax fool you.

Using the 3D Rect API: Client Code

Using our brand new API, we may write client-side code that creates, destroys, and accesses interfaces off the C3DRect object. Here is our custom API in action:

```
// Client side code (assume proper #includes...)
void main(void)
{
    bool retVal = false;
    IDraw* pDraw = NULL;
    IDraw3* pDraw3 = NULL;
    IShapeEdit* pShapeEdit = NULL;
    // Activate the 3DRect object.
    CreateThe3DRect();
    // Can I get the IDraw interface from object?
    retVal = GetInterfaceFrom3DRect(IDRAW, (void**)&pDraw);
    if(retVal)
        pDraw->Draw();
    // Get IShapeEdit from object?
    retVal = GetInterfaceFrom3DRect(ISHAPEEDIT, (void**)&pShapeEdit);
    if(retVal){
        pShapeEdit->Fill(POLKADOT);
        pShapeEdit->Inverse();
        pShapeEdit->Stretch(90);
    }
    // Does this object support IDraw3?
    retVal = GetInterfaceFrom3DRect(IDRAW3, (void**)&pDraw3);
    if(retVal)
        pDraw3->DrawToMetaFile();
    // Done.
    DestroyThe3DRect();
}    // End of main.
```

In this code sample, a client first must activate the global C3DRect object using the CreateThe3DRect() function. To access a given interface from this object, we call the

GetInterfaceFrom3DRect() function, passing in an interface ID and an empty pointer to a pointer (void**) to hold the acquired interface. Well, actually we don't send it a void** directly. We send in a pointer to the interface variable (by reference) we are looking for and cast it to a void** (this quiets down the compiler):

```
// Get IShapeEdit from object?
retVal = GetInterfaceFrom3DRect(ISHAPEEDIT, (void**)&pShapeEdit);
```

GetInterfaceFrom3DRect() returns a Boolean, which the client may test against; if this call succeeds, we have access to each method in the requested interface. Finally, when we are all done with our C3DRect object, we indirectly destroy it with a call to DestroyThe3DRect().

Strange new world, don't you agree? While interface-based programming can take a bit of getting used to, there is no escaping it when developing and using COM components. To finish up this chapter, you will be creating and extending the interface-based API we have just examined. After this, you have prepped considerably for "real COM" development, as you will see beginning in Chapter 3, and throughout the remainder of this book.

Lab 2-1: Interface-Based Programming

The purpose of this lab is to get you prepped for real COM development. As you will see, the separation of interface from implementation is what COM-based programming is all about. This lab will give you the chance to define some interfaces in C++ as well as develop two classes supporting a number of these interfaces. You will create your own API that creates, destroys, and extracts interface pointers from a given object. Finally, you will have a chance to work with interface hierarchies and functions which take interface pointers as parameters.

The solution for this lab can be found on your CD-ROM under:
Labs\Chapter 02\Shapes

Step One: Prepare the Project Workspace and Interface Design

This lab will get you comfortable creating and using objects that support multiple interfaces. Begin by creating a new Win32 Console Application (an empty project) named **Shapes**, and insert a new text file named **main.cpp**. In this file, define an empty main loop.

Next, insert another new text file which will be used to define the interfaces in this program. Save it as **interfaces.h**. Now, in this new header file, define the IDraw and IShapeEdit interfaces. Be sure to wrap your interface definitions in #ifndef/#define/#endif syntax to prevent redefinition errors, as numerous project files will include interfaces.h. Finally, create an enumeration for use by the Fill() method of IShapeEdit:

```
// Don't forget to #include <windows.h> to use the interface keyword!
#ifndef _IFACES
#define _IFACES
enum FILLTYPE { HATCH = 0, SOLID = 1, POLKADOT = 2 };
interface IDraw
{
    virtual void Draw() = 0;
};
```

```
interface IShapeEdit
{
    virtual void Fill (FILLTYPE fType) = 0;
    virtual void Inverse() = 0;
    virtual void Stretch(int factor) = 0;
};
#endif // _IFACES
```

Step Two: Implement the C3DRect Class

Insert a new C++ class into your project named **C3DRect**, which supports both the IDraw and IShapeEdit interfaces using standard C++ multiple inheritance:

```
// C3DRect supports IDraw and IShapeEdit.
class C3DRect : public IDraw, public IShapeEdit
{
public:
    C3DRect();
    virtual ~C3DRect();
    // IDraw
    virtual void Draw();
    // IShapeEdit
    virtual void Fill (FILLTYPE fType);
    virtual void Inverse();
    virtual void Stretch(int factor);
};
```

Go ahead and implement the inherited interface methods using simple cout statements. For example, here is a possible implementation of Fill():

```
// Print out the fill pattern.
void C3DRect::Fill(FILLTYPE fType)
{
    char* FillString[] = {"Hatch", "Solid", "Polkadot"};
    cout << "Filling a 3D Rect as: " << FillString[fType] << endl;
}
```

Use similar cout statements to implement Draw(), Inverse(), and Stretch(). You may also wish to place cout statements in the constructor and destructor of this class, which will be enlightening when running this lab later.

Step Three: Develop the Initial Rect API

We will be building our own API to create, destroy, and retrieve interface pointers from a C3DRect object. Insert another new file called **rectfunctions.h**. For simplicity, our API will only work with one object instance at a time, so go ahead and define a global level C3DRect pointer inside your new header file (yes this is contrived, but where better to be contrived than a lab?):

```
// Here is the global 3D rect.
C3DRect* ptheRect;
```

Now, add prototypes for the methods that activate and destroy the object on behalf of the client. Feel free to use the same signatures as used during this chapter:

```
// Functions to operate on the 3D rect.
void CreateThe3DRect();
void DestroyThe3DRect();
```

Implementing CreateThe3DRect() and DestroyThe3DRect() is trivial. Simply use the **new** and **delete** keywords to create and destroy the object:

```
// Creation function.
void CreateThe3DRect()
{
     // Create a 3d-rect.
     ptheRect = new C3DRect();
}
// Destroy the rectangle.
void DestroyThe3DRect()
{
     // See ya!
     delete ptheRect;
}
```

Now that we have provided a way to create and destroy the global rectangle, we need to provide a way to grab interfaces from an activated object. GetInterfaceFrom3DRect() needs to return an interface pointer to the client, based on an interface identifier. This function may be prototyped as:

```
// Global function used to fetch interface pointers.
bool GetInterfaceFrom3DRect(INTERFACEID iid, void** iFacePtr);
```

Add a new enumeration to your interfaces.h file called **INTERFACEID**. Assign a numerical cookie for the IDraw and IShapeEdit interfaces:

```
// Custom enumeration to identify each interface.
enum INTERFACEID { IDRAW = 0, ISHAPEEDIT = 1};
```

To implement GetInterfaceFrom3DRect(), examine the incoming interface ID, and perform an explicit cast against your global C3DRect object. Set the client's void** parameter to the result of this cast. For example:

```
// If we support the interface, fill the void** with the interface pointer.
*iFacePtr = (IShapeEdit*)ptheRect;
```

Be sure that your implementation of GetInterfaceFrom3DRect() returns a Boolean, which the client may test against before calling the methods of the requested interface. Again, here is a possible implementation of GetInterfaceFrom3DRect():

```
// This method returns interfaces to the client.
bool GetInterfaceFrom3DRect(INTERFACEID iid, void** iFacePtr)
{
     if(ptheRect == NULL){
          cout << "You forgot to create the 3DRect!" << endl;
          return false;
     }
     if(iid == IDRAW){      // They want access to IDraw.
          // Cast the client's pointer to the IDraw interface of ptheRect.
          *iFacePtr = (IDraw*) ptheRect;
          return true;
     }
     if(iid == ISHAPEEDIT) {// They want access to IShapeEdit.
          // Cast the client's pointer to the IShapeEdit interface of ptheRect.
          *iFacePtr = (IShapeEdit*) ptheRect;
          return true;
     }
```

```
        // I have no clue what they want.
        *iFacePtr = NULL;        // Just to be safe.
        cout << "C3DRect does not support interface ID: " << iid << endl<< endl;
        return false;
}
```

Step Four: Code the Initial Client

Let's take our C3DRect class out for a spin. Add code in your main loop to perform the following tasks:

```
// Fill up your main loop as so...
void main()
{
        // 1) Call CreateThe3DRect().
        // 2) Request interface pointers from the object by calling
        //    GetInterfaceFrom3DRect(). Ask the object
        //    for each interface defined in the INTERFACEID enumeration.
        // 3) Call the methods off the acquired interface pointer.
        // 4) Call DestroyThe3DRect() when you are finished.
}
```

This code was seen previously in the chapter, so take a look if you get stuck. When you have succeeded, move onto the next step where we will work with a versioned rectangle.

Step Five: Version an Existing Interface

Let's insert another new class into our existing project called **C3DRectEx**. This class will support a number of versioned interfaces: IDraw, IDraw2, and IDraw3. First off, define IDraw2 and IDraw3 in your interfaces.h file using interface inheritance. Using the interface hierarchy in Figure 2-11 as your guide, add in whichever extra interface methods you wish for IDraw2 and IDraw3 (in this lab I will assume the same interface methods described in the chapter text).

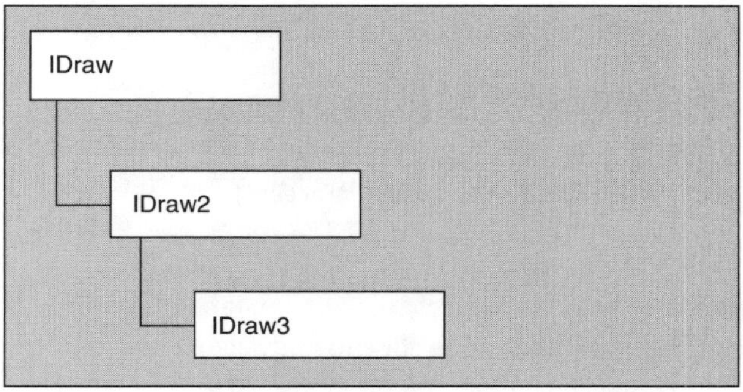

Figure 2-11: Drawing interface hierarchy.

```
// Additional interfaces in the drawing hierarchy.
interface IDraw2 : public IDraw
{
        virtual    void DrawToMemory() = 0;
        virtual    void DrawToPrinter() = 0;
};
interface IDraw3 : public IDraw2
{
```

```
      virtual     void DrawToMetaFile() = 0;
};
```

Next, update your INTERFACEID enumeration to identify these additional interfaces:

```
// A client could ask an object for any of the following interfaces.
enum INTERFACEID { IDRAW = 0, ISHAPEEDIT = 1, IDRAW2 = 2, IDRAW3 = 3};
```

Derive C3DRectEx directly from IDraw3. Remember—IDraw3 inherits the pure virtual methods from IDraw2 and IDraw as well. Therefore, your new rectangle class must support each and every method defined up the chain:

```
// C3DRectEx supports three interfaces.
class C3DRectEx : public IDraw3    // Brings in layout of IDraw3, IDraw2 & IDraw.
{
public:
    C3DRectEx();
    virtual ~C3DRectEx();
    // IDraw
    virtual void Draw();
    // IDraw2
    virtual void DrawToMemory();
    virtual void DrawToPrinter();
    // IDraw3
    virtual void DrawToMetaFile();
};
```

As we did for C3DRect, implement each method using simple cout statements. For example:

```
// Be sure each method of C3DRectEx identifies the method name and class
// in the cout statement.
void C3DRectEx::DrawToMemory()
{
    cout << "C3DRectEx::DrawToMemory" << endl;
}
```

Go ahead and build the application once C3DRectEx is fully assembled.

Step Six: Update the Rectangles API

As we now have two types of rectangles to worry about, we need to extend our custom API to work with C3DRectEx objects as well. Add the following functionality to your current rectfunctions.h file:

■ Declare a global C3DRectEx pointer.
■ Create a global function to set this pointer to a new instance.
■ Create another global function to destroy this instance.
■ Implement a function to test this object for the IDraw, IDraw2, and IDraw3 interfaces.

The prototypes mimic what we already have for the original C3DRect object:

```
// Here is the global 3DRectEx.
C3DRectEx* ptheRectEx;
// Functions to operate on the 3DRectEx object.
bool GetInterfaceFrom3DRectEx(INTERFACEID iid, void** iFacePtr);
void CreateThe3DRectEx();
void DestroyThe3DRectEx();
```

The GetInterfaceFrom3DRectEx() function must be able to return interface pointers to each version of IDraw. Go ahead and implement each new API function. As much of this code will be similar to your existing functions, feel free to leverage clipboard inheritance (just be very careful of copy/paste typos!). Here is the relevant code:

```
// The updated rectangle API functions.
void CreateThe3DRectEx()
{
    // Create a 3d-rect EX.
    ptheRectEx = new C3DRectEx();
}
void DestroyThe3DRectEx()
{
    // See ya.
    delete ptheRectEx;
}
bool GetInterfaceFrom3DRectEx(INTERFACEID iid, void** iFacePtr)
{
    if(ptheRectEx == NULL){
        cout << "You forgot to create the 3DRectEx!" << endl;
        return false;
    }
    if(iid == IDRAW){
        *iFacePtr = (IDraw*)ptheRectEx;
        return true;
    }
    if(iid == IDRAW2){
        *iFacePtr = (IDraw2*)ptheRectEx;
        return true;
    }
    if(iid == IDRAW3){
        *iFacePtr = (IDraw3*)ptheRectEx;
        return true;
    }
    // I have no clue what they want.
    *iFacePtr = NULL;
    cout << "C3DRectEX does not support interface ID: " << iid << endl << endl;
    return false;
}
```

Step Seven: Update the Client

With our new interfaces, class, and API methods in place, update main() to work with your C3DRectEx object and execute the program. Here is some possible client-side code to get you going:

```
// Interface client version two.
void main(void)
{
...
    // Make a 3DRectEx
    CreateThe3DRectEx();
    // Get interfaces from the RectEx object.
    GetInterfaceFrom3DRectEx(IDRAW, (void**)&pDraw);
    GetInterfaceFrom3DRectEx(IDRAW2, (void**)&pDraw2);
    GetInterfaceFrom3DRectEx(IDRAW3, (void**)&pDraw3);
```

```
// Use the interfaces!
pDraw2->DrawToMemory();
pDraw2->DrawToPrinter();
pDraw3->DrawToMetaFile();
pDraw->Draw();
// Kill the rectangle.
DestroyThe3DRectEx();
...
}
```

The new program should run like a champ (see Figure 2-12). We can now create objects supporting multiple interfaces and manipulate them with the Rect API. When we are all done with the object's functionality, we clean up by calling the correct DestroyXXX() method.

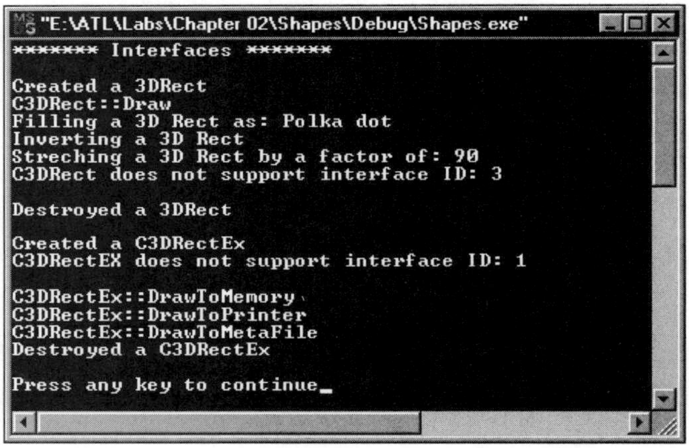

Figure 2-12:
Interface client
version two.

In the final step of this lab, we will extend the API with one final function that can work on any object supporting the IDraw interface. After this, it is on to "real COM" from here on out.

Step Eight: Interface-Based Polymorphism (or fun with pointers)

Recall that we achieve polymorphism through interface pointers. To test this behavior for yourself, add one final function to the Rect API that will draw any object supporting the IDraw interface:

```
// I am just waiting to draw something...
void ExerciseRect(IDraw* pDraw)
{
    cout << endl << "Drawing some IDraw compatible object..." << endl;
    pDraw->Draw();
    cout << endl;
}
```

Now, go back into your existing main loop, and send it the IDraw pointer you received from C3DRect to ExerciseRect() (before you call DestroyThe3DRect() of course):

```
// Get IDraw from Object.
retVal = GetInterfaceFrom3DRect(IDRAW, (void**)&pDraw);
// Draw it.
ExerciseRect(pDraw);
```

Next, send in the IDraw interface from the C3DRectEx object using the IDraw2 pointer:

```
// Take a valid IDraw2 pointer and cast it to an IDraw*.
ExerciseRect((IDraw*)pDraw2);
```

Here is the final output for the Shapes.exe lab (your run may look a bit different, depending on your cout statements and the order of method invocations):

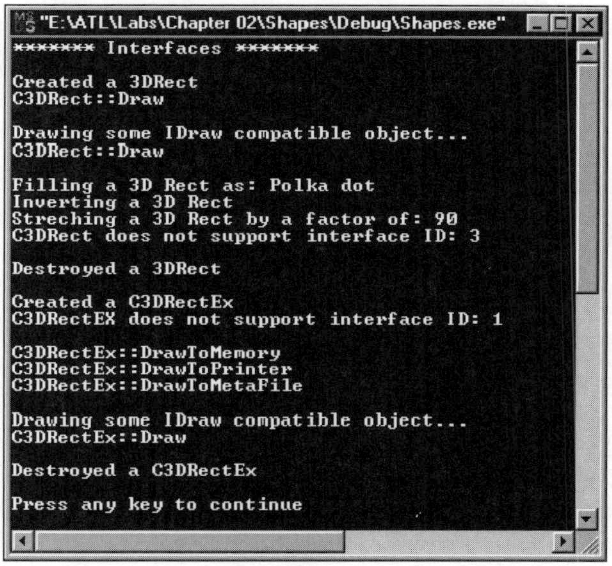

Figure 2-13:
The final client.

```
"E:\ATL\Labs\Chapter 02\Shapes\Debug\Shapes.exe"
******* Interfaces *******

Created a 3DRect
C3DRect::Draw

Drawing some IDraw compatible object...
C3DRect::Draw

Filling a 3D Rect as: Polka dot
Inverting a 3D Rect
Streching a 3D Rect by a factor of: 90
C3DRect does not support interface ID: 3

Destroyed a 3DRect

Created a C3DRectEx
C3DRectEX does not support interface ID: 1

C3DRectEx::DrawToMemory
C3DRectEx::DrawToPrinter
C3DRectEx::DrawToMetaFile

Drawing some IDraw compatible object...
C3DRectEx::Draw

Destroyed a C3DRectEx

Press any key to continue
```

Here is one possible iteration of the main() function:

```
// Your implementation may vary!
int main(void)
{
    bool retVal = false;
    cout << "******* Interfaces *******" << endl << endl;
    // Create an object to work with.
    CreateThe3DRect();
    IDraw* pDraw = NULL;
    IDraw2* pDraw2 = NULL;
    IDraw3* pDraw3 = NULL;
    IShapeEdit* pShapeEdit = NULL;
    // Get IDraw from Object.
    retVal = GetInterfaceFrom3DRect(IDRAW, (void**)&pDraw);
    if(retVal)
    {
        pDraw->Draw();
        ExerciseRect(pDraw);    // Send in a rect.
    }
    // Get IShapeEdit from object.
    retVal = GetInterfaceFrom3DRect(ISHAPEEDIT, (void**)&pShapeEdit);
    if(retVal)
    {
        pShapeEdit->Fill(POLKADOT);
```

```
        pShapeEdit->Inverse();
        pShapeEdit->Stretch(90);
}
// Get IDraw3?
retVal = GetInterfaceFrom3DRect(IDRAW3, (void**)&pDraw3);
if(retVal)
{
        pDraw3->DrawToMetaFile();
}
// Done.
DestroyThe3DRect();
// Now make a RectEx
CreateThe3DRectEx();
// Get interfaces
GetInterfaceFrom3DRectEx(IDRAW, (void**)&pDraw);
GetInterfaceFrom3DRectEx(IDRAW2, (void**)&pDraw2);
GetInterfaceFrom3DRectEx(IDRAW3, (void**)&pDraw3);
GetInterfaceFrom3DRectEx(ISHAPEEDIT, (void**)&pShapeEdit);
pDraw2->DrawToMemory();
pDraw2->DrawToPrinter();
pDraw3->DrawToMetaFile();
ExerciseRect((IDraw*)pDraw2);
DestroyThe3DRectEx();
return 0;
}
```

This lab has shown you how to create and implement interfaces in C++. What is missing, however, is a way to allow clients to make any number of objects (currently they can only work with a single global instance of either). Also, we do not have a tight connection between the global functions and the objects on which they operate. There is a lot of redundancy in our current API, which would rapidly grow out of control if we were to add more objects. These are just some of the issues COM resolves.

Chapter Summary

Interface-based programming is a refinement of classical OOP, and the foundation for all things COM. Logically, an interface is a collection of semantically related functions describing a specific behavior. Physically, interfaces are a named set of pure virtual functions. This new programming discipline marks a clear distinction between interface and implementation.

You have learned that interfaces provide deeper encapsulation than traditional OOP, as a client holding an interface pointer is in reality holding a pointer to the class's vPtr. By building custom APIs that are capable of creating, destroying, and retrieving interface pointers for clients, we have further isolated the client from numerous implementation details. As well, the interface provides us with polymorphism, as any class supporting a given interface may define how the interface methods are implemented. To a client, however, if an object supports a named interface, it can be treated the same way.

Finally, you learned that interfaces specify a "contract" between the client and object. This contract also provides us with a roadmap as to how we can version interfaces safely and adapt a class with the latest and greatest interface updates, as well as build interface hierarchies.

Part 2

Core COM

Chapter 3

The Component Object Model

Objectives:

■ Understand the benefits of the COM architecture.

■ Give your objects identity with IUnknown.

■ Develop COM interfaces, coclasses, and component housing.

■ Learn to manipulate string data in COM.

■ Understand COM class factories and IClassFactory.

■ Develop COM clients using the COM library.

■ Learn how to debug COM-based DLLs.

Microsoft's Component Object Model (COM) takes what you already know about objects and interfaces and extends them into the binary arena. Thus, everything you have read up to this point has prepared you to develop and use "real COM" components. In this chapter, you will learn exactly what the COM architecture is and the many benefits it provides. Next, you will have the chance to build an in-process COM server from the ground up using 100% straight C++. While you might see this as a slightly painstaking endeavor, it will provide a solid foundation for understanding ATL. Finally, you will learn about the various COM runtime services (the COM library, the service control manager, and the system registry) that provide the necessary run-time environment to create COM clients.

A Working Definition of the Component Object Model

As with most things, exact definitions of a specific thing vary depending on whom you ask (and often when you ask it). While this is also true when one attempts to describe the Component Object Model (COM), we will define COM as the following:

■ COM is an object-oriented, interface-based programming architecture.

■ COM is a set of run-time services.

First and foremost, COM is a programming architecture. When developers create software entities adhering to the COM specification, the end result is highly scaleable, reusable, and accessible binary objects. For example, all COM objects have the ability to be accessed by numerous languages, at various physical locations around the enterprise. Furthermore, developers may choose their *lingua franca* to develop the objects themselves. This allows developers skilled in a given language to stick to their language of choice when implementing and using COM components (management approval pending, of course).

 The companion CD contains Microsoft's official COM Specification. This white paper is regarded as the centerpiece of all COM literature. Be sure to check it out.

COM is not only a programming specification, but also a set of run-time services. COM provides a rich API called the COM library. The numerous services, functions, and data types defined in the COM library bootstrap the COM environment, much like our custom Rect API developed in Chapter 2. Unlike the Rect API, however, the COM library works with any COM-compliant object in a generic (a.k.a. polymorphic) manner. In addition to the COM library, the Service Control Manager (abbreviated SCM and pronounced "scum") and the system registry provide further COM run-time services.

The Benefits of COM

As noted, a COM-compliant object has a number of appealing traits. The following is a brief description of numerous COM benefits, which will be fully discussed throughout this book. Hopefully after reading this section, you will agree that COM is a very good thing indeed.

COM is Language Independent

COM is <u>not</u> a programming language. In fact, COM components may be written in any number of them. Although this book focuses on the use of C++ and ATL (a C++ COM template library), developers can create COM objects in C, Visual Basic, Delphi, Java, Visual FoxPro, COBOL, and so on. The only true requirement a language must satisfy in order to build COM-based solutions is that it is able to generate the binary layout (vTable) of a COM object.

Not only can developers build COM objects in any language, but the objects themselves may be accessed from any COM-enabled language. For example, you may have a team of hotshot C++ developers accessing COM objects written with Java. Web developers may use VBScript to access COM objects written in Delphi. COM encapsulates the inner implementation details of an object, including which language it was written in. All the COM object user sees is a set of well-defined interfaces supported by the object.

COM Provides Location Transparency

Before we can understand location transparency, we need to add three key concepts to our COM lexicon. COM objects and COM object users may be physically arranged in one of three ways. The "distance" between the two can be determined with help from the following terms:

- **Process:** In Win32 programming, a *process* can be defined as a partition of memory containing a running application (i.e., an active main thread) along with any necessary system resources or external binaries required by the application.
- **Client:** In COM, we define a *client* to be any piece of software using a COM object. In previous chapters of this book, we referred to the client as the "object user." From here on out, let's stick to the term "client."

- **Server:** In COM, we define the *server* to be a binary package (DLL or EXE) containing any number of COM objects. Typically, a single server is the home to many related COM objects, each one supporting any number of interfaces.

Keep in mind that the distinction between a client and server can become blurred just a bit. It is very possible (and quite common) for a client to use a server, which is itself a client to another server! Consider an application composed of a Visual Basic (VB) client making use of a COM-based DLL. Here, the VB front end is the client, while the DLL is playing the role of the server. Now, what if this DLL COM server makes use of another COM-based DLL to help get its work done? In this case the original DLL is a client to the second DLL, as illustrated in Figure 3-1:

Figure 3-1: Client and server relationships.

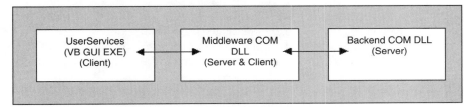

With these key terms in place (process, client, and server), we are now able to distinguish between the three possible relationships a client and server may have:

- An in-process relationship.
- An out-of-process relationship.
- A remote relationship.

Understanding the In-Process Relationship

This relationship is also abbreviated in-proc. In-proc servers are loaded into the same memory partition (process) as the client they are servicing. The key benefit of in-process relationships is speed. Clients may access the functionality of an in-proc server just about as quickly as making a local function call, as the client and object are communicating directly through interface pointers.

The biggest drawback of in-proc servers is their low level of fault tolerance (robustness). If a bug exists in the server, and that bug is hit, the entire process is taken down—client and all. Another potential problem with in-process servers is they always take on the security context of the client they are loaded into.

Figure 3-2 illustrates the in-process relationship:

Figure 3-2: The in-process relationship.

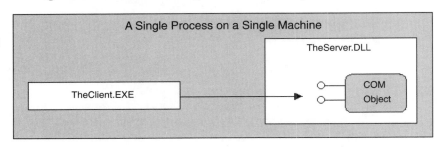

Note: If a client and in-proc server reside in different threading models, a direct interface connection is not achieved (more on this in Chapter 7).

Understanding the Out-of-Process Relationship

This relationship is also termed the *local* relationship. Here, the client and server are on the same physical machine but are loaded into two distinct memory partitions (processes), each with their own security context. One benefit of this relationship is a higher level of robustness. This time, if a bug shows up in the server, and this crashes the server's process, the client is still up and running. As long as that client has intelligent error handling on its end, its process is safe.

The down side of local servers is speed, as information from one process must be packaged, sent, and unpackaged between process boundaries. While COM will generally take care of this on your behalf (through a technique called universal marshaling), this process is time consuming.

Here is a representation of a local client/server relationship:

Figure 3-3:
The local (out-of-process) relationship.

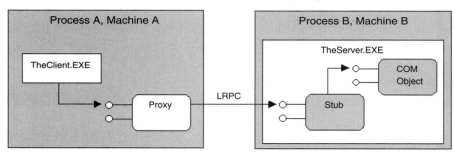

As shown in Figure 3-3, COM uses Lightweight Remote Procedure Calls (LRPC) to send information between COM components on the same machine but in different processes. LRPC is a proprietary communication protocol used under the hood by the COM runtime. In the local relationship, the client and server do not communicate directly with each other, but instead transmit data between stubs and proxies. As far as the client is concerned, the proxy is the COM object and can program against it as if it was in-process.

We will examine the inner workings of stubs and proxies later in Chapter 5. For the time being, just make a mental note that stubs and proxies are used whenever there is a local COM relationship.

Understanding the Remote Relationship

A remote server physically resides on a separate machine from the client. This is a core requirement of any enterprise-based solution, where user services, business rules, and data retrieval objects may be placed on any number of networked machines. Remote servers are the slowest of all possible COM client/server relationships, as not only do we need to marshal data between processes through stubs and proxies, but we must be aware of bandwidth and latency issues as well (sorry, COM cannot encapsulate you from the laws of physics).

Remote communication is established through the Distributed COM (DCOM) protocol, which uses Remote Procedure Calls (RPCs) to forward information between machines.

The remote relationship may be diagrammed as such:

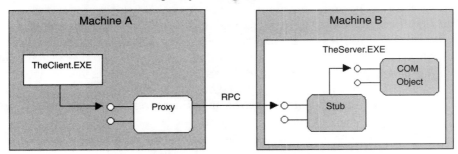

It is interesting to note that remote (or local) COM objects may be housed in either DLL or EXE servers. Legacy COM-based DLLs may be remoted using a special DLL surrogate utility named dllhost.exe (provided with NT SP 2.0 and greater). EXE server types were the "classic" way to remote a server, and at times this might still prove a decent solution, especially where small in-house LANs are involved.

Note: Of course, the new contender in the world of enterprise COM development is Microsoft Transaction Server (MTS). MTS is a "super surrogate," which will host (only) COM-based DLLs, and take care of the gory details of threading concurrency, atomic transactions, and so on.

Now then, back to location transparency! This benefit of COM states that the client-side code used to access the interfaces of a COM object <u>need not change based on the server's physical location</u>. Stubs and proxies provide a level of encapsulation, as the client is able to treat the proxy object as the "real object" and program against it as if the object itself were in its own process. Likewise, the COM object believes the stub is the "real client," leaving the server code unaltered.

The promise of location transparency does not mean your code could <u>never</u> change. The COM library does provide a number of methods and data structures to help optimize remote access. But these are optional. Using configuration utilities such as dcomcnfg.exe, you may redirect your client to access a server on any machine on the network without altering a single line of code.

These utilities and library extensions provide a far cleaner approach than we had before location transparency. At that time, developers needed to use different (and unrelated) APIs to move information between in-proc, local, and remote servers. As a COM developer, you do <u>not</u> write different code bases for client access to remote objects, local objects, or in-proc objects. Clients just see interfaces, and location transparency allows that client to be blissfully unaware of the exact location of the server.

COM is Object Oriented

OK now, relax. I am sure many of you have been told that COM is not as object oriented as it "could be." Recall from our review of OOP that every OO-based language must contend with encapsulation, polymorphism, and inheritance. Let's see how COM itself deals with these pillars of object technology:

- **Encapsulation:** COM provides very deep encapsulation of implementation details. First off, the only way a client may access a COM object's functionality is through an interface pointer. Given your knowledge of interfaces thus far, I think you see why this already provides encapsulation services. Now, on top of that, COM clients are working with the objects contained in the server at a binary level. Unless you want to disassemble the server and read some hex, you are <u>really</u> encapsulated from the details.

- **Polymorphism:** Again, as we have seen from our examination of interface-based programming, the interface allows any number of objects to implement the same interface in its own unique way (as we saw in the Shapes lab of Chapter 2). COM provides ad hoc polymorphism via the interface.

- **Inheritance:** If you read the above section on polymorphism carefully, you should guess by now that COM does not support classical inheritance of binary objects. In other words, you cannot say that "COM object A derives from COM object B." Now be careful here. We most certainly can use interface inheritance when we are creating the objects in a server (for example, C3DRect used interface inheritance to bring in the definitions of IDraw and IShapeEdit). What we cannot do with COM is something along the lines of the following:

```
// This is not possible in COM.
// Assume BLOB is a new keyword that defines a new binary COM object.
BLOB MyServer.NewBlob.EXE : public MyOtherServer.OldBlob.DLL
{
    ...
};
```

COM Containment and Aggregation

We can, however, reuse behaviors (a.k.a. interfaces) across binary COM objects via containment and aggregation. The key reason COM does not support classical inheritance is to allow objects to be as self-sufficient as possible. When using classical inheritance, if anything changes in a base class, the subclass has the potential of breaking. Given that a base class in COM would be a binary server containing any number of COM objects, how would we understand what to change in our derived class? COM sidesteps these complexities altogether by avoiding classical inheritance.

We do, however, have binary reuse in COM, using containment and delegation. A COM object may create and use other COM objects, allowing access to the inner object's interfaces via *delegation*. Clients are unaware that the outer object is composed of other inner objects. This is very much like the code-based containment we saw in our OO review; however, this time the outer class builds any inner objects with the COM library. Figure 3-5 illustrates the notion of containment and delegation. Notice that CoHotRod is an "outer class" that creates and maintains an "inner class" named CoCar. CoHotRod supports the IDrive interface, which has methods that forward calls to the inner object.

Figure 3-5: CoCar is contained by CoHotRod.

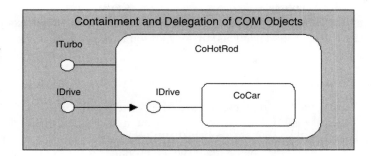

COM does offer another form of binary reuse, called *aggregation*. Here a COM object creates inner COM objects (just like the containment/delegation model). This time, however, the outer object <u>directly</u> extends its own set of interfaces with the interfaces of the inner objects. This gives clients the illusion that the object they are working with is composed of more interfaces than it really is, as shown in Figure 3-6.

Figure 3-6: CoHotRod exposing the inner object's interfaces as its own.

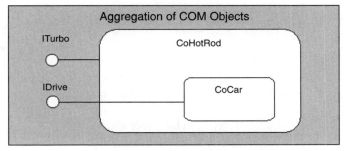

In aggregation, the outer object does not "forward" calls via delegation, as the inner object's interfaces are directly exposed as part of the outer object. We will detail the implementation of COM containment and aggregation later in Chapter 8, so we will hold off on the specifics for now.

COM Provides Clean Versioning of Components

We have seen that interfaces may be safely versioned by using interface inheritance. COM uses these same versioning techniques. As we have already seen, when an object implements a given interface, it may not alter that interface in any way or else it risks breaking clients. The COM interface is the key to robust versioning.

The COM, OLE, and ActiveX Relationship

COM is the backbone of each and every ActiveX and OLE technology. Pick up your current issue of *Microsoft Systems Journal*, and I'd bet a paycheck that at least one article discusses a new set of COM interfaces, COM service, or some other COM advancement. The point here (other than I can keep my paycheck to myself) is that COM technologies are bombarding us left and right. These days, any new software item coming from those kind folks in Redmond is delivered as a set of COM extensions—not a C-based API.

Before we can really appreciate the full set of COM-based technologies examined throughout this book, a brief (and painless) history lesson is in order, beginning with OLE 1.0.

OLE 1.0

OLE 1.0 was a 16-bit technology that appeared on the scene circa 1991. This technology enabled software applications to share information through linking and embedding. As you may know, certain applications may export visual objects to other applications. A host application may embed this object inside itself (which produced a copy of the original data) or reference it through a link (which is a connection to the original data source). The classic example of this technology is an MS Word document containing an embedded MS Excel spreadsheet. Under the hood, OLE 1.0 was not based on the COM we know today, but rather the clunky Dynamic Data Exchange (DDE) protocol. At this time, OLE was a technology specifically used for object linking and embedding.

OLE 2.0

Around 1993, 16-bit OLE 2.0 was released for the Windows 3.x OS. This marked a huge directional change for OLE, as the underpinnings of DDE were beginning to be stripped away and replaced with the COM infrastructure. With the release of Windows NT 3.51, OLE 2.0 was moved into 32 bits. The major additions to the existing 16-bit technology set was the full support for Unicode string handling, as well as tweaking COM itself to run completely on top of Microsoft's variation of the Open Software Foundation's Remote Procedure Call (OSF RPC) paradigm, rather than the older DDE paradigm.

Linking and embedding technology was still a core service of OLE 2.0—however, it did not stop there. OLE 2.0 introduced a whole slew of COM-related technologies. The key to OLE 2.0 was the extendable COM architecture. Given this, we will never see an OLE 3.0. Instead, we'll see more COM-related technologies. Thus, the terms OLE 1.0 and OLE 2.0 are not much more than historical footnotes in COM's family history.

ActiveX

ActiveX is the current blanket name for any COM-based technology. At one time, ActiveX referred to only web-specific COM technologies; however, these days most things COM are dubbed "ActiveX" something or other (ActiveX controls, ActiveX documents, ActiveX servers, and so on). To make things a bit more confusing, Microsoft occasionally uses the legacy term "OLE" to name some newer COM-based services, such as OLE DB (which really should have been ActiveX-DB to be consistent). We will see many ActiveX services pop up throughout the remainder of this book. Just realize that all ActiveX/OLE technologies are built off the COM protocol.

Standard and Custom Interfaces

COM is all about interfaces. The only way in which clients and servers can communicate is through COM interfaces. In the previous chapter, we examined interface-based programming from a C++ perspective. Each and every interface developed in that chapter (IDraw, IShapeEdit, and so forth) was developed from scratch to specify a possible behavior some class (C3DRect, C3DRectEx) may support. You discovered that C++ classes may support custom interfaces using standard multiple inheritance (MI), and through hand-rolled APIs we were able to retrieve interface pointers for the client. We defined an interface to be the following:

An *interface* is a collection of semantically related functions, which describe a single and unique behavior that may be supported by a class.

This same definition works almost perfectly in the world of COM. However, COM interfaces fall under two distinct categories. Under the hood, each type of interface is exactly the same: a collection of semantically related functions—no state, no implementation.

Furthermore, every COM interface (standard or custom) must ultimately derive from the core COM interface: IUnknown. We will examine IUnknown in detail in just a moment, but for now just regard this interface as the top-most node in any interface hierarchy which defines exactly three methods: QueryInterface(), AddRef(), and Release().

As any master node in a hierarchy, IUnknown provides basic COM-related functionality to all interface descendents, and thus all implementing classes. With this said, a COM interface may fall into one of two camps:

1. **Custom Interfaces:** These would be interfaces developed to solve an individual programming problem. We may create custom interfaces as C++ abstract classes, and extend them through numerical versioning. Every custom interface must directly or indirectly derive from IUnknown. For example, IDraw would be an official COM interface if and only if it was specified as so:

```
// Could also derive from another IUnknown derived interface as well.
interface IDraw : public IUnknown
{
    // Brings in pure virtual definitions of QueryInterface(), AddRef() and Release().
    virtual void Draw() = 0;
};
```

The above code suggests that the vTable of IDraw is colored by the methods defined in IUnknown. This is very true indeed. Any COM-based interface will always have the methods of IUnknown as the first three members; thus, any class implementing a COM interface will always have to contend with these three methods of IUnknown. Be aware that in interface inheritance, you are not required to explicitly relist inherited pure virtual methods in the derived interface. You may choose to relist the inherited pure virtual methods of IUnknown in your IDraw interface if you wish to be extremely clear; however, the compiler could care less. The class implementing IDraw would (of course) need to provide definitions for all four virtual functions.

Given that IUnknown is a mandatory requirement of any COM object, it holds a special place in COM notation. The IUnknown interface is always represented as the lollipop extending from the top of a COM class (see Figure 3-7).

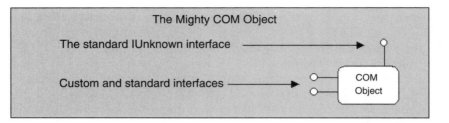

2. **Standard Interfaces:** These are predesigned and well-known interfaces useful in COM development (such as IUnknown). Every standard interface must also derive from IUnknown or another IUnknown-derived interface.

Having a set of standard interfaces is useful, as they provide a large surface area of behaviors necessary for a component-based distributed architecture such as COM. In fact, what makes one COM-based technology different from another is the set of standard interfaces supported by the given object. ActiveX controls support a number of interfaces not found in automation servers. ActiveX documents have a number of interfaces not found in COM drag and drop. This does not mean all aforementioned COM technologies are mutually exclusive. As you learn more about the set of standard COM interfaces, you will see sets of interfaces providing rendering, persistence, and other standard behaviors that tend to be implemented by numerous COM technologies.

Understanding Interface Identifiers (IIDs)

Interfaces must be named. In the previous chapter, we created a custom enumeration called INTERFACEID, which served as a way to uniquely identify the interfaces used in our mini-system. This technique worked just fine for us, as the interfaces developed were only used in the context of a single C++ application. In real life, COM objects and their interfaces may be remoted around the world (quite literally). Simple numerical identifiers such as {0, 1, 2, 3} are bound to introduce name clashes (as would string names—how many developers out there think IDataBase sounds like a good name for an interface?).

In COM development, every interface (standard or custom) is tagged with a Globally Unique Identifier (GUID, pronounced *goo-wid*), which is guaranteed to mark an interface as an individual entity for all space and time. The GUID is a 128-bit number, generated based on a unique network address coupled with the exact time (down to 100 nanoseconds!) it was requested. When a GUID is referring to a COM interface, we call this number an *interface identifier*, or IID. COM uses the GUID to uniquely identify COM classes (CLSIDs), type libraries (LIBIDs), COM executables (AppIDs), and numerous other COM items. A GUID is, in reality, a four-field structure:

```
// The GUID is represented as a structure defined in <winnt.h>.
typedef struct _GUID{    unsigned long Data1;
                         unsigned short Data2;
                         unsigned short Data3;
                         unsigned char Data4[8];} GUID;
```

The COM library provides a set of useful functions and types for working with GUIDs programmatically. Many COM library functions take GUIDs as parameters, and given that a 128-bit number might be a bit hefty to pass by value, a number of system defines (found in <wtypes.h>) are provided to pass these structures around by reference:

```
// <wtypes.h> lists a number of defines to work with GUIDs programmatically.
#define REFGUID      const GUID * const
#define REFIID       const IID * const
#define REFCLSID     const CLSID * const
```

We are also given a set of COM library functions to do comparisons of two existing GUIDs:

```
// Defined in <objbase.h>
BOOL IsEqualGUID(REFGUID g1, REFGUID g2);
BOOL IsEqualIID(REFIID i1, REFIID i2);
BOOL IsEqualCLSID(CLSID c1, CLSID c2);
```

Each function performs a memcmp() of the two structures, and returns a Boolean as the result of the comparison. Here is the implementation of IsEqualGUID:

```
// IsEqualGUID can be used to determine if two GUIDs are identical.
BOOL IsEqualGUID(REFGUID rguid1, REFGUID rguid2)
{
     return !memcmp(&rguid1, &rguid2, sizeof(GUID));
}
```

Note: An inlined version of IsEqualGUID() is also provided: InlineIsEqualGUID(). Use with care, as you know that inlined functions can bloat your code.

In addition to IsEqualGUID(), the COM library has overridden the C++ equality operator (==) and the not equal operator (!=), allowing you to compare two GUIDs as the following:

```
// We may also use == and != with two existing GUIDs, as
// we have overloaded operators at our disposal.
if(g1 == g2)     {...}      // GUIDs are the same, so do something.
if(g1 != g2)     {...}      // GUIDs are different, so do something else.
```

The implementation of the == operator function calls IsEqualGUID(), while the != operator implementation simply leverages the == operator:

```
// The overloaded operators simply call IsEqualGUID()
BOOL operator == (const GUID& guidOne, const GUID& guidOther)
{
     return IsEqualGUID(guidOne,guidOther);
}
BOOL operator != (const GUID& guidOne, const GUID& guidOther)
{
     return !(guidOne == guidOther);
}
```

Creating Custom GUIDs

Every standard COM interface already has been assigned a unique IID. For example, IUnknown has the IID of {00000000-0000-0000-C000-000000000046}. When you develop custom interfaces in C++, the job of associating a new GUID to your interface is up to you. Visual Studio provides a helpful utility, guidgen.exe, which creates new GUIDs through a friendly user interface (Figure 3-8).

You will find guidgen.exe installed under your <drive>:\ Program Files\Microsoft Visual Studio\Common\Tools directory (provided you used the default install paths):

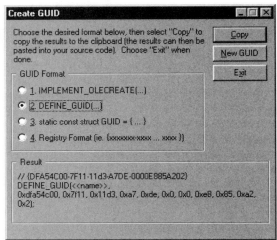

> **Note:**   For those among you who still love the DOS prompt, a command line version of this tool is also provided: uuidgen.exe. Run this tool from a command prompt with the -? switch for a full description of options.

Guidgen.exe defines four possible formats for a new GUID. The first format is an MFC-specific macro, which defines a GUID for an MFC-based class factory (we don't need that format here, so forget it even exists). Format 4 is helpful when writing Interface Definition Language (IDL) files (as we will see in the next chapter). Format 3 is what the DEFINE_GUID macro basically expands to, which leaves the final format, the DEFINE_GUID macro. This macro allows you to associate a human readable constant to the newly generated 128-bit number, much like our custom enumeration (INTERFACEID) from the previous chapter. When you paste the new GUID from the clipboard using the DEFINE_GUID format, you will see the following:

```
// {4B475690-DE06-11d2-AAF4-00A0C9312D57}
DEFINE_GUID(<<name>>,
0x4b475690, 0xde06, 0x11d2, 0xaa, 0xf4, 0x0, 0xa0, 0xc9, 0x31, 0x2d, 0x57);
```

You select the <<name>> parameter, and type in the constant used to refer to the underlying GUID. For example, here is a GUID and defined constant for the IDraw interface:

```
// {4B475690-DE06-11d2-AAF4-00A0C9312D57}
DEFINE_GUID(IID_IDraw,
0x4b475690, 0xde06, 0x11d2, 0xaa, 0xf4, 0x0, 0xa0, 0xc9, 0x31, 0x2d, 0x57);
```

> **Note:**   By convention, the human readable interface constant assigned to a GUID is prefixed with IID_ followed by the actual name of the interface.

Now, even if another developer has created an interface named IDraw, this particular version will be unique in the COM universe, given the unique IID.

DEFINE_GUID expands to the following constant. Note how the long, word, and byte parameters are simply sent into the GUID structure fields. Also note that the first parameter to this macro becomes the name of the new structure:

```
// The DEFINE_GUID macro creates a new GUID structure of some name.
#define DEFINE_GUID(name, l, w1, w2, b1, b2, b3, b4, b5, b6, b7, b8) \
  EXTERN_C const GUID name \
      = { l, w1, w2, { b1, b2, b3, b4, b5, b6, b7, b8 } }
```

In this chapter we will use the DEFINE_GUID macro when we create new GUIDs to identify our COM items. To do so, your projects must make a preprocessor include to the <initguid.h> header file in order to obtain the DEFINE_GUID macro definition. We will be creating interface header files in the upcoming labs, but just remember you can't use DEFINE_GUID without including <initguid.h> in your project.

On a final GUID-related note, the COM library function CoCreateGuid() may be used to create a GUID programmatically. Just send in a reference to a GUID, and it will stuff the fields:

```
// If you ever need to create a GUID on the fly...
HRESULT CoCreateGuid(GUID *pguid);
```

> **Note:**   Because the use of guidgen.exe is so common in COM and ATL programming, you may wish to create a custom menu item in the Visual C++ IDE to access it. To do so, select the Tools | Customize... menu selection and from the resulting dialog box, select the Tools tab. Type in a name for this custom menu item using the Menu Contents list box and map a path to guidgen.exe from the Command edit box (i.e., C:\Program Files\Microsoft Visual Studio\Common\Tools\Guidgen.exe). Select the Close button and examine your Tools menu. You will see your custom menu item is now visible and can be selected to run guidgen.exe.

The De Facto COM Interface: IUnknown

So far in this chapter, we have thrown around the terms IUnknown, COM object, and COM class quite liberally, without providing clear definitions. Let's fix these omissions right now:

- A *COM class* is the definition of a UDT implementing at least IUnknown. Often termed a *coclass*.
- A *COM object* is an instance of a coclass.
- *IUnknown* is the standard COM interface from which all others ultimately derive. Thus, the first three members of any COM interface will be the three inherited methods of IUnknown. Here is a streamlined version, which is fully defined in <unknwn.h>:

```
// The core COM interface.
interface IUnknown
```

```
        {
                virtual HRESULT QueryInterface(REFIID riid, void** ppv) = 0;
                virtual ULONG AddRef() = 0;
                virtual ULONG Release() = 0;
        };
```

The actual definition of IUnknown is wrapped in a number of COM macros, allowing for the correct expansion on various platforms (also found in <unknwn.h> is the C language equivalent of IUnknown). We will examine these COM macros later, but will ignore them for now so they don't cloud the fact that IUnknown is just like any other interface seen thus far: a collection of pure virtual functions.

IUnknown provides two services to every COM object. First, QueryInterface() allows a client to gain a pointer to any interface implemented on the object (including IUnknown itself) from another valid interface pointer. Second, the AddRef() and Release() methods provide a mechanism to control the lifetime management of the object. We will drill down into the details of these methods momentarily.

When creating COM classes in C++, you may support COM interfaces using either MI or nested classes. In this respect, things seem much like our C3DRect class of Chapter 2. In COM, however, we also must account for IUnknown. Thus, if we derive our custom IDraw interface from IUnknown, and implement IDraw in a coclass named CoHexagon, we would need to implement a total of four methods:

```
// IDraw derives from IUnknown,
// therefore CoHexagon must implement four methods.
class CoHexagon : public IDraw
{
public:
        // Constructor and destructor...
        // IUnknown.
        HRESULT QueryInterface(REFIID riid, void** ppv);
        ULONG AddRef();
        ULONG Release();
        // IDraw.
        void Draw();
};
```

COM Object Lifetime Management Using AddRef() and Release()

In COM programming, the client and coclass share the burden of the object's lifetime management. Every COM object maintains an internal *reference count*, representing the number of outstanding interface pointers currently in use. When this reference count drops to exactly zero, the object deallocates itself from memory. This joint venture of the object's lifetime management is critical, as a single object may be used by numerous clients at a single time. If client A is finished using a given object, and were to directly delete the COM object from memory, that would more than likely deeply offend the other active clients. This possibility is avoided altogether in COM by the use of an object's reference counter. The AddRef() and Release() methods of IUnknown are the two methods necessary to control the memory allocation of a COM object.

So when are AddRef() and Release() called? When a client asks for a given interface pointer through QueryInterface(), the COM object will call AddRef() if and only if it implements the interface in question. When a client is finished using that interface pointer, the client must call Release() to inform the object it has one less client. Implementing AddRef() and Release() is very simple, and extremely boilerplate. If you are not worried about thread safety, just increment or decrement the private reference counter (which of course you should set to zero in the class constructor):

```
// AddRef() is used to increase the internal reference count of the object.
ULONG CoHexagon::AddRef()
{
      return ++m_refCount;          // Private unsigned long defined in CoHexagon.
}
```

In the implementation of Release(), check the reference counter for the final release, and delete the object:

```
// Release() is called to decrement the internal reference count on the object.
// If (and only if) the final reference to the object has been released, the coclass
// removes itself from memory.
ULONG CoHexagon::Release()
{
      --m_refCount;
      // Did I lose my final connection?
      if(m_refCount == 0)
      {
            // Final Release! Remove coclass from memory.
            delete this;
            return 0;
      }
      return m_refCount;
}
```

Notice that both AddRef() and Release() return the current number of outstanding interface pointers to the client. Never use this value for any purpose other than general debugging. The COM specification does not state that this returned reference count is a perfect reflection of the object's number of clients. Although a client can examine this return value to get a general feel of the object in use, it should never use this value in production code.

If you are concerned with a thread-safe implementation of AddRef() and Release(), you should make calls to the Win32 functions InterlockedIncrement() and InterlockedDecrement(), rather than the C++ increment and decrement operators. Here is a thread-safe implementation of AddRef() and Release():

```
// The increment operator (++) is not thread safe.
// InterlockedIncrement() will safely increment a variable by one.
ULONG CoHexagon::AddRef()
{
      return InterlockedIncrement(&m_refCount);
}
ULONG CoHexagon::Release()
{
      InterlockedDecrement(&m_refCount);
      // Did I lose my final connection?
      if(m_refCount == 0)
      {
            // Final Release! Remove coclass from memory.
            delete this;
```

```
        return 0;
    }
    return m_refCount;
}
```

We have much more to say about thread safety and your COM objects in Chapter 7. The point here is to understand that AddRef() and Release() are the two methods of IUnknown that control the lifetime management of each and every COM object.

Understanding AddRef() and Release() Rules

Now that we understand the functionality of AddRef() and Release(), we need to understand the exact circumstances in which to call them. Proper reference counting can be broken down into the following small set of rules:

■ A COM object calls AddRef() on itself whenever it successfully hands out an interface pointer to the client, typically during a QueryInterface() invocation. We will see this rule in action in the next topic section.

■ When a client has successfully received an interface pointer (through a COM library call or some interface method), the client must assume that AddRef() has been called by the object, and must call Release() when finished with the acquired pointer:

```
// Assume the following method returns an interface pointer.
IDraw* pDraw = NULL;
if (GoGetIDraw(&pDraw))        // Success? The object has been AddRef-ed.
{
    pDraw -> Draw();
    pDraw -> Release();        // If this is the only reference, the object is now
                              // destroyed.
}
```

■ If a client (or server for that matter) makes a copy of an interface pointer, the client should call AddRef() on that copy explicitly:

```
// Assume we have fetched some interfaces and now set one equal to the other.
pIFaceTwo = pIFaceOne;
pIFaceTwo -> AddRef();
```

■ Functions that take interface pointers as parameters should AddRef() and Release() the interface during the method invocation:

```
// This method draws any IDraw compatible object.
HRESULT DrawMe(IDraw* pDrawingObject)
{
    pDrawingObject -> AddRef();        // We are using this object.
    pDrawingObject -> Draw();
    pDrawingObject -> Release();       // All done.
}
```

At times, these calls may seem redundant, although technically correct. You can minimize AddRef() and Release() calls under a few circumstances; however, with these rules fixed in your head, you can be assured objects are deleted from memory as efficiently as possible. It is far better to add in explicit AddRef() and Release() calls (even if things seem a bit redundant) rather than have objects hanging around in memory longer than necessary.

In COM, the objects we activate with COM library calls are responsible for removing themselves from memory when they are no longer wanted. This is in contrast to our

Shapes lab from the previous chapter where we indirectly deallocated our C3DRect using a custom API call (DestroyThe3DRect()). This is not the case in COM. As long as you abide by the AddRef() and Release() rules, you can rest assured that your objects take care of themselves.

Handing Out Interface Pointers with QueryInterface()

The final method of IUnknown, QueryInterface(), provides the functionality that allows a client to request an interface pointer from the object from an existing interface pointer. Recall the custom Rect API method, GetInterfaceFrom3DRect(). If the object supported the requested INTERFACEID, we received (through the void** parameter) a pointer to the given interface:

```
// Our custom rectangle API function mimicked QueryInterface() but
// this method was global, and was not tightly bound to the object it operated on.
bool GetInterfaceFrom3DRect(INTERFACEID iid, void** iFacePtr)
{
    ...
    if(iid == IDRAW)        // They want access to IDraw.
    {
        *iFacePtr = (IDraw*)theRect;
        return true;
    }
    ...
}
```

A standard implementation of QueryInterface() mimics our hand-rolled API almost exactly. Rather than sending in an arbitrary numerical identifier, we send in the GUID of the interface we are requesting by reference. As the object itself is performing the cast, we make use of the this pointer rather than a named object (such as our global C3DRect). Finally, rather than returning a simple Boolean, we return the de facto HRESULT return type. Here is the implementation of QueryInterface() for CoHexagon (take note of the AddRef() call, if the object supports the requested interface):

```
// QueryInterface() is implemented by each and every coclass, and provides
// a way to return an interface pointer to the client.
HRESULT CoHexagon::QueryInterface(REFIID riid, void** ppv)
{
    // Which interface does the client want?
    if(riid == IID_IUnknown)          // Human readable version of GUID
        *ppv = (IUnknown*)this;
    else if(riid == IID_IDraw)
        *ppv = (IDraw*)this;          // Generalized "*ppv = (IDraw*)theRect"
    if(*ppv)                          // Did we have the IID?
    {
        // Must call AddRef() if we hand out an interface.
        ((IUnknown*)(*ppv))->AddRef();
        return S_OK;
    }
    *ppv = NULL;            // NULL pointer if we do not have the interface.
    return E_NOINTERFACE;   // Standard return if we don't support the IID.
}
```

Note: Recall every standard interface already has a GUID assigned to it. As well, every standard interface has a human readable constant, using the IID_ prefix convention (for example, IID_IUnknown, IID_IMalloc, IID_IClassFactory, and so on).

Implementing QueryInterface(), like maintaining an object reference count, is also a very mechanical process. Basically, each interface supported on the object requires an additional two lines of code:

```
// Each interface supported by a COM object entails these two lines of code.
if(riid == interface ID)                    // If you want this...
    *ppv = (interface name*)this;           //...you get this.
```

When implementing QI, remember the basics of reference counting: If an object hands off an interface pointer to the client, the object must AddRef() itself. Every implementation of QI will have code the equivalent of the following after all IIDs have been checked (if we do not support the IID, return E_NOINTERFACE):

```
// Be sure to AddRef() the object if you have found the requested interface.
if(*ppv)
{
    ((IUnknown*)(*ppv))->AddRef();    // We have another active client.
    return S_OK;            // Informs the client we supported the requested IID.
}
```

Implementing QueryInterface() Using static_cast<>

As an alternative to traditional C++ casting, you may find other implementations of QueryInterface() making use of static_cast<>. One advantage of this approach is that compile-time errors will be generated if an illegal cast is attempted. Functionally, however, each approach yields the same result: returning a portion of the object to the interested client (i.e., casting the **this** pointer).

If we were to rewrite CoHexagon's QueryInterface() implementation using static_cast<>, we would see the following:

```
// QueryInterface() à la static_cast<>
HRESULT CoHexagon::QueryInterface(REFIID riid, void** ppv)
{
    if(riid == IID_IUnknown)
        *ppv = static_cast<IUnknown*>(this);
    else if(riid == IID_IDraw)
        *ppv = static_cast<IDraw*>(this);
    if(*ppv)
    {
        ((IUnknown*)(*ppv))->AddRef();
        return S_OK;
    }
    *ppv = NULL;
    return E_NOINTERFACE;
}
```

IUnknown Establishes an Object's Identity

You have seen that this single COM interface is responsible for the basic riggings of a COM class: object lifetime and handing out interface pointers. QueryInterface() has been defined by the COM specification with the following requirement in mind:

If a client has some interface pointer, the client must be able to navigate to <u>any other</u> interface on the object from that pointer.

In other words, QueryInterface() must ensure the rules of reflexivity, symmetry, and transitivity. This breaks down to the following set of guidelines:

- **Reflexivity:** If a client has an interface pointer, pA, a client must be able to query pA for itself.

- **Symmetry:** If a client can navigate from an interface pointer, pA, to another interface pointer, pB, the client must be able to navigate from pB back to pA.

- **Transitivity:** If a client can navigate from pA to pB, and from pB to pC, the client must be able to return from pC to pA.

What these rules mean to a client is simple: "From a valid interface pointer I can get to any other interface on the object."

In order to ensure your coclasses support each of these rules, be sure each custom interface derives from an IUnknown-derived interface, and in the implementation of QueryInterface() include a provision for each and every interface on the object. Be extra careful to ensure that if your coclass supports a versioned interface (IDraw, IDraw2), a provision for each version is supported in your QueryInterface() logic, not a single test for the most derived interface.

The De Facto COM Return Type: HRESULT

All of your COM interface methods should return the standard HRESULT return type. In the vast land of COM, only a tiny handful of interface methods (such as AddRef() and Release()) return otherwise, and that is only for quick and dirty debugging by the client. While nothing is syntactically preventing you from returning something other than an HRESULT from an interface method, you should get in the habit of always returning an HRESULT.

> **Note:**   Any interface that may be remotely accessed must return an HRESULT.

The HRESULT return type allows your client to investigate if the method invocation succeeded, and if not, why. The HRESULT is a 32-bit value, logically partitioned into discrete sectors. The most significant bit of the HRESULT (bit 31) is used to determine if a call succeeded or failed. Bits 30-29 are reserved, while 28-16 define the "facility" of the error. The remaining bits define specific information concerning the error. Here is the physical layout of an HRESULT:

Figure 3-9:
Fields of the
32-bit
HRESULT.

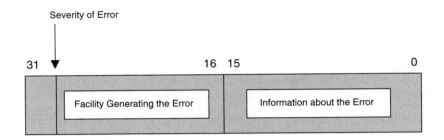

We have already seen some predefined COM HRESULT types, such as S_OK and
E_NOINTERFACE. Here is a brief list of some of the more common existing HRESULTs
(we will see more as necessary):

Standard HRESULT	Meaning in Life
S_OK	The method invocation returned successfully.
E_NOTIMPL	A member function of an interface is not implemented.
E_NOINTERFACE	Coclass does not support the requested interface.
E_OUTOFMEMORY	The coclass failed to allocate some memory.
E_FAIL	Something, in general, failed.

Clients are typically only really interested in the success or failure of the method invocation. For this purpose, COM provides two macros: SUCCEEDED and FAILED. These
macros simply test the most significant bit of the HRESULT on your behalf and return
true or false. Just send in an HRESULT to either macro, and it will return a Boolean. For
example, assume a client has an interface pointer to IUnknown, and wishes to see if a call
to QueryInterface() succeeded. Typical client-side COM code would be as follows:

```
// The SUCCEEDED macro tests the most significant bit of the HRESULT.
// In the code below, assume we have already obtained an IUnknown pointer,
// and now wish to grab IDraw off the object.
IDraw* pDraw = NULL;
HRESULT hr;
hr = pUnk -> QueryInterface(IID_IDraw, (void**)&pDraw);
// Did the QI call work? (i.e., does the object have an IDraw interface?)
if(SUCCEEDED(hr))
        pDraw->Draw();
// Clients must release all interface pointers when finished.
pUnk->Release();       // Done with IUnknown pointer.
pDraw->Release();      // Done drawing.
```

Analyzing an HRESULT

Beyond simply testing for the success or failure of a given interface method invocation, we
can extract more specific information about the error in a number of ways. First of all,
<winerror.h> defines all standard HRESULT errors, with a text description explaining

exactly what went wrong. Here is the information for HRESULT number 0x80040111 (or the more readable CLASS_E_CLASSNOTAVAILABLE):

```
// MessageId: CLASS_E_CLASSNOTAVAILABLE
// MessageText:
// ClassFactory cannot supply requested class
#define CLASS_E_CLASSNOTAVAILABLE
_HRESULT_TYPEDEF_(0x80040111L)
```

If you don't like the idea of looking up HRESULTs by examining <winerror.h>, you can make use of a CASE tool supplied by DevStudio. From the Tools menu, select Error Lookup. You may paste in any HRESULT (which can be copied directly from the build tab of the Visual C++ output window), and look up the error information as shown in Figure 3-10:

Figure 3-10:
The Error
Lookup utility.

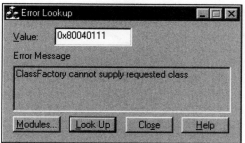

Finally, if you wish to examine the error description programmatically, you may use the Win32 FormatMessage() function. The parameters to this function are a bit hefty, but provide maximum flexibility (see online help for complete details). Here is an example of this function taking an HRESULT and storing the text message in a local buffer:

```
// The FormatMessage() function will programmatically grab the textual message for a
// given HRESULT.
HRESULT hr;
hr = CoCreateInstance(...);        // COM library function.
char buff[100];
BOOL bRet = FormatMessage( FORMAT_MESSAGE_FROM_SYSTEM,
                           0, hr, 0, buff, sizeof(buff), 0);
cout << buff << endl;
// Code on...
```

Defining COM Interfaces Using Standard COM Macros

When developing COM interfaces, you could decide to use straight C++ and build an interface using the **class**, **interface**, or **struct** keywords. However, these interface definitions will be far less robust than the same interface defined using the set of COM-specific interface macros. When we discuss the Interface Definition Language (IDL) in the next chapter, we will see how the Microsoft IDL compiler (MIDL) generates C/C++ interface code using COM macros automatically. Real COM developers always begin with IDL, but for the time being, we will make direct use of the COM macros directly.

   If you were to examine the exact definition of IUnknown as seen in <unknwn.h>, what you would really see is the following:

```
// Standard COM interfaces are wrapped by numerous COM macros.
MIDL_INTERFACE("00000000-0000-0000-C000-000000000046")
IUnknown
{
public:
```

```
BEGIN_INTERFACE
    virtual HRESULT STDMETHODCALLTYPE QueryInterface(
    /* [in] */ REFIID riid,
    /* [iid_is][out] */ void __RPC_FAR *__RPC_FAR *ppvObject) = 0;
    virtual ULONG STDMETHODCALLTYPE AddRef(void) = 0;
    virtual ULONG STDMETHODCALLTYPE Release(void) = 0;
END_INTERFACE
};
```

The BEGIN_INTERFACE and END_INTERFACE expand to nothing on Win32 platforms, and to keep things simple, we will not be using these macros in our interface definitions. The MIDL_INTERFACE macro resolves to the **struct** keyword and (if compiled on VC 5.0 or greater) a declspec allowing an IID to be directly attached to the interface:

```
// The MIDL_INTERFACE macro, defined in <rpcndr.h>
#if _MSC_VER >= 1100
#define MIDL_INTERFACE(x)   struct __declspec(uuid(x)) __declspec(novtable)
#else
#define MIDL_INTERFACE(x)   struct
#endif
```

The justification to use these COM macros amounts to correct expansion of your interface on different platforms. Thus, the IDraw interface will be interpreted a bit differently on a Macintosh than it would on the various Windows platforms (based on calling conventions, pointer logic, and whatnot). The good news is you do not need to know the exact differences needed for a given platform; simply use the set of COM macros and they will expand correctly based on preprocessor logic.

There are two basic sets of COM interface macros. One set is used when defining the interface itself (for example: IDraw), another for the coclass implementing the interfaces (for example: CoHexagon). Each set has two variations, depending on the physical return value of the interface method, thus giving us a total of four basic macros defined in <objbase.h>: STDMETHOD, STDMETHOD_, STDMETHODIMP, and STDMETHODIMP_.

Defining Interfaces Using COM Standard Macros

When you are defining a COM interface (such as IDraw) in C++, use the STDMETHOD or STDMETHOD_ macros. If your interface method returns an HRESULT, use STDMETHOD. The only parameter to STDMETHOD is the name of the method. Here is the expansion of STDMETHOD on Win32:

```
// Use STDMETHOD when defining a method which returns an HRESULT
#define STDMETHOD(method) virtual HRESULT STDMETHODCALLTYPE method
```

If you return anything other than HRESULT (including void), use STDMETHOD_. Here you must pass two arguments to the macro, the return type and method name:

```
// STDMETHOD_ is used if your method returns anything other than an HRESULT.
#define STDMETHOD_(type,method) virtual type STDMETHODCALLTYPE method
```

Notice that these two macros make use of yet another macro, STDMETHODCALLTYPE, which is defined in <winnt.h> simply as:

```
// Under Win32, STDMETHODCALLTYPE resolves to __stdcall
#define STDMETHODCALLTYPE       __stdcall
```

Let's rewrite IShapeEdit, this time using the correct COM interface macros:

```
// IShapeEdit using the COM macros.
interface IShapeEdit : public IUnknown
{
    STDMETHOD_(void, Fill) (FILLTYPE fType) = 0;
    STDMETHOD_(void, Inverse) () = 0;
    STDMETHOD_(void, Stretch) (int factor) = 0;
};
```

To be even more COM compliant, we really should return the standard HRESULT instead of void. Let's rewrite IShapeEdit again using the COM return value of choice (note the substitution of STDMETHOD for STDMETHOD_):

```
// A even more COM savvy version of IShapeEdit.
interface IShapeEdit : public IUnknown
{
    STDMETHOD(Fill) (FILLTYPE fType) = 0;
    STDMETHOD(Inverse) () = 0;
    STDMETHOD(Stretch) (int factor) = 0;
};
```

When defining COM interfaces using the set of macros, we do have some other helper items defined in <objbase.h>:

```
// Additional, but not core, COM macros.
#define PURE       = 0
#define DECLARE_INTERFACE(iface)   interface iface
#define DECLARE_INTERFACE_(iface, baseiface)   interface iface : public baseiface
```

The PURE macro evaluates to the =0 suffix of a pure virtual function definition. The DECLARE_INTERFACE variations allow you to send in interface names and any base interface as parameters. These macros are not necessary, but can help streamline interface definitions. Here would be a final variation of IShapeEdit using these optional macros:

```
// A very COM compliant interface definition.
DECLARE_INTERFACE_(IShapeEdit, IUnknown)
{
    STDMETHOD(Fill) (FILLTYPE fType) PURE;
    STDMETHOD(Inverse) () PURE;
    STDMETHOD(Stretch) (int factor) PURE;
};
```

With the above interface definition, we can rest assured that the macros expand correctly on a given platform. This is becoming more and more important, as COM is being ported to many flavors of UNIX, IBM variations, and so forth. If you write COM interface definitions in C++, get in the habit of learning these macros and sticking to them. Better yet, use IDL and let the MIDL compiler add them for you automatically (as we will do beginning in Chapter 4).

Implementing Interfaces Using COM Standard Macros

When you are creating interfaces defined with the STDMETHOD and STDMETHOD_ macros, you will need to use a corresponding set in the implementing coclass: STDMETHODIMP and STDMETHODIMP_. The presence or absence of the underscore is also determined by the interface method return type (HRESULT or anything else). These two macros are defined as follows:

```
// The COM class implementing a COM interface makes use of these macros.
#define STDMETHODIMP            HRESULT STDMETHODCALLTYPE
#define STDMETHODIMP_(type)     type STDMETHODCALLTYPE
```

Each macro simply complements the calling conventions used in the interface definition, and removes the **virtual** keyword from the expansion. If our CoHexagon class implements the IShapeEdit and IDraw interfaces (both defined with the COM interface macros), we would write the following:

```
// As our custom interfaces used the STDMETHOD macros, our coclass
// must make use of the corresponding STDMETHODIMP macros.
class CoHexagon : public IShapeEdit, public IDraw
{
public:
...
     STDMETHODIMP QueryInterface(REFIID riid, void** pIFace);
     STDMETHODIMP_(ULONG)AddRef();
     STDMETHODIMP_(ULONG)Release();
     STDMETHODIMP Draw();
     STDMETHODIMP Fill(FILLTYPE fType);
     STDMETHODIMP Inverse();
     STDMETHODIMP Stretch();
private:
     ULONG m_refCount;         // Initialize to zero in constructor.
};
```

In CoHexagon's *.cpp file, we would implement methods using the same IMP macros as used in the coclass's header file. AddRef() would be implemented as the following:

```
// Need IMP_ as AddRef() does not return an HRESULT.
STDMETHODIMP_(ULONG) CoHexagon::AddRef()
{
     return ++m_refCount;
}
```

QueryInterface() would be implemented with STDMETHODIMP, as QueryInterface() returns the standard HRESULT:

```
// Need IMP as QueryInterface() does return an HRESULT.
STDMETHODIMP CoHexagon::QueryInterface(REFIID riid, void** ppv)
{
     if(riid == IID_IUnknown)
          *ppv = (IUnknown*)(IDraw*)this;    // See below...
     else if(riid == IID_IDraw)
          *ppv = (IDraw*)this;
     else if(riid == IID_IShapeEdit)
          *ppv = (IShapeEdit*)this;
     if(*ppv)
     {
          ((IUnknown*)(*ppv))->AddRef();
          return S_OK;
     }
     return E_NOINTERFACE;
}
```

Notice the extra cast for the IUnknown provision. As both IDraw and IShapeEdit derive from IUnknown, we get an ambiguity error if we cast directly to IUnknown*. This extra cast keeps the compiler happy (we could have used any interface supported by the coclass as part of this cast, not just IDraw). All we are doing here is taking some IUnknown-derived interface and sucking out the "IUnknown-ness" from it.

> **Note:**   There is some inconsistency regarding the correct use of the IMP macros in the COM literature. Sometimes you will find the IMP macro set used in both the method prototypes (*.h files) and implementation in the coclass (*.cpp) as we have seen here. Other times, you will see STDMETHOD used in both the interface definition and again in the coclass method prototypes, leaving the corresponding IMP macro in the *.cpp file only. Although the use of either STDMETHOD or STDMETHODIMP macros in the coclass header file will compile just fine, the justification of sticking to the IMP set in both the prototype and implementation is, when expanded, the virtual keyword is removed, and is technically more correct.

Strings in COM

This might seem like a slightly out of place topic at this point in the book. However, in our next lab, we will begin porting the CarInCPP application from Chapter 1 into a COM server, and given that CCar uses text data, we need to examine the standard COM string data types: OLECHARs and the Basic String (BSTR).

Let me forewarn you: COM string manipulation can be tricky. Because COM is a language-independent programming discipline, we must contend with the following reality: Not all languages represent strings as NULL-terminated character arrays. Period. For example, VB considers a string to be a byte length prefixed, NULL-terminated set of characters. While COM syntactically allows you to pass around traditional C character arrays as interface method parameters, VB, VBScript, and Java clients will have little clue what to do with them.

Furthermore, given that COM is gaining ground as a platform-neutral protocol, realize that different platforms represent strings on different levels as well. WinNT is completely Unicode under the hood. Win9x is not. Furthermore, since the release of 32-bit OLE, all strings in the COM universe are considered 100% Unicode. This means all strings you pass into COM library functions and as textual interface parameters should be 100% Unicode.

What these points suggest is that COM strings should somehow be defined such that all languages and all platforms can understand. This universal string type is the BSTR. However, before we examine this de facto COM string type, we will begin with the OLECHAR primitive.

Understanding the OLECHAR Data Type

The OLECHAR data type (defined in <wtypes.h>) is the standard C++ centric COM character type. A good majority of COM library functions that take text parameters expect to be sent an array of OLECHAR types. OLECHAR will expand to either a char (ANSI) or wchar_t (Unicode) character, depending on your target platform:

```
// OLECHAR expands to wchar_t or char.
// Below, WCHAR is a simple typedef to wchar_t.
#if defined(_WIN32) && !defined(OLE2ANSI)
     typedef WCHAR OLECHAR;
#else
     typedef char OLECHAR;
#endif
```

The OLECHAR data type is used to hold a single COM character (e.g., the letter "H"). When you need an array of these types (e.g., "Hello World!") you will typically declare a variable of type LPOLESTR (an OLECHAR pointer), or if the string should remain constant, an LPCOLESTR (a const OLECHAR pointer). These typedefs resolve to char* or wchar_t* (either with or without the **const** keyword):

```
// An array of OLECHARs can be defined with the LPOLESTR or LPCOLESTR
// typedefs.
#if defined(_WIN32) && !defined(OLE2ANSI)
     typedef OLECHAR*          LPOLESTR;
     typedef const OLECHAR*    LPCOLESTR;
#else
     typedef LPSTR             LPOLESTR;
     typedef LPCSTR            LPCOLESTR;
#endif
```

Before we learn how to create a COM string with these new types, we have one further item to consider: the OLESTR macro. So, what is the OLESTR macro all about? Well, recall that some platforms use Unicode under the hood and some don't. When we prefix a text literal with L we force the creation of a Unicode string, and thus we could create a Unicode character array as so:

```
// This will only work on Unicode savvy platforms.
OLECHAR* pOLEStr;              // Could use LPOLESTR or LPCOLESTR as well.
pOLEStr = L"Fred Flintstone";
```

If we did this, however, we could have problems on non-Unicode environments such as Win9x. The other option is to create an array of OLECHARs without the "L" prefix to force an array of char types. This would work on all platforms, but would also force NT to perform an internal conversion (which can slow things down). To account for these differences, OLESTR prefixes "L" if compiled under a Unicode build, and omits it otherwise:

```
// OLESTR will conditionally expand to a Unicode or char* string.
#if defined(_WIN32) && !defined(OLE2ANSI)
     #define OLESTR(str) L##str
else
     #define OLESTR(str) str
#endif
```

Always initialize OLECHAR arrays with the OLESTR macro and everybody is happy. Well, almost everyone. Always remember that if you create custom interface methods that define OLECHAR arrays, <u>you have limited the use of your COM object to C and C++ clients only</u>.

Understanding the BSTR Data Type

Most COM language mappings do not work with simple NULL-terminated character arrays (Unicode or not). Visual Basic, Java, VBScript, and JScript all expect strings to be byte length prefixed as well. The BSTR data type is a Unicode, byte length prefixed, NULL-terminated string that all COM-compatible languages understand. Although all COM mappings understand the BSTR, each language has its own unique way to manipulate it. VB developers create BSTRs whenever they write code such as:

```
' VB developer made a BSTR.
'
Dim name as String
name = "Fred Flintstone"
```

As C++ developers, we create BSTR data types and manipulate them with a small set of COM library functions. Each BSTR method has a "Sys-" prefix to help identify it as a BSTR specific function (system string). It is interesting to note that the BSTR data type is defined as a typedef of OLECHAR*, again being an array of OLECHAR characters:

```
// Behold the BSTR (<wtypes.h>).
typedef OLECHAR*     BSTR;
```

It is through the use of the system string functions where the real difference (prefixing the byte length) is made. The following is a rundown of the most common system string functions and when to use them.

Creating a Brand New BSTR in C++

When you need to create a brand new BSTR in C++, you must make use of SysAllocString(). This API function automatically calculates the length of the string and sets the underlying buffer. For example, here we send in a Unicode text literal, and cache the returned BSTR in a variable named bstrName:

```
// SysAllocString() creates a BSTR.
BSTR bstrName;
bstrName = SysAllocString(L"Fred Flintstone");
```

Of course, many times you may not wish to initialize a BSTR using a hard-coded text literal, but would rather work with some variable data. Thus, you can allocate a BSTR with an existing OLECHAR* variable (using the OLESTR macro to ensure the correct underlying data type):

```
// Create a BSTR using an array of OLECHAR types (could be char or wchar_t).
OLECHAR* pOLEStr;
pOLEStr = OLESTR("Fred Flinstone");
BSTR bstrName;
bstrName = SysAllocString(pOLEStr);
```

Manipulating an Existing BSTR

Once you have created a BSTR, the chances are good you will need to reassign it to another value during the life of your program. If you have a current BSTR that you wish to modify, use SysReAllocString(), which frees the existing memory, recalculates the length, and resets the buffer:

```
// Change existing bstrName to 'Mr. Slate'
SysReAllocString(&bstrName, L"Mr. Slate");
```

The system string functions also provide a way to obtain the current length of a given BSTR buffer, using SysStringLen():

```
// Mr. Slate == 9
int length = SysStringLen(bstrName);
```

Most importantly, any BSTR directly created by SysAllocString() must be destroyed with a corresponding call to SysFreeString(). Any BSTR you receive back from an interface method must also be freed using SysFreeString():

```
// All done with the string.
SysFreeString(bstrName);
```

> **Note:**   Forgetting to free a BSTR with SysFreeString() will lead to hard-to-find memory leaks! This is just as important as calling delete on memory acquired via new in C++.

Additional BSTR API Functions

While SysAllocString(), SysStringLen(), and SysFreeString() are a good start for most BSTR manipulations, the system string API does define a number of other methods. Here is the complete set of BSTR manipulation functions as found in <oleauto.h>, each of which are further documented in online help:

BSTR Function	Meaning in Life
SysAllocString()	Creates a new BSTR.
SysReAllocString()	Reallocates an existing BSTR.
SysStringLen()	Returns the character length of a BSTR.
SysFreeString()	Destroys an existing BSTR.
SysReAllocStringLen()	Used to create a BSTR based on some length of characters.
SysStringByteLen()	Returns the length (in bytes) of a BSTR. Win32 only.
SysAllocStringByteLen()	This function is provided to create BSTRs that contain binary data. You can use this type of BSTR only in situations where it will not be translated from ANSI to Unicode, or vice versa. Win32 only.

Unicode to ANSI Conversions

Even if we can all agree on the use of the BSTR type (in order to gain the greatest level of language independence), we still have one remaining problem. Win32 API functions that take textual parameters typically <u>seem</u> to require ANSI strings. For example, the MessageBox() method we all know and love is typically understood to look like the following:

```
// This is the MessageBox() method we think we know...
MessageBox (HWND hWnd , LPCSTR lpText, LPCSTR lpCaption, UINT uType);
```

Given the prototype above, it looks as though we need to supply two constant char arrays (LPCSTR = long pointer to a constant string). Reality can often be a strange thing, however. Truth be told, there is no MessageBox() function in the Win32 API(!). Actually, this method (or any Win32 method that takes textual parameters) is defined to be one of two possibilities:

```
// Every Win32 function which takes text strings has an ANSI (A) or Unicode(W)
// variation.
#ifdef UNICODE
      #define MessageBox MessageBoxW
#else
      #define MessageBox MessageBoxA
#endif // !UNICODE
```

Under WinNT, the UNICODE preprocessor symbol is defined when you configure a Unicode build of your current project (this may be done from the Project | Settings menu selection). In this case, each and every API function will automatically expand to the "wide" version. For MessageBox(), this breaks down as:

```
// Under Unicode builds, all strings come through as an array of constant wchar_t.
MessageBoxW( HWND hWnd, LPCWSTR lpText,
            LPCWSTR lpCaption, UINT uType);
```

Under non-Unicode builds, MessageBox() expands to the following ANSI version:

```
// ANSI builds use const char arrays.
MessageBoxA (HWND hWnd , LPCSTR lpText, LPCSTR lpCaption, UINT uType);
```

The dilemma is, if we configure Unicode-only builds, our project will only run correctly under WinNT. If we do not configure a Unicode build, we will run under all platforms, although Unicode platforms (such as NT) will need to internally convert the ANSI strings to Unicode (which as mentioned can slow things down).

Conversion Functions

Win32 defines two rather hefty functions that allow you to translate ANSI strings into Unicode, and Unicode strings into ANSI. While these Win32 API functions provide you with maximum flexibility, they can often be seen as overkill given their parameter set (as you may agree when we see them in use in the next lab):

■ **MultiByteToWideChar()**: Converts an ANSI string to a Unicode equivalent.

■ **WideCharToMultiByte()**: Converts a Unicode string to an ANSI equivalent.

As an alternative, the C run-time (CRT) library provides simpler, streamlined, and platform-independent conversion functions. If you have a Unicode string (such as a BSTR) and want the ANSI equivalent, make a call to wcstombs() (Wide Character String to Multibyte String):

```
// wcstombs( char *ANSIString, wchar_t *UNICODEString, size_t count );
char buff[MAX_LENGTH];
BSTR bstr = SysAllocString(L"How did strings get so ugly?");
wcstombs(buff, bstr, MAX_LENGTH);      // P3 = size of target buffer.
cout << buff << endl;                  // Pump to console.
SysFreeString(bstr);
```

If you want to take an existing ANSI string and convert it into Unicode, call mbstowcs() (Multi Byte String to Wide Character String), prototyped below:

```
// Transform an existing char* (ANSI) into a wchar_t* (Unicode)
mbstowcs( wchar_t *UNICODEString , char *ANSIString, size_t count );
```

When we move our COM efforts into ATL, we are given a whole slew of conversion macros that streamline the process of translating between Unicode and ANSI strings, allowing us to more or less forget about these four conversion functions. As well, the CComBSTR class of ATL shields you from many of the ugly details of the system string functions. For now, we will take the long road and use the system string and various conversion functions.

A COM Text Example: COM Interface Methods Using BSTRs

To pull together all the information concerning COM string manipulation thus far, let's implement a very simple interface called IText. To ensure all COM language mappings can make use of this interface, we will stick to the preferred BSTR data type:

```
// IText contains methods which work with the COM string of choice.
DECLARE_INTERFACE_(IText, IUnknown)
{
      STDMETHOD(Speak) (BSTR bstrMessage)      PURE;
      STDMETHOD(GiveMeABSTR) (BSTR* bstr)      PURE;
};
```

The companion CD-ROM contains the CoTextServer project and a C++ client application (CoTextClient). Although these projects are making use of some material not yet covered (class factories, registry entries, and so forth), feel free to examine the source code.

The Speak() method receives a BSTR created by the client and makes use of it internally. Given that the BSTR is a Unicode string, we will need to convert it into a char* in order to send it into any text savvy Win32 API function (unless we configure a 100% Unicode build, which binds us to NT). GiveMeABSTR() is called by a client to receive a new BSTR created by the coclass. As the client will receive a Unicode string, it will also need to convert the string to ANSI if it intends to use any text savvy API function (again, unless it is a 100% Unicode build).

Assume we have implemented IText within a coclass named CoText. This coclass maintains a private BSTR data member, which is created and destroyed in the constructor and destructor of the coclass using the correct system string function:

```
// CoText maintains a private BSTR, which is manipulated by the IText interface.
class CoText : public IText
{
      // Private underlying BSTR.
      BSTR m_bstr;
      ULONG m_refCount;
public:
      CoText()
      {
            m_refCount = 0;
            m_bstr = SysAllocString(L"");
      }
      ~CoText()
```

```
    {
         if (m_bstr)
              SysFreeString(m_bstr);
    }
    // Assume standard IUnknown implementation...
    // IText methods.
    STDMETHODIMP Speak (BSTR bstrMessage);
    STDMETHODIMP GiveMeABSTR (BSTR* bstr);
};
```

The implementation of Speak() will take an incoming client-supplied BSTR (which is Unicode), and convert it into an ANSI string:

```
// Because we are not in a Unicode build, we need to flip between string types.
STDMETHODIMP CoText::Speak(BSTR bstrMessage)
{
    char buff[80];
    // Transform the Unicode BSTR into an ANSI char*
    WideCharToMultiByte(CP_ACP, NULL, bstrMessage,
                    -1, buff, 80, NULL, NULL);
    // Now put ANSI string (buff) into a message box.
    MessageBox(NULL, buff, "The BSTR is...",
                MB_OK | MB_SETFOREGROUND);
    return S_OK;
}
```

GiveMeABSTR() will simply return the internal buffer to the client. To do so requires that we make a copy of the buffer, as the client is responsible for destroying the BSTR when finished. We don't want to give the client direct access to our buffer; that's our business, and we will destroy it when we are released!

```
// GiveMeABSTR() creates a copy of the internal underlying BSTR.
STDMETHODIMP CoText::GiveMeABSTR(BSTR *bstrMessage)
{
    *bstrMessage = SysAllocString(m_bstr);          // Client frees the memory.
    return S_OK;
}
```

Now assume that a client has obtained a valid IText interface. It may exercise the methods as follows. Remember that any BSTR we allocate, or is allocated for us, must be freed using SysFreeString():

```
// First, create a BSTR and send it into the object.
BSTR bstr;
bstr = SysAllocString(L"Is anybody out there?!");
pText-> Speak (bstr);          // Server pops up a message box.
SysFreeString(bstr);          // I made it, I free it.
// Now, we are asking the object for a new BSTR, which is allocated for us.
BSTR bstr2;
pText -> GiveMeABSTR(&bstr2);
// As the BSTR is Unicode, we can convert to ANSI using wcstombs().
char buff[80];
wcstombs(buff, bstr2, 80);   // Convert to ANSI for cout.
cout << "\'" << buff << "\' " << " is what the server said!" << endl;
SysFreeString(bstr2);          // It was made for me, I free it.
pText->Release();              // Done with interface.
```

So then, remember the following: When you create your COM interface methods, always use the BSTR data type in order to ensure that every COM savvy language can make use of your objects. If you choose to use OLECHAR types as interface method parameters, you have limited yourself to C++ only solutions. To work with the BSTR, you must make use of the set of system string functions to correctly manage the underlying memory. Most importantly, remember that COM clients are always responsible for freeing BSTRs returned by COM objects (as well as BSTRs they create themselves).

Debugging Unicode Strings

As a final note concerning COM text programming, you need to know that Visual C++ has an odd default IDE option, which prevents you from seeing the actual text a given Unicode string holds. You may change this option from the Tools | Options menu. Be sure to select the Display Unicode Strings option from the Debug tab, and you will be able to examine the real text in a Unicode string (and that means BSTRs too):

Figure 3-11: Configuration to view Unicode strings.

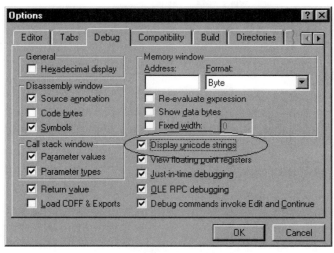

Once this configuration is set, you may examine the underlying buffer of the Unicode string during debugging sessions. Here is a look inside our BSTR data types using the Variables window in the VC IDE:

Figure 3-12: The result of enabling Unicode string debugging.

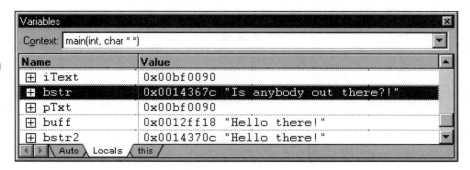

A Summary of Developing COM Interfaces and COM Classes in C++

To summarize the information covered so far in this chapter, when you are creating COM interfaces and coclasses using C++, follow the steps below:

1. Create any custom interfaces using the STDMETHOD macro family, and be sure to derive each interface from IUnknown (directly or indirectly). If you wish, you may use the DECLARE_INTERFACE macros when writing your interface definitions.

2. Using guidgen.exe, assign a new GUID for your interface using the DEFINE_GUID format. Substitute a human readable constant in place of the <<name>> marker.

3. Create the coclass, deriving from all standard or custom interfaces using C++ multiple inheritance.

4. Use the STDMETHODIMP/STDMETHODIMP_ macros in the coclass method implementation.

5. Implement the three methods of IUnknown (AddRef(), QueryInterface(), and Release()) as well as any additional interface methods.

6. When creating COM interface methods manipulating text data, stick to the BSTR data type to allow maximum usage of your coclass. Remember: OLECHAR data types are only usable by C and C++ clients.

Got all that? Let's move onto the next lab and put together what we have learned.

Lab 3-1: COM as a Better C++

In order to get you comfortable with GUIDs, HRESULTs, reference counting, COM strings, and IUnknown logic, we will develop CoCarApp.exe. This application is not an official COM client/server yet. Rather the COM object will be created and manipulated directly inside a single executable (consider this lab "COM as a better C++").

The CoCar coclass we build here will be reused in the next lab, where we place the COM class into a binary DLL home, which is then accessed by a COM client. As well, the global activation function created in this lab will mimic the behavior of a COM class factory almost exactly. As we will see after this lab, the IClassFactory interface is a standard COM mechanism, which allows COM clients to create COM objects in a language-independent and location-neutral manner.

 The solution for this lab can be found on your CD-ROM under:
Labs\Chapter 03\CoCarApp

Step One: Interface Design

Begin by creating a brand new Win32 Console Application project workspace, selecting **empty application**. We will be creating a coclass that supports three custom interfaces. Recall from Chapter 1 that the CCar class exported all functionality of the automobile through the single default public interface. If you looked carefully, you might have noticed that this single interface could have been partitioned into logical groupings (interfaces). Create a new header file named **interfaces.h** and define three new interfaces to model the behaviors of an automobile:

```
// IStats is used to retrieve the pet name of the automobile, as well as display
// all of the stats of the implementing object.
```

```
DECLARE_INTERFACE_(IStats, IUnknown)
{
    STDMETHOD(DisplayStats)() PURE;
    STDMETHOD(GetPetName)(BSTR* petName) PURE;
};
// IEngine models the behavior of an engine. We can speed it up, grab the
// maximum speed as well as get the current speed.
DECLARE_INTERFACE_(IEngine, IUnknown)
{
    STDMETHOD(SpeedUp)() PURE;
    STDMETHOD(GetMaxSpeed)(int* maxSpeed) PURE;
    STDMETHOD(GetCurSpeed)(int* curSpeed) PURE;
};
// ICreateCar is used to set the pet name and the maximum speed of the
// implementing object.
DECLARE_INTERFACE_(ICreateCar, IUnknown)
{
    STDMETHOD(SetPetName)(BSTR petName) PURE;
    STDMETHOD(SetMaxSpeed)(int maxSp) PURE;
};
```

Recall that all custom COM interfaces must derive from IUnknown, so be sure to #include <windows.h> in the interfaces.h file. As well, you should wrap up the interface definition with preprocessor #ifndef/#define/#endif calls, to prevent multiple redefinition errors.

Next up, we need to assign GUIDs to each custom interface. Create another new header file named **iid.h** which will hold all DEFINE_GUID macro listings. Using guidgen.exe, create three new GUIDs with corresponding constants (using the IID_ prefix). Here are possible GUIDs for each interface (yours will be different of course):

```
// {A533DA30-D372-11d2-B8CF-0020781238D4}
DEFINE_GUID(IID_IEngine,
0xa533da30, 0xd372, 0x11d2, 0xb8, 0xcf, 0x0, 0x20, 0x78, 0x12, 0x38, 0xd4);
// {A533DA31-D372-11d2-B8CF-0020781238D4}
DEFINE_GUID(IID_IStats,
0xa533da31, 0xd372, 0x11d2, 0xb8, 0xcf, 0x0, 0x20, 0x78, 0x12, 0x38, 0xd4);
// {A533DA32-D372-11d2-B8CF-0020781238D4}
DEFINE_GUID(IID_ICreateCar,
0xa533da32, 0xd372, 0x11d2, 0xb8, 0xcf, 0x0, 0x20, 0x78, 0x12, 0x38, 0xd4);
```

Now, create another new file named **iid.cpp**. All this file needs to do is make the following #includes. Be sure to insert this file into the project workspace (just like any implementation file, use the **Project | Add To Project | Files...** menu selection):

```
// IID.cpp
#include <windows.h>        // For the good COM stuff.
#include <initguid.h>       // For definition of DEFINE_GUID.
#include "iid.h"            // The IIDs.
```

Having a centralized header file for your application's GUIDs can be very helpful down the road when you need to include the definitions into other projects. The benefit of having a corresponding *.cpp file for your interface IDs is to ensure that <initguid.h> is called automatically before your header file (a necessary step!) rather than relying on the end user of your IIDs to do so.

Step Two: Implement IUnknown

Insert a new C++ class named **CoCar**, which derives from the IEngine, IStats, and
ICreateCar interfaces. As every COM interface derives from IUnknown, you will need to
be sure to implement not only the methods of each custom interface, but also the three
methods of IUnknown. Here is the initial header file of CoCar:

```
// CoCar implements four COM interfaces.
#include "interfaces.h"
class CoCar : public IEngine, public ICreateCar, public IStats
{
public:
    CoCar();
    virtual ~CoCar();
    // IUnknown
    STDMETHODIMP QueryInterface(REFIID riid, void** pIFace);
    STDMETHODIMP_(ULONG)AddRef();
    STDMETHODIMP_(ULONG)Release();
    // IEngine
    STDMETHODIMP SpeedUp();
    STDMETHODIMP GetMaxSpeed(int* maxSpeed);
    STDMETHODIMP GetCurSpeed(int* curSpeed);
    // IStats
    STDMETHODIMP DisplayStats();
    STDMETHODIMP GetPetName(BSTR* petName);
    // ICreateCar
    STDMETHODIMP SetPetName(BSTR petName);
    STDMETHODIMP SetMaxSpeed(int maxSp);
};
```

Unlike the previous C++ version of Car, we will not be using cout to implement the interface methods. This time we make use of a simple Win32 API MessageBox() call. By doing
so now, we will be able to port this CoCar class into a binary DLL in the next lab without
being tied to a Win32 Console client!

Let's implement reference counting first. Add a private reference counter named
m_refCount (of type ULONG) to CoCar, and set it to zero in the constructor. AddRef()
will bump this counter by one, while Release() will decrement this counter by one and
check for the final release, at which time the object deallocates itself from memory using
"delete this" syntax:

```
// Establishing your object's reference counting schema.
STDMETHODIMP_(ULONG) CoCar::AddRef()
{
    return ++m_refCount;
}
STDMETHODIMP_(ULONG) CoCar::Release()
{
    if(--m_refCount == 0)
    {
        delete this;
        return 0;
    }
    else
        return m_refCount;
}
```

Next, implement QueryInterface() to return interface pointers for IUnknown, IStats, ICreateCar, and IEngine. Don't forget to call AddRef() if you hand out an interface pointer, and return E_NOINTERFACE to indicate no such support:

```
// QueryInterface() is responsible for scoping the 'this' pointer for a given client.
STDMETHODIMP CoCar::QueryInterface(REFIID riid, void** pIFace)
{
    // Which aspect of me do they want?
    if(riid == IID_IUnknown)
    {
        *pIFace = (IUnknown*)(IEngine*)this;
    }
    else if(riid == IID_IEngine)
    {
        *pIFace = (IEngine*)this;
    }
    else if(riid == IID_IStats)
    {
        *pIFace = (IStats*)this;
    }
    else if(riid == IID_ICreateCar)
    {
        *pIFace = (ICreateCar*)this;
    }
    else
    {
        *pIFace = NULL;
        return E_NOINTERFACE;
    }
    ((IUnknown*)(*pIFace))->AddRef();
    return S_OK;
}
```

Step Three: Implement the Custom Interface Methods

With IUnknown complete, we now need to implement the custom interfaces of CoCar. Add the following data members to the private sector, and initialize each item to a default value in the constructor. Be sure to use the correct system string functions when working with your BSTR:

```
// Private data of CoCar.
BSTR  m_petName;      // Initialize via SysAllocString(), kill with SysFreeString().
int   m_maxSpeed;     // The max speed of the CoCar.
int   m_currSpeed;    // The CoCar's current speed.
// CoCar's constructor and destructor.
CoCar::CoCar() : m_refCount(0), m_currSpeed(0), m_maxSpeed(0)
{
    m_petName = SysAllocString(L"Default Pet Name");
}
CoCar::~CoCar()
{
    if(m_petName)
        SysFreeString(m_petName);
}
```

The implementation of IEngine is trivial. SpeedUp() will increment the m_currSpeed data point by 10, and return S_OK. GetMaxSpeed() is a simple accessor for the m_maxSpeed variable, where GetCurSpeed() accesses m_currSpeed:

```
// IEngine implementation
STDMETHODIMP CoCar::SpeedUp()
{
    m_currSpeed += 10;
    return S_OK;
}
STDMETHODIMP CoCar::GetMaxSpeed(int* maxSpeed)
{
    *maxSpeed = m_maxSpeed;
    return S_OK;
}
STDMETHODIMP CoCar::GetCurSpeed(int* curSpeed)
{
    *curSpeed = m_currSpeed;
    return S_OK;
}
```

ICreateCar has two methods. SetPetName() takes a client-allocated BSTR, and sets it to the internal BSTR buffer using SysReAllocString(). SetMaxSpeed() does what it has always done: sets the maximum speed as long as the value is less than or equal to the MAX_SPEED constant (which you should define in the coclass header file):

```
// ICreateCar implementation.
STDMETHODIMP CoCar::SetPetName(BSTR petName)
{
    SysReAllocString(&m_petName, petName);
    return S_OK;
}
STDMETHODIMP CoCar::SetMaxSpeed(int maxSp)
{
    if(maxSp < MAX_SPEED)
        m_maxSpeed = maxSp;
    return S_OK;
}
```

Finally, we have IStats. GetPetName() returns a copy of our internal buffer to the client. You will want to use SysAllocString() for this purpose:

```
// Return to the client a copy of your internal BSTR buffer.
STDMETHODIMP CoCar::GetPetName(BSTR* petName)
{
    *petName = SysAllocString(m_petName);
    return S_OK;
}
```

DisplayStats() will simply pop up two message boxes to show the current speed and pet name. The only trick here is the Unicode to ANSI conversion:

```
// Place the state of the CoCar into a couple message boxes.
STDMETHODIMP CoCar::DisplayStats()
{
    // Need to transfer a BSTR to a char array.
    char buff[MAX_LENGTH];      // Another program defined const.
```

```
        WideCharToMultiByte(CP_ACP, NULL, m_petName, -1, buff,
                            MAX_LENGTH, NULL, NULL);
        MessageBox(NULL, buff, "Pet Name", MB_OK | MB_SETFOREGROUND);
        memset(buff, 0, sizeof(buff));
        sprintf(buff, "%d", m_maxSpeed);
        MessageBox(NULL, buff, "Max Speed", MB_OK| MB_SETFOREGROUND);
        return S_OK;
}
```

That wraps up the implementation of CoCar. Over the course of this book, we will add
more and more functionality to this COM object (including a more efficient set of interfaces). Go ahead and compile at this point to be sure your project is stable.

Step Four: Create a Bootstrapping Function

In real COM, objects are created with COM library calls. A standard COM interface,
IClassFactory, can be extracted from a server, and from it, a client can create a related
coclass. We will examine COM's creation mechanism after this lab wraps up. Be aware that
the code you are writing for the following global function will mimic the functionality of
IClassFactory::CreateInstance() almost exactly.

   For the time being, however, we will create a special function that knows how to make
CoCars and returns an IUnknown reference. Create a global function in your
CoCarApp.cpp file called CarFactory():

```
// This is a global function which knows how to create CoCars.
HRESULT CarFactory(void** pIFace);
```

This function is a more generic version of the Rect API function set. Recall from Chapter 2
that we had two distinct steps to create a C3DRect: call a creation method, and ask for an
interface pointer with another. Here, we always get back IUnknown to help the client get
up and running:

```
// The CarFactory() function is a global function, and not part of the CoCar.
// If we scoped this method to CoCar, we would have a 'dog chasing its tail'
// situation: We would have to create a car to create a car...
HRESULT CarFactory(void** pIFace)
{
    HRESULT hr;
    LPUNKNOWN pUnk = NULL; // System typedef for IUnknown*.
    // Dynamically allocate a new CoCar.
    CoCar *pCar = new CoCar();
    // Fetch IUnknown pointer from CoCar.
    hr = pCar->QueryInterface(IID_IUnknown, (void**)&pUnk);
    if(SUCCEEDED(hr))
    {
        *pIFace = pUnk;
        return S_OK;
    }
    else
    {
        delete pCar;
        return E_FAIL;
    }
}
```

What also makes this function unique from the Rect API is that we can now create any number of CoCars dynamically. The Rect API operated on only a single global object at a time. With this function complete, we now have one final step: creating the client-side code.

Step Five: Program the Client-Side Code

Finally, we need to add code to your main() function to perform the following:

1. Create a CoCar by making a call to CarFactory(). You will need to define an IUnknown* variable to send on in for this purpose:

```
// Go get IUnknown from a new CoCar.
IUnknown* pUnk;
HRESULT hr;
hr = CarFactory((void**) &pUnk);
```

2. From the resulting IUnknown pointer, attempt to obtain IID_ICreateCar, and if successful, exercise the interface methods:

```
// Create a CoCar
ICreateCar *pICreateCar;
pUnk->QueryInterface(IID_ICreateCar, (void**)&pICreateCar);
pICreateCar->SetMaxSpeed(30);
BSTR name = SysAllocString(OLESTR("Bertha"));
pICreateCar->SetPetName(name);
SysFreeString(name);
```

3. Obtain the IStats interface from the CoCar, and call DisplayStats(). You should see the CoCar's messages pop up when you run the program.

4. Now ask for IEngine. Given the laws of IUnknown, you may ask for IEngine from any valid pointer; thus, you may call QueryInterface() from your IUnknown or ICreateCar pointer. As before, rev the car until the engine block cracks. Use IStats::GetPetName() to return the pet name of the coclass, which we can format into an ANSI string using WideCharToMultiByte() or wcstombs() to inform the user of the car's demise:

```
// Rev it!
int curSp = 0;
int maxSp = 0;
pUnk->QueryInterface(IID_IEngine, (void**)&pIEngine);
pIEngine->GetMaxSpeed(&maxSp);
do
{
     pIEngine->SpeedUp();
     pIEngine->GetCurSpeed(&curSp);
     cout << "Speed is: " << curSp << endl;
}while(curSp <= maxSp);
// Convert to char array.
char buff[MAX_NAME_LENGTH];
BSTR bstr;
pStats->GetPetName(&bstr);
wcstombs(buff, bstr, MAX_NAME_LENGTH);
cout << buff << " has blown up! Lead Foot!" << endl << endl;
SysFreeString(bstr);
```

Be sure to Release() all interface pointers you have acquired to destroy the CoCar:

```
// Release any acquired interfaces to destroy the CoCar
// currently in memory.
if(pUnk) pUnk->Release();
if(pIEngine) pIEngine->Release();
if(pStats) pStats->Release();
if(pICreateCar) pICreateCar->Release();
```

When contrasting this lab with the Rect API, here we have bound together the lifetime management and interface retrieval into a single class (given the utility of IUnknown), rather than three global functions. So far so good! We have taken a C++ class, and factored it out into a number of COM interfaces, and implemented them in a coclass. However, CoCar is not a reusable binary object yet. We need to get our hands around class factories and component housing to reach that goal.

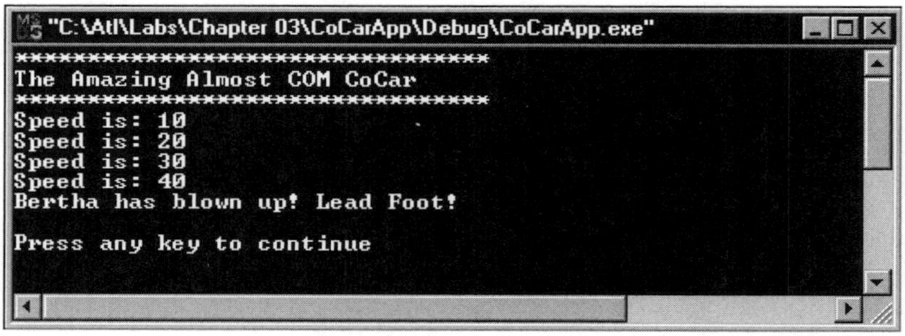

Figure 3-13: The "almost real COM" application.

Activating COM Objects

COM objects do not sit alone on your hard drive as simple *.obj files. COM objects are packaged up inside some type of "component housing." Recall earlier in this chapter we examined the various physical relationships between a client and COM server (in-process, local, and remote). These three relationships were determined, in part, by the type of binary packaging containing the COM objects (DLL or EXE). Given that your COM objects need to live in some sort of binary house (which could be located outside of the client's process), the first question you might ask is, "How can a client create the objects living within another binary?" A perfect question to ask, as we now turn our attention to the standard way to create COM objects residing in a binary server.

You know COM is a language-independent architecture, and therefore a client cannot create a COM object using a language-specific keyword. For example, the C++ **new** operator has no built-in ability to create a new instance of a binary object. As we will see in Chapter 4, the Visual Basic **New** keyword appears to automatically load and extract an object from a binary server, but this is just a language mapping issue. Under the hood VB makes the same set of COM library calls that the C++ developer makes by hand. Furthermore, the VB **New** keyword and the C++ **new** operator may look the same; however, the semantics behind them are specific to the respective language. Clearly, language-specific constraints will not help out much in a language-independent architecture such as COM.

In addition, a COM client can create a server that may reside at any location in the enterprise. The promise of location transparency allows the same set of client-side COM code to activate a COM object located on the same machine as the client, a machine down the hall, or a machine across the state. Given these two issues (locality and language independence), we need a language- and location-neutral way in which a client can create a COM object. There is such a way through (you guessed it) another standard COM interface named IClassFactory.

COM Class Objects and IClassFactory

The definition of IClassFactory is also found in <unknwn.h>, and looks like the following:

```
// IClassFactory is defined in <unknwn.h>.
MIDL_INTERFACE("00000001-0000-0000-C000-000000000046")
    IClassFactory : public IUnknown
    {
    public:
        virtual /* [local] */ HRESULT STDMETHODCALLTYPE CreateInstance(
            /* [unique][in] */ IUnknown __RPC_FAR *pUnkOuter,
            /* [in] */ REFIID riid,
            /* [iid_is][out] */ void __RPC_FAR * __RPC_FAR *ppvObject) = 0;
        virtual /* [local] */ HRESULT STDMETHODCALLTYPE LockServer(
            /* [in] */ BOOL fLock) = 0;
    };
```

IClassFactory specifies two methods that define a behavior for creating and monitoring COM objects in a language-independent and location-neutral manner. The core method is CreateInstance(), which will create a specific coclass on behalf of the calling client. LockServer() is used to hold the binary server itself in memory per client request (we will see why this can be helpful in just a moment). If we strip away the comments and standard COM macros, IClassFactory can be distilled down to the following:

```
// The core syntax of IClassFactory, stripped of comments and COM macros.
interface IClassFactory : public IUnknown
{
    virtual HRESULT CreateInstance(LPUNKNOWN pUnk, REFIID riid,
                                    void** ppv) = 0;
    virtual HRESULT LockServer(BOOL fLock) = 0;
};
```

It is important to point out that a secondary class factory interface, IClassFactory2, is also defined in COM. This interface extends the behavior of IClassFactory by supporting additional methods for licensing support. For example, you might have an ActiveX control that you do not want developers to use in their application until they provide (read: pay for) a valid *.lic (license) file. IClassFactory2 provides this functionality, and we will see details of this standard interface in Chapter 14. Now that we have an understanding of the behavior specified by IClassFactory(2), we can introduce a new COM term: the class object.

A *class object* is a COM object implementing the IClassFactory (or IClassFactory2) interface. Class objects are often called *class factories*.

Class objects exist only to create another type of COM object. This is how COM provides a language- and location-neutral means by which a client can create a coclass located in a binary server. If every COM-enabled language has some way to access the IClassFactory interface, every client is able to create the object they desire in a language-independent manner. Furthermore, as the actual implementation of the IClassFactory methods is hidden at the binary level, we (as the object creators) can use whatever language keywords we have at our disposal (such as the C++ **new** operator) to create the associated coclass. As they say, everything can be solved with another level of indirection!

COM class objects have a one-to-one correspondence with the object they are responsible for creating. In other words, every creatable COM object contained in a server has exactly one class object. Class objects are never responsible for creating a <u>set</u> of COM objects, no matter how related these objects appear to be. A server containing two creatable COM objects would break down like this:

Figure 3-14: Class objects create related coclasses.

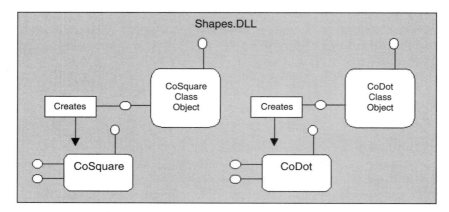

As suggested by Figure 3-14, class objects only implement the IUnknown and IClassFactory interfaces. Class objects <u>never</u>, <u>ever</u> implement interfaces supported by the object they are creating! The class factory simply creates the associated object, asks for a particular interface from the object, and returns it to the client. If you like, consider the COM class factory to be a language- and location-independent **new** operator.

Building a Class Factory

Let's develop a class object for the CoHexagon coclass defined earlier in this chapter. As you recall, CoHexagon implemented the IDraw and IShapeEdit interfaces. Our class factory, which we will call CoHexFactory, is responsible for creating CoHexagon objects for a client and returning some interface pointer from CoHexagon. The definition of CoHexFactory should appear straightforward:

```
// This class factory is in charge of creating CoHexagon objects.
class CoHexFactory : public IClassFactory
{
public:
    // constructor and destructor...
    // IUnknown methods.
    STDMETHODIMP QueryInterface(REFIID riid, void** pIFace);
    STDMETHODIMP_(ULONG)AddRef();
    STDMETHODIMP_(ULONG)Release();
    // IClassFactory methods.
    STDMETHODIMP CreateInstance( LPUNKNOWN pUnk, REFIID riid,
                                 void** pIFace);
    STDMETHODIMP LockServer(BOOL fLock);
```

```
private:
     ULONG m_refCount;
};
```

As with any COM object, the implementation of AddRef() and Release() for a class factory
will simply increment or decrement the internal reference counter, and check for the final
release to remove itself from memory:

```
// Class objects, being COM objects, maintain a reference count.
STDMETHODIMP_(ULONG) CoHexFactory::AddRef()
{
     return ++m_refCount;
}
STDMETHODIMP_(ULONG) CoHexFactory::Release()
{
     if(--m_refCount == 0)
     {
          delete this;
          return 0;
     }
     return m_refCount;
}
```

QueryInterface() will simply hand out pointers to the standard IUnknown or IClassFactory
interfaces:

```
// Every single 'generic' class object will have a QueryInterface() implementation
// which looks like the following. Again note that there are no provisions for
// the interfaces supported by the related coclass (CoHexagon).
STDMETHODIMP CoHexFactory::QueryInterface(REFIID riid, void** pIFace)
{
     if(riid == IID_IUnknown)
          *pIFace = (IUnknown*)this;
     else if(riid == IID_IClassFactory)
          *pIFace = (IClassFactory*)this;
     if(*pIFace){
          ((IUnknown*)(*pIFace))->AddRef();
          return S_OK;
     }
     *pIFace = NULL;
     return E_NOINTERFACE;
}
```

Implementing IClassFactory::CreateInstance()

So far, class objects look like any other COM object; however, class objects also support
the IClassFactory interface. CreateInstance() is responsible for creating a new instance of
the associated COM object, asking the object for the client-specified interface, and returning it to the client. As you examine the code behind CreateInstance(), think back to the
global CarFactory() method you developed in the previous lab. You should be able to see
the connection between the two. CarFactory() was also responsible for creating a coclass
and returning an interface to the caller. However, as we are now interested in moving
CoCar into the binary realm, we need a standard and well-known way for COM languages
to create the object (after all, what does Visual Basic know of the C++ centric
CarFactory() function?).

The first parameter of CreateInstance() is used in conjunction with COM aggregation. Recall that aggregation is one form of binary reuse in COM. We will not examine the details of aggregation until Chapter 8 and will assume this parameter to always be NULL (which specifies no aggregation support is being requested). The second parameter is the IID of the interface the client is interested in obtaining from the coclass once it has been created. As CoHexFactory creates CoHexagons, this parameter will more than likely be from the set {IID_IUnknown, IID_IDraw, IID_IShapeEdit}. The final parameter, void**, is a place to put the interface pointer fetched from the coclass. Without further ado, here is the implementation of CreateInstance():

```
// Looks a lot like the CarFactory(), does it not?
STDMETHODIMP CoHexFactory::CreateInstance(LPUNKNOWN pUnk, REFIID riid, void** pIFace)
{
    // We do not support aggregation in this class object.
    // If LPUNKNOWN is not NULL, return this standard HRESULT.
    if(pUnk != NULL)
        return CLASS_E_NOAGGREGATION;
    // CoHexFactory makes CoHexagons.
    CoHexagon* pHexObj = NULL;
    HRESULT hr;
    pHexObj = new CoHexagon;
    // Ask object for an interface.
    hr = pHexObj -> QueryInterface(riid, pIFace);
    // Problem? We must delete the memory we allocated!
    if (FAILED(hr))
        delete pHexObj;
    return hr;
}
```

Implementing IClassFactory::LockServer()

Finally, we need to address the LockServer() method of IClassFactory in order to finish up our CoHexagon class factory. LockServer() provides a way for a client to lock the server down in memory, even if there are currently no active objects in the server. The reason to do so is client optimization. Once a client obtains an IClassFactory pointer, it may call LockServer(TRUE), which will bump up a global level lock counter maintained by the server. When the COM runtime attempts to unload a server from memory, this lock count is consulted first. If the value of the global lock counter is not zero (which signifies no locks), COM will just stop by later and ask again.

For example, as a COM client, you may wish to load up your COM servers when the application first comes to life, but delay the creation of the actual COM objects until the time they are specifically needed. To prevent having to reload the server, you may lock it down upon startup, even though you do not intend to create any objects at this time. Again, remember that LockServer() is nothing more than an optimization technique, and a way to keep a server loaded into memory even when it contains no living, breathing COM objects.

Any client that calls LockServer(TRUE) must call LockServer(FALSE) before terminating in order to decrement the server's global lock counter. With that said, assume that somewhere in the server code is a globally declared ULONG named g_lockCount. This variable is used to represent the number of existing client locks. The LockServer() method of CoHexFactory may then be implemented as such:

```
// LockServer() simply increments or decrements the server level global lock counter.
STDMETHODIMP CoHexFactory::LockServer(BOOL fLock)
{
     if(fLock)
          ++g_lockCount;
     else
          --g_lockCount;
     return S_OK;
}
```

The next step is to package up CoHexagon and the CoHexFactory into a binary home.

Implementing DLL Component Housing

The last major hurdle facing us before CoHexagon is ready for client access is to create a binary home for itself and its class object to dwell. Assume you have created a Win32 DLL project workspace named Shapes, and wish to expose your COM objects from this in-process server. Every COM-based DLL gets its work done by exporting (through a standard DEF file) four necessary functions. Here is a breakdown of the functionality provided by each DLL export:

■ **DllGetClassObject()**: This method returns an IClassFactory pointer for a client, based off the CLSID of the object it is attempting to create. It is here that we create the class factory itself.

■ **DllCanUnloadNow()**: Remember the global lock counter? This is the function that will return "yes" or "no" to the question "Can I safely unload this DLL server from memory at this time?"

■ **DllRegisterServer()** and **DllUnregisterServer()**: Every well-behaved in-proc COM server should insert all necessary information into and out of the system registry when asked to do so. This is called *self-registration* of the server, and these two exports provide this very behavior.

As we have not yet looked into the COM runtime and the system registry, we will hold off on the details of DllRegisterServer() and DllUnregisterServer() for the moment, and concentrate on the other two required exports.

Exporting the Server's Class Objects: DllGetClassObject() and CLSIDs

The implementation of DllGetClassObject() creates a new class factory and returns the correct IClassFactory interface to the client. If your server contains a collection of coclasses, you will examine the incoming CLSID parameter of DllGetClassObject() to determine which class factory to create. This method has the following signature:

```
// Creates a given class factory for
// the client based on the CLSID of the coclass.
STDAPI DllGetClassObject(REFCLSID rclsid, REFIID riid, void** ppv);
```

Assume shapes.dll contains two coclasses (CoSquare and CoDot). You may visualize DllGetClassObject() as the following:

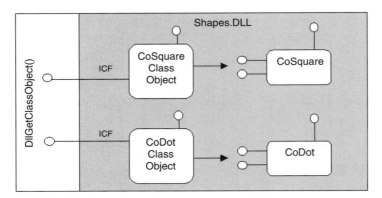

Figure 3-15: DllGetClass-Object() exposes class factories.

Every COM object contained in a binary package must be uniquely identified in the COM universe. In order to identify which coclass to create, we need to give our CoHexagon object a CLSID (which is simply a GUID). Again using the DEFINE_ GUID macro provided by guidgen.exe, we might specify CoHexagon as the following (the human readable constants of a coclass are prefixed with CLSID_ by convention):

```
// {F12327B0-DE3A-11d2-AAF4-00A0C9312D57}
DEFINE_GUID(CLSID_CoHexagon,
0xf12327b0, 0xde3a, 0x11d2, 0xaa, 0xf4, 0x0, 0xa0, 0xc9, 0x31, 0x2d, 0x57);
```

Every single coclass in the server will need a unique CLSID. Do note that the class factory itself does <u>not</u> receive a CLSID. Here is an implementation of the first server export, DllGetClassObject():

```
// DllGetClassObject() is in charge of creating a class factory, and returning the
// IClassFactory interface to the COM client.
STDAPI DllGetClassObject(REFCLSID rclsid, REFIID riid, void** ppv)
{
    HRESULT hr;
    CoHexFactory *pHFact = NULL;
    // We only know how to make CoHexagon objects in this house.
    if(rclsid != CLSID_CoHexagon)
        return CLASS_E_CLASSNOTAVAILABLE;
    // They want a CoHexagon, so create the hexagon factory.
    pHFact = new CoHexFactory;
    // Go get the interface from the Hex Factory (IClassFactory(2) or IUnknown)
    hr = pHFact -> QueryInterface(riid, ppv);
    if(FAILED(hr))
        delete pHFact;
    return hr;
}
```

This implementation of DllGetClassObject() is quite simple, as shapes.dll contains a single coclass (CoHexagon) and therefore a single class factory named CoHexFactory. As you might imagine, if our COM DLL server contained 20 different coclasses, that would be 20 different class factories that DllGetClassObject() could create for the client. We could set up simple if/else logic to test the CLSID and create the correct class object. As we build more elaborate servers during the course of this book, you will be given a chance to do this very thing (with the welcome help of ATL).

Managing Server Lifetime: DllCanUnloadNow()

We know that a given COM object is in charge of deleting itself from memory when the last client releases the final interface pointer. For example, CoHexagon's implementation of Release(), like all COM objects, looks like the following:

```
// Every object maintains an internal reference counter.
STDMETHODIMP_(ULONG) CoHexagon::Release()
{
    if(--m_refCount == 0)
    {
        delete this;
        return 0;
    }
    else
        return m_refCount;
}
```

However, we also must provide a way for the server itself to "know" how many active objects are living in the binary house at any given time. Just because the server might have an active CoHexagon object inside, a DLL itself has no innate ability to understand that important fact. In other words, a DLL has no clue that a client has created a CoHexagon. We must inform the DLL of this fact in order for the DLL to stay in memory as long as there is some active object in the server. In short, we must provide the hooks.

A common way to inform your DLL that it has some active objects is to provide another global level counter, which identifies the number of active objects in the server at any given time. Whenever a coclass (CoHexagon) or class object (CoHexFactory) is created, the given constructors of these classes should bump up this global object counter variable. Whenever a coclass (CoHexagon) or class object (CoHexFactory) is terminated, the destructor should decrement this global object counter. Here is the revised CoHexagon class, which properly adjusts the server-wide object counter (CoHexFactory would also need to be retrofitted in the same way):

```
// Every COM object in your DLL server needs to 'tell' the DLL when it has
// a new object coming to life, or when an object has died.
// Assume that g_objCount has been defined in some external file.
// Server gained an object.
CoHexagon::CoHexagon()
{
    g_objCount++;    // Also increment in class factory.
}
// Server lost an object.
CoHexagon::~CoHexagon
{
    g_objCount--;    // Also decrement in class factory.
}
```

So then, a given DLL has some global variables to worry about. As we have seen, one global counter maintains the number of outstanding locks. This global counter is adjusted by IClassFactory::LockServer(). The other global lock counter represents the number of active objects in the server at any given time, and is adjusted by the constructors and destructors of each and every COM object. Thus, a DLL can be unloaded safely by the COM runtime only if there are no server locks and no active objects. DllCanUnloadNow()

can check the two global variables maintaining this information, and return S_OK or S_FALSE accordingly:

```
// The DllCanUnloadNow() server export informs the COM runtime when it is
// safe to unload the DLL from memory.
ULONG g_lockCount = 0;              // Modified by ICF::LockServer.
ULONG g_objCount = 0;               // Modified by ctor & dtor of any coclass in the server.
STDAPI DllCanUnloadNow(void)
{
    if(g_lockCount == 0 && g_objCount == 0)
        return S_OK;                // Unload me.
    else
        return S_FALSE;             // Keep me alive.
}
```

> **Note:** Clients may force a call to DllCanUnloadNow() during idle item by invoking the COM library function CoFreeUnusedLibraries(). This call is not mandatory, but can be helpful to ensure our DLLs are not in memory longer than necessary.

You may wonder why we need to maintain two global counters in the DLL server. Could we not have a single global counter that is adjusted by LockServer() as well as the constructors and destructors of the objects? Sure, you bet. This is more or less a stylistic choice you can make as you develop your COM servers. In Chapter 5 we will take the "single counter in a server" approach. For now, we will stick with one counter for locking and another for the number of active objects, just to keep the details firm in your mind.

Exporting the Exports

Now that we have written DllGetClassObject() and DllCanUnloadNow(), we need to expose them to the outside world. To actually export these two DLL functions, you will need to assemble a standard Win32 DEF file, which must be included into your current project. The name of the library is the exact same name as your project workspace:

```
LIBRARY "SHAPES"
EXPORTS
    DllGetClassObject       @1      PRIVATE
    DllCanUnloadNow         @2      PRIVATE
```

As long as we wrote all this code in the context of a Win32 DLL project workspace, we can compile this COM server! However, before a client could create and use the object, we first must enter the correct information into the system registry.

The Service Control Manager (SCM) and the System Registry

In order for the COM runtime to locate and load a server into memory, the Service Control Manager (SCM) consults a utility known as the *system registry*. The registry is a local system database, which specifies (among other things) all the COM-centric information for a given computer. You may access the Registry Editor by running regedit.exe from the Windows Run command.

The registry is broken into a series of topmost nodes called *hives*. The most important hive for COM developers is HKEY_CLASSES_ROOT (abbreviate to simply HKCR). Figure 3-16 illustrates the hives found on a WinNT workstation installation:

Figure 3-16: The Registry Editor.

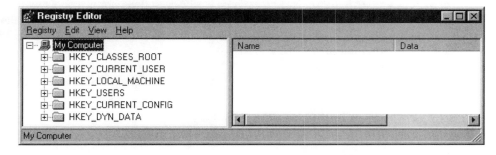

Entries under a hive are called *keys*, which may contain *subkeys*. A given key or subkey may contain string or numerical *values*. Entire books have been written about the layout and programming of the Windows registry, but luckily COM developers only need to understand a small subset of its overall functionality, beginning with the ProgID.

Programmatic Identifiers (ProgIDs)

Let's explore your computer's registry. The first thing listed under HKCR is a long list of file extensions, which we have no interest in at all. Scroll past this list until you find the first real text entry located after the final file extension. When you find that item (mine happens to be Access.Application), expand it:

Figure 3-17: ProgIDs map to CLSIDs.

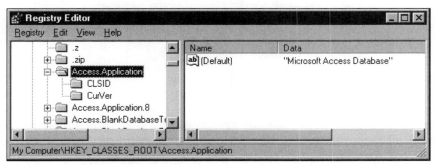

These strings <u>are</u> COM related, and are called Programmatic Identifiers (ProgIDs). ProgIDs are a text-based alternative used to refer to a COM object residing in some server. ProgIDs are simply text mappings for CLSIDs. As you can see, every ProgID listing has a subkey mapping to the corresponding CLSID value as well as an optional CurVer (current version) subkey. The standard format to follow when creating a ProgID for your coclass is ServerName.CoclassName.Version (the version is optional). ProgIDs are not guaranteed to be unique! If you get into the habit of beginning a ProgID with the name of your company, you are quite reasonably assured uniqueness. For example: MyCompany.Shapes.CoHexagon.1.

Why do we need ProgIDs? ProgIDs are useful for certain COM-enabled languages that have no ability to refer to the raw GUID associated to your coclass. In effect, a ProgID is a language-neutral way to identify a COM object. For example, VBScript needs the ProgID of a coclass to load the server into memory. VBScript does not provide a way to reference the raw 128-bit number of CoHexagon in the code. Visual Basic proper <u>does</u> allow a VB programmer to work with the real GUID, and ProgIDs are optional in modern VB (but not VBScript) programming.

The COM library provides two functions that allow us to obtain a ProgID given a CLSID, and vice versa. You may obtain the CLSID of a given ProgID using the COM library function CLSIDFromProgID():

```
// I have the ProgID, what was that CLSID again?
CLSID clsid;
CLSIDFromProgID(L"Shapes.CoHexagon.1", &clsid);
```

To fetch the ProgID given a CLSID, make a call to ProgIDFromCLSID():

```
// I have the GUID of the object, what was that ProgID again?
LPOLESTR progid;        // Array of OLECHARs
ProgIDFromCLSID(clsid, &progid);
```

In order to obtain a CLSID from a ProgID, the ProgID is located from HKCR, and the CLSID subkey is consulted.

A Critical Key: HKEY_CLASSES_ROOT\CLSID

The next point of interest is the CLSID key. The CLSID key is where SCM ultimately ends up when looking for the physical path to your COM server. Each subkey of HKCR\CLSID begins with the GUID for the entry. Figure 3-18 reveals the CLSID of Microsoft's Data Access Object's (DAO) DBEngine coclass:

Figure 3-18:
HKCR\CLSID maps to ProgIDs and the server's physical path.

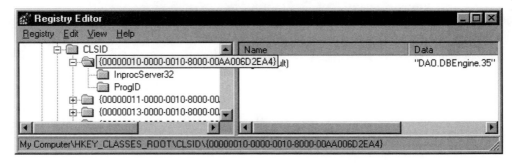

Under a given CLSID entry, you may find any of the following subkeys:

- **ProgID:** This key maps back to the ProgID associated with the coclass. When you call ProgIDFromCLSID(), SCM will examine the ProgID subkey of a given CLSID listing.

- **VersionIndependentProgID:** Same value as the ProgID key, without the version suffix. Recall that ProgIDs do not have to be versioned. Often, a developer may choose to register a version-independent and version-dependent ProgID for the same coclass.

Using the VersionIndependentProgID subkey allows SCM to reference each from the same CLSID subkey.

- **InprocServer32:** For in-process COM servers, this is the most important of all CLSID subkeys. This value is the physical path to the DLL server (for example, "C:\MyServers\Shapes\Debug\shapes.dll").

- **LocalServer32:** If you have COM objects that live in an EXE rather than a DLL, the value of LocalServer32 is the path to the COM executable (for example, "C:\MyServers\Shapes\Debug\shapes.exe"). We will work with this subkey in Chapter 5, where we create EXE component housing for a local (and remote) server.

There are other keys, subkeys, and values of HKCR that are useful for COM development; however, the above list is just right for now. At minimum, every COM class in your server (such as CoHexagon) needs a ProgID and CLSID entry in the system registry. So how do we stuff this information into the system registry?

Registering Your COM Servers

Recall that well-behaved in-proc servers export four well-known functions. Of these, DllRegisterServer() and DllUnregisterServer() are used to enter or remove the correct registry information for your server. These methods may be called by commercial installation programs, the regsvr32.exe utility, or programmatically with API calls. The implementations of these functions involve using a handful of Win32 Registry API functions, and to be honest, are about as much fun as discovering you have a computer virus. The code behind these methods is not impossible, but can be rather tricky.

COM development libraries, such as ATL, MFC, and Visual Basic, take care of the dirty work of implementing these functions for us. Until Chapter 6, where we begin using the Active Template Library to build our COM servers, we will take a shortcut ourselves. We will write our own registry scripts (REG file), which can be used to merge our server information into the registry automatically, bypassing the need to code DllRegisterServer() by hand. To create a REG file, we create a new text file and save it with an *.reg file extension. At the very least, this file should insert the following information into the system registry:

- A ProgID listing directly under HKCR, with a single subkey providing the CLSID.
- The CLSID of our coclass under HKCR\CLSID. Add in an InprocServer32 subkey (or LocalServer32 for EXE servers) that points to the physical path of our DLL (or EXE) server.

In order to get the correct CLSID format, you can copy the commented line from the DEFINE_GUID macro (guidgen.exe was kind enough to supply that for you):

```
// {F12327B0-DE3A-11d2-AAF4-00A0C9312D57}
DEFINE_GUID(CLSID_CoHexagon,
0xf12327b0, 0xde3a, 0x11d2, 0xaa, 0xf4, 0x0, 0xa0, 0xc9, 0x31, 0x2d, 0x57);
```

Here are some notes about REG file syntax: The REGEDIT tag is not optional and must be listed on the very first line. You <u>must</u> have a single space between each side of any assignment operator, and must <u>not</u> have spaces between keys and subkeys. To be sure, the devil is in the details. Here would be a minimal and complete REG file for our in-process shapes server:

```
REGEDIT
HKEY_CLASSES_ROOT\Shapes.CoHexagon\CLSID = {F12327B0-DE3A-11d2-AAF4-00A0C9312D57}
HKEY_CLASSES_ROOT\CLSID\{F12327B0-DE3A-11d2-AAF4-00A0C9312D57} = Shapes.CoHexagon
HKEY_CLASSES_ROOT\CLSID\{F12327B0-DE3A-11d2-AAF4-00A0C9312D57}\InprocServer32 =
C:\ILoveCOM\Shapes\Debug\shapes.dll
```

Once you save out this file, simply double-click on it from the Windows Explorer to merge
your information into the system registry. If your entries do not look something like the
following, you have problems with your REG file syntax. Here is the ProgID listing
entered from the shapes.reg file:

Figure 3-19:
ProgID listing
for CoHexagon.

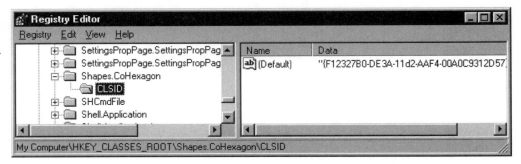

And here is the listing under the CLSID key:

Figure 3-20:
A path to
shapes.dll,
listed under
HKCR\CLSID.

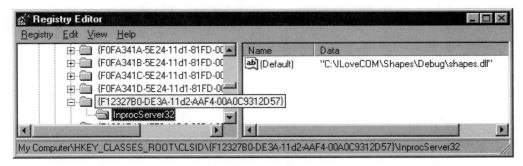

> **Note:**   Needless to say, the GUIDs, ProgIDs, and physical paths will always
> depend on your current COM project.

> **Note:**   Class factories are not entered into the system registry. Clients obtain
> IClassFactory interfaces using COM library functions.

Now, let's pull this knowledge together to create our first official COM server, using
straight C++. As mentioned, this process will prove both painful and edifying. However,
remember that ATL is just around the corner, and takes care of much of the necessary
COM boilerplate code on your behalf.

On a related note, ATL expects that the system registry, component housing, class objects, interfaces, and coclasses are nothing new to you. Taking the time to write some raw COM code will serve you well.

Lab 3-2: Developing an In-Process COM Server in C++

Here is your first real COM server. You will be taking the CoCar class created in Lab 3-1 and develop a class factory to activate it per client request. You will also place your new objects into a Win32 DLL, implement the minimal server exports (DllGetClassObject() and DllCanUnloadNow()), and create a registration file to merge your COM information into the system registry. This lab will pull together everything you have read up to this point in the book, and leave you with a reusable COM server.

Note: This lab will serve as the basis for Chapter 4, as well as Chapter 5.

The solution for this lab can be found on your CD-ROM under:
Labs\Chapter 03\CarInProcServer

Step One: Prepare the Project Workspace and Port CoCar

Begin by creating a new empty Win32 DLL project workspace named **CarInProcServer** (take care not to select an MFC-based DLL):

Figure 3-21:
New Win32 DLL
CASE tool.

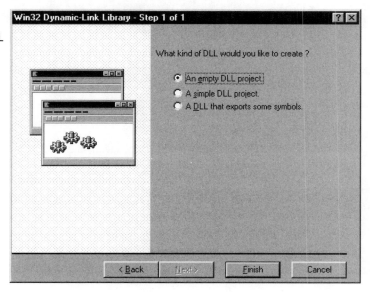

Add a brand new file named **CarInProcServer.cpp**. The functions and data points we will add to this file constitute the component housing for your DLL. First, define two global ULONG data types to represent the lock count and object count server variables. Be sure this new file is inserted into the project workspace:

```
// Add the following global data points to your component housing file.
#include <windows.h>
```

```
ULONG g_lockCount = 0;      // Number of client locks.
ULONG g_objCount = 0;       // Number of living objects in the house.
```

The CoCar coclass and the related interfaces defined in the previous lab can be easily reused in this current lab. Open the Windows Explorer, and copy the following files from your previous lab directory into the current project directory:

■ CoCar.h and CoCar.cpp: the Car coclass

■ iid.h and iid.cpp: GUID files

■ interfaces.h: custom interfaces

Insert each *.cpp file into the project workspace (using **Project | Add To Project | Files...**) and compile. You do not need to manually include header files, as they will be brought in automatically.

As this iteration of CoCar will be placed into a binary package, we need a CLSID to uniquely identity CoCar in the COM universe. Generate a new GUID (using guidgen.exe) to serve as the CLSID for CoCar. Specify the constant CLSID_CoCar as the first parameter to the DEFINE_GUID macro. Add this GUID to your existing iid.h file:

```
// {7AD2D539-EE35-11d2-B8DE-0020781238D4}
DEFINE_GUID(CLSID_CoCar,
0x7ad2d539, 0xee35, 0x11d2, 0xb8, 0xde, 0x0, 0x20, 0x78, 0x12, 0x38, 0xd4);
```

To finish this source code port, we need to increment and decrement the global object count in your CoCar constructor and destructor. Remember that we must provide hooks to inform the DLL server how many objects are currently living within it. Use the **extern** keyword to reference the globally defined g_objCount variable from within the CoCar class:

```
// cocar.cpp
extern ULONG g_objCount;
CoCar::CoCar() : m_refCount(0), m_currSpeed(0), m_maxSpeed(0)
{
     ++g_objCount;    // Other code...
}
CoCar::~CoCar()
{
     --g_objCount;    // Other code...
}
```

Finally, you might notice that your interface definitions do not show up in ClassView. The IDE has placed all your *.h files under the External Dependencies folder in FileView. You may relocate them to the Header Files folder (just by dragging and dropping) and once you do so, you will see your interfaces visible from ClassView.

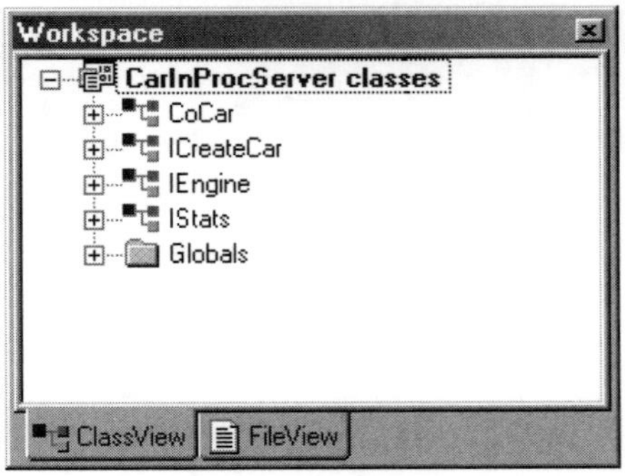

Figure 3-22:
The "repaired"
ClassView.

Step Two: Develop the CoCar Class Factory

Now we need to develop a class factory to create the CoCar. Insert a new class named CoCarClassFactory, deriving from IClassFactory <u>only</u>. Recall that a class object provides a language-neutral way to create COM objects. Here is the initial definition of your class object:

```
// The class object for your CoCar.
#include <windows.h>
class CoCarClassFactory : public IClassFactory
{
public:
     CoCarClassFactory();
     virtual ~CoCarClassFactory();
     // IUnknown
     STDMETHODIMP QueryInterface(REFIID riid, void** pIFace);
     STDMETHODIMP_(ULONG)AddRef();
     STDMETHODIMP_(ULONG)Release();
     // IClassFactory
     STDMETHODIMP LockServer(BOOL fLock);
     STDMETHODIMP CreateInstance(LPUNKNOWN pUnkOuter,
                                 REFIID riid, void** ppv);
private:
     ULONG m_refCount;        // Init to zero in constructor!
};
```

Begin by providing an implementation of the IUnknown methods AddRef(), Release(), and QueryInterface(). This code will be almost exactly like the IUnknown logic for CoCar, except this time your QueryInterface() will only be testing for IID_IUnknown and IID_IClassFactory:

```
// The class factory's IUnknown implementation.
STDMETHODIMP_(ULONG) CoCarClassFactory::AddRef()
{
     return ++m_refCount;
}
STDMETHODIMP_(ULONG) CoCarClassFactory::Release()
{
     if(--m_refCount == 0)
     {
          delete this;
          return 0;
     }
     return m_refCount;
}
// Remember! Class factories do not implement the interfaces of the coclass
// they are responsible for creating!
STDMETHODIMP CoCarClassFactory::QueryInterface(REFIID riid, void** ppv)
{
     // Which aspect of me do they want?
     if(riid == IID_IUnknown)
     {
          *ppv = (IUnknown*)this;
     }
     else if(riid == IID_IClassFactory)
     {
```

```
            *ppv = (IClassFactory*)this;
    }
    else
    {
            *ppv = NULL;
            return E_NOINTERFACE;
    }
    ((IUnknown*)(*ppv))->AddRef();
    return S_OK;
}
```

Next, implement IClassFactory::CreateInstance(). In this method, create a CoCar object and query it for the requested interface. Return an HRESULT that your client may test against. If anything fails in the CreateInstance() method, you must be sure to delete the memory given to the coclass:

```
// Create the CoCar!
STDMETHODIMP CoCarClassFactory::CreateInstance(LPUNKNOWN pUnkOuter,
                                         REFIID riid, void** ppv)
{
    // We do not support aggregation in this class object.
    if(pUnkOuter != NULL)
            return CLASS_E_NOAGGREGATION;
    CoCar* pCarObj = NULL;
    HRESULT hr;
    // Create the car.
    pCarObj = new CoCar;
    // Ask car for an interface.
    hr = pCarObj -> QueryInterface(riid, ppv);
    // Problem? We must delete the memory we allocated.
    if (FAILED(hr))
            delete pCarObj;
    return hr;
}
```

To finish up the class factory, implement IClassFactory::LockServer() to increment or decrement the server's global lock count. Also, in the constructor and destructor of your class object, adjust the global object count. In order to reference the global items defined in CarInProcServer.cpp, use the **extern** keyword in your class object's CPP file:

```
// Final details of the class factory.
extern ULONG g_lockCount;
extern ULONG g_objCount;
// Constructor.
CoCarClassFactory::CoCarClassFactory()
{
    m_refCount = 0;
    g_objCount++;
}
// Destructor.
CoCarClassFactory::~CoCarClassFactory()
{
    g_objCount--;
}
// Lock server.
STDMETHODIMP CoCarClassFactory::LockServer(BOOL fLock)
```

```
{
    if(fLock)
        ++g_lockCount;
    else
        --g_lockCount;
    return S_OK;
}
```

Beyond this, just be sure you are careful with including the correct files in your class factory source code (you're referencing CoCar in CreateInstance(), so be sure to include your CoCar header file). Compile again and clean up any resulting errors. The next step is to develop the minimal and complete set of server exports.

Step Three: Implement the DLL Component Housing

In your CarInProcServer.cpp file, implement DllGetClassObject() to perform the following functionality:

```
// This export exposes class factories to the Service Control Manager.
STDAPI DllGetClassObject(REFCLSID rclsid, REFIID riid, void** ppv)
{
    // 1. See if the CLSID is the same as CoCar, if not, return an error.
    // 2. Create the CoCarClassFactory object.
    // 3. Ask the new car class object for the REFIID parameter.
    // 4. Set HRESULT for client.
}
```

The final DLL export we will implement is DllCanUnloadNow():

```
// This export determines if the DLL can be unloaded from memory.
STDAPI DllCanUnloadNow()
{
    // If g_objCount and g_lockCount are both zero, return S_OK
    // otherwise return S_FALSE.
}
```

Here is the relevant code for each export:

```
// DLL Exports.
STDAPI DllCanUnloadNow()
{
    if(g_lockCount == 0 && g_objCount == 0)
        return S_OK;            // Unload me.
    else
        return S_FALSE;         // Keep me alive.
}
STDAPI DllGetClassObject(REFCLSID rclsid, REFIID riid, void** ppv)
{
    HRESULT hr;
    CoCarClassFactory *pCFact = NULL;
    // We only know how to make cars in this house.
    if(rclsid != CLSID_CoCar)
        return CLASS_E_CLASSNOTAVAILABLE;
    // They want a CoCarClassFactory
    pCFact = new CoCarClassFactory;
    // Go get the interface from the CoCarClassFactory
    hr = pCFact -> QueryInterface(riid, ppv);
    if(FAILED(hr))
```

```
        delete pCFact;
    return hr;
}
```

Next, create and insert a new file, **carinprocserver.def**, into your project to expose these two functions to the outside world. Be sure that the LIBRARY statement name is the same name of the project you are building:

```
LIBRARY "CARINPROCSERVER"
EXPORTS
    DllGetClassObject    @1    PRIVATE
    DllCanUnloadNow      @2    PRIVATE
```

Step Four: Provide Registry Information

To complete our DLL server, we need to create a REG file to merge the minimal and complete server information into the system registry. Create a ProgID for your coclass with a CLSID subkey. Enter this directly under HKCR. Next, enter your CLSID listing for your coclass, with an InprocServer32 subkey, pointing to the physical path of your DLL.

Remember that you <u>cannot</u> have spaces around slashes (\) and <u>must</u> have spaces around the assignment operator (=). Also recall that REGEDIT must be the very first line in the file. Here is a possible carinprocserver.reg file (be sure to use your CLSIDs and path, of course):

```
REGEDIT
HKEY_CLASSES_ROOT\CarInProcServer.CoCar\CLSID = {7AD2D539-EE35-11d2-B8DE-0020781238D4}
HKEY_CLASSES_ROOT\CLSID\{7AD2D539-EE35-11d2-B8DE-0020781238D4} = CarInProcServer.CoCar
HKEY_CLASSES_ROOT\CLSID\{7AD2D539-EE35-11d2-B8DE-0020781238D4}
\InprocServer32 = E:\ATL\Labs\Chapter 03\CarInProcServer\Debug\CarInProcServer.dll
```

When you have finished, double-click on the REG file using the Windows Explorer to merge this information into the registry. Use regedit.exe to ensure the entries are correct. You have just created a COM server in straight C++, no libraries, no help. Sit back and grin. Once you have savored your achievement, read on to learn how to build a C++ COM client that accesses this server.

Developing a COM Client

Now that you have implemented your first COM-based in-process server, we need to investigate the necessary COM library calls to access it. Regardless of the client's language, under the hood the same basic sequence of COM library calls is used. Some COM language mappings (such as VB) hide this process so well that the developer has little understanding of what is happening under the hood.

When COM developers make requests to SCM, they do so by calling COM library functions, which (for the most part) are contained in the granddaddy of all COM system DLLs, ole32.dll. This core system file is the gateway between your client code and the Service Control Manager (which by the way is a running service named rpcss.exe).

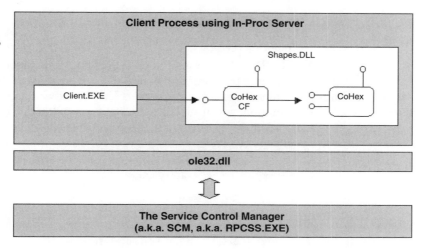

Figure 3-23: SCM, ole32.dll, the client, and your server.

Bootstrapping the COM Runtime

The very first thing COM clients must be sure to do is initialize the COM subsystem. Each and every thread using the COM libraries must make a call to CoInitialize() before making any further requests from the COM runtime. When that thread is finished with the COM subsystem, a complementing call to CoUninitialize() must be made to clean things up:

```
// Before a COM client can work with the COM runtime (SCM), it must
// load and initialize the COM libraries, and unload before termination.
void main(void)
{
    // This parameter is reserved, and should be NULL
    CoInitialize(NULL);
    CoUninitialize();
}
```

Activating COM Objects

Once the COM runtime is ready to receive our requests, clients typically make calls to one of two COM activation functions—CoGetClassObject() or CoCreateInstance()—to load a server and create a new COM object. We will examine the use of CoGetClassObject() first, as CoCreateInstance() is simply a helper function, wrapping the call to CoGetClassObject() on your behalf.

CoGetClassObject() tells SCM to locate, load, and retrieve the IClassFactory pointer for a given coclass. From this pointer, we can create an instance of the associated coclass (via CreateInstance()), and go to town. Here is the signature of CoGetClassObject():

```
// This activation function is used to return the IClassFactory pointer for a given
// class factory. Using this interface, the client can then create the corresponding class
// object.
HRESULT CoGetClassObject(REFCLSID rclsid,
                         DWORD dwClsContext,
```

```
                    COSERVERINFO * pServerInfo,
                    REFIID riid,
                    LPVOID * ppv);
```

The first parameter is the CLSID of the coclass you wish to create, for example
CLSID_CoHexagon. As we entered this information into the system registry, SCM knows
where to find the path to the binary and loads the server. The second parameter is a member from the CLSCTX enumeration, which specifies the class context of the server. You
know that COM offers us location transparency, and this parameter allows you to specify if
you wish an in-proc, local, or remote version of the server. The values of the CLSCTX can
be one of the following:

```
// The class context allows a COM client to specify which 'locale' they are interested in.
enum tagCLSCTX
{
    CLSCTX_INPROC_SERVER       = 0x1,       // In-proc server.
    CLSCTX_INPROC_HANDLER      = 0x2,       // NT service.
    CLSCTX_LOCAL_SERVER        = 0x4,       // Local server.
    CLSCTX_REMOTE_SERVER       = 0x10,      // Remote server
} CLSCTX;
```

You will specify CLSCTX_INPROC_SERVER if you desire in-proc servers, CLSCTX_
LOCAL_SERVER for local servers, or CLSCTX_REMOTE_SERVER for a remote server.
You may also combine any of the CLSCTX flags, and SCM will find the server closest to
the client. If you specify the predefined CLSCTX_ALL (which is an OR-ing together of
INPROC, LOCAL, and REMOTE), you can effectively say to SCM "Just give me the one
closest to me." If SCM finds an in-proc version, you will get this version. Next is local, followed by remote.

The third parameter, COSERVERINFO, is a structure that specifies useful information
about a remote server machine. Of course, if you are not accessing a remote COM server,
you can simply send in NULL for this parameter (which we will do until Chapter 5).

The fourth and fifth parameters should be quite familiar to you by now: the IID of the
interface you want from the coclass and a place to put it (void**). Let's write some client
code that loads up the Shapes.dll server and returns the IClassFactory pointer for the
CoHexFactory coclass (without excessive error checking):

```
// Client side C++ COM code.
// (Notice we need to include the GUID and interface definitions from the server project)
#include "iid.h"
#include "interfaces.h"
void main(void)
{
    HRESULT hr;
    IClassFactory* pCF = NULL;
    IDraw* pDraw = NULL;
    CoInitialize(NULL);      // Initialize the COM runtime.
    // Get the class factory pointer of CoHexagon:
    hr = CoGetClassObject(CLSID_CoHexagon, CLSCTX_INPROC_SERVER,
                        NULL, IID_IClassFactory, (void**)&pCF);
    // Make and render a CoHexagon.
    hr = pCF->CreateInstance(NULL, IID_IDraw, (void**)&pDraw);
    pDraw->Draw();
```

```
    // Get IShapeEdit pointer.
    IShapeEdit* pSE = NULL;
    pDraw ->QueryInterface(IID_IShapeEdit, (void**)&pSE);
    pSE -> Invert();
    // All done.
    pCF ->Release();         // ref count = 0. Destroys class factory.
    pDraw -> Release();      // ref count = 1
    pSE -> Release();        // ref count = 0. CoHexagon is destroyed.
    CoUninitialize();        // Terminate the COM runtime.
}
```

There you have it! We first grab the class object's IClassFactory pointer and create a CoHexagon via CreateInstance(), asking for IDraw. Also note that once we have used the IDraw interface, we can turn right around and ask IDraw for IShapeEdit given the laws of COM identity. Most importantly, call Release() on any acquired interface pointer when you are finished, to allow the coclasses to be destroyed and the server to be unloaded.

Accessing a Coclass Using CoCreateInstance()

Having seen CoGetClassObject() in action, we can now look at CoCreateInstance(). This function is useful if you only require a single instance of the coclass (CoHexagon in this example) and don't want to grab the IClassFactory directly. CoCreateInstance() finds the class object and calls CreateInstance() from the IClassFactory pointer automatically. All you do is pass in the CLSID and IID you are looking for:

```
// CoCreateInstance() creates the class factory for you automatically.
HRESULT CoCreateInstance(REFCLSID rclsid, LPUNKNOWN pUnkOuter,
                         DWORD dwClsContext, REFIID riid, LPVOID * ppv);
```

The only difference from CoGetClassObject() is the second parameter, pUnkOuter. This parameter is used only in COM aggregation. We will not worry about this now, and simply pass in NULL. Because CoCreateInstance() does not provide us direct access to IClassFactory, we can alter the client code using CoCreateInstance(), thus bypassing any reference to the class object:

```
// Using CoCreateInstance() the client does not need to access or worry about the
// IClassFactory interface when creating the coclass.
hr = CoCreateInstance(CLSID_CoHexagon, NULL, CLSCTX_INPROC_SERVER,
                      IID_IDraw, (void**)&pDraw);
pDraw -> Draw();
pDraw-> Release();
```

So, using this function looks a lot easier than CoGetClassObject(). So why would you not use CoCreateInstance() every time? Realize that when we use CoCreateInstance(), the class object is created and destroyed each and every time. Thus, if you are interested in creating, say, ten CoHexagon objects, CoCreateInstance() creates and destroys the class factory ten times. CoGetClassObject() is far more efficient when you wish to create a batch of objects, as you are directly holding the IClassFactory pointer.

Furthermore, as CoCreateInstance() does not give you back an IClassFactory pointer directly, your client could never lock the server. Whenever you wish to lock a server into memory, you must do so using an IClassFactory pointer, and thus must use CoGetClassObject(). Either way you go, this is typical COM client code.

Debugging In-Process COM Servers

Before we get to the final lab of this chapter (a C++ COM client) we need to look at a debugging technique for in-process servers. Recall that by definition, an in-proc server is a DLL that is always hosted by some other EXE. Therefore, when it comes time to debug your DLL servers, you will need to assign some EXE to host your server during the debug cycle.

Assume you have created a COM-based DLL. Also assume you have additionally created a COM-based client that is making use of the coclasses contained in the server. Once each project has been compiled, load the server project into Visual Studio and begin a debug session (F5). This will launch a small dialog box (Figure 3-24). Use the browse button to navigate to the location of the client project. For example, if we are interested in debugging the CoText server seen earlier in this chapter, navigate to the client EXE:

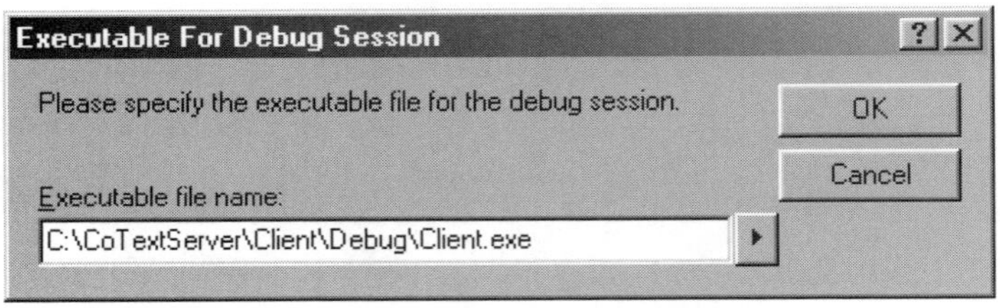

Figure 3-24: Specifying a COM DLL debugging host.

Once this association is made, any breakpoints will be triggered by the hosting COM client logic.

If you ever wish to change the hosting EXE, you can change the initial settings using the Project Settings dialog box. Select the Debug tab and edit the Executable for Debug Session edit box.

> **Note:**   The hosting EXE client does not need to be of the C++ variety. Recall that one of the great boons of COM development is its language-independent nature. In the next chapter you will learn how to create Visual Basic and Java/COM clients. This same debugging technique may be used to troubleshoot your COM-based DLLs using a COM client developed in any COM-aware language.

Lab 3-3: Developing a COM Client

In this lab we will be building an official COM client to use the CoCar COM server you created in Lab 3-2. You will make requests of SCM using the COM library, manage interface pointers, work with BSTRs, and exercise class factories. Once this lab is complete you will have ported your humble CoCar through the following iterations over the course of three chapters:

■   A struct in C operated on by a set of global functions.

■   A simple object in C++.

- A C++ object with multiple interfaces.
- A binary COM-based DLL.

The solution for this lab can be found on your CD-ROM under:
Labs\Chapter 03\CoCarClient

Step One: Prepare the Project Workspace

Begin by creating a new Win32 Console Application named CoCarClient. This time select
simple project. You will already see an empty main() loop provided for you. Before we can
use our CarInProcServer.dll, we need to bring in the following files to the client
workspace:

- iid.h and iid.cpp: We need the GUID constants to code against. Insert the CPP file into
  your project.
- interfaces.h: We need the interface names to define pointer variables to them.

Include the header files at the top of your cocarclient.cpp file:

```
// Once you have copied these files to your project sub directory, you are ready to code
// the client itself.
#include "interfaces.h"
#include "iid.h"
#include <iostream.h>
int main()
{
    return 0;
}
```

Step Two: Implement the main() Function

To pull together all your COM knowledge, add the following functionality to main():

```
// Your C++ client code.
int main(void)
{
    // Initialize the COM sub system.
    // Grab the IClassFactory pointer from CoCarClassFactory.
    // Call CreateInstance() from pICF, and ask for IID_ICreateCar from the CoCar.
    // Exercise ICreateCar.
    // Next ask for IID_IStats from your ICreateCar or IUnknown pointer.
    // Call DisplayStats() from pIStats.
    // QI for IEngine
    // Rev that engine until the engine block snaps in two!
    // Using pIStats->GetPetName(), print the BSTR to the console to inform the user
    // of the car's demise.
    // Release all acquired interface pointers.
    // Terminate the COM sub system.
    return 0;
}
```

Figure 3-25 shows the client output:

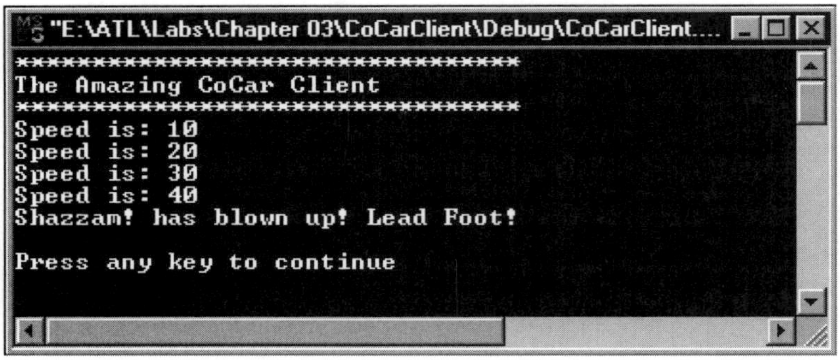

Figure 3-25:
Who says you
can't get
satisfaction?

```
"E:\ATL\Labs\Chapter 03\CoCarClient\Debug\CoCarClient....

**********************************
The Amazing CoCar Client
**********************************
Speed is: 10
Speed is: 20
Speed is: 30
Speed is: 40
Shazzam! has blown up! Lead Foot!

Press any key to continue
```

Much of this client code will be the same as your CoCarApp application (Lab 3-1). Here is the complete code listing:

```cpp
// The COM client logic.
int main()
{
    CoInitialize(NULL);
    HRESULT hr;
    IClassFactory* pCF = NULL;
    ICreateCar* pICreateCar = NULL;
    IStats* pStats = NULL;
    IEngine* pEngine = NULL;
    cout << "**********************************" << endl;
    cout << "The Amazing CoCar Client" << endl;
    cout << "**********************************" << endl;
    // Get the class factory pointer of CoCar.
    hr = CoGetClassObject(CLSID_CoCar, CLSCTX_INPROC_SERVER,
                          NULL, IID_IClassFactory, (void**)&pCF);
    // Make a CoCar & get ICreateCar.
    hr = pCF->CreateInstance(NULL, IID_ICreateCar, (void**)&pICreateCar);
    pCF->Release();
    if(SUCCEEDED(hr)){
        pICreateCar->SetMaxSpeed(30);
        BSTR petName = SysAllocString(L"Shazzam!");
        pICreateCar->SetPetName(petName);
        SysFreeString(petName);
        // Now get IStats
        hr = pICreateCar->QueryInterface(IID_IStats, (void**)&pStats);
        pICreateCar->Release();
    }
    if(SUCCEEDED(hr)){       // Show stats and get IEngine.
        pStats->DisplayStats();
        hr = pStats->QueryInterface(IID_IEngine, (void**)&pEngine);
    }
    // Zoom!
    if(SUCCEEDED(hr))
    {
        int curSp = 0;
        int maxSp = 0;
        pEngine->GetMaxSpeed(&maxSp);
        do{
            pEngine->SpeedUp();
```

```
        pEngine->GetCurSpeed(&curSp);
        cout << "Speed is: " << curSp << endl;
    }while(curSp <= maxSp);
    // Convert BSTR to char array.
    char buff[80];
    BSTR bstr;
    pStats->GetPetName(&bstr);
    WideCharToMultiByte(CP_ACP, NULL, bstr, -1, buff, 80, NULL, NULL);
    cout << buff << " has blown up! Lead Foot!" << endl << endl;
    // Final clean up.
    SysFreeString(bstr);
    if(pEngine)
        pEngine->Release();
    if(pStats)
        pStats->Release();
    }
    CoUninitialize();
    return 0;
}
```

With this, the COM CoCar server is complete. What we do not yet have is a way for other languages to access the functionality of our server. You could develop an MFC test client to use your current CoCar server, but again, MFC is still using the C++ programming language. How can other COM-aware languages such as Visual Basic and Java make use of CoCar? That is a job for type information, which is the subject of the next chapter.

Chapter Summary

In this chapter we began by looking at the core benefits of COM architecture: language independence, location transparency, object orientation, and robust versioning. We also had a very brief history lesson showing the general relationship between OLE 1.0, OLE 2.0, and ActiveX.

You learned how to create custom COM interfaces through a set of various standard COM macros to gain platform independence, and that each interface must derive from IUnknown and needs a custom GUID to identify it. We defined a coclass as an object implementing at the very least IUnknown, and typically a number of other COM interfaces (both standard and custom).

As you may agree, building a COM server by hand requires a good amount of boilerplate code. An in-process server needs class objects, coclasses, and a small handful of DLL exports. As well, we need to register CLSID and ProgID information into the system registry, allowing the COM runtime the necessary hooks to activate the objects. If you feel this level of understanding is unnecessary when using ATL, don't fool yourself.

Finally, we examined the COM library and client-side code. Using two COM library activation functions, CoGetClassObject() and CoCreateInstance(), we are able to activate the COM server, create the coclass, and use the interface functionality, thanks to SCM and ole32.dll.

Chapter 4

Type Information and Language Independence

Objectives:

■ **Understand the reasons for using the Interface Definition Language (IDL).**

■ **Examine the output files generated by the MIDL compiler.**

■ **Learn to define interfaces, coclasses, and type libraries using IDL.**

■ **Understand how to define custom enumerations in IDL.**

■ **Understand the Visual Basic and Java COM language mappings.**

■ **Use C++ smart pointers to simplify client-side COM code.**

There are two solid reasons why every COM-based project should begin with the Interface Definition Language (IDL): language independence and location transparency.

IDL is the "official" language of COM that provides a way to specify the functionality of a COM server such that all COM language mappings can access them. In this chapter we will investigate how to create type information for a COM server and how various target languages (specifically VB and Java) can make use of it. We also come to learn how to ease C++ client-side COM development using smart pointer technology.

As for the other benefit of IDL (location transparency), the COM architecture keeps a client encapsulated from a server's actual physical location using stubs and proxies, which are often created using MIDL-generated code, as we will see in Chapter 5.

Understanding Life without IDL

Up until this point in our journey, we have defined our COM interfaces in C++ using the **class**, **interface**, and **struct** keywords. We can ensure these interfaces expand correctly on various platforms using a small handful of COM macros (STDMETHOD, STDMETHOD_, STDMETHODIMP, and STDMETHODIMP_ being the most common). Sadly, despite the usefulness of these macros, we have still written COM interfaces that can only be implemented and accessed using the C++ language.

COM is a very inclusive club. A well-defined interface should be able to be implemented by, and accessed from, any COM-enlightened language. Currently, Visual Basic, C, or Java developers cannot create our coclasses or access any of our custom interfaces. For example, a VB developer cannot declare an IDraw variable, as IDraw was defined in C++ syntax. If a language can't create a variable of the correct type, it has no way to store the logical return value of QueryInterface(). The moral of the story is that interfaces defined in a given language are usable only from that language. Obviously this is a problem for a language-independent specification such as COM.

We have another even more insidious problem occurring here. Each COM-enabled language allows developers to assign GUIDs in language- and environment-specific ways. For example, if we wish to assign an IID in C++, we first create the interface definitions and then manually associate a GUID using the DEFINE_GUID macro (or another format provided by guidgen.exe).

VB, on the other hand, automatically associates a GUID to custom interfaces at compile time, without developer participation. Furthermore, a VB developer has no way to change the GUID generated by VB. To illustrate how this behavior can spell trouble, consider again the IShapeEdit interface defined in C++, now with an associated GUID constant:

```
// {442F32E2-E7EE-11d2-B8D2-0020781238D4}
DEFINE_GUID(IID_IShapeEdit,
0x442f32e2, 0xe7ee, 0x11d2, 0xb8, 0xd2, 0x0, 0x20, 0x78, 0x12, 0x38, 0xd4);
DECLARE_INTERFACE_(IShapeEdit, IUnknown)
{
     STDMETHOD(Fill) (FILLTYPE fType) PURE;
     STDMETHOD(Inverse) () PURE;
     STDMETHOD(Stretch) (int factor) PURE;
};
```

A savvy VB developer can create a COM interface named IShapeEdit as well, as shown in Figure 4-1 (VB supplies the necessary IUnknown methods behind the scenes):

Figure 4-1:
A VB definition of the custom IShapeEdit interface.

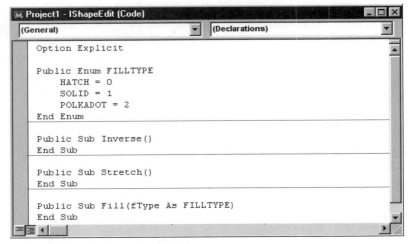

If we examine the GUID generated by VB for this definition of IShapeEdit (using the OLE/COM Object Viewer, which is mentioned later), we might find an assigned IID of {91D5CC38-E644-11D2-B8D1-0020781238D4}. If you are thinking, "I thought IShapeEdit was already assigned an IID of {442F32E2-E7EE-11d2-B8D2-0020781238D4}," you are beginning to see the problem.

If a VB developer (whom we'll call Frank) "just happened" to create a new interface named IShapeEdit without any knowledge of our existing C++ interface definition, all would be fine as far as COM is concerned. The separate GUIDs ensure a unique tag for each definition. If, however, Frank thought, "Hey! I want my VB object to support Gerta's IShapeEdit interface, I'll rewrite it in VB," then we have a huge problem. Frank did not want to create a <u>new</u> interface at all, but wanted to <u>reuse</u> an existing interface written in C++. If Frank and Gerta were members of the same development team, we have assigned two GUIDs to the same behavior. Imagine the problems injected into the COM mainstream if a C++ developer created a new coclass deriving from IUnknown, and in the process, assigned a new GUID to the IID_IUnknown constant! The same potential nightmare exists here.

What we need is a higher level metalanguage that we may use to define our COM items once and for all, and let developers use their language of choice to implement and work with the definitions (interfaces, types, coclasses, and so on). This metalanguage is Microsoft's Interface Definition Language, or simply MIDL.

The Origins of MIDL

Microsoft's Interface Definition Language (MIDL) is an extension of an older existing IDL standard. The IDL used in modern-day COM development is based off of the "Open Software Foundation Distributed Computing Environment Remote Procedure Call Interface Definition Language," which gives us one of the longer acronyms out there in the universe: OSF DCE RPC IDL. Let's just call this DCE IDL for short.

DCE IDL allows software developers to write descriptions of remote procedure calls (RPCs). It is important to note that DCE IDL had no support for object-based definitions. All DCE IDL code revolved around the tried and true structured programming (SP) paradigm, and the output of DCE IDL definitions was tailored to C and C++ language mappings (that would be "C++ as a better C," not OOP-based C++).

Microsoft IDL extends DCE IDL to support numerous items such as COM interfaces, interface inheritance, coclass definitions, and type information by introducing a handful of new keywords. Under the hood, MIDL still supports DCE IDL, as MIDL is an extension of DCE IDL's functionality.

> **Note:** From here on out, when mentioning IDL, assume we are referring to Microsoft's Interface Definition Language (MIDL) unless otherwise noted.

A Working Definition of IDL

IDL is a C-like language with the additional notion of *attributes*. Attributes are blocks of IDL keywords that remove any possibility of ambiguity from a COM definition. For example, there are attributes that assign GUIDs to COM interfaces, attributes that specify the direction of method parameters (necessary for effective marshaling), and attributes that specify the "default interface" of a coclass. We will see each of these IDL aspects in turn.

Real COM developers write IDL definitions to describe the full functionality of their COM server and send the *.idl file into the MIDL compiler (midl.exe). Midl.exe will generate a number of output files that may be consumed by COM object builders, as well as object users. These files are the keys to COM's language independence and location transparency.

> **Note:** You may have heard of the Object Definition Language, or ODL. This definition language is an older incarnation of MIDL, designed specifically to create type libraries for OLE automation servers using the MkTypLib.exe utility. MIDL 2.0 did not support type library generation, but generated stub and proxy code to marshal COM interfaces between apartment, machine, and process boundaries. Nowadays with MIDL 3.0, anything you could describe in ODL may be described in IDL (including type libraries). Unless you have inherited some legacy ODL definitions, you can safely ignore the older ODL syntax and stick to modern-day IDL.

What Does COM IDL Bring to the Table?

IDL is only a definition language. The syntax of IDL is modeled after C; however, you will find no support for looping constructs (for loops, while loops, and the like) or decision statements (if/else, switch, and so on). You will never (and could never) build an executable program such as MS Word using IDL code, and cannot implement coclasses with IDL either! So what exactly can you do with IDL? To understand the answer to this question, recall some of the problems we had without it:

- COM items defined in a given language are bound to that language.
- Many COM language mappings assign GUIDs automatically, which could result in duplication of interface behaviors (which may or may not be problematic).

When you describe your COM servers using IDL, we ensure the following:

- GUIDs are established once and for all for each COM item.
- We can remove any ambiguity from our definitions using IDL attributes.
- We provide a language-neutral way to allow COM-enabled languages to implement our interfaces and program against our coclasses.
- We automatically receive stub and proxy code to remotely access COM interfaces (this point is the subject of the next chapter, so put this on the back burner until then).

Configuring a Win32 Project to Compile IDL

Before we begin to write our own custom interfaces in IDL, we need to set up shop. Typically speaking, a given COM server project will have a single IDL file that specifies all COM items in the component housing. This is usually what we are looking for, as this will result in exactly one type library, one GUID file, one stub/proxy DLL, and one file containing C/C++ language bindings.

The Visual C++ IDE is an ideal place to write your IDL code. Once you insert an *.idl file into the project workspace, you may simply right-click on the file from FileView and select Compile, which will activate the MIDL compiler and automatically send the output files into your project directory (Visual Studio 6.0 or higher). The MIDL compiler will also run automatically when you build your projects, if you have inserted one or more *.idl files.

The MIDL compiler itself can be configured using the MIDL tab of the Project Settings dialog box (found under the Project | Settings... menu). By default, MIDL is set to the MkTypLib compatible option, which means all IDL code will be expected to conform under the older ODL syntax. Be sure to turn this feature off in your raw C++ COM projects:

Figure 4-2:
Be sure to
deselect the
MkTypLib
compatible
option.

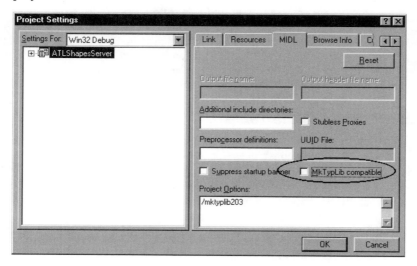

Note: ATL-based projects turn off this option by default. You only need to bother with this step if you are building a COM server from scratch.

Output of the MIDL Compiler

The IDL code you author to describe your interfaces and coclasses is processed by the midl.exe compiler. Assume we have written some IDL code in a file named shapes.idl (don't worry what that code might look like at this point). When the IDL file is sent into the MIDL compiler, a handful of new files will be dumped into our project's directory. These files may be grouped by related functionality, as shown in Figure 4-3. Note that the names of most of these MIDL-generated files are based on the initial name of the *.idl file:

Figure 4-3:
MIDL-generated
output files.

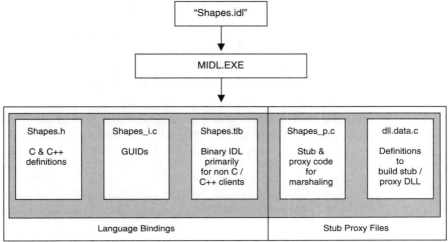

Many of these files serve the same purpose as the files we have been writing by hand up until now, which is another benefit of IDL—less typing on your part. So what do these files contain? Here is an overview of each MIDL-generated file:

■ **Shapes.h** now contains the C and C++ interface definitions. Previously we were writing our own header files (such as interfaces.h) using C++ syntax to build a given interface definition (IEngine, IStats, ICreateCar, and so forth). The MIDL-generated interface definitions make use of the COM interface macros you already know and love, helping to maintain platform independence.

■ **Shapes_i.c** contains all the C and C++ GUID definitions contained in your IDL code. This includes IIDs, CLSIDs, and LIBIDs. This file takes the place of the iid.h and iid.cpp files we have been maintaining ourselves in previous chapters. MIDL was even kind enough to add in the human readable constants for you using the standard IID_, CLSID_, and LIBID_ prefixes.

■ **Shapes.tlb** is the binary equivalent of the IDL code, which is termed a *type library*. This might be the most important file MIDL generates, as your server's type library is the key to COM's language independence. Languages other than C and C++ may access this file and "peek inside" your COM server to understand the coclasses, interfaces, and UDTs it contains. Various COM languages can include this file into their projects, allowing developers to implement your interfaces and use the coclasses in his or her *lingua franca*.

■ The final files (**shapes_p.c** and **dlldata.c**) are used to build stub and proxy DLLs for remotely accessing your COM interfaces. The COM remoting architecture revolves around stubs and proxies. As a COM developer, you do have choices as to where the stub and proxy DLL comes from. Thus, although MIDL generates these stub/proxy files automatically, we do not have to use them if you would rather leverage COM's type library marshaling. As this chapter is only concerned with language independence, we will revisit the proxy files and location transparency in Chapter 5.

The Core IDL Data Types

Now, I am sure you are anxious to see some IDL code with your own eyes. Before we get to that point, however, we need to examine the set of intrinsic data types provided by IDL. In the table below, you can see how the core set of IDL data types maps to the C and C++ programming languages (we will see some problems with this set in just a moment).

IDL Base Type	Bits	C/C++ Equivalent
boolean	8-bit	unsigned char
byte	8-bit	unsigned char
char	8-bit	unsigned char
small	8-bit	char
wchar_t	16-bit	wchar_t (e.g., unsigned short)
short	16-bit	short
int	32-bit	int
long	32-bit	long
void(*)	32-bit	void(*)
float	32-bit floating-point number	float
double	64-bit floating-point number (high-precision decimal number)	double

The signed and unsigned modifiers may be used with most of these core IDL data types. As well, each may be declared as a pointer. Furthermore, you may make enumerations, unions, arrays or structures of these types using the **enum**, **union**, **array**, and **struct** IDL keywords. In this light, the intrinsic data types of IDL seem to behave very much like those of C. This very point is part of the problem, with regards to COM's language independence.

Problems with the Core Set of IDL Data Types

You must be aware of this fact before you go any further: The core IDL data types just presented are <u>not</u> compatible among all COM-enabled languages. If you were to create C or C++ exclusive COM solutions, the above list would be perfect. From this list you could create structures based off these types, develop COM interfaces using these structures, marshal them between clients and servers without (too much) hassle, and life appears fine.

Until that day when your manager drops by and says, "We want you to develop a web-enabled front end to access this COM object." This one simple utterance will provide you with great pain and suffering, as web development typically means VBScript, and VBScript can't work with your nifty C/C++ centric types. VBScript cannot work with your NULL-terminated C strings, and VBScript will choke when working with hyper data points. Beyond VBScript, this set of core IDL data types will not perfectly map into the Visual Basic, JScript, and Java COM language mappings.

Note: The integration of types among COM-aware languages is improving all the time. For example, with the release of NT SP4, the system-provided marshaler has been upgraded to allow Visual Basic 6.0 to work with IDL structures as interface parameters (VBScript cannot). We will examine more elaborate IDL constructs (such as structures and arrays) in Chapter 11.

To be honest, when the COM specification came about (circa 1993), it was geared toward the C and C++ developers of the world. As COM matured, it became apparent that other popular languages wanted to get in on the binary reuse game; however, a problem cropped up. C++ types did not transfer directly into non-C++ languages (we have already seen this problem in the area of text representation). When you program against the COM specification, you need to remember that your COM object could be used in just about any programming language. I know that you are aware that a valid data type in one language may not be a valid data type in another. If COM is an open-arms, language-independent philosophy, we need to agree upon a set of valid data types that all COM languages understand and can work with.

Given this discrepancy, Microsoft crafted a set of "universal IDL data types" that everyone understood from their respective language mapping. The first language that wanted to play the COM game was Visual Basic, which supports a peculiar intrinsic data type called the *Variant*. Once you understand this VB data type, you will understand the set of "variant compliant" (e.g., universal) IDL data types.

The Visual Basic Variant Data Type

Visual Basic is not necessarily a strongly typed language. The intrinsic Variant data type can safely assume the identity of any other VB type, at anytime. For example, the following is completely valid VB code:

```
' Create a Variant data type and set it to various identities.
'
Dim v as Variant       ' Create a variable of type Variant
v = 12                 ' v is an integer
v = 3.88               ' v is a double
Set v = New CFoo       ' v is a reference to the default custom interface of CFoo
v = txtPetName.text    ' v is now a String
```

The Variant variable above starts out life as an integer. Along the way it transforms into a double, an interface reference, and a string value obtained from the txtPetName edit box. Notice in the second to last line of code v is assigned to what looks to be a new instance of the CFoo class (whatever that might be). What v is really pointing to is not an object instance but a reference to CFoo's "default interface." VB completely hides the fact that v is not an object at all, but an interface reference. Here's how it works: When we specify a coclass definition in IDL, we may designate one of the supported interfaces to serve as the "default." This allows certain COM language mappings to quickly return a specified interface to the developer free of charge.

As mentioned, the set of universal IDL data types is modeled after the intrinsic VB Variant data type. Thus, anything that can be described using a VB Variant can be represented by this alternative set of IDL types, called the variant compliant types. This set of data types not only accounts for the data types you would hope to find in a given language

(Booleans, shorts, and so forth) but a number of new types not natively supported in C and C++. These types, such as the BSTR, SAFEARRAY, and CURRENCY data types, are supported directly in Visual Basic, as a custom package for Java clients (J++), and as a set of APIs for C++ clients.

The Set of Variant Compliant IDL Data Types

If you conform your interface method parameters to use the set of variant compliant data types, all COM-enabled languages will be able to work with your interfaces and the implementing coclasses. As soon as you move outside of this agreed-upon subset, you will more likely than not develop a COM object which can only be used by C and C++ object consumers.

Working with variant compliant data types does have a very appealing side effect: You receive automatic marshaling support if your COM client is accessing a local or remote COM server. As we will see in Chapter 5, this is achieved by leveraging a system-supplied proxy/stub DLL (oleaut32.dll) that understands how to build stub/proxy code using your type information if (and only if) your interfaces make exclusive use of variant types.

As soon as you begin to work with interface parameters other than the variant compliant set, you cannot make use of oleaut32.dll and will need to build and register your own stub/proxy DLL to allow your objects to be accessed out of process. Finally, if you create dispinterface or dual interface coclasses, you <u>must</u> stick to variant compliant types (more on this later in Chapter 10).

In this book, we will leverage the set of variant compliant types as we build our COM servers to get the biggest bang for the buck. Furthermore, from here on out, we will be building a number of COM clients in languages other than C++ to illustrate COM's language-independent nature. The chart below illustrates how some core variant compliant IDL types map to VB, Java, and C++ primitives:

Variant Compliant IDL Type	Visual Basic Mapping	Java (J++) Mapping	C/C++ Mapping
VARIANT_BOOL	Boolean	boolean	VARIANT_BOOL
double	Double	double	double
float	Single	float	float
long	Long	int	long
short	Integer	short	short
BSTR	String	java.lang.String	BSTR
DATE	Date	double	DATE
IDispatch*	Object	java.lang.Object	IDispatch*
IUnknown*	Interface reference	com.ms.com.IUnknown	IUnknown*
VARIANT	Variant	com.ms.com.Variant	VARIANT
CY/CURRENCY	Currency	long	CY/CURRENCY
SAFEARRAY	Variant	com.ms.com.SafeArray	SAFEARRAY

> **Note:** Scripting clients (VBScript and JScript) interpret each of the variant compliant IDL types as a pure Variant. We will see examples of web-based COM clients beginning in Chapter 10.

Examining Our Favorite Interface Defined in IDL

Let's examine some real IDL code before writing our own. We have already seen the C++ definition of IUnknown as described in <unknwn.h>. What you might not have realized is that this file is actually a MIDL-generated file based off the <u>real</u> definition of IUnknown found in <unknwn.idl> (recall that the *.h file generated by Midl.exe contains C/C++ interface bindings). Here is the IDL code describing IUnknown:

```
// The real definition of IUnknown.
[local, object, uuid(00000000-0000-0000-C000-000000000046),
 pointer_default(unique)]
interface IUnknown
{
    typedef [unique] IUnknown *LPUNKNOWN;
    HRESULT QueryInterface([in] REFIID riid, [out, iid_is(riid)] void **ppvObject);
    ULONG AddRef();
    ULONG Release();
};
```

As you can see, QueryInterface(), AddRef(), and Release() are present as always. Recall that IDL uses attributes to remove any possible ambiguity from our COM definitions. Attributes are always contained in square brackets [ ] and refer to the IDL keyword immediately following the closing right bracket. For example, the attribute block [local, object, uuid(), pointer_default()] modifies the entire IUnknown interface. The parameters of QueryInterface() are modified by [in], [out], and [riid_is] attributes. To begin understanding the syntax of IDL, we start with the **typedef** keyword.

IDL Typedefs Statements

Notice how the IDL definition of IUnknown provides a typedef to IUnknown* (LPUNKNOWN). Most standard COM interfaces provide a similar definition, and your custom interface definitions are also free to do so as well. On a related note, you might wonder how ULONG is defined as the return value for AddRef() and Release(), given that they did not show up in our set of variant compliant IDL data types. <wtypes.idl> is a core IDL file that defines a number of common Windows types (such as ULONG) in IDL syntax. In reality, a ULONG is defined in IDL as:

```
// ULONG is a typedef for DWORD
typedef DWORD ULONG;
// DWORD is a typedef for an unsigned long
typedef unsigned long DWORD;
```

So, a ULONG is just a typedef for an unsigned long, which is just fine in IDL. The same story holds for the HRESULT return type. An HRESULT is defined in <wtypes.idl> as the following:

```
// HRESULT is just a typedef for LONG
typedef LONG HRESULT;
```

Similar twisted paths exist to define Windows types in IDL. Feel free to examine <wtypes.idl> yourself. You will find numerous definitions to support the Win32 COLOR-REF, POINT, SIZE, and RECT structures, metafiles, and HBITMAPS, to name just a few.

The IDL Import Keyword

The **import** keyword provides a way to bring existing IDL definitions to your custom IDL files. This is obviously very important, as all COM interfaces are derived from IUnknown, which is defined in <unknwn.idl>. The **import** keyword works much like the #include preprocessor directive:

```
/* C style comments are OK in IDL
*/
import "oaidl.idl";              // C++ comments also OK in IDL
```

Note that unlike the #include preprocessor directive, the IDL **import** keyword must end in a semicolon and does not begin with "#". You may use **import** to bring in any IDL file at all, including a core set of IDL files describing all system-level COM items. Unless you are working with traditional OLE, the only import you typically need is <oaidl.idl>, which includes <objidl.idl>, which then includes <unknwn.idl> and <wtypes.idl> for you. Here are some of the core IDL system files:

IDL System File	Meaning in Life
wtypes.idl	Defines basic Windows types.
unknwn.idl	IUnknown and IClassFactory definitions.
objidl.idl	The core COM interfaces (marshaling, COM persistence, monikers, structured storage, default enumerators, et.al.).
oleidl.idl	OLE Document interfaces.
oaidl.idl	Automation interfaces.

Defining Custom Interfaces in IDL

Every interface definition must at the very least be specified with the [object] attribute (which marks it as a COM interface, not a DCE IDL interface) and the [uuid()] attribute (which specifies, once and for all, the GUID for this interface). As we are building COM interfaces, you must derive your custom interfaces from IUnknown or some other interface ultimately deriving from IUnknown. The interface itself is declared using the **interface** keyword. Here is a basic skeleton for a custom IDL interface definition:

```
// Your custom IDL interface definitions will take on the following generic format.
import "oaidl.idl";              // Bring in definition of IUnknown & friends.
[
    object,                      // Marks interface as a COM interface.
    uuid( my IID )               // Get a GUID with guidgen.exe
]
interface IMyInterface : IUnknown  // Or any IUnknown derived interface
{
};
```

> **Note:** DCE IDL uniquely specifies items with universally unique IDs, or UUIDs. A GUID is just a UUID, and therefore Microsoft IDL recycled the existing DCE IDL (uuid), rather than introducing a new and redundant (guid) attribute.

To generate a new IID for your custom interfaces in IDL, use guidgen.exe. This time, however, do not select DEFINE_GUID but instead opt for the Registry Format option and remove the curly brackets ({ }) from the paste. If you already have an existing GUID declared using the DEFINE_GUID macro which you wish to define in IDL, you may simply paste in the guidgen.exe generated commented line as the [uuid()] attribute parameter:

```
// {442F32E2-E7EE-11d2-B8D2-0020781238D4}
DEFINE_GUID(IID_IShapeEdit,
0x442f32e2, 0xe7ee, 0x11d2, 0xb8, 0xd2, 0x0, 0x20, 0x78, 0x12, 0x38, 0xd4);
```

When you are creating IDL interface definitions, be aware that the COM macros are <u>not</u> part of an IDL interface definition, but are rather a <u>result</u> of the MIDL compilation. Here is the IDL definition for IShapeEdit (without any interface methods):

```
// ShapeServer.idl
[object, uuid(442F32E2-E7EE-11d2-B8D2-0020781238D4)]
interface IShapeEdit : IUnknown        // No 'public' keyword in IDL.
{
};
```

Note how we specify we are derived from IUnknown without use of a **public** keyword. If we mistakenly write an IDL definition for IShapeEdit as so:

```
// An incorrect IDL definition...
interface IShapeEdit : public IUnknown   // Nope!
{
};
```

we are issued errors from the MIDL compiler. As well, interface methods defined in IDL do <u>not</u> prefix **virtual** and suffix =0. All methods defined in IDL are considered pure virtual (as they must be, as IDL won't let you implement anything anyway).

Directional Parameter Attributes

Method parameters are also decorated with IDL attributes. IDL uses the [in], [out], and [in,out] attributes to tag a given parameter in an interface method. These attributes are used to help streamline the transmission of data between processes and machines during the marshaling process. As well, these same attributes help COM clients and servers understand exactly who is responsible for the allocation and deallocation of memory during the method invocation:

Parameter Attribute	Meaning in Life
[in]	Sent from the client to the server. The client allocates and frees the memory for this parameter. All parameters are defaulted to [in] unless specified otherwise.

Parameter Attribute	Meaning in Life
[out]	Sent from the server to the client. The client is responsible for freeing the retrieved data. [out] parameters are always pointers to some IDL type.
[in, out]	Sent from the client to the server. The client allocates and destroys the memory for this parameter; however, the server may optionally reallocate the memory during the method invocation.

With this, we can now define the methods of IShapeEdit in IDL:

```
// The complete IDL definition of IShapeEdit.
[object, uuid(4B475690-DE06-11d2-AAF4-00A0C9312D57)]
interface IShapeEdit : IUnknown
{
    HRESULT Fill( [in] FILLTYPE fType);
    HRESULT Inverse();
    HRESULT Stretch( [in] int factor);
};
```

When designing COM interfaces, we should always return HRESULTs as the physical return value of the method (when you wish to create logical return values, simply configure a number of [out] method parameters). Here is another example of a custom IDL-defined interface:

```
// IDraw in IDL syntax.
[ object, uuid(4B475690-DE06-11d2-AAF4-00A0C9312D57) ]
interface IDraw : IUnknown
{
    HRESULT Draw();        // no params.
};
```

Creating Enumerations in IDL

To fully port IShapeEdit into IDL syntax, we need to establish a custom FILLTYPE enumeration. IDL enumerations will correctly map into the C, C++, Visual Basic, and Java language mappings. IDL allows us to define enumerations in a C-like manner, and therefore IDL enums must make use of typedef syntax. IDL enumerations may take a GUID attribute to mark them as unique in all space and time. Here is the FILLTYPE enum:

```
// Creating enums in IDL is just about identical as C syntax.
[uuid(442F32E0-E7EE-11d2-B8D2-0020781238D4), v1_enum]
typedef enum FILLTYPE
{
    HATCH      = 0,
    SOLID      = 1,
    POLKADOT   = 2
} FILLTYPE;
```

Enumerations in IDL are defaulted as 16-bit. To transmit your IDL enums as 32-bit entities, be sure to declare the enumeration with the [v1_enum] attribute. Using the [v1_enum] attribute increases the efficiency of marshaling and unmarshaling data when the enumeration is embedded within an IDL structure or union. To that end, [v1_enum] is an optional attribute.

Self-Documenting IDL

IDL provides a number of ways to allow your IDL definitions to be self-describing. The first is an IDL attribute called [helpstring]. This attribute takes a text literal that can be used by various COM object browsers (as found in the VB and J++ IDEs) to help document what a given item is all about. This helpful text information becomes part of the binary type library (*.tlb) file.

The second way to document your IDL is by using the **cpp_quote()** IDL keyword. **cpp_quote()** also takes a string literal. However, these strings don't end up in your *.tlb file; they end up in the MIDL-generated C++ source code. Recall that the *.h file generated by MIDL holds the C and C++ language bindings. While you could add code for conditional compilation, pragma settings, and even "real code," it is safer to simply use **cpp_quote()** to add verbose comments to the MIDL-generated *.h file. For example, here is IShapeEdit making use of these new IDL conventions:

```
// Using the cpp_quote keyword and the helpstring attribute.
cpp_quote("// This is my custom enum")
[
    uuid(442F32E0-E7EE-11d2-B8D2-0020781238D4), v1_enum,
    helpstring("This is the FILLTYPE enumeration used with IShapeEdit")
]
typedef enum FILLTYPE
{
    HATCH = 0,
    SOLID = 1,
    POLKADOT = 2
} FILLTYPE;
[
    object, uuid(442F32E2-E7EE-11d2-B8D2-0020781238D4),
    helpstring("IShapeEdit allows you to modify a shape")
]
interface IShapeEdit : IUnknown
{
    [helpstring("Fill a shape")] HRESULT Fill([in] FILLTYPE fType);
    [helpstring("Invert a shape")] HRESULT Inverse();
    [helpstring("Stretch a shape by n")] HRESULT Stretch([in] int factor);
};
```

These [helpstrings] will be very useful in Visual Basic and Java client projects, as they will be integrated into the various Object Browser tools used by the IDE. This will allow your COM objects to be well documented, and hopefully more likely to be used (and purchased) by folks other than yourself. Get in the habit of using [helpstrings] and keep the COM universe a more understandable place.

Defining Library Statements in IDL

Now that you are familiar with defining COM interfaces, methods, and parameters in IDL, we need to learn how to define the coclasses that live inside the binary COM server. Remember that COM development languages and tools can make use of type information to discover the set of COM objects living in a component house (DLL or EXE server). In order to generate type information, we must define what is commonly called a *library statement* using the IDL **library** keyword.

Every library statement must have a [uuid] attribute and should have [version] and [helpstring] attributes as well. The name of the library is irrelevant as far as MIDL is concerned; however, it should have some bearing on the DLL or EXE itself. This said, here is an initial library statement for a server named Shapes.dll :

```
// A library statement contains all the coclasses found in your server, and
// the interfaces supported by each coclass.
[
    uuid(442F32E1-E7EE-11d2-B8D2-0020781238D4),
    version(1.0),
    helpstring("The Shapes Library")
]
library ShapesLibrary
{
    importlib("stdole32.tlb");   // importlib() must be the first item in a library.
};
```

The **importlib** keyword is very similar to the **import** keyword. However, rather than bringing in existing IDL code, **importlib** imports the compiled (binary) type libraries. Every library statement needs to import the standard OLE type library stdole32.tlb at a minimum, and must do so as the very first line of the library statement. When you include stdole32.tlb in your library statement, you ensure that the core COM definitions come along with your custom information. The [version] attribute allows you to incrementally add more and more functionality to a server—simply adjust the major and minor version with each new release.

Defining Coclasses in IDL

Every coclass in our server must be listed within the library statement. The only necessary IDL attribute a coclass must have is [uuid], which serves as the CLSID of the COM class. To declare a COM class in the library, use the **coclass** keyword. To inform the world that Shapes.dll contains a COM object named CoHexagon, we can write:

```
// The CoHexagon coclass is part of the shapes library.
[
    uuid(442F32E1-E7EE-11d2-B8D2-0020781238D4),   // LIBID
    version(1.0), helpstring("The Shapes Library")
]
library ShapesLibrary
{
    importlib("stdole32.tlb");
    [uuid(442F32E3-E7EE-11d2-B8D2-0020781238D4)]   // CLSID
    coclass CoHexagon
    {
    };
};
```

So far so good. However, we have not yet specified which interfaces the CoHexagon coclass implements. To specify that CoHexagon implements IDraw and IShapeEdit, use the **interface** keyword within the library statement:

```
// IDL uses the interface keyword to (a) define the interface and
// (b) bind it to a given coclass.
[uuid(442F32E3-E7EE-11d2-B8D2-0020781238D4)]
coclass CoHexagon
```

```
{
     interface IDraw;
     interface IShapeEdit;
};
```

Specifying the Default Interface

Some COM language mappings support what is known as a default interface. This simply means "What interface do I get for free when I create you?" and is only found in lazy COM language such as VB. C++ developers do not get a free interface when they create a coclass using the COM library—we need to ask up front using CoCreateInstance() or through a valid IClassFactory pointer returned by CoGetClassObject(). Every coclass defined in your IDL file should specify exactly one default interface using the [default] attribute. For example, if we were to assign IDraw as the default interface of CoHexagon, we could write:

```
// Marking a default interface of the coclass.
 [uuid(442F32E3-E7EE-11d2-B8D2-0020781238D4)]
coclass CoHexagon
{
     [default] interface IDraw;
     interface IShapeEdit;
};
```

VB developers access the default interface of a coclass automatically when they declare a new instance of the COM class. Under the hood, the hex variable really points to the default interface as defined by our type library. The VB developer may now use the dot operator to access any methods defined in IDraw:

```
' VB client code creating the CoHexagon.
'
Dim hex as New CoHexagon          ' I now have access to IDraw.
hex.Draw                          ' I want to draw the hexagon!
```

If we defined the IShapeEdit interface as the coclass default, the VB developer would have initial access to those methods from the hex object. When deciding which interface should be defaulted, use common sense and ask yourself which interface captures the "essence" of a coclass. If you do not speak your mind, MIDL will automatically designate the first interface listed by the coclass as the [default].

Physical and Logical Return Values: The [retval] Attribute

Interface methods should return an HRESULT which serves as the "physical" return value of the given method (by this, I mean the literal function return type). COM clients can test this return value to determine the success or failure of a given method invocation. But what if you need to return some "logical" values to your client, such as the result of a string concatenation or the result of adding two numbers? When you wish to return a logical return value you may decide to define [out] parameters (which are always pointers). Assume you are creating a very simple interface named IBasicMath that adds two numbers, and sends the result back to the client as an [out] parameter:

```
// Add has a physical return value of HRESULT, and a logical return value
// of int*
[ object, uuid(709EF655-E8A3-11d2-B8D2-0020781238D4) ]
```

```
interface IBasicMath : IUnknown
{
     HRESULT Add([in] int x, [in] int y, [out] int* answer);
};
```

C++ clients may utilize logical and physical return values as so:

```
// C and C++ clients have no problem using [out] parameters.
HRESULT hr;
int ans = 0;
...
hr = pIBasicMath->Add(20, 20, &ans);
if(SUCCEEDED(hr))
     cout << " 20 + 20 = " << ans << end;
```

In addition to [out] parameters, some COM mappings, such as Visual Basic, support the [retval] attribute which allows you to mark the final parameter of a method to serve as the physical return value. Here is the Add() method of IBasicMath now with a specific [out, retval] parameter:

```
// By marking a parameter as [out, retval] we enable a way to return useful
// information to [out] challenged COM languages mappings.
[ object, uuid(709EF655-E8A3-11d2-B8D2-0020781238D4) ]
interface IBasicMath : IUnknown
{
     HRESULT Add([in] long x, [in] long y, [out, retval] long * answer);
};
```

The final parameter of Add() will now behave as a physical return in COM language mappings that support [retval]. Assume we have a coclass named CoCalculator that specifies IBasicMath as the default interface. A VB client would work with IBasicMath as so:

```
' VB COM client code.
'
Dim c as New CoCalculator          ' Assess to [default] IBasicMath.
Dim ans as Integer
ans = c.Add (20, 20)               ' [out, retval] is mapped to physical return.
```

Languages that do not support [out, retval] parameters simply ignore [retval], and treat the parameter as a logical return (e.g., [out] only). A C++ client will make use of this interface as before:

```
// Raw C++ clients ignore [out, retval] parameters.
HRESULT hr;
int long = 0;
...
hr = pIBasicMath->Add(20, 20, &ans);
if(SUCCEEDED(hr))
     cout << " 20 + 20 = " << ans << end;
```

The Complete Shapes.idl Listing

To pull together the core IDL syntax examined thus far, here is the complete shapes.idl listing, defining IDraw, IShapeEdit, a custom enumeration, and CoHexagon:

```
// Shapes.idl
import "oaidl.idl";
```

```
cpp_quote("// This is my custom enum")
// The FILLTYPE enumeration.
[uuid(442F32E0-E7EE-11d2-B8D2-0020781238D4), v1_enum,
 helpstring("The FILLTYPE enumeration")]
typedef enum FILLTYPE
{
     HATCH = 0,
     SOLID = 1,
     POLKADOT = 2
} FILLTYPE;
// IShapeEdit.
[object, uuid(442F32E2-E7EE-11d2-B8D2-0020781238D4),
 helpstring("IShapeEdit allows you to modify a shape")]
interface IShapeEdit : IUnknown
{
     [helpstring("Fill a shape")] HRESULT Fill([in] FILLTYPE fType);
     [helpstring("Invert a shape")] HRESULT Inverse();
     [helpstring("Stretch a shape by n")] HRESULT Stretch([in] int factor);
};
// IDraw
[object, uuid(4B475690-DE06-11d2-AAF4-00A0C9312D57),
 helpstring("IDraw allows you to draw a shape")]
interface IDraw : IUnknown
{
     [helpstring("Draw Partner!")] HRESULT Draw();
};
// The Shapes Library.
[uuid(442F32E1-E7EE-11d2-B8D2-0020781238D4), version(1.0), helpstring("The Shapes Library")]
library ShapesLibrary
{
     importlib("stdole32.tlb");
     // CoHexagon.
     [uuid(442F32E3-E7EE-11d2-B8D2-0020781238D4)]
     coclass CoHexagon
     {
          [default] interface IDraw;
          interface IShapeEdit;
     };
};
```

Examining the MIDL-Generated Files

 The Midl.exe processed shapes.idl file can be found on the companion CD-ROM under the Labs\Chapter 04\ShapesIDL subfolder.

Now that we have a complete IDL file, let's send shapes.idl file into the MIDL compiler and see what is generated. As you will notice, all IDL attributes come through as comments, and all cpp_quote statements as C++ code. As well, IDL imports become a preprocessor #include. To begin, shapes.h defines the C and C++ language mappings. Here is how our custom enumeration comes through (note the result of cpp_quote):

```
// This is my custom enum
/* [helpstring][v1_enum][uuid] */
typedef enum FILLTYPE
{    HATCH      = 0,
     SOLID      = 1,
```

```
      POLKADOT   = 2
}     FILLTYPE;
```

IShapeEdit and IDraw are also defined in shapes.h and should look familiar given your knowledge of the COM macros. Recall that the MIDL_INTERFACE macro automatically inserts the **struct** keyword as part of the expansion. MIDL has generated both C++ and C language bindings. We won't be concerned with the C bindings. However, when you complete the next lab be sure to look them over (notice that the C++ compiler automatically generates a vTable). Here are the C++ definitions for each of the custom interfaces:

```
MIDL_INTERFACE("442F32E2-E7EE-11d2-B8D2-0020781238D4")
IShapeEdit : public IUnknown
{
public:
      virtual /* [helpstring] */
      HRESULT STDMETHODCALLTYPE Fill( /* [in] */ FILLTYPE fType) = 0;
      virtual /* [helpstring] */
      HRESULT STDMETHODCALLTYPE Inverse( void) = 0;
      virtual /* [helpstring] */
      HRESULT STDMETHODCALLTYPE Stretch( /* [in] */ int factor) = 0;
};
MIDL_INTERFACE("4B475690-DE06-11d2-AAF4-00A0C9312D57")
IDraw : public IUnknown
{
public:
      virtual /* [helpstring] */
      HRESULT STDMETHODCALLTYPE Draw( void) = 0;
};
```

shapes_i.c contains all the GUIDs defined in the IDL file. In our previous labs, you were maintaining a pair of IID files containing DEFINE_GUID macros. Using IDL, we have no need to do so, as we can simply #include the MIDL-generated *_i.c file whenever we need to refer to the GUID constants.

As you may have guessed, whenever MIDL encounters a [uuid] attribute, a new GUID constant is declared. Here are the IID, CLSID, and LIBID GUIDs:

```
const IID IID_IShapeEdit =
{0x442F32E2,0xE7EE,0x11d2,{0xB8,0xD2,0x00,0x20,0x78,0x12,0x38,0xD4}};
const IID IID_IDraw = {0x4B475690,0xDE06,0x11d2,{0xAA,0xF4,0x00,0xA0,0xC9,0x31,0x2D,0x57}};
const IID LIBID_ShapesLibrary =
{0x442F32E1,0xE7EE,0x11d2,{0xB8,0xD2,0x00,0x20,0x78,0x12,0x38,0xD4}};
const CLSID CLSID_CoHexagon =
{0x442F32E3,0xE7EE,0x11d2,{0xB8,0xD2,0x00,0x20,0x78,0x12,0x38,0xD4}};
```

Making Use of the MIDL-Generated Files

These two MIDL-generated files may be used in C or C++ based COM projects. In the server project we include shapes.h when creating coclass definitions:

```
// When you are creating your coclasses, include the MIDL-generated header
// file to grab the C++ interface definitions.
#include "shapes.h"
class CoHexagon : public IDraw, public IShapeEdit
{
      // Use STDMETHODIMP/STDMETHODIMP_ as before
};
```

Include shapes_i.c into the coclass implementation file to get the definition of IID_IShapeEdit and IID_IDraw for use in our QueryInterface() logic. As well, the server file which defines DllGetClassObject() will also need to reference this same file to get the correct CLSID constants.

In a COM client project, we need to include the same MIDL-generated files to allow us to make CoCreateInstance() calls as well as declare interface pointer variables:

```
// COM clients also make use of MIDL-generated files.
#include "shapes_i.c"        // Contains GUIDs.
#include "shapes.h"          // Contains interfaces definitions.
void main(void)
{
    IDraw* pDraw;
    ...
    CoCreateInstance(CLSID_CoHexagon, NULL, CLSCTX_INPROC_SERVER, IID_IDraw,
                     (void**)&pDraw);
    ...
}
```

So! As you can see, by defining all your COM servers in IDL, you are able to avoid having to maintain separate files which hold onto DEFINE_GUID statements and C++ interface definitions. Two of the MIDL-generated files can now be included in your COM server and COM client workspaces to get references to the correct GUIDs and interface definitions.

Summation of Core IDL Keywords

At this point, you have enough knowledge to create IDL interfaces, coclasses, and library statements. As you have seen, the MIDL-generated header *.h and *_i.c files provide the necessary C and C++ language bindings to build COM clients and COM servers. Before we begin working with our type information from the client's perception, here is a summary of all the IDL keywords examined so far.

IDL Keyword	Meaning in Life
cpp_quote	Injects C/C++ code into MIDL-generated header files.
enum, v1_enum	Used to create a custom enumeration of types. Use with the v1_enum attribute to transmit as 32-bit.
helpstring	Injects text descriptions into generated type libraries.
import	Used to bring in existing IDL definitions into the current IDL file.
importlib	Brings in binary type information into a library statement.
in, out, retval	Used to specify the direction of interface method parameters including a 'physical return' if the language mapping supports them.
interface	Used to declare a new COM interface (if colored by the uuid and object attributes)
library	Declares type information for the server.
object	Marks the interface as a COM interface, not a DCE-based interface
uuid	Binds a GUID to the given item.

Obviously Microsoft IDL is more sophisticated than this small set of keywords. Over the course of this book, we will see many additional aspects of IDL. For example, in Chapter 11 you will learn to build structures and arrays of IDL types. Do be aware that the full set of IDL keywords can be found in online help (do a keyword search for "MIDL Language Reference").

Now that we are able to describe the functionality of our COM server in a language-neutral manner, we will spend the remainder of this chapter examining how Visual Basic, Java, and C++ clients can access this type information. But first, we need to register a server's type information to allow these other languages to access its functionality.

Registering Your Type Information: HKEY_CLASSES_ROOT\TypeLib

The key to COM's language independence is the MIDL-generated *.tlb file, which is simply the binary equivalent of the associated IDL code. Before languages such as VB and Java can make use of a COM object, they must be able to reference a server's type information. HKEY_CLASSES_ROOT (HKCR) maintains a separate key named TypeLib which holds all the relevant information about your *.tlb files on your system.

To enter the correct information under HKCR\TypeLib, we will need to extend our server's REG file and remerge this file into the system registry. Of course, once we begin working with ATL, this process is automated on your behalf using the ATL registry scripting language and COM library calls.

To update a REG file to account for type information, you must specify the LIBID, current version, and a friendly text string describing the type information. The LIBID can be obtained from the [uuid] attribute of the library statement in your IDL file. The version information should match the value assigned in the [version] attribute. Here are the relevant pieces of your IDL file that need to be placed into the registry:

```
// We need the LIBID when building entries for HKCR\TypeLib.
[
     uuid(442F32E1-E7EE-11d2-B8D2-0020781238D4), version(1.0),
     helpstring("The Shapes Library")
]
library ShapesLibrary
{
...
}
```

To enter the LIBID and version, update the REG as the following:

```
; Format is: HKCR\TypeLib\{<guid>}\version = string name.
;
HKEY_CLASSES_ROOT\TypeLib\{442F32E1-E7EE-11d2-B8D2-0020781238D4}
\1.0 = Shapes Server Type Lib
```

Next, under "HKCR\TypeLib\{guid}\version" we need to add another subkey that specifies the language ID of the type library (that would be a human language, not a programming language). After this subkey is the Win32 path to the *.tlb file itself:

```
; Format is: HKCR\TypeLib\{<guid>}\version\language ID\Win32 = <path>
;
HKEY_CLASSES_ROOT\TypeLib\{442F32E1-E7EE-11d2-B8D2-0020781238D4}\1.0\0\Win32 = E:\Chapter
04\ShapeServer\Debug\ShapesServer.tlb
```

These two registry entries are all we technically need; however, most TypeLib listings also specify the optional Flags and HelpDir subkeys. Our server has no flags, and no help file, but for the sake of completion here are the final TypeLib entries (if it did have a help file, we would enter the path to that file):

```
; Optional TypeLib entries.
;
HKEY_CLASSES_ROOT\TypeLib\{442F32E1-E7EE-11d2-B8D2-0020781238D4}\1.0\FLAGS = 0
HKEY_CLASSES_ROOT\TypeLib\{442F32E1-E7EE-11d2-B8D2-0020781238D4}\1.0\HELPDIR
```

When you merge this updated *.reg file you will see the following listing under HKCR\TypeLib:

Figure 4-4: HKCR\TypeLib entries for our Shape server type information.

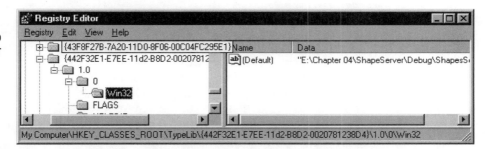

To fully merge our type information, we should go back to HKCR\CLSID and enter a TypeLib subkey. In this way, SCM can easily find the type information from within the scope of the COM object's CLSID. As a rule of thumb, always identify the correct type library for each and every coclass defined within the server:

```
; Your coclasses should specify which type library they are defined in.
;
HKEY_CLASSES_ROOT\CLSID\{442F32E3-E7EE-11d2-B8D2-0020781238D4}\TypeLib =
{442F32E1-E7EE-11d2-B8D2-0020781238D4}
```

Now that we have entered the relevant information for our server's type information into the registry, we are ready to allow other COM-enabled languages to access our functionality. But first, allow me to introduce RegEdit's big brother, the OLE/COM Object Viewer.

The OLE/COM Object Viewer

Visual C++ ships with a great IDE-neutral browsing tool named the OLE/COM Object Viewer. Using this tool you are able to examine the COM objects installed on your local machine. Open this tool from the Visual C++ IDE using the Tools menu. You will notice a number of nodes in the left-hand pane tree view control:

Figure 4-5:
The various
nodes of the
OLE/COM
Object Viewer.

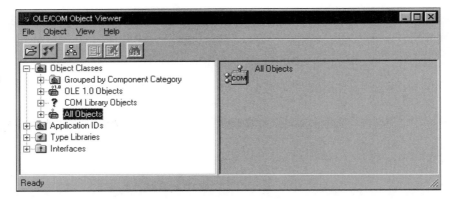

As you can see from Figure 4-5, you may view type information, interface information, component category information (which we will learn all about in Chapter 9), and so on. In your next lab, you will be adding type information to your CoCar server developed in Chapter 3. When you have done so, you can expand the All Objects node, and hunt down your coclass. For the sake of discussion, assume you have already added some type information to CoCar, and wish to use the OLE/COM Viewer to examine its attributes.

Figure 4-6:
Expanding on a
coclass will
activate the
object.

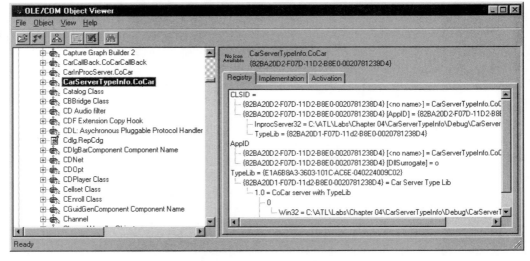

In Figure 4-6, the CoCar object has been selected. Do note that when you expand a coclass sub-node, you have literally activated the object! For example, if you placed a MessageBox() call in the constructor of CoCar, you will see it pop up from the context of the OLE/COM Viewer utility.

Beneath the CoCar is a listing of <u>registered</u> interfaces supported by the object. As we will see in the next chapter, a separate key of HKCR maintains information about the COM interfaces on your machine. Had we registered ICreateCar, IEngine, and IStats, we would see these listed as well. On the right-hand pane of the OLE/COM Object Viewer are a number of tabs, which allow you to examine registry information and implementation details, as well as set some security options for your coclass. Typically, you will make use of the dcomcnfg.exe utility to configure your COM objects; however, this tool allows you to establish certain security settings as well.

Using this tool is rather self-explanatory, and I will assume you will take the time to play with its functionality. One item is worth pointing out here and now: It is possible to examine the IDL code behind a given coclass. Most classes found from the All Objects node provide a context-sensitive View Type Information menu selection:

Figure 4-7: Preparing to examine an object's IDL code.

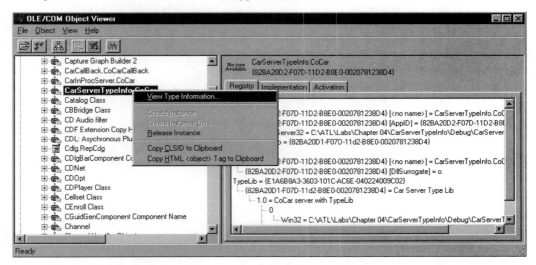

With this option selected, a separate window will appear, displaying the IDL code behind the COM object. As you can guess, this is a very handy way to learn about the IDL language (there are even copy/paste options in the tool to grab existing IDL code).

So now you can code, compile, and register type information for your C++ COM servers. If you are still looking for the major benefit of using IDL, the wait is over. The remainder of this chapter will examine how various programming languages (other than C++) can program against your coclasses using MIDL-generated type libraries.

Visual Basic's COM Language Mapping

In the dark days of Visual Basic, developers were only able to access a COM server's functionality through a standard interface named IDispatch. IDispatch provides an alternative way for clients who cannot directly reference our object's vTable interfaces (such as IDraw and IShapeEdit) to access the functionality of a COM object. IDispatch is most commonly used in scripting environments (such as VBScript); we will have much more to say about this interface in Chapter 10.

These days, Visual Basic developers may directly access our COM object's set of custom (vTable) interfaces as well as IDispatch. Before VB developers can do so, however, they must set a reference to the server's type information using the References dialog, accessed from the Project | References menu. Figure 4-8 illustrates how to include the shapes library into a VB project (notice the custom [helpstring] in action):

Figure 4-8:
The VB
References
dialog.

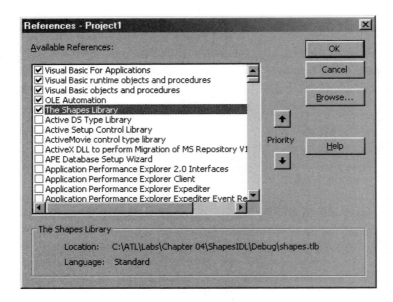

As you may suspect, the VB References dialog box will scan HKCR\TypeLib for all registered type libraries on your machine, and present them in a list box. Also notice the Browse... button. If we did not add the necessary TypeLib information to our server's REG file, the VB developer could make use of this button to manually navigate to the location of the *.tlb file. Be a thoughtful COM developer, however, and get in the habit of going that extra step. Register your type information.

Once a reference has been set to the type library, VB developers may examine the contents of a server using the VB Object Browser utility (F2 is the hot key). Figure 4-9 shows the type information VB extracted from our shapes.tlb file. As you can see, CoHexagon, IShapeEdit, and our custom FILLTYPE enum all come through. Notice we do not see an IDraw interface, as we declared it to be the [default] interface of CoHexagon:

Figure 4-9:
The VB Object
Browser.

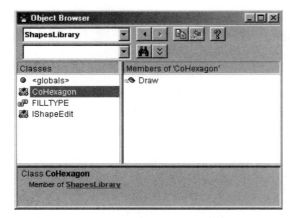

Creating Coclasses in VB

Visual Basic developers are free to make instances of our COM classes using the **New** keyword. The VB **New** keyword does quite a bit on your behalf under the hood. Here is what really happens when a VB programmer creates a new coclass like so:

```
' Once a reference to the Shapes.tlb file has been set,
' a VB developer may make use of CoHexagon as so.
'
Dim hex as New CoHexagon     ' Declare a new object type.
hex.Draw                     ' Access methods of [default] interface.
```

The code above wraps up all the steps we, as C++ developers, go through by hand:

1. VB reads the type information in our server and discovers the [default] interface.
2. VB calls CoCreateInstance() for CLSID_CoHexagon.
3. VB asks for the default interface, resulting in an AddRef() on CoHexagon.
4. VB stores the default interface in the CoHexagon variable.

At this point, the VB developer holds onto an IDraw* variable, although this is completely hidden from the VB language mapping. To unknowing VB developers, it looks as if they are holding onto an object reference. You know better. COM is all about interfaces. Even when it looks as if you don't have one, you do.

When a VB developer is finished with an interface pointer, the VB runtime will automatically call Release() on the interface when it falls out of scope. If you wish to call Release() before that time, you may explicitly set a reference to Nothing:

```
' An explicit Release().
'
Set hex = Nothing          ' The VB equivalent of pDraw->Release()
```

Calling QueryInterface() from Visual Basic

Now, if VB automatically grants access to the default interface of a coclass, the next logical question is "how can we query for the others?" Visual Basic 5.0 introduced the ability to navigate a coclass's set of supported custom interfaces using the **Set =** syntax. Here is how a VB client may query for interfaces beyond the default (note the implicit AddRef() calls):

```
' First create the coclass and grab the [default] interface.
'
Dim hex as New CoHexagon
hex.Draw                   ' AddRef has been called. [refcount = 1]
' Declare a variable of type IShapeEdit (can't 'New' interfaces!)
Dim itfSH as IShapeEdit
' Query hex for IID_IShapeEdit (e.g., hex.QueryInterface(IID_IShapeEdit, itfSH) )
Set itfSH = hex            ' AddRef has been called again. [refcount = 2]
```

The above code is great, but what if we wish to ensure the above QueryInterface() call succeeded before calling off the IShapeEdit pointer? In order to test if a QueryInterface() call succeeded, we may make use of the following VB syntax:

```
' Test before calling interface methods
'
Set itfSH = hex
```

```
If Not itfSH Is Nothing Then       ' Do we have the IShapeEdit interface?
    itfSH.Inverse
    itfSH.Stretch 20
    itfSH.Fill POLKADOT
End If
```

Again, the itfSH and the hex variable will eventually drop out of scope of the given function which calls Release() on the interfaces automatically. In VB we can force a Release() of an interface pointer as soon as possible by using the **Nothing** keyword:

```
' Explicitly releasing interfaces in VB.
'
Set itfSH = Nothing              ' Release() called.   [refcount = 1]
Set hex = Nothing                ' Object destroyed.   [refcount = 0]
```

AddRef() and Release() are so well hidden by the VB runtime, we seldom have to think about it at all. QueryInterface() in Visual Basic can be summed up with the following pseudo-code:

```
Dim CoClassVariable as New <CoClassYouWant>     ' Get the [default]
Dim InterfaceVariable as < InterfaceYouWant >   ' Declare interface variable
Set InterfaceVariable = CoClassVariable         ' Get another interface
```

This information is just enough to make you dangerous in the VB COM universe. In the next set of labs, you will be given a step-by-step VB client example, so don't panic if you are unfamiliar with VB syntax. The point here is not to develop professional VB applications, but to understand the basics of using VB to access our C++ COM servers. Next, let's see what it would take to use CoHexagon from within the Java language.

A Word on the Java/COM Language Mapping

J++ is Microsoft's Java IDE. Although you can create 100% pure Java code with J++, you will discover just by tinkering with the tool for a bit that it is (a) very Windows-centric and (b) has great support for COM technologies. To date, Visual J++ is the only Java IDE that supports COM development.

Not all Java Virtual Machines (JVM) support a COM to Java language mapping. Microsoft's JVM is the only virtual machine capable of working with the Java/COM language mapping. Keep in mind that when you choose to integrate COM and Java, you are losing Java's platform independence and become tied to the Microsoft Java interpreter.

Note: When you create any "unpure" Java solution with J++, you will be prompted with a few dialog boxes asking for your permission to import the necessary Java packages that will tie you to the Windows OS. Say "OK" and you are ready to go.

Including Your Type Information into a J++ Project Solution

Much like a VB client, a Java client must include the type information for the COM server it wishes to program against, using the COM Wrappers dialog box. You may include type information using the Project | Add COM Wrapper menu selection of the J++ IDE:

Figure 4-10:
J++ COM
Wrappers dialog
box.

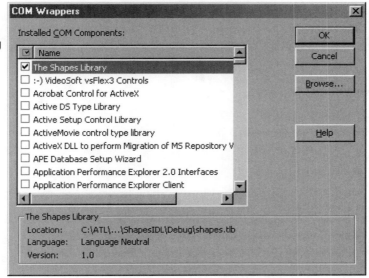

Once you select the desired *.tlb file, you will have a new Java package added to your current J++ solution space which contains all the interfaces, coclasses, and other COM definitions found in the type information, each of which is placed in a separate *.java file. These files contain Java to COM proxy wrappers, which map Java source code to various COM library calls. The bridge between the two is your friendly MS Java Virtual Machine. From the Project Explorer, you can see the contents of the shapes package:

Figure 4-11:
IDL constructs
end up as Java
proxy classes.

Again, much like Visual Basic, you may use the Java Object Browser (F2, provided you have a *.java file as the active window) to examine the type information of the COM server:

Figure 4-12:
The Java Object
Browser.

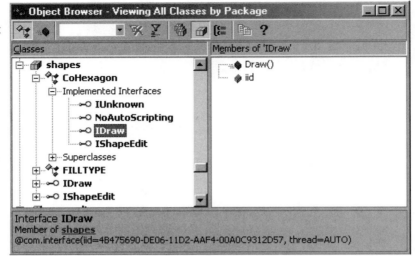

Examining the Generated Java Code

When you include type information using the COM Wrappers utility, you trigger a utility named jactivex.exe which engineers IDL types into corresponding Java classes. As things turn out, these classes are proxies to the real binary COM objects. Let's walk through the files brought in by jactivex.exe for the shapes project.

The FILLTYPE enumeration is realized in Java as a collection of "static final" types (Java has no enum keyword). Here is the content of the FILLTYPE.java file:

```
// The IDL enumeration is mapped to a collection of constant types.
public interface FILLTYPE
{
    public static final int HATCH = 0;
    public static final int SOLID = 1;
    public static final int POLKADOT = 2;
}
```

How about the custom interfaces? J++ makes use of a specific package (com.ms.com) to provide the necessary COM support. Jactivex.exe embeds the IID of the interface as a static final data member as part of the class definition (omitted for clarity). Here is our Java savvy IDraw interface (IShapeEdit appears similar):

```
// IDraw in Java.
public interface IDraw extends IUnknown
{
    public void Draw();
}
```

Next, we have the CoHexagon coclass itself. This is a creatable Java class which implements the IUnknown, IDraw, and IShapeEdit interfaces. All the method names come through as native, reminding us that we are developing an unpure Java solution:

```
// The J++ developer will create an instance of CoHexagon in the Java source code.
// Note the use of the Java 'implements' keyword.
public class CoHexagon implements IUnknown,
```

```
                              com.ms.com.NoAutoScripting,
                              shapes.IDraw,
                              shapes.IShapeEdit
{
     public native void Draw();
     public native void Fill(int fType);
     public native void Inverse();
     public native void Stretch(int factor);
}
```

The support for the NoAutoScripting interface marks this coclass as a non-automation based class (i.e., no support for IDispatch) accessible through the coclass vTable only. As the J++ developer, you can ignore the NoAutoScripting interface and just concentrate on creating a CoHexagon and accessing the IDraw and IShapeEdit interfaces. Before we see the Java code to do just this, here is some further information on the Java to COM mapping layer.

Getting @com in Java

When you examine the jactivex.exe generated code, you will find a number of source code comments using the @com prefix. These *prelimiters* are directives used by the MS JVM to map Java atoms to COM atoms during runtime (therefore <u>don't remove these comments</u>). Here is a breakdown of the most common MS JVM directives:

J++ COM Directive	Meaning in Life
@com.class	Specifies that this Java class maps to a COM coclass.
@com.interface	Marks a COM interface, including the GUID used to represent it.
@com.method	Used with @com.parameters to map universal COM types to Java types. Also marks the vTable offset for each method.
@com.struct	Maps a COM structure to a Java class (Java has no struct keyword).

Full commentary on the @com directives can be obtained from online help (MS Developer Network) under the Java/COM Attributes Reference section. Armed with this information, let's examine how JActivex.exe <u>really</u> defined IDraw:

```
// VTable-only interface IDraw
/** @com.interface(iid=4B475690-DE06-11D2-AAF4-00A0C9312D57, thread=AUTO) */
public interface IDraw extends IUnknown
{
     /** @com.method(vtoffset=0, addFlagsVtable=4)
         @com.parameters() */
     public void Draw();
public static final com.ms.com._Guid iid = new com.ms.com._Guid((int)0x4b475690,
(short)0xde06, (short)0x11d2, (byte)0xaa, (byte)0xf4, (byte)0x0, (byte)0xa0, (byte)0xc9,
(byte)0x31, (byte)0x2d, (byte)0x57);
}
```

Creating Coclasses and Accessing Interfaces from Java

The Java/COM language mapping is about as seamless as you can get. All calls to the COM library are hidden deep within COM-specific packages and MS JVM. To create an instance of your coclass, use the Java **new** operator. This will call CoCreateInstance() on your behalf. When you wish to obtain a given interface from the coclass, you perform an explicit Java style cast (which looks very much like a C++ style cast).

Assume you have created a new J++ Windows Application workspace, and have included the correct COM wrapper. Here is a Java class named ShapesConsumer making use of CoHexagon:

```
// Some Java code making use of CoHexagon.
import shapes.*;        // Must import files into a class referencing them.
public class ShapesConsumer
{
    // Create private member variables for the coclass & interfaces.
    private shapes.CoHexagon myHex;
    private shapes.IDraw itfDraw;
    private shapes.IShapeEdit itfSE;
    public static void main(String[] args)
    {
        // Make the CoHexagon
        myHex = new shapes.CoHexagon();
        itfDraw = (IDraw)myHex;       // QI for IDraw.
        itfDraw.Draw();
        itfSE = (IShapeEdit)myHex;    // QI for IShapeEdit.
        itfSE.Invert();
    }
}
```

The MS Java GC (garbage collector) automatically calls Release() on all interface references when necessary. Therefore, Java clients never see Release() calls at the Java source code level.

So then, at this point you can begin to use raw C++ COM objects from within the Visual Basic and Java languages, given the virtues of IDL. Not too bad! The last stop before a set of labs to try this all out for yourself is to see how type information can also be used to ease the burden of raw C++ client-side COM programming.

Using the Visual C++ COM Compiler Directives

Traditionally, C++ client-side COM code begins with CoInitialize() and ends with CoUninitialize(). Between these COM library functions are numerous calls to create coclasses, obtain interfaces, and go to town. This approach to COM client-side logic can place extra burdens on the C++ developer, especially with regard to managing the object's reference count. Since the release of Visual C++ 5.0, client-side COM programming has been simplified quite a bit using smart pointer technology. Although you are completely free to always do raw COM programming using the COM library directly, you can now make use of type information in your C++ client code as well.

Note: Complete documentation of the Visual C++ COM extensions can be found on MSDN. Look up "compiler COM support classes."

The #import directive, introduced in Visual C++ 5.0, is used to generate "smart pointer" wrappers based on a server's type information (i.e., the *.tlb file). This functionality is provided by the <comip.h> and <comdef.h> system files which define a number of new templates, data types, and magic macros to help the #import generated code perform its magic. You have no need to directly include these into your client projects, as they are already included within the #import generated files. We will see exactly what a "smart pointer" is soon enough. But first, let's get to know the #import statement.

#importing Type Information

Assume you have a new Win32 Console project (or an MFC project for that matter) and wish to access CoHexagon using the Visual C++ COM compiler directives. First, you would import the type information as so:

```
// To use the VC++ smart pointer technology in your C++ client side code,
// begin by importing the server's type information.
#import "E:\ShapesServer\Debug\shapes.tlb" no_namespace named_guid
```

The behavior of the #import directive can be modified using a handful of optional attributes such as no_namespace. This flag will place the server's COM definitions into the current namespace. The named_guid flag instructs the compiler to define the GUIDs contained in the *.tlb file using the CLSID_, LIBID_, and IID_ prefixes.

There are a total of 17 different #import attributes that may be used to control how a server's type information is included into your project. Look up "The #import Directive" from MSDN for a description of each option. For our purposes, no_namespace and named_guid will do just fine.

Now, when the VC compiler encounters the #import command, it will generate two new C++ files and place them into your project's Debug folder. Here is a breakdown of each generated file (note that the file extensions will be the same between projects; however, the name of the files will depend on the name of the imported file).

■ **shapes.tlh:** The type library header file contains smart pointer definitions of the IDL interface definitions. Also included in this file are the raw C++ equivalents of the generated smart pointers.

■ **shapes.tli:** The type library implementation file contains implementation code for the smart pointers defined by the related *.tlh file.

Understanding Smart Pointers

So then, what is a *smart pointer*? C++ COM folks have often looked for a way to minimize the AddRef(), QueryInterface(), and Release() calls necessary to work with COM objects. Some of these same folks have written custom wrapper classes around a given COM interface which automatically AddRefs and Releases itself through the wrapper's constructor set, various overloaded operators, and destructor. A smart pointer is not really a pointer at all, but an intelligent C++ class wrapped around a COM interface. If you examine a given *.tlh file you will see smart pointer definitions based on the *.tlb file. Each is established with the _COM_SMARTPTR_TYPEDEF macro:

```
// Shapes.tlh contains the smart pointer definitions for the interfaces defined in the
// shapes type library.
_COM_SMARTPTR_TYPEDEF(IDraw, __uuidof(IDraw));
_COM_SMARTPTR_TYPEDEF(IShapeEdit, __uuidof(IShapeEdit));
```

The _COM_SMARTPTR_TYPEDEF macro expands into a typedef for a new variable named XXXXPtr, where "XXXX" is the name of your interface (i.e., IDrawPtr, IShapeEditPtr, and so on). You make use of these types in your C++ COM client code to help ease the burden of raw COM development. The _COM_SMARTPTR_TYPEDEF macro is defined in <comdef.h> as the following:

```
// <comdef.h> defines the _COM_SMARTPTR_TYPEDEF macro.
#define _COM_SMARTPTR_TYPEDEF(Interface, IID) \
typedef _COM_SMARTPTR<_COM_SMARTPTR_LEVEL2<Interface, &IID> > \
Interface ## Ptr
```

The _com_ptr_t<> Template

The _COM_SMARTPTR_TYPEDEF macro eventually expands into a _com_ptr_t<> template, which is defined in <comip.h> as the following:

```
// _COM_SMARTPTR_TYPEDEF(IDraw, __uuidof(IDraw));
// Eventually ends up as:
template<typename _IIID> class _com_ptr_t { // Lots of cool methods to help you };
```

This template defines a number of methods having nothing to do with your custom interfaces directly, but provides numerous COM-like behaviors for the smart pointer. For example, _com_ptr_t<> supports a templatized version of QueryInterface() which creates a new smart pointer given an existing smart pointer.

The CreateInstance() method of _com_ptr_t<> makes the necessary COM library calls to find and activate a coclass on your behalf. Even better, the _com_ptr_t<> template defines a number of overloaded operators which you may use when working with smart pointer technology. Collectively, the methods of _com_ptr_t<> that are not specific to the interface being wrapped are called the *intrinsic* methods. Any of these intrinsic methods are accessed using the C++ dot operator.

Note: Check out com_ptr_t<> in online help to discover all the intrinsic methods of the Visual C++ smart pointer.

Client-Side COM Using Smart Pointers

When you wish to create a brand new COM object using smart pointers, you have a number of choices. You may elect to define a smart pointer variable and call the intrinsic CreateInstance() method of _com_ptr_t<>, passing in the CLSID of the object you wish to wrap (which we received by using the named_guids attribute):

```
// Creating CoHexagon using the CreateInstance() method of
// _com_ptr_t<>
IDrawPtr spDraw;                    // Make a smart pointer to IDraw
spDraw.CreateInstance(CLSID_CoHexagon); // Create the CoHexagon.
```

You may also choose to send in the CLSID of the coclass to the constructor of your smart pointer using the __uuidof() extension. The following code is simply another version of the preceding code:

```
// Another way to construct a CoHexagon with VC smart pointers.
IDrawPtr spDraw(__uuidof(CoHexagon));
```

Using Your New Smart Pointer

Once you have a smart pointer created (using either of the above techniques) you make use of the arrow operator to access the methods of the underlying smart pointer interface methods:

```
// When spDraw falls out of scope, Release is called.
spDraw->Draw();
```

Let's say you now want to access the IShapeEdit interface of CoHexagon from your current IDraw smart pointer. To call QueryInterface() from a valid smart pointer, use the overloaded assignment operator:

```
// QI for IID_IShapeEdit.
IShapeEditPtr spSEdit = spDraw;
spSEdit -> Invert(90);
```

The real bonus of using a smart pointer is that Release() will be called automatically when it drops out of scope; just be sure to set your smart pointers to NULL when finished. To pull this all together, here is a sample COM client using smart pointers to access the functionality of CoHexagon:

```
// A C++ COM client using a server's type information.
#import "E:\ShapesServer\Debug\shapes.tlb" no_namespace named_guid
void main(void)
{
     CoInitialize(NULL);
     // Create a smart pointer for IDraw.
     IDrawPtr spDraw(__uuidof(CoHexagon));
     spDraw->Draw();
     // Query for IShapeEdit.
     IShapeEditPtr spSEdit = spDraw;
     spSEdit -> Invert();
     spSEdit -> Release();
     // Clean up.
     spSEdit = NULL;
     spDraw = NULL;
     CoUninitialize();
}
```

Now that is quite a cleanup from traditional COM C++ client programming! As you spend more time with the _com_ptr_t<> template, you will see there are many ways to manipulate templates.

> **Note:** The ATL framework defines an alternative set of smart pointers (CComPtr<> and CComPtrQI<>) that are also used to help minimize client coding efforts. We will see some of these ATL smart pointers in use later in the book; however, a vast majority of the sample code will make use of straight COM library calls and IUnknown logic.

Additional Visual C++ COM Extensions

To finish up our investigation of the Visual C++ COM compiler support, let's examine how COM compiler support can also simplify our BSTR string manipulations. The _bstr_t data type may be used in place of the native BSTR. This shields you from the direct use of system string functions and provides a number of overloaded operators to manipulate the COM string of champions. For example, here is a code snippet using _bstr_t to access our CoCar's IStats functionality (note the overloaded << operator automatically converts the underlying BSTR to a char*):

```
// BSTR development as it should be.
_bstr_t bstrName;
bstrName = spStats->GetPetName();        // [out, retval] also supported!
cout << bstrName << " has blown up! Lead Foot!" << endl << endl;
```

The COM compiler directives also provide the _variant_t data type which wraps up the VARIANT data type and the various associated API functions. The VARIANT data type is a core aspect of IDispatch programming. If you plan to make heavy use of C++ IDispatch programming, be sure to check _variant_t.

You are also provided with the _com_error type that maps standard COM HRESULTs to C++ exceptions. As methods you call from a valid smart pointer can throw exceptions, the _com_error type provides detailed information concerning the nature of the error. Assume we called the Draw method from an IDraw smart pointer and wish to forward any COM error into a system MessageBox:

```
// The VC COM extensions support try/catch blocks to
// intercept COM HRESULTs.
try
{
    IDrawPtr spDraw( __uuidof(CoHexagon));
    spDraw -> Draw();
}
catch( _com_error e)
{
    // Extract error message from the _com_error object.
    MessageBox(NULL, e.ErrorMessage, "Oops!",
            MB_OK | MB_SETFOREGROUND);
}
```

Now that we have seen not only how to add type information to our COM servers but how various COM language mappings may use them, it is time for some serious lab work. After you complete this lab, it is off to location transparency and the world of Distributed COM (DCOM) computing.

Lab 4-1: Providing Type Information for CoCar

This lab will give you the chance to experiment with the language-independent nature of COM. Here, you will be extending the CarInProcServer.dll developed in Chapter 3 to support type information and make use of the MIDL-generated files. Once we retrofit the CoCar server, you will have the chance to build Visual Basic and Java clients, as well as a C++ client using the COM compiler directives.

The solution for this lab can be found on your CD-ROM under:
Labs\Chapter 04\CarServerTypeInfo
Labs\Chapter 04\CarServerTypeInfo\VB Client
Labs\Chapter 04\ CarServerTypeInfo\VJ Client
Labs\Chapter 04\ CarServerTypeInfo\CPP Import Client

Step One: Create the Type Information

In this lab you will be extending your previous CarInProcServer.dll lab by supplying type information. To begin, open the CarInProcServer workspace you developed in Chapter 3 (or make a copy of this project) and insert a new file (using **File | New...**) named **CarServerTypeInfo.idl** into the project. This single file will hold all interface, coclass, and library definitions for the server.

Note: The sample solution on your CD-ROM for this step of the lab is an entirely new server named CarServerTypeInfo. The CoCar class and DLL export logic have been ported over; however, the GUIDs have been changed to prevent clashes from the Chapter 3 lab solution.

In your new IDL file, import oaidl.idl. This file contains all the core COM data types and interface definitions. Begin by defining the IStats, IEngine, and ICreateCar interfaces in IDL syntax. When assigning IIDs for the [uuid()] attribute, simply copy the existing IIDs from your iid.h file.

Be sure to mark your method parameters with [in] and [out, retval] attributes and, to be kind, include a [helpstring] for each interface. Here is the IDL definition of the CoCar interfaces:

```
// Bring in core IDL files.
import "oaidl.idl";
// IStats
[object, uuid(A533DA31-D372-11d2-B8CF-0020781238D4),
  helpstring("Get info about this car")]
interface IStats : IUnknown
{
     HRESULT DisplayStats();
     HRESULT GetPetName([out, retval] BSTR* petName);
};
// IEngine
[object, uuid(A533DA30-D372-11d2-B8CF-0020781238D4),
  helpstring("Rev your car & slow it down")]
interface IEngine : IUnknown
{
     HRESULT SpeedUp();
     HRESULT GetMaxSpeed ([out, retval] int* maxSpeed);
     HRESULT GetCurSpeed ([out, retval] int* curSpeed);
};
// ICreateCar
[object, uuid(A533DA32-D372-11d2-B8CF-0020781238D4),
  helpstring("This lets you create a car")]
interface ICreateCar : IUnknown
{
     HRESULT SetPetName([in]BSTR petName);
     HRESULT SetMaxSpeed([in]int maxSp);
};
```

Next define a library statement marked with the [version] and [uuid] attribute. You will need to use guidgen.exe to obtain a new LIBID which uniquely identifies the *.tlb file. Be sure to add a [helpstring] for the library, as this will identify your type information in various IDE tools (such as the VB References dialog box). As well, be sure your library makes a call to:

```
importlib("stdole32.tlb");
```

In your library statement, define the CoCar class using your existing CLSID, which will also be found in your iid.h file. CoCar needs to support each custom interface. Pick one as the [default] interface for the coclass (for the purposes of this lab, assume ICreateCar to be the [default]). Here is the IDL:

```
// The library statement.
[uuid(82BA20D1-F07D-11d2-B8E0-0020781238D4), version(1.0),
    helpstring("CoCar server with TypeLib")]
library CarServer
{
    importlib("stdole32.tlb");
    [uuid(82BA20D2-F07D-11d2-B8E0-0020781238D4)]
    coclass CoCar
    {
        [default] interface ICreateCar;
        interface IStats;
        interface IEngine;
    };
};
```

Recall that the MIDL compiler will generate a number of C++ files used in your project, so we need to get rid of existing files we used for the same purpose. Before you proceed, remove the following files from your project workspace (using FileView):

- **iid.h/iid.cpp:** You do not need these files any more, as the MIDL-generated CarServerTypeInfo_i.c file will now contain your GUID definitions.
- **interfaces.h:** You do not need this file any more, as the C++ interface bindings will now be defined automatically by MIDL and stored in the CarServerTypeInfo.h file.

Next, be sure you update your existing source code files throughout your project by removing #includes to iid.h and interfaces.h and replacing them with the MIDL-generated *.h and *_i.c files. Knowing where to include the correct MIDL files can be a bit of a black art, so feel free to use the following guide (or examine the supplemental CD lab solution):

Project Source File	MIDL-Generated File to Include
CoCar.h	#include "carservertypeinfo.h"
CoCar.cpp	#include "carservertypeinfo_i.c"
CoCarClassFactory.h	No need to include MIDL-generated files.
CoCarClassFactory.cpp	No need to include MIDL-generated files.
CarInProcServer.cpp	#include "carservertypeinfo_i.c"

Now, recompile your project to allow the MIDL compiler to do its work. If you get any errors, you may have forgotten to turn off the MkTypLib Compatible option from the Project | Settings dialog.

This should convert your previous C++ specific CoCar to the language-independent variety. Be sure to check out the MIDL-generated files. Now that we have some type information, let's rework the REG file to enter the correct information into the system registry.

Step Two: Register Your Type Information

Technically this step is optional, as both the VB and J++ IDEs provide a way to manually navigate to a *.tlb file via the Browse button. However, to solidify your COM lifestyle, add the correct type library entries now. Here is what the full REG file should look like (just add your GUIDs and paths accordingly):

```
REGEDIT
HKEY_CLASSES_ROOT\CarServerTypeInfo.CoCar\CLSID = {82BA20D2-F07D-11d2-B8E0-0020781238D4}
HKEY_CLASSES_ROOT\CLSID\{82BA20D2-F07D-11d2-B8E0-0020781238D4} = CarServerTypeInfo.CoCar
HKEY_CLASSES_ROOT\CLSID\{82BA20D2-F07D-11d2-B8E0-0020781238D4}
\InprocServer32 = C:\ATL\Labs\Chapter 04\CarServerTypeInfo \Debug\CarServerTypeInfo.dll
HKEY_CLASSES_ROOT\CLSID\{82BA20D2-F07D-11d2-B8E0-0020781238D4}\TypeLib =
{82BA20D1-F07D-11d2-B8E0-0020781238D4}
HKEY_CLASSES_ROOT\TypeLib\{82BA20D1-F07D-11d2-B8E0-0020781238D4} = Car Server Type Lib
HKEY_CLASSES_ROOT\TypeLib\{82BA20D1-F07D-11d2-B8E0-0020781238D4}\1.0\0\Win32 =
C:\ATL\Labs\Chapter 04\CarServerTypeInfo\Debug\CarServerTypeInfo.tlb
HKEY_CLASSES_ROOT\TypeLib\{82BA20D1-F07D-11d2-B8E0-0020781238D4}\1.0\FLAGS = 0
HKEY_CLASSES_ROOT\TypeLib\{82BA20D1-F07D-11d2-B8E0-0020781238D4}\1.0\HELPDIR
```

When you have updated your REG file, be sure to remerge it into the registry, and confirm each update.

Step Three: A Visual Basic Client

Here, we will be building a Visual Basic COM client. Start up VB and select a new Standard EXE project workspace from the initial New Project dialog. The very first thing you

Figure 4-13: Bringing our type information into VB.

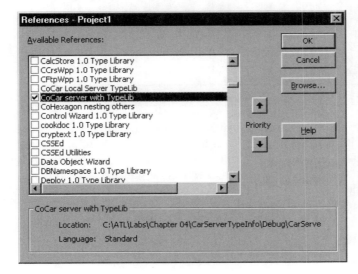

should do is add a reference to your CoCar type information. If you updated and merged the REG file, you should find your server listed automatically from the scrolling list box (look for the [helpstring] you added for your library statement). Otherwise use the Browse... button to navigate to the *.tlb file under your server's Debug folder.

Standard EXE projects will always provide you with one main Form object. This will serve as the main window of your VB application. Double-click anywhere on the Form to pull up the code window. Notice how you have landed in a Form_Load() event handler. Click above this stub code to enter the [General][Declaration] section.

Any variable defined in this namespace is available for use by the rest of the Form class. Create some global variables in your Form's [General][Declaration] section representing a CoCar, as well as IStats and IEngine interface variables:

```
' The [General][Declaration] section allows you to create some Form level variables.
'
Option Explicit
' The coclass exposing the [default] ICreateCar
Private mCar As CarServer.CoCar
' Extra interfaces on the coclass
Private itfEngine As CarServer.IEngine
Private itfStats As CarServer.IStats
```

Next, create a functional GUI to exercise your CoCar. Designing a VB form is much like creating a dialog using the Visual C++ dialog editor. Select a GUI widget from the VB toolbox, and draw the object onto the form. Here is a possible GUI implementation containing three CommandButtons, two TextBox objects, a single ListBox, and a few labels:

Figure 4-14:
The GUI design
of our VB client.

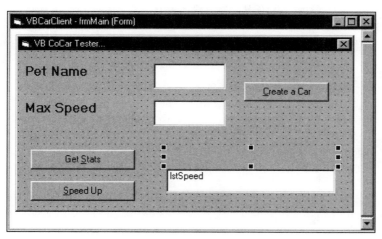

Give each widget a reasonable name using the Properties window (the Name property will be the very first item; the value you enter here will be used to refer to a given item in your code). The end user may enter a pet name and max speed using the TextBox objects. By clicking the Create a Car button, we will exercise the [default] ICreateCar interface. The following VB code creates the Form level CoCar and sends in some state data:

```
' When the user clicks the 'Create A Car' button, make the CoCar
' and use the information in the text boxes to set the pet name and max speed.
'
Private Sub btnCreate_Click()
      ' Create a car.
      Set mCar = New CoCar
```

```
' Set car via ICreateCar
mCar.SetMaxSpeed CLng(txtMaxSpeed)
mCar.SetPetName txtName
' Get IStats and set the label.
Set itfStats = mCar
lblCarName.Caption = "Speed of: " & itfStats.GetPetName
Set itfStats = Nothing
End Sub
```

The Get Stats button accesses the IStats interface and calls each method (you should see two message boxes pop up from the server):

```
' Show the state of this car.
'
Private Sub btnStats_Click()
    Set itfStats = mCar
    itfStats.DisplayStats
    Set itfStats = Nothing
End Sub
```

When the Speed Up button is clicked, we simulate the C++ client almost exactly: increase the current speed until we are 10 miles over the max speed. When the car blows up, use the VB MsgBox function to alert the user:

```
' Speed up the car, and place the current speed into the list box.
'
Private Sub btnSpeed_Click()
    Set itfEngine = mCar
    Set itfStats = mCar
    ' Rev that engine!
    Do While itfEngine.GetCurSpeed <= itfEngine.GetMaxSpeed
        itfEngine.SpeedUp
        lstSpeed.AddItem itfEngine.GetCurSpeed
    Loop
    ' Tell user car is dead.
    MsgBox itfStats.GetPetName & " has blown up! Lead foot!"
End Sub ' VB will release all references to CoCar as they fall out of scope...
```

You have now created a VB client, which is making use of the C++ COM server you created with your own blood, sweat, and tears. Feel free to extend and play with this VB client. Also, don't forget to open the VB Object Browser (F2) to examine the imported type information.

Step Four: A Java COM Client

Open up Visual J++ 6.0 and select a new Windows Application from the New Project dialog box:

Figure 4-15:
J++ New Project
workspace.

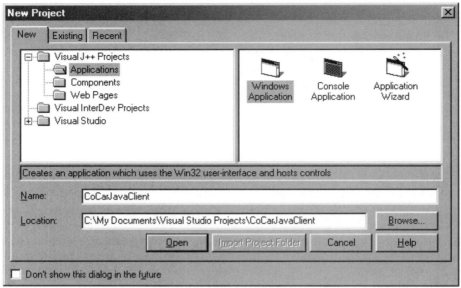

You will be given a new Java class named Form1, extending from the Windows Foundation Classes Form class (notice the imports to numerous com.ms.wfc packages which contain the Java Windows GUI classes). The J++ IDE is very similar to that of VB, so begin by creating a GUI to drive the CoCar server using the WFC Controls provided from the J++ Tool Box. For this lab, we will assemble the same sort of GUI layout as the previous VB client:

Figure 4-16:
J++ Form layout
for CoCar client.

Now, add a COM wrapper for your CoCar type information. You will see that jactivex.exe has added a number of new *.java files to your current project. Open them up and get a feel for the generated code (especially the @com directives which are used to map Java code into the MS JVM). Also open the J++ Object Browser (F2) and check out your CoCar's type information.

Now we need to tie the WFC controls on the form to Java code exercising our CoCar. If you are unfamiliar with the syntax of Java, just type along and look up specifics as you go. Begin by declaring some private data members in your Form1 class (double-click on the form to open the code window):

```
// Form1 will be making use of your CoCar.
import carservertypeinfo.*;        // Must have this!
public class Form1 extends Form
{
      // The coclass.
      private carservertypeinfo.CoCar m_Car;
      // All the interfaces of CoCar.
      private carservertypeinfo.ICreateCar itfCreate;
      private carservertypeinfo.IEngine itfEngine;
      private carservertypeinfo.IStats itfStats;
...
}
```

When the Create Car button is clicked, create a CoCar and access the ICreateCar interface to set the state of your COM object. Like the previous VB client, you will be reading the values of the edit boxes to grab the pet name and max speed:

```
// Create the CoCar and query for ICreateCar.
private void m_btnCreate_click(Object source, Event e)
{
      // Create a new CoCar.
      m_Car = new CoCar();
      // Query for ICreateCar by using a Java cast.
      itfCreate = (ICreateCar)m_Car;
      // Set the pet name by asking the text box for the pet name.
      itfCreate.SetPetName( m_txtName.getText() );
      // Ask for the max speed, and transform the text into an Integer.
      int sp = Integer.parseInt(m_txtMaxSpeed.getText());
      itfCreate.SetMaxSpeed(sp);
      // Now, ask for IStats, and set the label with the max speed.
      itfStats = (IStats)m_Car;
      m_lblSpeed.setText( "Speed of: " + itfStats.GetPetName() );
}
```

When Get Stats is selected, simply call DisplayStats() from an IStats interface:

```
// Show the state of the car.
private void m_btnStats_click(Object source, Event e)
{
      // Display everything.
      itfStats = (IStats)m_Car;
      itfStats.DisplayStats();
}
```

And finally, when Speed Up is clicked, rev the engine, send the current speed to the WFC ListBox object, and present a message box when the engine cracks in two:

```
// Speed things up!
private void m_btnSpeedUp_click(Object source, Event e)
{
```

```
int curSp = 0;
int maxSp = 0;
itfEngine = (IEngine)m_Car;
maxSp = itfEngine.GetMaxSpeed();
do     // Zoom!
{
     itfEngine.SpeedUp();
     curSp =itfEngine.GetCurSpeed();
     // Add cur speed to list box.
     String s;
     s = Integer.toString(itfEngine.GetCurSpeed());
     listBoxSpeed.addItem(s);
}while(curSp <= maxSp);
// Need to get IStats
itfStats = (IStats)m_Car;
// Tell user car blew up...
MessageBox.show(itfStats.GetPetName() + " Blew Up!", "Lead Foot!",
                  MessageBox.ICONEXCLAMATION);
}
```

Go ahead and run the application to see your Java client in action:

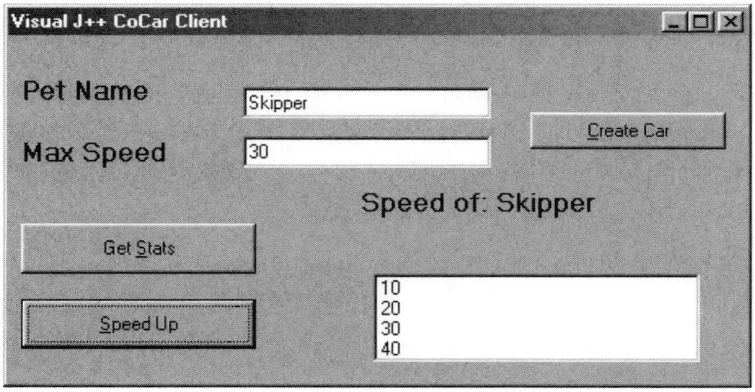

Figure 4-17: Java client using our C++ COM server.

In the final step of this lab, we will take the Visual C++ COM compiler extensions out for a test drive.

Step Five: A C++ Type Library Client

Create a new Win32 Console Application (a simple project will be fine). Add a new file called **main.cpp** and bring in your *.tlb file using the **import** directive. Compile the project. Here is some COM client code making use of smart pointers. Notice that we have no calls to QueryInterface(), AddRef(), or Release() (although we do set the smart pointers to NULL when finished to trigger the cleanup). Notice that we are making use of _bstr_t, which has an overloaded << operator to insert the buffer into the cout stream. Finally, be aware that the COM compiler support does honor the [retval] attribute:

```
// A C++ COM client using smart pointers.
#import "E:\ATL\Labs\Chapter 04\CarServerTypeInfo\Debug\CarServerTypeInfo.tlb" no_namespace
named_guids
int main(int argc, char* argv[])
```

```
{
    CoInitialize(NULL);
    cout << "*********************************" << endl;
    cout << "The Amazing CoCar Import Client" << endl;
    cout << "*********************************" << endl;
    ICreateCarPtr iCCar(CLSID_CoCar);
    IEnginePtr iEng(iCCar);
    IStatsPtr iStats(iCCar);
    _bstr_t name = "Greased Lighting!";
    spCCar->SetPetName(name);
    iCCar->SetMaxSpeed(50);
    // Show our state.
    iStats->DisplayStats();
    int curSp = 0; int maxSp = 0;
    maxSp = iEng->GetMaxSpeed();
    do    // Zoom!
    {
        iEng->SpeedUp();
        curSp = iEng->GetCurSpeed();        // [out, retval]
        cout << "Speed is: " << curSp << endl;
    }while(curSp <= maxSp);
    // Blown up!
    _bstr_t bstrName;                       // No conversions!
    bstrName = iStats->GetPetName();        // [out, retval]
    cout << bstrName << " has blown up! Lead Foot!" << endl << endl;
    iCCar = NULL;
    iStats= NULL;
    iEng = NULL;
    CoUninitialize();
    return 0;
}
```

At this point we have injected type information into an existing COM server. As you have seen, IDL and the MIDL-generated type library are the keys to COM's language independence.

Chapter Summary

This chapter has illustrated how COM fulfills the promise of language independence through type information and IDL. You have seen how the MIDL compiler generates language-neutral type libraries as well as C and C++ specific language bindings. Simply by describing our servers in IDL we suddenly are able to have Visual Basic, Java, C++, and numerous other languages access our coclasses.

You have seen how to create interface, coclass, and library definitions in IDL using attribute-based programming. This will serve as your baseline for more advanced IDL constructs introduced throughout the remainder of this book.

Furthermore, you have gained enough knowledge of VB and Java syntax (if you did not have it already) to allow you to build clients in these languages, as well as a better understanding of what is taking place under the hood.

In the next chapter you will learn how to make use of the remaining MIDL-generated output and create an out-of-proc (EXE) and remote (DCOM) version of your CoCar server.

Chapter 5

Type Information and Location Transparency

Objectives:

- ■ Understand the relationship between stubs, proxies, and marshaling.
- ■ Learn to run legacy COM DLLs in a surrogate process.
- ■ Understand the various marshaling options provided by COM.
- ■ Assemble local (EXE) component housing to host your coclasses.
- ■ Learn to securely access remote COM servers à la DCOM.

In Chapter 3, you learned about the nuts and bolts required to build COM-based DLLs using C++. In Chapter 4, you injected type information into an existing DLL, allowing your coclasses to be accessed from COM-aware languages such as Java and Visual Basic. In addition to language independence, location transparency is another virtue provided by the path of COM and IDL, the key to which are stubs and proxies.

Here, we dig into the inner workings of stubs and proxies and investigate COM's marshaling options. To illustrate location transparency, we will begin by loading an existing COM DLL into a surrogate process. Next, you will see how to configure class factories and coclasses to dwell within a COM-based EXE server. Finally, we learn how to use the DCOM protocol to securely access EXE servers located on a distant machine.

Reviewing Location Transparency

The notion of *location transparency* allows a COM client to access COM objects in such a way that the existing code base need not be altered, regardless of where the COM server is physically located (in-proc, local, or remote). Before COM, application developers needed to be concerned with creating unique code blocks (from different APIs) to access in-process, local, and remote binaries. The greatest drawback of this approach is the simple fact that three different APIs result in a rather large surface area the developer is responsible for understanding. In COM development, a single block of code is used to access a COM object, regardless of its physical proximity to the caller. In effect, COM encapsulates the activation and data transmission details from the client by providing the illusion that all interface method invocations are happening in the client's own address space (i.e., in-process).

Recall that clients and servers may have three relationships. First, we have the in-process relationship shown below. When a COM client has loaded an in-proc server and obtains an interface pointer on some object, the two entities talk directly through the acquired interface. This results in a very fast (but not very robust) connection.

Figure 5-1: In-proc servers offer a fast though less robust connection.

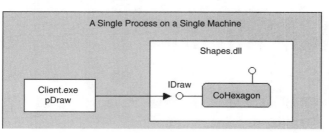

> **Note:**   Recall that if a client and in-proc server are running under different threading models, a client does not have direct access to the interface pointer. Instead, the client holds a pointer to a proxy object just as it does during local or remote access. We will examine the details of COM's threading models in Chapter 7. For the time being, it is safe to assume that the in-process relationship entails a direct connection to the interface.

Next, we have the local (or out-of-process) relationship. When a COM client obtains an interface pointer from a coclass residing in a local (EXE) server, the client does not have a direct connection to the acquired interface. Instead, the COM runtime secretly loads a "stub/proxy DLL". This DLL contains marshaling code for each custom interface defined in the server's IDL file, providing a safe bridge between the two collaborating processes. We will see where this stub/proxy DLL comes from soon enough.

A Win32 process is extremely protective of the memory it represents, and access between processes cannot occur without a safe and well-defined protocol (such as RPC). This is a good thing, as a given process cannot inadvertently invade another process and cause damage. So then, what exactly is a "stub" and "proxy"? We will define a stub and proxy as the following, and expand from here:

- **Proxy**: A COM object loaded into the client's process, which packages up client requests for any out-of-process (or out of apartment) method invocation.
- **Stub**: A COM object loaded into the server's process, which receives the client's requests, unpackages them, and hands them off to the "real COM object."

The figure at the top of the next page illustrates the local relationship. Assume the client has acquired an IDraw interface pointer and wishes to call the Draw() implementation of CoHexagon residing outside of its own process.

Because a proxy looks and feels like the "real COM interface" as far as the client can tell, the existing code base remains unaltered. As well, the server object regards the stub as "the real client" and thus the code in your coclass does not need to change in order to return information to clients located outside of its own process.

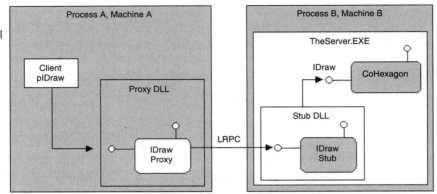

Figure 5-2: Clients and local servers communicate through stubs and proxies.

Note: This is the core of location transparency: provide the illusion that a COM client and COM objects are always communicating with an in-process entity.

Under the hood, processes have information transmitted between them using a procedure called *marshaling*. Marshaling is the process of packing, sending, and unpacking data between clients and local or remote servers, via stubs and proxies. Marshaling between local servers entails lightweight RPC (LRPC) calls. LRPC is a Microsoft extension to DCE RPC that includes support for marshaling interface pointers between stubs and proxies (among other things).

A given stub/proxy DLL contains marshaling code for every interface supported by the coclass. Recall that the MIDL compiler will generate a handful of files (most notably the *_p.c file) that define the stub/proxy code for all IDL-defined interfaces. With these files, you may build and register a stub/proxy DLL used in order to achieve local or remote method invocations.

Last but not least, we have the remote relationship. If a client and server are communicating across machine boundaries using DCOM, the client is once again really calling a proxy loaded into its memory partition, which communicates with a stub loaded in the memory partition of the remote process. This time, calls are made over the wire using full-blown RPC:

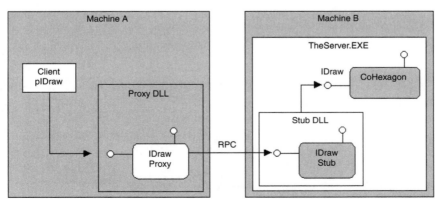

Figure 5-3: Remote invocations require DCOM's underlying RPC protocol.

Note: LRPC and RPC are often simply referred to as ORPC (Object RPC).

Dissecting a Proxy

Let's begin to better understand the role of the interface proxy. The very first thing to be aware of is that proxy objects are true-blue COM objects, which support standard COM interfaces to get the job done. Proxy objects reside in the client's process and have the same look and feel as the local or remote interface they pretend to be. As mentioned, this illusion is the backbone of location transparency, as the client assumes the IDraw interface is always right next door.

Every proxy object supports an additional standard COM interface beyond a given interface of the remote coclass: IRpcProxyBuffer. IRpcProxyBuffer contains two methods used by an entity called the proxy manager. These methods, Connect() and Disconnect(), provide a way for the proxy to communicate with yet another middleman between your client and distant object: the ORPC channel object. Here is the IDL definition of IRpcProxyBuffer, as defined in <objidl.idl>:

```
// IRpcProxyBuffer allows a proxy to connect to the ORPC channel object, when
// told to do so by the proxy manager.
[local, object, uuid(D5F56A34-593B-101A-B569-08002B2DBF7A)]
interface IRpcProxyBuffer : IUnknown
{
     HRESULT Connect( [in, unique]
                         IRpcChannelBuffer *pRpcChannelBuffer);
     void Disconnect(void);
};
```

Understanding the Channel Object

ORPC channel objects are COM objects that support the standard COM interface IRpcChannelBuffer (notice that the Connect() method of IRpcProxyBuffer takes an IRpcChannelBuffer interface pointer parameter). IRpcChannelBuffer has a handful of methods that make calls into the RPC layer in order to assemble a client's request packet and send it off into the stub. Channel objects are the worker bees of the COM marshaling process, and are responsible for pushing data between processes. IRpcChannelBuffer is defined in <objidl.idl> as the following:

```
// Channel objects implement IRpcChannelBuffer, which does the grunge
// work to move data between process boundaries.
[ local, object, uuid(D5F56B60-593B-101A-B569-08002B2DBF7A) ]
interface IRpcChannelBuffer : IUnknown
{
     HRESULT GetBuffer([in] RPCOLEMESSAGE *pMessage, [in] REFIID riid);
     HRESULT SendReceive ([in,out] RPCOLEMESSAGE *pMessage,
                         [out] ULONG *pStatus);
     HRESULT FreeBuffer([in] RPCOLEMESSAGE *pMessage);
     HRESULT GetDestCtx([out] DWORD *pdwDestContext,
                         [out] void **ppvDestContext);
     HRESULT IsConnected (void);
};
```

This orchestration between proxies and the ORPC channel sounds more complex than it really is. The good news is that the loading of stubs and proxies (and the implementation of these new standard interfaces) is taken care of automatically by the COM runtime and the MIDL-generated code. To reiterate the story thus far, two new COM interfaces are used to help move the client's request to the stub:

■ **IRpcProxyBuffer**: Implemented by the proxy and used by the proxy manager to connect or disconnect a proxy to the ORPC channel object.

■ **IRpcChannelBuffer**: Implemented by the channel object. Packages up the client requests and sends them to the stub using low-level ORPC calls.

With these two additional interfaces, we can get a more intimate look at what is really happening when a client calls into the proxy object, as illustrated below:

Figure 5-4:
Proxies support IRpcProxyBuffer, which allows them to communicate to the channel object. The channel object supports IRpcChannel-Buffer, which packages up method requests.

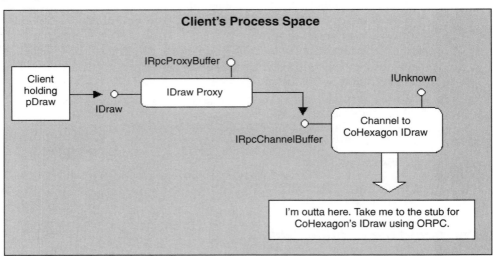

Understanding the Proxy Manager

The proxy manager is the acting chieftain for all proxies loaded in the client's process. Using the IRpcProxyBuffer interface, the proxy manager informs a given proxy object that it is up for duty by calling the Connect() method. This method takes a pointer to the channel object's IRpcChannelBuffer interface, allowing the proxy to send client requests into the channel. The proxy manager is responsible for assembling all loaded proxies into a unified whole, providing yet another illusion for the client, that the entire "real COM object" is right next door.

There is a one-to-one correspondence between a given out-of-process interface and a proxy. If the client has interface pointers to ten interfaces on some local or remote object, this results in ten proxies representing those interfaces, all maintained by the proxy manager. The proxy manager assembles each individual proxy into a collective using (of all things) COM aggregation, and provides an IUnknown implementation for the aggregated interfaces. Figure 5-5 illustrates the role of the proxy manager. Notice how the unified proxies look just like the remote CoHexagon object as far as the client is concerned:

Figure 5-5:
The proxy manager aggregates all proxies into a whole, simulating the distant coclass.

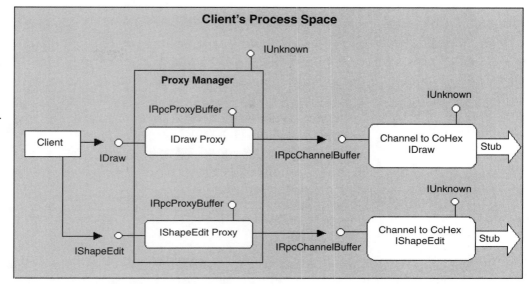

It is comforting to know that a given AddRef() or Release() call by the client does not result in an ORPC call until the final release has been detected. This of course results in a much more optimized scenario than one round trip per AddRef() and Release().

Dissecting a Stub

So then, the proxy manager provides the illusion that the distant object is an in-process entity. IRpcProxyBuffer and IRpcChannelBuffer do the grunge work of packing up the request and sending it over to the distant process using ORPC. Who, then, is waiting on the other side? The stub.

Recall that a stub is responsible for taking incoming request packets sent from a proxy and sending them to the real COM object. Each stub object implements a standard COM interface named IRpcStubBuffer which, like IRpcProxyBuffer, also supports Connect() and Disconnect() methods. IRpcStubBuffer is defined in <objidl.idl> as so:

```
// IRpcStubBuffer allows the stub to communicate with the channel object.
[ local, object, uuid(D5F56AFC-593B-101A-B569-08002B2DBF7A)]
interface IRpcStubBuffer : IUnknown
{
    HRESULT Connect( [in] IUnknown *pUnkServer);
    void Disconnect();
    HRESULT Invoke( [in] RPCOLEMESSAGE *_prpcmsg,
                    [in] IRpcChannelBuffer *_pRpcChannelBuffer);
    IRpcStubBuffer *IsIIDSupported( [in] REFIID riid );
    ULONG CountRefs (void);
    HRESULT DebugServerQueryInterface(void **ppv);
    void DebugServerRelease(void *pv);
}
```

The stub manager makes use of IRpcStubBuffer to receive the incoming request packets and forward the remote invocation to the distant COM object:

Figure 5-6:
Stubs
implement
IRpcStubBuffer
to unpackage
the request and
hand it off to the
real COM object.

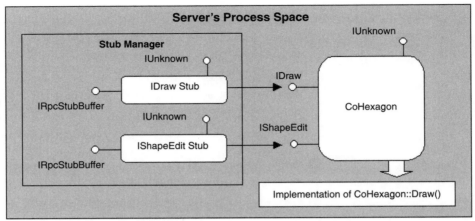

Unlike the proxy manager, the stub manager does not aggregate the stubs into a unified whole. Beyond taking the incoming request and passing it along to the "real object," stubs are also in charge of the task of assembling the object's response to the method invocation. This response may be a single HRESULT, as well as any [out] parameters that are defined by the interface's IDL.

All Together Now!

Under the hood we now see what stubs and proxies are all about. In essence, a proxy packages up a client's request for a local or remote method call. This request is sent to the stub via the intervening ORPC channel object. Once the request makes it to the server process, the request packet is intercepted by the stub manager and directed to the correct interface stub, and finally the correct information is sent to the coclass interface method. We can summarize this handshaking as follows (managers omitted for sanity):

Figure 5-7:
The movement
of remote
interface
method
invocations.

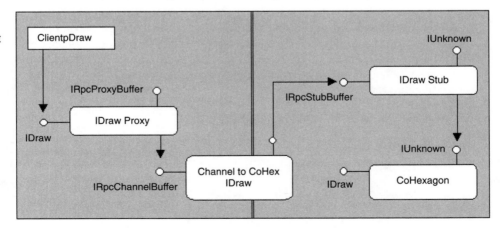

Now then, if stubs and proxies are so central to COM's remoting architecture, a logical question would be to ask how these objects are created in the first place. Sounds like another standard COM interface to me.

Creating Stubs and Proxies: IPSFactoryBuffer

The last item to note concerning stubs and proxies is that they are true COM objects that are created by a true COM class factory. Unlike your custom coclasses, a single class factory creates both the stub and proxy for a given interface using a special interface named IPSFactoryBuffer. As soon as a client requests access to a distant interface, the corresponding managers call the CreateProxy() or CreateStub() methods of IPSFactoryBuffer to load the stubs and proxy objects into the correct process:

```
// The class object responsible for creating stubs and proxies implements
// the IPSFactoryBuffer interface (defined in <objidl.idl>).
[ local, object, uuid(D5F569D0-593B-101A-B569-08002B2DBF7A)]
interface IPSFactoryBuffer : IUnknown
{
    HRESULT CreateProxy([in] IUnknown *pUnkOuter, [in] REFIID riid,
                        [out] IRpcProxyBuffer **ppProxy, [out] void **ppv );
    HRESULT CreateStub ([in] REFIID riid, [in, unique] IUnknown *pUnkServer,
                        [out] IRpcStubBuffer **ppStub);
}
```

In summary, the remoting architecture of COM involves four standard COM interfaces: IRpcProxyBuffer, IRpcStubBuffer, IRpcChannelBuffer, and IPSFactoryBuffer. So (you may be asking) why is it important to understand all these low-level COM interfaces? At the very least you should be able to see why (a) calling a remote or local server is slower than calling an in-proc server, (b) it is a good thing that COM provides automatic loading of stubs and proxies, and (c) it is a very good thing that MIDL generates the required stub/proxy code.

Hosting COM DLLs in a Surrogate Process

Before we examine the set of COM marshaling options, let's perform a little experiment to illustrate COM's location transparency and run our existing CarInProcServer.dll server in its own surrogate process. Follow along if you wish; just make sure you have completed the CarInProcServer lab from Chapter 4.

Since the release of NT SP2, we have had the ability to host legacy in-proc COM servers within an EXE shell, using a utility named dllhost.exe. This application provides the necessary hooks to allow existing COM DLLs to behave as a local (or remote) server by wrapping them into a surrogate process. There are a number of reasons a person may wish to do this:

■ You have a great set of coclasses dwelling in an existing DLL and you would rather not have to rewrite the component housing code to access them remotely.

■ You want to isolate the DLL from the client process to avoid hard crashes (recall that if a bug is hit in your DLL, the client's process goes down with it as well).

■ You wish to configure security options for the legacy DLL (by their nature, DLL servers always have the security settings of the client host).

The dllhost.exe utility will load your COM-based DLLs and expose its functionality from a distinct process on your behalf, leaving your server's code base unaltered. As you can probably guess, this requires altering the system registry to instruct SCM to load the in-process server into the dllhost.exe shell, rather than the client's process. This feat requires an understanding of yet another incarnation of the GUID—the AppID.

Understanding Application Identifiers (AppIDs)

In order to allow client access to distant COM servers (local or remote), we find yet another use for the omnipresent GUID, termed an *AppID* or *application identifier.* An AppID is assigned to the entire COM server and is used to describe security and activation settings for the application at large. Given this, you can correctly assume that a single AppID collectively identifies all the coclasses in a given executable. For convenience, a server's AppID can be assigned to the same GUID as a given CLSID contained in the server. The reasoning behind this is simple: Many legacy COM servers did not register an AppID as part of their installation process. Because AppIDs and CLSIDs are used under different circumstances, we can get away with a bit of creative GUID swapping.

Figure 5-8 illustrates the LocalShapes.exe server containing four COM objects, each of which has been assigned a unique CLSID. Now, assume for the sake of illustration that CoDot has a CLSID of {5D432C50-F507-11d2-B8E0-0020781238D4}. Next, assume the server itself is identified by a single AppID, which happens to be the same GUID as CoDot's CLSID:

Figure 5-8: AppIDs identify the entire COM application.

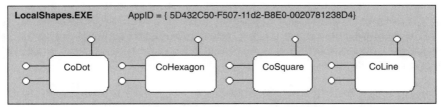

AppID Registry Settings: HKEY_CLASSES_ROOT\AppID

Now that we can collectively identify all coclasses held within a component home using an AppID, we may associate a number of attributes to the binary. In general, the AppID is used to associate activation and security attributes to the objects it contains. As you introduce the idea of remote access to your objects, security is injected into the picture. You do not need to be a full-fledged system administrator to configure COM security options, but it will be helpful to understand the basics. The system registry holds such information for every COM application under the AppID key of HKEY_CLASSES_ROOT:

Figure 5-9: HKCR\AppID holds all registered COM applications.

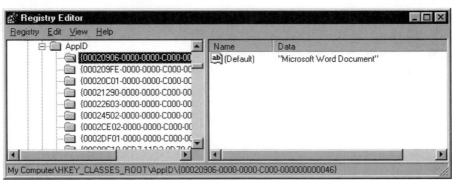

A given entry under HKCR\AppID can specify several named values which control how the COM application should be used. Here are some of the more common settings found under a single AppID listing:

AppID Value	Meaning in Life
AccessPermission	Sets up the access control list (ACL) of users that can access the server.
AuthenticationLevel	Sets the authentication level.
DllSurrogate	Names the correct surrogate to host a DLL. If blank, the default dllhost.exe will be used.
LaunchPermissions	Sets up the ACL of users that can launch this application.
RemoteServerName	Identifies the name of a remote server machine.

For this DLL surrogate experiment, we are only interested with the DllSurrogate value. Assume we have written a REG file to enter an AppID for CoCar, which has been merged into the registry. Notice that the AppID listing has an empty DllSurrogate value; this tells SCM to use the default dllhost.exe:

Figure 5-10: The DllSurrogate value under an AppID listing specifies who should host legacy in-proc servers.

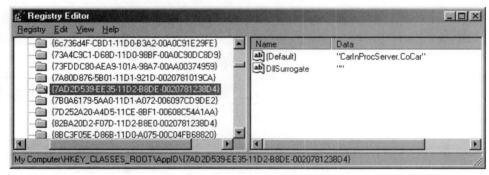

Beyond adding a listing for HKCR\AppID, you should also update your REG file to modify the HKCR\CLSID entry for each coclass in the COM application to specify the correct AppID. Recall that each coclass in the server points to the same AppID, thus each coclass in a given server will have an AppID value with the same GUID:

Figure 5-11: Each CLSID in a COM application maps to the same AppID.

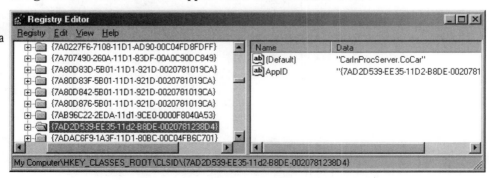

With the addition of two new registry entries (which we have yet to enter) we are now able to load a DLL into a separate process using dllhost.exe. To get these entries into the system registry, we can simply run the dcomcnfg.exe utility and get an AppID for free (no pain). This approach will generate an AppID for the server based on an existing CLSID. We will introduce dcomcnfg.exe later in this chapter.

Using other approaches, we could update our REG files by hand (some pain) or even enter the information programmatically using DllRegisterServer() (greater pain). We do, however, have another alternative for entering AppID information into the registry: Configure the AppID of a server using the OLE/COM Object Viewer and call it a day.

Configuring a Surrogate with the OLE/COM Object Viewer

If you launch the OLE/COM Object Viewer utility and locate your existing DLL server from the All Object category, you may configure it to run under the system surrogate. Doing so will merge the necessary AppID entries automatically. To do so, select the Use Surrogate Process option from the Implementation tab:

Figure 5-12:
Configuring a DLL to use dllhost.exe

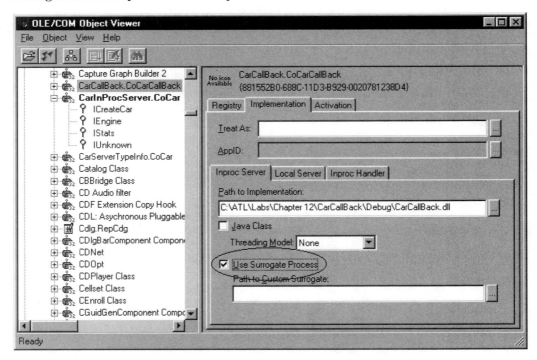

By selecting this option, the OLE/COM Object Viewer creates an HKCR\AppID listing for the DLL (using the first CLSID defined in the type library) and modifies each CLSID to point to the newly assigned AppID. To verify the OLE/COM viewer-generated entries, switch back to the Registry tab of the viewer and examine the registry entries (Figure 5-13):

Figure 5-13:
The generated
AppID entries.

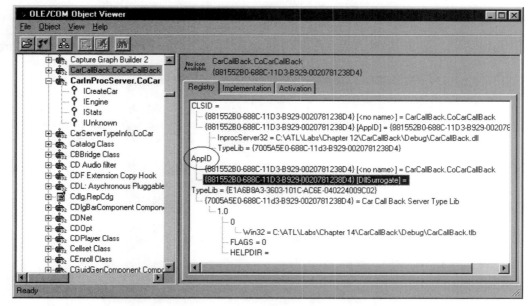

Note that the OLE/COM Object Viewer has modified your existing CLSID value with the AppID and created a new AppID listing for the server, using the creative GUID swapping approach mentioned earlier in this chapter. This is all you need to do in order to inform SCM to load your legacy DLL into the dllhost.exe surrogate process.

Programming a Surrogate Client

We do have one minor adjustment to make in the C++ client-side code. Open an existing C++ client project workspace, and modify your CLSCTX flag to specify a local, rather than an in-process, server:

```
// By asking for a LOCAL server instance of this DLL,
// we run the server within a surrogate process.
hr = CoGetClassObject(CLSID_CoCar, CLSCTX_LOCAL_SERVER,
                      NULL, IID_IClassFactory, (void**)&pCF);
// Create the CoCar. Access interfaces. Release interfaces.
```

We are now telling SCM to load our DLL into a surrogate. First SCM consults HKCR\CLSID for a given AppID entry. If such an entry exists, SCM then checks HKCR\AppID and discovers that it should use the default surrogate. Recompile and run the client. If you examine the NT Task Manager (CTRL + SHIFT + ESC) you will see your CoCarClient program is loaded as well as an instance of dllhost.exe:

Figure 5-14: A running surrogate process and launching client.

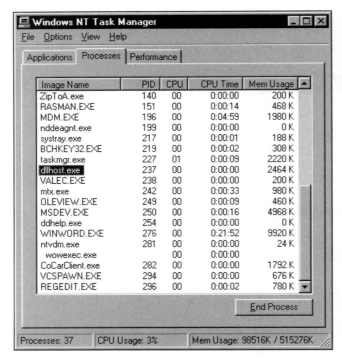

So there you have it! We have just launched a DLL COM server in its own protected process. Remember the promise of location transparency: Clients can activate objects at various locations without reworking their code base. So did I lie? After all, we did need to change the CLSCTX flag. OK, you've got me. At times we will modify an occasional flag or send in an extra parameter to some COM library function to achieve location transparency. But think about the benefits of changing a flag versus writing DDE or sockets code! Later in this chapter we will use the dcomcnfg.exe utility to redirect SCM to access a remote server without any code adjustments at all (see, I'm honest).

COM's Marshaling Options

While loading existing DLLs into a surrogate process is an interesting exercise, the $24,000 question is "How was information marshaled between the processes?" We have a number of different marshaling options as COM developers, so let's see the choices (for the record, we just leveraged the universal marshaler). You may choose between three basic marshaling options:

- **Custom marshaling**: Implement IMarshal by hand.
- **Standard marshaling**: Build and register your own custom stub/proxy DLL.
- **Universal marshaling**: Leverage a system-supplied stub/proxy DLL.

As with any choice made in programming we must weigh the pros and cons. One of the biggest issues to contend with in development overall seems to be the "speed of program execution" versus "approaching deadline" debate. For example, we should all agree by now that a very sophisticated UI can be assembled in Visual Basic in a fraction of the time than one in MFC. Although this is true, if you want absolute speed and control, you should opt to drop straight to the Win32 API and the C language. Although we all have our favorite development environment, the smart developer is willing to put aside personal preferences to save a failing deadline.

Choosing between the COM marshaling options presents a similar issue. Beyond the "speed of execution" versus "approaching deadline" debate you will need to wrestle with the "Wow this is easy!" versus "You have to be kidding!" groaning debate. COM provides a number of techniques to move information between stubs and proxies, each with varying complexity.

However, given our DLL surrogate example, you should already feel relatively confident that marshaling can be quite simple (add a registry entry and change the CLSCTX flag). Let's begin by quickly discussing the most complex (and therefore most flexible) way one can marshal information between processes.

Custom Marshaling

This form of marshaling is the backbone for COM's other two marshaling techniques, standard and universal marshaling. Developers who wish to utilize custom marshaling begin by implementing the IMarshal interface on a given coclass. This standard COM interface contains a number of methods that allow you to define exactly how information is sent between the coclass and the proxies. When a client is activating your coclass, SCM will query for the IMarshal interface. IMarshal is defined as the following:

```
// When you want complete control of object communication.
[local, object, uuid(00000003-0000-0000-C000-000000000046)]
interface IMarshal : IUnknown
{
    HRESULT GetUnmarshalClass ([in] REFIID riid, [in, unique] void *pv,
        [in] DWORD dwDestContext, [in, unique] void *pvDestContext,
        [in] DWORD mshlflags, [out] CLSID *pCid );
    HRESULT GetMarshalSizeMax ( [in] REFIID riid, [in, unique] void *pv,
        [in] DWORD dwDestContext, [in, unique] void *pvDestContext,
        [in] DWORD mshlflags, [out] DWORD *pSize );
    HRESULT MarshalInterface ( [in, unique] IStream *pStm, [in] REFIID riid,
        [in, unique] void *pv, [in] DWORD dwDestContext,
        [in, unique] void *pvDestContext, [in] DWORD mshlflags);
    HRESULT UnmarshalInterface ( [in, unique] IStream *pStm, [in] REFIID riid,
        [out] void **ppv );
    HRESULT ReleaseMarshalData ( [in, unique] IStream *pStm );
    HRESULT DisconnectObject ( [in] DWORD dwReserved);
};
```

If your coclass returns an IMarshal interface pointer to SCM, it will be used to move information between processes. If SCM cannot extract an IMarshal pointer from your coclass, SCM assumes you do not support custom marshaling and instead will be making use of standard or universal marshaling.

When you implement custom marshaling, you get to decide what that transport layer will be (and leverage it yourself). Beyond the implementation of IMarshal on your coclass, you will code up the packaging and sending of your interface method parameters. If this is your wish, you must implement your own marshaling code (something we will not be doing in this book).

Standard Marshaling

A far simpler approach is to use what is called *standard marshaling*, which is based upon the ORPC protocol examined earlier in this chapter. If you decide to use COM's standard marshaling support, you need to build and register your own stub/proxy DLL (using those MIDL-generated files I keep referring to). Do note that stub and proxy DLLs are used to marshal your <u>custom</u> interfaces. Standard COM interfaces are marshaled by the system-provided ole32.dll.

Assume that the shapes.idl file (defined in Chapter 4) has been sent through the MIDL compiler. The generated shapes_p.c file contains stub and proxy definitions for each method of every interface defined in the IDL file. To illustrate, if you were to insert the shapes_p.c file into a project workspace, you will see the given stub and proxy functions appear in the Globals folder:

Figure 5-15: The global methods of your *_p.c MIDL-generated file.

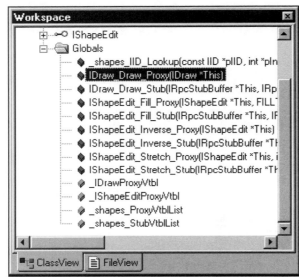

Recall that each interface method is defined by a _Proxy() and _Stub() method. From Figure 5-15, you can see that the IDraw interface has stub/proxy code defined in the IDraw_Draw_Proxy() and IDraw_Draw_Stub() method pair. Notice the stub methods take an IRpcStubBuffer interface pointer as a method parameter, allowing the stub object to communicate with the ORPC channel.

Beyond your *_p.c file, the other marshaling related file generated by MIDL is dlldata.c. Within this file you will see a listing for the following macro:

```
// This macro is listed in the MIDL-generated dlldata.c file.
DLLDATA_ROUTINES( aProxyFileList, GET_DLL_CLSID )
```

The DLLDATA_ROUTINES macro expands into a handful of other macros, each bringing in support for the following core DLL exports as well as a few others used to define the required class factories (supporting the IPSFactoryBuffer interface). DLLDATA_ROUTINES expands to the following macros:

- **DllRegisterServer**: Via the DLLREGISTRY_ROUTINES macro.
- **DllUnregisterServer**: Also via DLLREGISTRY_ROUTINES.
- **DllGetClassObject**: Via the DLLGETCLASSOBJECTROUTINE macro.
- **DllCanUnloadNow**: Via the DLLCANUNLOADNOW macro.

The good news is MIDL writes all of this standard marshaling code on your behalf (which you may ignore entirely), leaving building and registering the stub/proxy DLL as your only task.

Building a Custom Stub/Proxy DLL

To build your stub and proxy DLL, open up a brand new (simple) Win32 DLL project workspace (we will name our sample DLL ShapesPS.dll) and insert the MIDL-generated shapes_i.c, shapes.h, shapes_p.c, and dlldata.c into the current project. Recall these

MIDL-generated files define the GUIDs, proxy code, and DLL exports, respectively. The next step is to create a standard DEF file for the DLL and insert it into the project workspace. If this looks familiar to you, it should. Stub/proxy DLLs are COM-based in-process servers, and therefore they must export the same set of methods as a custom in-proc COM server:

```
LIBRARY      SHAPESPS.DLL
EXPORTS
        DllGetClassObject        @1        PRIVATE
        DllCanUnloadNow          @2        PRIVATE
        DllRegisterServer        @3        PRIVATE
        DllUnregisterServer      @4        PRIVATE
```

Recall that dlldata.c defines a set of macros that supply self-registration support. This means we do not need to write custom REG files for our stub/proxy DLLs, as the DllRegisterServer() and DllUnregisterServer() functions will insert and delete all necessary registry entries.

For this self-registration code to be compiled into your project, you must go into the Project Settings dialog box (select Project|Settings), navigate to the C/C++ tab, and add the REGISTER_PROXY_DLL and _WIN32_DCOM flags to the Preprocessor Definitions field, as shown below:

Figure 5-16: Configuring the preprocessor to build your stub and proxy.

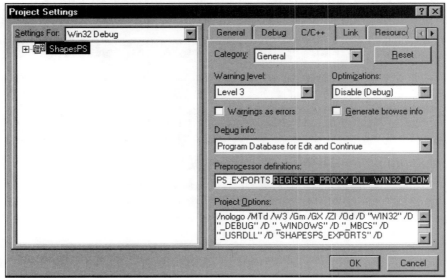

Finally, before we can successfully build this project, we must link to the libraries that define all the RPC functions used by the MIDL-generated shapes_p.c file. Go into the Project Settings dialog box and select the Link tab. Specify linkage to rpcndr.lib, rpcns4.lib, and rpcrt4.lib, as shown in Figure 5-17:

Figure 5-17:
Linking to the
RPC libraries.

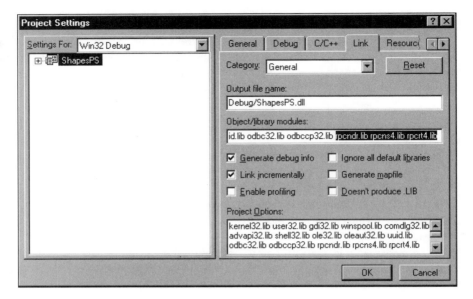

You can now compile your DLL and register it using the Tools | Register Control
command:

Figure 5-18:
Registering
your stub and
proxy DLL.

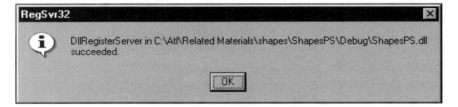

Building a Stub/Proxy DLL à la ATL

On a related note, when you use the ATL framework to build your COM servers, you will
find that one of the ATL COM AppWizard generated files ends with the *.mk file extension. This file can be used to build your custom stub/proxy DLL with considerably less
work than the by hand approach we have just examined.

   To do so, navigate to your project directory using a command prompt window and send
in the ATL generated *.mk file as a parameter to the nmake.exe utility. This will build the
stub and proxy DLL in a single step, bypassing the need to create and configure a new
Win32 DLL project workspace. From there, you can register your new stub/proxy DLL as
usual.

Registry Entries for Stub/Proxy DLLs: HKEY_CLASSES_ROOT\Interface

So the next question is "What was registered?" In order for SCM to load and create the
stubs and proxies for your custom interfaces, it needs to be able to locate the correct
stub/proxy DLL. Allow me to introduce you to yet another core key under HKCR, the
Interface key. This key maintains information for each interface on your machine that may
be marshaled between process, machine, or apartment boundaries.

Recall that the COM servers we constructed in Chapters 3 and 4 did not require you to enter any information into the registry for the ICreateCar, IStats, and IEngine interfaces. The reason is simple: These COM servers were in-process, and therefore no stubs and proxies were necessary (therefore SCM did not need to locate these interfaces from HKCR\Interface\{<guid>}). As soon as you plan to allow your interfaces to be accessed from outside of the client's process, you will need to enter interface information into the registry. Here are some valid interface entry subkeys:

HKCR\Interface Subkey	Meaning in Life
BaseInterface	Lists the direct base interface from which an interface derives.
NumMethods	The number of methods in the interface, including inherited methods.
ProxyStubClsid32	The CLSID of the stub/proxy DLL used to marshal this interface.
ProxyStubClsid	16-bit version of stub/proxy DLL (if any).
TypeLib	The LIBID for the type library that describes this interface.

When you opt to use standard marshaling, you will need to add in the correct registry entries for <u>each and every</u> custom interface defined by the server to allow SCM to find the necessary stub/proxy DLL. For example, here is the HKCR\Interface listing for a well-known workhorse in COM, IClassFactory:

Figure 5-19:
HKCR\Interface
listing for
IClassFactory.

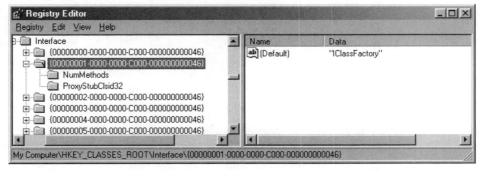

The ProxyStubClsid32 subkey specifies the CLSID of the stub/proxy DLL. As these stub/proxy DLLs are loaded and maintained by the COM runtime, you will not find ProgID equivalents. The value stored under ProxyStubClsid32 for IClassFactory is {00000320-0000-0000-C000-000000000046}, which maps to a listing under HKCR\CLSID revealing ole32.dll (recall, standard COM interfaces have marshaling code defined in the system-provided ole32.dll):

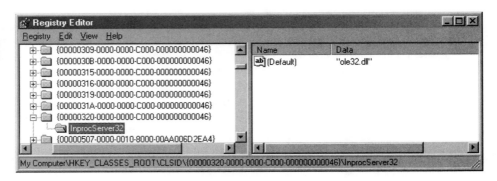

Figure 5-20:
Ole32.dll: The core standard interface marshaler.

Type Library Marshaling

This brings us to the final (and simplest) technique used to marshal data between stubs and proxies. *Type library marshaling* (sometimes called *universal marshaling*) is an approach that leverages another system-provided stub/proxy DLL named oleaut32.dll. Yes, the "_aut_" infix does suggest OLE automation; however, this does not imply what you may be thinking.

The universal marshaler was developed to provide automatic marshaling support for the IDispatch interface, which makes exclusive use of variant compliant data types we examined in the previous chapter. However, using type library marshaling does not imply in any way that the interface being marshaled must derive from IDispatch. You may leverage the system-provided universal marshaler for any custom interface you create (such as IStats, IDraw55, IShapeEdit) provided that <u>all your interface method parameters are variant compatible</u>.

Type library marshaling has very appealing side effects. You will have no need to compile your own custom stub/proxy DLL. This means you will have one less file to distribute and register on machines using your COM server. Configuring your custom interfaces to leverage the universal marshaler entails an understanding of the [oleautomation] IDL attribute.

Configuring Your Interfaces to Use the Universal Marshaler

If you wish to use oleaut32.dll as your marshaler, you have a small handful of steps to take in your server code. First off, you should mark each of your interfaces with the [oleautomation] attribute. This informs the MIDL compiler that all parameters in the interface are variant compatible. For example, here is IDraw, marked as "OLE-OK":

```
// Every custom interface which wishes to use the universal marshaler must
// be marked with the [oleautomation] attribute.
[ object, uuid(4B475690-DE06-11d2-AAF4-00A0C9312D57), oleautomation ]
interface IDraw : IUnknown
{
    [helpstring("Draw Partner!")]
    HRESULT Draw();
};
```

Another very critical step is to make sure that your type library information is registered in the system registry. The universal marshaler makes use of your type information in order to build the stub and proxy DLL on the fly, and therefore it needs to know where to find the server's type library (*.tlb) file. As we have seen in Chapter 4, LIBID entries end up under HKCR\TypeLib.

As well, you must register each interface defined in your IDL file under HKCR\Interface subkey. To mark your custom interfaces as a consumer of oleaut32.dll, they must have the value of ProxyStubClsid32 set to the CLSID of the universal marshaler: {00020424-0000-0000-C000-000000000046}.

If you then examine the HKCR\CLSID listing for {00020424-0000-0000-C000-000000000046}, you will see the correct mapping to oleaut32.dll:

Figure 5-21: CLSID of the universal marshaler.

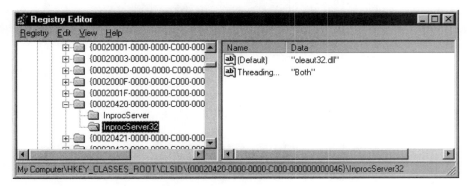

As a final step to access the universal marshaler, each HKCR\Interface listing must provide a TypeLib subkey mapping to the type library that holds the interface definitions. Here is a listing under HKCR\Interface for an interface that should give you warm-fuzzies by now.

Figure 5-22: A custom interface registered under HKCR\Interface.

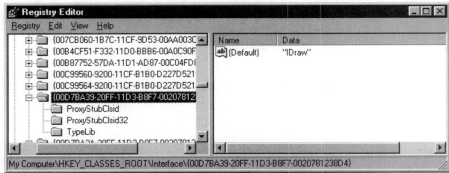

If you like the idea of using the system-supplied universal marshaler, but shudder at the thought of writing a massive REG file for each of your interfaces, help is just around the corner.

Simplifying Interface and Type Library Registration

Rather than writing a massive REG file that enters all interface and type information into the system registry, you will find it far simpler to make use of a COM library function that does so automatically. The LoadTypeLibEx() function is equipped to load up a type library and provide access to its contents programmatically using an ITypeLib pointer. When calling LoadTypeLibEx(), you send in the REGKIND_REGISTER flag to request automatic registration of your interfaces and type library. Obvious places to call this COM library function would be in DllRegisterServer(), or from within a WinMain() implementation. LoadTypeLibEx() takes a total of three parameters:

```
// LoadTypeLibEx() allows you to programmatically register the interfaces defined in
// your server's type library, as well as the library itself.
LoadTypeLibEx(LPOLESTR szFile,        // Name of TLB file.
              REGKIND regKind,        // REGKING flag.
              ITypeLib** ppTlib);     // [out] parameter.
```

The REGKIND flag must be set to REGKIND_REGISTER to force the necessary information to be placed into the system registry. The following code loads up the shapes.tlb type library, and programmatically registers the interfaces and type library into the registry:

```
// Automatically register your type and interface information as so...
ITypeLib* pTLib = NULL;
LoadTypeLibEx(L"Shapes.tlb", REGKIND_REGISTER, &pTLib);
pTLib->Release();
```

Notice that we must send in an ITypeLib pointer to LoadTypeLibEx(), even though we have no intention of using it. This pointer has been AddRef-ed, and therefore we must release it. With these three little lines of code, you receive the following registry entries automatically (assuming your interfaces have been tagged with the [oleautomation] attribute):

- HCKR\TypeLib\{your LIBID}\1.0
- HCKR\TypeLib\{your LIBID}\1.0\0\win32 = <path to your *.tlb file>
- HCKR\TypeLib\{your LIBID}\Flags
- HCKR\TypeLib\{your LIBID}\1.0\Helpdir
- HKCR\Interface\{your IID}
- HKCR\Interface\ProxyStubClsid = <CLSID of oleaut32.dll>
- HKCR\Interface\ProxyStubClsid32 = <CLSID of oleaut32.dll>
- HKCR\Interface\TypeLib = <LIBID of *.tlb file describing the interfaces>

If you configured your interfaces with the [oleautomation] attribute, the ProxyStubClsid32 subkey points to the universal marshaler. Nice, huh? Once the correct registry information is entered into the system, you can now safely cross process boundaries using oleaut32.dll (a.k.a. {00020424-0000-0000-C000-000000000046}).

Building a Local COM Server

Now that you understand stubs, proxies, and your marshaling options we need some information to marshal and a process to marshal from. Recall that marshaling is usually not necessary for in-process servers, as communication happens directly through interface pointers. Our next task is to learn how to create a local (EXE) server. Once we create a local component home for CoHexagon and its class factory we leverage our knowledge of the LoadTypeLibEx() function to automatically register the necessary library and interface information to make use of the universal marshaler (therefore we do not need to build and register our own stub/proxy DLL).

When we create COM servers of the EXE variety, we have some new issues to contend with. Most notably, we do not have a way to export functions from an EXE, such as DllGetClassObject(), DllCanUnloadNow(), DllRegisterServer(), or DllUnregisterServer(). As you know, the functionality provided by these four exports is core to a COM DLL's implementation, as they provide a way to install and remove registry information, create class objects, and unload the server when it is no longer in use.

How, then, can we expose this same functionality from an EXE? Unlike a COM DLL, EXE servers have a single entry point: WinMain(). As we will see, the logic of registration and class object creation is handled based on command line parameters. Furthermore, EXE servers are in charge of unloading themselves from memory (rather than being unloaded by the COM runtime).

Exposing Class Factories from a Local Server

Because SCM needs to locate IClassFactory pointers for a client regardless of the binary packaging, local COM servers advertise their class objects using two COM library functions, rather than implementing DllGetClassObject(). CoRegisterClassObject() is used to register a given class factory with an entity named the *class object table*. CoRegisterClassObject() takes five parameters:

```
// Used to register a class factory from a local server.
STDAPI CoRegisterClassObject(
  REFCLSID rclsid,          // Class identifier (CLSID) to be registered.
  IUnknown * pUnk,          // Pointer to the class object.
  DWORD dwClsContext,       // Context for running executable code.
  DWORD flags,              // How to connect to the class object.
  LPDWORD lpdwRegister);    // Registration ID.
```

The first and second parameters are and should be self-explanatory: the CLSID of the coclass created by a given class factory (parameter 1) and the IClassFactory interface of the associated class factory (parameter 2). The third and fourth parameters are used in conjunction to describe the exact behavior of the class factory. For example, do we want to have our class factory create objects exclusively for external clients, or can the server process itself create instances as well? Do we want to have a single server work with multiple clients, or should the class factory launch a new server process for each? These issues are addressed with various combinations of the CLSCTX and REGCLS flags. These combinations can be hairy, so let's look at the most practical combinations.

If the third parameter is set to CLSCTX_INPROC_SERVER, we inform SCM that only the server itself can access the posted class factory. If the third parameter is CLSCTX_LOCAL_SERVER, this allows a class object to be used only by external clients. Thus, in remote or locally accessed EXE coclasses, this flag is a must. But what if you want the best of both worlds? What if you want to allow the server to create objects for its own use, while still allowing clients to access them? Simple. Just OR together each of the CLSCTX flags as the third parameter.

Parameter 4 is a member of the REGCLS enumeration used to specify how the class factory creates the related coclasses. The REGCLS enumeration defines the following activation flags:

```
// The REGCLS enumeration specifies how a class factory is created for a client.
typedef enum tagREGCLS
{
    REGCLS_SINGLEUSE      = 0,
    REGCLS_MULTIPLEUSE    = 1,
    REGCLS_MULTI_SEPARATE = 2,
    REGCLS_SUSPENDED      = 4,
    REGCLS_SURROGATE      = 8
} REGCLS;
```

We have indirectly already used the REGCLS_SURROGATE flag, as this was the value used when dllhost.exe posted our server's class object. You will never have to use REGCLS_SURROGATE in your own EXE component housing, unless you are creating your own custom surrogate. REGCLS_SINGLEUSE informs SCM to launch a new instance of the server for each client request. REGCLS_MULTIPLE_SEPARATE specifies that any number of clients can share a single server until the class object is revoked from the class table by the EXE using CoRevokeClassObject().

The fifth and final parameter to CoRegisterClassObject() is a COM-provided registration ID (a numerical cookie). Be sure to hold onto this value, as it allows you to tell SCM when a given class object has left the stage and is no longer taking client requests. Here is a common way to register a class factory using CoRegisterClassObject(), allowing both the server and the client to share a single instance of the CoHexClassFactory:

```
// To post your class factories to the class table, call CoRegisterClassObject()
CoHexClassFactory HexFact;
DWORD hexID;
CoRegisterClassObject(CLSID_CoHexagon,
                      (IClassFactory*)&HexFact,
                      CLSCTX_LOCAL_SERVER | CLSCTX_INPROC_SERVER,
                      REGCLS_MULTIPLE_SEPARATE, &hexID);
```

Because this above combination of flags is so common, a shorthand notation may be used. The call above to CoRegisterClassObject() can be replaced by the following:

```
// This is the most standard way to register your class objects from an
// EXE server. Both the server and external clients can create the objects
// and a single EXE is used for all active clients.
CoRegisterClassObject(CLSID_CoHexagon,
                      (IClassFactory*)&HexFact,
                      CLSCTX_LOCAL_SERVER,
                      REGCLS_MULTIPLEUSE, &hexID);
```

Revoking Your Class Objects

When your EXE application is about to shut down, you will need to call CoRevokeClassObject() before WinMain() terminates. This informs SCM that a given class object is no longer available, and removes the factory from the class table. The sole parameter to this COM library function is the registration ID obtained by the final parameter of CoRegisterClassObject():

```
// Clients can no longer create hexagons.
CoRevokeClassObject(hexID);
```

Registering Multiple Class Factories

Recall what a typical implementation of DllGetClassObject() looks like under the hood. A class factory contained in a server can be created given the correct CLSID, after which we hand off the IClassFactory pointer to a client. From this pointer, clients can create a given coclass instance using CreateInstance(). Let's assume Shapes.dll server contains two creatable objects:

```
// In-process servers export DllGetClassObject() to allow SCM to grab IClassFactory
// pointers on behalf of a COM client.
// The implementation may test the REFCLSID parameter to determine which
// class factory to create.
STDAPI DllGetClassObject(REFCLSID rclsid, REFIID riid, void** ppv)
{
     HRESULT hr;
     CoHexClassFactory *pHexFact = NULL;
     CoParallelogramClassFactory *pPGramFact = NULL;
     // Which coclass is the client trying to create?
     if(rclsid == CLSID_CoHexagon ){
          pHexFact = new CoHexClassFactory();
          hr = pHexFact -> QueryInterface(riid, ppv);
          if(FAILED(hr)
          {
               delete pHexFact;
               return hr;
          }
     }
     else if (rclsid == CLSID_CoPGram ){
          pPGramFact = new CoParallelogramClassFactory ();
          hr = pPGramFact -> QueryInterface(riid, ppv);
          if(FAILED(hr)
          {
               delete pPGramFact;
               return hr;
          }
     }
     else
          return CLASS_E_CLASSNOTAVAILABLE;
}
```

Local servers register class objects if and only if they are told to do so by SCM. SCM sends a command line argument through the LPSTR parameter of WinMain(). If this string contains the "-Embedding" or "/Embedding" substrings, you are being launched by COM

and you need to register your class objects. The following implementation of WinMain()
re-creates the logic used by DllGetClassObject() with in-process servers:

```
// EXE servers do not export a function to register class factories, but rather test the
// LPSTR parameter of WinMain(), and call CoRegisterClassObject()
// accordingly.
int APIENTRY WinMain( HINSTANCE hInstance, HINSTANCE hPrevInstance,
                      LPSTR lpCmdLine, int nCmdShow)
{
    // Let's see if COM started us.
    if(strstr(lpCmdLine, "/Embedding") || strstr(lpCmdLine, "-Embedding"))
    {
        CoInitialize(NULL);
        // Here are the class objects.
        CoHexClassFactory HexFact;
        CoParallelogramClassFactory PGramFact;
        // Tokens identifying the registration ID
        DWORD hexID;
        DWORD PGramID;
        // Post the class factories with SCM.
        CoRegisterClassObject(CLSID_CoHexagon,
            (IClassFactory*)&HexFact, CLSCTX_LOCAL_SERVER,
            REGCLS_MULTIPLEUSE, &hexID);
        CoRegisterClassObject(CLSID_CoPGram,
            (IClassFactory*)&ParallelogramClassFactory,
            CLSCTX_LOCAL_SERVER, REGCLS_MULTIPLEUSE,
            &PGramID);
        // ^^^^^ OK, now what? ^^^^^ //
        // Remove class factories from class object table.
        CoRevokeClassObject(hexID);
        CoRevokeClassObject(PGramID);
        CoUninitialize();
        return 0;
    }
    // Not launched by COM, so do whatever.
    return 0;
};
```

Well, this seems to be a step in the right direction. Each class object contained in this EXE
is registered with the class object table, after which it is shut down instantaneously.
We better have some really fast clients, as they only have nanoseconds to call
CreateInstance() from the IClassFactory pointer before the class objects are dead! Of
course we need a bit more boilerplate code here to allow a client to make calls to "posted"
class objects.

The Ultimate Breakpoint: GetMessage()

Unlike a DLL server, an EXE server is responsible for shutting itself down when detecting
there are no active objects and no server locks. Until that point, the EXE server must
remain loaded in memory. The easiest way to ensure our server stays in memory is to create a dummy message pump in the implementation of WinMain(), right after registering
the class factories:

```
// Once all class objects are registered just wait...
MSG ms;
```

```
while(GetMessage(&ms, 0, 0, 0))
{
    TranslateMessage(&ms);
    DispatchMessage(&ms);
}
```

GetMessage() will now whirl away until a quit message has been posted to the message queue. This ensures that our factories are made available throughout the server's lifetime. Next question: How to terminate the EXE when we have no active objects.

Understanding Object Lifetime in EXE Servers

We have seen that an in-process server returns S_OK from DllCanUnloadNow() whenever the lock count and object count are both at zero. This informs SCM that the DLL may be safely unloaded from memory, as it has no active objects and no client locks. The in-proc class objects adjust the lock count via LockServer() while each coclass and class factory adjust the object count in their constructors and destructors. This deactivation strategy changes just a bit when implementing a local server.

Coclasses contained in EXE servers act the same as an in-process implementation and can simply increment or decrement the global object count accordingly. The class factories, however, must be accessible as long as the dummy message pump is whirling away. As we have created a locally scoped class object in WinMain() we should not "delete this" during the final release. Furthermore, the constructors and destructors of a class object do not adjust the global object count in their constructors and destructors, as they are typically created in the scope of WinMain() and must remain in existence until the final coclass fades away.

In effect, class factories created in local function scope are not really using the internal reference count to monitor self-destruction (this little fact is hidden from our client). Class factories used within an EXE can return fixed values from AddRef() and Release() to pacify any client that happens to examine the returned ULONG. Here is how we can modify CoHexClassFactory's reference counting scheme for use in our EXE server:

```
// EXE class factories do not destroy themselves when the reference count reaches
// zero, but are removed from the class object table when the server is shutting down.
STDMETHODIMP_(ULONG) CoHexClassFactory::AddRef()
{
    return 10;      // ++m_refCount;
}
STDMETHODIMP_(ULONG) CoHexClassFactory::Release()
{
    // We are not 'deleting this' here, as
    // the class factory is scoped to WinMain().
    return 20;      // --m_refCount;
}
```

The next trick used when implementing a local server is to ensure that when the global object count and global lock count are both at zero, a WM_QUIT message is posted, which will cause our dummy message loop to fail. This in turn revokes the class objects and shuts down the server. To simplify this process, it is helpful to create some global functions that all class factories and custom coclasses may access. Furthermore, it is often easier to have a single server-wide counter to represent the combination of locks and active objects, as opposed to two unique counters:

```
// Locks.cpp
ULONG g_allLocks;        // Server locks + active objects.
void Lock()              // Called by coclass constructors and LockServer(TRUE)
{
     ++g_allLocks;
}
void UnLock()            // Called by coclass destructors and LockServer(FALSE)
{
     --g_allLocks;
     if(g_allLocks == 0)
          PostQuitMessage(0);        // Kill the message pump!
}
```

Registering Local COM Servers

Once you have assembled your component housing for a COM EXE, you need to ensure that the corresponding REG file is modified to specify a LocalServer32 subkey rather than InprocServer32. Recall that COM-based DLLs use InprocServer32 to point to the physical path to the dll in question (e.g., C:\MyDLL.dll). Local EXE servers must also direct SCM to the correct physical path using LocalServer32 (e.g., C:\MyEXE.exe). For example:

```
; Be sure your EXEs specify LocalServer32!
;
HKEY_CLASSES_ROOT\LocalShapes.CoHexagon\CLSID = {<guid>}
HKEY_CLASSES_ROOT\CLSID\{<guid>} = LocalShapes.CoHexagon
HKEY_CLASSES_ROOT\CLSID\{<guid>}\LocalServer32 = C:\LocalShapes\Debug\LocalShapes.exe
```

The next lab will allow you to assemble your own EXE server, which will be accessed from a remote COM client later in this chapter.

Lab 5-1: Developing a Local Server in C++

In this lab, we continue on towards the initial promise of Chapter 1: porting a C program into a remote DCOM server. Here, you will be building a local component house (EXE) to hold your existing CoCar and the retrofitted class factory. This will give you a chance to work with CoRegisterClassObject() and CoRevokeClassObject() as well as programmatic manipulation of type information. This lab will also allow you to configure your custom interfaces to make use of the universal marshaler. Once this lab is completed, you will be able to reuse this EXE as a remote server later in the chapter.

The solution for this lab can be found on your CD-ROM under:
Labs\Chapter 05\CoCarEXE
Labs\Chapter 05\CoCarEXE\VBClient

Step One: Create the Project Workspace

Fire up Visual C++ and create a new Win32 Application workspace, selecting a simple application named **CoCarEXE**. This will give you a default implementation of WinMain() as well as precompiled headers (stdafx.h and stdafx.cpp). Locate your previous CoCarInProcServer project folder (from Chapter 4) from the Windows Explorer and copy over the CoCar, CoCarClassFactory, and CoCarInProcServer.idl files. Insert the *.cpp and *.idl files into your new project workspace. Now, update each custom interface to make use of the [oleautomation] attribute:

```
// Because we will be leveraging the universal marshaler, we must mark our interfaces
// as variant compliant.
[object, uuid(A533DA31-D372-11d2-B8CF-0020781238D4),
 oleautomation, helpstring("Get info about this car")]
interface IStats : IUnknown
{
     HRESULT DisplayStats();
     HRESULT GetPetName([out, retval] BSTR* petName);
};
[object, uuid(A533DA30-D372-11d2-B8CF-0020781238D4),
 oleautomation, helpstring("Rev your car & slow it down")]
interface IEngine : IUnknown
{
     HRESULT SpeedUp();
     HRESULT GetMaxSpeed ([out, retval] int* maxSpeed);
     HRESULT GetCurSpeed ([out, retval] int* curSpeed);
};
[object, uuid(A533DA32-D372-11d2-B8CF-0020781238D4),
 oleautomation, helpstring("This lets you create a car")]
interface ICreateCar : IUnknown
{
     HRESULT SetPetName([in]BSTR petName);
     HRESULT SetMaxSpeed([in]int maxSp);
};
```

Next, bring over your REG existing file from CoCarInProcServer. We do not need to list any LIBID or Interface entries in the *.reg file, as we will do this step programmatically. However, modify the path for this new server, and change the listing from InprocServer32 to LocalServer32 (recall that EXE servers make use of the LocalServer32 subkey when specifying their path):

```
REGEDIT
HKEY_CLASSES_ROOT\CoCarEXE.CoCar\CLSID =
{C8376C06-F1FA-11d2-B8E0-0020781238D4}
HKEY_CLASSES_ROOT\CLSID\{C8376C06-F1FA-11d2-B8E0-0020781238D4}
= CoCarEXE.CoCar
HKEY_CLASSES_ROOT\CLSID\{C8376C06-F1FA-11d2-B8E0-0020781238D4}
\LocalServer32 = <your path>\Debug\CoCarEXE.exe
```

Go ahead and merge this file into the system right now. As a final step, be sure you modify the behavior of your car's class factory such that AddRef() and Release() return simple fixed values and that the implementation of Release() does not "delete this."

```
// Update the class factory.
//
STDMETHODIMP_(ULONG) CoCarClassFactory::AddRef()
{
     return 10;        // ++m_refCount;
}
STDMETHODIMP_(ULONG) CoCarClassFactory::Release()
{
     // We are not 'deleting this' here, as
     // the class object is scoped to WinMain!
     return 20;        // --m_refCount;
}
```

Step Two: Assemble the EXE Component Housing

When you call CoRegisterClassObject() from within an EXE server, this informs SCM
your CoCarClassFactory is ready to take client requests. In your WinMain() loop, check
the LPSTR parameter for the "Embedding" substring and register your class factory only
if launched by COM:

```
// include <string.h> to use the strstr() function!
// Don't forget to call CoInitialize() from within WinMain().
if(strstr(lpCmdLine, "/Embedding") || strstr(lpCmdLine, "-Embedding"))
{
    // Create the class factory.
    CoCarClassFactory CarClassFactory;
    // Registration cookie.
    DWORD regID = 0;
    // Post the class factory.
    CoRegisterClassObject(CLSID_CoCar, (IClassFactory*)&CarClassFactory,
    CLSCTX_LOCAL_SERVER, REGCLS_MULTIPLEUSE, &regID);
}
```

Next, create a dummy message pump. The purpose of this loop is to keep your EXE
server alive as long as we have active objects and/or server locks. After declaring the message pump, remove your class factory using CoRevokeClassObject(), passing in the
DWORD cookie obtained from CoRegisterClassObject():

```
// This message pump will process messages until you post a WM_QUIT message.
MSG ms;
while(GetMessage(&ms, 0, 0, 0))
{
    TranslateMessage(&ms);
    DispatchMessage(&ms);
}
CoRevokeClassObject(regID);  // Server dying, so remove class object.
```

As a final administrative duty for the local server, we need to register your server's type
library and interface information to make use of the universal marshaler. Configure your
server to register these entries automatically by making a call to LoadTypeLibEx(), just
before the command line test:

```
// Automatic interface and type library registration!
ITypeLib* pTLib = NULL;
LoadTypeLibEx( L"CarServerEXETypeInfo.tlb",          // Your file name may vary!
            REGKIND_REGISTER, &pTLib);
pTLib->Release();
```

Recall that you could choose to check for the –regserver and /regserver command line
parameters and register your type information only if told to do so. Here we ensure all
necessary entries are always registered each time the application runs. Here is a complete
implementation of your EXE's component housing:

```
// The EXE component housing.
int APIENTRY WinMain(HINSTANCE hInstance, HINSTANCE hPrevInstance,
                LPSTR lpCmdLine, int nCmdShow)
{
    // Initialize COM.
    CoInitialize(NULL);
    // Let's register the type library and interfaces.
```

```
ITypeLib* pTLib = NULL;
LoadTypeLibEx(L"CoCarEXETypeInfo.tlb",
            REGKIND_REGISTER, &pTLib);
pTLib->Release();
// Let's see if we were started by SCM.
if(strstr(lpCmdLine, "/Embedding") || strstr(lpCmdLine, "-Embedding"))
{
      // Create the Car class factory.
      CoCarClassFactory CarClassFactory;
      // Register the Car class factory.
      DWORD regID = 0;
      CoRegisterClassObject(CLSID_CoCar,
                        (IClassFactory*)&CarClassFactory,
                        CLSCTX_LOCAL_SERVER,
                        REGCLS_MULTIPLEUSE, &regID);
      // Now just run until a quit message is sent.
      MSG ms;
      while(GetMessage(&ms, 0, 0, 0))
      {
            TranslateMessage(&ms);
            DispatchMessage(&ms);
      }
      // All done, so remove class object.
      CoRevokeClassObject(regID);
}
// Terminate COM.
CoUninitialize();
return 0;
}
```

Step Three: Create and Utilize Global Locking Functions

Local servers need to unload themselves from memory when they detect no active objects
and no server locks. Create a brand new header file named locks.h that defines two global
function prototypes:

```
// Locks.h
#ifndef _MYLOCKS
#define _MYLOCKS
      void Lock();          // Increment lock.
      void UnLock();        // Decrement lock.
#endif                      // _MYLOCKS
```

Now create a corresponding locks.cpp file, which implements these functions and defines a
single global variable that holds the sum of all locks and active objects in the server. Be
sure that your UnLock() method posts a WM_QUIT message into the message pump
when the final release has occurred:

```
// Locks.cpp
#include "stdafx.h"         // For precompiled headers.
#include "locks.h"
ULONG g_allLocks;           // locks + objects
// Called by cocar constructor and LockServer(TRUE)
void Lock()
{
      ++g_allLocks;
}
```

```
// Called by cocar destructor and LockServer(FALSE)
void UnLock()
{
     --g_allLocks;
     // Shut down the dummy message pump.
     if(g_allLocks == 0)
          PostQuitMessage(0);
}
```

The constructor of CoCar as well as LockServer(TRUE) each must call the global Lock() method. The destructors of CoCar as well as LockServer(FALSE) must call UnLock():

```
// Modifications to the coclass.
CoCar::CoCar() : m_refCount(0), m_currSpeed(0), m_maxSpeed(0)
{
     m_petName = SysAllocString(L"Default Pet Name");
     // Bump up the 'all locks' counter.
     Lock();
}
CoCar::~CoCar()
{
     // Take down the 'all locks' counter.
     UnLock();
     if(m_petName)
          SysFreeString(m_petName);
}
// Modifications to the class factory.
STDMETHODIMP CoCarClassFactory::LockServer(BOOL fLock)
{
     if(fLock)
          Lock();
     else
          UnLock();
     return S_OK;
}
```

Now, compile and run your server once to enter the type information into the registry. Take the time to hunt down the entries made for you by the LoadTypeLibEx() function under HKCR\Interface and HKCR\TypeLib.

As well, remember that once we have registered our custom interfaces, the OLE/COM Object Viewer is able to display each supported interface by name.

Also recall that we have configured our server to use type library marshaling, and therefore we do not need to build a custom stub/proxy DLL.

This completes the EXE server-side programming. If you are unable to find the correct entries in the registry, be sure you have run your EXE once to hit the LoadTypeLibEx() logic.

Step Four: Build a Client for the Local Server

In the previous chapter we examined how to create Java, Visual Basic, and C++ smart pointer clients. Any of these languages would do in order to test our local server and you may pick your language of choice in this step (the CD solution uses a VB front end). If you create a C++ client, be sure to specify a local class context:

```
// To access an EXE server, use the CLSCTX_LOCAL_SERVER flag.
hr = CoCreateInstance(CLSID_CoCar, NULL, CLSCTX_LOCAL_SERVER,
                      IID_ICreateCar, (void**)&pCCar);
```

If you pick Java or VB as your target client, just be sure to select the correct *.tlb file from your current project directory, for example:

Figure 5-23: Referencing our local CoCar from VB.

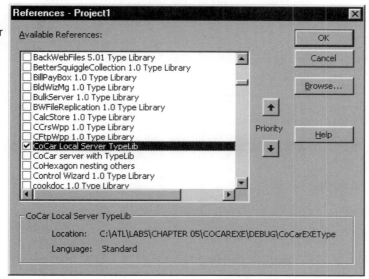

Next, it's time to learn how to remotely access your new local car server à la DCOM.

If((DCOM == COM) && (COM == DCOM)) return S_OK;

Everything you know about COM applies directly to DCOM. DCOM is not necessarily a "new way" to do COM, and it is not necessarily a modification to traditional COM. In essence DCOM is an evolution, providing the ability for a client to access servers located on another machine. A developer may configure a client to access a remote server by taking two approaches, both achieving the same end result of remote activation:

1. Use the DCOM configuration utility (dcomcnfg.exe) to redirect all client requests on a given machine to a named remote machine hosting the server. This is the "no-code" approach.

2. Program a client to always access a named remote machine using DCOM-centric COM library calls and structures. The approach always overrides any settings specified by the dcomcnfg.exe utility.

Both approaches require that the server information is correctly registered on each machine, including entries for ProgIDs, CLSIDs, AppIDs, LIBIDs, and IIDs. Each approach requires configuring the remote server with the desired security attributes to determine which clients can access the server and exactly how they may do so. We will access our CoCar EXE server using both techniques, starting with the dcomcnfg.exe utility. But first, a little more detail is needed on how our objects are created remotely.

Local SCM to Remote SCM Communications

Communication between a client and remote server is established by the SCM on the client machine asking the SCM on the server machine to find, load, and return an interface pointer from a remote COM object. We already know that if a client requests an interface from a COM object on the same machine (in-proc or local), SCM consults the system registry to find the exact location of the component home based off the InprocServer32 or LocalServer32 subkeys of HKCR\CLSID.

In remote activation, the SCM on the client's machine reads the local registry and discovers the path of the object maps to some other named machine. The red flag that alerts a SCM to "go remote," is the presence of the RemoteServerName entry in the AppID of the local registry (Figure 5-24). This realization results in the local SCM making a call to the remote SCM, which in turn looks up the path to the binary in the remote registry. This SCM to SCM contact is accomplished again by ORPC calls.

Figure 5-24: A given AppID may have a RemoteServer-Name value specifying a remote machine.

As you recall, an AppID should have a listing under the corresponding CLSIDs for each coclass in the server:

Figure 5-25: CLSID listing should have a corresponding AppID value.

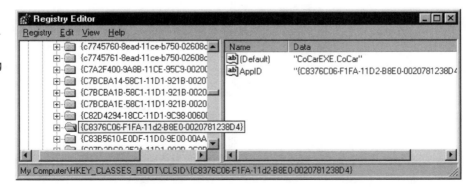

With these two registry tweaks (and assuming the server has been actually registered on the remote machine) your client requests will now be sent to the named machine, without a single line of code changed in the client. Rather than making these adjustments by hand or via a REG file, you may make use of the dcomcnfg.exe utility to enter or remove them using a friendly GUI environment.

As mentioned, dcomcnfg.exe is not the only way to access a remote server. If you choose to alter your client's code base to launch a remote server, you have a handful of new COM library items to help you get across the wire. For example, the CoCreateInstanceEx() function takes as one of its parameters a COSERVERINFO structure. One of these fields specifies the name of the remote machine.

Note: SCM will always honor explicit creation calls above any RemoteServerName registry entries.

What is DCOMCNFG?

The dcomcnfg.exe utility that ships with Windows NT is an administrative tool used to redirect client requests to a remote machine without affecting the existing code base. This same tool is used to configure the security attributes for a given COM application on the remote machine on a server-by-server basis. Configuring a remote connection requires administration details for each computer involved in the experience of this long-distance relationship. This is a frustrating aspect of DCOM, as it can tend to require a good deal of running around the office to configure everyone's machine properly.

DCOM is available for Win95/98 as well. However, as these operating systems are not enterprise-level systems you will find many options unavailable, most notably in the area of COM security. Under NT workstations, you will find more security options than you can shake a stick at, and all servers are allowed to be launched when asked to do so by an authenticated client.

Note: The DCOM lab presented at the end of this chapter assumes a Windows NT configuration.

An Overview of DCOMCNFG

When you first run dcomcnfg.exe, you will see four individual tabs (using NT SP4; SP3 does not supply the Default Protocols tab). The leftmost Applications tab lists all coclasses on a given machine (Figure 5-26). If the server has registered a ProgID you will find it listed alphabetically; if not, you will find the less-than-friendly CLSID listings.

Figure 5-26:
The Applications tab allows you to edit the security and activation values for a given COM application.

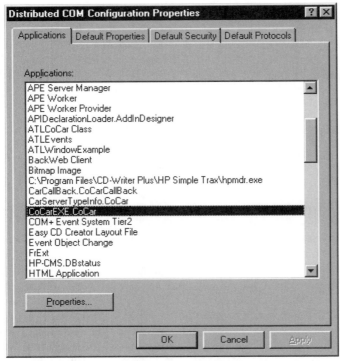

Figure 5-27:
You may specify default client security checks using the Default Properties tab.

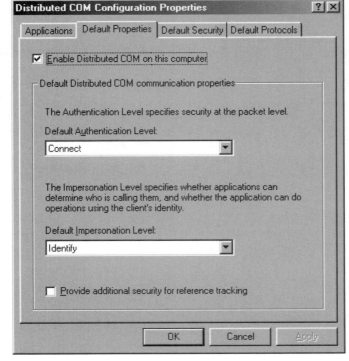

As an interesting side note, whenever dcomcnfg.exe is launched, it will automatically discover any COM applications that do not currently have an AppID listing and assign one automatically, using the first CLSID encountered in the server's type library (again, this is a good thing, as many legacy COM servers never registered AppIDs). Assume we want to configure LocalShapes.CoHexagon using dcomcnfg.exe. Even if we do not edit our REG file to configure a specific AppID, the AppID assigned to LocalShapes.CoHexagon will be identical to the CLSID of CoHexagon.

When you double-click any AppID entry (or select an item and hit the Properties button), you will launch another tabbed dialog which allows you to set the activation and security settings of that particular AppID (such as LocalShapes.CoHexagon). We will see this in just a moment, but let's finish discussing the remaining tabs of the main dialog.

The Default Properties tab (Figure 5-27) allows you to configure how DCOM will generally behave on a given machine. First off, you have the option of enabling or disabling DCOM itself on the current machine. The other options allow you to establish machine-wide default authentication and impersonation levels (which we discuss shortly). If a given AppID does not specify otherwise, these settings will be used when accessing the remote server.

Figure 5-28:
You may apply machine-wide DCOM security settings with dcomcnfg.

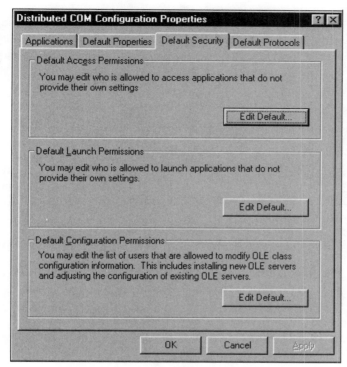

The Default Security tab (Figure 5-28) allows you to configure how this machine will allow remote users to launch and access the COM applications residing here. This same tab allows you to modify the set of users allowed to configure COM applications on this machine (read: "who can install new COM servers and configure existing ones").

The final tab, Default Protocols, lists each network protocol currently used by DCOM. This tab allows you to configure the current protocols, add new ones, and remove existing ones (which you should typically <u>not</u> do).

A New Hive: HKEY_LOCAL_MACHINE

Keep in mind that the values set with the Default Properties, Default Security, and Default Protocols tabs are used only if a given AppID does not specify otherwise. Typically you will want to configure an AppID yourself and override many of these default settings. Your system registry holds the value of each DCOM-centric default under HKEY_LOCAL_MACHINE\SOFTWARE\Microsoft\Ole, as shown below:

Figure 5-29:
Location of all default security settings for a particular machine.

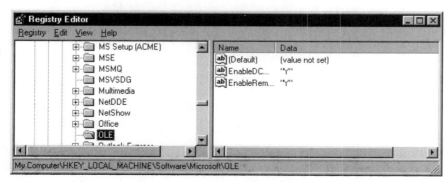

As you can see, many of these entries revolve around secure access to the COM servers. Therefore, we need to get the basics of COM security under our belts before going remote.

COM Security Basics

Now that a client machine can redirect all activation requests to a remote host using the RemoteServerName value, we need to address the issue of COM security. Just because we have registered a COM server on some remote machine does not mean clients can come breaking down the doors whenever they desire. While a client machine uses dcomcnfg.exe to redirect clients to a remote server, the remote machine also uses dcomcnfg.exe to configure how a given COM application deals with its security issues.

COM security can be configured using two approaches, both achieving the same end result (more or less). First, you may elect to use *declarative security*. This approach stores a server's security settings in the local system registry. Declarative security is typically done using dcomcnfg.exe on an AppID-by-AppID basis (or by using the default DCOM security settings mentioned earlier).

Programmatic security, on the other hand, makes use of a number of COM security interfaces and security-related COM library calls. As you may suspect, this gives you more control over security measures than declarative settings. The core library function in the COM security suite is CoInitializeSecurity(), which sets the security for a given process at run time. If a given process sets programmatic security, any declarative entries in the registry are ignored. In fact, the COM runtime calls CoInitializeSecurity() automatically using the declarative entries you made with dcomcnfg.exe.

COM's security is based on the NT security model. Every time a user logs onto an NT workstation, he or she is required to supply a user name and password, collectively termed a *user account*. NT assigns a security ID (SID) to each user account, which may then be added to local or global groups such as Administrators, Users, and Power Users. The User Manager utility supplied with Windows NT allows system administrators to edit these groups.

SIDs can also be used to establish security settings for a given resource. NT maintains the master list of "who can do what to whom" using a Discretionary Access Control List, or DACL. The DACL is used to establish the three fundamental COM security traits:

- **Authentication**: Are you who you claim you are?
- **Access Control**: Who can use and/or launch this COM server?
- **Server Identity**: Sets identity for running the remote server.

Setting the Authentication Level

Authentication is the act of verifying the identity of a DCOM client. A DCOM server needs to be certain that a remote client is who it claims to be before it allows any further activity (such as activation or access to currently active objects). NT provides authentication services through a Security Support Provider (SSP) OS layer such as the NT 4 Lan Manager (NTLM).

The authentication of a remote client takes place at the packet level, and therefore the packet is the unit of measurement used to determine how often the SSP should perform authentication logic. Here are the various authentication levels supported by COM:

Authentication Level	Meaning in Life
None	Absolutely no client authentication performed whatsoever.
Connect	Verify client identity at initial RPC connection only.
Call	Verify client identity for the first packet sent.
Packet	Verify client identity for each packet sent.
Packet Integrity	Packet level authentication plus a signed payload to ensure no tampering has taken place during transmission.
Packet Privacy	Packet Integrity level plus encryption to ensure that no "along the wire" peeking can take place.

Recall that the Default Properties tab of dcomcnfg.exe can be used to set the default level of authentication. NT SP4 also allows you to set the authentication level on an AppID basis under the General tab of a given AppID. This configuration will override any authentication level set at the machine level. For example, we may establish the default authentication level of our CoCar server as shown in Figure 5-30:

Figure 5-30: Managing authentication at the AppID level.

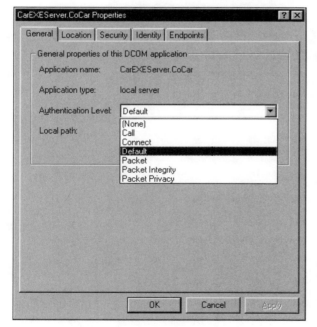

Access Control

Like authentication settings, access control may be set at the machine-wide or AppID level using dcomcnfg.exe. Each AppID maintains an Access Control List (ACL), specifying which groups or individual users can access, launch, and configure the underlying COM server. If you wish to establish a default machine-wide access control level, you may do so from the Default Security tab. If you wish to specify control access for a given COM application, you may select an AppID and create unique ACLs for the following access categories:

- **Access permissions**: Users included in the Access ACL may invoke methods on the remote server. If they are not on the list, they cannot access a running COM server.

- **Launch permissions**: Users contained in this ACL have the rights to start up a new instance of a COM server. Any user that has launch permissions should also have access permission; however, the reverse situation is not always true. You may block out some users from launching a new instance of the COM server while allowing them to access running servers.

- **Configuration permissions**: Specifies who is able to change these ACL lists for a given AppID. Chances are you do not want Fred from accounting to configure your COM servers, and using configuration levels, you may block him out.

Figure 5-31 illustrates the dcomcnfg.exe ACL editor used for launch permissions. Access and configuration settings use a similar ACL editor.

Figure 5-31:
ACLs may be established for access, launch, and configuration permissions using dcomcnfg.exe. You have the choice of default machine-wide settings or AppID-specific setting.

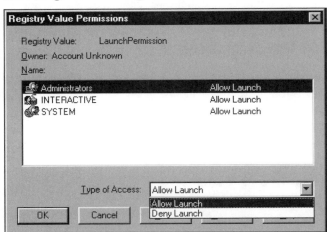

Information concerning a COM application's ACL lists are held in the registry as named values, under HKCR\AppID:

Figure 5-32:
Access control for HKEY_CLASSES_ROOT\ AppID\{C8376C06-F1FA-11d2-B8E0-0020781238D4} (CoCar).

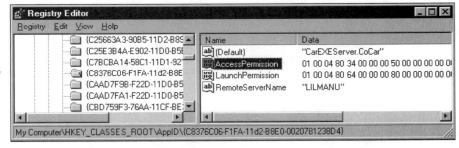

Server Identity Settings

The final issue we need to address has to do with server identity. Once a SID has passed the authentication, launch, and access security checks, COM needs to know under which "identity" to launch the server, meaning "what is the SID for the user who is using me?" The choices are controlled from the Identity tab and may take the following values, which are used to set the RunAs value for a given AppID:

■ **The Interactive User:** This is really only useful during COM debugging sessions. All COM servers run under the identity of the user logged on at the server NT workstation. This would mean if your buddy logged onto your machine after hours under her account, she has the identity rights for this server. This is the only identity setting that permits a server to launch any UI elements contained in the server.

■ **The Launching User:** This is the default (and worst) choice. Here you give identity rights for your COM server based off the user that launched it. This has the unappealing side effect of SCM launching a new instance of your server for each remote client.

■ **This User:** For any production application, this is the correct setting. You may establish a user account for the COM application. As long as you add in the correct users and groups to this ACL, you ensure a select group around the enterprise is the "identity" of the COM server.

Going Remote Using DCOMCNFG: Setting up the Client and Server Machines

Now that you have an understanding of these four tabs and basic DCOM security options, let's investigate how to configure our CoCar EXE server to run on a remote host. First, you must be connected to at least one other machine (just had to mention that).

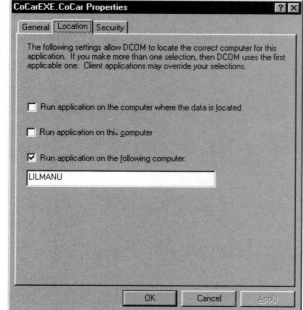

Figure 5-33: Editing the RemoteServer-Name value for a given AppID.

Now let's begin by configuring the client machine. Begin by launching dcomcnfg.exe. From the Applications tab, double-click the AppID entry for CoCarEXE. Under the Location tab you specify the machine on which SCM should look for the remote server. This entry automatically enters a RemoteServerName value under HKCR\AppID (see Figure 5-33).

Notice that it is possible to configure a single AppID with what seems to be more than one location. If you were to check both the On this Computer and On the Following Computer options, SCM will activate the server at the closest proximity from the client. When we learn how to access a remote computer programmatically with the COM library, these settings will be overridden by the client's code base.

Now we need to set up security options on the server machine. Open dcomcnfg.exe on the server computer and locate CoCar (if you can't find it, you may have forgotten to register the server). Under the Security tab, you must make sure that your server's ACL allows the remote client to access and activate the server. Using the ACL editor, it is often easiest to specify members of the Everyone group during testing and debugging:

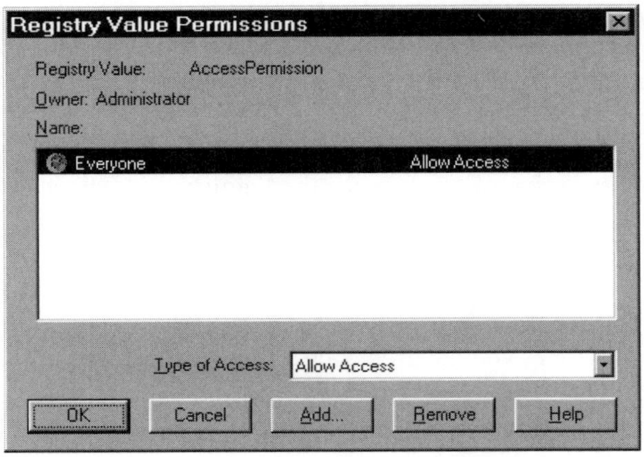

Figure 5-34: Setting universal access to a COM server.

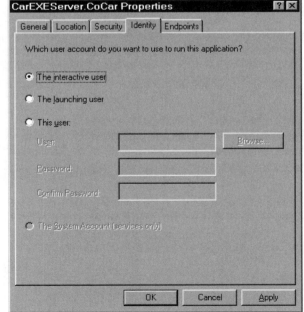

Finally, if your server displays any user interface elements (including message boxes) you must set the server's identity as the Interactive User (Figure 5-35). If you forget to do so, when the server item launches a UI, it will not be displayed and your server will appear to hang (as the GUI is waiting for some user interaction). In the real world, you would want to create a specific This User account to assume the identity of the launch and would not establish either Interactive or Launching user identities.

Figure 5-35: The Interactive User is the only identity that allows the server to show any GUI element.

Programmatic DCOM Library Function Calls

There are times when the best choice for remote access is to hard code a remote server in your client code. Imagine that the end user may select a number of options from a drop-down list box. Based on the selection, you might have to access information located across the enterprise on numerous remote machines. Clearly you need more flexibility than the RemoteServerName AppID value. You need code. The COM library supplies a small set of functions and data structures to help streamline remote access. Before you can use any of the following DCOM-specific COM library calls, you must define the following constant in your program <u>before</u> including <windows.h>:

```
// This includes all DCOM centric definitions.
#define _WIN32_DCOM
#include <windows.h>
```

If you do not do so, you will have a number of errors, as the DCOM-centric definitions have been conditionally omitted from your compile. With that detail out of the way, the first new DCOM related item at our disposal is the COSERVERINFO structure, used to specify the named remote server:

```
// COSERVERINFO is used to specify the characteristics of a remote connection.
typedef struct _COSERVERINFO
{
    DWORD dwReserved1;          // Reserved (Set to NULL)
    LPWSTR pwszName;            // Remote computer name.
    COAUTHINFO *pAuthInfo;      // Authentication settings.
    DWORD dwReserved2;          // Reserved (Set to NULL)
} COSERVERINFO;
```

Beyond the two reserved fields, the LPWSTR field specifies the remote server machine. This may be in the form of a UNC, DNS, or IP address. COAUTHINFO is another structure which allows for programmatically setting security authentication levels. For our purposes, we will send in NULL for this parameter and use the default authentication established by dcomcnfg.exe

The COSERVERINFO structure is used as a parameter to another DCOM-centric item, CoCreateInstanceEx(). This function is very unique in that it allows you to specify a *batch* of interfaces you want to acquire from the server in a single round trip. To do so, you need to create and establish a MULTI_QI structure.

MULTI_QI allows you to specify any number of required interfaces using a fixed array. When the RPC returns, you may check the HRESULT for each QI attempt, and see which (if any) interfaces were unsupported by the remote object. Here is how MULTI_QI breaks down:

```
// MULTI_QI is a structure which allows you to obtain a batch of remote
// interfaces in a single round trip.
typedef struct _MULTI_QI
{
    const IID* pIID; // The IID you are looking for.
    IUnknown * pItf; // Storage for interface pointer.
    HRESULT hr;      // Error code for a given QueryInterface() invocation.
} MULTI_QI;
```

To illustrate using these new DCOM-centric items, here is some sample code using all three DCOM items to access a remote server:

```
// Programmatically accessing a remote CoHexagon.
void main()
{
...
        // These are parameters to CoCreateInstanceEx().
        COSERVERINFO csi = {0};        // null out all fields.
        MULTI_QI qi[2] = {0};          // null out all fields.
        // Set the name of the remote server.
        csi.pwszName = L"SERVERMACHINE";        // Must be Unicode.
        // Here are the interfaces I want from the CoHexagon.
        qi[0].pIID = &IID_IShapeEdit;
        qi[1].pIID = &IID_IDraw;
        // Create the remote CoHexagon.
        CoCreateInstanceEx(CLSID_Hexagon,              // CLSID of object.
                        NULL,
                        CLSCTX_REMOTE_SERVER,          // CLSCTX
                        &csi,                          // Machine information.
                        2,                             // Items in MULTI_QI array.
                        qi);                           // MULTI_QI array.
        // Assign interface pointers to fetched results
        // (could check each HRESULT...)
        IDraw* pDraw = (IDraw*)qi[0].pItf;
        IShapeEdit* pSE = (IShapeEdit*)qi[1].pItf;
        pDraw->Draw();
...
}
```

Time for a lab that will give you a chance to work with dcomcnfg.exe and programmatic remote activation. When you have finished this lab, it is time to rejoice, as you will no longer be subjected to raw COM development using C++, REG files, or nasty source code ports. From here on out it is all about ATL (for the most part). I guarantee your hard work over the last five chapters will serve you well in all your future COM and ATL endeavors.

Lab 5-2: Accessing a Remote Server Using DCOM

This lab will give you the chance to experiment with remote server access. First off, you will configure a server on a remote machine, specifying various security settings using dcomcnfg.exe. Next you will access your remote server with an existing C++ client using both approaches discussed in this chapter (configuration and code). Needless to say, you must be connected to one other computer to work through this lab.

 The solution for this lab can be found on your CD-ROM under:
Labs\Chapter 05\CPP Remote Client

Step One: Register the Server on the Remote Machine

Create a folder on the remote server machine to hold the required files. Copy the following files from the client machine to the server's folder:

■ The server's REG file.

■ The server's type library file (*.tlb).

■ The server binary you created in Lab 5-1 (CoCarEXE.exe).

Next, run the server once on the remote machine to force a call to LoadTypeLibEx(). This will ensure your server's interfaces and type information are registered on the remote host. Verify you have the correct HKCR\Interface and HKCR\TypeLib entries using regedit.exe.

Next, open the REG file on the remote machine for editing. Be sure that the LocalServer32 key points to the correct path on the server machine (if not, make the necessary edits now before merging). Merge this file into the system registry and verify the correct ProgID and CLSID listings, again using regedit.exe.

Now that your remote server has been properly registered with the system, we need to assign some security options to the EXE.

Step Two: Secure the Server on the Remote Machine

We will not add any high-level security measures to the remote CoCar server, but instead take the low road, and opt for easy configuration (perfect for a lab). Open up dcomcnfg.exe on the server machine, locate your ProgID from the Applications tab, and pull up the corresponding AppID property page by double-clicking on the ProgID.

Using the Security tab, edit the ACL for both launch and access permissions to include the name of your remote client. Again, to keep it simple, simply add **Everyone** into each ACL.

Under the Identity tab, be sure you select the **Interactive User.** Although this is not recommended for production-level COM servers, this option is often essential for debugging. This is especially true in this case, since we must be able to view message boxes on the remote machine, and the Interactive User is the only setting that will allow a COM server to display a GUI.

This finishes up the server configuration. Now, change keyboards, and return to your development (client) machine.

Step Three: Configure the Client Machine

Begin by launching dcomcnfg.exe. The first step is to redirect the client machine to go remote. Locate the AppID for your CoCar EXE server and launch its property page. Under the Location tab, specify the name of the remote machine (whatever that may be), and deselect the Run application on this computer setting:

Figure 5-36:
Specifying the
remote server.

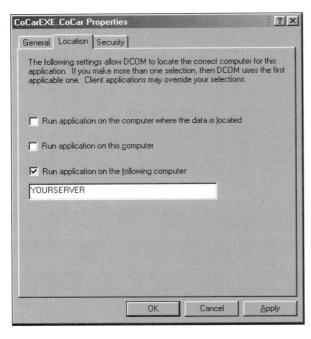

Recall that this modification will be
held under the RemoteServerName
value of the COM object's AppID.

Now, run your existing client
from Lab 5-1 (or assemble a simple
VB client). You should hear some
whirling away on each machine, followed by the two message boxes
appearing on the remote monitor,
courtesy of your IStats interface.
This is location transparency at its
finest. We had no need to alter a single line of code. The universal
marshaler took us from point A to
point B automatically.

Step Four: Programmatic Access to your Remote Server

As the final step of this lab, we will change our client's code base to make use of the
DCOM-centric COM library items. Before you do, open up dcomcnfg.exe one more time
and "roll back" the client changes you have just made.

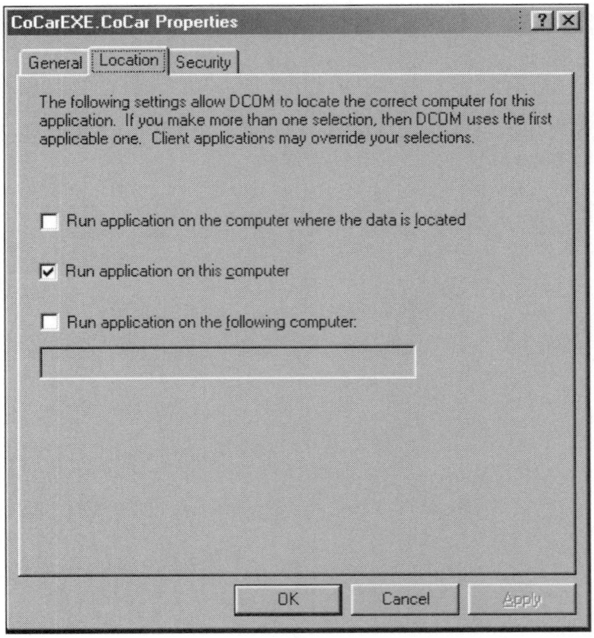

Figure 5-37:
Reset the
location of the
DCOM server.

Run the client again and verify that
CarEXEServer.exe has launched on
your local machine. Remember, programmatic DCOM will always
overwrite any RemoteServerName
values. Therefore, there is no need
to set a RemoteServerName value
when writing DCOM code in the
raw.

Now open up a C++ client project workspace, and modify (or
create) main() to behave as follows:

1. Create a COSERVERINFO structure, and set the pwszName field to be the name of your remote host.

2. Create an array of MULTI_QI structures to hold each interface you wish to fetch. Set the pIID fields to each index in the array to your named IID values.

3. Call CoCreateInstanceEx(), passing in your structures and other parameters. Be sure to set the CLSCTX flag to CLSCTX_REMOTE_SERVER.

4. If CoCreateInstanceEx() succeeds, assign fetch interface pointers to a local interface variable (don't forget that MULTI_QI returns the HRESULTs for each QueryInterface() attempt).

Here is the complete C++ client code, front to back:

```
//The steps above equate to the following code:
#define _WIN32_DCOM
#include <windows.h>
#include "CarServerEXETypeInfo_i.c"      // MIDL file.
#include "CarServerEXETypeInfo.h"        // MIDL file.
int main(int argc, char* argv[])
{
    CoInitialize(NULL);
    COSERVERINFO csi = {0};
    // -> ADD YOUR SERVER NAME HERE!!!!!!!! <-
    csi.pwszName = L"YOURSERVER";
    // Here are the interfaces I want.
    MULTI_QI qi[3] = {0};
    qi[0].pIID = &IID_IEngine;
    qi[1].pIID = &IID_IStats;
    qi[2].pIID = &IID_ICreateCar;
    // Create the remote CoCar.
    CoCreateInstanceEx(CLSID_CoCar, NULL, CLSCTX_REMOTE_SERVER, &csi, 3, qi);
    // Assign interface pointers to fetched results.
    IEngine* pEngine = (IEngine*)qi[0].pItf;
    IStats* pStats = (IStats*)qi[1].pItf;
    ICreateCar* pCCar = (ICreateCar*)qi[2].pItf;
    // Exercise the car.
    BSTR name;
    name = SysAllocString(L"Cindy");
    pCCar->SetPetName(name);
    pCCar->SetMaxSpeed(40);
    pStats->DisplayStats();
    SysFreeString(name);
    // Clean up.
    pCCar->Release();
    pStats->Release();
    pEngine->Release();
    CoUninitialize();
    return 0;
}
```

Now, run the program on the client machine. You should see the same message boxes pop up on the remote server, this time using programmatic DCOM. The patiently waiting client is shown in Figure 5-38.

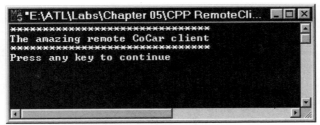

Figure 5-38: From C structure to DCOM server in five easy chapters.

If you have remained diligent and worked through these first five chapters, you have most certainly developed a solid understanding of core COM. As you have most likely realized, doing raw COM development can be a long and winding road. Although it is completely possible, creating COM servers is straight C++ and IDL can be an error-prone experience.

The Active Template Library (ATL) provides the help you need to remain focused on your application's logic by providing framework support for the necessary "COM goo." Now that you have a firm background in the basics of COM development using IDL and C++, it is time to turn to the world of ATL.

Chapter Summary

This chapter gave you the lowdown on COM's location transparency. We began by reviewing the three relationships a client and server may take: in-proc, local, and remote. From here, we discovered that stubs and proxies are the keys to making a server's physical location an unnecessary detail in a client's mind. We dug into the stub/proxy architecture, and discovered a set of new COM interfaces and the associated managers that help stubs and proxies communicate with the RPC layer.

Next we examined COM's marshaling options. Custom marshaling allows you to have complete control over the process of moving data between processes using the IMarshal interface. Standard marshaling is almost free when you write your interfaces in IDL, leaving you to the task of creating the DLL for this stub/proxy. Universal marshaling is as free as you can get, as you have no need to worry about a separate DLL to distribute; however, you must constrict all your interfaces to use variant compliant parameters, and configure each interface to point to the CLSID of the universal marshaler.

We examined how to create a local server. As you have seen, this requires a new way to work with server lifetime management, as class factories must remain active as long as there is a connected client. We then examined the AppID, and saw the various ways that we can configure security contexts for our servers. Finally, you learned how to use the dcomcnfg.exe utility to configure and access remote servers, and wrapped up by examining remote access on the programmatic level using the COM library.

Part 3

Core ATL

Chapter 6

An Introduction to the Active Template Library

Objectives:

- **Generate component housing with the ATL COM AppWizard.**
- **Insert coclasses using the ATL Object Wizard.**
- **Understand ATL's registry scripting language.**
- **Populate your interfaces with methods à la ATL.**
- **Learn to add properties to a COM interface.**
- **Leverage ATL's support for COM text manipulation.**
- **Understand ATL's debugging options.**

So far, this book has focused on the development of COM DLLs and EXEs using IDL and the C++ programming language. As you may have noticed, writing your COM servers without framework support is a "labor of love" and is often not the best approach for a large-scale COM project, given the sheer amount of repeat code. On the upside, however, ATL is of little use to developers who lack a firm understanding of the underpinnings of COM, which you have gained during the previous five chapters. The purpose of this chapter is to get you up and running with ATL and the common CASE tools used during the development process. In this chapter we will not be diving in too deeply into the underlying internals of ATL, leaving that task for the remainder of the book.

The Need for ATL

Up until this point in your COM journey, you have been writing every line of source code from scratch. Chapters 3, 4, and 5 were devoted to illustrating what can be done with "raw COM" using C++ and IDL. I hope you have found that although COM can be a bit much to swallow in one session, it can eventually be digested into fairly clear pieces. However, I would also imagine you noticed the following points about implementing COM servers "in the raw":

- Implementing component housing requires similar code for every DLL server. In essence, what really changes is the code behind DllGetClassObject(). Based on a CLSID, create the correct class factory and return an interface pointer to the client. EXE servers are just about the same in this regard. Call CoRegisterClassObject() *n* times for *n* number of class factories, revoking them when WinMain() is shutting down.
- COM class factories are all very similar. A class object basically requires modifying IClassFactory::CreateInstance() to specify the name of the coclass you are creating.
- All COM objects implement IUnknown, which basically means two lines of code for every interface supported by the object, as well as hooks for reference counting.
- Adding the correct registry entries for a COM server is (to put it kindly) a pain. Typically, servers register AppID, ProgID, CLSID, TypeLib, and interface information.

In short, COM requires lots of boilerplate code. These days, no sane developer would begin a new COM project from scratch—unless you need to learn the basic building blocks of COM. After that point, you really should adopt a component framework to help you with the repeat code demanded by COM.

The Active Template Library (ATL) supplies the help you have been longing for. This collection of C++ templates, macros, and classes is aimed at helping you develop very small and very fast COM servers. ATL contains code to assist you when developing traditional COM objects, ActiveX controls, Automation servers, MTS components, and MMC Snap Ins as well as full-blown Windows executables. As an added bonus, ATL 3.0 has extended the number of CASE tools, giving you just about as much flexibility and support as MFC developers have grown accustomed to.

Much like MFC, ATL projects begin by accessing CASE tools to provide a minimal and complete code base for the project at hand. The ATL COM AppWizard is used to create the component housing for your COM server and is typically followed by using the ATL Object Wizard to insert any number of coclasses into their new home.

Unlike MFC, ATL has much slimmer support for Windows application development. This does not imply you could not use ATL to build the next version of Microsoft Word or a high-profile graphics application. What this does imply is that ATL does not offer you the full set of wizards, data structures, and helper classes found in a Windows application framework such as MFC.

For example, there is no Dialog Data Exchange (DDX) support in ATL. You do not have utility classes (such as CPoint, CRect, CPen, and so forth) wrapping Windows drawing primitives. ATL is a component framework aimed at helping you build robust COM servers. To this end, if you are a C++ developer, ATL is the absolute best choice around. Specifically, ATL is here to help you with the following aspects of your COM server development (among others):

- ATL supplies all necessary component housing code for DLL and EXE COM servers.
- ATL provides support for IUnknown using a table-driven implementation of QueryInterface().
- ATL provides a default class factory for every ATL coclass. If you require a more sophisticated class object, ATL will help you develop your own.
- ATL provides server self-registration, avoiding messy REG file maintenance.

■ ATL also offers support for a number of COM services we have yet to discover: rich error information, dual interfaces, and connection points, as well as support for COM threading models and object aggregation.

I'm sure this partial list has you sold already, so let's begin to get our hands around the Active Template Library.

What Exactly is ATL?

Physically, ATL is not much more than a number of header files (and a few CPP files) installed under the ATL\Include subdirectory of MS Visual Studio (see Figure 6-1).

Figure 6-1:
Behold ATL.

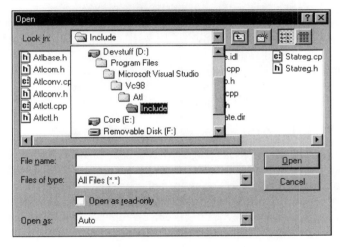

As we will be digging into a number of these files throughout the remainder of this book, the following table presents a roadmap describing the sort of code you can expect to find in the ATL file set (grouped by related functionality):

ATL Source Code File	Meaning in Life
<atlwin.h> <atlwin.cpp> <atlhost.h>	ATL's support for window and dialog development. <atlhost.h> is new to ATL 3.0, which defines support for building ActiveX control host windows.
<atldb.h> <atldbcli.h> <atldbsch.h>	OLE DB support.
<atlsnap.h>	ATL's support for MMC Snap In development.
<atlctl.h> <atlctl.cpp>	ATL's support for ActiveX control development.
<atliface.idl> <atliface.h>	IDL code for ATL-defined COM interfaces and the MIDL-generated header file.
<altconv.h> <atlconv.cpp>	Defines a number of conversion functions and macros to work with COM string manipulation.
<atldef.h>	ATL preprocessor symbols (#defines).

ATL Source Code File	Meaning in Life
<statreg.h> <statreg.cpp>	ATL support for self-registration.
<atlbase.h>	The core ATL file that defines the framework support for your COM servers, COM wrapper classes, and debugging aids.
<atlcom.h>	Support for IUnknown, automation, enumerators, and COM persistence. Aggregation support, default class objects, and COM map macros are also defined in <atlcom.h>.
<atlimpl.cpp>	Implementations of various ATL classes. Heap allocation operators (used if you choose not to link to the C runtime).

For the most part, the correct files will be included into your project based on the configuration of the ATL COM AppWizard and the type of coclass selected from the ATL Object Wizard. At times, however, you will need to include various files manually, as ATL attempts to include the minimal and complete set of header files. For example, unless you are developing an inherently GUI-based coclass (such as an ActiveX control), you cannot access the Windows support provided by <atlwin.h> until you include this file in your precompiled header.

The Division of Labor: ATL and You

When developers make the choice to leverage existing code provided by a framework, the first task is to understand where the framework support ends and your work begins. ATL is a component framework comprised of a number of wizards, C++ templates, classes, and macros. The framework provides implementations for many standard COM interfaces, server housing support, and various types of coclasses. Furthermore, a coclass may support any number of ATL-supplied COM services, such as connection points, COM error support, threading models, and so on.

However, ATL can only take you half the way home. ATL has little idea what your specific programming tasks will entail. Therefore, while ATL can most certainly provide support for the necessary COM goo most solutions require, you pick up the ball and extend the wizard-generated code to finalize your COM project for your specific needs.

You will still be required to provide the following: First off, you cannot escape a solid understanding of COM itself. If you read the first five chapters in this book, you are in a perfect position to leverage ATL. Next, ATL does not remove you from writing IDL code. While the ATL wizards set up minimal IDL code in many ways, you will still need to define all your COM interfaces in IDL syntax.

Finally, as you have made the choice to leverage a component framework, you now have an additional responsibility: You need to understand the ATL framework. As previously mentioned, this chapter gives you the minimal and complete set of tools to build ATL COM servers. The next several chapters will dive headlong into the inner workings of ATL, as well as introduce more advanced COM and ATL topics.

Creating Component Housing with the ATL COM AppWizard

Your ATL projects begin by accessing the ATL COM AppWizard located under the File | New menu selection of the Visual C++ IDE (see Figure 6-2).

Figure 6-2:
Creating a new
ATL project
workspace.

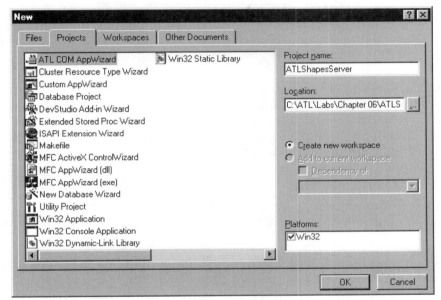

Once you provide the name of your ATL project, you will be presented with a one-step CASE tool named the ATL COM AppWizard, as shown in Figure 6-3. Based on your initial selections, you will receive a number of starter files representing your component housing.

Figure 6-3:
The ATL COM
AppWizard is
used to
generate
boilerplate code
for your
component
housing.

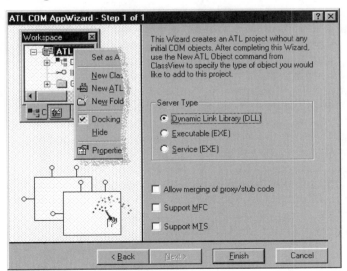

The ATL COM AppWizard offers four configuration choices used in constructing your component home. Below is an overview of the ATL COM AppWizard selections.

 In this chapter we will be investigating an in-process server named ATLShapesServer.dll with <u>no</u> support for MFC, MTS, or merging of stub/proxy code. This project is included on the companion CD under the Labs\Chapter 06 subdirectory.

Specifying the Type of Server Housing

The Server Type section allows you to specify how you wish to package your COM objects. As we have already written in-proc, local, and remote servers in the first part of this book, these choices should be relatively clear.

■ **Dynamic Link Library:** The ATL COM AppWizard will generate component housing for a COM-based DLL (in-proc) server. All DLL export functions will be fully implemented, and exposed through an associated DEF file.

■ **Executable:** The ATL COM AppWizard will generate component housing for a COM-based EXE. A WinMain() implementation will be provided on your behalf.

■ **Service:** The ATL COM AppWizard will generate component housing code for an EXE server which may be run as an NT service, a local server, or a remote server.

Once you have decided on the type of component housing, you have three remaining choices to make before beginning to insert coclasses into the AppWizard-generated code.

> **Note:** Each of the remaining options are only available when you create in-process (DLL) servers. Although it is possible to implement an EXE server using these options, you will be making the necessary modifications by hand.

Allow Merging of Proxy/Stub Code

You already know quite a bit about the role stubs and proxies play in COM development. Recall that if you restrict your COM servers to use only VARIANT compliant types, you can leverage the universal (type library) marshaler, and will not need a custom proxy/stub DLL at all. If you plan to use [oleautomation] restricted interfaces (as well as dual interfaces, which we address later), there is no need to check this box, as you will end up with a small amount of code bloat that is not actually required.

If you plan to build interfaces falling <u>outside</u> of the range of VARIANT compliant types, checking this option will add the necessary hooks to allow the custom proxy/stub code to be bundled inside of your DLL server, resulting in one less file to distribute. Of course, keep in mind that you are <u>never required</u> to merge your stub/proxy DLL into your in-proc server (every DLL server will work just fine if this option is unselected). This is just another design step to consider as you build your COM servers.

If you do select this option, the ATL COM AppWizard will generate two extra files for your project: dlldatax.h and dlldatax.c. As you recall, every COM-based DLL server must export DllCanUnloadNow(), DllRegisterServer(), DllUnregisterServer(), and DllGetClassObject() to interact with the COM runtime. In order to circumvent the name clashes resulting from two sets of DLL entry points (your server DLL and the stub/proxy DLL), dlldatax.c adjusts the entry points for the stub/proxy DLL:

```
// dlldatax.c
// Server exports            stub/proxy exports
#define DllMain              PrxDllMain
#define DllRegisterServer    PrxDllRegisterServer
#define DllUnregisterServer  PrxDllUnregisterServer
#define DllGetClassObject    PrxDllGetClassObject
#define DllCanUnloadNow      PrxDllCanUnloadNow
```

Dlldatax.h prototypes each "Prx-" function, which are implemented as in dlldatax.c as simple stub code. For example, here is the stub code for PrxDllCanUnloadNow():

```
// 'Prx-' functions are implemented as stub code to avoid name clashes
// resulting from two sets of DLL export functions.
STDAPI PrxDllCanUnloadNow(void)
{
    return S_OK;
}
```

The remaining "Prx-" methods are implemented with similar stub code. In this way, the server is able to define one set of DLL exports. Now, although these files have been included into your project workspace, you must manually configure them before the stub and proxy code is actually merged into your server DLL. This three-step process begins by right-clicking on dlldatax.c (from FileView) and selecting Settings from the resulting context menu. From the General tab of the Project Settings dialog box, uncheck the Exclude file from build option:

Figure 6-4:
Including
dlldatax.c into
your project's
build.

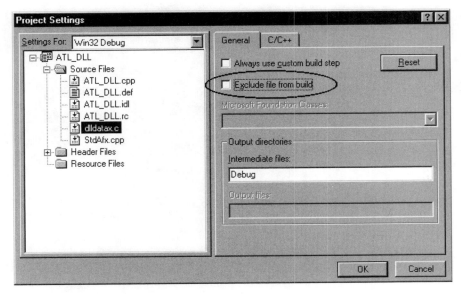

Next, from the C/C++ tab, configure dlldatax.c with the Not using precompiled headers option, from the Precompiled Headers category (see Figure 6-5):

Figure 6-5:
Removing
precompiled
header
dependencies
from dlldatax.c.

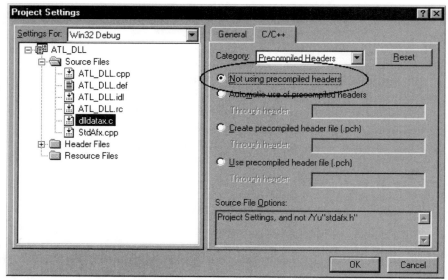

Finally, define the _MERGE_PROXYSTUB symbol for your program from the C/C++ tab under the Preprocessor category:

Figure 6-6:
The final step to
merge your
stub/proxy DLL:
define the
preprocessor
symbol
MERGE
PROXYSTUB.

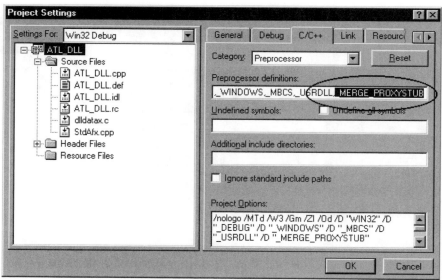

At this point, your stub/proxy code will be merged into your DLL server. Doing so, however, is left to your discretion, as we will not do so in this book.

Note: You must have at least one ATL coclass in your project before compiling a project merging stub and proxy code, as dlldatax.c is including dlldata.c, which will not exist until the MIDL compiler is run!

Support MFC (just say no)

This choice allows your ATL project to leverage the Microsoft Foundation Class (MFC) library. The chances of you needing to select this option should be slim to none. By doing so, you tie your ATL code to the MFC runtime library, and therefore must ensure the MFC runtime DLL is installed (and shipped) along with your ATL COM server. Most developers who feel compelled to select this option reason that there are a handful of MFC classes that they simply cannot live without (CString being the biggest offender). Resist this temptation! Although the CComBSTR class provided by ATL is not as robust as MFC's CString, it does provide you with a subset of the same functionality. With a bit of extra coding on your part, you can avoid dependency upon the MFC runtime DLL (which is approximately 970K in size). To illustrate:

```
// This string cost me 970K, enough said.
CString strWasItWorthIt;
strWasItWorthIt = "no";
```

In all fairness, there are times when linking to the MFC runtime might be beneficial. If you are developing a COM server which is only to be used by some legacy MFC application, you may wish to support MFC. Even then, however, you may wish to create an MFC COM server from the onset, as MFC COM servers can be easier to develop than ATL COM servers (more often than not).

Support Microsoft Transaction Server (MTS)

Checking this option will configure your project to access and interact with the MTS runtime by linking your project with the MTS libraries (mtx.lib and mtxguid.lib). MTS is a "super surrogate" that will host your COM-based DLL servers and provide a robust runtime environment, which we will not concern ourselves with at this time.

Confirming the New Project

The New Project Information dialog, shown in Figure 6-7, summarizes your selections. Once you select the component type and configure support for MFC, MTS, and merging of stub/proxy code, the wizard will whirl away for a moment, and dump a handful of new files into your project subdirectory.

Figure 6-7:
New Project
confirmation
dialog.

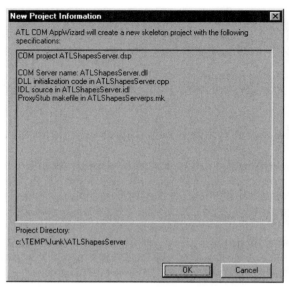

At this point you can fully compile your DLL or EXE server; however, you will have a very lonely dwelling as no COM objects have yet been invited to the party. COM objects are inserted into ATL component housing using another CASE tool, the ATL Object Wizard. Before we begin inserting coclasses, let's examine the files generated by the ATL COM AppWizard.

Examining the Initial ATL DLL Project Files

If you examine the ClassView tab for your new ATL DLL project, you will see a number of familiar-looking functions located under the Globals folder:

Figure 6-8:
Your initial ATL
DLL project.

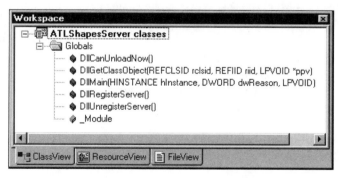

After the initial compile (which automatically runs MIDL), you will have the complete set of files representing your component housing. The following table lists your new files, grouped by related functionality.

> **Note:**   Of course, the names of many of these files will depend on the name given to your ATL project.

AppWizard Generated Files	Meaning in Life
stdafx.h stdafx.cpp	Precompiled header files. Includes the core ATL files into your current project.
ATLShapesServer.cpp	Implements the DLL export functions for this server enlisting help from the ATL class, CComModule. Also defines a DllMain() implementation to initialize and terminate the CComModule instance and declares the server's OBJECT_MAP.
ATLShapesServer.def	Exports your DLL functions.
ATLShapesServer.idl	Your project's IDL file, doing nothing more at this point than declaring an empty library statement.
ATLShapesServer.h ATLShapesServer_i.c ATLShapesServer_p.c dlldata.c ATLShapesServer.tlb	MIDL-generated files to hold your C/C++ interface bindings, GUID definitions, proxy/stub code (including DLL exports), and the binary type library. Dlldata.c and ATLShapesServer_p.c are generated after you insert an ATL coclass and rerun MIDL.
ATLShapesServerps.mk ATLShapesServerps.def	ATL generated makefile and DEF file to build your stub/proxy DLL using the nmake.exe utility (and thus removing the need to create a separate DLL project to build the stub/proxy DLL).
resource.h ATLShapesServer.rc	Minimal resource files for this project.

The MIDL-generated files (ATLShapesServer.h, ATLShapesServer_i.c, ATLShapes-Server_p.c, ATLShapesServer.tlb, and dlldata.c) should be no surprise to you at this point, so we will not comment on them further. The following is a more detailed look at the remaining AppWizard generated files.

Initial Project Resources

ATL projects do contain some minimal resources, as defined by your resource.h and ATLShapesServer.rc files. If you expand the subfolders from the ResourceView tab (Figure 6-9) you will see support for a project-wide string table as well as a version information resource.

Figure 6-9: Default ATL resources.

> **Note:** Much like MFC's CString class, ATL's CComBSTR provides a LoadString() method which reads a string resource from the project's String Table.

To insert additional resources into your ATL projects, go under the Insert | Resource menu selection and select the required resource from the resulting dialog box. Just like an MFC project, each additional resource type results in a new subdirectory.

Precompiled Header Files

Much like an MFC project, ATL provides you with stdafx.h and stdafx.cpp files, working as your project's precompiled headers. Here is a peek inside stdafx.h:

```
// stdafx.h file
#ifndef _WIN32_WINNT
#define _WIN32_WINNT 0x0400
#endif
#define _ATL_APARTMENT_THREADED
#include <atlbase.h>
extern CComModule _Module;
#include <atlcom.h>
```

The _ATL_APARTMENT_THREADED symbol marks the default threading model for this server (more on threading in Chapter 7). Note the extern reference to _Module. This object is an instance of ATL's CComModule class that is the backbone for your component housing implementation. This object <u>must</u> be named _Module, as a number of ATL header files (such as <atlcom.h>) reference it by name.

> **Note:** By way of a friendly reminder, be aware that each and every *.cpp file in your ATL projects (including those you create by hand) must include stdafx.h as the very first line, or else you will get the dreaded: "fatal error C1010: unexpected end of file while looking for precompiled header directive" compiler error.

The Skeleton IDL File

The generated IDL file contains just enough code to force MIDL to generate an empty type library for the server. Notice that you have already been provided with a LIBID for the type library, which you are free to change if need be:

```
// The initial IDL file for ATL COM AppWizard projects.
import "oaidl.idl";
import "ocidl.idl";
[
    uuid(4A01DCF1-066C-11D3-B8E5-0020781238D4),
    version(1.0),
    helpstring("ATLShapesServer 1.0 Type Library")
]
library ATLSHAPESSERVERLib
{
```

```
    importlib("stdole32.tlb");
    importlib("stdole2.tlb");
};
```

The various ATL wizards maintain this file for you in many respects. When you use the ATL Object Wizard to insert coclasses into the component home, the IDL file is automatically updated. However, you will need to edit this file by hand when you wish to define new COM interfaces and/or modify the wizard-generated IDL code.

Your Component Housing File: ATLShapesServer.cpp

The major workhorse in the new project is ATLShapesServer.cpp, which implements the DLL exports for the server. ATL has already included a corresponding DEF file into your project, so the detail of exposing the DLL export functions is of no concern to you. Each of your DLL exports is implemented with help from the ATL class CComModule. Many methods of CComModule make use of an ATL object map.

We have much to say about the object map at a later time; however, for now just understand that each coclass contained in your server <u>must</u> be listed in this map, or else it cannot be created or registered by the ATL framework. Many methods of CComModule will iterate over the object map in order to create class factories, as well as ask a coclass to (un)register itself into the system.

> **Note:** The CComModule class of ATL provides a similar service as the CWinApp class in MFC. Both classes are used to encapsulate the details of the necessary "goo" for DLL and EXE projects.

Located at the top of ATLShapesServer.cpp is the global instance of the CComModule class and its related object map:

```
// ATLShapesServer.cpp
// _Module encapsulates the details of DLL and EXE server housing.
CComModule _Module;
// The object map maintains a list of all coclasses contained in the server.
BEGIN_OBJECT_MAP(ObjectMap)
END_OBJECT_MAP()
```

After the definition of your CComModule object you find the DLL export functions. The CarInProcServer.dll server we created "in the raw," did not require a DllMain() entry point, as we had no server-level initialization or termination related code. As far as COM is concerned, this DLL export is strictly optional.

In ATL, DllMain() is used to initialize and destroy the CComModule object. When a client process is connecting to the server, the dwReason parameter of DllMain() will be set to DLL_PROCESS_ATTACH. On the other hand, if the DLL is being unloaded, the dwReason parameter is set to DLL_PROCESS_DETACH. Based on this value, CComModule is configured by a call to Init() or Term(), respectively:

```
// Initialize or terminate the CComModule object based on dwReason.
BOOL WINAPI DllMain(    HINSTANCE hInstance,
                        DWORD dwReason,
                        LPVOID /*lpReserved*/)
{
    ...
```

```
        if (dwReason == DLL_PROCESS_ATTACH)
        {
                // Prep the internal state of the CComModule object.
                _Module.Init(    ObjectMap, hInstance,
                                 &LIBID_ATLSHAPESSERVERLib);
        }
        // Clean up the CComModule object.
        else if (dwReason == DLL_PROCESS_DETACH)
                _Module.Term();
        return TRUE; // ok
}
```

The remainder of ATLShapesServer.cpp contains implementation code for the DLL
exports. Given what you already know, you should feel comfortable with the signatures of
these methods, and understand when they are called. DllCanUnloadNow() is implemented
by a single call to CComModule::GetLockCount(), which returns the number of server
locks and active objects in the server:

```
// Returns S_OK if server contains no active objects and no server locks.
STDAPI DllCanUnloadNow(void)
{
        return (_Module.GetLockCount() == 0) ? S_OK : S_FALSE;
}
```

DllGetClassObject() is implemented by calling the GetClassObject() method of
CComModule. GetClassObject() consults the server's object map in order to determine
which class factory to create for the client:

```
// Return a class object pointer (IClassFactory) to the client.
STDAPI DllGetClassObject(REFCLSID rclsid, REFIID riid, LPVOID* ppv)
{
        return _Module.GetClassObject(rclsid, riid, ppv);
}
```

Finally, ATL in-process servers export the DllRegisterServer() and DllUnregisterServer()
functions. When a COM server provides registration logic to the outside world, the server
is termed *self-registering*. Our CarInProcServer.dll server did not implement these functions, but instead relied on a REG file to install the correct registry listings. Not so in
ATL! The CComModule class provides methods that automatically install or remove the
server's type information: RegisterServer() and UnregisterServer().

```
// Enter all necessary registry entries into the system registry.
STDAPI DllRegisterServer(void)
{
        // Registers coclasses, typelib, and all interfaces (if marked with
        // the [oleautomation] attribute) as defined in the type library
        return _Module.RegisterServer(TRUE);
}
// Remove all necessary registry entries from the system registry.
STDAPI DllUnregisterServer(void)
{
        return _Module.UnregisterServer(TRUE);
}
```

Registering Self-Registering Servers

One question that should strike you at this point is "who calls these self-registration functions?" First off, ATL projects automatically register DLL and EXE projects as part of the build process, so your COM servers are always available for you to test against on your development machine. When it comes time to ship the server to another machine, you may opt to register your servers with the aid of a professional installation program. These tools have vendor-specific means to register DLL and EXE servers. If your COM servers are part of a larger stand-alone Windows application, this is sure to be the option for you.

Another approach used to register your COM servers is to use the regsvr32.exe utility. From a command prompt window, navigate to the directory containing the DLL server you wish to register, and send in the name of the DLL as a command line argument (Figure 6-10). If successful, you will see a resulting confirmation message box. You may unregister a server by providing the -u switch (e.g., regsvr32 -u atlshapesserver.dll).

Figure 6-10:
Registering a
DLL with
regsvr32.exe

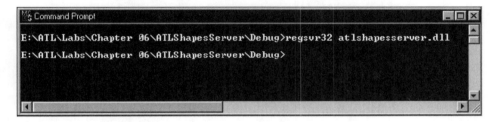

```
Command Prompt                                                        _ □ X

E:\ATL\Labs\Chapter  06\ATLShapesServer\Debug>regsvr32 atlshapesserver.dll

E:\ATL\Labs\Chapter  06\ATLShapesServer\Debug>
```

EXE servers are not registered with the regsvr32.exe utility. Instead, WinMain() is implemented to check for the -regserver or -unregserver command line arguments (proper EXE servers also check for /regserver or /unregserver). Again, from a command prompt, navigate to the directory containing the EXE server you wish to register, and execute it with the appropriate flag:

Figure 6-11:
Registering an
EXE server at
the command
line.

```
Command Prompt                                                        _ □ X

E:\ATL\Labs\Chapter  06\ATLEXEShapesServer\Debug>atlexeshapesserver.exe -regserver

E:\ATL\Labs\Chapter  06\ATLEXEShapesServer\Debug>
```

Testing for the -regserver or -unregserver arguments in a WinMain implementation is no problem at all. Simply do a string compare between WinMain()'s LPSTR parameter and the token strings. If you find either, make calls into the Win32 registry API to install or remove the correct registry settings:

```
// Check LPSTR parameter to determine (un)registration command.
int APIENTRY WinMain(HINSTANCE hInstance, HINSTANCE hPrevInstance,
                  LPSTR lpCmdLine, int nCmdShow)
{
      if(strstr(lpCmdLine, "/regserver") || strstr(lpCmdLine, "-regserver"))
            // Stuff information into registry.
```

```
if(strstr(lpCmdLine, "/unregserver") || strstr(lpCmdLine, "-unregserver"))
    // Remove information from registry.
...
}
```

The ATL Object Wizard

Once you have created the component housing using the ATL COM AppWizard, you need to insert the coclasses themselves. To insert ATL-based COM classes into your project, you access the ATL Object Wizard. Activate this tool by right-clicking on your project node from ClassView, and select New ATL Object from the context menu (this tool is also available from the Insert | New ATL Object menu selection as well as the ATL toolbar).

Figure 6-12: Accessing the Object Wizard.

> **Note:**   Many of ATL's wizards are accessed from the ClassView tab. If you are not in the habit of using this aspect of the VC++ IDE, begin doing so now.

The Object Wizard specifies four categories of COM objects that you may insert into your component home, as shown in Figure 6-13. While you use the ATL COM AppWizard once per project, the Object Wizard is used numerous times throughout the development of your ATL COM servers. A single server may contain any number of, and types of, ATL objects. Be aware, however, that some objects make little sense in the context of EXE servers (such as ActiveX controls, which are always loaded in-proc).

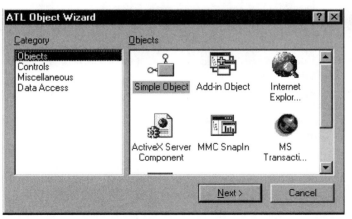

Figure 6-13: The ATL Object Wizard allows you to insert COM objects into component housing generated by the ATL COM AppWizard.

Following is a breakdown of each object type.

The Objects Category

The Objects category allow you to insert "traditional" object types as well as more specialized COM items such as MMC Snap Ins. In general, selections from the Objects category do not provide much by way of an interactive user interface, but instead focus on COM-based "business objects" (i.e., no GUI and all logic). Here is a rundown of each selection from the Objects category:

■ **Simple Object:** If you are interested in creating a COM "business object" containing no user interface, this will be your object of choice. These objects are equipped with an IUnknown implementation and a default class factory. This is the "minimal and complete" coclass.

■ **Add-in Object:** This selection allows you to create a COM component that integrates into the Visual C++ IDE, complete with a toolbar button and event handling support, allowing your coclass to respond to various Visual Studio commands. Objects of this type support and implement the IDSAddIn interface which provides the methods for the VC IDE and your object to communicate.

■ **Internet Explorer Object:** A coclass with the necessary interfaces required by Internet Explorer, but without a UI. This coclass implements the IObjectWithSite interface, which provides a lightweight way to "site" your object in the container, allowing the object to communicate with IE. ATL provides an implementation of this interface with the IObjectWithSiteImpl<> template.

■ **ActiveX Server Component:** A non-GUI server-side coclass equipped to run in an Active Server Page (ASP) under Internet Information Server (IIS). Allows the object to handle Request, Session, Response, Application, and Server objects.

■ **MMC SnapIn:** Creates a COM framework used to create an extension to the Microsoft Management Console (MMC). Provides support for object persistence as well as the required COM interfaces used to communicate with the MMC GUI shell (such as menus, property sheets, and toolbars).

■ **MTS Component:** Creates a new coclass configured to run under control of the Microsoft Transaction Server (MTS) runtime. The property sheet for MTS objects provides an option to support the IObjectControl interface which allows an object running under the MTS runtime to do any necessary initialization or clean up when it is activated or deactivated by the MTS runtime.

■ **Component Registrar Object:** Creates a coclass supporting the IComponentRegistrar interface. This allows you to develop an object providing programmatic control over the process of registering and unregistering components in your server. ATL projects already provide default registration support operating on every coclass defined in the object map; however, if you wish to selectively register or unregister <u>individual</u> objects in a server, this is the option for you.

The Controls Category

The next set of options comes by way of the Controls category as shown in Figure 6-14.

Figure 6-14: Types of ActiveX controls supported by ATL 3.0.

Here you will find three different variations of GUI-based ActiveX controls, each providing a Lite and Full version. Full controls support the entire set of necessary COM interfaces needed to function in any ActiveX-compliant container. The only down side of Full controls is you may end up with implementation code you will never access (depending on the requirements of the container), resulting in some marginal code bloat.

Lite controls are slimmed-down versions of their Full counterparts and do offer a smaller footprint; however, they are not guaranteed to function in each and every ActiveX control container. For example, Lite controls will not function correctly if placed inside MS Office 97 containers. Chances are, you can live with a small amount of code bloat for the resulting peace of mind. Here are the choices provided by the Controls section:

- **Full/Lite Controls:** A traditional ActiveX control. Supports the required COM interfaces for screen rendering, property persistence, and in-place activation.
- **Full/Lite Composite Controls:** ActiveX controls which may contain other ActiveX controls as part of their makeup. Visual Basic developers (since the release of VB 5) have been given the ability to create ActiveX controls in a drag-and-drop environment. ATL composite controls provide similar support for C++ developers.
- **Full/Lite HTML Controls:** Creates a control project supporting DHTML. This ATL object type allows you to create controls that can access the IE object model, which in turn provides access to the rendering, scripting, and browsing support provided by the container.
- **Property Page:** Although not an ActiveX control, property pages are also found under the Controls category, as they provide a design-time mechanism used to configure ActiveX controls.

Remaining Object Wizard Selections

As for the remaining two Object Wizard selections, the Miscellaneous category currently provides only a single selection: dialog box. This option allows you to insert a traditional Windows dialog box into your server project. These dialogs are implemented with help from ATL base classes, but provide no COM-related functionality (for example, ATL dialog boxes do not implement any COM interfaces). Just to remind you, ATL dialogs do not offer the same level of support as found in MFC, and are basically a thin C++ wrapper around the Win32 APIs.

Finally, the Data Access category gives you the option to create ATL objects using the OLE DB (OLE database) protocol. OLE DB supports the vision of *universal data access* whereby a database client (called *data consumers* in OLE DB-speak) can access data held in numerous formats through a set of COM interfaces. From this tab you may create OLE DB providers or OLE DB consumers. We will not be covering data access object types in this book. OLE DB is a book (or two) in its own right.

Inserting a Simple Object

Each object you select from the Object Wizard will launch a unique property sheet allowing you to configure various attributes for your new coclass. The number of tabs (and what they allow you to specify) for an object's property sheet will vary depending on the type of object you have selected. Let's insert a Simple Object named CoHexagon into the ATLShapesServer.dll project. Simple objects have two configuration tabs: Names and Attributes. Figure 6-15 illustrates the Names tab:

Figure 6-15:
Configuration options for an ATL Simple Object.

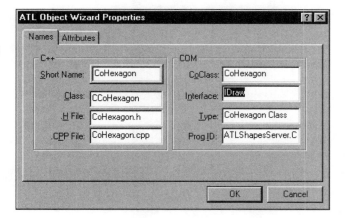

From this tab, you configure the C++ source code names (class name, header file, and CPP file) and the COM-related names. All choices are based on the Short Name edit box, and may be modified to your liking. The *.h and *.cpp files for the coclass will be named according to the .H File and .CPP File edit boxes. The name of the class is controlled (of course) from the Class field.

The COM names selections allow you to configure the name of the first interface supported by the coclass. Most often you will want to change the interface field, as this too is based on the "short name." Thus, the initial interface name for CoHexagon is set to ICoHexagon, which we will edit to be our good friend IDraw instead. Also notice that the ProgID is built using standard <ServerName.Coclass.Version> syntax. The Type field will be used to provide a simple string description of the COM object, which may be accessed by various object browser tools.

The Attributes tab (Figure 6-16) allows you to configure your object's threading model, aggregation support, and interface type. You can also specify whether your object supports the COM event protocol (Support Connection Points) and/or extended error information (Support ISupportErrorInfo). We examine these topics at a later time. CoHexagon will support a Custom interface, as this corresponds to the COM vTable interfaces we have been creating thus far. As well, we will support the default aggregation (Yes) and the Apartment threading model options.

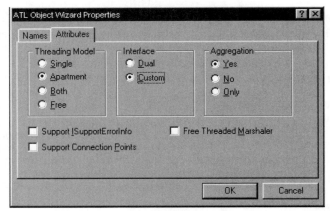

> **Note:** The default interface configuration is for a Dual, not Custom, interface. If you forget to check Custom, you will find your ATL coclass is derived from IDispatchImpl<> and the IDL definition is quite different. This option is used to configure scriptable COM objects, and will be fully detailed in Chapter 10.

When you hit the OK button, the ATL Object Wizard will insert a new Simple Object into your component housing. Figure 6-17 shows our new CoHexagon class from the ClassView tab. Notice that we see two IDraw interface jacks. The IDraw lollipop listed directly under the CCoHexagon class is used to navigate to the C++ implementations of the IDraw interface methods (currently none). The IDraw lollipop coming off the project node is used to navigate to the IDL code defining the interface methods (also currently none).

Figure 6-17:
Navigating ATL
source code
with the
ClassView tab.

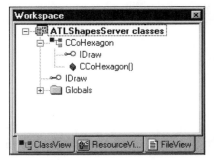

Removing an ATL Coclass

The ATL Object Wizard is a great way to insert new coclasses into your project; however, this tool is completely clueless about how to remove a coclass. Sometimes you may wish to remove a class from an ATL project, and no matter how hard you look, you will not find a "Remove Coclass Wizard." When you wish to remove a coclass inserted by the wizard, you will need to follow these steps.

Assume you have added CoOops into your project using the ATL Object Wizard, and now wish to remove this from your project. First, you will need to edit your project's object map. Open your server's implementation file, and comment out (or remove) the offending map entry. As well, in this same file, comment out (or remove) the preprocessor #include call for the coclass's header file:

```
// Comment out the header file and OBJECT_ENTRY listing for the
// class you wish to remove from your project.
#include "stdafx.h"
#include "resource.h"
#include <initguid.h>
#include "ATLShapesServer.h"
#include " ATLShapesServer_i.c"
// #include "CoOops.h"
CComModule _Module;
BEGIN_OBJECT_MAP(ObjectMap)
    // OBJECT_ENTRY(CLSID_CoOops, CCoOops)
END_OBJECT_MAP()
```

Now you will need to delete the code inserted into your IDL file. The Object Wizard will automatically write an interface definition for the [default] interface, as well as add a coclass definition to your library statement. Go into your IDL file and remove the offending code.

Next, you will need to edit your project's *.rc file. The simplest way to do so is to open this file from WordPad, and locate the section beginning with the REGISTRY comment. Carefully select the entire line of the offending resource (shown in bold below) and delete.

```
// REGISTRY
IDR_COSTRINGREADER      REGISTRY DISCARDABLE "CoStringReader.rgs"
IDR_COOOPS              REGISTRY DISCARDABLE "CoOops.rgs"
```

Finally, you will need to remove the *.cpp, *.h, and *.rgs files from your project workspace. Open up your FileView tab, select the *.cpp file from the Source Files subdirectory and delete the file. Do the same for the header file and RGS file. You may also wish to go under the Windows Explorer and delete the CoOops.h, CoOops.cpp, and CoOops.rgs from your hard drive. Recompile the project, and code on.

Examining the Updated Project

Before we learn how to add methods to our IDraw interface, as well as support additional interfaces, we need to examine the changes made to the existing ATLShapesServer project. Because CoHexagon is a creatable COM object, you will find that your OBJECT_MAP has been updated with an OBJECT_ENTRY listing. The first parameter to this macro is the CLSID of the coclass (which ATL has supplied for you). The second parameter is the name of the C++ class representing your COM class:

```
// Recall the object map holds a list of all creatable coclasses in the server.
BEGIN_OBJECT_MAP(ObjectMap)
    OBJECT_ENTRY(CLSID_CoHexagon, CCoHexagon)
END_OBJECT_MAP()
```

The ATL Object Wizard also updated your IDL file, providing an empty definition of the IDraw interface (with a new IID) and a coclass listing (with a new CLSID) in the server's library statement. The first interface added to a coclass is set to be the [default] for the coclass; however, you are always free to change this after the fact. Here are the relevant changes to our IDL file, after inserting CoHexagon:

Note: Unlike MFC wizard-generated ODL code, you can rip apart ATL IDL generated code to your heart's content (within the syntactic constraints of IDL!) without breaking the tools.

```
// Updated IDL file.
// The IDraw Interface.
[    object, uuid(4A01DD02-066C-11D3-B8E5-0020781238D4),
     helpstring("IDraw Interface"),
     oleautomation,    /*added to enforce interface registration */
     pointer_default(unique)
]
interface IDraw : IUnknown
{
};
// This coclass definition will appear within your library statement.
[
     uuid(4A01DD03-066C-11D3-B8E5-0020781238D4),
     helpstring("CoHexagon Class")
]
coclass CoHexagon
{
     [default] interface IDraw;
};
```

As you would expect, the MIDL-generated files will also be updated with the next build, defining GUIDs, interface bindings, type information, and stub/proxy code as dictated by the CoHexagon coclass.

New Project Files

With the addition of a Simple Object, the ATL Object Wizard has added three new files to your project workspace:

1. CoHexagon.h   The header file for CoHexagon.
2. CoHexagon.cpp   The implementation file for CoHexagon.
3. CoHexagon.rgs   The registry script file for CoHexagon.

Before examining the source code, let's recap the basics of what ATL will be supplying for us:

■ ATL will provide a default implementation of IUnknown for your coclasses. This support is provided by CComObjectRootBase, CComObjectRootEx<>, and your class's COM map.

■ ATL will provide a generic class factory to create your objects. CComCoClass<> defines a generic class factory for this purpose.

■ ATL will provide self-registration support for each coclass in the server. This is achieved with your server's registry script file, CComModule, and a handful of registration macros.

Examining CCoHexagon.h

Here is the header file for our ATL-ized CoHexagon coclass:

```
// A typical header file for an ATL Simple Object.
class ATL_NO_VTABLE CCoHexagon :
     public CComObjectRootEx<CComSingleThreadModel>,
     public CComCoClass<CCoHexagon, &CLSID_CoHexagon>,
     public IDraw
{
public:
     CCoHexagon()
     {
     }
DECLARE_REGISTRY_RESOURCEID(IDR_COHEXAGON)
DECLARE_PROTECT_FINAL_CONSTRUCT()
BEGIN_COM_MAP(CCoHexagon)
     COM_INTERFACE_ENTRY(IDraw)
END_COM_MAP()
// IDraw
public:
};
```

Notice that your simple CoHexagon derives directly from two ATL templates. These ATL templates specify CoHexagon's threading model, level of aggregation support, and the associated class factory as well as support for IUnknown. Here is a rundown of the functionality provided by these base classes, which we will explore in much greater detail in later chapters:

An Overview of CComObjectRootEx<>

Although you can't tell from your class's inheritance chain, CComObjectRootEx<> is derived from another ATL class, CComObjectRootBase. These two ATL classes are used to provide helper functions called by the IUnknown implementation for your coclass. As we will see later in this section, your coclass is <u>not</u> the most derived class, but is actually passed as a template parameter to another ATL class (most often CComObject<>) which implements the three methods of IUnknown.

CComObjectRootBase and CComObjectRootEx<> provide member functions that are accessed by CComObject<> to finalize the implementation of QueryInterface(), AddRef(), and Release(). CComObjectRootBase defines the "look and feel" for QueryInterface(). CComObjectRootEx<> fills out the IUnknown specification by adding helper functions used for the implementation of AddRef() and Release().

The single template parameter given to CComObjectRootEx<> is one of a handful of threading model classes defined by ATL. Using this parameter, your object's reference counting implementation will specified with just enough thread safety. We will cover COM threading in Chapter 7, but realize that the template parameter used by CComObjectRootEx<> is determined by your threading model selection from the Attribute tab of the ATL Object Wizard.

An Overview of the ATL COM Map

In order for ATL's IUnknown implementation to function correctly, your coclass must define a *COM map*. The COM map is established with the BEGIN_COM_MAP and

END_COM_MAP macro set. An object's COM map contains a list of all interfaces supported by the coclass. Keep in mind that if you do not list an interface in the COM map, a client will not be able to access it via QueryInterface. IUnknown is the exception with the COM map, as the IUnknown pointer is calculated indirectly using the first entry in the COM map and therefore you will not explicitly find a listing. As you can see, the ATL Object Wizard has already listed support for IDraw with the COM_INTERFACE_ENTRY macro:

```
// ATL COM maps provide a look-up table defining each supported interface
// in the coclass. CComObjectRootBase must find this map in your derived class.
BEGIN_COM_MAP(CCoHexagon)
    COM_INTERFACE_ENTRY(IDraw)
END_COM_MAP()
```

The ATL COM map may be populated by 17 different interface macros (which we cover in Chapter 8). Many of these are only useful when building a coclass using some advanced COM techniques such as aggregation or tear-off interfaces. By and large, the most common entry is COM_INTERFACE_ENTRY, which will return the vPtr for the specified interface.

> **Note:**   Note that the COM_INTERFACE_ENTRY macro takes the IDL name of the interface (IDraw, IShapeEdit, IStats, and so forth), and not the IID associated to it.

An Overview of CComCoClass<>

The second ATL template from which you derive specifies the class object for the class. The definition of CComCoClass<> specifies the DECLARE_CLASSFACTORY macro, which expands to define a default class factory implementing IClassFactory. As well, CComCoClass<> specifies how CoHexagon should behave if it is asked by another object to serve as an aggregate. Recall that aggregation is a COM reuse mechanism, by which an "outer" object creates and maintains an "inner" object. The inner object's interfaces are exposed by the outer object, providing the illusion that the outer object is composed of more interfaces than it actually is. We will revisit COM aggregation (and discover why you might want to do this) later in Chapter 8. For now, just realize that CComCoClass<> defines the DECLARE_AGGREGATABLE macro which tells the world that CoHexagon can function as an aggregated object if asked to do so, but is not required to do so.

Examining CCoHexagon.cpp

Your CoHexagon implementation file is completely empty as of now (beyond #include statements), as we have not yet fleshed out the methods of IDraw:

```
// CoHexagon.cpp : Implementation of CCoHexagon
#include "stdafx.h"
#include "ATLShapesServer.h"
#include "CoHexagon.h"
```

Examining CoHexagon.rgs

As mentioned, a *self-registering* COM server understands what to do when told to register and unregister itself. In ATL, CComModule is the class in charge of entering (or removing) the necessary registry information for each coclass listed in the object map. When performing registration duties, CComModule will be on the lookout for the DECLARE_REG-

Figure 6-18: The "REGISTRY" resource holds the RGS binaries for an ATL server.

ISTRY_RESOURCEID macro in your class's header file. This macro expands to provide an implementation of the UpdateRegistry() method, and is called by CComModule during the registration and unregistration of your coclasses. The sole parameter to DECLARE_REGISTRY_ RESOURCEID is the resource ID of your server's binary RGS file. If you examine your ResourceView tab, you will see a new custom resource ("REGISTRY") subfolder has appeared (Figure 6-18).

ATL's Registry Scripting Language

So what is an RGS (ReGistry Script) file? ATL supplies a simple and elegant scripting language to specify what to insert (or remove) into (or from) the system registry during the installation process. This registry scripting language removes the need to maintain a messy REG file to register your COM servers. By default, an RGS file specifies a version-dependent ProgID, and version-independent ProgID and CLSID entries. Your server's interfaces and TypeLib information are entered programmatically. Here is the RGS file for CoHexagon:

```
HKCR
{
    ATLShapesServer.CoHexagon.1 = s 'CoHexagon Class'
    {
        CLSID = s '{4A01DD03-066C-11D3-B8E5-0020781238D4}'
    }
    ATLShapesServer.CoHexagon = s 'CoHexagon Class'
    {
        CLSID = s '{4A01DD03-066C-11D3-B8E5-0020781238D4}'
        CurVer = s 'ATLShapesServer.CoHexagon.1'
    }
    NoRemove CLSID
    {
        ForceRemove {4A01DD03-066C-11D3-B8E5-0020781238D4} = s
        'CoHexagon Class'
        {
            ProgID = s 'ATLShapesServer.CoHexagon.1'
            VersionIndependentProgID = s 'ATLShapesServer.CoHexagon'
            InprocServer32 = s '%MODULE%'
            {
                val ThreadingModel = s 'Apartment'
            }
            'TypeLib' = s '{13AE1FB1-1582-11D3-B8F2-0020781238D4}'
        }
    }
}
```

As you can see, RGS syntax is modeled after a standard tree structure, with each node identified by an open/close bracket pair ({}). The topmost node (in this case HKCR) is used to identify which hive will be modified by the script. RGS syntax allows you to write to any hive in the registry, and may take any of the following values:

Hive Acronym	Meaning in Life
HKCR	HKEY_CLASSES_ROOT
HKCU	HKEY_CURRENT_USER
HKLM	HKEY_LOCAL_MACHINE
HKU	HKEY_USERS
HKPD	HKEY_PERFORMANCE_DATA
HKDD	HKEY_DYN_DATA
HKCC	HKEY_CURRENT_CONFIG

Subnodes may take modifiers. The CLSID node takes the NoRemove identifier, which is a very good thing, as any entries made to HKCR\CLSID needs to keep all other subkeys intact. On the other hand, the {<GUID>} entry for CoHexagon is marked with ForceRemove, which tells ATL to remove any previous entries under this subkey and replace as necessary. Finally, although not present in your initial RGS file, a node may take the Delete modifier, which is used to remove (but not replace) a given key.

As we have seen in Chapter 3, a subkey may contain numerous values. In RGS syntax, named values are marked with the val modifier. RGS syntax allows you to enter string (S), numerical (D, for DWORD), or binary (B) values. For example, the version-independent ProgID lists two default string values:

```
ATLShapesServer.CoHexagon = s 'CoHexagon Class'
{
    CLSID = s '{4A01DD03-066C-11D3-B8E5-0020781238D4}'
    CurVer = s 'ATLShapesServer.CoHexagon.1'
}
```

The final point of interest is the %MODULE% tag. RGS syntax allows you to define place-holder types, which are dynamically added to the script during the registration/unregistration process. %MODULE% is one such predefined placeholder, which resolves to a call to the Win32 GetModuleFileName() function. It is also possible to define your own custom placeholders, as we will see in Chapter 9.

That finishes up our examination of the ATL-generated files. As you can see, ATL has done quite an admirable job of providing component housing code, as well as basic COM riggings (a class factory, IUnknown implementation, and self-registration support). Of course, we still have quite a way to go before we understand exactly how ATL performs its magic. Rest assured we will dig into the gory details in upcoming chapters. But for now let's push onward and learn how to extend the wizard-generated code with interface methods and learn about interface "properties."

Populating Your Interfaces with Methods

Now that we have a coclass supporting IDraw, we need to learn how to add methods to the interface itself. To add a method to an interface, right-click on the interface from ClassView (Figure 6-19) to activate the Add Method Wizard.

Note: You may always choose to add support for a COM method by hand. The ATL wizards simply save you typing.

Figure 6-19: Accessing the Add Method Wizard.

This tool allows you to specify the name, return value, and method parameters for a given interface method. You will be writing IDL code when defining the method parameters, so don't forget to use the [in], [out], [in, out], and [out, retval] attributes. Figure 6-20 shows the setup for the Draw() method of IDraw:

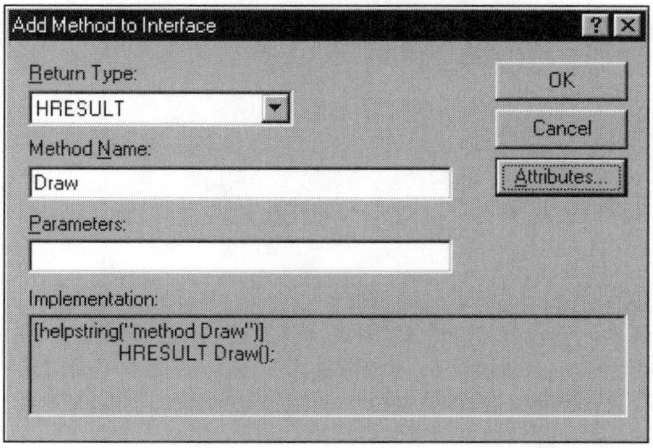

Figure 6-20: Adding methods to your interfaces.

The Attributes button allows you to specify additional attributes for an IDL method definition from a drop-down list box (Figure 6-21). Every method will automatically have a [helpstring] attribute. If you find that you wish to modify your IDL method definitions after closing down the Add Method Wizard, you will need to edit the IDL file by hand, as you cannot edit previously defined interface methods with this dialog box.

Figure 6-21:
Adding
additional
method
attributes.

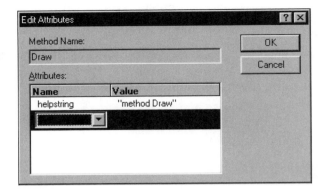

Once you hit the OK button, the Add Method Wizard will do the following on your behalf (which you can always elect to do by hand):

■ Update your IDL file to specify the new interface method.

■ Add a C++ prototype for the method in your coclass header file.

■ Add stub code for the method in your coclass implementation file.

Here is the updated IDraw IDL definition:

```
// Updated IDraw definition
interface IDraw : IUnknown
{
     [helpstring("method Draw")] HRESULT Draw();
};
```

Your CoHexagon definition and implementation file define the method in C++ syntax:

```
// Cohexagon.h
class ATL_NO_VTABLE CCoHexagon :
     public CComObjectRootEx<CComSingleThreadModel>,
     public CComCoClass<CCoHexagon, &CLSID_CoHexagon>,
     public IDraw
{
...
public:
     STDMETHOD(Draw)();
};
```

> **Note:**   The STDMETHOD macro will be used in your header file, as your class is not the most derived; therefore, the virtual suffix is still technically permissible. Our previous coclasses used STDMETHODIMP in the header and CPP files, as we <u>were</u> the most derived, and therefore did not need the virtual keyword.

```
// Cohexagon.cpp
STDMETHODIMP CCoHexagon::Draw()
{
     // TODO: Add your implementation code here
```

```
        return S_OK;
}
```

At this point, all you need to do is give your interface methods some implementation code. I always recommend calls to MessageBox():

```
// Cohexagon.cpp
STDMETHODIMP CCoHexagon::Draw()
{
        // De facto implementations begin with MessageBox.
        MessageBox(NULL, "I am drawing a hexagon", "CoHex Says",
                MB_OK | MB_SETFOREGROUND);
        return S_OK;
}
```

Adding Additional Interfaces

What would CoHexagon be without support for IShapeEdit? When you wish to add support for additional interfaces to an ATL coclass, you have two options. First, you may elect to make all code edits by hand. This is not a very painful process at all, and until ATL 3.0, this was the only choice you had. You may instead choose to make use of the Implement Interface Wizard. To illustrate what this wizard will do on your behalf, we will add support for IShapeEdit by hand and then turn our attention to the Implement Interface Wizard. Be sure you understand the following steps, as you will need to do them time and time again when developing ATL COM objects. Below are the steps to take to add a new COM interface to an existing ATL class.

Note: Both approaches require that you write (and understand) IDL code. There is no "Write All the IDL Code For Me" Wizard as of ATL 3.0.

Note: There is no "Remove the Interface I Just Added" Wizard. If you use the Implement Interface Wizard and then decide to remove it, you will need to do so by hand. Simply reverse the steps outlined below to do so.

Adding (or Removing) an Interface by Hand

1. Begin with the IDL. Open your project's IDL file and define a bare bones COM interface. As you remember, COM interfaces must at minimum have the [object] and [uuid] keywords. As before, use guidgen.exe to generate a new IID, and be sure to write the definition outside your library statement (this forces MIDL to generate the C and C++ language bindings). When you are finished, save the IDL file. You should see the new interface appear in the ClassView tab.

```
// Minimal IDL interface definition, curiosity of copy/paste reuse techniques.
//
[
        object, uuid(297B9B10-119D-11d3-B8F2-0020781238D4), oleautomation,
        pointer_default(unique), helpstring("IShapeEdit Interface")
]
interface IShapeEdit : IUnknown
```

```
{
};
```

2. At this point you can use the New Method Wizard to add the methods to your new interface. If you prefer, you can directly edit the IDL file rather than using the New Method
   Wizard. Assume this IDL code (with the FILLTYPE enumeration) is exactly the same as
   we saw from Chapter 4:

```
// Our little enum.
typedef
[uuid(442F32E0-E7EE-11d2-B8D2-0020781238D4), v1_enum]
enum FILLTYPE
{
        HATCH       = 0,
        SOLID       = 1,
        POLKADOT    = 2
} FILLTYPE;
[...]
interface IShapeEdit : IUnknown
{
        [helpstring("method Inverse")] HRESULT Inverse();
        [helpstring("method Stretch")] HRESULT Stretch([in] int factor);
        [helpstring("method Fill")] HRESULT Fill([in] FILLTYPE fType);
};
```

3. Next, edit your coclass's IDL definition to specify support for the new interface. You are
   free to change the [default] interface if you wish (the Object Wizard always marks the first
   interface as the [default]).

```
// Updated IDL coclass definition
[
        uuid(4A01DD03-066C-11D3-B8E5-0020781238D4),
        helpstring("CoHexagon Class")
]
coclass CoHexagon
{
        [default] interface IDraw;
        interface IShapeEdit;
};
```

4. Now that the IDL code has been completed, open up your coclass's header file and derive
   from your new interface. Next, add a COM_INTERFACE_ENTRY for this interface to your
   COM map and finally define the prototypes for the methods (using the STDMETHOD
   macro). Here are the relevant changes made to CoHexagon:

```
// Cohexagon.h
class ATL_NO_VTABLE CCoHexagon :
     public CComObjectRootEx<CComSingleThreadModel>,
     public CComCoClass<CCoHexagon, &CLSID_CoHexagon>,
     public IDraw,
     public IShapeEdit
{
...
BEGIN_COM_MAP(CCoHexagon)
     COM_INTERFACE_ENTRY(IDraw)
     COM_INTERFACE_ENTRY(IShapeEdit)
END_COM_MAP()
...
```

```
// IShapeEdit
    STDMETHOD(Stretch)(int factor);
    STDMETHOD(Fill)(FILLTYPE fType);   // FILLTYPE is defined in the
                                       // MIDL-generated header file.
    STDMETHOD(Inverse)();
};
```

5. Finally, implement each new interface method. For example:

```
// Cohexagon.cpp
STDMETHODIMP CCoHexagon::Stretch(int factor)
{
    for(int i = 0; i < factor; i++)
        MessageBox(NULL, "Stretching!", "CoHex Says", MB_OK | MB_SETFOREGROUND);
    return S_OK;
}
```

Not too bad, huh? The only thing you need to be on the lookout for is the dreaded copy and paste error. Be sure your header file uses the STDMETHOD macro, while your CPP file uses STDMETHODIMP (remember that the syntax of each macro is unique). If you copy your prototypes from the header file and do not readjust for the STDMETHODIMP syntax in your *.cpp files, you are bound to get a number of bizarre errors.

By the same token, be sure you remove the semicolon from the header file prototypes when pasting your interface methods into the implementation file (this one is very easy to forget). You will know you did forget to remove the semicolon if you see the following compile error:

```
error C2447: missing function header (old-style formal list?)
```

As mentioned, ATL 3.0 provides a second way to implement additional interfaces on a coclass, using the Implement Interface Wizard, which automates the above steps on your behalf. Let's check this tool out next.

Using the Implement Interface Wizard

This CASE tool, new to ATL 3.0, helps automate the process outlined above. As before, you begin by writing the minimal IDL code for the new interface and adding support for it in the coclass. To illustrate the Implement Interface Wizard, let's add support for a new interface named IErase. Here is the updated IDL file:

```
// Definition of, and support for, IErase.
[
    object, uuid(13AE1FBD-1582-11D3-B8F2-0020781238D4),
    helpstring("IErase Interface"), oleautomation,
    pointer_default(unique)
]
interface IErase : IUnknown
{
};
[...]
coclass CoHexagon
{
    [default] interface IDraw;
    interface IShapeEdit;
    interface IErase;
};
```

Next, you must recompile your IDL file to recompile the *.tlb file. If you do not refresh your type information, the Implement Interface Wizard cannot see your unimplemented interfaces.

> **Note:** When using the Implement Interface Wizard for your custom interfaces, do not add methods or properties to your interface until you have first run the wizard. Read on to see why.

Assuming all is well with your IDL code, right-click on the coclass from ClassView and select the Implement Interface menu selection. The resulting dialog box (Figure 6-22) will list all interfaces defined in your IDL file which are not currently supported by your coclass (notice that IDraw and IShapeEdit do not appear as options). If you have updated the IDL for a new interface but do not see it listed in the Interfaces pane, you forgot to recompile your type library. Check off the IErase interface and click OK.

Figure 6-22:
The Implement
Interface
Wizard.

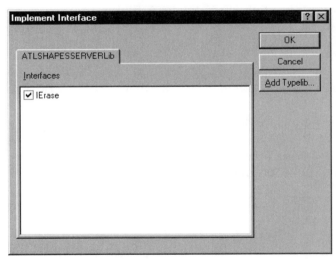

The Add Typelib button allows you to implement interfaces defined in other type libraries. As you may suspect, HKCR\TypeLib is consulted when you click this button (thus the slight delay). If you wish to implement, say, CoCar interfaces in your CoHexagon (which would most likely be a very bad design), just select the type lib from the list box. We will not do this, but Figure 6-23 illustrates the process:

Figure 6-23:
Implementing
interfaces
defined outside
your project.

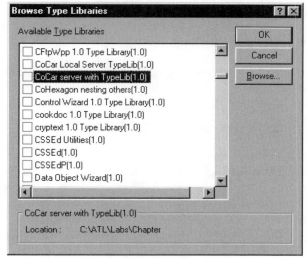

Wizard Generated Code

Here is the result of using the Implement Interface Wizard: Your coclass will be derived
from the new interface, and your COM map is automatically updated with a
COM_INTERFACE_ENTRY listing.

If you used this tool to implement an interface already containing IDL method definitions, each method in the interface will be listed inline in your header file. Assume that we
added an Erase() method to IErase <u>before using the wizard</u>. If this were the case, we
would see the following listed in the CoHexagon header file once we ran the tool:

```
// Implement Interface Wizard generated code
class ATL_NO_VTABLE CCoHexagon :
    public CComObjectRootEx<CComSingleThreadModel>,
    public CComCoClass<CCoHexagon, &CLSID_CoHexagon>,
    public IDraw,
    public IShapeEdit,
    public IErase
{
...
BEGIN_COM_MAP(CCoHexagon)
    COM_INTERFACE_ENTRY(IDraw)
    COM_INTERFACE_ENTRY(IShapeEdit)
    COM_INTERFACE_ENTRY(IErase)
END_COM_MAP()
...
// IErase
    // The Wizard will inline any methods found in the IDL interface definition.
    STDMETHOD(Clear)()
    {
        return E_NOTIMPL;
    }
};
```

If you do not define your methods before using this CASE tool, you may then use the Add Method tool after running the wizard. This will place prototypes in your header file and method stub code in your implementation file. You are free to mix and match both approaches in your projects. The best approach is to define an empty interface definition in your IDL, activate the Implement Interface Wizard, and then fill your interface with methods as usual.

Populating Your Interfaces with Properties

Up until this point we have created interfaces supporting a collection of semantically related methods. We have seen that most methods, when described in IDL, support a physical return value (HRESULT) as well as a logical return value ([out, retval]). Beyond this, many COM-enabled languages support the use of properties in an interface definition. Furthermore, some languages support class properties in the language itself.

For example, in Visual Basic, a class property (such as Name) is internally represented by a pair of Property Let and Property Get methods. The VB object user triggers the correct variation based on the object's calling syntax. If we, as a VB class builder, write the following code in a CLS file (named CEmployee), we can define a property (Name) for a single private String called m_name:

Figure 6-24:
A Visual Basic class defining a single property.

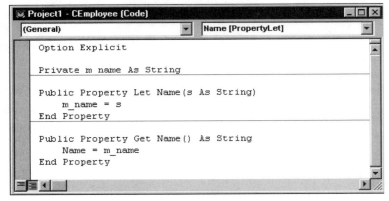

```
Option Explicit

Private m_name As String

Public Property Let Name(s As String)
    m_name = s
End Property

Public Property Get Name() As String
    Name = m_name
End Property
```

Note: Before you try this at home, realize that only Visual Basic 4.0 and higher support user-defined classes. A class is defined in VB by simple virtue of the CLS file extension; there is no VB keyword used to define a class.

Once the property is defined, as a VB object user you can now write the following:

```
' Form_Load is an event sent just before the VB form is about to be shown.
' This event is in response to a WM_CREATE message.
'
Private Sub Form_Load()
    Dim Fred as CEmployee
    Set Fred = New CEmployee
    Fred.Name = "Fred"                ' Calls Property Let    (C++ mutator)
```

```
      MsgBox "Name is " & Fred.Name      ' Calls Property Get      (C++ accessor)
End Sub
```

In Visual Basic, a *class* is seen as a collection of properties and methods (and events for that matter). Notice how the Name property in the VB example above seems to suggest the object user is directly using public data (which would break encapsulation). This is not true. Under the hood we are calling the VB equivalent of accessors and mutators.

In COM, we can equip our vTable interfaces (as well as dispinterfaces and dual interfaces which we examine later) to expose properties. With ATL, this process is automated with the Add Property Wizard, accessible by right-clicking on your coclass from the ClassView tab. Assume that CoHexagon supports a new interface named IShapeID that allows users to provide a friendly name to identify their CoHexagon. IShapeID contains a single BSTR property called Name. We can configure this property using the Add Property Wizard (see Figure 6-25).

Figure 6-25: The Add Property Wizard.

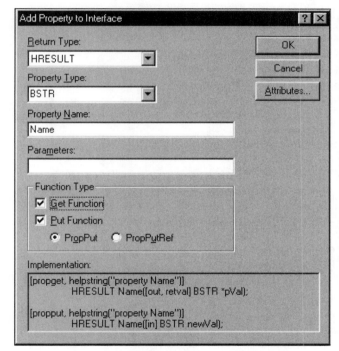

Notice that we can configure a property to be read-only or write-only by deselecting the appropriate Function Type check box. If you want a read-only property, deselect the Put Function option. If you want a write-only property, deselect Get Function. As you can see, it is possible for properties to take parameters; however, this is rare. It is always safe to ignore the Parameters edit box.

Note: For the record, if you should ever need to add (or remove) a property to an interface without the Add Property Wizard, the steps below may be implemented by hand. Always remember that wizards do little more than save you some typing.

IDL Syntax for Interface Properties

We can see that our single Name property has been mapped to two separate IDL function definitions. The [propget] attribute marks a method as an accessor function, whereas [propput] marks a mutator:

```
// IShapeID supports the Name property.
interface IShapeID : IUnknown
{
```

```
[propget, helpstring("property Name")]          // Accessor.
HRESULT Name([out, retval] BSTR *pVal);
[propput, helpstring("property Name")]          // Mutator.
HRESULT Name([in] BSTR newVal);
};
```

One important thing to keep in mind is that COM properties are always represented internally as methods. Interfaces can <u>only</u> contain methods, and the fact that some languages support properties is not much more than "syntactic sugar" provided by the target language. If we examine the header file for CoHexagon, we can see that in C++ syntax the Name property has been prototyped by the wizard as the following:

```
// Cohexagon.h
// A single property resolves to "get" and "put" functions.
STDMETHOD(get_Name)(/*[out, retval]*/ BSTR *pVal);
STDMETHOD(put_Name)(/*[in]*/ BSTR newVal);
```

From an implementation point of view, a property is identical to fleshing out the details for a COM interface method. Assume we have added a private BSTR data member (named m_bstrName) to CoHexagon. We could then complete the Name property as so:

```
// [propget] Name implementation.
STDMETHODIMP CCoHexagon::get_Name(BSTR *pVal)
{
    // return private BSTR.
    *pVal = SysAllocString(m_bstrName);
    return S_OK;
}
// [propput] Name implementation.
STDMETHODIMP CCoHexagon::put_Name(BSTR newVal)
{
    // Reset the internal BSTR.
    SysReAllocString(&m_bstrName, newVal);
    return S_OK;
}
```

Properties: The Client's Point of View

Different COM language mappings interpret the [propput] and [propget] attributes in different ways. Clients using straight C++ access the Name property as any other interface method:

```
// Create a new CoHexagon named Fred.
BSTR hexName;
hexName = SysAllocString(L"Fred");
pShapeID -> put_Name(hexName);
SysFreeString(hexName);
// Print out name of my CoHex.
char buff[80];
pShapeID -> get_Name(&hexName);
WideCharToMultiByte(CP_ACP, NULL, hexName, -1, buff, 80, NULL, NULL);
cout << "Your CoHex is called" << buff << endl;
SysFreeString(hexName);
```

Visual Basic developers can get at the Name property as such:

```
' A little VB code illustrating property manipulation.
'
Dim myHex as New CoHexagon
Dim itfShapeID as IShapeID
Set itfShapeID = myHex
itfShapeID.Name = "Fred"                          ' [propput]
MsgBox itfShapeID.Name, , "My Hex is named..."    ' [propget]
```

> **Note:** If you have opted to use the C++ COM import statement (see Chapter 4), a C++ client can manipulate [propput] and [propget] in the same fashion as a VB developer.

And finally, a Java (J++) client can exercise the Name property as so. Notice how jactivex.exe prefixes "get" to [propget] functions and "set" to [propput] functions:

```
// A little bit of Java code.
CoHexagon myHex = new CoHexagon();
IShapeID itfShapeID;
itfShapeID = myHex;
// Get and Put the Name property.
itfShapeID.setName(new String("Fred"));
MessageBox.show( itfShapeID.getName(), "Your CoHex is named",
                MessageBox.ICONEXCLAMATION);
```

You may be wondering if there are times when a property is a better choice than a method, or vice versa. In many cases, this is just another design issue for you to contend with. COM properties allow your interfaces to mesh into a given language mapping more naturally if the language supports the [propget] and [propput] attributes.

Other times, properties are a completely bad idea. For example, if we have a coclass that allows the user to set the state of the object using properties, we might have to make five [propput] calls to configure a new instance. Now what if the object resided on a distant machine? That would, of course, mean five round trips. Obviously, COM properties make for lousy remotable interfaces. If you have a number of properties that are serving to set the state of a COM object (e.g., Name, ID, SSN, DeptID), you will be wise to define a single method (e.g., Create(BSTR, int, BSTR, int)) for remote access.

ATL and COM Text

In Chapter 3, we saw that text handling is a bit problematic in a multi-language, multi-platform system such as COM. Some systems are Unicode centric, some ANSI. Some languages want NULL-terminated character arrays and others want length prefixed. The solution we should agree on is the use of the BSTR data type, the string type of choice in COM development.

Working with BSTRs in C++ entails a small handful of system string functions (SysAllocString(), SysFreeString(), et. al.), as well as some functions to convert from ANSI to Unicode and visa versa. This was not all that difficult, but ATL can make your string chores much more rewarding.

First, ATL provides the CComBSTR class to help encapsulate the details of BSTR management. As well, ATL provides a number of conversion macros, which help you convert between the onslaught of string data types (wchar_t, BSTR, OLECHAR, char*, and so forth) bypassing direct API function calls. Here is a rundown of ATL's string support beginning with CComBSTR.

CComBSTR: Lovingly Wrapping a Raw BSTR

CComBSTR, defined in <atlbase.h>, is a C++ class wrapping an underlying BSTR data member named m_str. When you create an instance of CComBSTR, the underlying buffer is set to NULL. The destructor frees the m_str using SysFreeString():

```
// CComBSTR is here to help with painful BSTR maintenance.
class CComBSTR
{
public:
    BSTR m_str;                        // The underlying BSTR.
    CComBSTR()
    {
        m_str = NULL;                  // Set to NULL.
    }
    ~CComBSTR()
    {
        ::SysFreeString(m_str);        // Free underlying BSTR.
    }
...
};
```

> **Note:**   Notice that the default constructor of CComBSTR sets the underlying BSTR to NULL, not an empty string. If your coclass maintains a private CComBSTR, be sure to set it to a valid empty string, or your client program may crash if accessing the BSTR before making an assignment!

The public sector of CComBSTR provides a good number of methods to allow you to play with the underlying BSTR buffer. While this class is not as robust as MFC's CString or the _bstr_t compiler extension data type, it is a real improvement over raw BSTR manipulation. The functionality of CComBSTR may be grouped in the following high-level categories:

- A set of overloaded constructors, allowing you to set m_str based on existing ANSI and Unicode strings, as well as an existing REFGUID (which creates a string representation of the 128-bit number).

- Methods to copy (Copy()), concatenate (Append(), AppendBSTR()) and free (Empty(), Detach()), your underlying BSTR. ToUpper(), ToLower(), and Length() member functions are also defined. The LoadString() method allows you to stuff your underlying BSTR with data from your project's string table.

- A full set of overloaded operators to allow you to work with CComBSTR objects in an intelligent manner. Among the most interesting operators are concatenation (+ =) and assignment (=).

MSDN provides a listing for most of the methods of CComBSTR. Some (such as ToUpper() and ToLower()) are not found in online help, but do appear as a valid selection from the IntelliSense drop-down window of the Visual Studio IDE.

Here is the public interface of CComBSTR:

```
class CComBSTR
{
public:
     BSTR m_str;
     CComBSTR();
     CComBSTR(int nSize);
     CComBSTR(int nSize, LPCOLESTR sz);
     CComBSTR(LPCOLESTR pSrc);
     CComBSTR(const CComBSTR& src);
     CComBSTR(REFGUID src);
     CComBSTR& operator=(const CComBSTR& src);
     CComBSTR& operator=(LPCOLESTR pSrc);
     ~CComBSTR();
     unsigned int Length() const;
     operator BSTR() const;
     BSTR* operator&();
     BSTR Copy() const;
     HRESULT CopyTo(BSTR* pbstr);
     void Attach(BSTR src);
     BSTR Detach();
     void Empty();
     bool operator!() const;
     HRESULT Append(const CComBSTR& bstrSrc);
     HRESULT Append(LPCOLESTR lpsz);
     HRESULT AppendBSTR(BSTR p);
     HRESULT Append(LPCOLESTR lpsz, int nLen);
     HRESULT ToLower();
     HRESULT ToUpper();
     bool LoadString(HINSTANCE hInst, UINT nID);
     bool LoadString(UINT nID);
     CComBSTR& operator+=(const CComBSTR& bstrSrc);
     bool operator<(BSTR bstrSrc) const;
     bool operator==(BSTR bstrSrc) const;
     bool operator<(LPCSTR pszSrc) const;
     bool operator==(LPCSTR pszSrc) const;
     HRESULT WriteToStream(IStream* pStream);
     HRESULT ReadFromStream(IStream* pStream);
};
```

Using a CComBSTR Object

To illustrate CComBSTR in action, let's change the underlying implementation of the Name property provided by the IShapeID interface. First off, we will now want to maintain a private CComBSTR data type, as opposed to a raw BSTR. In CoHexagon's constructor, we can set the underlying m_str data member using CComBSTR's overloaded assignment operator, which has been implemented to work with existing CComBSTR objects or literal strings:

```
// CoHexagon working with the ATL CComBSTR data type.
class ATL_NO_VTABLE CCoHexagon :
```

```
        public CComObjectRootEx<CComSingleThreadModel>,
        public CComCoClass<CCoHexagon, &CLSID_CoHexagon>,
        public IDraw,
        public IShapeEdit,
        public IErase, ·
        public IShapeID
{
public:
        CCoHexagon()
        {
                m_bstrName = L"";        // Set to a empty string in constructor.
        }
...
private:
        CComBSTR m_bstrName;
};
```

We can now use the Copy() method to return a safe copy of the m_bstrName data member:

```
// Copy() safely returns a BSTR to the client.
STDMETHODIMP CCoHexagon::get_Name(BSTR *pVal)
{
        // Client wants a copy of the string.
        *pVal = m_bstrName.Copy();
        return S_OK;
}
```

When you want to return a BSTR to a client using CComBSTR you make a call to the Copy() method. This will call SysAllocStringLen() on your behalf and hand off the client a brand new BSTR which is identical to your own:

```
// CComBSTR::Copy()
BSTR Copy() const
{
        return ::SysAllocStringLen(m_str, ::SysStringLen(m_str));
}
```

In the put_Name implementation, use the overloaded operator=:

```
// Overloaded operator= will safely clean up m_str and reset it to newVal.
STDMETHODIMP CCoHexagon::put_Name(BSTR newVal)
{
        // Client wants to change the string.
        m_bstrName = newVal;
        return S_OK;
}
```

The assignment operator has been overloaded twice for CComBSTR. One version allows you to assign a text literal, the other allows you to set one CComBSTR to another. The version used for the put_Name function is as follows:

```
// Operator= Take One.
CComBSTR& operator=(LPCOLESTR pSrc)
{
        ::SysFreeString(m_str);
        m_str = ::SysAllocString(pSrc);
        return *this;
}
```

The other version of the overloaded assignment operator looks like so:

```
// Operator= Take Two.
CComBSTR& operator=(const CComBSTR& src)
{
    if (m_str != src.m_str)
    {
        if (m_str)
            ::SysFreeString(m_str);
        m_str = src.Copy();
    }
    return *this;
}
```

Notice that the assignment between two CComBSTR objects will not occur if the source is the same as the target. If you wish to examine the remaining methods of CComBSTR you may open <atlbase.h> (or online help) and take a look for yourself. Now that we have some help managing the de facto BSTR, let's see how ATL will help us work with string conversions.

ATL Conversion Macros

Beyond the CComBSTR data type, ATL defines a number of conversion macros to use in place of the Unicode to ANSI to Unicode API functions we examined in Chapter 3. Reading the macros without a roadmap is just about impossible, so we need a heads up. All conversion macros take a similar form: *X2Y*. Here, X identifies the type of string you have and Y is the string you want. All macros take a single argument, that being the "string you have." The end result of using these macros is a new string of the Y variety. X or Y may be composed of the following shorthand combinations:

Macro Conversion Symbol	Meaning in Life
C	Represents a C++ const tag.
BSTR	Represents a COM BSTR data type.
A	Represents an ANSI character pointer type (char* or LPSTR)
W	Represents a Unicode character pointer type (wchar_t* or LPWSTR).
T	Represents Win32 TCHAR or LPTSTR types.
OLE	Represents a LPOLESTR.

Armed with this knowledge, here is a listing of the ATL conversion macros:

ANSI to...	OLE to...	TCHAR to...	wchar_t to...
A2BSTR	OLE2A	T2A	W2A
A2COLE	OLE2BSTR	T2BSTR	W2BSTR
A2CT	OLE2CA	T2CA	W2CA
A2CW	OLE2CT	T2COLE	W2COLE

ANSI to...	OLE to...	TCHAR to...	wchar_t to...
A2OLE	OLE2CW	T2CW	W2CT
A2T	OLE2T	T2OLE	W2OLE
A2W	OLE2W	T2W	W2T

In order to convert from type X to type Y, these macros need to establish a set of temporary variables to hold and swap the string buffers. These variables are provided for you automatically when you specify the USES_CONVERSION macro <u>before</u> you use the conversion macros:

```
// This macro expands to define a number of temporary variables used by the numerous
// ATL conversion macros.
#define USES_CONVERSION int _convert = 0; _convert; UINT _acp = CP_ACP; \
    _acp; LPCWSTR _lpw = NULL; _lpw; LPCSTR _lpa = NULL; _lpa
```

Convention dictates that the USES_CONVERSION macro be the first line in some method scope. For example:

```
// This method takes an incoming BSTR and converts to ANSI using W2A.
STDMETHODIMP CMyATLClass::ChangeThisBSTRToANSI(BSTR bstr)
{
    USES_CONVERSION;
    MessageBox(NULL, W2A(bstr), "I converted a BSTR into a char*!", MB_OK);
    return S_OK;
}
```

Using the conversion macros and CComBSTR can most certainly make your COM text programming endeavors more productive and less painful. If you are interested in seeing what the ATL conversion macros resolve to, check out <atlconv.h>. Now that you have seen the basics of working with the ATL CASE tools, we will finish up this chapter by examining ATL's debugging support.

Debugging ATL Projects

Reading this section is completely optional, as COM development has now become easy and intuitive when using ATL. OK that's a lie. The truth is, ATL can add complexity to an already challenging architecture. To help ease our pain even further, ATL does provide a number of helpful debugging tricks, which we will now examine.

First of all, ATL does provide a macro for tracing the flow of execution in your code. When you wish to send diagnostic strings into the Visual C++ Debug window, use ATLTRACE. This macro will expand to either a call to AtlTrace() (for debug builds) or nothing (in non-debug builds). ATLTRACE is much like the MFC tracing macros, in that the calling syntax mimics the C printf() function. Assume you wish to display a string that reveals the FILLTYPE sent from a client:

```
// Making use of ATLTRACE.
STDMETHODIMP CCoHexagon::Fill(FILLTYPE fType)
{
    ATLTRACE("Client is using fill type number: %d\n", fType);
...
```

```
        return S_OK;
}
```

When you are in a debug session, you will see this formatted string appear in your Debug window:

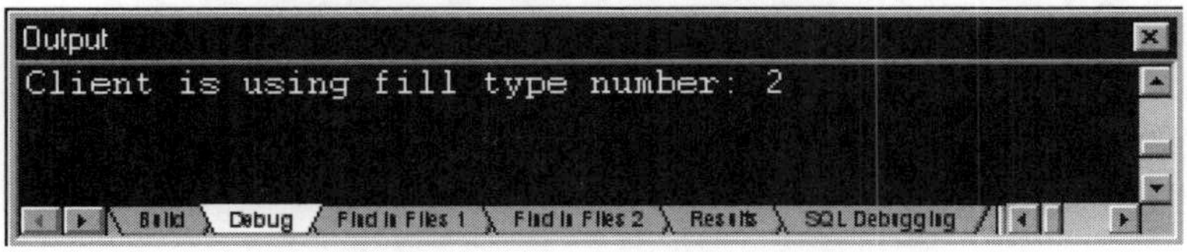

Figure 6-26:
ATLTRACE
output.

Another helpful debugging aid is the _ATL_DEBUG_QI preprocessor symbol. When this constant is defined in your project, you will be able to see the QueryInterface() calls sent to your coclasses during a debug session. To enable this functionality, you may add a #define entry in your stdafx.h file:

```
// stdafx.h
#define STRICT
#ifndef _WIN32_WINNT
#define _WIN32_WINNT 0x0400
#endif
#define _ATL_APARTMENT_THREADED
// Enable QI debugging support
#define _ATL_DEBUG_QI
```

In order to debug a COM DLL, you will have to select an EXE used to host the server at debug time. Assume a VB client project has been compiled and has been specified as the EXE to host ATLShapesServer.dll during a debug session (simply start a debug session for the DLL and navigate to the compiled EXE server from the resulting dialog box). Here is a possible output for CoHexagon's QI debug session:

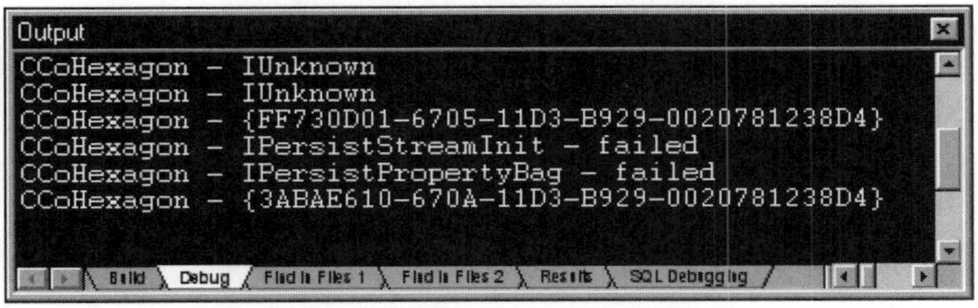

Figure 6-27:
_ATL_DEBUG_
QI output.

The GUIDs you see in Figure 6-27 specify IID_IDraw and IID_IErase. If you would rather see the friendly text names appear in the QI debug session (such as IUnknown), you will need to ensure your interfaces are registered under HKCR\Interface. Recall that if your COM interfaces are all VARIANT compliant, you may specify the [oleautomation] attribute to leverage the universal marshaler.

Also recall (from Chapter 5) that when you register your type information using the COM library, any interface marked with this attribute is automatically merged into the registry. If we were to add the [oleautomation] attribute to IDraw, IShapeEdit, IErase, and

IShapeID and rebuild the project (which will also reregister the server), we would find a more intuitive QI dump:

Figure 6-28:
_ATL_DEBUG_
QI only uses
friendly names
for registered
interfaces.

```
Output                                                          [X]
CComClassFactory - IClassFactory
CCoHexagon - IUnknown
CCoHexagon - IUnknown
CCoHexagon - IDraw
CCoHexagon - IPersistStreamInit - failed
CCoHexagon - IPersistPropertyBag - failed
CCoHexagon - IErase
  Build \ Debug / Find in Files 1 \ Find in Files 2 \ Results \ SQL Debugging /
```

The final bit of ATL debugging that can prove very helpful is the _ATL_DEBUG_INTERFACES. This preprocessor flag supercedes _ATL_DEBUG_QI in that you see not only the interface requested by a client, but the current reference count to the interfaces. If we were to edit stdafx.h to use _ATL_DEBUG_INTERFACES and recompile, here is a new debugging session output:

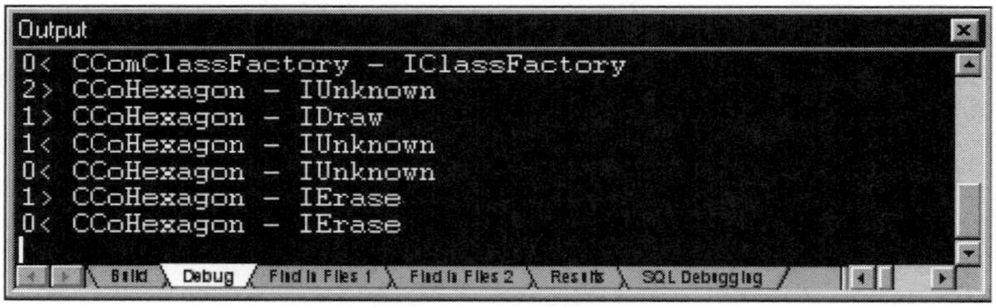

Figure 6-29:
_ATL_DEBUG_
INTERFACES
also displays
reference
counts.

```
Output                                                          [X]
0< CComClassFactory - IClassFactory
2> CCoHexagon - IUnknown
1> CCoHexagon - IDraw
1< CCoHexagon - IUnknown
0< CCoHexagon - IUnknown
1> CCoHexagon - IErase
0< CCoHexagon - IErase
  Build \ Debug / Find in Files 1 \ Find in Files 2 \ Results \ SQL Debugging /
```

The best thing about using _ATL_DEBUG_INTERFACES is that it is smart enough to detect mismanaged reference counting! Visual Basic will always ultimately call Release() on all acquired interfaces, so let's assume we have a C++ client that created CoHexagon and forgets to Release() the obtained IDraw interface. In a debug session, we would find the following listing:

```
INTERFACE LEAK: RefCount = 1, MaxRefCount = 1, {Allocation = 4} CCoHexagon - IDraw
```

So then, that wraps up our initial look at the Active Template Library. This chapter has you at a point where you can move around intelligently in the ATL environment, but there is a ton more to see. Move onto the next lab, and then to Chapter 7 to drill down deeper into the framework's support for COM classes.

Lab 6-1: ATL Car Server

This lab will allow you to work with the various tools and techniques introduced in this chapter including the ATL COM AppWizard, ATL Object Wizard, and Implement Interface Wizard. You will be creating an ATL version of the CoCar you know and love. Beyond implementing the ICreateCar, IStats, and IEngine interfaces, you will also be adding an additional interface containing COM properties.

Note: This lab will serve as the basis of numerous other labs throughout the book. When you have completed this lab, you may wish to make a complete copy of this project to use as a starting point in the future.

The solution for this lab can be found on your CD-ROM under:
Labs\Chapter 06\ATLCarServer
Labs\Chapter 06\ATLCarServer\VB Client

Step One: Develop the Component Housing and Code Examination.

Begin your lab by accessing the ATL COM AppWizard. Create an in-process server named **ATLCarServer,** with no support for MFC, MTS, or merging of proxy/stub code. Once you hit the Finish button you will be presented with a confirmation dialog. Hit **OK** and compile your new DLL.

Figure 6-30:
The initial
ATL COM
AppWizard
exports.

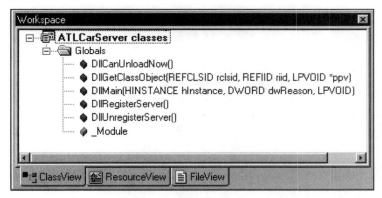

Expand the Globals folder from ClassView (Figure 6-30). Remember that the AppWizard is used to generate the necessary code for COM servers, and at this point you will have no coclasses in your project. ATL implements your DLL exports by calling various methods of your project-wide instance of CComModule, _Module. Examine the source code behind DllCanUnloadNow(), DllGetClassObject(), DllMain(), DllRegisterServer(), and DllUnregisterServer(). Take the time to look up CComModule from online help and investigate the various members of this class.

As you have seen, and will see much more of in Chapter 9, CComModule uses your project's object map to get much of its work accomplished (object creation and registration). Every COM object that you wish to allow a client to activate must be listed in your object map. Currently your map is empty, as we have not yet added any ATL coclasses to the project:

```
// Initial COM Map.
BEGIN_OBJECT_MAP(ObjectMap)
END_OBJECT_MAP()
```

Also recall that the ATL COM AppWizard will automatically include a DEF file into your project to export your DLL functions:

```
; ATLCarServer.def : Declares the module parameters.
LIBRARY "ATLCarServer.DLL"
EXPORTS
    DllCanUnloadNow         @1 PRIVATE
    DllGetClassObject       @2 PRIVATE
    DllRegisterServer       @3 PRIVATE
    DllUnregisterServer     @4 PRIVATE
```

Finally, examine your FileView subfolders. ATL projects always provide separate files for implementation code, class definitions, and project resources. MIDL-generated files are automatically placed in the External Dependencies folder. When you have finished examining the initial AppWizard generated files, move to step two.

Step Two: Insert a Simple Object

Access the ATL Object Wizard. Insert a Simple Object named **ATLCoCar**. Be sure to change the name of the initial interface to **ICreateCar**. Also be sure you select a **Custom** interface from the Attributes tab, leaving all other options as is.

Figure 6-31: Changing the suggested name for the [default] interface.

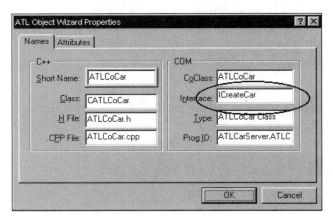

Once you have inserted this simple object, take a look at your class declaration. You will see that your ATL class derives from two ATL templates and your custom interface. CComObjectRootEx<> and its base class CComObjectRootBase provide helper functions used to implement the methods of IUnknown. CComCoClass<> defines a default class factory for your new coclass (via the DECLARE_CLASSFACTORY macro) as well as aggregation support (via the DECLARE_AGGREGATABLE macro).

```
// The initial CoCar.
class ATL_NO_VTABLE CATLCoCar :
    public CComObjectRootEx<CComSingleThreadModel>,
    public CComCoClass<CATLCoCar, &CLSID_ATLCoCar>,
    public ICreateCar
{
...
};
```

Locate your COM map. Recall the COM map is used to provide a table driven implementation of QueryInterface(). For each interface supported in your COM class you will need to be sure to add a COM_INTERFACE_ENTRY listing, or else clients will not be able to receive vPtrs for the requested interface. The Object Wizard has already added an entry for your [default] interface, and thus your COM map should appear as so:

```
// Updated COM Map.
BEGIN_COM_MAP(CATLCoCar)
    COM_INTERFACE_ENTRY(ICreateCar)
END_COM_MAP()
```

Now examine your project's IDL file. You should see the interface definition for ICreateCar as well as support for ICreateCar in your coclass statement. You may wish to add the [oleautomation] attribute to the initial IDL code to ensure interface registration. Last but not least, check out your RGS file. Recall that ATL servers are all self registering and the script contained in a coclass's RGS file will be entered or removed from the system registry.

Step Three: Implement the ICreateCar Interface

Access the Add Method Wizard by right-clicking on the ICreateCar interface from ClassView. Add the **SetPetName()** method, taking a single [in] BSTR as the sole parameter. Remember to define your parameters in IDL notation:

Figure 6-32:
Adding
methods à la
ATL.

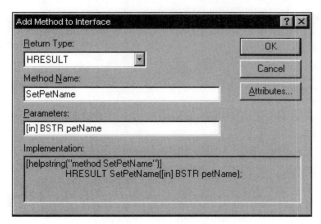

Open the Add Method Wizard once again, and add **SetMaxSpeed()** to ICreateCar. When you have added these methods, your interface definition will appear as so:

```
// The ICreateCar interface in IDL syntax.
interface ICreateCar : IUnknown
{
    [helpstring("method SetPetName")]
    HRESULT SetPetName([in] BSTR petName);
    [helpstring("method SetMaxSpeed")]
    HRESULT SetMaxSpeed([in] int maxSp);
};
```

Add a private CComBSTR to your class named **m_petName**, as well as a private integer named **m_maxSpeed**. In the constructor of your coclass, set each state variable to a default value (remember that CComBSTR objects are set to NULL, not an empty string!):

```
// Recall that CComBSTR does not set the underlying BSTR to an empty string!
CATLCoCar() : m_maxSpeed(0)
{
     // Set the BSTR to an empty string
     m_petName = "";
}
```

Use these two data members to implement the methods of ICreateCar. Because the Object Wizard has already added stub code to your implementation file, you can focus on the logic behind the interface. Be sure to set the car's maximum speed only if it is less than or equal to 500 MPH:

```
// Same as it ever was...
STDMETHODIMP CATLCoCar::SetMaxSpeed(int maxSp)
{
     // Assume MAX_SPEED is a class level const,
     // i.e., const int MAX_SPEED = 500;
     if(maxSp < MAX_SPEED)
          m_maxSpeed = maxSp;
     return S_OK;
}
```

SetPetName can make use of the overloaded assignment operator of CComBSTR. Remember that CComBSTR is making the same system string function calls you were making by hand in previous labs:

```
// Using overloaded operators of CComBSTR.
STDMETHODIMP CATLCoCar::SetPetName(BSTR petName)
{
     // operator= is a good thing!
     m_petName = petName;
     return S_OK;
}
```

Go ahead and compile the project, just to be sure you come out clean.

Step Four: Add an Interface by Hand

Wizards are good tools when you want to save yourself some typing. The problem is if you click on too many CASE tools without understanding what is being done on your behalf, you are sure to get burned (not to mention what to do if the CASE tool breaks). To avoid that pitfall, we will now add support for IStats by hand.

Begin by opening up your IDL file and define a bare bones interface definition. Use guidgen.exe to grab a new IID for IStats (be sure to select the registry format option):

```
// You can't escape understanding IDL when using ATL.
[object, uuid(A533DA31-D372-11d2-B8CF-0020781238D4), oleautomation,
helpstring("Get info about this car")]
interface IStats : IUnknown
{
};
```

Next, add this new interface to your coclass definition in the project's library statement:

```
// Manually add support for your new interfaces.
coclass ATLCoCar
{
     [default] interface ICreateCar;
```

```
    interface IStats;
};
```

Go ahead and save the IDL file. You should see IStats appear in ClassView.

Now open up your coclass's header file and derive your ATL CoCar from IStats. Next, add an entry for IStats to your COM map. This step is critical.

```
// The COM_INTERFACE_ENTRY macro spits out a vPtr for a given interface.
BEGIN_COM_MAP(CATLCoCar)
    COM_INTERFACE_ENTRY(ICreateCar)
    COM_INTERFACE_ENTRY(IStats)
END_COM_MAP()
```

Go ahead and save everything and recompile.

In this chapter you were told about the true "by hand" approach. After this point you would type the IDL method definitions, add prototypes to the header file (by hand), and then implement the methods in the CPP file. But here is a shortcut. Now that you have an empty IDL interface definition and a COM map entry, simply right-click on the IStats interface from ClassView and add the **DisplayStats()** method using the New Method Wizard (recall this method takes no parameters). When you click OK, you will see that the CASE tool has automatically added a prototype and stub code on your behalf:

```
// ATL Wizard starter code.
STDMETHODIMP CATLCoCar::DisplayStats()
{
    // TODO: Add your implementation code here
    return S_OK;
}
```

I thought you might like that cheat. Now, finish off the IDL definition by adding the **GetPetName()** method:

Figure 6-33: Don't forget to specify parameter attributes!

GetPetName() will be using the Copy() method of CComBSTR rather than raw system string functions:

```
// Using the overloaded Copy method.
STDMETHODIMP CATLCoCar::GetPetName(BSTR *petName)
```

```
{
    *petName = m_petName.Copy();
    return S_OK;
}
```

DisplayStats() will be trimmed down a bit, as we can now make use of the ATL conversion macros. Define the USES_CONVERSION macro within the method, and transform your BSTR into a char* using W2A. Format the string into a message box and exit the function:

```
// Using ATL conversion macros.
STDMETHODIMP CATLCoCar::DisplayStats()
{
    // Use the ATL conversion macros.
    USES_CONVERSION;
    MessageBox(NULL, W2A(m_petName), "Pet Name",
               MB_OK | MB_SETFOREGROUND);
    char buff[MAX_NAME_LENGTH];
    memset(buff, 0, sizeof(buff));
    sprintf(buff, "%d", m_maxSpeed);
    MessageBox(NULL, buff, "Max Speed",
               MB_OK | MB_SETFOREGROUND);
    return S_OK;
}
```

Compile the server and move on to the next step.

Step Five: Use the Implement Interface Wizard

Next, we must add support for IEngine. Begin by writing an empty IDL interface definition for IEngine. Next, add support for your new interface in the coclass definition and recompile the project. Now, right-click on CATLCoCar from ClassView, and select the Implement Interface Wizard. You will see IEngine listed from the tool, as your class does not yet support this interface. Select it and click **OK**.

Figure 6-34:
Don't forget to recompile your type library first.

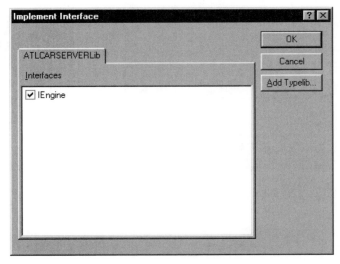

This tool will derive your class from IEngine as well as add an entry to your COM map. Now use the Add Method Wizard as usual to define the methods of IEngine. When you have finished, your IDL should appear as such:

```
[object, uuid(A533DA30-D372-11d2-B8CF-0020781238D4), oleautomation,
helpstring("Rev your car & slow it down")]
interface IEngine : IUnknown
{
     [helpstring("method SpeedUp")]
     HRESULT SpeedUp();
     [helpstring("method GetMaxSpeed")]
     HRESULT GetMaxSpeed([out, retval] int* maxSpeed);
     [helpstring("method GetCurSpeed")]
     HRESULT GetCurSpeed([out, retval] int* curSpeed);
};
```

Finally, implement these three methods. Add a private integer to hold the current speed, and code SpeedUp(), GetMaxSpeed(), and GetCurSpeed() as usual:

```
// IEngine implementation.
STDMETHODIMP CATLCoCar::SpeedUp()
{
     m_currSpeed += 10;
     return S_OK;
}
STDMETHODIMP CATLCoCar::GetMaxSpeed(int *maxSpeed)
{
     *maxSpeed = m_maxSpeed;
     return S_OK;
}
STDMETHODIMP CATLCoCar::GetCurSpeed(int *curSpeed)
{
     *curSpeed = m_currSpeed;
     return S_OK;
}
```

Compile your ATL server. You may wish to whip together a quick Visual Basic test client at this point (or simply recycle an existing VB car tester). Before you move onto the next chapter, however, we have one additional step...

Step Six: An Interface with Properties

We are going to extend the functionality of our CoCar by maintaining information about the current owner. Define an IDL interface named **IOwnerInfo** and use the Implement Interface Wizard to add support for this interface to ATLCoCar. Next, right-click on this new interface from ClassView and access the Add Property Wizard. Define two properties to keep track of the name and address of the car owner. Your IDL will appear as such:

```
// Using [propput] and [propget].
[object, uuid(530D7320-333E-11d3-B904-0020781238D4), oleautomation,
helpstring("Information about the owner of this car")]
interface IOwnerInfo : IUnknown
{
     [propget, helpstring("property Name")]
     HRESULT Name([out, retval] BSTR *pVal);
     [propput, helpstring("property Name")]
```

```
HRESULT Name([in] BSTR newVal);
[propget, helpstring("property Address")]
HRESULT Address([out, retval] BSTR *pVal);
[propput, helpstring("property Address")]
HRESULT Address([in] BSTR newVal);
};
```

Add two CComBSTRs to your CoCar, and implement the four methods as necessary. Coding a property pair is identical to a traditional COM interface method. Here is the Name property to get you started:

```
// IDL Properties map to get_ and put_ methods.
STDMETHODIMP CATLCoCar::get_Name(BSTR *pVal)
{
    *pVal = m_ownerName.Copy();
    return S_OK;
}
STDMETHODIMP CATLCoCar::put_Name(BSTR newVal)
{
    m_ownerName = newVal;
    return S_OK;
}
```

Again, create a simple Visual Basic (or Java or C++) tester to exercise your new interface. The point here is to understand that properties are a nicety C++ developers give to COM developers using kinder, gentler languages such as VB:

```
' Don't forget to include a reference to this type information.
'
Private Sub Form_Load()
    Dim MyCar As New ATLCoCar
    MyCar.SetMaxSpeed 40
    MyCar.SetPetName "JoJo"
    Dim itfOwner As IOwnerInfo
    Set itfOwner = MyCar
    itfOwner.Name = "Manu"
    MsgBox itfOwner.Name
    itfOwner.Address = "123 Happy Lane"
    MsgBox itfOwner.Address
End Sub
```

There you have it! I am sure you agree that this iteration of the CoCar was substantially simpler to implement with the help of the ATL framework. In the next chapter, we will build on your current understanding of the ATL framework and investigate just how ATL provides core services to a COM class.

Chapter Summary

The goal of this chapter was to introduce you to the basic process of building an ATL COM server. ATL projects begin by accessing the ATL COM AppWizard, which provides support for your component housing. CComModule is the ATL class that encapsulates the inner details common to EXE and DLL servers. The object map is used by CComModule to register and create your coclass, and contains an entry for each COM object contained in the server.

The ATL Object Wizard is used to insert coclasses into a component house. In this chapter, we examined a Simple Object and took a look at the basic functionality provided by the framework. CComObjectRootEx<> and its base class CComObjectRootBase provide the basic hooks for your IUnknown implementation. CComCoClass<> defines a default class factory for your coclass, as well as defines how your coclass will behave as an aggregate. In the next several chapters, we will take a look at exactly how ATL provides this support.

Finally, we examined a set of CASE tools that can help make your ATL development even easier. New interfaces can be added to an existing ATL coclass using the Implement Interface Wizard. Properties and methods may be added to existing interfaces using the Add Property and Add Method tools, respectively.

Chapter 7

ATL COM Objects and COM Exceptions

Objectives:

- **Understand ATL's support for the various threading models of COM.**
- **Understand ATL's support for IUnknown.**
- **Understand the various CComObject<> templates.**
- **Understand the derivation of an ATL Simple Object.**
- **Examine the ATL COM map.**
- **Learn to throw and receive COM exceptions.**

Although the previous chapter got you up and running with the ATL environment, this chapter will begin to drill down into the architecture of the ATL framework in greater detail. We begin this chapter with an overview of multithreaded programming, and quickly see how the concept of numerous paths of execution in a Win32 process can affect the COM developer. Next, we examine the options ATL provides to equip your coclasses to run within single-threaded and multithreaded apartments.

We will then examine the derivation of an ATL Simple Object and learn about the functionality supplied by CComObjectRootBase, CComObjectRootEx<>, and CComCo-Class<>. During this process, we will understand how ATL provides support for IUnknown, learn about the inner workings of the ATL COM map, and investigate the various CComObject<> templates. We wrap up this chapter by learning how a coclass can return rich error information to both C++ and Visual Basic COM clients.

Just In Case You Didn't Know...

In this chapter we will be digging into the ATL source code. Although this chapter (and others that follow) illustrates the relevant pieces of the code under discussion, you may wish to take a look for yourself. The Visual C++ IDE has a very nice browsing tool to help you navigate around your code; however, it is turned off by default (given that this option can increase your build times). To enable project browsing support, access the Project Settings dialog from the Project | Settings menu selection. Go under the Browse Info tab and select the Build browse info file option:

Figure 7-1: Enabling project browsing.

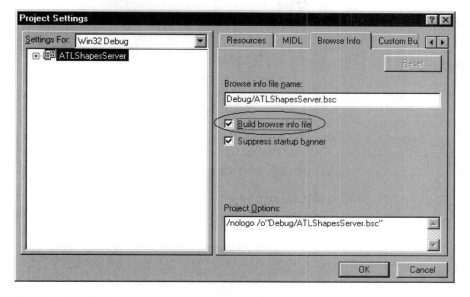

Once this option is enabled (and your project is recompiled), you will be able to right-click on class names, macro entries, data types, or whatnot and select Go to Definition of... from the resulting context pop-up menu.

For example, if you want to see what BEGIN_COM_MAP is all about, right-click on this macro and select "Go To Definition of BEGIN_COM_MAP"; the IDE will open the correct ATL source file containing this definition, placing your cursor at the formal definition.

Once you have enabled project browsing, you may also access the options provided by the Browse toolbar. From here, you may examine files, base classes, derived classes, and so forth (Figure 7-2). One odd annoyance with this tool is that it will close down automati-

Figure 7-2: The Developers Studio Browse window.

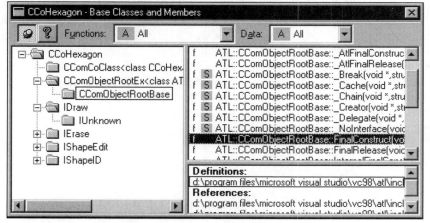

cally when you double-click on a given entry (which opens the correct file). To keep your browser window open at all times, select the thumb tack icon.

> **Note:** Needless to say (but I'll say it anyway), be very careful when examining the ATL source files. If you edit and save, this could entail a reinstallation of Visual C++.

An Overview of Win32 Threads

As you know, the 32-bit Windows OS manages processes. For each EXE loaded into memory, the operating system creates a separate and isolated memory partition (process) for use during its lifetime. By default, every process has at least one main thread which is the entry point for the program—known as WinMain() in a traditional Windows application or main() in a console application. A *thread* is a path of execution within a process, and is owned by the same process during its entire lifetime.

Many developers are completely happy to write software containing a single path of execution within the process, and do so quite successfully. This developer's life is generally quite peaceful, as he or she is unconcerned with ensuring the program's data is thread safe given the fact that there is only one thread to worry about at any given time. On the down side, a single-threaded application can be a bit unresponsive to user input requests if that single thread is performing a complex operation (such as printing out a lengthy text file).

Other developers demand more work from a process. Under Win32, it is possible for a developer to create multiple threads within a single process, using a handful of thread API functions such as CreateThread(). Each thread becomes a unique path of execution in the process, and has concurrent access to all data in that process. As you may have guessed, developers typically create additional threads in a process to help improve the program's overall responsiveness.

A thread savvy developer may create a background worker thread to perform a labor-intensive calculation (again, such as printing a large text file). As this secondary thread is churning away, the main thread is still responsive to user interaction, which gives the entire process the potential of delivering greater performance. However, this is only a possibility. Too many threads in a single process can actually degrade performance, as the CPU must switch between the active threads in the process (which takes time).

Multithreading is often a simple illusion provided by the operating system. Machines that host a single CPU do not have the ability to literally handle multiple threads at the same exact time. Rather, a single CPU will execute one thread for a unit of time (called a *time slice*) based on the thread's priority level. When a thread's time slice is up, the existing thread is suspended to allow the other thread to perform its business. In order for a thread to remember what was happening before it was kicked out of the way, each thread is given the ability to write to Thread Local Storage (TLS) and provided a separate call stack, as illustrated by Figure 7-3:

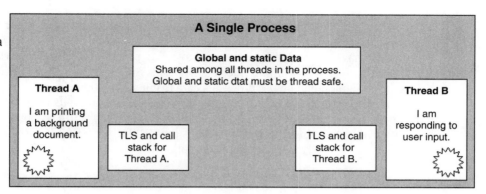

Figure 7-3: Each thread in a process receives local storage but shares global data.

The Problem of Concurrency and Thread Synchronization

Machines supporting multiple CPUs can enjoy very responsive multithreaded programs, as threads can be assigned to individual CPUs by the operating system, as opposed to time slices on a single CPU. Machines with a single CPU will have threads swapped around by the Windows' thread scheduler. Beyond taking time, the process of switching between threads can cause additional problems. For example, assume a given thread is accessing a point of data, and in the process begins to modify it. Now assume that the first thread is told to wait, to allow another thread to access the same point of data. If the first thread was not finished with its task, the second thread may be modifying data that is in an unstable state.

To protect the application's data from corruption, the developer must make use of any number of Win32 threading primitives such as critical sections, mutexes, or semaphores to synchronize access to shared data. A common primitive (and the default provided by ATL) is the critical section, represented by the CRITICAL_SECTION structure.

When using this approach to make blocks of code thread safe, you must initialize and terminate your CRITICAL_SECTION using Win32 API thread calls. Once the critical section is ready to go, you enter the initialized section, perform any calculations, and exit the critical section. As an example, assume you wish to write a thread-safe function that operates on a private member variable using a CRITICAL_SECTION. You may write code as so:

```
// This member function adjusts a private integer in a thread-safe
// manner using a CRITICAL_SECTION.
STDMETHODIMP CCoClass::FooBar()
{
    CRITICAL_SECTION cs;
    InitializeCriticalSection(&cs);
    EnterCriticalSection(&cs);
        m_theInt = m_theInt + 10;    // Thread safe!
        if(m_theInt >= 3000)         // Thread safe!
            m_theInt = 0;            // I'm still thread safe!
    LeaveCriticalSection(&cs);
    DeleteCriticalSection(&cs);
    return S_OK;
}
```

Of course, you could declare a private CRITICAL_SECTION data member for use by the entire class, but I'm sure you get the general idea.

So, as we have thread loving and thread avoiding programmers in the world, we end up with single-threaded and multithreaded applications. Single-threaded applications are typically easier to implement, as the process's data is inherently thread safe.

Multithreaded applications are tougher to engineer, as numerous threads can operate on the application's data at the same time. Unless the developer has accounted for this possibility using threading primitives (such as the CRITICAL_SECTION), the program may end up with a good amount of data corruption.

A Complete Threading Example

Before we add the complexity of COM threading into your life, let's look at a COM-free threading example. Assume you have a Win32 console application that defines a structure named FOOFIGHTER which contains two fields. Also assume the program has declared a single global instance of this item:

```
// An application wide global structure.
struct FOOFIGHTER
{
     int one;
     int two;
} Foo;
int main(int argc, char* argv[])
{
     return 0;
}
```

The primary thread of this application is the program's entry point: main(). When a thread wishes to spawn additional threads, the developer can make use of the CreateThread() function. The parameters of this function break down as so:

```
// A thread can create another thread using this Win32 API call.
HANDLE CreateThread(
  LPSECURITY_ATTRIBUTES lpThreadAttributes,    // Security attributes
  DWORD dwStackSize,                           // Initial thread stack size
  LPTHREAD_START_ROUTINE lpStartAddress,       // Pointer to thread function
  LPVOID lpParameter,                          // Argument for new thread
  DWORD dwCreationFlags,                       // Creation flags
  LPDWORD lpThreadId);                         // Pointer to receive thread ID
```

To illustrate how multiple threads can lead to data corruption, let's set up main() to create some additional threads, all of which will access the shared global FOOFIGHTER structure. Notice in the code below how CreateThread() returns a HANDLE. This handle will be sent into CloseHandle() to clean up, so be sure to hold onto this value:

```
// Main thread.
int main(int argc, char* argv[])
{
     // Make some secondary threads.
     for(int i = 0; i < 5; i++)
     {
```

```
        DWORD dw;
        HANDLE h = CreateThread(NULL, 0, ThreadProc, (void*)i, 0, &dw);
        CloseHandle(h);
    }
    return 0;
}
```

The third parameter of CreateThread() specifies the name of the function that will perform the work of the new secondary threads; here it is ThreadProc(). The name of this function can be anything at all but must have the correct signature. Our thread procedure will increment each field of the FOOFIGHTER structure by one and print out the results. To simulate a lengthy task, the Sleep() method is called between field access:

```
// The thread procedure.
DWORD WINAPI ThreadProc(void *p)
{
    // Access field one.
    cout<< "[S] Foo.one++ is: " << Foo.one++ << endl;
    Sleep(500);
    // Access field two.
    cout<< "[S] Foo.two++ is: " << Foo.two++ << endl;
    Sleep(500);
    return 0;
}
```

Now, to illustrate the problem of multiple threads accessing the same point of data, the primary thread (main()) will also increment the fields of FOOFIGHTER by one:

```
// Main thread will now access the same data as the secondary threads.
int main(int argc, char* argv[])
{
    for(int i = 0; i < 5; i++)
    {
        // Access field one.
        cout<< "[P] Foo.one++ is: " << Foo.one++ << endl;
        Sleep(500);
        // Access field two.
        cout<< "[P] Foo.two++ is: " << Foo.two++ << endl;
        Sleep(500);
        // Make a new thread.
        DWORD dw;
        HANDLE h = CreateThread(NULL, 0, ThreadProc, (void*)i, 0, &dw);
        CloseHandle(h);
    }
    // Wait for all threads to finish.
    Sleep(5000);
    return 0;
}
```

If we run the program, we suddenly have a number of threads all accessing the same single global instance of FOOFIGHTER. The Windows scheduler will swap between active threads, giving ample time for data corruption. Here is some possible output:

Figure 7-4:
When multiple threads access global data not secured by a Win32 locking primitive, bad things happen.

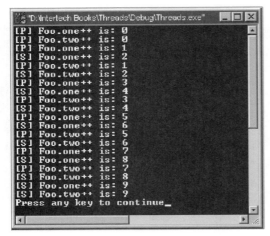

```
"D:\Intertech Books\Threads\Debug\Threads.exe"
[P] Foo.one++ is: 0
[P] Foo.two++ is: 0
[P] Foo.one++ is: 1
[S] Foo.one++ is: 2
[P] Foo.two++ is: 1
[S] Foo.two++ is: 2
[P] Foo.one++ is: 3
[S] Foo.one++ is: 4
[P] Foo.two++ is: 3
[S] Foo.two++ is: 4
[P] Foo.one++ is: 5
[S] Foo.one++ is: 6
[P] Foo.two++ is: 5
[S] Foo.two++ is: 6
[P] Foo.one++ is: 7
[S] Foo.one++ is: 8
[P] Foo.two++ is: 7
[S] Foo.two++ is: 8
[S] Foo.one++ is: 9
[S] Foo.two++ is: 9
Press any key to continue_
```

One would hope to see access to the fields of FOOFIGHTER incremented safely, but the job of doing so is up to the Windows developer. In other words, we need to secure our shared data using a Win32 locking primitive, such as the CRITICAL_SECTION.

Locking Down the FOOFIGHTER

To provide safe data access to the FOOFIGHTER structure among multiple threads, we can wrap a CRITICAL_SECTION around the field manipulation logic. Working with a critical section requires the use of four Win32 functions:

CRITICAL_SECTION Function	Meaning in Life
InitializeCriticalSection()	Initializes a CRITICAL_SECTION structure for use by the program.
DeleteCriticalSection()	Destroys a CRITICAL_SECTION.
EnterCriticalSection()	Locks down a block of code for safe data access.
LeaveCriticalSection()	Unlocks a block of code from safe data access.

Here is an updated version of the previous program, which wraps access to the FOOFIGHTER structure using a Win32 critical section. To make it more interesting, the primary thread asks whether safe or unsafe data access is desired. Based on this flag, we will either safely lock access to the fields of FOOFIGHTER or allow all threads to mangle the data accordingly:

```
// Safe data access tester.
CRITICAL_SECTION cs;          // A global critical section.
int ans;                      // Stores safe or mangled access request.
DWORD WINAPI ThreadProc(void *p)
```

```
    {
        // Enter the safety of a critical section.
        if(ans == 1)
            EnterCriticalSection(&cs);
            cout<< "[S] Foo.one++ is: " << Foo.one++ << endl;
            Sleep(500);
            cout<< "[S] Foo.two++ is: " << Foo.two++ << endl;
            Sleep(500);
        // All done with accessing FOOFIGHTER, leave critical section.
        if(ans == 1)
            LeaveCriticalSection(&cs);
        return 0;
    }
    int main(int argc, char* argv[])
    {
        // Ask user what type of access they want.
        cout<< "Preserve (1) or Mangle (0) data? ";
        cin >> ans;
        cout << endl << endl;
        // Initialize critical section on startup.
        if(ans == 1)
            InitializeCriticalSection(&cs);
        // Make some secondary threads and access FOOFIGHTER.
        for(int i = 0; i < 5; i++)
        {
            // Enter the safety of a critical section.
            if(ans == 1)
                EnterCriticalSection(&cs);
                cout<< "[P] Foo.one++ is: " << Foo.one++ << endl;
                Sleep(500);
                cout<< "[P] Foo.two++ is: " << Foo.two++ << endl;
                Sleep(500);
            // All done with accessing FOOFIGHTER, leave critical section.
            if(ans == 1)
                LeaveCriticalSection(&cs);
            DWORD dw;
            HANDLE h = CreateThread(NULL, 0, ThreadProc, (void*)i, 0, &dw);
            CloseHandle(h);
        }
        Sleep(5000);
        // Kill critical section on shutdown.
        if(ans == 1)
            DeleteCriticalSection(&cs);
        return 0;
    }
```

If the user now elects to preserve data access using a CRITICAL_SECTION, the output would look like the following:

Figure 7-5:
The thread-safe
FOOFIGHTER.

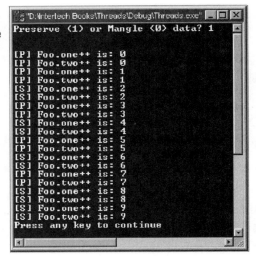

```
"D:\Intertech Books\Threads\Debug\Threads.exe"
Preserve (1) or Mangle (0) data? 1

[P] Foo.one++ is: 0
[P] Foo.two++ is: 0
[P] Foo.one++ is: 1
[P] Foo.two++ is: 1
[S] Foo.one++ is: 2
[S] Foo.two++ is: 2
[P] Foo.one++ is: 3
[P] Foo.two++ is: 3
[S] Foo.one++ is: 4
[S] Foo.two++ is: 4
[P] Foo.one++ is: 5
[P] Foo.two++ is: 5
[S] Foo.one++ is: 6
[S] Foo.two++ is: 6
[P] Foo.one++ is: 7
[P] Foo.two++ is: 7
[S] Foo.one++ is: 8
[S] Foo.two++ is: 8
[S] Foo.one++ is: 9
[S] Foo.two++ is: 9
Press any key to continue
```

As you can see, the FOOFIGHTER structure is now safely wrapped by a CRITICAL_SECTION, which provides safe access by multiple threads. When developers create applications with numerous threads of execution, all shared data must be locked in a similar manner.

The FOOFIGHTER example program is included on your CD-ROM under the Labs\Chapter 07\Threads subdirectory.

Threads and the COM Developer

As a COM developer, you need to accept the fact that your object may be loaded into a process which has numerous threads running around, many of which might be coming to attack an instance of your coclass. For example, what if the Threads program was not accessing a FOOFIGHTER structure, but the IDraw interface of CoHexagon?

If you do not take the steps to provide your COM object with the correct armor, your data may be mangled, as numerous threads are attempting to change the state of your object at more or less the same time. To protect your COM objects from the violent world of multithreaded clients, you too must protect your data using any number of threading primitives such as critical sections, semaphores, or mutexes.

You should also be prepared for a single-threaded process to create and use your COM objects. In this case, all is well, and you may rest assured that a single thread will access your object at any given time. Under this condition, you do not have to worry about writing enormous amounts of code to keep your data safe (you should still ensure shared global and static data is thread safe).

Nevertheless, you cannot control which type of client (single-threaded or multithreaded) will load your server and access the COM objects it contains. You can, however, advertise how you wish your objects to be handled under diverse threading conditions.

On a related note, a COM client should not need to worry if your object is thread safe. In other words, if a process containing ten threads wishes to create and use an instance of CoHexagon, the client assumes the object is ready to fend for itself. It would be a bother indeed if a COM client was only able to work with objects supporting the correct threading model. The Component Object Model would fail miserably if multithreaded clients could only use COM objects explicitly coded to work with multithreaded clients. It would be an additional bother if COM developers needed to create thread-safe and thread-oblivious versions of the same object to account for the possible threading option of the client. In order to account for the fact that multithreaded or single-threaded clients may load an object that may or may not be thread safe, COM provides a level of abstraction called an apartment.

Understanding COM Apartments

To understand what a COM apartment is, let's begin by learning what it is not. An apartment is <u>not</u> a process. An apartment is <u>not</u> a thread. An *apartment* is a conceptual entity which defines an execution context within a process. Apartments provide an environment for COM objects to live, based on their own level of thread awareness. When identifying the apartment model of a COM object, we are able to instruct the COM subsystem how we wish our objects to be handled under various threading conditions. Thus, it is possible to allow objects and clients to mingle together, regardless of each entity's level of thread awareness. COM apartments currently come in two varieties: single threaded (STA) or multithreaded (MTA).

The Single-Threaded Apartment (STA)

A single-threaded apartment (STA) contains exactly one thread (not too much of a stretch there, huh?). If your coclass supports this threading model, you instruct COM to ensure that only a single thread may access it at any given time. The end result of this model is that the developer of this object (that would be you) will not need to synchronize access to your object's state data, as COM ensures that thread access takes place using a queue. This is accomplished by the automatic creation of an invisible window used to serialize client access into the object through an associated message pump.

Note: Objects living in an STA should still protect any global or static data from concurrent access using a Win32 locking primitive (CRITICAL_SECTION, et.al.).

Each STA in a process has a hidden window message pump controlling synchronized access to the COM objects it contains (this invisible window is based off the OleMainThreadWndClass window class). Therefore, if requests are coming to your object from numerous threads, they must form a line at the queue and wait for the former thread to finish up its business. As you can tell, the STA is a very safe place for a COM object to live. However, if multiple threads attempt to use your object, access can be less responsive. You may visualize the STA as the following:

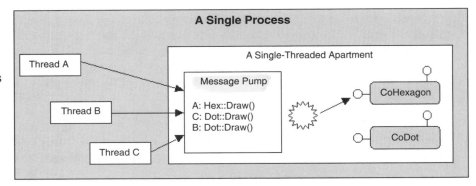

Figure 7-6: Multiple threads must wait in line to access objects in an STA.

In Figure 7-6, we can see that COM objects configured to live in an STA are protected from multiple clients (threads). The hidden window and the associated message pump force each thread to wait in line, as all requests are sent through the message pump in the apartment. For example, thread C is second in the queue, and cannot have its Draw() request honored until client A is finished with its Draw() request. Likewise, thread B is dead last in line, and must wait for C and A to finish up before it gets a chance to ask for CoDot to be rendered.

So, the STA is a safe place for COM objects to live, as the majority of the synchronization effort is provided automatically by the COM subsystem. However, you can suffer a performance hit if multiple clients are attempting to access an object. To allow faster access by multiple threads COM provides the multithreaded apartment (MTA).

The Multithreaded Apartment (MTA)

The multithreaded apartment (MTA) can contain any number of threads. Rather than providing serialized access via a background message pump, the MTA allows individual client requests to execute on a separate thread. COM objects supporting this model must be programmed to be accessed by multiple threads in a safe manner, thus the developer must write thread savvy code to ensure the state data in the object is protected from a possible bombardment of simultaneous requests. The MTA may be visualized as so:

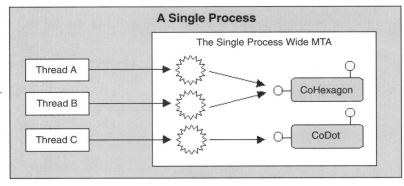

Figure 7-7: Objects in the MTA can be accessed by multiple threads at once.

In Figure 7-7, we have three threads accessing two COM objects loaded into the MTA. As the objects are residing in the MTA, they make the bold assertion that they are ready to

take any number of client requests from any number of threads, and have been programmed accordingly. Threads A and B are both coming to ask CoHexagon to perform
some action. If CoHexagon has its internal data protected by a critical section (or similar
threading primitive), we have a thread-safe coclass. If not, we have data corruption.

Entering an Apartment

Understand that a single process may contain numerous apartments in various combinations. To be specific, a process may contain the following types of (and number of)
apartments:

- A process may contain exactly one MTA or no MTA at all.
- A process may have zero or more STAs in addition to a single MTA.

The very first STA created in a process is called the main STA. Legacy COM objects that
do not advertise a threading model (as there were no threading issues to contend with at
the time) are loaded into the main STA automatically. An object in the main STA is completely safe from any threading issues, as COM ensures a single thread may access all
state, global, and static data at a given time.

A logical question at this point is "How are these apartments created?" COM library
functions, of course! As you know, when a client is preparing to use a coclass, the client
must first call CoInitialize() before any further work can be done. This method is a legacy
function of the COM library that initializes the COM libraries, and automatically specifies
that the launching thread is about to join a new STA. Under the hood, CoInitialize() actually maps to a call to CoInitializeEx(). CoInitializeEx() allows a calling thread to specify
which type of apartment it wishes to join via the dwCoInit parameter (the first parameter
is reserved, and must be NULL):

```
// CoInitialize() is really mapped to CoInitializeEx().
// CoInitializeEx() allows a thread to join an STA or MTA.
HRESULT CoInitializeEx(LPVOID pvReserved, DWORD dwCoInit);
```

> **Note:**   Beware! You cannot use this COM library function until you define the
> _WIN32_DCOM symbol in your current project.

Assume a COM client wishes to use CoHexagon. Before doing so, the client must specify
which apartment the calling thread is about to join. As you recall, a process always has a
single main thread; thus, if your main thread wants to join the single process-wide MTA,
you can write the following:

```
// Send the main thread into the process wide MTA.
#define _WIN32_DCOM      // A must have!
#include <windows.h>
int main(int argc, char* argv[])
{
    CoInitializeEx(NULL, COINIT_MULTITHREADED);
    // Do some COM stuff...
    CoUninitialize();
    return 0;
}
```

If the client would rather enter an STA, you may simply call CoInitialize(), or alternatively use CoInitializeEx() specifying COINIT_APARTMENTTHREADED:

```
// Sent the main thread into an STA.
#define _WIN32_DCOM      // Still a must have!
#include <windows.h>
int main(int argc, char* argv[])
{
     // This call to CoInitializeEx() is equivalent to CoInitialize(NULL).
     CoInitializeEx(NULL, COINIT_APARTMENTTHREADED);
     // Do some other COM stuff...
     CoUninitialize();
     return 0;
}
```

Specifying a Threading Model for EXE Servers

To make things more interesting, EXE COM servers also specify the apartment they wish to join by calling CoInitializeEx() (or the legacy CoInitialize()). When we developed our EXE COM server in Chapter 5, WinMain() began its life by joining a new STA:

```
// EXE servers get to specify the apartment they wish to join.
int APIENTRY WinMain(HINSTANCE hInstance, HINSTANCE hPrevInstance,
                     LPSTR lpCmdLine, int nCmdShow)
{
     // The objects in this server are not thread safe, so enter an STA.
     CoInitialize(NULL);
     // Register class objects...
     // Start a message pump...
     CoUninitialize();
     return 0;
}
```

If you have an EXE server that contains thread-safe coclasses, you may opt to enter the MTA:

```
// EXE servers get to specify the apartment they belong to.
int APIENTRY WinMain(HINSTANCE hInstance, HINSTANCE hPrevInstance,
                     LPSTR lpCmdLine, int nCmdShow)
{
     // Objects are thread safe, so let's join the MTA.
     CoInitializeEx(NULL, COINIT_MULTITHREADED);
     // Register class objects...
     // Start a message pump...
     CoUninitialize();
     return 0;
}
```

As you can see, every thread that is using COM must specify an apartment it wishes to join. This is true for both COM clients and EXE servers. If you are developing a COM client that spawns additional threads beyond the primary thread, they must all make a call to CoInitializeEx() before working with COM objects, and call CoUninitialize() when the worker thread has exited.

Specifying a Threading Model for DLL Servers

Now, we need to examine how coclasses living in DLLs get to advertise the type of apartment they wish to join. You may have noticed that the in-proc servers we have developed never called CoInitialize(), CoInitializeEx(), or CoUninitialize(). The reason is that in-proc servers always live in the context of the client, as the client has already called CoInitialize[Ex]().

To instruct COM how to handle the objects contained in an in-proc server, each coclass in the server is marked in the registry with the ThreadingModel value. This value is added to the InprocServer32 subkey of HKCR\CLSID\{guid}. For example, here is the ThreadingModel value of the ATL CoCar created in Chapter 6:

Figure 7-8: In-process servers advertise their threading preference with the Threading-Model value.

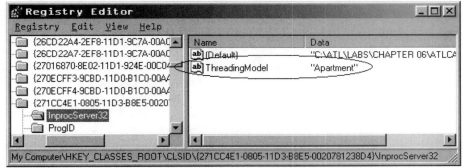

If you go back and examine the RGS file for CoCar, you will see the syntax responsible for this entry:

```
ForceRemove {4DE3E4A3-16C6-11D3-B8F3-0020781238D4} = s 'CoCar Class'
{
     ProgID = s 'ATLCoCar.CoCar.1'
     VersionIndependentProgID = s 'ATLCoCar.CoCar'
     InprocServer32 = s '%MODULE%'
     {
          val ThreadingModel = s 'Apartment'
     }
     'TypeLib' = s '{4DE3E496-16C6-11D3-B8F3-0020781238D4}'
}
```

The ThreadingModel value may take one of four settings, each of which is used to instruct COM how to treat your in-process objects with regard to matters of thread awareness:

- **(none)**: If there is an empty ThreadingModel value in the registry for an in-process coclass, COM assumes this object must join the very first STA created in a process. Recall, the first STA created in a process is called the main STA. An object in the main STA is 100% thread safe (including access to global and static data).

- **Apartment**: Objects will load into some STA in the process. This ensures all instance data is thread safe, as every STA has serialized access provided by the hidden message pump. Your global and static data must still be made thread safe, as multiple objects of this type would share the same global data.

- **Free:** Free threading is just another way to refer to the MTA. Objects marked as Free wish to be loaded into the process-wide MTA. These objects had better be 100% thread safe, as COM will not serialize thread requests through a hidden message pump. The job of creating thread-safe code is your responsibility.
- **Both:** If the ApartmentModel value has been set to Both, your object is safe to work in either an STA or the MTA, based on the threading preferences of the client. Your objects must still be 100% thread safe.

Marshaling Revisited

If you recall the discussion of COM marshaling from Chapter 5, you remember that when a COM client wishes to access a COM object outside of its own process, it does so using stubs and proxies. It is through stubs and proxies that location transparency is achieved as both parties believe they are always communicating with an in-process entity. While this is technically correct, we did not address a very important aspect of COM's marshaling layer: Calls across apartments <u>also</u> entail the loading of stub and proxies. Therefore, not only are client requests marshaled across process and machine boundaries, but during intra-apartment calls as well. Keep the following situations in mind:

- If a process has multiple STAs, and an object in one STA wishes to access a COM object in another STA, stubs and proxies are loaded.
- If an object in the process-wide MTA wishes to work with an object in an STA, stubs and proxies are loaded.
- If two objects in the same STA want to communicate, stubs and proxies are <u>not</u> loaded.
- If two objects in the process-wide MTA wish to communicate, stubs and proxies are <u>not</u> loaded.

Figure 7-9 sums up some possible interactions between a process and its apartments, stubs (S), and proxies (P):

Figure 7-9: Intra-apartment calls entail stubs and proxies.

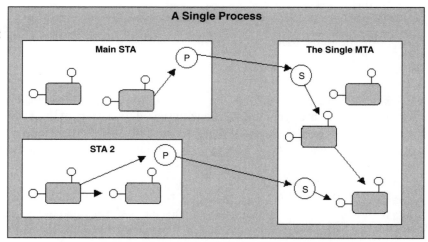

> **Note:** If a client's threading model is incompatible with the coclass's threading model, COM will automatically create stubs and proxies when appropriate. The COM runtime will never refuse to create an object due to incompatible threading.

That concludes our primer of the threading models of COM. Remember that the apartment is a conceptual unit that allows objects written with different levels of thread awareness to live together peacefully. In fact, the apartment is yet another application of location transparency. With this bit of theory behind us, we now turn our attention to the support ATL provides to create thread-aware as well as thread-oblivious coclasses.

Specifying an Object's Threading Model à la ATL

The ATL Object Wizard allows you to specify a COM object's level of thread safety from the Attributes tab. Leaving aside the free threaded marshaler, you are presented with a total of four selections, as seen in Figure 7-10:

Figure 7-10: ATL coclasses support all of COM's threading models.

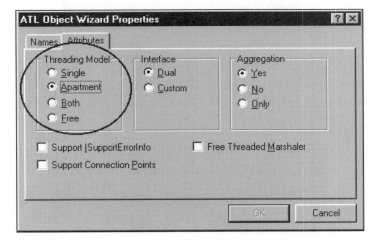

Among other things, these four options map to the possible values placed in the registry to mark a coclass's level of thread awareness. Realize, however, that the ATL naming conventions do not perfectly map to the ThreadingModel value. Assume that we have placed four coclasses in a given DLL server, each one supporting a possible ATL threading option (Single, Apartment, Both, and Free). If we were to examine the generated RGS file for each one, we can see the resulting registry entry.

A coclass marked with the Single threading model will map to (none), and therefore the ThreadingModel value will be empty. Recall that coclasses that do not specify a ThreadingModel value will only be loaded into the initial STA:

```
ForceRemove {D241B77E-29DF-11D3-B900-0020781238D4} = s 'CoSingle Class'
{
    ProgID = s 'Threading.CoSingle.1'
    VersionIndependentProgID = s 'Threading.CoSingle'
    InprocServer32 = s '%MODULE%'
```

```
        {
        }
    'TypeLib' = s '{D241B771-29DF-11D3-B900-0020781238D4}'
}
```

ATL coclasses marked as Apartment will load into some STA in the process:

```
ForceRemove {D241B780-29DF-11D3-B900-0020781238D4} = s 'CoApt Class'
{
    ProgID = s 'Threading.CoApt.1'
    VersionIndependentProgID = s 'Threading.CoApt'
    ForceRemove 'Programmable'
    InprocServer32 = s '%MODULE%'
    {
        val ThreadingModel = s 'Apartment'
    }
    'TypeLib' = s '{D241B771-29DF-11D3-B900-0020781238D4}'
}
```

Coclasses marked as Both or Free will have one of the following lines substituted in their RGS file, and advertise they prefer to be loaded into the process-wide MTA:

```
val ThreadingModel = s 'Free'
val ThreadingModel = s 'Both'
```

ATL's Core Threading Classes

ATL provides a number of major high-level classes to help you write thread savvy COM objects. Here are two key players, which show up as the parameter passed into CComObjectRootEx< >:

- **CComSingleThreadModel:** For objects designed for life in the STA.
- **CComMultiThreadModel:** For objects designed for life in the MTA.

Each class defines a number of methods that provide the correct level of threading support for your coclass. The public interface of both classes is identical and you may therefore program against them in the same way. This is very helpful should you ever decide to change your coclass's level of thread awareness. You can simply change the threading template parameter of CComObjectRootEx< > and leave your existing code base unaltered.

Each class provides the Increment() and Decrement() methods to adjust your object's reference counter (m_dwRef) with the appropriate level of thread safety. Each class also provides three typedefs (AutoCriticalSection, CriticalSection, and ThreadModelNoCS) wrapping a Win32 CRITICAL_SECTION (or not, in the case of ThreadModelNoCS) to synchronize your data.

ATL Support for Objects in the STA

ATL objects marked as Single or Apartment will make use of CComSingleThreadModel, specifying the coclass as a member of an STA:

```
// Coclasses marked as Single or Apartment will be parameterized based off
// CComSingleThreadModel.
class ATL_NO_VTABLE CCoHexagon :
    public CComObjectRootEx<CComSingleThreadModel>,
    public CComCoClass< CCoHexagon, &CLSID_CoHexagon >,
    public IDraw
{ ... };
```

CComSingleThreadModel is defined in <atlbase.h> as the following:

```
// Provides support for the STA threading model.
class CComSingleThreadModel
{
public:
    // Used to adjust your object's reference count.
    static ULONG WINAPI Increment(LPLONG p) {return ++(*p);}
    static ULONG WINAPI Decrement(LPLONG p) {return --(*p);}
    // Typedefs used to wrap a critical section.
    // These do nothing in an STA...
    typedef CComFakeCriticalSection AutoCriticalSection;
    typedef CComFakeCriticalSection CriticalSection;
    typedef CComSingleThreadModel ThreadModelNoCS;
};
```

Notice that the Increment() and Decrement() methods of CComSingleThreadModel adjust the object's reference count without regard to thread safety using the C increment (++) and decrement (--) operators. This is a good thing, as objects living in the STA are guaranteed to have a single thread accessing them at any given time, and thus do not need any additional overhead of Win32 atomic locking functions.

CComSingleThreadModel and CComMultiThreadModel each define three typedefs that provide three different ways to work with the underlying CRITICAL_SECTION (or not, if using the ThreadModelNoCS typedef). Exactly what these typedefs map to will depend on the threading model of the coclass.

The first typedef (AutoCriticalSection) is used when you wish to have your critical section automatically initialized and terminated using the constructor and destructor of the typedef-ed class. The CriticalSection typedef forces you to take control over the lifetime of the critical section by calling the Init() and Term() methods manually. Finally, ThreadModelNoCS provides a way to protect your code using a synchronization primitive other than the Win32 CRITICAL_SECTION.

As objects living in the STA have no real interest in thread-safe code, CComSingleThreadModel defines "dummy" critical sections for the AutoCriticalSection and CriticalSection typedefs, represented by CComFakeCriticalSection, which, as you would expect, does nothing:

```
// Dummy implementations of a critical section for objects in the STA.
class CComFakeCriticalSection
{
public:
    void Lock() {}
    void Unlock() {}
    void Init() {}
    void Term() {}
};
```

When CComSingleThreadModel is passed into CComObjectRootEx<>, the typedefs are used to adjust the CRITICAL_SECTION data member maintained by CComObjectRootEx<>:

```
// How CComObjectRootEx<> makes use of CComSingleThreadModel.
template <>
class CComObjectRootEx<CComSingleThreadModel> : public CComObjectRootBase
{
```

```
public:
    typedef CComSingleThreadModel _ThreadModel;
    typedef _ThreadModel::AutoCriticalSection _CritSec;
    typedef CComObjectLockT<_ThreadModel> ObjectLock;
    ...
    void Lock() {}
    void Unlock() {}
};
```

The Lock() and Unlock() methods your ATL coclasses inherit make use of the AutoCriticalSection typedef and could now be used to create a thread-safe block of ATL code:

```
// STA objects use a fake critical section.
STDMETHODIMP CCoClass::FooBar()
{
    // A thread-safe function that uses a fake CRITICAL_SECTION.
    Lock();
        m_theInt = m_theInt + 10;
        if(m_theInt >= 3000)
            m_theInt = 0;
    Unlock();
    return S_OK;
}
```

Of course, Lock() and Unlock() do nothing if your object is living in the STA. However, as both CComSingleThreadModel and CComMultiThreadModel have the same public interface, if you suddenly wish to change the threading model of a coclass, the Lock() and Unlock() methods take on a whole new life. Let's take a look at how ATL provides support for objects choosing to live in the frantic world of the MTA.

ATL Support for Objects in the MTA

If your coclass has been marked as Free or Both you need to be thread safe; hence, your coclass will be parameterized using CComMultiThreadModel:

```
// Coclasses marked as Free or Both will be parameterized based off
// CComMultiThreadModel.
class ATL_NO_VTABLE CCoThreadSavvyHexagon :
    public CComObjectRootEx< CComMultiThreadModel >,
    public CComCoClass< CCoThreadSavvyHexagon,
                        &CLSID_CoThreadSavvyHexagon >,
    public IDraw
{ ... };
```

CComMultiThreadModel is defined in <atlbase.h> as the following. Note this class has the same public interface as CComSingleThreadModel:

```
// For thread savvy COM objects in the MTA.
class CComMultiThreadModel
{
public:
    static ULONG WINAPI Increment(LPLONG p)
        {return InterlockedIncrement(p);}
    static ULONG WINAPI Decrement(LPLONG p)
        {return InterlockedDecrement(p);}
    typedef CComAutoCriticalSection AutoCriticalSection;
```

```
        typedef CComCriticalSection CriticalSection;
        typedef CComMultiThreadModelNoCS ThreadModelNoCS;
};
```

Here, the Win32 API InterlockedIncrement() and InterlockedDecrement() methods are used to adjust the reference count for the coclass in a thread-safe (atomic) manner rather than the more efficient (but less safe) increment and decrement operators. As we do care a great deal about thread safety when we belong to the MTA, the AutoCriticalSection typedef resolves to a true CRITICAL_SECTION à la CComAutoCriticalSection:

```
// Objects in the MTA receive a "real" critical section which operate on the
// CRITICAL_SECTION data member.
class CComAutoCriticalSection
{
public:
    void Lock() {EnterCriticalSection(&m_sec);}
    void Unlock() {LeaveCriticalSection(&m_sec);}
    CComAutoCriticalSection() {InitializeCriticalSection(&m_sec);}
    ~CComAutoCriticalSection() {DeleteCriticalSection(&m_sec);}
    CRITICAL_SECTION m_sec;
};
```

Using CComMultiThreadModel, Lock() and Unlock() operate on a true critical section:

```
// Locking down our critical data using ATL.
STDMETHODIMP CCoClass::FooBar()
{
    // A thread-safe function using a CRITICAL_SECTION.
    Lock();
        m_theInt = m_theInt + 10;
        if(m_theInt >= 3000)
            m_theInt = 0;
    Unlock();
    return S_OK;
}
```

So then to recap, ATL provides a number of threading classes that provide the most efficient reference counting scheme for your coclass, based on the object's level of thread awareness. Objects in the STA will use the ++ and -- operators, while objects in the MTA will make use of InterlockedIncrement() and InterlockedDecrement().

As well, your coclass will receive the Lock() and Unlock() methods to protect your state data from concurrency issues. The implementation of these methods depends on the parameter of CComObjectRootEx<>. CComSingleThreadModel defines a no-op critical section via CComFakeCriticalSection. CComMultiThreadModel defines a "real" critical section using CComAutoCriticalSection.

Understand that ATL source code is "thread safe enough" as well. As an ATL developer, you will never need to concern yourself with the thread safety of framework code. ATL state and global data is protected from access by multiple threads, using CComGlobalsThreadModel. This is not a new class, but a typedef that resolves to either CComSingleThreadModel or CComMultiThreadModel, based on the default threading of the ATL server.

An ATL Server's Default Threading Support

Every project generated using the ATL COM AppWizard maintains what is known as the "default threading model" for the server. This default is used to account for all threading details you don't directly have too much concern over (such as how ATL locks its global data). If you examine your precompiled header (stdafx.h) you will see the default ATL threading classes are determined based on a handful of ATL defined constants. These flags are used to specify which ATL classes will be used by the framework to work with global and ATL state data, as seen in <atlbase.h>:

```
// These flags are used to determine how ATL should take care of its own data.
//
#if defined(_ATL_SINGLE_THREADED)
    typedef CComSingleThreadModel CComObjectThreadModel;
    typedef CComSingleThreadModel CComGlobalsThreadModel;
#elif defined(_ATL_APARTMENT_THREADED)
    typedef CComSingleThreadModel CComObjectThreadModel;
    typedef CComMultiThreadModel CComGlobalsThreadModel;
#else // _ATL_FREE_THREADED
    typedef CComMultiThreadModel CComObjectThreadModel;
    typedef CComMultiThreadModel CComGlobalsThreadModel;
#endif
```

As you can guess, if you replace the initial flag found in your precompiled header file (_ATL_APARTMENT_THREADED) you would change how ATL should handle these matters. If you have any MTA-aware objects in your server, you should change this flag to _ATL_FREE_THREADED to force ATL to use more thread savvy classes to handle access to ATL's global and static data.

Threading Summary

Threading is a complex issue, even in a typical Win32 application using no COM objects whatsoever. As we have seen, a single process always has a primary thread (WinMain()) which may spawn additional threads using CreateThread() or a similar threading function. When a process has multiple threads, the developer must ensure that all shared data is thread safe, making use of a locking mechanism such as the CRITICAL_SECTION.

Once you inject COM into the picture, threading becomes even more complex. Given the fact that your COM objects can be used by single-threaded or multithreaded processes, we must ensure our coclasses are thread safe as well. However, in COM, the concept of an apartment helps ensure that COM objects receive automatic synchronization if the object is marked to live in the STA. If an object is marked to live in the MTA, it is again the responsibility of the developer to ensure all shared data is thread safe. As you have also seen, stubs and proxies are loaded for any intra-apartment calls.

Finally, when you use ATL to build your coclasses, you receive Lock() and Unlock() methods that operate on a true CRITICAL_SECTION (for objects in the MTA) or a fake critical section (for objects in the STA). If you have no interest (or time) to create thread savvy coclasses, mark your objects as apartment threaded. Your performance is still reasonably good. If you love threads (or have lots of spare time), set up your objects to live in the MTA, and Lock() and Unlock() accordingly.

ATL Coclasses are Abstract Base Classes

Now that we have a better understanding of ATL's threading support, we are in a good position to examine the architecture of a typical ATL coclass. For the purpose of this discussion, assume we have created an in-process server named ATLShapesServer.dll, which contains a single ATL Simple Object named CoRectangle. The name of the [default] custom interface is IDraw.

As we drill into the anatomy of CoRectangle, keep in mind that ATL was designed to produce the smallest and fastest COM objects around. To achieve this goal, ATL uses some rather bizarre coding conventions, which introduce a number of surprises to the uninitiated developer. Here is the first such surprise: CoRectangle is an *abstract base class* at this point and cannot be directly created. Recall that abstract base classes contain at least one pure virtual function. Therefore the following will not compile:

```
// Can't create abstract base classes!
CCoRectangle *pRect = new CCoRectangle();      // Compiler error.
```

Truth be told, CoRectangle does not yet have an implementation of the IUnknown interface. As you may have guessed (or are already aware) CoRectangle is not the most derived class in the ATL inheritance chain. ATL objects are in fact passed as a parameter to one of the various CComObject<> templates. These ATL templates are responsible for providing a specific implementation of IUnknown for your coclass.

So, why does the ATL framework choose to specify the implementation of IUnknown "one level below" your coclass? Independence. COM objects may be created under a number of circumstances: on the stack, on the heap, as part of an aggregate, as a tear-off interface, and so forth (if some of these terms are unfamiliar to you at this point, keep reading). Each of these variations will require a slightly different implementation of the IUnknown interface.

The CComObject<> Templates

Rather than hard coding a specific IUnknown implementation directly into your coclass (such as CoRectangle), ATL provides a number of variations of CComObject<> templates which are used to assemble your coclass's IUnknown implementation under a number of different circumstances, keeping your ATL source code far more portable. For example, CoRectangle can be created as an object that does influence the server's object count or as an object that does not alter the server's object count, without altering the code base in CoRectangle. Instead, simply pass the ATL coclass into the correct variation of the CComObject<> template:

```
// Create a CoRectangle which keeps the server in memory.
CComObject< CCoRectangle >*pRect = NULL;
CComObject< CCoRectangle >::CreateInstance(&pRect);
// Create a CoRectangle which does not keep the server in memory.
CComObjectNoLock< CCoRectangle>*pRect =
    new CComObjectNoLock <CCoRectangle>;
```

Recall from Chapter 5 that class factories dwelling in EXEs should not alter the server-wide object count. Class factories in DLLs must adjust the server object count. This forced us to create two versions of the CoCar class factory, which differed only in the way they adjusted the server's global object counter. ATL abstracts away these minor differences by resolving the implementation of such details outside of the coclass itself.

The most common CComObject<> template is CComObject<> itself, which creates a heap-based, non-aggregated object. When passing an ATL coclass into CComObject<>, you should call the static CreateInstance() method, which ensures the framework triggers FinalConstruct() (we will see this shortly). If you do use the **new** keyword directly (as seen above with CComObjectNoLock<>), FinalConstruct() is not called, although you still do have a usable ATL COM object. Some of the most common variations of CComObject<> are seen below and are formally found in <atlcom.h>:

CComObject<> Template	Meaning in Life
CComObject<>	Creates a non-aggregated, heap-based object which affects the server's object count (m_nLockCnt).
CComObjectNoLock<>	Creates non-aggregated objects that do not adjust the server's object count (m_nLockCnt).
CComAggObject<>	Used to create classes that can work as an aggregate.
CComObjectStack<>	Creates objects whose lifetime is limited to some function scope.
CComObjectGlobal<>	Creates objects whose lifetime is dependent upon the lifetime of the server. Thus, the object's reference counter is based off CComModule::m_nLockCnt.
CComPolyObject<>	Creates objects that may or may not work as an aggregate.
CComTearOffObject<>	Creates an object that implements a tear-off interface.

Most of the time, you will not need to make use of these ATL templates directly, as the framework will use the correct variation when assembling your objects. In Chapter 8, we will begin to examine the full set of ATL's COM map macros. As you will see, many of these macros (when expanded) make use of these CComObject<> alternatives on your behalf.

For example, if you are exposing an interface as a tear-off, your COM map will have a listing for COM_INTERFACE_ENTRY_TEAR_OFF, which makes use of CComTearOffObject<>:

```
// Many ATL COM map macros used CComObject<> templates
// on your behalf.
#define COM_INTERFACE_ENTRY_TEAR_OFF(iid, x)\
    {&iid,\
    (DWORD)&_CComCreatorData<\
        CComInternalCreator< CComTearOffObject< x > >\
        >::data,\
    _Creator},
```

If you ever need to create an instance of an ATL coclass from within an ATL coclass (i.e., create an ATL object defined within your project) you would need to do so by hand and pass the coclass in question into one of the ATL CComObject<> templates. For the time being, we will only concern ourselves with CComObject<> and wait until Chapter 8 to examine the various alternatives.

Drilling into an ATL Simple Object

In addition to the support provided by the CComObject<> templates, CoRectangle receives a good deal of base class functionality. Figure 7-11 illustrates the derivation for CoRectangle. We will examine each level in turn, so just attempt to absorb the big picture for now:

Figure 7-11:
The derivation
of an ATL
Simple Object.

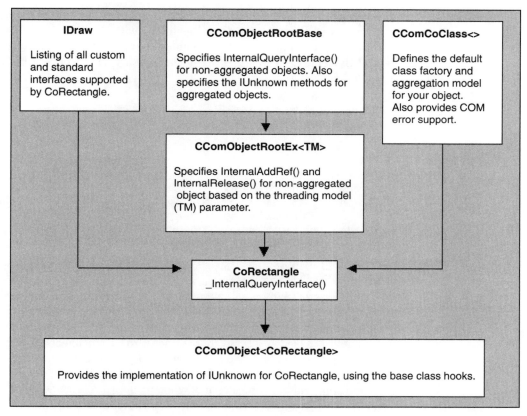

First off, each ATL coclass will derive from the set of interfaces that it supports. In the case of CoRectangle, this is IDraw (which in turn derives from IUnknown).

Beyond this, ATL Simple Objects derive from three framework base classes: CComObjectRootBase, CComObjectRootEx<>, and CComCoClass<>. Here is the initial code listing for CoRectangle:

```
// The CoRectangle Simple Object.
class ATL_NO_VTABLE CCoRectangle :
    public CComObjectRootEx<CComSingleThreadModel>,
    public CComCoClass<CCoRectangle, &CLSID_CoRectangle>,
    public IDraw
{
public:
    CCoRectangle()
    {}
// We will examine this macro in Chapter 9...
```

```
DECLARE_REGISTRY_RESOURCEID(IDR_CORECTANGLE)
BEGIN_COM_MAP(CCoRectangle
    COM_INTERFACE_ENTRY(IDraw)
END_COM_MAP()
};
```

The ATL_NO_VTABLE Class Declaration Tag

To better understand how ATL assembles a coclass, let's drill into the functionality provided by the framework from the top down, beginning with the ATL_NO_VTABLE class tag. If COM is all about handing out vTable pointers to interested clients, what could this possibly mean? By default, ATL classes are declared using ATL_NO_VTABLE, which is defined as the following:

```
// This class tag is nothing more than an optimization.
#ifdef _ATL_DISABLE_NO_VTABLE
    #define ATL_NO_VTABLE
#else
    #define ATL_NO_VTABLE __declspec(novtable)
#endif
```

> **Note:** If your project defines the _ATL_DISABLE_NO_VTABLE symbol (which you may do from the Project Settings dialog), _ATL_NO_VTABLE resolves to nothing, effectively disabling this option for every ATL coclass in the project.

This compiler optimization prevents the vPtr for a class from being initialized in the constructor and destructor of the class. Of course, after the constructor call, you do have a valid vPtr at your disposal. Why might we want to do this? Well, initializing a vPtr takes time. Technically speaking, the only time a derived class needs a proper vPtr is when it is the most derived class in the hierarchy. We have just seen that ATL objects are not the most derived, but are passed as a template parameter to CComObject<> and friends. ATL is doing everything it can to create zippy, lightweight COM objects, and this is just one example of how it is doing so.

There is one point you must be aware of when using the ATL_NO_VTABLE optimization. As you have no vPtr to work with in your constructor and destructor blocks, you cannot safely call any virtual or pure virtual methods of your base classes in their implementations! How then can you leverage base class functionality? Glad you asked.

The FinalConstruct() and FinalRelease() Methods

CComObjectRootBase defines two methods, which allow your class to safely perform any instance level initialization and termination code, as well as access base class functionality. Rather than accessing base class functionality in your constructor, use FinalConstruct(). If you need to perform any cleanup, use FinalRelease() rather than the destructor. These methods are given a default implementation in CComObjectRootBase as follows:

```
// Secondary creation call.
HRESULT FinalConstruct()
{
    return S_OK;
}
```

```
// Pre-destruction call.
void FinalRelease()
{
}
```

As you can see, these methods are implemented as simple stubs. Your derived class (such as CoRectangle) can override these methods in order to do any post-constructor and/or pre-destructor calls. FinalConstruct() will be called by the ATL framework right after the call to your coclass constructor. In this method you may safely access any base class functionality and create any inner objects (which we will do later), as well as initialize your own internal state data.

FinalRelease() will be called just before your object is about to be destroyed, and allows you to perform any cleanup required by the class. Using FinalConstruct() and FinalRelease() in your derived coclass is trivial:

```
// Overriding FinalConstruct() and FinalRelease().
//
class ATL_NO_VTABLE CCoRectangle :
    public CComObjectRootEx<CComSingleThreadModel>,
    public CComCoClass<CCoRectangle, &CLSID_CoRectangle>,
    public IDraw
{
...
    // Safe to access parents.
    HRESULT FinalConstruct()
    {
        MessageBox(NULL, "I have arrived!", "CoRect!",
                MB_OK | MB_SETFOREGROUND);
        return S_OK;
    }
    // Clean up after CoRectangle.
    void FinalRelease()
    {
        MessageBox(NULL, "I'm outta here", " CoRect!",
                MB_OK | MB_SETFOREGROUND);
    }
...
};
```

Now that the ATL_NO_VTABLE tag has been demystified, the next order of business is to examine CComObjectRootBase in some greater detail.

CComObjectRootBase: Providing IUnknown Helpers

Although you do not see mention of this class directly in your inheritance chain, CComObjectRootBase (defined in <atlcom.h>) is at the very top of an ATL coclass hierarchy. Beyond defining FinalConstruct() and FinalRelease(), CComObjectRootBase maintains a reference counting variable (m_dwRef) for an ATL coclass. This public data member is initialized to zero in the constructor of the class:

```
// m_dwRef is your object's reference counter. That is why we do not need to provide
// a private reference counter in our ATL coclasses. The framework maintains this on
// your behalf.
CComObjectRootBase()
{
```

```
        m_dwRef = 0L;
}
```

In addition to specifying the m_dwRef data member to represent your object's reference count, CComObjectRootBase also defines a method named InternalQueryInterface() which is used to obtain interface pointers for non-aggregated COM objects.

When your COM object is passed into the CComObject<> template, the "real" implementation of IUnknown::QueryInterface() will eventually call InternalQueryInterface(). This method in turn calls a helper method which performs the grunt work to see if a given interface is supported by your coclass:

```
// InternalQueryInterface() is used to discover if your coclass supports a given interface.
class CComObjectRootBase
{
public:
...
    static HRESULT WINAPI InternalQueryInterface(void* pThis,
        const _ATL_INTMAP_ENTRY* pEntries, REFIID iid,
        void** ppvObject)
    {
        ...
        HRESULT hRes = AtlInternalQueryInterface(pThis, pEntries, iid, ppvObject);
        ...
    }
};
```

InternalQueryInterface() takes a number of parameters: a pointer to the class itself (*pThis), the class's COM map (*pEntries), the GUID of the interface to be found (iid), and a place to store the interface pointer (**ppvObject). As we will see a bit later in this chapter, the ATL COM map defines an array of _ATL_INTMAP_ENTRY structures. Each structure in this array contains vital information about how to calculate the vPtr for a given interface supported by the coclass.

InternalQueryInterface() delegates the bulk of the work to a helper function named AtlInternalQueryInterface(). This method iterates over the COM map, testing for a given IID, until a NULL entry is discovered which signifies the end of the COM map.

We will see the code behind AtlInternalQueryInterface() a bit later in this chapter. Do understand, however, that this is the method responsible for obtaining interface pointers for any interested clients based on your coclass's COM map.

CComObjectRootBase: Support for Aggregation

CComObjectRootBase also defines methods used for tear-off interfaces and COM aggregation. ATL provides a set of "outer" IUnknown methods for this purpose, as well as a public IUnknown pointer (m_pOuterUnknown) used by the aggregated class. We will discuss aggregation and tear-off interfaces in Chapter 8, but since we are examining CComObjectRootBase at the moment, here are the outer IUnknown members:

```
// The 'outer' methods are used only for aggregation and tear-off relationships.
class CComObjectRootBase
{
public:
...
    ULONG OuterAddRef()
    {
```

```
            return m_pOuterUnknown->AddRef();
    }
    ULONG OuterRelease()
    {
            return m_pOuterUnknown->Release();
    }
    HRESULT OuterQueryInterface(REFIID iid, void ** ppvObject)
    {
            return m_pOuterUnknown->QueryInterface(iid, ppvObject);
    }
    // Pointer to the aggregating object's IUnknown.
    IUnknown* m_pOuterUnknown;
...
};
```

CComObjectRootBase: COM Map Macro Helpers

Finally, CComObjectRootBase defines six internal helper functions (_Chain(), _Break(), _NoInterface(), _Cache(), _Delegate(), and _Creator()) that are used by various ATL COM map macros to help calculate the vPtr for a given interface which is not supported using multiple inheritance. Here is a breakdown of when each of these internal helper methods are called:

CComObjectRootBase Helper Method	Meaning in Life
_Break()	Called internally by COM_INTERFACE_ENTRY_BREAK to issue a debug break.
_NoInterface()	Called internally by COM_INTERFACE_ENTRY_NOINTERFACE. Automatically returns E_NOINTERFACE for a requested interface.
_Creator()	Called internally by COM_INTERFACE_ENTRY_TEAR_OFF to create an instance of the tear-off class.
_Delegate()	Called internally by the non-auto aggregation macros COM_INTERFACE_ENTRY_AGGREGATE and COM_INTERFACE_ENTRY_AGGREGATE_BLIND to query an aggregated object for a given interface.
_Chain()	Called internally by COM_INTERFACE_ENTRY_CHAIN to forward a QueryInterface() call to a base class COM map.
_Cache()	Called by the ATL auto-aggregation macros as well as by COM_INTERFACE_ENTRY_CACHED_TEAR_OFF to create a cached tear-off class.

Much like the alternative CComObject<> templates, you should not need to interact with these helper functions directly. The framework will call these methods where appropriate. Take, for example, the COM_INTERFACE_ENTRY_NOINTERFACE macro. When expanded, a call to CComObjectRootBase::_NoInterface() is made automatically:

```
// Many of the more exotic COM map macros call these CComObjectRootBase helper
// functions to calculate a vPtr for an interface (or not).
#define COM_INTERFACE_ENTRY_NOINTERFACE(x)\
```

```
{& ATL_IIDOF(x), \
NULL, \
_NoInterface},
```

The implementation of _NoInterface() does what you might expect:

```
// COM_INTERFACE_ENTRY_NOINTERFACE calls _NoInterface() to explicitly
// inform a client that the coclass does not support the interface in question.
static HRESULT WINAPI _NoInterface(void* /* pv */, REFIID /* iid */, void** /* ppvObject */,
DWORD /* dw */)
{
    return E_NOINTERFACE;
}
```

Each of these internal helper functions, and the macros that call them, are found in
<atlcom.h>. Again, we will detail these alternative COM map macros and helper functions
in Chapter 8.

CComObjectRootEx<>: Establishing a Threading Behavior

So much for CComObjectRootBase. Let's take a look at the first direct parent to
CoRectangle, CComObjectRootEx<>:

```
// The sole parameter to CComObjectRootEx<> specifies a threading model for the
// coclass.
class ATL_NO_VTABLE CCoRectangle :
    public CComObjectRootEx<CComSingleThreadModel>,
    public CComCoClass<CCoRectangle, &CLSID_CoRectangle>,
    public IDraw
{ ... };
```

As we have seen earlier in this chapter, the parameter to CComObjectRootEx<> specifies
the level of threading support for a given coclass using CComSingleThreadModel (STA) or
CComMultiThreadModel (MTA).

CComObjectRootEx<> is a very lightweight class, providing exactly four methods
and a critical section typedef. This typedef is assembled based on the threading class
passed in as a template parameter. The first two methods, Lock() and Unlock(), are used in
your coclass to enter or leave a critical section (which as you recall is a "fake" critical section for objects in the STA).

The next two methods, InternalAddRef() and InternalRelease(), are used to adjust the
reference counter of non-aggregated objects and to define how the coclass should implement reference counting with regard to the appropriate level of thread safety.

Here is the definition of CComObjectRootEx<> as defined in <atlcom.h>:

```
// Your object's reference counting scheme will be "thread safe enough."
template <class ThreadModel>
class CComObjectRootEx : public CComObjectRootBase
{
public:
    // Threading model typedefs.
    typedef ThreadModel _ThreadModel;
    typedef _ThreadModel::AutoCriticalSection _CritSec;
...
    // ++ or InterlockedIncrement()
    ULONG InternalAddRef()
    {
```

```
                    return _ThreadModel::Increment(&m_dwRef);
              }
              // -- or InterlockedDecrement()
              ULONG InternalRelease()
              {
                    return _ThreadModel::Decrement(&m_dwRef);
              }
              // Do nothing or enter a critical section.
              void Lock()
              {
                    m_critsec.Lock();
              }
              // Do nothing or leave a critical section.
              void Unlock()
              {
                    m_critsec.Unlock();
              }
private:
              // CComFakeCriticalSection or CComAutoCriticalSection.
              _CritSec m_critsec;
};
```

CComCoClass<>: Class Factories, Aggregation and Error Handling

The final base class, CComCoClass< >, is found towards the end of CoRectangle's inheritance chain:

```
// The final core ATL base class.
class ATL_NO_VTABLE CCoRectangle :
      public CComObjectRootEx<CComSingleThreadModel>,
      public CComCoClass<CCoRectangle, &CLSID_CoRectangle>,
      public IDraw
{
      ...
};
```

This class is used to establish two critical aspects for your ATL object. First of all, CComCoClass< > defines the default level of aggregation support for the coclass. Next, CComCoClass< > supplies a default class factory used to specify how to create the CoRectangle. Both of these details are defined using ATL-specific macros:

```
// CoRectangle's aggregation support and class object are defined using ATL macros
// within the CComCoClass template.
template <class T, const CLSID* pclsid = &CLSID_NULL>
class CComCoClass
{
...
public:
      // Provides a generic class factory.
      DECLARE_CLASSFACTORY()
      // Sets up default aggregation support.
      DECLARE_AGGREGATABLE(T)
...
};
```

The DECLARE_CLASSFACTORY macro expands to define the ATL class implementing IClassFactory. By default, this class is CComClassFactory. We will have much to say about

CComClassFactory, as well as how to override this default behavior in Chapter 9. Just realize at this point that the reason ATL does not require you to create a class factory by hand is that the DECLARE_CLASSFACTORY macro gives you a generic class factory for free.

CComCoClass also defines the DECLARE_AGGREGATABLE macro to instruct the ATL framework how CoRectangle should respond if asked to become aggregated by another object. The DECLARE_AGGREGATABLE macro allows CoRectangle to function correctly as a stand-alone object <u>or</u> as an aggregated object. We will examine aggregation in greater detail in Chapter 8.

Beyond establishing a class object and aggregation support, CComCoClass specifies a number of overloaded Error() methods dealing with COM exceptions. Your ATL coclasses may make use of these methods to return rich error information to a COM client beyond the standard HRESULT. We will see how to do so later in this chapter.

CComObject<>: The Final Destination

So far we have seen the functionality given to CoRectangle from three core base classes:

- CComObjectRootBase provides a number of methods to support COM aggregation and interface resolution and defines the object's internal reference counter (m_dwRef).
- CComObjectRootEx<> supports a "thread safe enough" reference counting scheme, as well as providing Lock() and Unlock() methods.
- CComCoClass<> provides a class factory for the object, as well as sets up the object's level of "aggregation awareness" and the ability to throw COM exceptions.

At this point, CoRectangle will be passed into the correct CComObject<> template, which provides a specific implementation of IUnknown. The constructor of CComObject<> increases the global object counter variable (m_nLockCnt), while the destructor calls FinalRelease() and decrements the same variable. This logic ensures your server remains loaded as long as there is an instance of CoRectangle in use:

```
// Recall the name of your CComModule instance is _Module.
template <class Base>
class CComObject : public Base
{
public:
...
    // Increment m_nLockCnt.
    CComObject(void* = NULL)
    {
        _Module.Lock();
    }
    // Call FinalRelease() and decrement m_nLockCnt.
    ~CComObject()
    {
        FinalRelease();
        _Module.Unlock();
    }
...
};
```

CComObject<> is responsible for providing the actual implementation of your coclass's IUnknown interface. Here at long last we see the markings of a true COM object:

QueryInterface(), AddRef(), and Release(). Notice how the implementation of each method makes calls on the "internal" IUnknown methods defined by CComObjectRootBase and CComObjectRootEx< >:

```
// CComObject<> creates non-aggregated, heap-based objects.
template <class Base>
class CComObject : public Base
{
public:
...
      // InternalAddRef() is defined in CComObjectRootEx<>
      STDMETHOD_(ULONG, AddRef)()
      {
            return InternalAddRef();
      }
      // InternalRelease() is also defined in CComObjectRootEx<>
      STDMETHOD_(ULONG, Release)()
      {
            ULONG l = InternalRelease();
            if (l == 0)
                  delete this;
            return l;
      }
      // _InternalQueryInterface() is a helper function
      // defined by your COM map, which in turn calls
      // CComObjectRootBase::InternalQueryInterface()
      STDMETHOD(QueryInterface)(REFIID iid, void ** ppvObject)
      {
            return _InternalQueryInterface(iid, ppvObject);
      }
};
```

CComObject::CreateInstance()

Another important aspect of CComObject< > is the static CreateInstance() method. When you need to create an ATL COM object from within your ATL project (meaning both objects are in the same binary server) you should call CreateInstance() to allocate your object and ensure a call to FinalConstruct(). For example:

```
// Create an ATL COM object from within an ATL project.
CComObject<CCoRectangle> *pRect;
CComObject<CCoRectangle>::CreateInstance(&pRect);
```

Here is the implementation of CComObject::CreateInstance():

```
// CreateInstance() ensures FinalConstruct() is called.
template <class Base>
HRESULT WINAPI CComObject<Base>::CreateInstance(CComObject<Base>** pp)
{
      ATLASSERT(pp != NULL);
      HRESULT hRes = E_OUTOFMEMORY;
      CComObject<Base>* p = NULL;
      ATLTRY(p = new CComObject<Base>())
      if (p != NULL)
      {
...
            hRes = p->FinalConstruct();
```

```
...
            if (hRes != S_OK)
            {
                    delete p;
                    p = NULL;
            }
        }
        *pp = p;
        return hRes;
}
```

That brings us to the end of the CoRectangle hierarchy! While having a better understanding of what ATL is doing to represent your COM objects is certainly helpful, you have to agree the road is long and winding.

In a nutshell, the ATL base classes work together to provide your coclass with the correct level of thread safety, a default class factory, aggregation support, and a full implementation of IUnknown. Now that we have peeked into the framework support for CoRectangle, let's turn our attention to the details of the ATL COM_MAP structure.

Understanding the ATL COM Map

The ATL COM map is a data structure used by the framework to determine if your coclass has a requested interface, and if so, to determine how to return a reference to the client. When a client is attempting to obtain an interface from an ATL coclass, the framework responds with the following sequence of events:

1. CComObject<>::QueryInterface() is called by the framework.
2. CComObject<>::QueryInterface() calls _InternalQueryInterface(). As we will see, this helper method is supplied by the BEGIN_COM_MAP macro.
3. _InternalQueryInterface() then calls CComObjectRootBase::InternalQueryInterface().
4. Finally, CComObjectRootBase::InternalQueryInterface() calls a helper function named AtlInternalQueryInterface(), which interrogates the COM map to obtain a given interface.

Every ATL coclass maintains a COM map, which is established using the BEGIN_COM_MAP and END_COM_MAP macros. The ATL Object Wizard always includes support for the initial default interface (as specified by the Names tab) with the COM_INTERFACE_ENTRY macro. As we specified IDraw as the default interface for CoRectangle, our initial COM map looks like the following:

```
// The COM map is ATL's way to provide a lookup table for your coclass's
// set of supported interfaces.
class ATL_NO_VTABLE CCoRectangle :
     public CComObjectRootEx<CComSingleThreadModel>,
     public CComCoClass<CCoRectangle, &CLSID_CoRectangle>,
     public IDraw
{
...
BEGIN_COM_MAP(CCoRectangle)
     COM_INTERFACE_ENTRY(IDraw)
END_COM_MAP()
...
};
```

Some aspects of the COM map should be clear by now. First, if you do not have a listing for your custom interfaces in this map (typically using COM_INTERFACE_ENTRY), external clients will not be able to obtain an interface reference. Forgetting to add a listing in your COM map is just as offensive as forgetting to add an if(riid == IID_XXX) provision in a raw C++ QueryInterface() implementation.

However, understanding exactly what these magic macros are doing is not altogether obvious. To begin, let's look at the BEGIN_COM_MAP macro.

The BEGIN_COM_MAP Macro

This macro is used to begin the definition of your map. Notice that the only parameter is the name of the defining class (CCoRectangle). When the BEGIN_COM_MAP macro expands, a number of new methods and data members are inserted into your class's public sector. Here is a brief description of each item:

Item Inserted by BEGIN_COM_MAP	Meaning in Life
typedef x	Your class (in this case CCoRectangle) is typedef-ed to _ComMapClass.
_GetRawUnknown() GetUnknown()	These methods are used to fetch the IUnknown interface for a given coclass.
_InternalQueryInterface()	This is a helper method called by CComObject<>, which in turn calls InternalQueryInterface().
_entries[]	An array of _ATL_INTMAP_ENTRY structures.
_GetEntries()	This helper function returns the array of _ATL_INTMAP_ENTRY structures.

Armed with this overview, here is the definition of BEGIN_COM_MAP (<atlcom.h>):

```
// The parameter to this macro is the name of the class defining the map.
#define BEGIN_COM_MAP(x) public: \
    // Friendly typedef of your class. \
    typedef x _ComMapClass; \
    // Function to extract raw IUnknown pointer. \
    IUnknown* _GetRawUnknown() \
    { ATLASSERT(_GetEntries()[0].pFunc == _ATL_SIMPLEMAPENTRY); \
        return (IUnknown*)((int)this+_GetEntries()->dw); } \
    IUnknown* GetUnknown() {return _GetRawUnknown(); } \
    // Tests for a given IID by calling InternalQueryInterface(). \
    HRESULT _InternalQueryInterface(REFIID iid, void** ppvObject) \
    { return InternalQueryInterface(this, _GetEntries(), iid, ppvObject); } \
    // Define an array of _ATL_INTMAP_ENTRY structures, \
    // and a method to return this array.\
    const static _ATL_INTMAP_ENTRY* WINAPI _GetEntries() { \
    static const _ATL_INTMAP_ENTRY _entries[] = { DEBUG_QI_ENTRY(x)
```

The _ATL_INTMAP_ENTRY Array

A COM map is, in reality, a NULL-terminated array of _ATL_INTMAP_ENTRY structures. Each structure in the array provides detailed information used to determine the vPtr for a given interface. The _ATL_INTMAP_ENTRY array is used by AtlInternal-QueryInterface() to test for a given interface ID and return the associated vPtr to the calling client. The BEGIN_COM_MAP macro names this array of structures _entries[]. Here is the _ATL_INTMAP_ENTRY structure, as defined in <atlbase.h>:

```
// A COM map is essentially an array of _ATL_INTMAP_ENTRY structures.
struct _ATL_INTMAP_ENTRY
{
    const IID* piid;              // The GUID of this interface.
    DWORD dw;                     // Offset to vPtr.
    _ATL_CREATORARGFUNC* pFunc;   // How do I find the offset?
};
```

The first field of _ATL_INTMAP_ENTRY is the REFIID for the given interface, for example &IID_IDraw. The second DWORD field contains the offset to the vPtr for a given interface. This offset is calculated in various ways based off the final field, pFunc, which will usually be set to the default value of _ATL_SIMPLEMAPENTRY (#defined as 1). If pFunc is equal to _ATL_SIMPLEMAPENTRY, this informs the framework to calculate the offset to the vPtr using the coclass's this pointer.

If pFunc is not set to _ATL_SIMPLEMAPENTRY, this instructs the framework to call the "function pointed to" by pFunc to calculate the offset to the vPtr. These alternative helper functions will be used to find a vPtr if the interface in question is implemented using more exotic techniques such as tear-off interfaces, aggregation, or interface chaining.

We have already seen that CComObjectRootBase does provide a small set of helper functions (_Chain(), _Break(), _NoInterface(), _Cache(), _Delegate(), and _Creator()) for these purposes, but for the time being we will assume that pFunc is set to _ATL_SIMPLEMAPENTRY.

The _GetEntries() Helper Method

BEGIN_COM_MAP also defines the _GetEntries() method, which returns the array of _ATL_INTMAP_ENTRY structures (a.k.a. _entries[]):

```
// _GetEntries() returns the _entries[] array.
const static _ATL_INTMAP_ENTRY* WINAPI _GetEntries() { \
static const _ATL_INTMAP_ENTRY _entries[] = { DEBUG_QI_ENTRY(x)
```

The _InternalQueryInterface() Method

The COM map adds a method named _InternalQueryInterface() which delegates to CComObjectRootBase::InternalQueryInterface(). _InternalQueryInterface() passes the _ATL_INTMAP_ENTRY array (via a call to _GetEntries()), the REFIID of the interface, and an [out] parameter to hold the vPtr of the interface in question:

```
// Your COM map defines _InternalQueryInterface() which passes the _entries array
// to InternalQueryInterface() via _GetEntries().
HRESULT _InternalQueryInterface(REFIID iid, void** ppvObject) \
{ return InternalQueryInterface(this, _GetEntries(), iid, ppvObject); } \
```

Finding your IUnknown: The _GetRawUnknown() and GetUnknown() Methods

Finally, BEGIN_COM_MAP provides a function called _GetRawUnknown(), which returns the IUnknown pointer for the coclass. _GetRawUnknown() first retrieves the array of _ATL_INTMAP_ENTRY structures with a call to _GetEntries(). A check is made to ensure that the first entry in the COM map is a simple map entry. Using the DWORD field of the first index in the array, _GetRawUnknown() adjusts the pointer offset to return the correct vPtr for IUnknown. If you ever have a need to fetch your own IUnknown pointer, call GetUnknown():

```
// The very first entry in the COM map is used to determine the offset to your
// IUnknown pointer.
IUnknown* _GetRawUnknown() \
{ ATLASSERT(_GetEntries()[0].pFunc == _ATL_SIMPLEMAPENTRY); \
return (IUnknown*)((int)this+_GetEntries()->dw); } \
IUnknown* GetUnknown() {return _GetRawUnknown(); } \
```

Finding IUnknown for External COM Clients

Because the first entry in the COM map is used to calculate the vPtr for IID_IUnknown, you will not find an explicit COM_INTERFACE_ENTRY listing for IUnknown. AtlInternalQueryInterface() will examine the first entry of your class's COM map to return IUnknown to the outside world. To ensure this will not fail, be sure the very first entry in your COM map is COM_INTERFACE_ENTRY, COM_INTERFACE_ENTRY2, COM_INTERFACE_ENTRY_IID, or COM_INTERFACE_ENTRY2_IID. Collectively, these four COM map macros are called *simple entries* in that they all specify pFunc as _ATL_SIMPLEMAPENTRY:

```
// The ATL "simple" COM map macros all specify pFunc as
// _ATL_SIMPLEMAPENTRY. Be sure the very first listing in your COM map is one
// of the following macros, or else your IUnknown* will not be calculated correctly.
#define COM_INTERFACE_ENTRY(x)\
      {&_ATL_IIDOF(x), \
      offsetofclass(x, _ComMapClass), \
      _ATL_SIMPLEMAPENTRY},
#define COM_INTERFACE_ENTRY_IID(iid, x)\
      {&iid,\
      offsetofclass(x, _ComMapClass),\
      _ATL_SIMPLEMAPENTRY},
#define COM_INTERFACE_ENTRY2(x, x2)\
      {&_ATL_IIDOF(x),\
      (DWORD)((x*)(x2*)((_ComMapClass*)8))-8,\
      _ATL_SIMPLEMAPENTRY},
#define COM_INTERFACE_ENTRY2_IID(iid, x, x2)\
      {&iid,\
      (DWORD)((x*)(x2*)((_ComMapClass*)8))-8,\
      _ATL_SIMPLEMAPENTRY},
```

Here is a peek into AtlInternalQueryInterface():

```
// AtlInternalQueryInterface() finds IUnknown based on the first entry in the map.
ATLINLINE ATLAPI AtlInternalQueryInterface(void* pThis,
      const _ATL_INTMAP_ENTRY* pEntries, REFIID iid, void** ppvObject)
{
```

```
ATLASSERT(pEntries->pFunc == _ATL_SIMPLEMAPENTRY);
...
// Find IUnknown based off of the first entry in the map.
if (InlineIsEqualUnknown(iid))
{
    IUnknown* pUnk = (IUnknown*)((int)pThis+pEntries->dw);
    pUnk->AddRef();
    *ppvObject = pUnk;
    return S_OK;
}
...
}
```

The END_COM_MAP Macro

The END_COM_MAP macro adds in a final _ATL_INTMAP_ENTRY structure to the
array containing all NULL fields, signaling the end of the map has been reached. As
AtlInternalQueryInterface() iterates over your class's COM map to test for and calculate a
vPtr for a COM client, it knows it has reached the end when it encounters all NULL fields:

```
// Your _entries[] array is terminated with a NULL entry provided by
// the END_COM_MAP macro.
#define END_COM_MAP() {NULL, 0, 0}}; return _entries;}
```

So, as you can see, the BEGIN_COM_MAP and END_COM_MAP macros dump quite a bit
of information into your coclass's header file. The core pieces to keep in mind are the array
of _ATL_INTMAP_ENTRY structures, the _GetEntries() helper function, and the
_InternalQueryInterface() method. A partial expansion of an empty COM map would look
as so:

```
// An empty COM map for CoRectangle.
class ATL_NO_VTABLE CCoRectangle:
    public CComObjectRootEx<CComSingleThreadModel>,
    public CComCoClass<CCoRectangle, &CLSID_CoRectangle >,
    public IDraw
{
public:
...
    HRESULT _InternalQueryInterface(REFIID iid, void** ppvObject)
    {
        return InternalQueryInterface(this, _GetEntries(), iid, ppvObject);
    }
    const static _ATL_INTMAP_ENTRY* WINAPI _GetEntries()
    {
        static const _ATL_INTMAP_ENTRY _entries[] =
        {
            {NULL, 0, 0}
        };
    return _entries;
    }
};
```

An empty COM map is no fun at all for clients, as this signals our COM object has no
interfaces to return. Obviously, we need to examine how to populate the array of
_ATL_INTMAP_ENTRY structures with the necessary information for our CoRectangle.
This work is simplified by a number of additional COM map macros.

The COM_INTERFACE_ENTRY Macro: Populating the COM Map

Although your COM map may be populated by numerous macros, the good news is that the COM_INTERFACE_ENTRY macro will do just about everything you need to do for a standard ATL coclass. Just to jog your memory, here is the _ATL_INTMAP_ENTRY structure one more time:

```
// Recall, this structure holds information for a given interface supported by our coclass.
//
struct _ATL_INTMAP_ENTRY
{
    const IID* piid;                // The GUID of this interface.
    DWORD dw;                       // Offset to the vPtr.
    _ATL_CREATORARGFUNC* pFunc;     // Where do I find the offset?
};
```

Each of the various COM map macros provided by ATL will fill the fields of the _ATL_INTMAP_ENTRY structure in its own unique way. In the case of IDraw, the vPtr is calculated using the COM_INTERFACE_ENTRY macro, defined in <atlcom.h> as the following:

```
// All of the COM map macros are used to fill the fields of an _ATL_INTMAP_ENTRY
// structure.
#define COM_INTERFACE_ENTRY(x)\
    {&_ATL_IIDOF(x), \                    // IID of interface.
    offsetofclass(x, _ComMapClass), \     // Offset to vPtr held in DWORD.
    _ATL_SIMPLEMAPENTRY},                 // Where to find the offset.
```

Note that the only parameter to this macro is the name of the interface supported by the coclass. The first field of the structure is the GUID of the named interface, which is determined by the _ATL_IIDOF macro. This macro simply evaluates to __uuidof():

```
// The first field of the _ATL_INTMAP_ENTRY array is the GUID of the supported
// interface.
#define _ATL_IIDOF(x) __uuidof(x)
```

The second field of the structure is the offset of the interface's vPtr from the base. In the case of the COM _INTERFACE_ENTRY macro, the base is the supporting class (CoRectangle). The offsetofclass() macro is used to determine this offset, given the interface (IDraw) and supporting class (CoRectangle).

The third and final field of the _ATL_INTMAP_ENTRY structure specifies a function pointer used to calculate the offset of the vPtr. As COM_INTERFACE_ENTRY automatically sets this field to _ATL_SIMPLEMAPENTRY, we use the coclass itself to calculate the offset.

To help pull this new information together, here is what CoRectangle would look like after the populated COM map has expanded:

```
// The magic COM map macros define an array of _ATL_INTMAP_ENTRY
// structures, which specify how to determine the vPtr for a given interface.
class ATL_NO_VTABLE CCoRectangle :
    public CComObjectRootEx<CComSingleThreadModel>,
    public CComCoClass<CCoRectangle, &CLSID_CoRectangle>,
    public IDraw
{
...
// BEGIN_COM_MAP(CCoRectangle)
```

```
//    COM_INTERFACE_ENTRY(IDraw)
// END_COM_MAP()
     // The essence of the COM map.
     HRESULT _InternalQueryInterface(REFIID iid, void** ppvObject)
     {
          return InternalQueryInterface(this, _GetEntries(), iid, ppvObject);
     }
     const static _ATL_INTMAP_ENTRY* WINAPI _GetEntries()
     {
          static const _ATL_INTMAP_ENTRY _entries[] =
          {
               { &IID_IDraw, offsetofclass(IDraw, CCoRectangle),
               _ATL_SIMPLEMAPENTRY},
               {NULL, 0, 0}
          };
          return _entries;
     };
...
};
```

AtlInternalQueryInterface() : Walking the COM Map

Again, when a client is interested in obtaining an interface from your ATL coclass, the framework passes your COM map to the AtlInternalQueryInterface() method to test for a given interface and fill the client-supplied pointer. Here is the definition of AtlInternalQueryInterface(), as seen in <atlbase.h>:

```
// AtlInternalQueryInterface() finds interface pointers by examining the COM map.
ATLINLINE ATLAPI AtlInternalQueryInterface(void* pThis,
     const _ATL_INTMAP_ENTRY* pEntries, REFIID iid, void** ppvObject)
{
     // Remember! The first entry must be a 'simple entry'
     ATLASSERT(pEntries->pFunc == _ATL_SIMPLEMAPENTRY);
     ...
     // Find IUnknown based off of the first entry in the map.
     if (InlineIsEqualUnknown(iid)) // use first interface
     {
          IUnknown* pUnk = (IUnknown*)((int)pThis+pEntries->dw);
          pUnk->AddRef();
          *ppvObject = pUnk;
          return S_OK;
     }
     // Loop over the COM map until we find a NULL entry.
     while (pEntries->pFunc != NULL)
     {
          // Is this entry the requested IID?
          BOOL bBlind = (pEntries->piid == NULL);
          if (bBlind || InlineIsEqualGUID(*(pEntries->piid), iid))
          {
               // If we are a simple entry, use 'this' pointer to get vPtr.
               if (pEntries->pFunc == _ATL_SIMPLEMAPENTRY)
               {
                    ATLASSERT(!bBlind);
                    IUnknown* pUnk = (IUnknown*)
                                        ((int)pThis+pEntries->dw);
                    pUnk->AddRef();
```

```
                        *ppvObject = pUnk;
                        return S_OK;
                }
                // Not a simple entry, call helper function to get the vPtr.
                else
                {
                        HRESULT hRes = pEntries->pFunc(pThis,
                                iid, ppvObject, pEntries->dw);
                        if (hRes == S_OK || (!bBlind && FAILED(hRes)))
                                return hRes;
                }
        }
        pEntries++; // Go to next entry.
}
return E_NOINTERFACE;  // Did not have the requested IID.
}
```

COM Error Handling

That brings us to the end of our examination of CoRectangle. Hopefully you now have a better idea how the ATL framework is composing your objects. To close this chapter, we will switch gears completely, and revisit CComCoClass< >. As you recall, this class defines a number of overloaded Error() methods that can be used to send out COM exceptions.

You are aware by now that each method contained in a COM interface should return the de facto HRESULT. When a COM client has obtained some interface pointer off your coclass, the HRESULT is often tested to determine the success or failure of the method invocation. The HRESULT is useful in that a COM client can quickly determine if a given interface method responded as hoped:

```
// The SUCCEEDED and FAILED macros test for the
// most significant bit of the HRESULT.
HRESULT hr;
hr = pUnk->QueryInterface(IID_IDraw, (void**)&pDraw);
if(SUCCEEDED(hr))
{
        // Things worked so start drawing.
        pDraw->Draw();
        pDraw->Release();
}
pUnk->Release();
```

When a method does fail, it would be helpful to explain to the client exactly what went wrong. For example, assume our CoRectangle was able to return a text string describing why the request to render itself failed. Furthermore, what if the offending interface method was able to return to the client a path to a Windows help file, the ProgID of the failing COM object, and more? This very sort of rich error handling is an intrinsic service of the COM architecture.

This facility is often termed *COM exceptions* and is supported by three standard interfaces and three COM library functions. Some are used by the coclass to raise the error; others are used by the client to catch the error. As a COM developer, you may be tempted to devise your own set of custom error interfaces. For example, you might have a custom interface that always returns a single text string describing what caused a given method to fail. You may then configure your COM clients to ask for this custom interface whenever they read a failed HRESULT. While this is a valid approach, the problem is that your custom error interface is unique to your given solution(s), and perhaps even specific to a given language.

COM offers a standard and generic mechanism to return useful error information to COM clients. As this approach is well known and established through a set of standard interfaces and COM library calls, each COM-aware language is able to respond to these exceptions in their respective language mapping in a location-transparent manner. In other words, COM exceptions are the error reporting mechanism that every COM language mapping understands without any infrastructure work on your part.

Raising a COM exception using ATL is as simple as calling one of the Error() methods you have inherited from CComCoClass< >. However, before we see just how easy this can be, we will begin by examining what a raw C++ coclass would need to do in order to support standard COM error handling. We will then see how Visual Basic and C++ clients catch the exception, and then see how ATL makes throwing a COM exception a piece of cake.

Standard Error Interfaces and COM Library Functions

To support COM exceptions, three standard interfaces have been defined in <oaidl.idl>:

Standard COM Interface	Meaning in Life
ISupportErrorInfo	This interface is implemented by the coclass. A client may obtain a pointer to this interface and determine which interfaces supported by the coclass are capable of returning rich error information.
ICreateErrorInfo	The COM object that wishes to send out rich error information uses this interface to describe the error that occurred.
IErrorInfo	This interface is used by the recipient of the error. From an IErrorInfo pointer, a client is able to interpret the COM exception.

To work with these standard error interfaces, we have three related COM library functions at our disposal:

COM Library Function	Meaning in Life
CreateErrorInfo()	This function is used to create a COM exception. The function returns a pointer to a "live" ICreateErrorInfo interface, from which a coclass may begin describing the error itself.
SetErrorInfo()	Once the error has been defined, this function is used to send the error to the current thread of execution (i.e., back to the client).
GetErrorInfo()	Used by the client to "catch" the COM exception, and discover what went wrong.

Configuring a Coclass to Support COM Exceptions in Raw C++

For the sake of argument, assume we have written CoRectangle using straight C++, and avoided (for some bizarre reason) the ATL framework. We might have the following initial definition:

```
// A CoRectangle à la C++.
class CoRectangle : public IDraw
{
public:
     CoRectangle() { m_ref = 0;}
     // IUnknown implementation...
     // IDraw implementation...
private:
     ULONG m_ref;
};
```

If we wish CoRectangle to support COM exceptions, the first step is to add ISupportErrorInfo to our inheritance chain:

```
// A CoRectangle à la C++ supporting COM exceptions.
class CoRectangle : public IDraw, public ISupportErrorInfo
{
public:
     CoRectangle() { m_ref = 0;}
     // IUnknown implementation...
     // IDraw implementation...
     // ISupportErrorInfo implementation...
private:
     ULONG m_ref;
};
```

ISupportErrorInfo is used by a COM client for exactly one reason: determining which interfaces supported on the coclass are able to return COM exceptions. As a coclass developer, you are able to specify which interfaces will participate in rich error information. This may be each and every interface, or a subset of all possible interfaces. This standard COM interface contains one method. Here is the IDL:

```
// Clients make use of this interface to discover which interfaces supported
// by the coclass provide rich error information.
[ object, uuid(DF0B3D60-548F-101B-8E65-08002B2BD119)]
interface ISupportErrorInfo: IUnknown
{
     HRESULT InterfaceSupportsErrorInfo([in] REFIID riid);
};
```

The implementation of InterfaceSupportsErrorInfo() is trivial. Once you decide which interfaces will be providing rich error information to COM clients, test the incoming IID and return S_OK or E_FAIL accordingly. Thus, to let the world know that IDraw supports rich error information when implemented by CoRectangle:

```
// Return S_OK if the client asks for an interface providing COM exceptions.
STDMETHODIMP CoRectangle::InterfaceSupportsErrorInfo(REFIID riid)
{
     if(riid == IID_IDraw)
          return S_OK;
```

```
        return E_FAIL;
}
```

Realize, of course, that when you inform a COM client that a given interface can return COM exceptions, you will want to throw your error from within a method of the given interface. For CoRectangle, this is simple, as we only have the Draw() method to contend with. Also realize that a coclass supporting numerous interfaces can specify any number of interfaces from within InterfaceSupportsErrorInfo(). Recall the original C++ CoCar developed in Chapter 3. If we wish to return COM exceptions from IEngine and IStats but not ICreateCar, we may implement InterfaceSupportsErrorInfo() as so:

```
// Specifying multiple interfaces that are capable of throwing COM
// exceptions.
STDMETHODIMP CoCar::InterfaceSupportsErrorInfo(REFIID riid)
{
    if((riid == IID_IEngine) || (riid == IID_IStats))
        return S_OK;
    return E_FAIL;
}
```

Throwing a COM Exception

When a coclass has determined that some error of interest has occurred, and wishes to inform the client of the situation, the method issuing the error will make use of the CreateErrorInfo() COM library function. Assume that the Draw() method of CoRectangle is attempting to allocate a ton of memory during the scope of the function. Perhaps this memory is needed to render the image in an offscreen buffer. If this memory allocation fails, CoRectangle wishes to raise a COM exception that informs the client about the specifics of the error. Here is a possible implementation:

```
// The Draw method attempts to allocate lots of memory.
// If it fails, we will return E_FAIL to the client and issue a COM exception,
// otherwise return S_OK and all is fine...
STDMETHODIMP CoRectangle::Draw()
{
    HRESULT hr;
    bool b = false;
    // Go attempt to grab a ton of memory.
    b = GetTonsOfMemory();
    if(b == false)          // A SNAFU has occurred.
    {
        ICreateErrorInfo *pCER;
        // Go create an "error object" and set a description of the error.
        if(SUCCEEDED(CreateErrorInfo(&pCER)))
            pCER->SetDescription(L"I can't get that much memory!!");
        // Ask the error object for the IErrorInfo interface.
        IErrorInfo *pEI;
        pCER->QueryInterface(IID_IErrorInfo, (void**)&pEI);
        // Now send the error object back to the current thread.
        SetErrorInfo(NULL, pEI);
        // Clean up our end.
        pCER->Release();
        pEI->Release();
        return E_FAIL;
    }
}
```

```
        else
            // No error, so draw a rectangle.
            GoDrawARectangle();
        return S_OK;
}
```

The sequence of events is very boilerplate. A method determines if it needs to raise a COM exception, and if so, it creates a COM error object using the CreateErrorInfo() COM library function. If this call is successful, the fetched ICreateErrorInfo interface may be used to establish the information that identifies the error. ICreateErrorInfo has a number of mutator functions which may be called to fully define the error in question (note that you are not required to set each item of the error object). Here is the IDL:

```
// ICreateErrorInfo allows a coclass to define the scope of a COM exception.
[ object, uuid(22F03340-547D-101B-8E65-08002B2BD119)]
interface ICreateErrorInfo: IUnknown
{
    // IID of the offender.
    HRESULT SetGUID( [in] REFGUID rguid );
    // ProgID of the offender.
    HRESULT SetSource( [in] LPOLESTR szSource );
    // Custom string describing what happened.
    HRESULT SetDescription( [in] LPOLESTR szDescription );
    // Path to any help file.
    HRESULT SetHelpFile( [in] LPOLESTR szHelpFile );
    // Help context identifier.
    HRESULT SetHelpContext( [in] DWORD dwHelpContext);
};
```

Once the error has been described, we need to raise the error using SetErrorInfo(). Note that we must ask our error object for its IErrorInfo interface, as this interface will be used by the client to catch the exception.

Catching a COM Exception: A C++ Client

Assume we have a C++ client that has created a CoRectangle object, obtained a pointer to IDraw, and is attempting to draw accordingly. Being a good COM citizen, the client tests the HRESULT for success or failure. If the returned HRESULT is set to a failure, the C++ client may go through the following steps to catch the COM exception:

■ Query the object for IID_ISupportErrorInfo. If this is successful, you know the coclass supports COM exceptions.

■ From the retrieved ISupportErrorInfo pointer, call InterfaceSupportsErrorInfo(), passing in the IID of the interface that offended you.

■ If that call succeeded, the interface supports COM exceptions. Call GetErrorInfo() and use the acquired IErrorInfo interface pointer to make sense of the error.

The IErrorInfo interface has methods that complement ICreateErrorInfo. Rather than a set of mutator methods, IErrorInfo holds the accessors for the COM exception. Here is the IDL:

```
// IErrorInfo contains all the information thrown by the coclass.
[ object, uuid(1CF2B120-547D-101B-8E65-08002B2BD119)]
interface IErrorInfo: IUnknown
{
```

```
        HRESULT GetGUID( [out] GUID * pGUID );
        HRESULT GetSource( [out] BSTR * pBstrSource );
        HRESULT GetDescription( [out] BSTR * pBstrDescription );
        HRESULT GetHelpFile( [out] BSTR * pBstrHelpFile );
        HRESULT GetHelpContext( [out] DWORD * pdwHelpContext );
    };
```

Now, if our C++ client has detected that the Draw() method has failed, it may catch the exception as so (see Figure 7-12 for output):

```
// Get the exception thrown by the coclass.
HRESULT hr;
hr = pDraw->Draw();
if(FAILED(hr))
{
    ISupportErrorInfo *pISER;
    // Does CoRectangle have COM exceptions for me?
    hr = pDraw->QueryInterface(IID_ISupportErrorInfo, (void**)&pISER);
    if(SUCCEEDED(hr))
    {
        // Does IDraw have COM exception support?
        if(SUCCEEDED(pISER->InterfaceSupportsErrorInfo(IID_IDraw)));
        // Great! Get the exception.
        IErrorInfo *pEI;
        if(SUCCEEDED(GetErrorInfo(NULL, &pEI)))
        {
            BSTR desc;
            pEI->GetDescription(&desc);
            char buff [80];
            WideCharToMultiByte(CP_ACP, NULL, desc, -1, buff,
                                80, NULL, NULL);
            cout << desc << endl;
            SysFreeString(desc);
            pEI->Release();
        }
    }
    pISER->Release();
}
```

Figure 7-12:
C++ client
catching our
COM exception.

Again, the code used by a COM client is very boilerplate in nature. The client tests the HRESULT for a failed invocation. If something went wrong, the client first asks the object if it supports COM exceptions by querying for ISupportErrorInfo. If that call is successful, the client then determines if the offending interface supports COM exceptions by calling InterfaceSupportsErrorInfo(). If that is also successful, the client catches the exception using the GetErrorInfo() COM library call, and calls methods off the fetched IErrorInfo interface.

To be sure, writing C++ error handling code can be a drag, given the amount of repeat code on both ends. To help streamline your code, you would do well to create global helper functions that you can call whenever you detect a non-successful HRESULT (client side) or need to throw the error (server side).

For example, we could create a function called ParseError() to help the C++ client deal with the COM exception. Whenever a COM method fails, send in the offending interface pointer and its associated IID. This function could then do all the grunt work of determining if the interface supports error information, and dump the exception to a file, list box, message box, or whatever mechanism you require. You will have a chance to do this very thing in your next lab.

Catching a COM Exception: A Visual Basic Client

As you may suspect, catching a COM exception in Visual Basic is substantially easier than in C++, because that VB includes an intrinsic Err object, which may be used to extract the details of the COM exception. Before we examine the Err object, however, we need to learn how VB handles errors as a whole. Generally speaking, VB error trapping happens on the method level. Thus, if we wish to equip a function to respond to any possible error, we begin by defining an error label within the function using the On Error GoTo syntax:

```
' Generic VB error handling.
'
Private Sub btnDoIt_Click()
On Error GoTo OOPS
      ' Write your VB code here. If an error occurs, the flow of logic
      ' will jump to the label below.
Exit Sub
' Error trap
OOPS:
      ' Process the error here using the Err object.
Resume Next
End Sub
```

Once you have defined the label to catch the error, you need to be sure to explicitly tell the flow of logic to exit the subroutine once the function is about to exit successfully, or you will fall into the error trap again! Also notice the optional Resume Next syntax that informs VB to continue executing the subroutine, as the error has been caught.

Within the scope of the error label you will want to make use of the intrinsic Err object to extract the information about the error, including any COM exceptions thrown by a COM object. The Err object contains a small set of properties which, as you may have guessed, map to the same methods of IErrorInfo. Armed with this information, here is some simple VB client-side code that can catch the COM exception thrown by CoRectangle and displays it in a message box (see Figure 7-13):

```
' Trap and use the COM exception à la VB.
'
Private Sub btnDoIt_Click()
On Error GoTo OOPS
      ' Create your CoRectangle
      Dim r as New CoRectangle
      ' Throws an exception if the object cannot grab enough memory.
      r.Draw
```

```
Exit Sub
' Error trap
OOPS:
        ' Process the error here using the Err object.
        MessageBox Err.Description, , "Message from the CoRectangle"
Resume Next
End Sub
```

Figure 7-13:
VB client
catching our
COM exception.

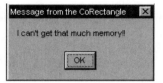

ATL's Support for ISupportErrorInfo

Now that you have seen what it takes to configure a raw C++ server to send out COM
error objects, let's see what ATL can do to help ease the necessary COM goo. When you
are inserting a new coclass with the ATL Object Wizard, one of the options you have is to
allow ATL to provide an implementation of ISupportErrorInfo for you. This option is available
from the Attributes tab:

Figure 7-14:
Specifying ATL
support for
COM
exceptions.

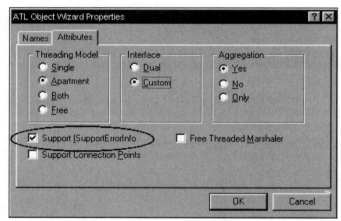

If you have legacy ATL objects that were not initially equipped with this option, it is very
easy to retrofit your coclass. To do so, let's see what ATL will do for you when you select
the Support ISupportErrorInfo checkbox. First off, your new coclass will derive from
ISupportErrorInfo as well as the necessary framework templates and your initial [default]
interface:

```
// The Object Wizard automatically adds support for ISupportErrorInfo if
// asked to do so...
class ATL_NO_VTABLE CCoRectangle:
    public CComObjectRootEx<CComSingleThreadModel>,
    public CComCoClass< CCoRectangle, &CLSID_CCoRectangle >,
    public ISupportErrorInfo,
    public IDraw
```

```
{
...
};
```

Next, you will find that your COM map has been updated, which allows a COM client to retrieve a pointer to ISupportErrorInfo:

```
// The wizard also automatically updates your COM map.
BEGIN_COM_MAP(CCoRectangle)
    COM_INTERFACE_ENTRY(IDraw)
    COM_INTERFACE_ENTRY(ISupportErrorInfo)
END_COM_MAP()
```

Finally, ATL will implement the sole method of ISupportErrorInfo on your behalf. Initially, InterfaceSupportsErrorInfo() will only return S_OK for your initial [default] interface. As you add more interfaces to your coclass, you will have to come back to this implementation and add an entry to the IID array by hand. Here is the initial code:

```
// ATL's implementation of InterfaceSupportsErrorInfo() performs a lookup
// using an extendable array of IIDs.
STDMETHODIMP CCoRectangle::InterfaceSupportsErrorInfo(REFIID riid)
{
    static const IID* arr[] =
    {
        &IID_IDraw
    };
    for (int i=0; i < sizeof(arr)/sizeof(arr[0]); i++)
    {
        if (InlineIsEqualGUID(*arr[i],riid))
            return S_OK;
    }
    return S_FALSE;
}
```

ATL's implementation takes an incoming GUID and performs an inline comparison between it and each member of the static IID array. To illustrate extending this array, assume that your CoRectangle also supports the IShapeEdit interface, and you wish to allow clients to receive COM exceptions from a valid IShapeEdit pointer:

```
// Extending the initial implementations.
STDMETHODIMP CCoRectangle::InterfaceSupportsErrorInfo(REFIID riid)
{
    static const IID* arr[] =
    {
        &IID_IDraw,
        &IID_IShapeEdit
    };
    for (int i=0; i < sizeof(arr)/sizeof(arr[0]); i++)
    {
        if (InlineIsEqualGUID(*arr[i],riid))
            return S_OK;
    }
    return S_FALSE;
}
```

ATL's Support for Raising COM Exceptions

As we learned earlier in this chapter, CComCoClass<> defines a number of overloaded Error() methods, which may be used by your ATL COM objects whenever they wish to throw a COM exception. The implementation of each Error() method delegates to an ATL helper function named AtlReportError(); however, the set of parameters will depend on how fully you wish to define the error. Here are the prototypes:

```
// ATL allows you to throw a COM exception with a single function call.
template <class T, const CLSID* pclsid = &CLSID_NULL>
class CComCoClass
{
public:
...
    static HRESULT WINAPI Error(LPCOLESTR lpszDesc,
        const IID& iid = GUID_NULL, HRESULT hRes = 0);
    static HRESULT WINAPI Error(LPCOLESTR lpszDesc, DWORD dwHelpID,
        LPCOLESTR lpszHelpFile, const IID& iid = GUID_NULL, HRESULT
        hRes = 0);
    static HRESULT WINAPI Error(UINT nID, const IID& iid = GUID_NULL,
        HRESULT hRes = 0,
        HINSTANCE hInst = _Module.GetResourceInstance());
    static HRESULT WINAPI Error(UINT nID, DWORD dwHelpID,
        LPCOLESTR lpszHelpFile, const IID& iid = GUID_NULL,
        HRESULT hRes = 0,
        HINSTANCE hInst = _Module.GetResourceInstance());
    static HRESULT WINAPI Error(LPCSTR lpszDesc,
        const IID& iid = GUID_NULL, HRESULT hRes = 0);
    static HRESULT WINAPI Error(LPCSTR lpszDesc, DWORD dwHelpID,
        LPCSTR lpszHelpFile, const IID& iid = GUID_NULL,
    HRESULT hRes = 0);
...
};
```

To throw a COM exception from within the ATL framework is a no-brainer. Simply call the Error() method when some condition fails. If we were to rewrite CoRectangle::Draw() using ATL's Error methods, we could save ourselves the trouble of having to create the error object, establish the error context, and send the error to the calling thread:

```
// The Error method creates and sends the exception in a single call.
STDMETHODIMP CCoRectangle::Draw()
{
    HRESULT hr;
    bool b = false;
    // Go attempt to grab a ton of memory.
    b = GetTonsOfMemory();
    if(b == false)
    {
        // Throw ATL error.
        Error("I can't get that much memory!!");
        return E_FAIL;
    }
    else
```

```
            GoDrawARectangle();
        return S_OK;
}
```

The VB and C++ clients would continue to work as before.

> **Note:** If you would like to see the real work behind the Error() methods, look at the code behind AtlSetErrorInfo(), which can be found in <atlbase.h>. This helper function is doing the exact same thing we did when throwing a raw C++ exception.

Lab 7-1: Sending and Receiving COM Exceptions

ATL makes throwing COM exceptions painfully easy, which is a good thing. Rather than having you select the correct Object Wizard option and call an Error() method, in this lab you will take your existing raw C++ CoCar developed in Chapter 4 and add support for COM error handling. This will drill the architecture of COM exceptions into your mind, and let you appreciate the work ATL is doing on your behalf. As well, you will be creating a C++ and Visual Basic client to catch the error you raise from within your coclass.

The solution for this lab can be found on your CD-ROM under:
Labs\Chapter 07\RawErrors
Labs\Chapter 07\RawErrors\VB Client
Labs\Chapter 07\RawErrors\CPP Client

Step One: Support ISupportErrorInfo

Open up your CarServerTypeInfo project from Chapter 4 (or make a copy of this project and begin there). We will adding in the necessary infrastructure to support COM error handling from your CoCar object. Start by opening the header file for CoCar, derive from ISupportErrorInfo, and add a QueryInterface() provision for IID_ISupportErrorInfo. Recall that this COM interface allows a client to figure out which interfaces support error information. In your class definition, prototype the **InterfaceSupportsErrorInfo()** method:

```
// Any coclass which can throw COM errors must implement ISupportErrorInfo
class CoCar :
    public IEngine,
    public ICreateCar,
    public IStats,
    public ISupportErrorInfo
{
public:
...
    // ISupportErrorInfo
    STDMETHODIMP InterfaceSupportsErrorInfo(REFIID riid);
};
```

Next, let's implement InterfaceSupportsErrorInfo() to specify IEngine is capable of returning COM errors:

```
// List the interfaces that can return error information here...
STDMETHODIMP CoCar::InterfaceSupportsErrorInfo(REFIID riid)
{
```

```
        if(riid == IID_IEngine)
            return S_OK;
        return E_FAIL;
}
```

Step Two: Throw a COM Exception

Your previous COM clients using CoCar had to monitor when the current speed was greater than the maximum speed and react accordingly. As an example, a VB client using our raw CoCar might have code like the following:

```
' An ugly form of client-side error handling.
'
Private Sub btnSpeed_Click()
    Set itfEngine = mCar
    Set itfStats = mCar
    ' Rev that engine and check for error.
    Do While itfEngine.GetCurSpeed <= itfEngine.GetMaxSpeed
        itfEngine.SpeedUp
        lstSpeed.AddItem itfEngine.GetCurSpeed
    Loop
        MsgBox itfStats.GetPetName & " is has blown up! Lead foot!"
End Sub
```

A far better design would be to allow CoCar to let the object inform the client when the engine has exploded through a COM exception. Go to the current implementation of SpeedUp() and throw a COM exception whenever the current speed is greater than the maximum speed. The general flow is as follows:

1. Call CreateErrorInfo() to receive a pointer to a COM error object via the ICreateErrorInfo interface.
2. From the acquired interface call any mutator methods (i.e., SetXXX()) to set the information about the error.
3. Now, ask the error object for the IErrorInfo interface and send the error using SetErrorInfo().
4. Release all acquired interfaces and return E_FAIL.

Here is some sample code that sets the description of the error:

```
// Sending an error in straight C++.
STDMETHODIMP CoCar::SpeedUp()
{
    m_currSpeed += 10;
    if(m_currSpeed > m_maxSpeed)
    {
        ICreateErrorInfo *pCER;
        // Go create an 'error object' and set a description of the error.
        if(SUCCEEDED(CreateErrorInfo(&pCER)))
            pCER->SetDescription(L"Engine block has exploded!!");
        // Ask the error object for the IErrorInfo interface.
        IErrorInfo *pEI;
        pCER->QueryInterface(IID_IErrorInfo, (void**)&pEI);
        // Now send the error object back to the current thread.
        SetErrorInfo(NULL, pEI);
        pCER->Release();
        pEI->Release();
```

```
        return E_FAIL;
    }
    else
        return S_OK;
}
```

If we were building an ATL object supporting COM exceptions, the code above could be replaced with a single line:

```
// Throwing a COM error using ATL.
STDMETHODIMP CoCar::SpeedUp()
{
    m_currSpeed += 10;
    if(m_currSpeed > m_maxSpeed)
    {
        Error("Engine block has exploded!!");
        return E_FAIL;
    }
    else
        return S_OK;
}
```

Go ahead and recompile your project, and move on to create some test clients.

Step Three: A C++ Client

Catching a COM exception from a C++ client entails lots of repeat code. To help out, we will be creating a global level helper function that the C++ client can call whenever it detects a failed HRESULT. First, create a new Win32 Console Application project (a simple project). In your initial CPP file, prototype a global function named **ParseError**() which takes the following parameters:

```
// A custom client-side error handler.
void ParseError(IUnknown* pInterface, REFIID riid);
```

A full, production level implementation of this helper method would need to acquire the IErrorInfo pointer using GetErrorInfo() and extract fully the state of the error object. For this lab, we will only extract the description of the error. Implement the method to perform the following tasks:

1. AddRef() the incoming interface pointer.
2. Query the incoming interface for IID_ISupportErrorInfo. If this is successful, call InterfaceSupportsErrorInfo(), passing in the GUID parameter.
3. If this succeeded, call GetErrorInfo() and use the acquired IErrorInfo pointer to call GetDescription().
4. Release any interfaces.

Here is the necessary code:

```
// A generic COM error handler function.
void ParseError(IUnknown* pInterface, REFIID riid)
{
    pInterface->AddRef();
    ISupportErrorInfo *pISER;
    HRESULT hr;
    // Does this object have COM exceptions for me?
    hr = pInterface->QueryInterface(IID_ISupportErrorInfo, (void**)&pISER);
```

```
        if(SUCCEEDED(hr))
        {
            // Does this interface have COM exception support?
            if(SUCCEEDED(pISER->InterfaceSupportsErrorInfo(riid)))
            {
                // Great! Get the exception & dump description.
                IErrorInfo *pEI;
                if(SUCCEEDED(GetErrorInfo(NULL, &pEI)))
                {
                    BSTR desc;
                    pEI->GetDescription(&desc);
                    char buff [80];
                    WideCharToMultiByte(CP_ACP, NULL, desc, -1, buff,
                                        80, NULL, NULL);
                    cout << buff << endl;
                    SysFreeString(desc);
                    pEI->Release();
                }
            }
            pISER->Release();
        }
        pInterface->Release();
}
```

Now we need to code main() to make use of our new error facility. Using standard COM calls, create your CoCar and set the maximum speed from an ICreateCar pointer. Next, acquire an IEngine interface:

```
// Create the CoCar and grab some interfaces.
int main(int argc, char* argv[])
{
    CoInitialize(NULL);
    IEngine *pEngine;
    ICreateCar *pCCar;
    // Make the car.
    CoCreateInstance(CLSID_CoCarErrors, NULL, CLSCTX_SERVER,
                     IID_ICreateCar, (void**)&pCCar);
    pCCar->SetMaxSpeed(20);
    pCCar->QueryInterface(IID_IEngine, (void**)&pEngine);
    pCCar->Release();
...
}
```

From the IEngine interface, call SpeedUp() a number of times to trigger the COM error, each time making use of the ParseError() method:

```
// Speed up to cause error
if(FAILED(pEngine->SpeedUp()))
    ParseError(pEngine, IID_IEngine);
```

Once you call SpeedUp() one too many times (i.e., 10 miles over the maximum) you should see output from your server showing the text description of the problem.

Step Four: A VB Client

To test the language-independent nature of the COM error protocol, open up Visual Basic and create a new Standard EXE project. Create a really simple GUI which allows you to create a CoCar and catch the error in a single button click. Recall that VB supplies the Err object to receive the COM exception. Set up an error handler within the button's Clicked event and place the description into a message box:

```
' Don't forget to set a reference to your type library!
'
Private Sub btnDoIt_Click()
On Error GoTo OOPS
     ' Create a new car
     Dim o As New CoCarErrors
     o.SetMaxSpeed 30
     ' Get IEngine interface.
     Dim i As IEngine
     Set i = o
     ' Destroy the automobile.
     i.SpeedUp
     i.SpeedUp
     i.SpeedUp
     i.SpeedUp
Exit Sub
' Error trap. Use Err object to suck out information.
OOPS:
     MsgBox Err.Description, , "Message from the Car"
End Sub
```

Very good! In the next chapter we will continue to look into the ATL framework by examining further uses of the COM map and the notion of object identity.

Chapter Summary

As you have seen in this chapter, the ATL framework is focused on creating an "as generic as possible" implementation of COM objects. The CComObjectRootEx<> template is used to equip your coclass with the appropriate level of threading support based on your configuration of the ATL Object Wizard. Objects living in the STA will make use of CComSingleThreadModel, whereas objects designed to live in the MTA will make use of CComMultiThreadModel. As the public interface of each is identical, you may swap between these classes to create thread-safe or thread-oblivious COM classes.

ATL objects support a table driven approach to QueryInterface(). The COM map resolves to an array of _ATL_INTMAP_ENTRY structures, each of which contains the information needed to return a vPtr to the client. The most common entry in the map is the COM_INTERFACE_ENTRY macro, which is considered a "simple" entry in that the vPtr is calculated using the coclass itself. Other ATL COM map macros determine the vPtr by accessing helper functions provided by base class templates.

Finally, this chapter has shown you a generic manner in which COM objects can report language-independent and location-transparent exceptions. To do so requires working with three standard COM interfaces, and three COM library functions, all of which are hidden from view when using the set of ATL Error() methods.

Chapter 8

COM Object Identity and ATL

Objectives:

- Learn to implement interfaces using nested classes.
- Resolve interface method name clashes.
- Examine alternative ATL COM map macros.
- Understand "tear-off" interfaces and how to implement them.
- Build coclasses using COM containment.
- Build coclasses using COM aggregation.

As you know, a COM object expresses itself through QueryInterface(). Typically your implementation of this method will simply check the incoming REFIID and return a vTable pointer if the interface is supported. To support each implemented interface, most coclasses developed using C++ make use of public multiple inheritance (MI). Another interface implementation technique is the use of *nested classes*, which as we will see, can be very helpful when resolving interface method name clashes.

Beyond multiple inheritance and nested classes, COM does allow for a number of interesting identity tricks that C++ developers can employ to develop more sophisticated coclasses. In this chapter we will examine a number of these COM identity tricks, and see how ATL offers a helping hand by way of a number of additional COM map macros, beyond the de facto COM_INTERFACE_ENTRY.

The Basic ATL COM Map

When developing coclasses with ATL, you become dependent upon a table driven implementation of QueryInterface(). As we have seen in Chapter 7, the COM map is a NULL-terminated array of _ATL_INTMAP_ENTRY structures. Most of the time this array is populated by the COM_INTERFACE_ENTRY macro, used whenever you are supporting a COM interface using C++ multiple inheritance:

```
// A typical COM map.
BEGIN_COM_MAP(CoSalesEmployee)
    COM_INTERFACE_ENTRY(ICalcCommission)
    COM_INTERFACE_ENTRY(ISmileAlot)
```

```
        COM_INTERFACE_ENTRY(IPersonalInfo)
END_COM_MAP()
```

COM_INTERFACE_ENTRY makes use of the offsetofclass() macro to calculate the correct vPtr for a given COM interface:

```
// The de facto ATL COM map macro.
#define COM_INTERFACE_ENTRY(x)\
    {&_ATL_IIDOF(x), \
    offsetofclass(x, _ComMapClass), \
    _ATL_SIMPLEMAPENTRY},
```

This chapter discusses a number of additional coclass implementation techniques (and related COM map macros) beyond simple multiple inheritance. We begin by examining some advanced topics such as nested classes, tear-off interfaces, and resolution of method name clashes. To wrap up this chapter, you will learn how to achieve binary reuse using COM containment and COM aggregation.

Variations on the ATL COM Map Macros

<atlcom.h> defines the entire set of COM map macros provided by ATL 3.0. If you examine these macros, you will see a total of 17 different variations. Don't lose heart, however, as many of these macros are grouped by related functionality. For example, four of the macros deal with COM aggregation. Three are used to resolve base interface ambiguities. That brings our count down to ten. The story gets brighter still, as two of the COM map macros are no longer necessary as of ATL 3.0:

```
// The 'impl' macros are now obsolete as of ATL 3.0.
#define COM_INTERFACE_ENTRY_IMPL(x)\
    COM_INTERFACE_ENTRY_IID(_ATL_IIDOF(x), x##Impl<_ComMapClass>)
#define COM_INTERFACE_ENTRY_IMPL_IID(iid, x)\
    COM_INTERFACE_ENTRY_IID(iid, x##Impl<_ComMapClass>)
```

These macros were used in ATL 2.0 as a way to provide debugging support for interface reference counting; however, interface debugging has changed with the release of ATL 3.0. Legacy ATL code that makes use of these older COM map macros will still compile just fine under ATL 3.0, as the _IMPL macros are redefined to the more useful COM_INTERFACE_ENTRY_IID.

The remaining COM map macros will be examined throughout this chapter, as well as suggestions on when they might actually be useful. To help you keep your bearings, the following table lists the full set of ATL COM macros, grouped by related functionality:

ATL COM Map Macro	Meaning in Life
COM_INTERFACE_ENTRY	The most common macro. Used for standard interface support.
COM_INTERFACE_ENTRY_IID COM_INTERFACE_ENTRY2 COM_INTERFACE_ENTRY2_IID	Used to resolve ambiguities in your interface hierarchies.

ATL COM Map Macro	Meaning in Life
COM_INTERFACE_ENTRY_AGGREGATE COM_INTERFACE_ENTRY_AGGREGATE_BLIND COM_INTERFACE_ENTRY_AUTOAGGREGATE COM_INTERFACE_ENTRY_AUTOAGGREGATE_BLIND	This set is used to allow an outer coclass to reuse inner coclasses via COM aggregation.
COM_INTERFACE_ENTRY_TEAR_OFF COM_INTERFACE_ENTRY_CACHED_TEAR_OFF	These macros are used to support tear-off interfaces.
COM_INTERFACE_ENTRY_NOINTERFACE	Returns E_NOINTERFACE for the specified IID. Useful if you want to automatically exclude an interface from your coclass.
COM_INTERFACE_ENTRY_BREAK	Forces a break to occur during a debug cycle if this interface is queried for.
COM_INTERFACE_ENTRY_CHAIN	Allows a subclass to "inherit" the COM map of a base class.
COM_INTERFACE_ENTRY_FUNC COM_INTERFACE_ENTRY_FUNC_BLIND	Used to force ATL to jump to a custom function when a given interface is queried for. These macros allow you to extend the ATL COM map to your liking.

Implementing a Coclass Using C++ Multiple Inheritance

To get to know these new COM map macro entries, we first need to understand the pros and cons of standard C++ multiple inheritance (MI). All of the COM objects developed thus far have had one thing in common: heavy use of standard C++ multiple inheritance. If we were to create a class declaration for the following COM object (Figure 8-1):

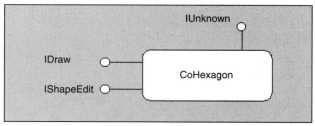

Figure 8-1: A familiar-looking coclass, exposing three interfaces.

We could create a C++ header file representing this notation as so:

```
// Building CoHexagon using C++ multiple inheritance.
class CoHexagon : public IDraw, public IShapeEdit
{
public:
        CoHexagon();
        virtual ~CoHexagon();
        // IUnknown methods.
        // IDraw methods.
        // IShapeEdit methods.
```

```
private:
    ULONG m_refCount;
};
```

As you know, IUnknown is the only COM compliant interface which does not derive from any other interface. Every standard and custom interface beyond IUnknown must derive either directly or indirectly from IUnknown, and thus ensures the first three members of an interface's vTable will be the first three methods of IUnknown. But have you stopped to notice that although every COM interface derives from IUnknown, we only need supply a single implementation of QueryInterface(), AddRef(), and Release() for a given coclass?

Given the current incarnation of CoHexagon, it looks as if we have brought in the methods of IUnknown twice: once for IDraw and another time for IShapeEdit. How then can we provide a single implementation of IUnknown in the coclass without causing a number of unresolved external compiler errors?

The best thing about using standard C++ multiple inheritance to support numerous COM interfaces is that the C++ compiler and linker will politely fill the vTable entries for each interface to point to the same (shared) implementation of IUnknown. Typically this is exactly what we want. When using MI, we ensure that all of our COM compliant interfaces can share the same implementation of IUnknown. For example:

```
// Each calls CoHexagon::QueryInterface()
pDraw -> QueryInterface(IID_IShapeEdit, (void**)&pShapeEdit);
pShapeEdit -> QueryInterface(IID_IUnknown, (void**)&pUnk);
pShapeEdit -> Release();      // Each calls CoHexagon::Release()
pUnk -> Release();
pDraw -> Release();
```

Implementing a COM Object Using Nested Classes

Multiple inheritance is not the only way to build a coclass. Other frameworks, such as MFC, support multiple interfaces on a coclass using a technique called *nested classes*. Here, the coclass under construction (that would be CoHexagon) derives from IUnknown exclusively. A unique inner class represents an interface the outer class wishes to support. While MFC provides a number of framework-specific macros to facilitate writing inner classes, we can do the same in straight C++. To create CoHexagon using nested classes, we begin by deriving the outer class from IUnknown:

```
// The outer class derives from IUnknown, and provides the
// master implementation for all inner classes.
class CoHexagon : public IUnknown
{
public:
    CoHexagon();
    virtual ~CoHexagon();
    // Master IUnknown methods.
    STDMETHODIMP_(ULONG) AddRef();
    STDMETHODIMP_(ULONG) Release();
    STDMETHODIMP QueryInterface(REFIID riid, void** ppv);
private:
    ULONG m_refCount;
};
```

The implementation of AddRef() and Release() for the outer class (CoHexagon) would be as usual; simply adjust the internal reference count and check for the final release:

```
// The use of nested classes will not affect the outer class's reference counting logic.
STDMETHODIMP_(ULONG) CoHexagon::AddRef()
{
    return ++m_refCount;
}
STDMETHODIMP_(ULONG) CoHexagon::Release()
{
    if(--m_refCount == 0)
    {
        delete this;
        return 0;
    }
    return m_refCount;
}
```

QueryInterface(), however, is implemented differently for an outer class making use of nested classes (we will see exactly how so momentarily).

Defining an Inner Class

When you wish to define an inner class to represent an implemented interface, declare the class definition directly within the outer class. Each inner class will derive directly from the interface it represents, and provide implementations for each method of the custom interface, as well as its own implementation of IUnknown. The good news is that inner classes can instead call the master IUnknown methods on the outer object to do most of the real work. Allowing the inner class to communicate with the outer class requires that each inner class maintain a pointer back to its parent. This back pointer can be represented as a member variable of the inner class. Here, then, is CoHexagon supporting IDraw as a nested class:

```
// CoHexagon using nested classes as opposed to MI.
class CoHexagon : public IUnknown
{
public:
...
    // IDrawImpl is a nested class.
    struct IDrawImpl : public IDraw
    {
        // Inner IUnknown methods.
        STDMETHODIMP_(ULONG) AddRef();
        STDMETHODIMP_(ULONG) Release();
        STDMETHODIMP QueryInterface(REFIID riid, void** ppv);
        // IDraw methods.
        STDMETHODIMP Draw();
        // Pointer to parent.
        CoHexagon* m_pParent;
    };
    // Master IUnknown methods.
    STDMETHODIMP_(ULONG) AddRef();
    STDMETHODIMP_(ULONG) Release();
    STDMETHODIMP QueryInterface(REFIID riid, void** ppv);
private:
```

```
        ULONG m_refCount;
        IDrawImpl m_drawImpl;   // Hold onto instance of inner class.
};
```

As you can see, the outer class maintains a member variable for each inner class it maintains (currently IDrawImpl). When the outer class is created, it sets the back pointer of the nested class. Assume CoHexagon defines another inner class (IShapeEditImpl) to support the IShapeEdit interface. During construction, CoHexagon tells each inner object how to report back to it:

```
// The outer object sets the back pointer during construction.
CoHexagon::CoHexagon()
{
    m_refCount = 0;
    // Tell each nested class who the parent is (set the back pointer).
    m_drawImpl.m_pParent = this;
    m_shapeEditImpl.m_pParent = this;
}
```

The reason inner classes need to point back to the parent becomes clear when we examine how to implement the IUnknown interface for each inner object: Inner objects use this back pointer to call the master IUnknown implementation. Furthermore, if the outer class defines public helper methods (which are not rigged up to a COM interface, but simply exist to help the class get work accomplished) the inner objects may call these helper functions using the same back pointer.

Implementing an Inner Class

When implementing the methods of an inner nested class, we must make use of double scope resolution syntax. Recall that a standard C++ class uses the scope resolution operator to implement the methods prototyped in its header file, using the following syntax:

```
// ReturnType ClassName::FunctionName()
ULONG CoHexagon::AddRef(){...}
```

When implementing a nested class, the inner must be scoped to the context of the outer. For example:

```
// ReturnType OuterClassName::InnerClassName::FunctionName()
ULONG CoHexagon::IDrawImpl::AddRef(){...}
```

Here then, is the implementation for the inner IDrawImpl nested class. Notice that the inner object's IUnknown implementation simply calls back to the parent class using the m_pParent pointer. The implementation of the Draw() method is as expected.

```
// IDrawImpl implements IUnknown using the parent pointer.
STDMETHODIMP_(ULONG) CoHexagon::IDrawImpl::AddRef()
{
    return m_pParent->AddRef();
}
STDMETHODIMP_(ULONG) CoHexagon::IDrawImpl::Release()
{
    return m_pParent->Release();
}
STDMETHODIMP CoHexagon::IDrawImpl::QueryInterface(REFIID riid, void** ppv)
{
```

```
        return m_pParent->QueryInterface(riid, ppv);
}
STDMETHODIMP CoHexagon::IDrawImpl::Draw()
{
        MessageBox(NULL, "CoHexagon::IDrawImpl::Draw", "Inner Class",
                MB_OK | MB_SETFOREGROUND);
        return S_OK;
}
```

IShapeEditImpl would be implemented using the same approach. Use the back pointer to
implement IUnknown and provide code for each custom method of IShapeEdit.

Implementing the Outer QueryInterface()

The last step is to finish the IUnknown implementation for the outer class. As we have
seen, AddRef() and Release() need no modifications whatsoever for an outer class.
QueryInterface() will be modified such that if the client asks for any interface other than
IUnknown, we hand off a reference to the correct inner class:

```
// QueryInterface hands off interface pointers as always,
// this time using the inner members.
STDMETHODIMP CoHexagon::QueryInterface(REFIID riid, void** ppv)
{
        if (riid == IID_IUnknown)
        {
                *ppv = (IUnknown*)this;
        }
        else if (riid == IID_IDraw)
        {
                *ppv = (IDraw*)&m_drawImpl;
        }
        else if(riid == IID_IShapeID)
        {
                *ppv = (IShapeID*)&m_shapeIDImpl;
        }
        else
        {
                *ppv = NULL;
                return E_NOINTERFACE;
        }
        ((IUnknown*)(*ppv))->AddRef();
        return S_OK;
}
```

Making Use of a Nested Class

A COM client could care less that the coclass has chosen to supply interface pointers using
nested classes as opposed to standard multiple inheritance. Here is a Visual Basic client
obtaining access to the [default] IDraw interface and asking for IShapeEdit:

```
' A VB client using a coclass
' constructed with nested class composition.
'
Private Sub Form_Load()
        ' Make outer object and get IDraw.
        Dim hex As New CoHexagon
```

```
    hex.Draw
    ' Query for IID_IShapeEdit
    Dim itfSE As IShapeEdit
    Set itfSE = hex
    itfSE.Invert
End Sub
```

Nested classes provide an alternative to standard C++ multiple inheritance. If you are using MFC to build custom COM objects, this is the road you tend to take. As you have just seen, inner classes derive from the COM interface that they represent, which entails a unique implementation of IUnknown for each inner class. The outer class assembles QueryInterface() to hand off references to the inner class instances.

I am sure you all agree that multiple inheritance is a far simpler approach. So why then did we even bother to examine nested classes? Nested classes can be used to resolve method name clashes. Before we see how nested classes can help with this issue, the next lab gives you a chance to work with nested classes firsthand.

Lab 8-1: Building a Coclass with Nested Classes

Although C++ multiple inheritance is a far simpler approach than nested classes, both techniques yield the same result of a COM-compliant binary layout. In this lab you will be given the chance to assemble an in-proc server that makes use of nested classes. Beyond building character, this lab will get you into the necessary mindset to understand how the nested class technique allows you to resolve interface method name clashes in a coclass.

 The solution for this lab can be found on your CD-ROM under:
Labs\Chapter 08\RawNested
Labs\Chapter 08\RawNested\VB Client

Step One: Develop the Initial Project and IDL

The goal of this lab is to let you build a coclass that implements a set of interfaces using nested classes. If you are up to the challenge, begin by creating a brand new Win32 DLL project named **RawNested** (an empty DLL is fine).

Insert a new file named **rawnested.idl** and be sure you deselect the **MkTypLib Compatible** option from your project settings. In your new IDL file, define your good friend, IDraw. Next, define an interface named IShapeID. This interface allows you to refer to your shapes by a numerical identifier. Finally, define the CoHexagon coclass that supports each interface. Here is the complete IDL code:

```
// Bring in core IDL files.
import "oaidl.idl";
// IDraw
[object, uuid(A533DA31-D372-11d2-B8CF-0020781238D4)]
interface IDraw : IUnknown
{
    HRESULT Draw();
};
// IShapeID
[object, uuid(DD900363-2C02-11d3-B901-0020781238D4)]
interface IShapeID : IUnknown
{
```

```
     [propput] HRESULT ID([in] int ShapeId);
     [propget] HRESULT ID([out, retval] int* ShapeId);
};
// Library statement.
[uuid(AD454EA3-2C15-11d3-B901-0020781238D4), version(1.0),
helpstring("CoHexagon nesting others")]]
library RawNested
{
     importlib("stdole32.tlb");
     [uuid(AD454EA0-2C15-11d3-B901-0020781238D4)]
     coclass CoHexagon
     {
          [default] interface IDraw;
          interface IShapeID;
     };
};
```

Insert this file into your project workspace and compile your IDL file to ensure there are no syntactical problems.

Step Two: Implement CoHexagon Using Nested Classes

CoHexagon is a COM object supporting the IDraw and IShapeID interfaces, this time using nested classes rather than C++ MI. Begin by defining the class definition of CoHexagon. Recall that outer classes derive directly from IUnknown:

```
// CoHexagon using nested classes as opposed to MI.
class CoHexagon : public IUnknown
{
public:
     CoHexagon();
     virtual ~CoHexagon();
     // Master IUnknown implementation.
     STDMETHODIMP_(ULONG) AddRef();
     STDMETHODIMP_(ULONG) Release();
     STDMETHODIMP QueryInterface(REFIID riid, void** ppv);
private:
     ULONG m_refCount;
};
```

Implement your AddRef() and Release() methods as usual, remembering to set your internal reference counter (m_refCount) to zero in the constructor of CoHexagon.

Next, we will be adding support for IDraw using a nested class. Inside the definition of CoHexagon, define an inner class deriving from IDraw, named IDrawImpl. Also define a CoHexagon pointer member variable in the inner class, allowing the child class to communicate with the parent:

```
// Inner classes maintain a pointer to the parent, for use in its own
// IUnknown implementation.
class CoHexagon : public IUnknown
{
public:
     CoHexagon();
     virtual ~CoHexagon();
     // This inner class implements IDraw.
     struct IDrawImpl : public IDraw
```

```
        {
                // IUnknown methods.
                STDMETHODIMP_(ULONG) AddRef();
                STDMETHODIMP_(ULONG) Release();
                STDMETHODIMP QueryInterface(REFIID riid, void** ppv);
                // IDraw methods.
                STDMETHODIMP Draw();
                // Pointer to parent.
                CoHexagon* m_pParent;
        };
...
};
```

Now do the same for IShapeID using another nested class called IShapeIDImpl:

```
// The second inner class, also defined within the scope of CoHexagon.
struct IShapeIDImpl : public IShapeID
{
        // IUnknown methods.
        STDMETHODIMP_(ULONG) AddRef();
        STDMETHODIMP_(ULONG) Release();
        STDMETHODIMP QueryInterface(REFIID riid, void** ppv);
        // IShapeID methods.
        STDMETHODIMP put_ID(int id);
        STDMETHODIMP get_ID(int* id);
        // Pointer to parent.
        CoHexagon* m_pParent;
};
```

Before we begin implementing the inner methods of each nested class, let's finish up the definition of CoHexagon by declaring an instance of both IDrawImpl and IShapeIDImpl, and set each m_pParent pointer in CoHexagon's constructor:

```
// In the constructor of the outer class, set each inner class's back pointer.
m_drawImpl.m_pParent = this;
m_shapeIDImpl.m_pParent = this;
```

Now, we can complete the implementation of CoHexagon's IUnknown. In your QueryInterface() method, test the incoming REFIID parameter and return IUnknown, IDraw, and IShapeID pointers. In the case of the nested classes, stuff the (void**) parameter with a reference to the correct inner object:

```
// The outer class's QI hands out references to the inner objects.
STDMETHODIMP CoHexagon::QueryInterface(REFIID riid, void** ppv)
{
        if (riid == IID_IUnknown)
        {
                *ppv = (IUnknown*)this;
        }
        else if (riid == IID_IDraw)
        {
                *ppv = (IDraw*)&m_drawImpl;
        }
        else if(riid == IID_IShapeID)
        {
                *ppv = (IShapeID*)&m_shapeIDImpl;
        }
        else
```

```
    {
        *ppv = NULL;
        return E_NOINTERFACE;
    }
    ((IUnknown*)(*ppv))->AddRef();
    return S_OK;
}
```

To finish up the implementation of CoHexagon, we need to implement IDrawImpl as well as IShapeIDImpl. Start by implementing IUnknown for IDrawImpl. Recall that your inner classes maintain a pointer back to the parent, which allows it to call any method in the parent's public sector. Use this back pointer to flesh out the details of AddRef(), Release(), and QueryInterface() using double scope resolution syntax:

```
// IDrawImpl
STDMETHODIMP_(ULONG) CoHexagon::IDrawImpl::AddRef()
{
    return m_pParent->AddRef();
}
STDMETHODIMP_(ULONG) CoHexagon::IDrawImpl::Release()
{
    return m_pParent->Release();
}
STDMETHODIMP CoHexagon::IDrawImpl::QueryInterface(REFIID riid, void** ppv)
{
    return m_pParent->QueryInterface(riid, ppv);
}
```

As for Draw() itself, I still always recommend calls to MessageBox:

```
// Draw your inner object.
STDMETHODIMP CoHexagon::IDrawImpl::Draw()
{
    MessageBox(NULL, "CoHexagon::IDrawImpl::Draw", "Inner Class",
               MB_OK | MB_SETFOREGROUND );
    return S_OK;
}
```

To implement IShapeIDImpl, start by adding a public integer data member to CoHexagon named m_ID, and set it to zero in the constructor. This will be used by the put_ID and get_ID methods of IShapeID. Next, implement the IUnknown methods for IShapeIDImpl in the same way you did for IDrawImpl. As IShapeID defines a single property, we have two final methods to implement. Here is the code for get_ID and put_ID. Notice the use of the back pointer:

```
// IShapeIDImpl
STDMETHODIMP CoHexagon::IShapeIDImpl::put_ID(int shapeID)
{
    m_pParent->m_ID = shapeID;    // Set parent's m_ID.
    return S_OK;
}
STDMETHODIMP CoHexagon::IShapeIDImpl::get_ID(int* shapeID)
{
    *shapeID = m_pParent->m_ID;  // Get parent's m_ID.
    return S_OK;
}
```

Recall that the m_ID data member defined in CoHexagon is public and therefore we can access it directly from the scope of an inner class. If you would rather, feel free to create your own accessor and mutator for a private m_ID, or declare a friendship (e.g., the **friend** keyword) between the outer and inner classes. Regardless of which path you choose, you should see how to equip an inner class to communicate to the outer parent.

Go ahead and compile.

Step Three: Build a Class Factory

Developing a class factory for your COM objects is a very redundant operation. Feel free to steal the files from a previous raw C++ project. As you know, a typical class factory derives from IClassFactory. In your CreateInstance() implementation, create a new CoHexagon as usual:

```
// Yet another class factory.
STDMETHODIMP CoHexFactory::CreateInstance(LPUNKNOWN pUnkOuter, REFIID riid, void** ppv)
{
    if(pUnkOuter != NULL)
        return CLASS_E_NOAGGREGATION;
    CoHexagon* pHexObj = NULL;
    HRESULT hr;
    // Create the object.
    pHexObj = new CoHexagon;
    hr = pHexObj -> QueryInterface(riid, ppv);
    if (FAILED(hr))
        delete pHexObj;
    return hr;
}
```

To implement LockServer(), you will need to add a global lock counter, which you may assume for the moment is defined in another file. Likewise, be sure the constructor and destructor of the class factory adjust the server-wide object count. AddRef(), Release(), and QueryInterface() are the same as they would be for any class factory. Finally, be sure to adjust the object counter in the constructor and destructor of CoHexagon.

Step Four: Assemble the Component Housing

Like class factories, in-proc server export functions are also very boilerplate in nature. Feel free to reuse a previous implementation. You know the drill:

```
// Exports.
STDAPI DllCanUnloadNow()
{
    if(g_lockCount == 0 && g_objCount == 0)
        return S_OK;          // Unload me.
    else
        return S_FALSE;       // Keep me alive.
}
STDAPI DllGetClassObject(REFCLSID rclsid, REFIID riid, void** ppv)
{
    HRESULT hr;
    CoHexFactory *pCFact = NULL;
    // We only know how to make CoHexagon objects in this house.
    if(rclsid == CLSID_CoHexagon)
```

```
{
        pCFact = new CoHexFactory;
        hr = pCFact -> QueryInterface(riid, ppv);
        if(FAILED(hr))
                delete pCFact;
    }
    else
        return CLASS_E_CLASSNOTAVAILABLE;
    return hr;
}
```

Finally, create (and insert) a DEF file into the project and build (and merge) a minimal REG file specifying the ProgID and CLSID for CoHexagon. Go ahead and compile your new DLL. You should come through nice and clean.

Step Five: A Simple Visual Basic Client

Fire up VB, set a reference to your server's type library, and create a simple client to test your server. Figure 8-2 shows a possible sample GUI:

Figure 8-2:
Making use of
nested classes.

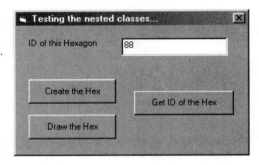

Here is the VB code that exercises CoHexagon. Notice that the client has no idea the coclass is composed of nested classes rather than C++ multiple inheritance:

```
' [General][Declarations]
'
Option Explicit
Private mTheHex As CoHexagon
Private mItfShapeID As IShapeID
Private Sub btnCreate_Click()
        ' Make the Hex.
        Set mTheHex = New CoHexagon
        ' Set ID.
        Set mItfShapeID = mTheHex
        mItfShapeID.ID = CInt(txtID.Text)
        ' Enable buttons
        btnDraw.Enabled = True
        btnID.Enabled = True
End Sub
Private Sub btnDraw_Click()
        ' Draw the hex.
        mTheHex.Draw
End Sub
Private Sub btnID_Click()
```

```
        ' Echo ID.
        MsgBox mItfShapeID.ID, , "The ID is..."
End Sub
Private Sub Form_Load()
        btnDraw.Enabled = False
        btnID.Enabled = False
End Sub
```

So, now that you have written a coclass using nested classes, you may be wondering exactly why one might want to do this. After all, nested classes entail more work than multiple inheritance. Well, read on and let's examine one situation where C++ multiple inheritance can leave much to be desired, and how the nested class technique can be used to remedy the situation.

Resolving Interface Method Name Clashes

Using standard multiple inheritance to support COM interfaces is simple: derive and implement. The compiler and linker will automatically direct each interface's IUnknown methods to a common, shared implementation. This behavior is great for IUnknown, but not so great if we have a coclass deriving from two (or more) interfaces with the same method names. For example, let's say a colleague has just designed a new COM interface that draws any shape with a 3-D look and feel:

```
// I3DRender
[object, uuid(DD900360-2C02-11d3-B901-0020781238D4)]
interface I3DRender : IUnknown
{
        HRESULT Draw();
};
```

This new interface gets us excited, and we want a shape to render itself in both 2-D as well as vivid 3-D. Using multiple inheritance, we design Co3DHexagon accordingly:

```
// This shape can be drawn in 2-D or 3-D.
class Co3DHexagon : public IDraw, public I3DRender
{
public:
        Co3DHexagon();
        virtual ~Co3DHexagon();
        // IUnknown methods.
        // IDraw methods.
        // I3DRender methods.
...
};
```

As you know by now, IDraw defines the sole method Draw(). I3DRender also defines a single method named Draw(). Therefore, the C++ compiler and linker will, again, direct both Draw() methods to the <u>same implementation</u>. In this case, we don't appreciate the compiler and linker as much as we did when they shared the common methods of IUnknown. However, just as we can use nested classes to provide a specific implementation for an interface's IUnknown we can also use nested classes to resolve name clashes. Whenever you have a COM interface containing methods with the same signature of another interface supported by the coclass, create a nested class to resolve the name clash.

For example, to allow Co3DHexagon to provide unique implementations for each Draw() method, we begin by deriving from each custom interface <u>excluding</u> the offending I3DRender. Next, we define an inner class to represent the implementation of I3DRender, setting its back pointer in Co3DHexagon's constructor:

```
// Using a nested class to resolve interface method name clashes.
class Co3DHexagon : public IDraw   // Not deriving from I3DRender...
{
public:
    Co3DHexagon()
    {
        m_refCount = 0;
        m_3dRenderImpl.m_pParent = this;
    }
    virtual ~Co3DHexagon();
    // Master IUnknown
    STDMETHODIMP_(ULONG) AddRef();
    STDMETHODIMP_(ULONG) Release();
    STDMETHODIMP QueryInterface(REFIID riid, void** ppv);
    // IDraw::Draw
    STDMETHODIMP Draw();
    // I3DRender is represented by a nested class.
    struct I3DRenderImpl : public I3DRender
    {
        // IUnknown methods.
        STDMETHODIMP_(ULONG) AddRef();
        STDMETHODIMP_(ULONG) Release();
        STDMETHODIMP QueryInterface(REFIID riid, void** ppv);
        // I3DRender methods.
        STDMETHODIMP Draw();
        // Pointer to parent.
        Co3DHexagon* m_pParent;
    };
private:
    // Instance of inner class.
    I3DRenderImpl m_3dRenderImpl;
    ULONG m_refCount;
};
```

The outer class's IUnknown::QueryInterface() will provide a static cast to IUnknown and IShapeEdit, but return a reference to m_3dRenderImpl if asked for I3DRender:

```
// Master QueryInterface() logic.
STDMETHODIMP Co3DHexagon::QueryInterface(REFIID riid, void** ppv)
{
    if (riid == IID_IUnknown)
    {
        *ppv = (IUnknown*)(IDraw*)this;
    }
    else if (riid == IID_IDraw)
    {
        *ppv = (IDraw*)this;
    }
    else if(riid == IID_I3DRender)
    {
        *ppv = (I3DRender*)&m_3dRenderImpl;
```

```
        }
        else
        {
                *ppv = NULL;
                return E_NOINTERFACE;
        }
        ((IUnknown*)(*ppv))->AddRef();
        return S_OK;
}
```

To finish up our inner class, we will use double scope resolution to provide implementations of IUnknown (which as before simply forwards the call to Co3DHexagon's implementation) as well as an implementation of I3DRender::Draw():

```
// I3DHexagon::Draw()
STDMETHODIMP Co3DHexagon::I3DRenderImpl::Draw()
{
        MessageBox(NULL, "Drawing a lovely 3D hexagon", "Inner Class",
                        MB_OK | MB_SETFOREGROUND);
        return S_OK;
}
```

IDraw's version of Draw() will be implemented as usual:

```
// IDraw::Draw()
STDMETHODIMP Co3DHexagon::Draw()
{
        MessageBox(NULL, "Drawing a boring 2D hexagon", "Outer Class",
                        MB_OK | MB_SETFOREGROUND);
        return S_OK;
}
```

Again, the COM client has no idea of our C++ handiwork:

```
' A simple VB client using a coclass
' constructed with nested class composition.
'
Private Sub Form_Load()
        Dim threeDHex As New Co3DHexagon
        ' Draw in 2D.
        threeDHex.Draw
        ' Now draw in 3D
        Dim itf3D As I3DRender
        Set itf3D = threeDHex
        itf3D.Draw
End Sub
```

 If you would like to investigate the code behind a raw C++ name clash, your CD-ROM contains the Co3DHexagon project under the Labs\Chapter 08\RawNameClash subdirectory.

Resolving Name Clashes in ATL

Let's examine the same problem of clashing method names in ATL. To begin, assume we have an in-proc server named ATLNameClash, containing Co3DHexagon which supports the default IDraw interface. Next, assume we have written the IDL code for I3DRender in our project's IDL file and added a single method named Draw(). If we were to now use the Implement Interface Wizard, ATL would do the following:

- Add I3DRender to our inheritance chain.
- Add a COM_INTERFACE_ENTRY for I3DRender.

What ATL would <u>not</u> do is create a nested class for I3DRender::Draw(). In fact, as IDraw already defines a Draw() method, ATL does not write a single line of stub code. If we were to compile and test the project, a COM client would indeed be able to ask for I3DRender and IDraw independently; however, each Draw() method would call the shared implementation. Here is the story thus far:

```
// ATL class with unique methods mapping to a shared implementation.
class ATL_NO_VTABLE CCo3DHexagon :
    public CComObjectRootEx<CComSingleThreadModel>,
    public CComCoClass<CCo3DHexagon, &CLSID_Co3DHexagon>,
    public IDraw,
    public I3DRender
{
public:
...
BEGIN_COM_MAP(CCo3DHexagon)
    COM_INTERFACE_ENTRY(IDraw)
    COM_INTERFACE_ENTRY(I3DRender)
END_COM_MAP()
public:
    STDMETHOD(Draw)();
};
// Shared implementation.
STDMETHODIMP CCo3DHexagon::Draw()
{
    MessageBox(NULL, "I don't know what to do!!", "Panic!", MB_OK);
    return S_OK;
}
```

Remedying the name clash in ATL will require a similar but not completely identical approach to the nested class example used in straight C++. The reason we cannot just carry over the previous example has to do with how ATL handles QueryInterface(). The COM map is ATL's way to provide a table driven approach to return interfaces to clients. While this works great, it does hide the standard implementation of QueryInterface() we know and love (if...else...if...else). Therefore, we have no obvious way to tweak the QueryInterface() logic to hand out references to a nested class.

In ATL, we can resolve method name clashes by creating wrapper classes around the offending interfaces, and intercept the ambiguity before our coclass is aware the clash exists. The trick is to provide an implementation of the clashing methods within the wrapper, which in turn call <u>unique</u> methods on the supporting class. Our first step, then, is to create the wrapper classes. Assume you have inserted a new file (wrappers.h) into your project and define the following:

```
// Here we provide an implementation of I3DRender::Draw(), which calls
// a uniquely named method in the coclass (the name of the method is arbitrary).
// Note the wrapper methods are pure virtual, as the coclass will provide a distinct
// implementation.
struct I3DRenderImpl : public I3DRender
```

```
{
    STDMETHODIMP Draw()
    {
        return Draw3DHex();
    }
    STDMETHOD(Draw3DHex)() = 0;
};
struct IDrawImpl : public IDraw
{
    STDMETHODIMP Draw()
    {
        return Draw2DHex();
    }
    STDMETHOD(Draw2DHex)() = 0;
};
```

> **Note:**   Recall that the STDMETHOD macro inserts the virtual keyword, while STDMETHODIMP does not. Do not use STDMETHODIMP for the uniquely named methods, as these will be implemented by the coclass, and must be pure virtual.

We can now go back to the ATL coclass, and rather than deriving from IDraw and I3DRender directly, derive from the wrapper classes.

```
// Deriving from the wrapper classes will not affect your COM map.
class ATL_NO_VTABLE CCo3DHexagon :
    public CComObjectRootEx<CComSingleThreadModel>,
    public CComCoClass<CCo3DHexagon, &CLSID_Co3DHexagon>,
    public IDrawImpl,
    public I3DRenderImpl
{
...
// COM map stays the same.
BEGIN_COM_MAP(CCo3DHexagon)
    COM_INTERFACE_ENTRY(IDraw)
    COM_INTERFACE_ENTRY(I3DRender)
END_COM_MAP()
...
public:
    // These are inherited from the wrappers.
    STDMETHOD(Draw2DHex)();
    STDMETHOD(Draw3DHex)();
...
};
```

Now, if a client calls Draw() from an IDraw pointer, the wrapper class (IDrawImpl) in turn calls a unique method by the coclass. Likewise for I3DRenderImpl. Although each interface has a Draw() method, the name clash is avoided as they have each provided an implementation in a separate wrapper class, not twice in a single class. All we have left to do is flesh out the pure virtual methods in our derived class:

```
// To each their own.
STDMETHODIMP CCo3DHexagon::Draw3DRect()
{
```

```
        MessageBox(NULL, "3D!!", "Better!", MB_OK | MB_SETFOREGROUND);
        return S_OK;
}
STDMETHODIMP CCo3DHexagon::Draw2DRect()
{
        MessageBox(NULL, "2D!!", "Better!", MB_OK | MB_SETFOREGROUND);
        return S_OK;
}
```

When you are writing your wrapper classes for conflicting interfaces, you only need to forward the clashing methods to a unique member in the coclass. In other words, if IDraw and I3DRender each had additional members that do not introduce a name clash:

```
// Each interface has an offending method as well as a non-offending method.
interface IDraw : IUnknown
{
        HRESULT Draw();                   // Offensive.
        HRESULT AnotherIDrawMethod();     // Non-offensive.
};
interface I3DRender : IUnknown
{
        HRESULT Draw();                   // Offensive.
        HRESULT AnotherI3DRenderMethod(); // Non-offensive.
};
```

Your wrappers will only need to account for Draw(). The non-offending methods would be implemented as usual in the Co3DHexagon coclass.

Lab 8-2: Dealing with Interface Name Clashes in ATL

As you develop more sophisticated coclasses, you are bound to run into the situation where two interfaces each define a method with the same name and signature. This lab will give you the chance to explore some ways to circumvent this sort of name clash using ATL.

The solution for this lab can be found on your CD-ROM under:
Labs\Chapter 08\ATLNameClash
Labs\Chapter 08\ATLNameClash\VB Client

Step One: Create a Name Clash

Before we create wrapper classes for offending interface method names, we need to create a name clash to illustrate the problem. Begin your lab by accessing the ATL COM AppWizard. Create an in-proc server named **ATLNameClash**. Open the Object Wizard and insert a Simple Object named **Co3DHexagon**, supporting a single custom interface named **IDraw**. Add a single method to the IDraw interface (I bet you can guess the name) called **Draw()**. Implement Draw() however you desire:

```
// Draw method A.
STDMETHODIMP CCo3DHexagon::Draw()
{
        MessageBox(NULL, "Drawing a 2D Hex", "CoHex says...",
                   MB_OK | MB_SETFOREGROUND);
        return S_OK;
}
```

Now, edit your IDL file to add support for a new interface named I3DRender, which also supports a single method named Draw():

```
// Draw method B.
[object, uuid(DD900360-2C02-11d3-B901-0020781238D4)]
interface I3DRender : IUnknown
{
    [helpstring("Draw in 3D")] HRESULT Draw();
};
...
coclass Co3DHexagon
{
    [default] interface IDraw;
    interface I3DRender;
};
```

Next, support this interface in your ATL coclass with or without the aid of the Implement Interface Wizard. Either way, you will have a COM map that now looks like the following:

```
// Clients can get a pointer to IDraw and I3DRender, however
// each Draw() method calls the same shared implementation.
BEGIN_COM_MAP(CCo3DHexagon)
    OM_INTERFACE_ENTRY(IDraw)
    OM_INTERFACE_ENTRY(I3DRender)
END_COM_MAP()
```

At this point, build a simple Visual Basic test client. You will be able to obtain each interface from the coclass; however, they each call the same shared implementation of Draw(). There is the name clash. What we really want is to have the Draw() method of each interface respond in a unique manner.

Step Two: Resolve the Name Clash

The first point to be aware of when resolving a method name clash with ATL is that you must create a wrapper for each interface involved in the name clash. You cannot simply trap one of the ambiguous interfaces and leave the other(s) alone. Insert a new file named **wrappers.h**. In this file, create a wrapper class around the I3DRender and IDraw interfaces using the same approach as outlined in this chapter: Intercept the offending method, and call a uniquely named method implemented by the coclass:

```
// This IMPL class wraps the offending
// Draw method of the I3DRender interface.
struct I3DRenderImpl : I3DRender
{
    STDMETHODIMP Draw()
    {
        return Draw3DHex();
    }
    // This method is implemented by the coclass.
    STDMETHOD(Draw3DHex)() = 0;
};
struct IDrawImpl: IDraw
{
    STDMETHODIMP Draw()
    {
        return Draw2DHex();
```

```
        }
        // This method is also implemented by the coclass.
        STDMETHOD(Draw2DHex)() = 0;
};
```

Now that we have created wrapper classes to resolve the name clash, we need to retrofit Co3DHexagon to use them. Edit your inheritance chain to derive <u>only</u> from the wrapper classes, and comment out (or remove) the original IDraw and I3DRender interfaces (your COM map will remain unaltered):

```
// Derive from your wrapper classes.
class ATL_NO_VTABLE CCo3DHexagon :
    public CComObjectRootEx<CComSingleThreadModel>,
    public CComCoClass<CCo3DHexagon, &CLSID_Co3DHexagon>,
    // public IDraw,
    // public I3DRender,
    public IDrawImpl,
    public I3DRenderImpl
{
...
};
```

Recall that the wrapper classes each define a pure virtual function that needs to be implemented by the supporting coclass. In the class definition of Co3DHexagon, remove the existing Draw() prototype and implementation code, and add a prototype for **Draw2DHex()** and **Draw3DHex()**:

```
// These were defined by the wrappers.
STDMETHOD(Draw2DRect)();
STDMETHOD(Draw3DRect)();
```

Now, we will implement the wrappers to define a unique implementation for each Draw() method:

```
// Give a custom implementation for each wrapper.
STDMETHODIMP CCo3DHexagon::Draw3DRect()
{
    MessageBox(NULL, " Stunning 3D!!", " CoHex says",
            MB_OK | MB_SETFOREGROUND);
    return S_OK;
}
STDMETHODIMP CCo3DHexagon::Draw2DRect()
{
    MessageBox(NULL, "Drawing a 2D Hex", "CoHex says",
            MB_OK | MB_SETFOREGROUND);
    return S_OK;
}
```

Compile the project and run the VB test client again. You should now see a unique response for each Draw() method, depending on the interface!

Also recall that if an interface has additional methods defined which do not cause a name clash, nothing needs to be accounted for in the wrapper. For example, assume that IDraw has an additional (and unique) method:

```
// A non-clashing method.
interface IDraw : IUnknown
```

```
{
    [helpstring("Draw in 2D")] HRESULT Draw();
    HRESULT DrawBold();
};
```

Your wrapper class (IDrawImpl) would be unaffected, and would still simply be in charge of trapping the offending Draw() method. Co3DHexagon would provide an implementation of DrawBold() as usual.

Ambiguities within Interface Hierarchies

Back in Chapter 2, you were introduced to the idea of interface hierarchies. Let's extend the example briefly mentioned at that point, and create a set of related interfaces modeling automobile behaviors:

Figure 8-3: A hierarchy of related interfaces.

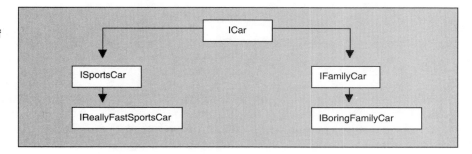

Now that we are knee-deep in COM, we know that ICar must derive from IUnknown directly (as it is the topmost node). The IDL code to capture this interface hierarchy would be as so:

```
// ICar is the master interface.
[ object, uuid(8945C9D5-2C00-11D3-B901-0020781238D4)]
interface ICar : IUnknown
{
    // Behavior for any car.
};
// ISportsCar is derived from ICar.
[ object, uuid(2B622560-2C42-11d3-B901-0020781238D4)]
interface ISportsCar : ICar
{
    // Behavior for a standard sports car.
};
// IReallyFastSportsCar is derived from ISportsCar.
[ object, uuid(2B622561-2C42-11d3-B901-0020781238D4)]
interface IReallyFastSportsCar : ISportsCar
{
    // Turbo boost support, water-cooled engine.
};
// IFamilyCar is derived from ICar.
[ object, uuid(2B622562-2C42-11d3-B901-0020781238D4)]
interface IFamilyCar : ICar
{
    // Practical and clean.
```

```
};
// IBoringFamilyCar is derived from IFamilyCar.
[ object, uuid(2B622563-2C42-11d3-B901-0020781238D4)]
interface IBoringFamilyCar : IFamilyCar
{
        // Practical, clean and at least one sliding door.
};
```

Again, I will allow you to imagine the properties and methods that populate these interfaces. Assume we design an ATL coclass named CoSportsSedan that implements the ICar, IFamilyCar, and ISportsCar interfaces:

Figure 8-4: CoSportsSedan supports two interfaces derived from ICar.

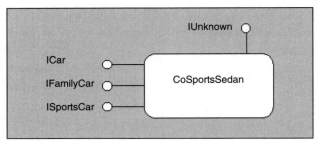

Recall that objects only directly derive from the *nth* most interfaces in an interface hierarchy. The pure virtual methods of the base interfaces are inherited automatically. Therefore, our ATL Simple Object would derive directly from IFamilyCar and ISportsCar, but not directly from ICar (or IUnknown), as these interfaces are base interfaces of each:

```
// ATL CoSportsSedan
class ATL_NO_VTABLE CCoSportsSedan :
        public CComObjectRootEx<CComSingleThreadModel>,
        public CComCoClass<CCoSportsSedan, &CLSID_CoSportsSedan>,
        public IFamilyCar,
        public ISportsCar
{
public:
...
// ICar methods.
// IFamilyCar methods.
// ISportsCar methods.
};
```

As we wish to allow COM clients to ask for ICar, IFamilyCar, and ISportsCar interfaces, we update our COM map as so:

```
// CoSportsSedan's COM map.
BEGIN_COM_MAP(CCoSportsSedan)
        COM_INTERFACE_ENTRY(ICar)
        COM_INTERFACE_ENTRY(IFamilyCar)
        COM_INTERFACE_ENTRY(ISportsCar)
END_COM_MAP()
```

Sadly, once we compile, we are issued the following error:

```
error C2594: 'static_cast' : ambiguous conversions from 'class CCoSportsSedan *' to 'struct ICar *'
```

The problem is that we have two custom interfaces (IFamilyCar and ISportsCar) with the same base interface (ICar). Ambiguity arises as a vPtr for ICar can be obtained from two subinterfaces, and we need to pick which branch the compiler should follow.

We have seen this same problem before. Recall that when we had at least two custom interfaces on a coclass we also had to tell the compiler how to cast for the IUnknown pointer:

```
// Resolving IUnknown ambiguities.
if(riid == IID_IUnknown)
    *ppv = (IUnknown*)(ISomeInterface*)this;
```

ATL provides three COM map macros beyond COM_INTERFACE_ENTRY to resolve this sort of base interface ambiguity:

- COM_INTERFACE_ENTRY_IID
- COM_INTERFACE_ENTRY2
- COM_INTERFACE_ENTRY2_IID

The COM_INTERFACE_ENTRY_IID Macro

When you have a coclass supporting interfaces descending from a common base interface, you will need to pick a specific subinterface the compiler can cast against. For example, as both IFamilyCar and ISportsCar derive from ICar, the compiler is confused as it sees two different definitions for ICar. We must tell the compiler to pick either IFamilyCar or ISportsCar as the class to cast against when fetching the ICar interface for a COM client. The COM_INTERFACE_ENTRY_IID macro is used for this very purpose:

```
// One of three COM map macros used to resolve method ambiguities.
#define COM_INTERFACE_ENTRY_IID(iid, x)\
    {&iid,\
    offsetofclass(x, _ComMapClass),\
    _ATL_SIMPLEMAPENTRY},
```

The COM_INTERFACE_ENTRY_IID macro takes two parameters: the GUID of the common base interface (in this case ICar) and the name of a derived interface used to resolve the ambiguity (which can be any interface deriving from ICar). If we update our COM map to use COM_INTERFACE_ENTRY_IID, we will compile clean as we have specified which subinterface will be used to determine the ICar pointer:

```
// This COM map resolves the ambiguity of a common base interface
// by using COM_INTERFACE_ENTRY_IID
BEGIN_COM_MAP(CCoSportsSedan)
    COM_INTERFACE_ENTRY(IFamilyCar)
    COM_INTERFACE_ENTRY(ISportsCar)
    COM_INTERFACE_ENTRY_IID(IID_ICar, ISportsCar)
END_COM_MAP()
```

The COM_INTERFACE_ENTRY2 Macro

This ATL COM map macro is also useful when dealing with base interface ambiguities. Functionally it serves the same purpose as COM_INTERFACE_ENTRY_IID, but this time you send in the IDL name of each interface (the common base interface and a derived interface):

```
// Another COM map macro used to resolve method ambiguities.
#define COM_INTERFACE_ENTRY2(x, x2)\
    {&_ATL_IIDOF(x),\
    (DWORD)((x*)(x2*)((_ComMapClass*)8))-8,\
    _ATL_SIMPLEMAPENTRY},
```

We could use this COM map macro in our CoSportsSedan as follows:

```
// This COM map resolves the ambiguity of a common base interface
// by using COM_INTERFACE_ENTRY2
BEGIN_COM_MAP(CCoSportsSedan)
    COM_INTERFACE_ENTRY(IFamilyCar)
    COM_INTERFACE_ENTRY(ISportsCar)
    // Use ISportsCar to fetch ICar.
    COM_INTERFACE_ENTRY2(ICar, ISportsCar)
END_COM_MAP()
```

The COM_INTERFACE_ENTRY2_IID Macro

The final macro ATL provides to resolve common base interface ambiguities is COM_INTERFACE_ENTRY2_IID. This macro takes three parameters: the GUID of the common base interface, the name of the common base interface, and the name of the subinterface used to resolve the ambiguity:

```
// The final ATL ambiguity macro.
#define COM_INTERFACE_ENTRY2_IID(iid, x, x2)\
    {&iid,\
    (DWORD)((x*)(x2*)((_ComMapClass*)8))-8,\
    _ATL_SIMPLEMAPENTRY},
```

We could again rewrite our COM map as follows:

```
// This COM map resolves the ambiguity of a common base interface
// by using COM_INTERFACE_ENTRY2_IID
BEGIN_COM_MAP(CCoSportsSedan)
    COM_INTERFACE_ENTRY(IFamilyCar)
    COM_INTERFACE_ENTRY(ISportsCar)
    COM_INTERFACE_ENTRY2_IID(IID_ICar, ICar, ISportsCar)
END_COM_MAP()
```

Functionally, COM_INTERFACE_ENTRY_IID, COM_INTERFACE_ENTRY2, and COM_INTERFACE_ENTRY2_IID are exactly the same. These COM map macros are used to help resolve the ambiguities arising from two (or more) interfaces with a common base interface.

Note: In order for the ATL framework to calculate the offset to your class's IUnknown interface, ensure the very first listing of your COM map is COM_INTERFACE_ENTRY, COM_INTERFACE_ENTRY_IID, COM_INTERFACE_ENTRY2, or COM_INTERFACE_ENTRY2_IID. These macros are often called the *simple entries*.

Understanding "Tear-Off" Interfaces

Most often, when a coclass supports a given set of interfaces, the assumption is made that a client will ask, and ask often, for access to these interfaces. In other words, if we create a coclass supporting a set of interfaces such as {IDraw, IShapeEdit, IDoubleBuffer} we naturally assume clients will ask for them as they manipulate the object. However, some coclasses may support a subset of interfaces that are rarely accessed by clients. This behavior often happens as a coclass matures, and acquires the "latest and greatest" interfaces which may overshadow existing functionality. Of course, the ability to know which interfaces are accessed less frequently than others is more an art than a science (furthermore, this art may be nothing more than a developer's educated guess).

Imagine you have a coclass named CoMyATLExperience supporting the IAmDrowningInMacros interface. You created this interface when you first began to examine ATL, and created an interface to express your pain in a well-defined set of methods. Time has progressed, and you now love ATL macros. Given the laws of COM identity, you know that you are bound by the interface contract. Once a client is able to acquire an interface from your object via QueryInterface(), the client must <u>always</u> be able to acquire that same interface. This is often termed the "law of predictability."

Therefore, as existing clients expect to obtain an IAmDrowningInMacros pointer, you cannot remove this outdated interface from your ATL COM map. For the sake of this discussion, here is the ATL coclass in question:

```
// Here is a coclass that you suspect contains interfaces of little use to most clients.
class ATL_NO_VTABLE CoMyATLExperience :
    public CComObjectRootEx<CComSingleThreadModel>,
    public CComCoClass< CoMyATLExperience,
                        &CLSID_CoMyATLExperience >,
    public IAmDrowningInMacros,       // Never used.
    public IDontTrustFrameworks,      // Never used.
    public IGuessThisIsOK,            // Used every now and then.
    public IThinkILikeThis,           // Used every now and then.
    public IAmAnATLJunkie,            // Often used.
    public IOnlyOpenATLWorkspaces     // Often used.
{
    ...
};
```

As you suspect most clients will only ask for the final two interfaces, you may wish to set up CoMyATLExperience in such a way that when an instance of this class is created, only the IAmAnATLJunkie and IOnlyCreateATLWorkspaces vPtrs are initialized. The remaining interfaces (which you assume to be of little use to most clients) will not have their vPtrs initialized until a client <u>explicitly</u> asks for access to these interfaces. The ability for a COM class to create vPtrs on demand can be visualized as "tearing off an interface," and hence the term *tear-off interfaces*.

Tear-off interfaces allow the coclass to be created more quickly (as fewer vPtrs need to spring to life) and leave a smaller code footprint if no clients are using the tear-offs (as vPtrs take up space, 4 bytes per interface).

A tear-off interface is implemented as a separate C++ class, and thus, the vPtr for less frequently used interfaces is not initialized until the object is created. The end result is avoiding overhead that may not actually be needed.

A Tear-Off Example in C++

Before we examine ATL's support for tear-off interfaces, it will be helpful to see how this might be set up in straight C++. To facilitate a simpler discussion than we would have with CoMyATLExperience, assume we have a C++ coclass named CoOldObject, which currently supports IOldInterface and INewFancyInterface.

The goal here is to implement IOldInterface as a tear-off using C++, as we suspect this interface is of little use to the outside world. Here is the IDL code describing each interface supported by CoOldObject:

```
// This interface has served its purpose.
[ object, uuid(1A928153-238F-11D3-B8F8-0020781238D4)]
interface IOldInterface : IUnknown
{
     HRESULT NoOneCallsAnymore();
};
// All the cool coclasses support this interface!
[ object, uuid(362BD920-2397-11d3-B8F8-0020781238D4)]
interface INewFancyInterface : IUnknown
{
     HRESULT IAmLovedByClients();
};
```

Here is the pre-tear-off implementation of CoOldObject. This is straight C++ COM, and should raise no eyebrows:

```
// This coclass supports two non tear-off interfaces.
class CoOldObject : public IOldInterface, public INewFancyInterface
{
public:
...
     STDMETHODIMP(NoOneCallsAnymore)()
     {
          MessageBox(NULL, "Someone DOES love me!",
                    "I am so lonely", MB_OK | MB_SETFOREGROUND);
     }
     STDMETHODIMP(IAmLovedByClients)()
     {
          MessageBox(NULL, "EVERYONE loves me!",
                    "I am so happy", MB_OK | MB_SETFOREGROUND);
     }
     STDMETHODIMP_(ULONG )AddRef()       {...}
     STDMETHODIMP_(ULONG )Release()      {...}
     STDMETHODIMP QueryInterface(REFIID riid, void** ppv)
     {
          if(riid == IID_INewFancyInterface)
               *ppv = (INewFancyInterface *)this;
          else if(riid == IID_IUnknown)
               *ppv = (IUnknown*)( INewFancyInterface*)this;
          else if(riid == IID_IOldInterface)
               *ppv = (IOldInterface*)this;
          else
          {
               *ppv = NULL;
               return E_NOINTERFACE;
          }
```

```
                    ((IUnknown*)(*ppv))->AddRef();
                    return S_OK;
            }
    ...
};
```

Implementing the Tear-Off Interface

A class exposing a tear-off interface is termed the *owner class*. The class implementing the outdated interface is termed the *tear-off class*. A separate C++ class will represent each interface you wish to expose as a tear-off. This should make sense, as we are trying to delay the creation of a vPtr until explicitly asked to do so. This tear-off class will derive from, and implement the methods of, the interface in question. The first step, then, is to create a new class implementing IOldInterface:

```
// This tear-off class implements the IOldInterface interface.
class COldInterfaceTearOff : public IOldInterface
{
public:
    // IOldInterface implementation.
    STDMETHODIMP(NoOneCallsAnymore)()
    {
            MessageBox(NULL, "Someone DOES love me!",
                        "I am so lonely", MB_OK | MB_SETFOREGROUND);
            return S_OK;
    }
...
};
```

The way in which the tear-off class implements IUnknown is unique. Because a client may acquire a tear-off interface (such as IOldInterface), the client must be able to query for additional interfaces found on the <u>owner</u> (INewFancyInterface). In short, the tear-off must be able to query for interfaces implemented by the owner. To permit the tear-off class to call methods implemented by the owner (such as QueryInterface()), the tear-off class maintains a pointer back to the owning class (much like the nested class technique):

```
// Forward declare owner class to quiet down the compiler.
class CCoOldObject;
// When the owner class creates a tear-off, it will pass in its own address which
// we store in a private member variable.
class COldInterfaceTearOff : public IOldInterface
{
private:
    // A tear-off interface maintains a pointer back to the owner.
    CoOldObject *m_pRealObject;
public:
    // The constructor of the tear-off sets the back pointer.
    COldInterfaceTearOff(CoOldObject *pThis)
          : m_pRealObject(pThis)
    {
        m_ref = 0;
        // The constructor should call AddRef() on the 'real' object.
        m_pRealObject -> AddRef();
    }
    ~ COldInterfaceTearOff()
```

```
    {
        // The destructor should call Release() on the 'real' object.
        m_pRealObject -> Release();
    }
    STDMETHODIMP(NoOneCallsAnymore)()
    {
        MessageBox(NULL, "Someone DOES love me!",
                   "I am so lonely", MB_OK | MB_SETFOREGROUND);
        return S_OK;
    }
private:
    ULONG m_ref;        // Tear-offs still maintain a reference count!
};
```

As mentioned, it is important to ensure that the tear-off class is careful about its implementation of QueryInterface(). For example, if a client has a pointer to IOldInterface, they will expect to obtain any other interface the coclass supports:

```
// COldInterfaceTearOff does not implement INewFancyInterface!
pOld -> QueryInterface(IID_INewFancyInterface, (void**)&pFancy);
```

We need to set up the QueryInterface() logic for the tear-off to give back a copy of an existing IOldInterface pointer and forward all other interface requests to the owner:

```
// Be sure your tear-off intercepts requests for the interface it implements!
// Use the cached back pointer for all other queries.
STDMETHODIMP COldInterfaceTearOff::QueryInterface(REFIID riid, void** ppv)
{
    // If they ask for any other interface than IID_IOldInterface, send the
    // request back to the real object, because that is where that interface may
    // be obtained.
    if(riid != IID_IOldInterface)
        return m_pRealObject->QueryInterface(riid, ppv);
    // They want IID_IOldInterface, so just give back a reference to self.
    if(riid == IID_IOldInterface)
        *ppv = (IOldInterface*)this;
    ...
}
```

To finish up the tear-off class implementation, we would create a standard implementation for AddRef() and Release(). Tear-off classes are still bound to maintain a reference count and remove themselves when their reference count is at zero.

That completes the implementation of the tear-off object. To sum things up, a tear-off class will derive from the outdated interface in question, and provide a standard reference count. The constructor of the tear-off class will allow the class to maintain a reference to the owner, and use this interface pointer to redirect QueryInterface() calls.

Changing the Owner Coclass

As for the owner class, we will need to retrofit CoOldObject as follows:

1. Remove IOldInterface from CoOldObject's inheritance chain. The owner class never directly derives from the tear-off interface:

```
// The creatable class should not derive from the tear-off interface.
class CoOldObject : public /* IOldInterface, */ INewFancyInterface
{
```

```
    ...
};
```

2. Declare COldInterfaceTearOff to be a friend class of CoOldObject. We need to ensure the tear-off class is able to access methods of the owner class:

```
// The tear-off interface should be declared as a friend of the 'real' class.
class CoOldObject : public /* IOldInterface, */ INewFancyInterface
{
...
private:
    friend class COldInterfaceTearOff;
};
```

3. Reengineer CoOldObject's implementation of QueryInterface() to create a new instance of the tear-off class if (and only if) the requested IID is indeed IID_IOldInterface:

```
// The owner class should dynamically allocate the tear-off class.
STDMETHODIMP CoOldObject::QueryInterface(REFIID riid, void** ppv)
{
    // Give out non tear-off references as usual.
    if(riid == IID_IUnknown)
        *ppv = (IUnknown*)( INewFancyInterface*)this;
    else if(riid == IID_INewFancyInterface)
        *ppv = ( INewFancyInterface *)this;
    // If the user asks for IOldInterface, create a new instance of the tear-off.
    else if(riid == IID_IOldInterface)
        *ppv = (IOldInterface*)new COldInterfaceTearOff(this);
    else
    {
        *ppv = NULL;
        return E_NOINTERFACE;
    }
    ((IUnknown*)(*ppv))->AddRef();
    return S_OK;
}
```

One problem with this implementation of QueryInterface() is that it will create a new instance of the tear-off object whenever IID_IOldInterface is queried for. A better solution would be to cache the initial COldInterfaceTearOff class, and hand out additional references accordingly. ATL provides a macro for this very behavior, as we will see shortly.

Using the Tear-Off

So what is the end result of this extra effort? As mentioned, our coclass now is able to save 4 bytes for each tear-off interface it supports. In this very simple example, the extra work to implement a tear-off may not be worth it. Nevertheless, here is some client code accessing this revised CoOldObject coclass. Notice how the client code is completely oblivious to the fact that the coclass is dynamically creating an IOldInterface reference:

```
// Tear-off clients have no clue they are using a tear-off interface.
// (assume proper #includes for GUIDs and interface definitions).
int main(int argc, char* argv[])
{
    CoInitialize(NULL);
    IOldInterface* pOld = NULL;
    INewFancyInterface * pNew = NULL;
```

```
HRESULT hr;
hr = CoCreateInstance(CLSID_CoOldObject, NULL, CLSCTX_SERVER,
                      IID_INewFancyInterface, (void**)&pNew);
if(SUCCEEDED(hr))
{
     pNew->IAmLovedByClients();
     // Coclass will dynamically create the tear off.
     hr = pNew->QueryInterface(IID_IOldInterface, (void**)&pOld);
     pNew->Release();
     if(SUCCEEDED(hr))
     {
          pOld->NoOneCallsAnymore();
          pOld->Release();
     }
}
CoUninitialize();
return 0;
}
```

Creating a Tear-Off Interface Using ATL

ATL does offer framework support to implement tear-off interfaces. This support comes by way of two COM map macro entries and a few new ATL templates. To see how to use these new items, we will reengineer the previous raw C++ example using ATL.

When you wish to create a tear-off class with ATL, you will begin by creating a new class deriving from CComTearOffObjectBase<>. The parameters given to this template are the name of the owner class and the tear-off's threading model. Here is the full definition defined in <atlcom.h>:

```
// Your tear-off interface class will derive from CComTearOffObjectBase<>.
template <class Owner, class ThreadModel = CComObjectThreadModel>
class CComTearOffObjectBase : public CComObjectRootEx<ThreadModel>
{
public:
     typedef Owner _OwnerClass;
     CComObject<Owner>* m_pOwner;
     CComTearOffObjectBase() {m_pOwner = NULL;}
};
```

Notice how the CComTearOffObjectBase<> template already holds onto a pointer to the owner class. The tear-off class makes use of m_pOwner to access data members and methods of the owner class. This is very helpful when your tear-off needs data maintained in the owner to help implement methods of its own (we will see this in action in the next lab).

A tear-off class built using ATL will also derive from the COM interface that it is representing (in this case IOldInterface) and implement the interface methods. Finally, you will need to provide a standard COM map, with an entry for the tear-off interface. Here is the ATL version of the tear-off class:

```
// Still need to forward declare owner to shut up compiler.
class CCoOldObject;
// The ATL version of a tear-off class.
class ATL_NO_VTABLE CoOldInterfaceTearOff :
public CComTearOffObjectBase<CCoOldObject, CComSingleThreadModel>,
public IOldInterface
```

```
{
public:
    STDMETHOD(NoOneCallsAnymore)()
        MessageBox(NULL, "Someone DOES love me!",
                    "I am so lonely", MB_OK | MB_SETFOREGROUND);
        return S_OK;
    }
BEGIN_COM_MAP(CoOldInterfaceTearOff)
    COM_INTERFACE_ENTRY(IOldInterface)
END_COM_MAP()
};
```

Implementing the Owner Class in ATL

As mentioned, ATL provides two COM map macros to support tear-off interfaces. Let's start with COM_INTERFACE_ENTRY_TEAR_OFF. This macro requires two parameters: the GUID of the interface and the name of the CComTearOffObjectBase<> derived class that supports it (note the call to CComObjectRootBase::_Creator()):

```
// Used to create a non-cached tear-off interface.
#define COM_INTERFACE_ENTRY_TEAR_OFF(iid, x)\
    {&iid,\
    (DWORD)& _CComCreatorData<\
        CComInternalCreator< CComTearOffObject< x > >\
        >::data,\
    _Creator},
```

To create a tear-off owner class in ATL, you will still take care not to derive from the outdated interface (such as IOldInterface). You will still need to declare the tear-off class as a friend of the owning class. The good news is that the new COM map macros will wrap up all the inner logic necessary to keep QueryInterface() functioning correctly. Here is the ATL version of the CoOldObject coclass:

```
// ATL's version of CoOldObject
class ATL_NO_VTABLE CCoOldObject :
    public CComObjectRootEx<CComSingleThreadModel>,
    public CComCoClass<CCoOldObject, &CLSID_CoOldObject>,
    // public IOldObject, not anymore!
    public INewFancyInterface
{
public:
...
// Your COM map will now make use of the tear-off macro.
BEGIN_COM_MAP(CCoOldObject)
    COM_INTERFACE_ENTRY(INewFancyInterface)
    COM_INTERFACE_ENTRY_TEAR_OFF(IID_IOldInterface, CoOldInterfaceTearOff)
END_COM_MAP()
public:
    STDMETHOD(IAmLovedByClients)();
    friend class CoOldInterfaceTearOff;
};
```

The COM_INTERFACE_ENTRY_CACHED_TEAR_OFF Macro

Like the previous C++ tear-off example, there is one slight problem with the current implementation of the owner class. COM_INTERFACE_ENTRY_TEAR_OFF is designed to create a new instance of the tear-off class each time a client queries for the interface in question. This behavior happens regardless of whether or not the client currently holds a valid IOldInterface pointer. For example, if a Visual Basic client were to acquire two references to IOldInterface, the coclass creates two instances of the tear-off class:

```
' Grab two references to IOldInterface.
'
Private Sub btnDoIt_Click()
    Dim o As New CoOldObject
    o.IAmLovedByClients
    Dim i As IOldInterface
    Set i = o                  ' Creates a tear-off.
    i.NoOneCallsAnymore
    Dim i2 As IOldInterface
    Set i2 = o                 ' Creates another tear-off.
    i.NoOneCallsAnymore
End Sub
```

To prevent this behavior, ATL provides an alternative tear-off macro named COM_INTERFACE_ENTRY_CACHED_TEAR_OFF. Using this interface, COM_INTERFACE_ENTRY_CACHED_TEAR_OFF can check if a previous version of the tear-off exists. If so, a new instance of the tear-off will not be created, but the existing instance will be referenced again.

This macro requires an extra parameter beyond the IID of the outdated interface and name of the tear-off class. You must also specify the IUnknown interface of the owner. Notice how this alternative macro makes use of CComCachedTearOffObject<>:

```
// This time create the tear-off class using CComCachedTearOffObject.
#define COM_INTERFACE_ENTRY_CACHED_TEAR_OFF(iid, x, punk)\
    {&iid,\
    (DWORD)&_CComCacheData<\
        CComCreator< CComCachedTearOffObject< x > >,\
        (DWORD)offsetof(_ComMapClass, punk)\
        >::data,\
    _Cache},
```

The call to CComObjectRootBase::_Cache() ensures only a single instance of the tear-off class is created:

```
// CComObjectRootBase helper function.
static HRESULT WINAPI _Cache(void* pv, REFIID iid,
                             void** ppvObject, DWORD dw)
{
    HRESULT hRes = E_NOINTERFACE;
    _ATL_CACHEDATA* pcd = (_ATL_CACHEDATA*)dw;
    IUnknown** pp = (IUnknown**)((DWORD)pv + pcd->dwOffsetVar);
    if (*pp == NULL)
        hRes = pcd->pFunc(pv, IID_IUnknown, (void**)pp);
    if (*pp != NULL)
        hRes = (*pp)->QueryInterface(iid, ppvObject);
    return hRes;
}
```

Specifying the Owner's IUnknown

For a cached tear-off to work correctly, the tear-off object needs to communicate with the owner using an IUnknown pointer. DECLARE_GET_CONTROLLING_UNKNOWN is an ATL macro that expands to define a method named GetControllingUnknown(). This method is used to calculate the offset to the IUnknown pointer for an ATL coclass:

```
// ATL helper macro which returns your coclass's IUnknown*
#define DECLARE_GET_CONTROLLING_UNKNOWN() public:\
virtual IUnknown* GetControllingUnknown() {return GetUnknown();}
```

CComCachedTearOffObject calls GetControllingUnknown(), and stores the owner's IUnknown pointer in the m_pOwner member variable defined by CComTearOff-ObjectBase<>:

```
// To create a cached tear-off, we need to supply a reference to the outer IUnknown.
template <class contained>
class CComCachedTearOffObject :
    public IUnknown,
    public CComObjectRootEx<contained::_ThreadModel::ThreadModelNoCS>
{
public:
    typedef contained _BaseClass;
    CComCachedTearOffObject(void* pv) :
        m_contained(((contained::_OwnerClass*)pv)->
                        GetControllingUnknown())
    {
        ATLASSERT(m_contained.m_pOwner == NULL);
        m_contained.m_pOwner =
            reinterpret_cast<CComObject<contained::_OwnerClass>*>(pv);
    }
...
}
```

So then, by adding the DECLARE_GET_CONTROLLING_UNKNOWN macro to your owner's class definition, CComCachedTearOffObject can communicate with the owner class to see if a previous instance of the tear-off exists.

Here is the updated ATL owner class making use of a cached tear-off interface. The implementation of the tear-off class itself is unchanged. However, the owner must directly pass in its own IUnknown to the tear-off using the GetControllingUnknown() method, and Release() it accordingly during the owner's FinalRelease() call:

```
// A cached tear-off à la ATL.
class ATL_NO_VTABLE CCoOldObject :
    public CComObjectRootEx<CComSingleThreadModel>,
    public CComCoClass<CCoOldObject, &CLSID_CoOldObject>,
    public INewFancyInterface
{
public:
    CCoOldObject() : m_pUnk(NULL)
    { }
...
// This will insert the GetControllingUnknown() method into our class.
DECLARE_GET_CONTROLLING_UNKNOWN()
// Make use of a cached tear-off.
BEGIN_COM_MAP(CCoOldObject)
```

```
        COM_INTERFACE_ENTRY(INewFancyInterface)
        COM_INTERFACE_ENTRY_CACHED_TEAR_OFF(IID_IOldInterface,
                    CoOldInterfaceTearOff, m_pUnk)
END_COM_MAP()
void FinalRelease()
{
    if(m_pUnk)
        m_pUnk->Release();
}
public:
    STDMETHOD(IAmLovedByClients)();
    friend class CoOldInterfaceTearOff;
    // Used to hold the IUnknown pointer.
    IUnknown* m_pUnk;
};
```

So with this, a single instance of the tear-off class is used to represent any number of interface references.

Think You're Sold on the Tear-Off?

Before you retrofit all your coclasses to use tear-off interfaces, you must be absolutely sure the offending interfaces are truly rarely used. The reason is simple: When a client does use a tear-off, your server's total size will swell by 12 bytes! That's 4 for the tear-off interface vPtr plus 4 for the tear-off class plus 4 for the owner's IUnknown pointer (not to mention the reference counter used by the tear-off).

The reasoning behind using tear-offs is that if we are willing to gamble that an interface has served its usefulness, we could save 4 bytes. Understand that if a client really does use the interface you have paid a greater penalty than you would have by just supporting the out-of-fashion interface in the first place.

Always remember that this technique is nothing more than a way to attempt to create a smaller, faster COM object and is <u>always optional</u>. You need to decide which (if any) interfaces may need to be implemented as a tear-off, and if you choose to do so, write the CComTearOffObjectBase<> derived class, and use one of the two COM map macros in the owner class.

That wraps up our discussion of tear-off interfaces, and how ATL can make it easier. The next lab will allow you to try each approach to tear-offs (cached and non-cached) on your own.

Lab 8-3: Building a Tear-Off Interface Using ATL

Even though tear-offs do have a dark side there are times when they can help build more efficient coclasses. As mentioned, as a coclass matures, interfaces that seemed like a good idea at the time may be replaced by the latest and greatest versions. In this lab you will be taking your current ATL CoCar developed in Chapter 6 and implement a tear-off, resulting in a more efficient manner to create your CoCar.

The solution for this lab can be found on your CD-ROM under:
Labs\Chapter 08\ATLTearOff
Labs\Chapter 08\ATLTearOff \VB Client

Step One: Add a New Interface to CoCar

As objects mature (and as COM developers learn better tricks) it is possible that interfaces which seemed like a good idea (or good design) at the time are now considered outdated. Open a copy of your ATLCoCar project (Lab 6-1) and examine the interface methods your coclass currently supports:

```
// IOwnerInfo
      STDMETHOD(get_Address)(/*[out, retval]*/ BSTR *pVal);
      STDMETHOD(put_Address)(/*[in]*/ BSTR newVal);
      STDMETHOD(get_Name)(/*[out, retval]*/ BSTR *pVal);
      STDMETHOD(put_Name)(/*[in]*/ BSTR newVal);
// IEngine
      STDMETHOD(GetCurSpeed)(/*[out, retval]*/ int* curSpeed);
      STDMETHOD(GetMaxSpeed)(/*[out, retval]*/ int* maxSpeed);
      STDMETHOD(SpeedUp)();
// IStats
      STDMETHOD(GetPetName)(/*[out, retval]*/ BSTR* petName);
      STDMETHOD(DisplayStats)();
// ICreateCar
      STDMETHOD(SetMaxSpeed)(/*[in]*/ int maxSp);
      STDMETHOD(SetPetName)(/*[in]*/ BSTR petName);
```

Notice that the ICreateCar interface defines two methods to set the attributes of a CoCar, and IOwnerInfo defines two properties to set the information of the owner. Therefore, it takes four calls (on two interfaces) to set the state of an ATLCoCar object. This is not a very optimized approach. For example, what if your CoCar was part of a distributed system? That would mean four RPC calls would be required to set up a single object. ICreateCar (and IOwnerInfo, for that matter) might be a good candidate for a tear-off interface.

Let's modify the existing Chapter 6 lab to support a tear-off interface for ICreateCar, and introduce a new interface that allows a COM client to set the state of a CoCar in a single round trip. Begin by typing in the IDL code for a new COM interface named ICreate. Use the Implement Interface Wizard to support ICreate, and then add a single method named **Create()**. Here is the IDL:

```
// ICreate allows the user to set the state of the CoCar in a single round trip.
[ object,uuid(1FB21BF0-3CCE-11d3-B910-0020781238D4), oleautomation,
helpstring("ICreate Interface"), pointer_default(unique)
]
interface ICreate : IUnknown
{
      [helpstring("This is the NEW Create")]
      HRESULT Create([in] BSTR ownerName, [in] BSTR ownerAddress,
                  [in] BSTR petName, [in] int maxSp);
};
...
coclass ATLCoCar
{
      [default] interface ICreate;            // Let's make the new ICreate the [default]
      interface ICreateCar;
      interface IStats;
      interface IEngine;
      interface IOwnerInfo;
};
```

Your COM map should now look something like this:

```
BEGIN_COM_MAP(CATLCoCar)
    COM_INTERFACE_ENTRY(ICreateCar)
    COM_INTERFACE_ENTRY(IStats)
    COM_INTERFACE_ENTRY(IEngine)
    COM_INTERFACE_ENTRY(IOwnerInfo)
    COM_INTERFACE_ENTRY(ICreate)
END_COM_MAP()
```

To implement your Create() method, you can just make use of your current private data members. Take the incoming parameters and assign them to your member variables:

```
// This one call does it all!
STDMETHODIMP CATLCoCar::Create(BSTR ownerName, BSTR ownerAddress,
                               BSTR petName, int maxSp)
{
    m_petName = petName;
    m_ownerName = ownerName;
    m_ownerAddress = ownerAddress;
    if(maxSp < MAX_SPEED)
        m_maxSpeed = maxSp;
    return S_OK;
}
```

Go ahead and compile to be sure you have not introduced any errors.

Now that we have a more efficient way to allow clients to establish the state of our ATL CoCar, we need to retrofit the outdated ICreateCar into a tear-off interface.

Step Two: Create the Tear-Off Class

Insert a new header file into your project named **ICC_TearOff.h** and an implementation file named **ICC_TearOff.cpp**. In your header file, create a new class named **CCreateCar_TearOff**, which derives from CComTearOffObjectBase<> as well as the outdated ICreateCar. To keep the compiler happy, you will need to forward declare your owner class before the tear-off definition:

```
// Need to forward declare to keep the compiler hushed up.
class CATLCoCar;
class ATL_NO_VTABLE CCreateCar_TearOff :
    public CComTearOffObjectBase<CATLCoCar, CComSingleThreadModel>,
    public ICreateCar
{
};
```

Next, create a COM map for the class, and support the ICreateCar interface using the COM_INTERFACE_ENTRY macro:

```
// Tear-off objects only return an interface pointer for the outdated interface.
BEGIN_COM_MAP(CCreateCar_TearOff)
    COM_INTERFACE_ENTRY(ICreateCar)
END_COM_MAP()
```

Add prototypes for the methods of **ICreateCar** and override **FinalConstruct()** and **FinalRelease()**, placing a message in each method. This will be helpful when we examine the differences between a standard and cached tear-off:

```
// Just a simple test.
HRESULT FinalConstruct()
{
    MessageBox(NULL, "Created tear-off", "Notice!",
                MB_OK | MB_SETFOREGROUND);
    return S_OK;
}
void FinalRelease()
{
    MessageBox(NULL, "The tear-off is destroyed", "Notice!",
                MB_OK | MB_SETFOREGROUND);
}
// Methods of outdated ICreateCar.
STDMETHOD(SetMaxSpeed)(int maxSp);
STDMETHOD(SetPetName)(BSTR petName);
```

In your implementation file, we need to supply code for **SetMaxSpeed()** as well as **SetPetName()**. Recall that CComTearOffObjectBase<> maintains a pointer to the owner, which is stored in the m_pOwner member variable. Use this data member to call the correct method of the owner class:

```
#include "stdafx.h"
#include "icc_tearoff.h"
#include "atlcocar.h"
// Use the pointer to your parent to set the state.
STDMETHODIMP CCreateCar_TearOff::SetMaxSpeed(int maxSp)
{
    if(maxSp < MAX_SPEED)
        m_pOwner->m_maxSpeed = maxSp;
    return S_OK;
}
STDMETHODIMP CCreateCar_TearOff::SetPetName(BSTR petName)
{
    return m_pOwner->SetPetName(petName);
}
```

This finishes up the tear-off class. If you wish, you may also create a tear-off for the IOwnerInfo interface as well, given that ICreate overshadows its functionality.

Step Three: Update the Owner Class

The coclass exposing the tear-off does not derive from the interface in question, but will dynamically create an instance of the tear-off class when necessary. Open your CATLCoCar.h file, remove ICreateCar from your inheritance list, and remove the COM map entry for this interface:

```
// Owner classes do not derive from the interface implemented by a tear-off.
class ATL_NO_VTABLE CATLCoCar :
    public CComObjectRootEx<CComSingleThreadModel>,
    public CComCoClass<CATLCoCar, &CLSID_ATLCoCar>,
    // public ICreateCar,
    public IStats,
    public IEngine,
    public IOwnerInfo,
    public ICreate
{
```

```
...
BEGIN_COM_MAP(CATLCoCar)
     // COM_INTERFACE_ENTRY(ICreateCar)
     COM_INTERFACE_ENTRY(IStats)
     COM_INTERFACE_ENTRY(IEngine)
     COM_INTERFACE_ENTRY(IOwnerInfo)
     COM_INTERFACE_ENTRY(ICreate)
END_COM_MAP()
...
};
```

Next, to allow your tear-off to access the private sector of your class, declare a friendship with the tear-off (you may place the following anywhere within your class declaration):

```
// Allow CCreateCar_TearOff to access the private data of CATL_CoCar.
friend class CCreateCar_TearOff;
```

Finally, we need to update CATLCoCar's COM map to support a tear-off version of ICreateCar. We will make use of the COM_INTERFACE_ENTRY_TEAR_OFF macro to create a non-cached solution. Edit the COM map by adding the following entry:

```
// Send in the GUID of the outdated interface and the name of the tear-off class.
COM_INTERFACE_ENTRY_TEAR_OFF(IID_ICreateCar, CCreateCar_TearOff)
```

Go ahead and compile your new version of the ATL CoCar. If you are error free, you are ready to create a client and see the pitfalls of a non-cached tear-off.

Note: Remember! The very first entry of your COM map must be a "simple" entry to allow ATL to calculate the offset to your IUnknown interface. Don't list the tear-off macro as the first entry!

Step Four: A Non-Cached Tear-Off Client

Assemble a simple Visual Basic client to test your new ICreate interface. Recall this new interface allows the user to set the state of the coclass in a single call. I am sure you can hack together a functional GUI by now, so here is the code in question:

```
' [General][Declarations]
'
Private mCar As ATLCoCar
Private mitfStats As ATLTEAROFFLib.IStats
Private mitfOwner As IOwnerInfo
Private Sub btnCreate_Click()
     Set mCar = New ATLCoCar
     mCar.Create txtOwnerName, txtOwnerAddress, txtPetName, txtMaxSpeed
End Sub
Private Sub btnStats_Click()
     Set mitfStats = mCar
     mitfStats.DisplayStats
     Set mitfOwner = mCar
     MsgBox mitfOwner.Name, , "Owner Name"
     MsgBox mitfOwner.Address, , "Owner Address"
End Sub
```

Now, exercise the tear-off. You should see the messages from the tear-offs FinalConstruct() and FinalRelease():

```
' Use the tear-off.
'
Private Sub btnOldWay_Click()
    Dim oldCar As New ATLCoCar
    Dim itfCCar As ICreateCar
    Set itfCCar = oldCar          ' Create tear-off interface.
    itfCCar.SetMaxSpeed 40
    itfCCar.SetPetName "JoJo"
End Sub
```

Recall that non-cached tear-offs spawn a new instance of the class for each reference. To illustrate this behavior, set a second reference to the ICreateCar interface:

```
' Set another reference to the tear-off.
'
Private Sub btnOldWay_Click()
    Dim oldCar As New ATLCoCar
    Dim itfCCar As ICreateCar
    Set itfCCar = oldCar          ' Create tear-off interface.
    itfCCar.SetMaxSpeed 40
    itfCCar.SetPetName "JoJo"
    Dim itfCCar2 As ICreateCar
    Set itfCCar2 = oldCar          ' Create another tear-off interface.
    itfCCar2.SetPetName "JoJo Jr."
End Sub
```

When you run the program, you will see two message boxes pop up from FinalConstruct() and FinalRelease(), as you have indirectly created two tear-offs! To change this behavior, we need to set up CoCar to make use of a cached tear-off.

Step Five: A Cached Tear-Off

Recall that when we wish to work with a cached tear-off, we must be sure to use the DECLARE_GET_CONTROLLING_UNKNOWN macro in the owner class. This macro expands to define the GetControllingUnknown() method for your coclass, which is accessed during the creation of your cached tear-off. To update your owner coclass, following these steps:

1. Add the DECLARE_GET_CONTROLLING_UNKNOWN macro in your header file.
2. Declare a public IUnknown* member variable and initialize it to NULL in your constructor. In your coclass's FinalRelease() method, release this IUnknown pointer.
3. Remove the COM_INTERFACE_ENTRY_TEAR_OFF entry from your COM map, and replace it with a COM_INTERFACE_ENTRY_CACHED_TEAR_OFF entry:

```
// Use a cached tear-off!
COM_INTERFACE_ENTRY_CACHED_TEAR_OFF(IID_ICreateCar,
                                    CCreateCar_TearOff,
                                    m_pUnk)
```

Your tear-off class will require no changes. Go ahead and recompile and test with your VB client once again. This time you will see only a single tear-off instance has been created, even though you have two references to ICreateCar.

COM Reuse Mechanisms: Containment and Aggregation

When you have two COM objects that seem to naturally work together, reuse is achieved when one of the coclasses accounts for the interfaces of another. What makes this form of reuse extremely interesting is that you are reusing a COM object at the binary level. Therefore it is completely possible for a coclass developed in Visual Basic to use a coclass developed in Delphi, Java, or C++. COM provides two ways to allow one object to reuse another: containment and aggregation.

Containment and Delegation in C++

One approach to achieve binary reuse is COM *containment*. This is a very flexible technique, as a COM object can contain other COM objects contained in EXE or DLL servers (aggregation is more restrictive, as we will see). As a C++ developer, you use containment so often that you most likely don't even notice it. Consider a simple C++ class named CCar, using no COM whatsoever. As you are creating this class, you wish to account for the fact that the CCar "has a" CRadio. This relationship may be coded in C++ as the following:

```
// Here is a radio.
class CRadio
{
public:
     void On();
     void Off();
     IncreaseVolume(int db);
};
// A car "has-a" radio.
class CCar
{
public:
     void TurnOnRadio(bool state);
     IncreaseVolume(int db);
     void Accelerate();
     void Stop();
private:
     CRadio m_theRadio;
};
```

As the CRadio object is a private data member of CCar, object users cannot access the methods of CRadio directly. Instead, the object user indirectly manipulates the inner object by accessing methods of the outer object (CCar). This is where *delegation* comes into play. When you establish a Has-A relationship among your objects, you decide how the outer class exposes the functionality of the inner class(es). For example, you may implement CCar::TurnOnRadio() as the following:

```
// The TurnOnRadio method manipulates the inner CRadio object.
// Clients have no clue that CCar operates internally on a CRadio instance.
void CCar::TurnOnRadio(bool state)
{
     if(state == true)
          m_theRadio.On();
     else
```

```
        m_theRadio.Off();
}
```

The important thing to notice here is that we did not extend the public interface of CCar with On() and Off() methods, although we would be free to do so. Instead, we have a single method (TurnOnRadio()) that accesses two methods of CRadio. When delegating, we may choose to have a one-to-one correspondence between the inner and outer methods as so:

```
// Just forward the call to the inner object.
void CCar::IncreaseVolume(int db)
{
        m_theRadio.IncreaseVolume(db);
}
```

Finally, we can implement methods of outer classes that make no use at all of any inner objects:

```
// This method of CCar makes no use of the inner CRadio.
void CCar::Accelerate ()
{
        // Accelerate logic.
}
```

What does this have to do with COM containment, you ask? Everything. In C++, inner objects are created using the member initialization list (or by an automatic call to the inner class's default constructor if you forgo the member initialization list). In COM, inner objects are created with COM library calls. The outer COM object has the same choices as the outer C++ object we have just examined, in that it may (or may not) make use of the inner object for a given interface method. The outer COM object may (or may not) expose the same interface as the inner object(s). In short, COM containment allows an outer class to create and use inner classes to help it get its work done.

Containment and Delegation in COM

COM containment allows an outer class to leverage the interfaces of an inner class that is contained in another binary COM server. The outer class is responsible for controlling the lifetime management of the inner objects it is using, as well as deciding how to expose its interfaces of the contained objects to the outside world (if necessary). In many ways, COM containment illustrates the classic Has-A relationship.

Assume that CoHexagon (an outer object) wishes to reuse another COM object named CoColor. CoColor can be found in another binary server (ColorServer.exe) and defines a single method on the default interface: SetRGB(). Here is the IDL:

```
// The [default] interface of CoColor.
[object, uuid(DDF18635-24F6-11D3-B8F9-0020781238D4), oleautomation]
interface IColor : IUnknown
{
        HRESULT SetRGB([in] short red, [in] short green, [in] short blue);
};
```

The first design choice we face is to decide how we wish to expose the inner object's functionality from a CoHexagon instance. One choice is to simply create the inner object and make calls to the inner object behind the scenes, without directly exposing the IColor interface to the outside world. In this light, CoColor is a private helper object of the outer class. This would be analogous to a standard C++ class called CEmployee that contains an internal private CString object to represent the name of an instantiated object. The user of CEmployee has no idea it is maintaining a private CString.

Another approach is to configure CoHexagon to support the interface(s) of the inner object(s). When the outer object implements the methods of the given interfaces, it simply delegates to the implementation of the inner object. For the sake of illustration, assume we have configured CoHexagon to support the IColor interface. When we implement the SetRGB() method, we delegate the call to the inner object. Conceptually, the relationship looks like the following:

Figure 8-5: CoColor is contained by CoHexagon.

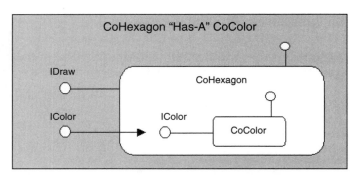

A Containment/Delegation Example

Creating a contained object is as simple as making a call to CoCreateInstance() or CoGetClassObject(). In the ATL framework, the safest place to create contained objects is within the FinalConstruct() method of the outer class. When we create the inner object, we should ask for any interfaces we require and cache the returned interfaces in private member variables. As well, we will need to release the acquired interfaces during FinalRelease().

```
// CoHexagon "has-a" CoColor.
class ATL_NO_VTABLE CCoHexagon :
    public CComObjectRootEx<CComSingleThreadModel>,
    public CComCoClass<CCoHexagon, &CLSID_CoHexagon>,
    public IDraw,
    public IColor
{
public:
    CCoHexagon() : m_pColor(NULL)
    { }
...
    // Create the inner object and get the interfaces we need.
    HRESULT FinalConstruct()
    {
        return CoCreateInstance(CLSID_CoColor, NULL, CLSCTX_SERVER,
                        IID_IColor, (void**)&m_pColor);
    }
    // Release the interfaces we have.
    void FinalRelease()
    {
```

```
            if(m_pColor) m_pColor->Release();
    }
public:
    // Storage for the IColor pointer.
    IColor* m_pColor;
    // The outer class defines IColor, but the implementation details
    // are held in the inner object.
    STDMETHOD(SetRGB)( short red, short green, short blue)
    {
        // Delegate to inner object.
        m_pColor->SetRGB(red, green, blue);
        return S_OK;
    }
};
```

Containment is a very common way to reuse COM objects, as the inner and outer objects may be contained in either DLL or EXE servers. The key point to note is that an outer object is in control of how "visible" the inner object is to the outside world. Here, CoColor has a single method from a single interface. If CoColor supported five different interfaces, it is up to the outer object to determine which interfaces are directly exposed and which are simply used internally to help the outer object get some work done.

Using a Contained Object

To make use of the contained object, assume we have a simple VB tester. The VB client has no clue that CoHexagon is delegating calls to an inner object.

```
' Make a red hex.
'
Private Sub btnSetColor_Click()
    Dim o As New CoHexagon
    Dim i As IColor
    Set i = o
    i.SetRGB 255, 0, 0
End Sub
```

COM containment is very easy to implement, yet it does have a down side. If you have an outer object using (for example) five interfaces of an inner object, you may end up with a lot of code that looks like the following:

```
// Containment can create lots of delegation code
void COuterClass::SomeMethodOnOuterObject()
{
    m_pInnerOne->SomeMethodOnInnerObject();
}
```

Before we examine COM aggregation, the next lab allows you to use containment to develop a new automobile class that leverages your existing CoCar.

Lab 8-4: COM Containment

The Has-A relationship is expressed when an outer (containing) coclass creates, maintains, and destroys an inner (contained) object. In this lab you will create a new coclass named CoMiniVan, which makes use of COM containment to help complete its implementation. This lab will also serve as the basis for the next lab in this chapter, where we will be creating hot rods and Jeeps using COM aggregation.

The solution for this lab can be found on your CD-ROM under:
Labs\Chapter 08\ATLVehicles
Labs\Chapter 08\ATLVehicles\VB Client

Step One: Create the Initial Containing Coclass

Create a brand new ATL project workspace named **ATLVehicles** (this lab assumes an in-proc server, but a local server would be just fine). Insert a new Simple Object named **CoMiniVan**, which supports a [default] interface named IMiniVan (be sure to choose a Custom interface). Use the Add Method Wizard to add a single method to the IMiniVan interface named **CreateMiniVan()**:

```
// We will implement this method in a later step...
[object, uuid(E8A4D620-3E44-11d3-B910-0020781238D4), oleautomation]
interface IMiniVan : IUnknown
{
    HRESULT CreateMiniVan([in] BSTR petName, [in] int maxSpeed,
                          [in] BSTR ownerName, [in] BSTR ownerAddress,
                          [in] int numberOfDoors);
};
```

Notice that this looks quite a bit like the Create() method of the ICreate interface we developed in our tear-off lab, except for the final parameter which represents the number of doors. As you may be guessing, IMiniVan::CreateMiniVan() will simply delegate to ICreate::Create().

Next, add a single property named **NumberOfDoors**, which will be used to get and set a private short maintained by the minivan (m_numberOfDoors). Be sure to initialize this variable to a safe value in the constructor and implement your new property.

Step Two: Create the Contained Coclass

Now we will add the code to create a contained CoCar. To begin this process, we need to copy over some files from our ATLTearOff project, and place them in our current project directory. Go into the Windows Explorer, and copy the MIDL-generated ATLTearOff.h, ATLTearOff_i.c, and ATLTearOff.idl files into your current project folder. When the CoMiniVan object is created, we in turn create our tear-off version of the ATL CoCar and obtain a number of interfaces from the inner object. To hold these interfaces, add the following member variables to CoMiniVan:

```
private:
    // These hold private interfaces on the 'inner' object.
    IUnknown* m_pCarUnk;
    ICreate* m_pCreate;
    IEngine* m_pEngine;
    IStats* m_pStats;
```

Override the FinalConstruct() method in your CoMiniVan coclass. When using COM containment, you select which interfaces of the inner object you wish to manipulate. We will be creating our ATLCoCar within this method, and obtain ICreate, IEngine, and IStats pointers:

```
// Have the containing class grab interfaces of the inner class.
HRESULT FinalConstruct()
{
    HRESULT hr;
    hr = CoCreateInstance(CLSID_ATLCoCar, NULL, CLSCTX_SERVER,
                     IID_IUnknown, (void**)&m_pCarUnk);
    if(SUCCEEDED(hr))
    {
        MessageBox(NULL, "Created contained car",
            "Message from Minivan", MB_OK | MB_SETFOREGROUND);
        m_pCarUnk->QueryInterface(IID_ICreate, (void**)&m_pCreate);
        m_pCarUnk->QueryInterface(IID_IEngine, (void**)&m_pEngine);
        m_pCarUnk->QueryInterface(IID_IStats, (void**)&m_pStats);
    }
    else
        return E_FAIL;   // Don't let them make minivan
                         // if we can't make a car.
    return hr;
}
```

Of course, we need to call Release() on all acquired interfaces when the CoMiniVan is destroyed. Override your FinalRelease() method to do so:

```
// Free up the inner class.
void FinalRelease()
{
    m_pCarUnk->Release();  m_pCreate->Release();
    m_pEngine->Release();  m_pStats->Release();
}
```

This code correctly models a contained relationship among COM objects. When a client creates a CoMiniVan, you turn around and create the ATLCoCar. Notice, however, that we have not provided a way for the outside world to make use of these internal interfaces. That is a job for delegation.

Step Three: Delegate to the Inner Object

To expose the functionality of the inner object to COM clients, we will derive from the obtained interfaces of the inner object, add entries to the outer object's COM map, and delegate accordingly.

Let's set up CoMiniVan to only allow clients to access the IStats and IEngine interfaces directly, while maintaining the ICreate interface for private internal use. Derive CoMiniVan from IStats and IEngine, and add an entry for each in your COM map:

```
// Mimic the inner object's interfaces.
class ATL_NO_VTABLE CCoMiniVan :
    public CComObjectRootEx<CComSingleThreadModel>,
    public CComCoClass<CCoMiniVan, &CLSID_CoMiniVan>,
    public IMiniVan,
    public IEngine,
    public IStats
{
public:
...
BEGIN_COM_MAP(CCoMiniVan)
    COM_INTERFACE_ENTRY(IMiniVan)
```

```
        COM_INTERFACE_ENTRY(IEngine)
        COM_INTERFACE_ENTRY(IStats)
END_COM_MAP()
...
};
```

Recall that IEngine and IStats define the following members, which you will now need to implement in your CoMiniVan. Here are the prototypes:

```
// IEngine.
        STDMETHOD(GetCurSpeed)(/*[out, retval]*/ int* curSpeed);
        STDMETHOD(GetMaxSpeed)(/*[out, retval]*/ int* maxSpeed);
        STDMETHOD(SpeedUp)();
// IStats
        STDMETHOD(GetPetName)(/*[out, retval]*/ BSTR* petName);
        STDMETHOD(DisplayStats)();
```

The implementation of the IEngine interface will be easy. Simply call the same method on your m_pEngine interface pointer. Here is CoMiniVan::GetCurSpeed() to get you started (do the same type of delegation for GetMaxSpeed() and SpeedUp()):

```
// We will delegate all methods to the inner object using the correct interface pointer.
STDMETHODIMP CCoMiniVan::GetCurSpeed(int *curSpeed)
{
        return m_pEngine->GetCurSpeed(curSpeed);
}
```

IStats works the same exact way. This time, implement each method, making use of your m_pStats pointer. For example:

```
// If a client asks me to display stats, I ask the inner object to do so...
STDMETHODIMP CCoMiniVan::DisplayStats()
{
        return m_pStats->DisplayStats();
}
```

The final item to implement on CoMiniVan is the CreateMiniVan() method of IMiniVan. Here we will make use of the private ICreate interface pointer, and set the private m_NumberOfDoors variable we are maintaining ourselves:

```
// CreateMiniVan() also delegates.
STDMETHODIMP CCoMiniVan::CreateMiniVan(BSTR petName, int maxSpeed,
      BSTR ownerName, BSTR ownerAddress, int numberOfDoors)
{
        // Tell the car to create itself.
        m_pCreate-> Create(ownerName, ownerAddress, petName, maxSpeed);
        // This is my state data, so I have to hold onto it...
        m_numberOfDoors = numberOfDoors;
        return S_OK;
}
```

With this, the CoMiniVan is complete. If you are using a C++ client, your work is done. Typically C++ clients do not need to access a *.tlb file to create your objects. But think for a moment about the VB or Java clients of the world. Even though we have added support to CoMiniVan for the IEngine and IStats interface, how is a type library-dependent client able to create variables of these interfaces?

```
' Help! I can't do this unless IStats is in a type library!
'
Dim itfStats as IStats
```

The answer is they can't do so until we update our IDL file. That realization brings us to
the final step of this lab.

Step Four: Update Your IDL

Although this task sounds trivial, remember you are attempting to support IDL interfaces
defined in another IDL file! Luckily we did copy over ATLTearOff.idl in the first part of this
lab, so we may import this file as part of our own. Edit your ATLVehicles.idl file as so:

```
// Need to import the IDL file that defines the inner object's interfaces.
import "ATLTearOff.idl";
```

Now, to force the MIDL compiler to publish IEngine and IStats in CoMiniVan's type library,
we must forward declare these interfaces in the library statement. Here is the updated
IDL:

```
// Forward declare interfaces to include them in your type information.
[ uuid(DDF18619-24F6-11D3-B8F9-0020781238D4), version(1.0),
helpstring("ATLVehicles 1.0 Type Library") ]
library ATLVEHICLESLib
{
    importlib("stdole32.tlb");
    importlib("stdole2.tlb");
    interface IStats;
    interface IEngine;
    [ uuid(DDF18626-24F6-11D3-B8F9-0020781238D4),
      helpstring("CoMiniVan Class") ]
    coclass CoMiniVan
    {
        [default] interface IMiniVan;
        interface IStats;
        interface IEngine;
    };
};
```

Note that we do not list ICreate, as we do not wish external COM clients to query for this
interface from a CoMiniVan instance. We are only using ICreate internally to help with the
implementation of CreateMiniVan().

Figure 8-6:
The result of
our IDL
configuration.

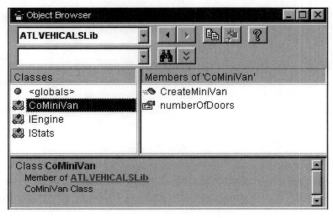

Recompile the server and set a
reference to your type library
using Visual Basic, and examine your objects (Figure 8-6).
You will see things have turned
out just fine. Go ahead and create a client of your choice, and
move on to the wonderful
world of COM aggregation.

Understanding COM Aggregation

Aggregation is the other binary reuse technique used in COM. Here, the outer object exposes the inner object's interfaces <u>directly</u>. Unlike containment, there is no need for the outer object to implement the interface(s) of the inner object. There is no need to delegate interface calls from the outer object to the inner object, as the inner object's interfaces are directly available to external clients. Conceptually, aggregation looks like the following:

Figure 8-7: COM aggregation.

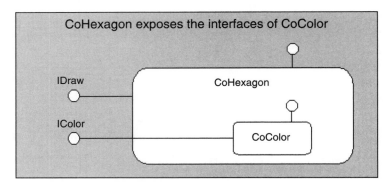

As far as the client is concerned, the inner and outer objects appear to be one seamless coclass. Thus, to a client, CoHexagon supports IDraw, IColor, and IUnknown. The client has no idea that the set of interfaces exposed are in fact provided, in part, by an inner object.

COM objects (such as CoColor) must be preprogrammed to support the ability to be aggregated by another object. Therefore, unless a COM object has been equipped with the correct infrastructure, an outer object cannot aggregate it. Contrast this to a contained inner object, which requires no extra code to behave correctly.

Also understand that not all COM objects are able to participate in COM aggregation even with the correct internal riggings. Specifically, only COM objects that are contained within in-process servers can be aggregated and even then, the inner and outer objects must be in the same apartment (i.e., execution context).

> **Note:**   Again, only objects housed within in-proc servers may be aggregated. You cannot aggregate objects living in EXE servers (local or remote).

The outer object and any aggregated inner objects must work together to uphold the rules of COM identity. As both the inner and outer objects maintain a unique implementation of QueryInterface(), a good deal of work needs to be done to allow a client to traverse among the interfaces of the inner and outer objects. Thankfully, ATL provides full and complete support for COM aggregation, which takes care of all the details for both the inner and outer object's implementation.

ATL's Support for COM Aggregation

When you insert a COM object using the ATL Object Wizard, one of the choices you need to specify is the object's level of "aggregation awareness." Assume we are creating an ATL-centric CoColor object, which is residing in ATLAggServer.dll. Based upon your selection from the Attributes tab (Figure 8-8), the ATL Object Wizard will configure your object with the proper level of aggregation support using ATL macros. Here again is a rundown of each choice:

Figure 8-8: Configuring aggregation support.

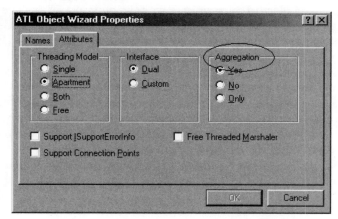

- **Yes:** Your object will be able to work either as a stand-alone (outer) object or an aggregated (inner) object. If you select this option, you will inherit the default functionality specified by the DECLARE_AGGREGATABLE macro defined in CComCoClass< >.

- **No:** Your object will <u>only</u> be able to function as a stand-alone (outer) object. If you choose this option, the Object Wizard will include the DECLARE_NOT_AGGREGATABLE macro in your coclass's header file.

- **Only:** This option ensures your object will never function as a stand-alone object, but <u>must</u> be part of an aggregate to function. The Object Wizard will include the DECLARE_ONLY_AGGREGATABLE macro in your coclass's header file.

Most of the time, you will want your object to behave as either an outer or inner object, and will therefore leave the default Yes selection. As we have seen earlier in Chapter 7, CComCoClass< > defines this macro by default:

```
// By default, all ATL objects are equipped to be aggregated.
template <class T, const CLSID* pclsid = &CLSID_NULL>
class CComCoClass
{
public:
...
    DECLARE_AGGREGATABLE(T)
...
};
```

Configuring the Outer Object

COM objects that aggregate other objects are responsible for creating them. Much like COM containment, FinalConstruct() is the safest place to create your inner objects. The whole idea behind aggregation is to provide the illusion that the outer coclass is composed of more interfaces than it really is. The interfaces of the inner object are obtainable directly from the QueryInterface() logic of the outer class. As well, the inner object must be able to navigate to the outer object to forward QueryInterface() requests.

In order for the inner object to communicate with the outer object, we need to send in an IUnknown to the aggregated object. This is accomplished again using the GetControllingUnknown() method provided by the DECLARE_GET_CONTROLLING_UNKNOWN macro. When we are creating the inner object, we will send in the outer object's IUnknown as the second parameter to CoCreateInstance(). This will allow the inner object to forward QueryInterface() calls to the outer class.

Likewise, the outer class needs to have an IUnknown pointer to the aggregated object to forward QueryInterface() calls to the inner object. We can store this fetched interface pointer in a private member variable (m_pInnerUnk). Here is the initial bit of code which illustrates how inner and outer objects exchange IUnknown pointers:

```
// An ATL-centric CoHexagon aggregating CoColor.
class ATL_NO_VTABLE CCoHexagon :
      public CComObjectRootEx<CComSingleThreadModel>,
      public CComCoClass<CCoHexagon, &CLSID_CoHexagon>,
      public IDraw
{
public:
      CCoHexagon() : m_pInnerUnk(NULL) { }
// Need this to gain IUnknown*.
DECLARE_GET_CONTROLLING_UNKNOWN()
HRESULT FinalConstruct()
{
      // We want to create the CoColor aggregate.
      HRESULT hr;
      hr = CoCreateInstance(CLSID_CoColor, GetControllingUnknown(),
                            CLSCTX_INPROC_SERVER,
                            IID_IUnknown, (void**)&m_pInnerUnk);
      return hr;
}
void FinalRelease()
{
      if(pColor)
      {
            m_pInnerUnk ->Release();
      }
}
BEGIN_COM_MAP(CCoHexagon)
      COM_INTERFACE_ENTRY(IDraw)
END_COM_MAP()
// IDraw
public:
      STDMETHOD(Draw)();
private:
```

```
        // Interface pointer of inner object.
        IUnknown* m_pInnerUnk;
};
```

With the above configuration, CoHexagon will create the CoColor object upon startup and destroy it upon shutdown. As well, CoColor now has a pointer back to CoHexagon (via the IUnknown pointer sent in using GetControllingUnknown()), while we have a pointer to the inner object.

Our next task is to decide which of the interfaces supported by CoColor we wish to expose as interfaces of CoHexagon. This is an easy choice, as CoColor only supports IColor. In general, for each interface of the inner object you wish to expose from the outer object, add a COM_INTERFACE_ENTRY_AGGREGATE entry to the outer class's COM map. For example:

```
// CoHexagon's updated COM map.
BEGIN_COM_MAP(CCoHexagon)
    COM_INTERFACE_ENTRY(IDraw)
    COM_INTERFACE_ENTRY_AGGREGATE (IID_IColor, m_pInnerUnk)
END_COM_MAP()
```

For the sake of discussion, assume CoColor supported a total of three color-related interfaces {IColor, IGradient, IBlend}. As the outer object, we may select which interfaces of the inner object(s) we wish to expose. If we wish to expose IColor as well as IBlend, CoHexagon's COM map would be updated as:

```
// CoHexagon's updated COM map.
BEGIN_COM_MAP(CCoHexagon)
    COM_INTERFACE_ENTRY(IDraw)
    COM_INTERFACE_ENTRY_AGGREGATE (IID_IColor, m_pInnerUnk)
    COM_INTERFACE_ENTRY_AGGREGATE (IID_IBlend, m_pInnerUnk)
END_COM_MAP()
```

With the above additions, we have fully implemented an outer and inner object using the ATL framework. To summarize how to aggregate with ATL:

- **Inner Objects:** Inner objects are configured automatically when using the ATL Object Wizard. From the Attributes tab, you may specify the level of aggregation support. By default, ATL objects leverage the DECLARE_AGGREGATABLE macro provided by CComCoClass<>.

- **Outer Objects:** ATL objects that aggregate other objects begin by constructing the inner object from within FinalConstruct(), and cache the fetched interface. To send in the IUnknown of the outer object, add the DECLARE_GET_CONTROL-LING_UNKNOWN macro to your coclass, and use the GetControllingUnknown() helper function as the second parameter to CoCreateInstance(). Finally, update your COM map using COM_INTERFACE_ENTRY_AGGREGATE for each interface you wish to expose as your own.

Alternative COM Map Aggregation Entries

While COM_INTERFACE_ENTRY_AGGREGATE is the most common COM map entry when working with aggregates, ATL does provide three others, which we will now discuss before wrapping up our discussion of containment and aggregation.

When your outer class makes use of the COM_INTERFACE_ENTRY_AGGREGATE COM map macro, you get to select exactly which interfaces of the inner object are available to external clients. This approach is called *selective aggregation*, and gives the outer object the final say on how it appears to the outside world. Another possibility is *blind aggregation*. This approach is more of a commando tactic, as the outer object calls the inner object's InternalQueryInterface() for any interface the outer object does not support. In raw C++, it would look something like the following:

```
// Blind aggregation.
STDMETHODIMP CoHexagon::QueryInterface(REFIID, riid, void** ppv)
{
...
    if( riid == IID_IUnknown)
        *ppv = (IUnknown*)(IDraw*)this;
    else if(riid == IID_IDraw)
        *ppv = (IDraw*)this;
    // Forward all other requests to the inner object!
    else
        hr = m_pInnerUnk -> QueryInterface(riid, ppv);
...
}
```

ATL provides the COM_INTERFACE_ENTRY_AGGREGATE_BLIND macro to support blind aggregation. In this case, you will not use COM_INTERFACE_ENTRY_AGGREGATE on an interface-by-interface basis, but rather send in the inner object's IUnknown as the sole parameter:

```
// CoHexagon is now blindly forwarding all calls it does not understand
// into CoColor.
BEGIN_COM_MAP(CCoHexagon)
    COM_INTERFACE_ENTRY(IDraw)
    COM_INTERFACE_ENTRY_AGGREGATE_BLIND(m_pInnerUnk)
END_COM_MAP()
```

As you can imagine, selective aggregation is preferred to blind, in that the outer object has more control over the process. Using blind aggregation, CoHexagon might very well ask CoColor for ICreateCar, IStats, or IEngine! The common approach is to use selective aggregation and the COM_INTERFACE_ENTRY_AGGREGATE macro for each interface you wish to support on the outer object.

ATL's Auto Aggregation COM Map Entries

The final aggregation macros allow you to both create and expose the internal interfaces without explicitly creating the inner objects. COM_INTERFACE_ENTRY_AUTOAGGREGATE and COM_INTERFACE_ENTRY_AUTOAGGREGATE_BLIND are interesting in that the aggregated object is only created when the client explicitly asks for an interface of the aggregated object.

In our previous design, CoHexagon created CoColor in its FinalConstruct() method using standard COM library calls. As the ATL framework calls FinalConstruct() as part of the object's creation, CoHexagon will load the server holding CoColor, regardless of whether the external client ever asks for IColor or not. If we configured CoHexagon to use the auto aggregation macros, we could clean up CoHexagon just a bit, and ensure the server housing the aggregated object is not loaded until absolutely required. Here is CoHexagon using auto aggregation:

```
// Auto aggregation delays the creation of the aggregated object until
// absolutely necessary.
class ATL_NO_VTABLE CCoHexagon :
     public CComObjectRootEx<CComSingleThreadModel>,
     public CComCoClass<CCoHexagon, &CLSID_CoHexagon>,
     public IDraw
{
public:
     CCoHexagon() : m_pInnerUnk(NULL) { }
...
DECLARE_GET_CONTROLLING_UNKNOWN()
void FinalRelease()
{
     if(m_pColor) m_pInnerUnk ->Release();
}
BEGIN_COM_MAP(CCoHexagon)
     COM_INTERFACE_ENTRY(IDraw)
     COM_INTERFACE_ENTRY_AUTOAGGREGATE (IID_IColor,
          m_pInnerUnk, CLSID_CoColor)
END_COM_MAP()
public:
     STDMETHOD(Draw)();
     IUnknown* m_pInnerUnk;
};
```

Notice how our call to FinalConstruct() has been removed, as the CoColor instance will be created automatically whenever the first request for IID_IColor is issued.

Lab 8-5: COM Aggregation with ATL

In the previous lab you were introduced to reuse of COM objects using containment. This final lab of the chapter will give you a chance to work with an alternative form of binary reuse, COM aggregation. Here, you will add to the objects housed within the ATLVehicles server to include a Jeep and hot rod, each aggregating your original ATLCoCar using the ATL framework.

The solution for this lab can be found on your CD-ROM under:
Labs\Chapter 08\ATLVehicles
Labs\Chapter 08\ATLVehicles\VB Client
Labs\Chapter 08\ATLVehicles\CPP Client

Step One: Create the Aggregated Object

Open the ATLVehicles project developed in the previous lab. Using the ATL Object Wizard, insert another Simple Object named **CoHotRod**. Change the name of the initial interface to **IDragRace,** and be sure to select a **Custom** interface. All other options may be left at their defaults.

Your new CoHotRod will make use of COM aggregation in order to reuse the ATLCoCar coclass. Begin by adding the DECLARE_GET_CONTROLLING_UNKNOWN()

macro to your cohotrod.h file. Recall this macro expands to define a method named GetControllingUnknown(), which returns the IUnknown pointer for your coclass.

```
// CoHotRod will reuse CoCar using aggregation.
class ATL_NO_VTABLE CCoHotRod :
    public CComObjectRootEx<CComSingleThreadModel>,
    public CComCoClass<CCoHotRod, &CLSID_CoHotRod>,
    public IDragRace
{
public:
    CCoHotRod()
    {
    }
DECLARE_REGISTRY_RESOURCEID(IDR_COHOTROD)
DECLARE_PROTECT_FINAL_CONSTRUCT()
DECLARE_GET_CONTROLLING_UNKNOWN()
...
};
```

Next, override **FinalConstruct**(), and make a call to CoCreateInstance() to create the inner aggregated CoCar (don't forget to #include atltearoff.h). Make use of the GetControllingUnknown() method in your CoCreateInstance() call. Ask up front for the inner object's IUnknown pointer, and store this in a public IUnknown pointer maintained by CoHotRod. You may also wish to add a friendly message box, which will be helpful during the testing phase:

```
// Create the aggregate.
HRESULT FinalConstruct()
{
    MessageBox(NULL, "Created a ATLCoCar using aggregation!",
            "Message from hotrod", MB_OK | MB_SETFOREGROUND);
    HRESULT hr;
    hr = CoCreateInstance(CLSID_ATLCoCar, GetControllingUnknown(),
            CLSCTX_SERVER, IID_IUnknown, (void**)&pUnkInnerCar);
    return hr;
}
```

In your class's FinalRelease(), dispose of the inner object's IUnknown pointer, and again, display a friendly message box:

```
// Kill the inner object within FinalRelease()
void FinalRelease()
{
    pUnkInnerCar->Release();
    MessageBox(NULL, "The HOTROD is dead!",
            "Message from hotrod", MB_OK | MB_SETFOREGROUND);
}
```

Step Two: Expose the Inner Object's Interfaces

Next, we will need to edit our COM map to expose interfaces of the inner object from the outer object. Let's equip CoHotRod to make use of the IEngine, IOwner, IOwnerInfo, and ICreateCar interfaces (recall that we revamped CoCar to support ICreateCar as a tear-off). Using the most standard ATL aggregation macro, COM_INTERFACE_ENTRY_AGGREGATE, update your COM map as follows:

```
// Don't forget that the first entry of your map should be a 'simple' entry such as
// COM_INTERFACE_ENTRY, as ATL uses this to calculate the offset to your
// IUnknown.
BEGIN_COM_MAP(CCoHotRod)
    COM_INTERFACE_ENTRY(IDragRace)
    COM_INTERFACE_ENTRY_AGGREGATE(IID_ICreateCar, pUnkInnerCar)
    COM_INTERFACE_ENTRY_AGGREGATE(IID_IStats, pUnkInnerCar)
    COM_INTERFACE_ENTRY_AGGREGATE(IID_IEngine, pUnkInnerCar)
    COM_INTERFACE_ENTRY_AGGREGATE(IID_IOwnerInfo, pUnkInnerCar)
END_COM_MAP()
```

Finish up the C++ implementation of CoHotRod by adding a single method to the [default] IDragRace interface named **DragRace()**. Give an implementation suited to a high-performance automobile:

```
// HotRods always win...
STDMETHODIMP CCoHotRod::DragRace()
{
    MessageBox(NULL, " Done! Dude, this is a fast car.",
              "Hot Rod message", MB_OK | MB_SETFOREGROUND);
    return S_OK;
}
```

Go ahead and compile. Remember that coclasses that aggregate other COM objects do not derive from the interfaces of the inner object. Therefore, your inheritance chain for CoHotRod will only derive from IDragRace, beyond the ATL framework templates:

```
// Outer objects do not derive from the interfaces of the aggregated objects.
class ATL_NO_VTABLE CCoHotRod :
    public CComObjectRootEx<CComSingleThreadModel>,
    public CComCoClass<CCoHotRod, &CLSID_CoHotRod>,
    public IDragRace
{
...
};
```

Step Three: Clean Up the IDL

As in the case with the contained ATLCoCar, we must update our coclass statement to ensure that type library-dependent COM language mappings can "see" our interfaces. Open the project's IDL file, and edit your coclass statement to support the following interfaces of the inner object. For ease of use by the object user, set ICreateCar to be the [default]:

```
// Expose interfaces.
[ uuid(DDF18628-24F6-11D3-B8F9-0020781238D4), helpstring("CoHotRod Class")]
coclass CoHotRod
{
    [default] interface ICreateCar;    // Inner object.
    interface IDragRace;               // Outer object.
    interface IStats;                  // Inner object.
    interface IEngine;                 // Inner object.
    interface IOwnerInfo;              // Inner object.
};
```

With these edits, we are able to present CoHotRod as a COM object supporting five distinct interfaces, even though four of these come from an aggregated inner object.

Step Four: Blind Auto Aggregation

Recall that the COM_INTERFACE_ENTRY_AUTOAGGREGATE_BLIND macro may be used to forward all client interface requests to the inner object, as well as automatically create the aggregated object when queried for. This ATL macro removes the need for your outer class to explicitly call CoCreateInstance(). Use the ATL Object Wizard to insert a new Simple Object named **CoJeep**, with support for a custom vTable interface. Once you bring in your new ATL vehicle, remove the generated ICoJeep from your COM map, IDL file, and inheritance chain (thus removing this interface from your project). Add support for IDragRace to CoJeep, and provide a prototype of the **DragRace()** method. Your CoJeep header file should appear as so:

```
// For all the off-roaders in the room.
class ATL_NO_VTABLE CCoJeep :
    public CComObjectRootEx<CComSingleThreadModel>,
    public CComCoClass<CCoJeep, &CLSID_CoJeep>,
    public IDragRace
{
public:
    CCoJeep()
    {
    }
BEGIN_COM_MAP(CCoJeep)
    COM_INTERFACE_ENTRY(IDragRace)
END_COM_MAP()
...
    STDMETHOD(DragRace)();
};
```

Your IDL file should have no mention of ICoJeep, while the DragRace() method should provide an implementation appropriate to a fine Jeep:

```
// Jeeps don't drag race much...
STDMETHODIMP CCoJeep::DragRace()
{
    MessageBox(NULL, "Dude! I'm goin' offroadin'.",
                "Jeep message", MB_OK | MB_SETFOREGROUND);
    return S_OK;
}
```

Now we need to aggregate the inner ATL CoCar. Include your atltearoff.h file and add a public IUnknown pointer to CoJeep. When using automatic blind aggregation, you will still need to add the DECLARE_GET_CONTROLLING_UNKNOWN() macro to your outer class, and you will still need to Release() the public IUnknown interface in your FinalRelease(). What you will not need to do is create the inner object yourself. Simply by using the COM_INTERFACE_ENTRY_AUTOAGGREGATE_BLIND macro in your COM map, the framework creates the inner object for you using CoCreateInstance(). Update your CoJeep as so:

```
// Using automatic blind aggregation.
class ATL_NO_VTABLE CCoJeep :
    public CComObjectRootEx<CComSingleThreadModel>,
    public CComCoClass<CCoJeep, &CLSID_CoJeep>,
    public IDragRace
{
```

```
public:
    CCoJeep() : pUnkInnerCar(NULL) { }
DECLARE_GET_CONTROLLING_UNKNOWN()
...
    // Kill the inner object within FinalRelease()
    void FinalRelease()
    {
        if(pUnkInnerCar)
            pUnkInnerCar->Release();
    }
BEGIN_COM_MAP(CCoJeep)
    COM_INTERFACE_ENTRY(IDragRace)
    COM_INTERFACE_ENTRY_AUTOAGGREGATE_BLIND(pUnkInnerCar, CLSID_ATLCoCar)
END_COM_MAP()
public:
    STDMETHOD(DragRace)();
    IUnknown *pUnkInnerCar;
};
```

And finally, update the IDL code for your CoJeep by listing the following interfaces of the inner object:

```
// Expose interfaces to object browsers.
coclass CoJeep
{
    [default] interface ICreate;
    interface IStats;
    interface IDragRace;
    interface IEngine;
    interface IOwnerInfo;
};
```

Step Five: Update CoMiniVan

In this step, we will add support for the IDragRace interface to the CoMiniVan object. You may wish to use the Implement Interface Wizard for this purpose, or make the necessary edits by hand. Either way, provide an implementation of **DragRace**() for your minivan:

```
// No offense, but...
STDMETHODIMP CCoMiniVan::DragRace()
{
MessageBox(NULL, "Dude, You have a minivan. You can't drag race.",
"Minivan message", MB_OK | MB_SETFOREGROUND);
return S_OK;
}
```

Now then! Let's recap what we have been working through in this ATLVehicles project. First we made use of COM containment by building a CoMiniVan object which contained the ATLCoCar object. Next, we added two COM objects (CoJeep and CoHotRod), each using COM aggregation to reuse the inner ATLCoCar. All of the coclasses defined in the ATLVehicles project support the IDragRace interface and expose various interfaces of the inner contained/aggregated CoCar.

Step Six: Update Your VB Client

To finish up, we will illustrate interface-based polymorphism from within a VB client. Open your previous VB tester, and create a simple GUI to create a CoJeep (and exercise some interfaces), a CoHotRod (and exercise some interfaces), and a separate button named DragRace (see Figure 8-9).

The code of interest here is what is behind the Drag Race click event. As each coclass supports the IDragRace interface, we can treat them in the same way (that's polymorphism). So, add some VB code to create an array of IDragRace pointers, and set each to one of your ATL vehicles. You may then loop over this array, and ask each car to participate:

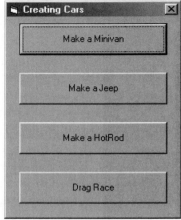

Figure 8-9: Start your engines!

```
' Interface-based polymorphism in VB.
'
Private Sub btnDragRace_Click()
     Dim ardrag(2) As IDragRace
     Set ardrag(0) = New CoHotRod
     Set ardrag(1) = New CoJeep
     Set ardrag(2) = New CoMiniVan
     Dim i As Integer
     For i = 0 To 2
          ardrag(i).DragRace
     Next i
End Sub
```

This same effect can be achieved in C++ as so:

```
// Interface-based polymorphism in C++.
int main(int argc, char* argv[])
{
     CoInitialize(NULL);
     IDragRace* pDragRace[3] = {NULL};
     // Make some cars.
     CoCreateInstance(CLSID_CoHotRod, NULL, CLSCTX_SERVER,
                    IID_IDragRace, (void**)&(pDragRace[0]));
     CoCreateInstance(CLSID_CoMiniVan, NULL, CLSCTX_SERVER,
                    IID_IDragRace, (void**)&(pDragRace[1]));
     CoCreateInstance(CLSID_CoJeep, NULL, CLSCTX_SERVER,
                    IID_IDragRace, (void**)&(pDragRace[2]));
     // Drag race!
     for(int i = 0; i < 3; i++)
          pDragRace[i]->DragRace();
     for(i = 0; i < 3; i++)
          pDragRace[i]->Release();
     CoUninitialize();
     return 0;
}
```

The Final COM Map Macros

To wrap up this chapter, we have a handful of remaining ATL COM map macros to examine. First, we have COM_INTERFACE_ENTRY_BREAK. This macro may be placed in your COM map to force the debugger to break if the interface in question is queried for by a client. Here is the expansion:

```
// Force a break in the debugger if interface 'x' is ever queried for.
#define COM_INTERFACE_ENTRY_BREAK(x)\
    {& ATL_IIDOF(x), \
    NULL, \
    _Break},
```

As you can see, the final field of the _ATL_INTMAP_ENTRY structure is pointed to the _Break() helper function provided by CComObjectRootBase. This method issues the break by calling DebugBreak():

```
// Recall CComObjectRootBase supplies a small batch of helper functions used
// by various COM map macros.
static HRESULT WINAPI _Break(void* /* pv */, REFIID iid, void** /* ppvObject */, DWORD /*
dw */)
{
    iid;
    _ATLDUMPIID(iid, _T("Break due to QI for interface "), S_OK);
    DebugBreak();
    return S_FALSE;
}
```

Next up is the COM_INTERFACE_ENTRY_NOINTERFACE macro. This macro exists to explicitly tell the world your coclass does <u>not</u> support the interface in question:

```
// When you need to bar an interface from working in your coclass...
#define COM_INTERFACE_ENTRY_NOINTERFACE(x)\
    {& ATL_IIDOF(x), \
    NULL, \
    _NoInterface},
```

_NoInterface() which is also provided by CComObjectRootBase, simply returns the appropriate HRESULT, E_NOINTERFACE:

```
// Issue an HRESULT.
static HRESULT WINAPI _NoInterface(void* /* pv */, REFIID /* iid */, void** /* ppvObject */,
DWORD /* dw */)
{
    return E_NOINTERFACE;
}
```

Rolling Your Own Mapping Functions

The next two ATL COM map macros are used when you wish to trigger the invocation of a specific custom function, as a result of a QueryInterface() call. The COM_INTERFACE_ENTRY_FUNC macro may be used to call a custom method in your coclass for a specific IID. COM_INTERFACE_ENTRY_FUNC_BLIND may be used to call an alternative function for <u>any</u> IID. Both macros take a DWORD parameter, which in turn is placed in the second field of the _ATL_INTMAP_ENTRY structure. Here are the expansions:

```
// These macros allow you to create a custom function which should be called in
// response to a given interface (or all interfaces).
#define COM_INTERFACE_ENTRY_FUNC(iid, dw, func)\
     {&iid, \
     dw, \
     func},
#define COM_INTERFACE_ENTRY_FUNC_BLIND(dw, func)\
     {NULL, \
     dw, \
     func},
```

Notice that the final field of the _ATL_INTMAP_ENTRY structure is func. This method is
actually the name of the custom method. The name can be anything at all, but must have
the following signature:

```
// The parameters of your custom method must be as so...
HRESULT WINAPI CallWhenQIed(void* pv, REFIID riid, LPVOID* ppv, DWORD dw)
{
     return S_OK;      // Signals that the custom function has found the interface.
}
```

The parameters to this custom global method are the class object (*pv), the GUID of the
interface (REFIID), a place to hold the vPtr (void**), and finally a DWORD which is the
value of the second parameter of the FUNC macros. This allows you to send in any specific
information to the custom function. Note that the custom function returns an HRESULT. If
the custom function has found (and set) the interface pointer, return S_OK. If not, return
S_FALSE to return to the COM map.

For example, assume you have an ATL coclass that supports some number of interfaces. Beyond handing out vPtrs for each, you might wish to call a custom helper function
during each client-side query. This would entail a custom global function and the
COM_INTERFACE_ENTRY_FUNC_BLIND macro:

```
// This method is called with every QI.
// Returning S_FALSE tells the function to return to the COM map to find the
// interface. S_OK signals that the custom function has already set the void**.
HRESULT WINAPI CallWhenQIed(void* pv, REFIID riid, LPVOID* ppv, DWORD dw)
{
     ATLTRACE("Someone wants to get an interface\n");
     ATLTRACE("DWORD param is %d\n", dw);
     return S_FALSE;
}
// Just for a simple example, 888 is sent in as DWORD data. This is realized as the 4th
// parameter of our custom function.
BEGIN_COM_MAP(CFinalMacros)
     COM_INTERFACE_ENTRY(IFinalMacros)
     COM_INTERFACE_ENTRY(IOther)
     COM_INTERFACE_ENTRY(IBaaz)
     COM_INTERFACE_ENTRY_FUNC_BLIND(888, CallWhenQIed)
END_COM_MAP()
```

So onto the big question: *Why?* The ATL _FUNC macros exist to allow developers to
extend the functionality of the COM map should the functionality of the core COM map
macros fall short of your needs.

The Last Stand: COM_INTERFACE_ENTRY_CHAIN

Last of all, we have the COM_INTERFACE_ENTRY_CHAIN macro. This macro is used to link your derived ATL coclass into the COM map of a base ATL coclass. In other words, this macro allows you to "inherit" the COM map of another class and include it as part of your own. Here is the definition:

```
// If you derive an ATL class from another ATL base class, you may chain
// each map together. This allows your subclass to direct QueryInterface() calls
// to the base class.
#define COM_INTERFACE_ENTRY_CHAIN(classname)\
      {NULL,\
      (DWORD)&_CComChainData<classname, _ComMapClass>::data,\
      _Chain},
```

The _Chain() helper function is used to calculate the location of the parent class and call InternalQueryInterface() accordingly:

```
// Another helper function supplied by CComObjectRootBase.
static HRESULT WINAPI _Chain(void* pv, REFIID iid, void** ppvObject, DWORD dw)
{
      _ATL_CHAINDATA* pcd = (_ATL_CHAINDATA*)dw;
      void* p = (void*)((DWORD)pv + pcd->dwOffset);
      return InternalQueryInterface(p, pcd->pFunc(), iid, ppvObject);
}
```

That's a wrap, folks. This chapter dove headlong into the ATL COM map macros. In the next chapter, we will dig into how the ATL framework supports component housing, and learn a number of advanced COM topics along the way such as component categories, object models, and custom registration à la ATL.

Chapter Summary

ATL's COM map is a rich playground for the C++ developer to romp around in. Typically the COM_INTERFACE_ENTRY macro is all you need to concern yourself with; however, this chapter has examined a number of additional macros and when you might want to use them.

Nested classes may be used as an interface implementation technique and are quite helpful when dealing with name clashes resulting from COM interfaces with duplicate method names. We examined how to use ATL to create wrapper classes which resolve the name clash before it becomes a problem in the supporting coclass.

Tear-off interfaces are a technique that allows the COM developer to make an educated guess. If you feel some of your COM interfaces are used infrequently, you may help reduce the overall size of the object by delaying the creation of vPtrs until explicitly asked by a COM client. Recall that if the client happens to ask for the interface you assume is no longer necessary, you will end up with a larger footprint than if you simply supported the interface in the first place. Use with caution.

Finally, we examined COM's binary reuse mechanisms: containment and aggregation. Containment maps quite well to the C++ techniques you are already comfortable with. Aggregation is not as common as containment; however, ATL provides a number of COM map macros to facilitate aggregation.

Chapter 9

Component Housing and ATL

Objectives:

- **Review the functionality provided by CComModule.**
- **Dissect the ATL Object Map and the _ATL_OBJMAP_ENTRY structure.**
- **Implement alternative class factories for ATL coclasses.**
- **Learn to customize your server's registration duties.**
- **Distinguish between creatable and non-creatable coclasses.**
- **Understand (and use) COM categories.**

In this chapter, you will spend some time digging deeper into ATL's support for COM servers. Although you already understand that the ATL COM AppWizard can be used to quickly put together a component home, we have yet to understand the details of exactly how the ATL framework is managing this. We begin by examining a number of methods of CComModule, and will quickly see that CComModule can't do much without an object map close by. The bulk of this chapter will be spent coming to understand exactly what this map is up to.

You will learn how to create customized registration of your ATL coclasses, as well as examine a number of more advanced COM topics, such as COM categories (CATIDs) and non-creatable coclasses, and how to develop a more sophisticated class factory than the framework provided default.

A Recap of COM Server Responsibilities

This chapter will examine ATL's support for component housing in far greater detail than Chapter 6. During the initial chapters of this book you were given the chance to build in-process and local servers from the ground up. Although COM-based DLL and EXE servers are implemented in slightly different ways, each is responsible for providing the following services:

- A COM server must provide a mechanism to expose class factories to the COM runtime. DLL servers expose their class factories using DllGetClassObject(). EXE servers post class factories to the class table using CoRegisterClassObject().

- A COM server must manage its lifetime. DLL servers maintain a lock counter (e.g., active objects + server locks), which can be obtained using DllCanUnloadNow(). If the lock count is at zero, SCM may unload the server from memory (as well, a client can invoke DllCanUnloadNow() indirectly using CoFreeUnusedLibraries()). EXE servers also maintain a server-wide lock counter; however, they are responsible for shutting themselves down when the count has reached zero. In a typical implementation, WinMain() establishes a dummy message loop to keep the server in memory that will fail upon receiving a WM_QUIT message sent when the lock count has transitioned to zero.
- A well-behaved COM server should register and unregister essential information into (or out of) the system registry when asked to do so. COM is very dependent upon the registry, and therefore a proper server should be able to insert (or delete) ProgIDs, AppIDs, CLSIDs, LIBIDs, and IIDs upon demand. DLL servers export two well-known functions to support self-registration: DllRegisterServer() and DllUnregister-Server(). EXE servers provide the same functionality as these DLL export functions by testing for the -regserver or -unregserver command line parameters.

While coding your component housing "by hand" is not impossible by any means, it can be a chore to reinvent the wheel time and time again. Using the ATL COM AppWizard, you can receive component housing with the click (or two) of a button. Regardless of how you choose to package your COM objects (DLL or EXE), CComModule and the server's object map provide the core support for your server's housing details. Our first task, then, is to review the basics of CComModule.

CComModule: Your Server's Housekeeper

This single ATL class contains methods and data members centered on the creation and registration details of the coclasses in the component housing. Most of the methods of CComModule make use of the server-wide object map to register, unregister, and create your objects. The basic functionality supplied by CComModule can be broken down into the following categories:

- Secondary creation and post destruction calls for the CComModule instance.
- Maintaining the number of server locks and active objects in the server.
- Performing registration and unregistration duties.
- Retrieving class factories for clients.

Creation and Termination of the CComModule Object

Every ATL COM server contains a single global instance of CComModule named _Module. ATL's implementation of DllMain() calls CComModule::Init() or CComModule::Term() based on the reason for the method invocation:

```
// ATL in-proc servers initialize and terminate _Module via DllMain()
BOOL WINAPI DllMain(HINSTANCE hInstance, DWORD dwReason, LPVOID)
{
    if (dwReason == DLL_PROCESS_ATTACH)
    {
        _Module.Init(ObjectMap, hInstance, &LIBID_ATLSHAPESLib);
```

```
                    DisableThreadLibraryCalls(hInstance);
        }
        else if (dwReason == DLL_PROCESS_DETACH)
        {
                _Module.Term();
        }
        return TRUE; // ok
}
```

ATL EXE servers call the same methods within the scope of _tWinMain(). Regardless of the type of component housing, these methods are used to set the internal state of the global level CComModule object (_Module) and deallocate any acquired resources.

CComModule::Init() takes three parameters: the object map (which is an array of _ATL_OBJMAP_ENTRY structures, hence _ATL_OBJMAP_ENTRY*), the instance of the DLL or EXE module, and the LIBID that defines the classes and interfaces defined in the server. If the LIBID is NULL, ATL assumes the *.tlb defined by your project contains the necessary information:

```
// Pass in object map, DLL/EXE instance, and LIBID to the CComModule object.
HRESULT Init( _ATL_OBJMAP_ENTRY* p,    // The object map.
    HINSTANCE h,                       // Module instance.
    const GUID* plibid = NULL)         // LIBID.
```

CComModule::Term() takes no parameters, and is called when the server itself (DLL or EXE) is being removed from memory:

```
// Clean up CComModule instance when server is going down.
void Term( );
```

Monitoring Active Locks and Active Objects

CComModule provides a number of methods used to monitor the number of server locks and currently active objects. When we were building in-proc servers by hand, we maintained two global counters for these purposes. When we were building our local server in Chapter 5, we combined these two counters into a single global variable. This is the approach of ATL. All of these locking methods are internally implemented to manipulate the public m_nLockCnt data member. When m_nLockCnt reaches zero, the server has no active objects and no server locks and can therefore be unloaded. Lock() and Unlock() calls are automatically called by the ATL framework; however, you may call them yourself if necessary:

```
// Active object/lock methods of CComModule.
LONG Lock();                   // Increments m_nLockCnt.
LONG Unlock();                 // Decrements m_nLockCnt.
LONG GetLockCount();           // Returns current value of m_nLockCnt.
LONG m_nLockCnt;               // Active objects + server locks.
```

As we have seen, ATL DLLs make use of GetLockCount() from within the DllCanUnloadNow() export:

```
// The lock count is represented by m_nLockCnt and obtained via GetLockCount().
STDAPI DllCanUnloadNow(void)
{
    return (_Module.GetLockCount()==0) ? S_OK : S_FALSE;
}
```

Registration Duties

Registration of your COM server is also handled by methods of CComModule. Both CComModule::RegisterServer() and CComModule::UnregisterServer() define a defaulted NULL LPCLSID parameter, which informs ATL to enter (or remove) registry information for every coclass contained in the server-wide object map.

ATL allows you to tweak the behavior of the server's (un)registration. If you wish to insert or remove registry information on a more selective coclass-by-coclass basis, set the default NULL LPCLSID parameter to a specific CLSID. Furthermore, the BOOL parameter is used to determine if the type library itself is to be registered as part of the process:

```
// Enter/remove server information for each entry in the object map.
HRESULT RegisterServer(BOOL bRegTypeLib = FALSE, CLSID* pCLSID = NULL );
HRESULT UnregisterServer(BOOL bUnRegTypeLib, const CLSID* pCLSID = NULL);
```

For in-proc servers, these methods are called from the DllRegisterServer() and DllUnregisterServer() exports:

```
// DllRegisterServer - Adds entries to the system registry
STDAPI DllRegisterServer(void)
{
    // Registers object, typelib, and all interfaces in typelib
    return _Module.RegisterServer(TRUE);
}
// DllUnregisterServer - Removes entries from the system registry
STDAPI DllUnregisterServer(void)
{
    return _Module.UnregisterServer(TRUE);
}
```

Creating Class Factories

A handful of CComModule methods are used to create class factories per client request. Given what you already know about class factories created by DLL and EXE servers, I'd bet you could decipher the following CComModule methods:

```
// Return an IClassFactory pointer for a client (DLL servers only)
HRESULT GetClassObject( REFCLSID rclsid, REFIID riid, LPVOID* ppv );
// Register a class object to the class table (EXE servers only)
HRESULT RegisterClassObjects( DWORD dwClsContext, DWORD dwFlags );
// Remove a class object from the class table (EXE servers only)
HRESULT RevokeClassObjects( );
```

The Default CComModule Instance

As mentioned, the ATL COM AppWizard will always generate a global instance of CComModule named _Module. Don't start to get clever and attempt to rename this instance, as ATL source code is looking for this object by name. DLL servers create an instance of CComModule like so:

```
// The single CComModule instance (DLL servers).
CComModule _Module;
```

EXE servers do not create an instance of CComModule directly. Rather, the ATL COM AppWizard will create an instance of a class named CExeModule, which is derived from CComModule. CExeModule inherits the core functionality of CComModule, and extends it by adding EXE-specific functionality:

```
// The single CExeModule instance (EXE servers).
CExeModule _Module;
```

The reason ATL subclasses a new class from CComModule is to keep the amount of boilerplate code to a minimum. If CComModule contained EXE-centric methods, DLL servers would lug around code they do not actually need! This wraps up our initial investigation of CComModule's public sector (see online help for the set of remaining CComModule methods). As mentioned earlier, a CComModule object cannot function by itself, but must have access to the server's object map.

Understanding the Object Map

The ATL object map contains critical information for each coclass contained in the server. By making use of this map, the global CComModule instance (_Module) is able to iterate over each object hosted by the server and request some action from the coclass. Possible actions include duties such as registration, unregistration, and the creation of the coclass's class factory. The object map is also used to perform some additional duties we have not yet encountered, such as providing access to the object's "category map," performing object initialization and termination as well as retrieving a self-describing registration string. We will be examining each of these duties throughout the remainder of this chapter.

Assume we have an empty server generated with the ATL COM AppWizard named ATLShapesServer.dll. The object map is completely devoid of entries at this point, and looks like the following:

```
// An empty object map, as generated by the ATL COM AppWizard.
BEGIN_OBJECT_MAP(ObjectMap)
END_OBJECT_MAP()
```

Note: ATL object maps are constructed in the same manner and provide the same basic services for both DLL and EXE servers.

Building an Object Map

The BEGIN_OBJECT_MAP macro (defined in <atlcom.h>) expands to define an array of _ATL_OBJMAP_ENTRY structures. The sole parameter that is sent into BEGIN_OBJECT_MAP becomes the <u>name</u> of the resulting _ATL_OBJMAP_ENTRY array:

```
// Declare an array of _ATL_OBJMAP_ENTRY structures named x. The name of
// the ATL COM AppWizard-generated array is ObjectMap.
//
#define BEGIN_OBJECT_MAP(x) static _ATL_OBJMAP_ENTRY x[] = {
```

The END_OBJECT_MAP macro simply terminates this array by providing all NULL entries for an _ATL_OBJMAP_ENTRY structure. As the CComModule instance iterates over the map, it knows the end of the map has been reached when it encounters all NULL entries:

```
// Terminate the _ATL_OBJMAP_ENTRY array.
#define END_OBJECT_MAP() {NULL, NULL, NULL, NULL,\
                          NULL, NULL, NULL, NULL} };
```

At this point, our server's empty object map expands to nothing more than a one-item array of _ATL_OBJMAP_ENTRY structures named ObjectMap:

```
// What the BEGIN_OBJECT_MAP and END_OBJECT_MAP macros resolve to.
static _ATL_OBJMAP_ENTRY ObjectMap[] =
{
     {NULL, NULL, NULL, NULL, NULL, NULL, NULL, NULL}
};
```

The _ATL_OBJMAP_ENTRY Structure

Now for the big question on your mind: What exactly is the _ATL_OBJMAP_ENTRY structure? This ATL structure is used to fully describe the creation and registration characteristics for every coclass contained in the server. Keep in mind that if you do not include a coclass in the object map, clients will not be able to create an instance using the COM library (e.g., CoCreateInstance()) and the ATL framework will not be able to register it into the system registry. From a high level, the _ATL_OBJMAP_ENTRY structure specifies the following information:

- The CLSID of the coclass.
- Pointer to the function that registers the type information of this coclass.
- Pointer to the function used to create the coclass's class factory.
- Pointer to the function used to create an instance of the coclass.
- Pointer to the class factory for the coclass.
- The DWORD ID returned from CoRegisterClassObject().
- Pointer to the function returning an object's string description.
- Pointer to the function returning an object's category map.
- Pointer to the function responsible for initializing the object.

I would guess the functionality of the first six items look familiar to you by now. You will get to know the remaining three by the end of this chapter.

Many of the fields of the _ATL_OBJMAP_ENTRY structure are pointers to a specific function. These functions are either supplied directly by your coclass or from one of its base classes. ATL understands which function to reference when filling a given field based on the function's signature (i.e., the return type, name, and argument list).

Many of these signatures have a corresponding ATL typedef used to identify them. For example, the function in your coclass (or base class) marked with the _ATL_CATMAPFUNC typedef will be used to fill the field pointing to your coclass's GetCategoryMap() function. Here are some of the ATL function signature typedefs, as found in <atlbase.h>:

```
// Specifies a "creator" function.
typedef HRESULT (WINAPI _ATL_CREATORFUNC)(void* pv, REFIID riid, LPVOID* ppv);
// Specifies a function returning your object's string description.
typedef LPCTSTR (WINAPI _ATL_DESCRIPTIONFUNC)();
```

```
// Signature for the function returning your coclass's category map.
// As you will see, _ATL_CATMAP_ENTRY is an array used to define
// the "category map" for your coclass.
typedef const struct _ATL_CATMAP_ENTRY* (_ATL_CATMAPFUNC)();
```

Armed with this knowledge, here is the full definition of the _ATL_OBJMAP_ENTRY structure, also defined in <atlbase.h>:

```
// Each entry in the OBJECT_MAP is a _ATL_OBJMAP_ENTRY structure.
// Take a note of the various function signature typedefs.
struct _ATL_OBJMAP_ENTRY
{
    const CLSID* pclsid;
    HRESULT (WINAPI *pfnUpdateRegistry)(BOOL bRegister);
    _ATL_CREATORFUNC* pfnGetClassObject;
    _ATL_CREATORFUNC* pfnCreateInstance;
    IUnknown* pCF;
    DWORD dwRegister;
    _ATL_DESCRIPTIONFUNC* pfnGetObjectDescription;
    _ATL_CATMAPFUNC* pfnGetCategoryMap;
    void (WINAPI *pfnObjectMain)(bool bStarting);
};
```

The following table should help you begin to make some initial sense of these fields. By the way, "pfn" is Hungarian notation for "pointer to a function":

_ATL_OBJMAP_ENTRY Field	Meaning in Life
pclsid	This holds the CLSID of the coclass.
pfnUpdateRegistry	Function used to update the registry with coclass-specific information.
pfnGetClassObject	Function used to create the class factory for the associated coclass.
pfnCreateInstance	Function used to create the coclass identified by the pclsid member.
pCF	Pointer to the class factory for a given coclass.
dwRegister	Numerical identifier returned by CoRegisterClass-Object(). Used to remove a class factory from class table upon EXE shutdown.
pfnGetObjectDescription	Function that provides the "object description" string for the coclass.
pfnGetCategoryMap	Function returning the "category map" for the coclass.
pfnObjectMain	Function used to initialize and terminate an instance of the coclass during the loading and unloading of the server.

The OBJECT_ENTRY Macro

Now that we have a better understanding of the _ATL_OBJMAP_ENTRY structure, we need to know how to fill it with coclass-specific information. As you may have suspected, this task is delegated to additional ATL macros. The most common entry found in the object map is the OBJECT_ENTRY macro, which is used to specify an externally creatable coclass. There is an additional object map macro, OBJECT_ENTRY_NON_CREATE-ABLE, used to define a non-creatable coclass that we examine later in this chapter during our discussion of server object models.

OBJECT_ENTRY takes two parameters: the CLSID of the coclass and the ATL-based class that implements it. Assume ATLShapesServer.dll contains the CoHexagon simple object. The object map would now look like the following:

```
// Our server contains a single creatable coclass named CoHexagon.
BEGIN_OBJECT_MAP(ObjectMap)
    OBJECT_ENTRY(CLSID_CoHexagon, CoHexagon)
END_OBJECT_MAP()
```

The OBJECT_ENTRY macro is defined in <atlcom.h> and is used to populate the fields of the _ATL_OBJMAP_ENTRY structure, given a C++ implementation class and the corresponding CLSID. Thus, each OBJECT_ENTRY entry increases the size of the _ATL_OBJMAP_ENTRY array by one. Here is the definition of the OBJECT_ENTRY macro, annotated with comments illustrating which function in the class (CoHexagon) sets the correct field of the _ATL_OBJMAP_ENTRY structure:

```
// The fields of an _ATL_OBJMAP_ENTRY structure are set by the
// OBJECT_ENTRY macro.
#define OBJECT_ENTRY(clsid, class) { \
&clsid, \                                            // [pclsid]
class::UpdateRegistry, \                             // [pfnUpdateRegistry]
class::_ClassFactoryCreatorClass::CreateInstance, \  // [pfnGetClassObject]
class::_CreatorClass::CreateInstance, \              // [pfnCreateInstance]
NULL, \                                              // Holds IUnknown* field.
0, \                                                 // Holds dwRegister field.
class::GetObjectDescription, \                       // [pfnGetObjectDescription]
class::GetCategoryMap, \                             // [pfnGetCategoryMap]
class::ObjectMain },                                 // [pfnObjectMain]
```

As you can see, the scope resolution operator is used to scope the class parameter to the correct function. However, if you examine the definition of CoHexagon you will fail to find any functions named GetObjectDescription(), UpdateRegistry(), ObjectMain(), and so forth:

```
// The functions required by the OBJECT_ENTRY macro appear to be missing...
class ATL_NO_VTABLE CCoHexagon :
    public CComObjectRootEx<CComSingleThreadModel>,
    public CComCoClass<CCoHexagon, &CLSID_CoHexagon>,
    public IDraw
{
public:
    CCoHexagon()
    {
    }
DECLARE_REGISTRY_RESOURCEID(IDR_COHEXAGON)
DECLARE_PROTECT_FINAL_CONSTRUCT()
BEGIN_COM_MAP(CCoHexagon)
    COM_INTERFACE_ENTRY(ICoHexagon)
END_COM_MAP()
};
```

Rest assured that these functions do exist; however, they are typically produced using a number of ATL macros. Some of these macros are specified directly in your coclass, while many others are inherited from one of your base classes. One of the nice things about the ATL framework is its ease of extendability. If you do not like the default support specified by one of your base classes, you are free to override that behavior, typically by inserting an ATL macro or two. Our next task is to investigate the following:

- Which ATL macros expand to define a given function referenced by an object map?
- Where are these macros initially declared?
- Can we override the default macros and when might we want to do so?

As we examine the functions of the ATL object map, be very aware that the ATL framework always provides you with default implementations for each. Much of the time you will want to use this default functionality, allowing you to quickly turn your attention to defining and implementing COM interfaces.

However, ATL does provide a way to override this default behavior to tailor-make your latest COM opus. That said, let's see exactly how a class such as CoHexagon provides the UpdateRegistry() method.

Specifying the UpdateRegistry() Method

The pfnUpdateRegistry field of the _ATL_OBJMAP_ENTRY structure points to your coclass's UpdateRegistry() method:

```
// Your class's UpdateRegistry() function is placed into the pfnUpdateRegistry
// field.
#define OBJECT_ENTRY(clsid, class) {
...
class::UpdateRegistry, \                              // [pfnUpdateRegistry]
...
```

The ATL framework will access this function whenever your server is told to register or unregister itself. Although you cannot find a method named UpdateRegistry() within CoHexagon, you will find the following default macro:

```
// The default implementation of UpdateRegistry() is specified using the
// DECLARE_REGISTRY_RESOURCEID macro.
class ATL_NO_VTABLE CCoHexagon :
    public CComObjectRootEx<CComSingleThreadModel>,
    public CComCoClass<CCoHexagon, &CLSID_CoHexagon>,
    public IDraw
{
...
    DECLARE_REGISTRY_RESOURCEID(IDR_COHEXAGON)
...
};
```

This macro is one of four possible ATL registration macros that expand to an implementation of UpdateRegistry(), all of which are defined in <atlcom.h>. Here is a rundown of each registration macro:

ATL Registration Macro	Meaning in Life
DECLARE_REGISTRY_RESOURCEID	The default macro. Used to register your coclasses based on the resource ID of the object's binary RGS file.
DECLARE_REGISTRY_RESOURCE	Also registers your coclass based on your RGS file. Takes a string name, rather than the resource ID.
DECLARE_NO_REGISTRY	Used to prevent any registration of the coclass. Often used for "non-creatable" coclasses.
DECLARE_REGISTRY	Bypasses the RGS file, and allows you to send in a minimal set of registration parameters.

Examining the ATL Registration Macros

DECLARE_REGISTRY_RESOURCEID takes a single parameter: the resource ID of the binary RGS file. Recall that all of your server's binary RGS resources are listed under the REGISTRY folder of the ResourceView tab, as shown in Figure 9-1:

Figure 9-1: The registration macros typically make use of resource IDs.

A closely related macro named DECLARE_REGISTRY_ RESOURCE takes the string name of the resource rather than the numerical resource ID. Both macros ultimately call CComModule::UpdateRegistryFromResource() which runs the registry script, registering or unregistering the coclass accordingly, based on the BOOL parameter. Here are the expansions of these first two ATL registration macros:

```
// Take the resource ID and pass into CComModule for processing.
#define DECLARE_REGISTRY_RESOURCEID(x)\
    static HRESULT WINAPI UpdateRegistry(BOOL bRegister)\
    {\
        return _Module.UpdateRegistryFromResource(x, bRegister);\
    }
// Take the string name of the resource and pass into CComModule for processing.
#define DECLARE_REGISTRY_RESOURCE(x)\
    static HRESULT WINAPI UpdateRegistry(BOOL bRegister)\
    {\
        return _Module.UpdateRegistryFromResource(_T(#x), bRegister);\
    }
```

The third ATL registry macro, DECLARE_NO_REGISTRY, is implemented as a simple no-op. This macro is commonly used when you have a "non-creatable" coclass and do not wish to specify any registry information (therefore preventing clients from directly instantiating any objects). Here is the definition of DECLARE_NO_REGISTRY:

```
// Defines a no-op version of UpdateRegistry.
#define DECLARE_NO_REGISTRY()\
    static HRESULT WINAPI UpdateRegistry(BOOL /*bRegister*/)\
    {return S_OK;}
```

Finally, we have the DECLARE_REGISTRY macro, which allows you to avoid registry scripts altogether, and specify the minimal set of registry information for a coclass (the CLSID, ProgIDs, object description string, and the threading model identifier).

This approach is not really recommended, as ATL's registry scripting language provides a much more fluid manner to register your server. Furthermore, most COM servers need more detailed registration information than the DECLARE_REGISTRY macro provides. Nevertheless, here is the definition of DECLARE_REGISTRY:

```
// If you want to bypass RGS files, you can use the DECLARE_REGISTRY
// macro.
#define DECLARE_REGISTRY(class, pid, vpid, nid, flags)\
    static HRESULT WINAPI UpdateRegistry(BOOL bRegister)\
    {\
        return _Module.UpdateRegistryClass(GetObjectCLSID(), pid, vpid, nid,\
            flags, bRegister);\
    }
```

By default, the ATL Object Wizard inserts the DECLARE_REGISTRY_RESOURCEID macro into your coclass header file. If you wish to use any other variations, you only need to substitute the desired macro in your coclass's header file. For example, if we wish to prevent the ATL framework from adding registry information for our CoHexagon class, we could write the following:

```
// To use a stock UpdateRegistry() method, simply define a given registry macro
// in your coclass's header file.
class ATL_NO_VTABLE CCoHexagon :
    public CComObjectRootEx<CComSingleThreadModel>,
    public CComCoClass<CCoHexagon, &CLSID_CoHexagon>,
    public IDraw
{
...
    // Nope... DECLARE_REGISTRY_RESOURCEID(IDR_COHEXAGON)
    DECLARE_NO_REGISTRY()
...
};
```

Customizing UpdateRegistry()

If you have some special registration needs, you are of course able to provide your own custom version of UpdateRegistry(). The only requirement is that your UpdateRegistry() implementation has the same function signature as found in the stock macros. Typically, you will want to be sure and call CComModule::UpdateRegistryFromResource() before you exit your custom implementation of UpdateRegistry(), allowing ATL to perform the default registration duties based on your RGS file. Here is a simple example:

```
// To provide your own implementation of UpdateRegistry(), remove all ATL
// registry macros and write it yourself.
class ATL_NO_VTABLE CCoHexagon :
    public CComObjectRootEx<CComSingleThreadModel>,
    public CComCoClass<CCoHexagon, &CLSID_CoHexagon>,
    public IDraw
{
...
    static HRESULT WINAPI UpdateRegistry(BOOL b)
    {
```

```
            if (b)
                    MessageBox(NULL, "Registering...", "Hey!", MB_OK);
            else
                    MessageBox(NULL, "Unregistering...", "Hey!", MB_OK);
            // Perform default registration based on RGS file.
            return _Module.UpdateRegistryFromResource(IDR_COHEXAGON, b);
    }
...
};
```

When is UpdateRegistry() Called?

To finish up our discussion of this first field of the _ATL_OBJMAP_ENTRY structure, we need to understand when UpdateRegistry() is called by the ATL framework. Recall that the ATL COM AppWizard has implemented DllRegisterServer() and DllUnregister-Server() with the help of CComModule:

```
// DLL exports which provide self-registration support.
//STDAPI DllRegisterServer(void)
{     return _Module.RegisterServer(TRUE);      }
STDAPI DllUnregisterServer(void)
{     return _Module.UnregisterServer(TRUE);    }
```

EXE servers will call RegisterServer() and UnregisterServer() based on the value of the LPTSTR command line parameter. The FindOneOf() helper function will scan a string for a set of tokens:

```
// EXE servers and the UpdateRegistry() invocation.
extern "C" int WINAPI _tWinMain(HINSTANCE hInstance,
HINSTANCE /*hPrevInstance*/, LPTSTR lpCmdLine, int /*nShowCmd*/)
{
    TCHAR szTokens[] = _T("-/");
    LPCTSTR lpszToken = FindOneOf(lpCmdLine, szTokens);
...
    if (lstrcmpi(lpszToken, _T("UnregServer"))==0)
    {
        nRet = _Module.UnregisterServer(TRUE);
...
    }
    if (lstrcmpi(lpszToken, _T("RegServer"))==0)
    {
        nRet = _Module.RegisterServer(TRUE);
...
    }
...
}
```

CComModule::RegisterServer() and CComModule::UnregisterServer() make calls to ATL helper functions (AtlModuleRegisterServer() and AtlModuleUnregisterServer() respectively) which iterate over the object map, calling UpdateRegistry() for each coclass in the object map:

```
// Your server's DllRegisterServer() method calls CComModule::RegisterServer()
// which in turn calls AtlModuleRegisterServer() which triggers each coclass's
// pfnUpdateRegistry method.
ATLINLINE ATLAPI AtlModuleRegisterServer(_ATL_MODULE* pM,
                BOOL bRegTypeLib, const CLSID* pCLSID)
```

```
{
...
      // Loop over the object map and call each class's UpdateRegistry() method.
      hRes = pEntry->pfnUpdateRegistry(TRUE);
...
}
```

Quite a winding path, yes? The good news is, all you need to worry about is providing an implementation of UpdateRegistry() in your coclass, and ATL will take care of the rest. As well, the UpdateRegistry() implementation defined by the DECLARE_REGISTRY_RE-SOURCEID macro is typically exactly what you require.

Later in our lab work, we will create a customized UpdateRegistry() method. Until then, let's move on and figure out how the pfnGetClassObject field is set, allowing ATL to create the class factory for your object. But first, a word about ATL creator classes.

Understanding ATL COM Creators

The ATL framework creates your class factories and coclasses in slightly different ways based off a number of COM influences. For example, in ATL, your coclasses are created based on your object's level of thread awareness and aggregation support. To help stream-line the differences between creating aggregated versus non-aggregated objects, traditional class factories versus custom class factories (and so on), ATL provides a level of abstraction called a *creator class*. An ATL creator will (for lack of a better word) create a given ATL object based off all the possible combinations of COM influences. In this chapter we will see the use of the CComCreator<> and CComCreator2<> creator templates.

Each ATL creator class has a single static method named CreateInstance(), which is used to assemble the object. The implementation of this method is determined by the con-figuration of the class under construction. A handy typedef will be used to represent the layout of the ATL creator, which helps clean up the object definition and reduces source code clutter. For example, the fields in the _ATL_OBJMAP_ENTRY structure that point to the function used to create a class factory and the related coclass are both called CreateInstance(); however, each is colored by the correct creator typedef (_ClassFactoryCreatorClass or _CreatorClass):

```
// _ClassFactoryCreatorClass and _CreatorClass are typedefs to the correct ATL
// creator class.
class::_ClassFactoryCreatorClass::CreateInstance, \ // [pfnGetClassObject]
class::_CreatorClass::CreateInstance, \              // [pfnCreateInstance]
```

Specifying the _ClassFactoryCreatorClass::CreateInstance() Method

Now that we have a feeling for these ATL creator classes, let's see one in action. The pfnGetClassObject field of the _ATL_OBJMAP_ENTRY structure points to the function used to create the class factory for a given coclass. The OBJECT_ENTRY macro sets this field using the correct creator typedef provided by your class, hence class::_ClassFactoryCreatorClass::CreateInstance:

```
// The _ClassFactoryCreatorClass::CreateInstance() function is
// held by the pfnGetClassObject field.
#define OBJECT_ENTRY(clsid, class) {
...
```

```
class::_ClassFactoryCreatorClass::CreateInstance, \  // [pfnGetClassObject]
...
```

If you have a DLL server, the ATL framework will access pfnGetClassObject during calls to DllGetClassObject() via CComModule::GetClassObject(). GetClassObject() in turn calls an ATL helper function named AtlModuleGetClassObject():

```
// DllGetClassObject is implemented by a call to CComModule::GetClassObject()
// which calls AtlModuleGetClassObject(). This ATL helper function accesses the
// pfnGetClassObject field of the _ATL_OBJMAP_ENTRY structure.
ATLINLINE ATLAPI AtlModuleGetClassObject(_ATL_MODULE* pM, REFCLSID rclsid,
                                         REFIID riid, LPVOID* ppv)
{
...
    if (pEntry->pCF == NULL)
        hRes = pEntry->pfnGetClassObject(pEntry->pfnCreateInstance,
            IID_IUnknown, (LPVOID*)&pEntry->pCF);
...
}
```

EXE servers access pfnGetClassObject via CComModule::RegisterClassObject(), which in turn accesses pfnGetClassObject to post class factories to the class table:

```
// ATL EXE servers access pfnGetClassObject via RegisterClassObject().
extern "C" int WINAPI _tWinMain(HINSTANCE hInstance,
   HINSTANCE /*hPrevInstance*/, LPTSTR lpCmdLine, int /*nShowCmd*/)
{
...
    hRes = _Module.RegisterClassObjects(CLSCTX_LOCAL_SERVER,
        REGCLS_MULTIPLEUSE | REGCLS_SUSPENDED);
...
}
```

Now that we have seen when this method is called, the next question is where this method is hiding. Your class's _ClassFactoryCreatorClass::CreateInstance() method is provided by a set of ATL class factory macros. Here is a rundown of the most common:

ATL Class Factory Creation Macro	Meaning in Life
DECLARE_CLASSFACTORY	The default macro. Provides a generic class factory implementing IClassFactory.
DECLARE_CLASSFACTORY_EX	Allows you to specify a custom class factory implementation.
DECLARE_CLASSFACTORY2	Allows you to create a licensed class factory supporting IClassFactory2.
DECLARE_CLASSFACTORY_SINGLETON	Allows you to construct a class factory which hands out multiple references to a single coclass.
DECLARE_CLASSFACTORY_AUTO_THREAD	Allows an EXE server to span objects which reside in multiple apartments.

ATL's Default Class Factory Support

To begin, recall that any creatable ATL class must derive from CComCoClass<>:

```
// CComCoClass defines a default implementation of
// _ClassFactoryCreatorClass::CreateInstance().
class ATL_NO_VTABLE CCoHexagon :
     public CComObjectRootEx<CComSingleThreadModel>,
     public CComCoClass<CCoHexagon, &CLSID_CoHexagon>,
     public IDraw
{ ... };
```

Among other things, this ATL template provides a default class factory. If we examine the definition of CComCoClass, we will find the following macro:

```
// The DECLARE_CLASSFACTORY macro expands to provide an implementation
// for _ClassFactoryCreatorClass::CreateInstance
template <class T, const CLSID* pclsid = &CLSID_NULL>
class CComCoClass
{
public:
     DECLARE_CLASSFACTORY()
...
};
```

Exactly what this macro expands to will depend upon the type of COM server you are working with. Recall that EXE servers typically do not want the class factory's reference count to influence the termination of the server, as the server is responsible for shutting itself down. DLL servers, on the other hand, must allow their reference count to influence the unloading of the server, as the DLL should not be unloaded until all clients are finished with all interface pointers.

In short, a class factory will be implemented in slightly different ways based off the type of component housing. ATL takes care of the differences between EXE and DLL class factories using the CComObjectCached<> and CComObjectNoLock<> templates, using the correct COM creator.

DECLARE_CLASSFACTORY and DECLARE_CLASSFACTORY_EX

The DECLARE_CLASSFACTORY macro will first make a preprocessor check for the _USRDLL flag. If _USRDLL has been defined by your project, you are building an in-proc server and therefore want ATL to create a class factory implementation that takes reference counting into account, using CComObjectCached<>.

If _USRDLL is not defined you are creating an EXE, and ATL will create a class factory which will not affect the server's object count, using CComObjectNoLock<>. As you can see, DECLARE_CLASSFACTORY expands to call another ATL class factory macro named DECLARE_CLASSFACTORY_EX:

```
// The class that implements the class factory depends on the _USRDLL flag.
#define DECLARE_CLASSFACTORY()
     DECLARE_CLASSFACTORY_EX(CComClassFactory)
// The class factories are living in a DLL, so use CComObjectCached<>.
#if defined(_WINDLL) | defined(_USRDLL)
#define DECLARE_CLASSFACTORY_EX(cf) \
typedef CComCreator< CComObjectCached< cf > > _ClassFactoryCreatorClass;
#else
// The class factories are living in an EXE, so use CComObjectNoLock<>.
#define DECLARE_CLASSFACTORY_EX(cf) \
typedef CComCreator< CComObjectNoLock< cf > > _ClassFactoryCreatorClass;
#endif
```

Notice that _ClassFactoryCreatorClass is the typedef of the creator class creating your class factory, based on its reference counting needs. ATL's CComClassFactory class is passed into the DECLARE_CLASSFACTORY_EX macro, which provides a default class implementing IClassFactory (more on this in a minute). The CComCreator<> template provides the actual static CreateInstance() method, which ends up being the function pointed to by the pfnGetClassObject field.

So to recap, DECLARE_CLASSFACTORY will expand in one of two ways based on the type of component home (DLL or EXE). CComCreator<> provides the CreateInstance() method. CComObjectCached<> (DLL) and CComObjectNoLock<> (EXE) are used to specify the reference counting behavior for your class factory:

```
// pfnGetClassObject is filled by one of these two implementations of
// _ClassFactoryCreatorClass::CreateInstance().
// DLL version.
CComCreator< CComObjectCached< CComClassFactory > >::CreateInstance()
// EXE version.
CComCreator< CComObjectNoLock< CComClassFactory > >::CreateInstance()
```

CComClassFactory: The Default Implementation of IClassFactory

CComClassFactory provides a default implementation of the IClassFactory interface. If you examine this class (<atlcom.h>) you will see it derives from IClassFactory, implements IClassFactory::CreateInstance() and IClassFactory::LockServer(), and provides a COM_MAP with an entry for IClassFactory. We will see what the SetVoid() and the _ATL_CREATORFUNC* member variable (m_pfnCreateInstance) are used for in just a moment. Here is the formal definition of CComClassFactory:

```
// CComClassFactory provides a standard implementation of IClassFactory.
class CComClassFactory :
     public IClassFactory,
     public CComObjectRootEx<CComGlobalsThreadModel>
{
public:
     BEGIN_COM_MAP(CComClassFactory)
          COM_INTERFACE_ENTRY(IClassFactory)
     END_COM_MAP()
     // IClassFactory methods
     STDMETHOD(CreateInstance)(LPUNKNOWN pUnkOuter, REFIID riid, void** ppvObj);
     STDMETHOD(LockServer)(BOOL fLock);
     // SetVoid() will assign CComClassFactory::m_pfnCreateInstance.
     void SetVoid(void* pv);
     // Used to store the pointer to the _ATL_OBJMAP_ENTRY
     // pfnCreateInstance field. Thus! Your class factory has a pointer to
     // the function used to create the correct coclass!
     _ATL_CREATORFUNC* m_pfnCreateInstance;
};
```

Implementing CComClassFactory::LockServer()

CComClassFactory::LockServer() is implemented with help from your global CComModule instance. As you would expect, the server's active object count needs to be adjusted based off the value of the incoming BOOL parameter:

```
// CComClassFactory::LockServer() adjusts the server's object count.
STDMETHOD(LockServer)(BOOL fLock)
```

```
{
    if (fLock)
        _Module.Lock();
    else
        _Module.Unlock();
    return S_OK;
}
```

Implementing CComClassFactory::CreateInstance()

CComClassFactory::CreateInstance() is implemented to operate on the internal m_pfnCreateInstance member variable. This public member variable points to the function used to create the corresponding coclass:

```
// CComClassFactory::CreateInstance() calls the function which creates the coclass, held
// in the m_pfnCreateInstance data member.
STDMETHOD(CreateInstance)(LPUNKNOWN pUnkOuter, REFIID riid,
                                      void** ppvObj)
{
    ATLASSERT(m_pfnCreateInstance != NULL);
    HRESULT hRes = E_POINTER;
    if (ppvObj != NULL)
    {
        *ppvObj = NULL;
        // Can't ask for anything other than IUnknown when aggregating
        if ((pUnkOuter != NULL) && !InlineIsEqualUnknown(riid))
        {
            hRes = CLASS_E_NOAGGREGATION;
        }
        else
            hRes = m_pfnCreateInstance(pUnkOuter, riid, ppvObj);
    }
        return hRes;
}
```

When the CComCreator<> class creates an instance of CComClassFactory, it will set this member variable to the m_pfnCreateInstance field of your _ATL_OBJMAP_ENTRY structure using the SetVoid() helper function. Recall that pfnCreateInstance is the field that creates the coclass itself (CoHexagon). Therefore, this data member points to the creator function of your coclass! Here is the relevant code behind CComCreator<>::Create-Instance():

```
// CComCreator:: CreateInstance() calls SetVoid(), which sets
// CComClassFactory::m_pfnCreateInstance.
template <class T1>
class CComCreator
{
public:
    static HRESULT WINAPI CreateInstance(void* pv, REFIID riid, LPVOID* ppv)
    {
        ATLASSERT(*ppv == NULL);
        HRESULT hRes = E_OUTOFMEMORY;
        T1* p = NULL;
        ATLTRY(p = new T1(pv))

        if (p != NULL)
        {
```

```
                    p->SetVoid(pv);
                    p->InternalFinalConstructAddRef();
                    hRes = p->FinalConstruct();
                    p->InternalFinalConstructRelease();
                    if (hRes == S_OK)
                        hRes = p->QueryInterface(riid, ppv);
                    if (hRes != S_OK)
                        delete p;
            }
            return hRes;
    }
};
```

Again, CComClassFactory::SetVoid() sets the m_pfnCreateInstance data member to the function used to create the associated coclass (the default implementation found in CComObjectRootBase does nothing):

```
// CComClassFactory overrides the default SetVoid() method defined in
// CComObjectRootBase.
void SetVoid(void* pv)
{
    m_pfnCreateInstance = (_ATL_CREATORFUNC*)pv;
}
```

Finally, we can see what CComClassFactory::CreateInstance() is all about. It calls a function to create your coclass, which happens to be the same function pointed to in the m_pfnCreateInstance field of the _ATL_OBJMAP_ENTRY structure.

Now the good news is your ATL coclasses will have a class factory supplied for free by the DECLARE_CLASSFACTORY macro defined in CComCoClass. It is edifying to have a better understanding of what ATL is doing under the hood; however, you can live a happy and productive life without it.

Before we move on, let's examine how we can override this default ATL class factory and why we might want to do so.

Licensed Class Factories and IClassFactory2

DECLARE_CLASSFACTORY provides a standard class factory for your coclass via CComClassFactory. If you wish to supply an alternative class factory for your coclass, you may override the default behavior specified in CComCoClass<> by supplying an alternative class factory macro in your coclass definition.

For example, sometimes you want to make money on your hard-won coclasses. Imagine you just created a fantastic new ActiveX control and want to sell it for $20 a pop. You would like to ensure that a given developer couldn't create the object until he or she can show proof of purchase. For this very reason COM allows you to implement a class factory using the IClassFactory2 interface. This interface derives from IClassFactory, and adds additional methods which allow you to locate and test for a valid license file (*.lic). As this support is most common among ActiveX controls, the IDL definition of IClassFactory2 is found in <ocidl.idl>:

```
// Implemented by a class factory which performs license checks
// before creating the coclass.
interface IClassFactory2 : IClassFactory
{
    HRESULT GetLicInfo([out] LICINFO * pLicInfo);
```

```
HRESULT RequestLicKey([in] DWORD dwReserved, [out] BSTR * pBstrKey );
HRESULT CreateInstanceLic([in] IUnknown * pUnkOuter,
                          [in] IUnknown * pUnkReserved,
                          [in] REFIID riid,
                          [in] BSTR bstrKey,
                          [out, iid_is(riid)] PVOID * ppvObj );
};
```

ATL provides the DECLARE_CLASSFACTORY2 macro to create a class factory deriving from (and implementing) IClassFactory2. This macro still leverages the DECLARE_CLASSFACTORY_EX macro to expose the correct CComCreator; however, this time, your class factory is represented by CComClassFactory2<>:

```
// Used to define a class factory with support for licensing.
#define DECLARE_CLASSFACTORY2(lic) \
    DECLARE_CLASSFACTORY_EX(CComClassFactory2<lic>)
```

The lic parameter is a C++ class (provided by you) that implements the licensing validation code. We will see an example of creating a licensed class factory in our discussion of ActiveX controls (Chapter 14), but for the sake of illustration, assume we have such a class named CMyLic. We could then create a licensed class object as so:

```
// CoHexagon: You've got to pay to play.
class ATL_NO_VTABLE CCoHexagon :
    public CComObjectRootEx<CComSingleThreadModel>,
    public CComCoClass<CCoHexagon, &CLSID_CoHexagon>,
    public IDraw,
    public IShapeEdit,
    public IErase,
    public IShapeID
{
public:
    ...
    DECLARE_CLASSFACTORY2(CMyLic)
    ...
};
```

Singleton Class Factories

Sometimes you may wish to design a class factory that creates a single instance of a coclass, regardless of how many clients may request a new instance. To do so would require tweaking the code behind IClassFactory::CreateInstance() such that all interface pointers are returned from a single object as opposed to a new object every time. ATL provides the DECLARE_CLASSFACTORY_SINGLETON macro for this very purpose.

When this macro expands, your class factory will be implemented using CComClassFactorySingleton<>:

```
// Create a singleton.
#define DECLARE_CLASSFACTORY_SINGLETON(obj)\
    DECLARE_CLASSFACTORY_EX(CComClassFactorySingleton<obj>)
```

CComClassFactorySingleton<> contains a private data member of type CComObjectGlobal<>. This data member represents the single instance of the associated coclass (for example, CoHexagon). Here is the formal definition. Notice that all references to the object are handed out using the single instance of the CComObjectGlobal<> member variable:

```
// Singletons are represented by CComClassFactorySingleton<>.
template <class T>
class CComClassFactorySingleton : public CComClassFactory
{
public:
    void FinalRelease()
    {
        CoDisconnectObject(m_Obj.GetUnknown(), 0);
    }
    // IClassFactory
    STDMETHOD(CreateInstance)(LPUNKNOWN pUnkOuter, REFIID riid, void** ppvObj)
    {
        HRESULT hRes = E_POINTER;
        if (ppvObj != NULL)
        {
            *ppvObj = NULL;
            // aggregation is not supported in Singletons.
            ATLASSERT(pUnkOuter == NULL);
            if (pUnkOuter != NULL)
                hRes = CLASS_E_NOAGGREGATION;
            else
            {
                if (m_Obj.m_hResFinalConstruct != S_OK)
                    hRes = m_Obj.m_hResFinalConstruct;
                else
                    hRes = m_Obj.QueryInterface(riid, ppvObj);
            }
        }
        return hRes;
    }
    CComObjectGlobal<T> m_Obj;    // A single instance of the coclass.
};
```

While a singleton might sound perfect in many situations, beware. Singleton class factories living in a DLL are only unique on a *per-process* basis. Thus, if ten clients are using a CoHexagon created by a singleton, this does not imply that all ten processes are using the same instance. EXE singletons are only unique for a given machine.

A better approach is to have a normal class factory that creates any number of new objects, and allow these objects to share instance data by use of some global utility object. This would require you to implement IClassFactory in such a way that when the class factory creates a new instance of the coclass, some secondary initialization is performed to "prep" the object to look like all the other existing coclasses. How, then, can we specify our own implementation of IClassFactory? Glad you asked.

A Class Factory of Your Very Own

If you want to create a customized class factory that will function within the ATL framework, you may use the DECLARE_CLASSFACTORY_EX macro and specify the name of your custom class implementing IClassFactory. This class will need to derive from CComClassFactory. As an example, if we wanted to create an implementation of IClassFactory that keeps a running count of how many CoHexagon objects have been created, we may create a custom class factory, declared as so:

```
// Every time we create a CoHexagon, we will increase a global counter.
class CMyCustomCF : public CComClassFactory
{
    ...
    STDMETHOD(CreateInstance)(LPUNKNOWN pUnkOuter, REFIID riid,
                              void** ppvObj)
    {
        ...
        ++g_HexCount;
        ...
    }
};
```

We would then specify this custom class factory in cohexagon.h using the
DECLARE_CLASSFACTORY_EX macro:

```
// Providing a custom class factory for CoHexagon.
class ATL_NO_VTABLE CCoHexagon :
    public CComObjectRootEx<CComSingleThreadModel>,
    public CComCoClass<CCoHexagon, &CLSID_CoHexagon>,
    public IDraw,
    public IShapeEdit,
    public IErase,
    public IShapeID
{
public:
    ...
    DECLARE_CLASSFACTORY_EX(CMyCustomCF)
    ...
};
```

To sum up ATL's class factory support, ATL coclasses automatically inherit a standard
class factory from CComCoClass< >, via the DECLARE_CLASSFACTORY macro. This
macro expands to parameterize the implementation of CComCreator::CreateInstance()
based off the class implementing IClassFactory(2) (CComClassFactory, CComClass-
Factory2, CComClassFactorySingleton), as well as the correct module locking support
(CComObjectCached or CComObjectNoLock).

If you wish to replace this default support, you may specify any of the alternative macros (DECLARE_CLASSFACTORY_EX, DECLARE_CLASSFACTORY_SINGLETON, or
DECLARE_CLASSFACTORY2) in your header file. As with most things, just because you
can does not mean you have to. The default class factory will serve your needs (almost)
every time.

Specifying the _CreatorClass::CreateInstance() Method

The _ATL_OBJMAP_ENTRY structure contains another parameterized CreateInstance()
method, again using a COM creator. This method, marked by the pfnCreateInstance field,
is used to specify which function to call to create the actual coclass (recall that your class
factory holds onto this function pointer):

```
// Your coclass's CreateInstance() function is placed into the pfnCreateInstance
// field.
#define OBJECT_ENTRY(clsid, class) {
    ...
```

```
class::_CreatorClass::CreateInstance, \          // [pfnCreateInstance]
...
```

You receive a default implementation of _CreatorClass::CreateInstance() from
CComCoClass<> using the DECLARE_AGGREGATABLE macro:

```
// DECLARE_AGGREGATABLE is defined in CComCoClass to implement
// the function used to create your coclass.
template <class T, const CLSID* pclsid = &CLSID_NULL>
class CComCoClass
{
public:
...
    DECLARE_AGGREGATABLE(T)
...
};
```

Beyond this default macro, ATL provides a number of alternatives. Here are some of the
most common:

ATL Coclass Creation Macro	Meaning in Life
DECLARE_AGGREGATABLE	Specifies that your coclass may work as an aggregated object, but is not required to.
DECLARE_NOT_AGGREGATABLE	Specifies that your coclass cannot work as an aggregated object.
DECLARE_ONLY_AGGREGATABLE	Specifies that your object cannot work as a stand-alone object, and must be part of an aggregate.

The DECLARE_AGGREGATABLE Macro and CComCreator2<>

DECLARE_AGGREGATABLE is defined in <atlcom.h>. As you recall, an ATL coclass
needs to specify how it wishes to be created with regard to aggregation. The
DECLARE_AGGREGATABLE macro states that your coclass can work as an aggregated
object or a stand-alone, non-aggregated object. This macro makes use of the
CComCreator2<> template, where the "2" signals the two possible creation behaviors
(aggregated or not).

If your coclass is working as an inner object, your class will be passed into
CComAggObject<>, which is then passed into CComCreator<>. This will implement the
necessary hooks to allow your coclass to work as an aggregate:

```
// Your object will work as an inner object.
CComCreator< CComAggObject< x > >
```

If your object will not work as an aggregate, you will be sent into the old familiar
CComObject<> template:

```
// Your object will not be an inner object.
CComCreator< CComObject< x > >
```

To allow one or the other of these creations to take place, each of the CComCreator<>
classes becomes a parameter to CComCreator2<>. The end result is a typedef to _Cre-
atorClass::CreateInstance(). Here then is the DECLARE_AGGREGATABLE macro:

```
// The default aggregation macro allows your coclass to work as an aggregate
// (CComCreator< CComAggObject< > > ) or not
// (CComCreator< CComObject< > > )
#define DECLARE_AGGREGATABLE(x) public:\
    typedef CComCreator2< CComCreator< CComObject< x > >, \
                          CComCreator< CComAggObject< x > > > > \
    _CreatorClass;
```

More often than not, this is exactly the behavior you want, and you can rest assured the ATL framework has provided you with the support your COM objects need.

Specifying Alternative Aggregation Support

Like the class factory macros, if you wish to change the level of aggregation support in your coclass, you have options. If you know which level of aggregation support you wish to specify at the time you are using the ATL Object Wizard, you may say so using the Attributes tab. Based on your selection, ATL will either leverage the default CComCoClass aggregation macro, or insert one of the following ATL macros in your coclass header file. If you change your mind after you have used the ATL Object Wizard, you may simply add the correct macro into your coclass after the fact.

The default option used to specify your level of aggregation is Yes, and therefore you automatically inherit the functionality of the DECLARE_AGGREGATABLE macro.

Choosing No will add DECLARE_NOT_AGGREGATABLE to your coclass header file, and Only will insert DECLARE_ONLY_AGGREGATABLE.

Specifying Non-Aggregatable Classes

If you select DECLARE_NOT_AGGREGATABLE, your coclass will not work as an aggregate and can only function as a stand-alone object. Here, your coclass will be created using either CComObject<> or CComFailCreator<> based on whether your class is being asked to function as an aggregate. CComFailCreator<> wraps up the logic for signaling the failed creation of a coclass:

```
// If you want to prevent your coclass from functioning as an aggregate, use the
// DECLARE_NOT_AGGREGATABLE macro.
#define DECLARE_NOT_AGGREGATABLE(x) public:\
    typedef CComCreator2< CComCreator< CComObject< x > >, \
        CComFailCreator<CLASS_E_NOAGGREGATION> > \
            _CreatorClass;
```

Specifying Only-Aggregatable Classes

The DECLARE_ONLY_AGGREGATABLE macro specifies that your coclass cannot function as a stand-alone object and <u>must</u> be aggregated. If you select this option, CCom-Creator2 will use CComAggObject<> for your aggregated implementation, and return E_FAIL (via CComFailCreator<>) if it is ever asked to work as a stand-alone object.

```
// If you wish to have a coclass which can only work as an aggregate,
// use the DECLARE_ONLY_AGGREGATABLE macro.
#define DECLARE_ONLY_AGGREGATABLE(x) public:\
    typedef CComCreator2< CComFailCreator<E_FAIL>, \
        CComCreator< CComAggObject< x > > > \
            _CreatorClass;
```

If you wish to change this default behavior, simply add an alternative aggregation macro to your coclass. For example, if we wish to ensure that CoHexagon can never be aggregated by another object, update the class definition as so:

```
// Change the default _CreatorClass::CreateInstance() method to ensure no one
// can ever aggregate CoHexagon
class ATL_NO_VTABLE CCoHexagon :
...
{
...
        DECLARE_NOT_AGGREGATABLE(CCoHexagon)
...
};
```

To sum up the pfnCreateInstance field of the _ATL_OBJMAP_ENTRY structure, pfnCreateInstance points to the CreateInstance() method configured by the correct COM creator via CComCreator2< >.

The creator understands exactly how to create your object with regard to the issue of aggregation. By default, ATL will provide you with the behavior defined by the DECLARE_AGGREGATABLE macro. If you want a new set of creators, just plug in the desired aggregation macro in your derived class.

Specifying the GetObjectDescription() Method

Those last two fields of the _ATL_OBJMAP_ENTRY structure may have caused your head to explode. This is a normal response. However, with that bit of nastiness behind us, we can look at some more intuitive function entry points. GetObjectDescription() is a method used to return a string which identifies your coclass, and is represented by the pfnGetObjectDescription field of the _ATL_OBJMAP_ENTRY structure.

```
// pfnGetObjectDescription points to your class's GetObjectDescription() method.
#define OBJECT_ENTRY(clsid, class) {
...
class::GetObjectDescription, \                          // [pfnGetObjectDescription]
...
```

CComCoClass< > provides a default implementation for this method, which returns a NULL string:

```
// The default implementation of GetObjectDescription() in CComCoClass<>
// does nothing.
static LPCTSTR WINAPI GetObjectDescription()
{
    return NULL;
}
```

GetObjectDescription() is a method that you will not need to worry about 99.9% of the time, allowing you to leverage the default implementation. Recall that when ATL is asked to register your objects, every coclass listed in the OBJECT_MAP will have its UpdateRegistry() method called. The point here is that _every_ coclass in the map will be registered.

If you wish to selectively register (or unregister) a subset of objects in your server, you need to create an object supporting the IComponentRegistrar interface (which is one possible choice from the ATL Object Wizard). This standard COM interface gives you the ability to selectively choose which coclasses should be registered.

If you obtain a pointer to an object implementing the IComponentRegistrar interface, you may call GetComponents(), which is used to call the GetObjectDescription() method defined in your coclass. If you want to go in this direction, you will need to provide a non-NULL return value for GetObjectDescription() using the DECLARE_OB-JECT_DESCRIPTION macro:

```
// CoHexagon is now providing its own description string.
class ATL_NO_VTABLE CCoHexagon :
...
{
...
    DECLARE_OBJECT_DESCRIPTION("The very independent CoHexagon")
...
};
```

As I am sure you guessed, the string parameter to this macro becomes the physical return value of GetObjectDescription():

```
// Allows your coclass to provide an object description string.
#define DECLARE_OBJECT_DESCRIPTION(x)\
static LPCTSTR WINAPI GetObjectDescription()\
{\
    return _T(x);\
}
```

So when is GetObjectDescription() called? When iterating over your _ATL_OBJMAP_ENTRY array, if a non-NULL return value is obtained from GetObjectDescription(), your coclass will <u>not</u> be registered by ATL, as it assumes a Component Registrar Object will be doing so on a more selective basis:

```
// Your class's GetObjectDescription() method is checked during the registration
// and unregistration of your server.
ATLINLINE ATLAPI AtlModuleRegisterServer(_ATL_MODULE* pM, BOOL bRegTypeLib,
                                         const CLSID* pCLSID)
{
...
    _ATL_OBJMAP_ENTRY* pEntry = pM->m_pObjMap;
    for (;pEntry->pclsid != NULL; pEntry = _NextObjectMapEntry(pM, pEntry))
    {
        if (pCLSID == NULL)
        {
            if (pEntry->pfnGetObjectDescription != NULL &&
                pEntry->pfnGetObjectDescription() != NULL)
                    continue;
        }
    ...
    }
...
}
```

Therefore what you are stating when you add the DECLARE_OBJECT_DESCRIPTION macro in your coclass is "Don't bother to register me. I'm taken care of." As mentioned, this is not a method you will need to worry about overwriting, but now you know how you can.

Understanding COM Categories

Before we can understand how ATL provides a pointer to your class's GetCategoryMap()
function, we need to understand COM categories. As you are well aware, a COM object
may support any number of interfaces, with each interface expressing a singular functionality. IDraw expresses the ability to be rendered, IShapeEdit expresses the ability to edit
an existing shape, and so on.

Now, what if you created a set of coclasses {CoHexagon, CoPoint, CoCone} all supporting the same set of interfaces. If each of these coclasses could belong to a named
group, a client could then work with any member of the set with the foreknowledge of how
they behave. This would be very helpful from a client's point of view if any member of this
set would do for the task at hand (e.g., "I just want to work with anything that can draw
something!") As well, if a client is able to understand what using a member of this set
requires, the client has an easy way to determine if it should bother to create the object
at all.

A coclass may specify a category to which it belongs. For example, we (as the object
developer) may decide that any object supporting the interface set {IDraw, IShapeEdit,
IErase, IShapeID} belongs to the category "Drawable." Once the category is defined (and
as long as we have a client that understands the implications of using objects belonging to
the Drawable category) we provide a way for the client to make an assumption about the
objects in the Drawable category: Drawable objects support four well-known drawing
related interfaces and can thus be treated the same way.

A coclass may specify the categories it belongs to during the registration process by
adding the correct settings under its HKCR\CLSID entry. Category information is logged
into the system registry under HKCR\Component Categories, which contains all registered categories on a given machine:

Figure 9-2:
The registry
holds all
component
categories in a
unique subkey.

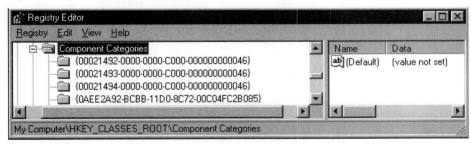

A COM category is identified by a GUID, termed a *CATID* (*category ID*). As you may
expect, there are a number of predefined categories (and corresponding CATIDs) that a
coclass may gain membership to. Many of these predefined CATIDs are defined in
<comcat.h>:

```
// Some predefined defined Category IDs.
EXTERN_C const CATID          CATID_Insertable;
EXTERN_C const CATID          CATID_Control;
EXTERN_C const CATID          CATID_Programmable;
EXTERN_C const CATID          CATID_IsShortcut;
EXTERN_C const CATID          CATID_NeverShowExt;
EXTERN_C const CATID          CATID_DocObject;
EXTERN_C const CATID          CATID_Printable;
```

```
EXTERN_C const CATID        CATID_RequiresDataPathHost;
EXTERN_C const CATID        CATID_PersistsToMoniker;
EXTERN_C const CATID        CATID_PersistsToStorage;
EXTERN_C const CATID        CATID_PersistsToStreamInit;
EXTERN_C const CATID        CATID_PersistsToStream;
EXTERN_C const CATID        CATID_PersistsToMemory;
EXTERN_C const CATID        CATID_PersistsToFile;
EXTERN_C const CATID        CATID_PersistsToPropertyBag;
EXTERN_C const CATID        CATID_InternetAware;
```

Viewing Registered Component Categories

The OLE/COM Object Viewer lists all Component Categories on your machine under the Grouped by Component Category node. When you expand a subnode, you will see the list of all coclasses supporting a given category:

Figure 9-3:
Registered COM
categories.

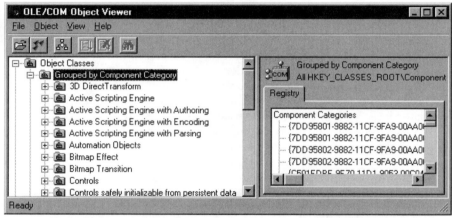

To learn exactly which CATIDs constitute a given COM category, select a subnode and examine the right-hand pane of the OLE/COM Object Viewer. As an example, here is the "safely scriptable" category:

Figure 9-4:
The safe for
scripting COM
category.

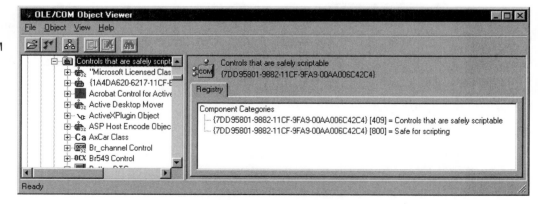

Categories of COM Categories

At the risk of sounding redundant, COM defines two categories of COM categories. If an object is a member of a category that assumes a client <u>must</u> be able to work with each interface expressed by the category, we say the coclass supports a "required category." For example, ActiveX controls typically support the "Control" category, which informs a client it should be able to work with all interfaces necessary for an ActiveX control, and can therefore be rendered, persisted, and so forth. On the other hand, if a coclass supports a category which does <u>not</u> require the client to work with the collection of interfaces expressing the category, we say the coclass defines an "implemented category." Implemented categories are more of a "heads-up" for the client.

An object choosing to belong to a given category needs to specify the full set of implemented or required categories, under HKCR\CLSID. For example, here is the Implemented Categories subkey for the Microsoft StatusBar Control:

Figure 9-5:
A given coclass lists the categories to which it belongs.

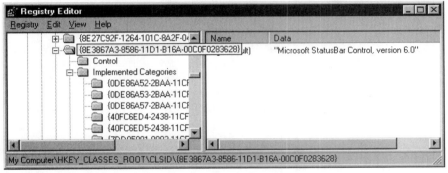

Assigning an ATL Coclass to a COM Category

So how can we use ATL to specify COM categories for a coclass? ATL defines a *category map* used to hold the set of all COM categories supported by a coclass. This map expands to provide the GetCategoryMap() method. Recall the pfnGetCategoryMap field of _ATL_OBJMAP_ENTRY is set to this method:

```
// pfnGetCategoryMap points to your class's GetCategoryMap() method.
#define OBJECT_ENTRY(clsid, class) {
...
class::GetCategoryMap, \                          // [pfnGetCategoryMap]
...
```

CComCoClass< > defines a default implementation of GetCategoryMap(), which simply returns NULL, signifying that your coclass has no COM categories to be registered:

```
// CComCoClass<> defines a default GetCategoryMap() method for your coclasses.
//
static const struct _ATL_CATMAP_ENTRY* GetCategoryMap()
{
    return NULL;
}
```

When you wish your coclass to supply a set of COM categories, you will need to override this default behavior and specify your own category map (and therefore your own

GetCategoryMap() implementation). There is no ATL wizard for this process, but doing so is quite simple.

Defining a Custom Category Map

A custom category map is established using the BEGIN_CATEGORY_MAP and END_CATEGORY_MAP macros. These macros expand to define an array of _ATL_CATMAP_ENTRY structures as well as the GetCategoryMap() method which returns this array:

```
// Declare an array of _ATL_CATMAP_ENTRY structures named 'pMap'
// and also define the GetCategoryMap() function to return an array of these
// structures.
#define BEGIN_CATEGORY_MAP(x)\
  static const struct _ATL_CATMAP_ENTRY* GetCategoryMap() {\
  static const struct _ATL_CATMAP_ENTRY pMap[] = {
// Terminate the array.
#define END_CATEGORY_MAP()\
  { _ATL_CATMAP_ENTRY_END, NULL } };\
  return( pMap ); }
```

Next, you must generate a GUID for your new CATID. It will behoove you to add a new header file to your project (wrapped in #ifndef/#endif logic) to hold all your CATIDs. In this way, you may include this file into each class making reference to the underlying GUIDs. Using guidgen.exe, choose the static const GUID option and substitute the <<name>> marker with your new CATID. By convention, all category IDs begin with the CATID_ prefix:

```
// A custom GUID for CATID_DRAWABLE
// {2134FA20-1B04-11d3-B8F4-0020781238D4}
static const GUID CATID_DRAWABLE =
{ 0x2134fa20, 0x1b04, 0x11d3, { 0xb8, 0xf4, 0x0, 0x20, 0x78, 0x12, 0x38, 0xd4 } };
```

Next, in your coclass's header file, define a category map with the corresponding category map macros. Populate this map using the IMPLEMENTED_CATEGORY and REQUIRED_CATEGORY macros. These macros make use of an ATL-provided flag marking the type of category:

```
// The macros used to fill your category map.
#define IMPLEMENTED_CATEGORY( catid ) \
{ _ATL_CATMAP_ENTRY_IMPLEMENTED, &catid },
#define REQUIRED_CATEGORY( catid ) \
{ _ATL_CATMAP_ENTRY_REQUIRED, &catid },
```

Here is our good friend CoHexagon, now a proud member of the Drawable category:

```
// If you wish to override the default implementation of GetCategoryMap() as
// defined by CoComCoClass<>, you must add a category map by hand.
#include "catids"// Defines the CATID_DRAWABLE constant.
class ATL_NO_VTABLE CCoHexagon :
...
{
...
    // A Category Map
    BEGIN_CATEGORY_MAP(CCoHexagon)
        IMPLEMENTED_CATEGORY(CATID_DRAWABLE)
    END_CATEGORY_MAP()
```

```
...
};
```

Finally, you will need to update your RGS file to update the Component Category key under HKCR with your new CATID. Although ATL will assign the correct category entries for the coclass by using the category map, ATL will not add the necessary HKCR\Component Categories listing (thus you need to update your RGS file):

```
HKCR
{
...
    NoRemove 'Component Categories'
    {
        {2134FA20-1B04-11d3-B8F4-0020781238D4}
        {
            val 409 = s 'Drawable Objects'
        }
    }
...
}
```

Once you recompile and reregister your server, ATL will update your CoHexagon registry information to support the new CATID. As you can see, since we used the IMPLEMENTED_CATEGORY macro entry in our category map, the ATL registrar added the Implemented Category subkey listing our custom CATID:

Figure 9-6:
Result of the custom category map.

The OLE/COM Object Viewer acknowledges the Drawable category as well. Assume ATLShapesServer.dll contains three coclasses, each belonging to the Drawable category:

Figure 9-7:
The drawable objects.

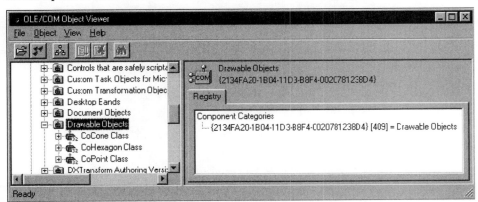

To sum up, the _ATL_OBJMAP_ENTRY's pfnGetCategoryMap field is set to your coclass's GetCategoryMap() method. CoComCoClass<> provides a default implementation that effectively returns an empty _ATL_CATMAP_ENTRY array, informing _Module that you have no categories to register.

If you wish to support COM categories, you must create a category map yourself. In this case, _Module will call your custom GetCategoryMap() method and iterate over your _ATL_CATMAP_ENTRY array during the registration process.

> **Note:** In the upcoming lab, we will also see how a COM client can obtain members of a given category at runtime using the Category Manager.

Specifying the ObjectMain() Method

The final field of the _ATL_OBJMAP_ENTRY structure, pfnObjectMain, is filled with an implementation of your class's ObjectMain() function:

```
// pfnObjectMain points to your class's ObjectMain() method.
#define OBJECT_ENTRY(clsid, class) {
...
class::ObjectMain },                      // [pfnObjectMain]
```

CComObjectRootBase provides an implementation, which you inherit by default:

```
// ObjectMain() is called during Module::Init() and Module::Term()
static void WINAPI ObjectMain(bool bStarting ) {}
```

This method will be called by the ATL framework under two conditions: When your server is loaded by the COM runtime, ATL will iterate over the object map, calling each coclass's ObjectMain() with the bStarting parameter set to true. In here, you may safely initialize your object's resources and so forth. When your server is unloaded, ObjectMain(false) will be called to allow you to deallocate any acquired resources.

If you wish to override the default behavior, simply provide an implementation in your coclass. There is not a helper macro to insert this method. It is a simple override:

```
// When an ATL server is loaded or unloaded, ObjectMain() is called for each coclass
// listed in the object map.
class ATL_NO_VTABLE CCoHexagon :
...
{
...
    static void WINAPI ObjectMain(bool starting)
    {
        if(starting)
            MessageBox(NULL, "The server is starting!",
                    "Hex ObjectMain() Says", MB_OK);
        else
            MessageBox(NULL, "The server is stopping!",
                    "Hex ObjectMain() Says", MB_OK);
    }
...
};
```

Building Server Object Models

We have now examined each field of the _ATL_OBJMAP_ENTRY structure. As you have seen, your object map is populated with the OBJECT_ENTRY macro; however, there is one additional option. Many COM servers (DLLs or EXEs) provide a relatively "flat" object model. In other words, the server provides a class factory for any number of top-level coclasses. Each of these coclasses is considered *creatable* in that they may be instantiated directly by a call to CoCreateInstance() and/or CoGetClassObject(). Assume ATLShapesServer.dll contains the following creatable coclasses (lollipops removed for clarity):

Figure 9-8:
A very flat object model.

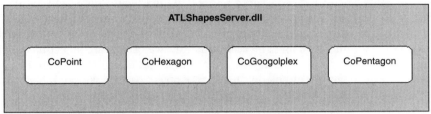

Each of these coclasses would have an entry in the server's object map:

```
// A server with four creatable objects.
BEGIN_OBJECT_MAP(ObjectMap)
    OBJECT_ENTRY(CLSID_CoHexagon, CCoHexagon)
    OBJECT_ENTRY(CLSID_CoPentagon, CCoPentagon)
    OBJECT_ENTRY(CLSID_CoPoint, CCoPoint)
    OBJECT_ENTRY(CLSID_CoGoogolplex, CCoGoogolplex)
END_OBJECT_MAP()
```

Other times, COM servers (DLLs or EXEs) may provide a more hierarchical object model within the binary home. To provide a level of depth, we may designate some objects in the hierarchy to be "topmost objects" creatable by COM library calls. Other objects in the server are not <u>directly</u> creatable by COM library calls, but must be created <u>indirectly</u> through another topmost object.

For example, assume that each topmost object in the server has an associated offscreen buffer object. If you are unfamiliar with graphics programming, an offscreen buffer is a region in memory to which you may render images, and then transfer the image (or a section of it) onto the screen. The idea here is that a client should not be able to have access to a buffer object until it has obtained a valid shape:

Figure 9-9:
A slightly deeper object model.

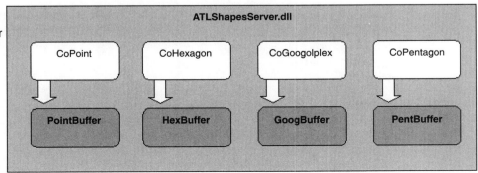

For objects that are "visible" by the client but not directly creatable, ATL provides the OBJECT_ENTRY_NON_CREATEABLE macro.

OBJECT_ENTRY_NON_CREATEABLE: Defining "Non-Creatable" Coclasses

This macro is not available using the ATL Object Wizard, and must be entered by hand if you wish to make use of it. This macro declares a "visible but not directly creatable" coclass, which can be very useful if you are creating an object hierarchy. Let's revisit the question "Why would we wish to define a coclass that is not directly creatable by a client?"

Assume CoHexagon contains a method in the [default] interface, returning an interface to a non-creatable coclass named HexBuffer. Again, the idea here is that a client should not be allowed to directly create a HexBuffer object, but must obtain an interface pointer from some drawable object. In this way, we can create object models that define a "front line" of creatable objects and a "back line" set of objects that are returned indirectly to the client. If we wish to model this sort of object design, we can modify our object map to look like the following:

```
// A server with one creatable object and one non-creatable object.
BEGIN_OBJECT_MAP(ObjectMap)
    OBJECT_ENTRY(CLSID_CoHexagon, CoHexagon)
    OBJECT_ENTRY_NON_CREATEABLE(HexBuffer)
END_OBJECT_MAP()
```

The OBJECT_ENTRY_NON_CREATEABLE macro ensures that the object is non-creatable by providing a NULL entry for the pfnGetClassObject and pfnCreateInstance fields of the _ATL_OBJMAP_ENTRY structure:

```
// This object map macro only specifies the registry, category map, and initialization
// function.
#define OBJECT_ENTRY_NON_CREATEABLE(class) \
{&CLSID_NULL, \
class::UpdateRegistry, \
NULL, NULL, NULL, 0, NULL, \
class::GetCategoryMap, \
class::ObjectMain },
```

Beyond listing HexBuffer with the OBJECT_ENTRY_NON_CREATEABLE macro, to complete the implementation of a non-creatable coclass, you should edit your IDL file to specify the [noncreatable] attribute on the coclass definition. This informs various high-level COM language mappings (such as Visual Basic) to issue a runtime error if the user attempts to create the object directly. Here is the IDL:

```
// Non-creatable coclasses should be identified as such with the [noncreatable] attribute.
// Note the spelling discrepancy! IDL says 'creatable', while ATL says 'createable'.
[
    uuid(4A01DD03-066C-11D3-B8E5-0020761438D4),
    helpstring("HexBuffer Class"),
    noncreatable
]
coclass HexBuffer
{
    [default] interface IHexBuffer;
};
```

As a final tweak, we should also add the DECLARE_NO_REGISTRY macro to the HexBuffer coclass to ensure the ProgIDs and CLSIDs are not entered into the registry. In the following lab, you will see exactly how to return a reference to a [noncreatable] object to an interested client.

Object Map Summary

So then! The BEGIN_OBJECT_MAP and END_OBJECT_MAP macros expand to define an array of _ATL_OBJMAP_ENTRY structures. We have examined (in detail) what a given entry in the object map resolves to. This structure contains a ton of relevant information regarding the creation and registration of the coclass, most in the form of pointers to functions.

We have seen how a coclass (in this case CoHexagon) or one of its base classes will provide a specific macro which expands to an implementation of these functions. The OBJECT_ENTRY and OBJECT_ENTRY_NON_CREATEABLE macros are used to pair up a specific function from an ATL coclass to the correct field of the _ATL_OBJMAP_ENTRY structure.

To wrap up this chapter, the following lab will give you a chance to extend the default ATL COM AppWizard-generated component house with a number of bells and whistles.

Lab 9-1: Heavy-Duty ATL Component Housing

The purpose of this lab is to give you a chance to try some of the new tricks introduced throughout this chapter. You will be building a small object hierarchy consisting of creatable and non-creatable objects. The topmost objects will all belong to a custom-implemented COM category.

You will also get to specify some custom registry information for each creatable object. As a final bonus, you will examine some C++ clients that make use of your custom COM category.

 The solution for this lab can be found on your CD-ROM under:
Labs\Chapter 09\ATLShapes
Labs\Chapter 09\ATLShapes\VB Client
Labs\Chapter 09\ATLShapes\CPP Client
Labs\Chapter 09\ATLShapes\MFC Client

Step One: Create the Initial Server

Create a new DLL server named **ATLShapes.dll** using the ATL COM AppWizard (all of the default settings will be fine). You will be developing two directly creatable coclasses: CoHexagon and CoLine, both supporting the IDraw and IShapeID interfaces. To begin, insert a Simple Object named **CoHexagon** using the ATL Object Wizard. Change the name of the [default] interface to **IDraw**, and be sure you select a custom interface (the remaining attributes may be left to their defaults). <u>Do not add methods to this interface just yet</u>. Go ahead and compile to get up and running.

Now insert **CoLine**. Note that the [default] interface found in the Names tab will be automatically named ICoLine. Change this to IDraw as well, and be sure that you select a custom interface from the Attributes tab. When you examine ClassView, you will see a problem: Two definitions of IDraw will be found in your IDL file (see Figure 9-10):

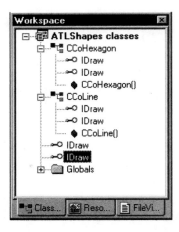

To remedy this problem, delete the IDL definition for one of the two IDraw interfaces and all associated attributes (it does not matter which one, as they are both empty at this point). Add the [oleautomation] attribute to the remaining IDraw interface. Save the IDL file and examine ClassView again; things should have cleaned up just fine.

Now, right-click on the IDL IDraw lollipop from ClassView and select the Add Method Wizard. Add a single method named **Draw**(), returning an HRESULT and taking no parameters. When you select OK, go look at ClassView again; notice how <u>both</u> CoLine and CoHexagon have been given stub code for Draw()! Cool, huh? You can use this same trick whenever your server defines a single interface supported by multiple objects. In the implementation of each coclass, simply display a message box identifying which shape is being drawn:

```
// Draw the hexagon.
STDMETHODIMP CCoHexagon::Draw()
{
    MessageBox(NULL, "I am drawing a hexagon", "IDraw::Draw",
            MB_OK | MB_SETFOREGROUND);
    return S_OK;
}
```

Now we will define the IShapeID interface. Open your IDL file and define an empty interface named **IShapeID**:

```
// This interface allows the user to give a unique ID to a given shape.
[ object, uuid(88A294F0-2127-11d3-B8F7-0020781238D4), oleautomation]
interface IShapeID : IUnknown
{
};
```

Next, add support for this interface to both coclasses in the library statement of your IDL file. Save and compile your IDL, right-click on your CoHexagon class from ClassView, and use the Implement Interface Wizard to add support for IShapeID. Do the same for CoLine.

Add a single BSTR property to IShapeID named **ShapeName**. When you click OK, notice again that both CoHexagon and CoLine have been given get_ShapeName and put_ShapeName method stub code.

Each class should maintain a private CComBSTR that will hold the name for a given shape. Set the CComBSTR member variable to an empty string in the constructor of each coclass. For each [propput], assign the incoming BSTR parameter to your private CComBSTR object. For each [propget], set the BSTR* parameter to a copy of your CComBSTR's underlying buffer. For example:

```
// Return the shape's name.
STDMETHODIMP CCoLine::get_ShapeName(BSTR *pVal)
{
    *pVal = m_name.Copy();
    return S_OK;
}
STDMETHODIMP CCoLine::put_ShapeName(BSTR newVal)
{
```

```
        m_name = newVal;
        return S_OK;
}
```

Step Two: Define a Custom COM Category

Given that CoHexagon and CoLine both support the same interfaces (and thus provide the same functionality), it would be nice to introduce a COM category for objects that support IDraw and IShapeID.

Insert a new text file into your project, saved as **catids.h**. Use guidgen.exe to create a new GUID for a COM category named CATID_NamedShape. Be sure to wrap your GUID in #ifndef, #define, #endif syntax, as both CoHexagon and CoLine will need to include this file (if you forget, you will get multiple redefinition errors):

```
#ifndef _CAT
#define _CAT
// {E5A9E920-2129-11d3-B8F7-0020781238D4}
static const GUID CATID_NamedShape =
{ 0xe5a9e920, 0x2129, 0x11d3, { 0xb8, 0xf7, 0x0, 0x20, 0x78, 0x12, 0x38, 0xd4 } };
#endif // _CAT
```

Include this file in cohexagon.h and coline.h. Now we need to override the default GetCategoryMap() method we have inherited from CComCoClass<>. Add a category map to CoHexagon which specifies a single Implemented Category using your new CATID:

```
// The Category Map (don't forget to #include catids.h)
BEGIN_CATEGORY_MAP(CCoHexagon)
    IMPLEMENTED_CATEGORY(CATID_NamedShape)
END_CATEGORY_MAP()
```

Do the same for CoLine:

```
// The Category Map
BEGIN_CATEGORY_MAP(CoLine)
    IMPLEMENTED_CATEGORY(CATID_NamedShape)
END_CATEGORY_MAP()
```

As you recall, ATL will use the category map to ensure your coclass is registered with the correct category subkeys. Therefore, if you examine the CLSID entries for each object (after a recompile) you will find an Implemented Category subkey has been inserted (thanks to the category map and ATL registration).

However, we need to edit our RGS file to specify the Component Category listing to insert under HKCR\Component Category. Open one of your RGS files (it does not matter which one) and add the following scripting code. Be sure the GUID you enter is the same as the CATID generated by guidgen.exe. Let's call our category "Named Drawing Objects." Be extra careful when adding RGS scripts. For example, be sure there are no spaces between your curly brackets and the GUID, and there are spaces between the assignment operators:

```
HKCR
{
...
    NoRemove 'Component Categories'
    {
        {E5A9E920-2129-11d3-B8F7-0020781238D4}
        {
```

```
                  val 409 = s 'Named Drawing Objects'
              }
        }
        ...
}
```

When you have recompiled, open the OLE/COM Object Viewer and expand the Grouped by Component Category node. You should see CoHexagon and CoLine strutting their stuff under the Named Drawing Objects subnode:

Figure 9-11:
The Named
Drawing Objects.

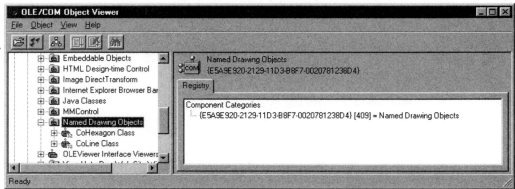

Later in this lab we will build some C++ clients that are able to discover the members of the Named Drawing Objects category at run time.

Step Three: Custom Registration

This chapter has shown you how the _ATL_OBJMAP_ENTRY structure maintains the pfnUpdateRegistry field to point to a coclass's UpdateRegistry() method. CoLine and CoHexagon automatically inherit an implementation of this method via the DECLARE_REGISTRY_RESOURCEID macro listed in each class's header file.

We are going to specialize the registration of our shape objects, so comment out the DECLARE_REGISTRY_RESOURCEID macro in each class and provide a new listing for UpdateRegistry() for both (call UpdateRegistryFromResource() to force ATL to perform the default registration duties):

```
// Put in each class's header file.
static HRESULT WINAPI UpdateRegistry(BOOL b)
{
    // Be sure your resource ID is correct for the given coclass!
    return _Module.UpdateRegistryFromResource(IDR_COLINE, b);
}
```

The task here is to add custom installation information which identifies the time the coclass was installed on a given machine. We will do this by defining a custom registry script placeholder (much like the framework provided "%MODULE%"). Add the following functionality to the UpdateRegistry() functions:

```
// We will add the time that this class was installed
// as part of our custom registration.
```

```
static HRESULT WINAPI UpdateRegistry(BOOL b)
{
    USES_CONVERSION;
    char time[50];
    SYSTEMTIME sysTime;
    GetLocalTime(&sysTime);
    // Format the time into the char array.
    sprintf(time, "Hour %.2d : Min %.2d : Second %.2d : MS %.2d",
        sysTime.wHour, sysTime.wMinute,
        sysTime.wSecond, sysTime.wMilliseconds);
    // Now we need to create a special tag to use in the RGS script.
    _ATL_REGMAP_ENTRY regMap[] =
    {
        { OLESTR("INSTALLTIME"), A2W(time)},
        {0, 0}
    };
    // Do default processing of RGS file.
    return _Module.UpdateRegistryFromResource(IDR_COLINE, b, regMap);
}
```

ATL makes it possible to extend the syntax of RGS files to serve your own needs. Notice the declaration of an _ATL_REGMAP_ENTRY array. The _ATL_REGMAP_ENTRY array is terminated by NULL entries, hence the {0, 0} entry.

This array is an optional parameter to CComModule::UpdateRegistryFromResource(), and is used to send in additional "%...%" tags above and beyond the framework defaults (such as %MODULE%).

Here, we have created a two-item array for a tag named INSTALLTIME, which maps to the current system time. We obtain this time using the Win32 GetLocalTime() function. This function takes a SYSTEMTIME structure, and will populate the fields of this structure with time and date information.

Finally, we need to edit the RGS file for each coclass in our server making use of this placeholder (i.e., every coclass that has supplied a custom UpdateRegistry() method). We get to choose where this entry will be made, and what the name of the subkey should be. Let's say that the ProgIDs for each coclass will include an extra subkey called InstallTime. Here is coline.rgs to get you started. Do the same for CoHexagon.

```
ATLShapes.CoLine.1 = s 'CoLine Class'
{
    CLSID = s '{00D7BA29-20FF-11D3-B8F7-0020781238D4}'
    InstallTime = s '%INSTALLTIME%'
}

ATLShapes.CoLine = s 'CoLine Class'
{
    CLSID = s '{00D7BA29-20FF-11D3-B8F7-0020781238D4}'
    CurVer = s 'ATLShapes.CoLine.1'
    InstallTime = s '%INSTALLTIME%'
}
```

Go ahead and recompile your project. This will automatically register your server. Use regedit.exe to hunt down the ProgIDs for each server. You should see something similar to Figure 9-12:

Figure 9-12:
Results of our
custom
UpdateRegistry()
logic.

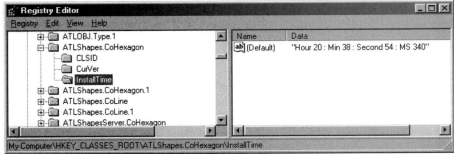

You are free to add as many registry symbols as you feel necessary to register your server. Just extend the _ATL_REGMAP_ENTRY array with *n* number of entries, and be sure you have a terminating {0, 0} entry.

If you are up for it, try to add another custom entry that identifies the name of the developer who created this object (your solution shows the necessary logic, so take a peek if you get stuck).

Step Four: Define a Non-Creatable Class

Recall that object maps may specify creatable and non-creatable objects. At first, the idea of a non-creatable object seems quite odd. However, the principle of topmost creating subclass objects is extremely common. Just look at the object model for the Data Access Objects (DAO) or Microsoft Excel (among others). Let's provide the ability for CoLine and CoHexagon to create a non-creatable sub object for a client and return the [default] interface of the new object.

Insert a new Simple Object named **COSBuffer** (Off Screen Buffer). Go ahead and use all defaults from the Name tab; however, be sure to set the Interface type to Custom. As this class is not creatable, we do not need any registry information placed in the system registry. Add the **DECLARE_NO_REGISTRY** macro in your new class's header file, and comment out the existing registration macro.

Now add a single method to the [default] IOSBuffer interface called **RenderTo-Memory**() and implement accordingly:

```
STDMETHODIMP COSBuffer::RenderToMemory()
{
    // Simulate bit blitting to memory.
    MessageBox(NULL, "I am rendering to memory", "Off Screen Buffer Says...",
            MB_OK | MB_SETFOREGROUND);
    return S_OK;
}
```

The ATL Object Wizard will always update your object map with OBJECT_ENTRY macros, which are used to identify creatable classes. Go into the object map and remove the wizard-generated entry for COSBuffer, and replace it with the correct OBJECT_ENTRY_NON_CREATEABLE macro. Your object map should now look like the following:

```
// Specifying a non-creatable object.
BEGIN_OBJECT_MAP(ObjectMap)
    OBJECT_ENTRY(CLSID_CoHexagon, CCoHexagon)
    OBJECT_ENTRY(CLSID_CoLine, CCoLine)
```

```
    OBJECT_ENTRY_NON_CREATEABLE(COSBuffer)
END_OBJECT_MAP()
```

Recall that every non-creatable class should be marked as such in the IDL code. Open up the project's IDL file, and add the [noncreatable] attribute to your coclass statement (also recall the inconsistent spelling—this is <u>not</u> a typo in the book).

```
// Recall this will force many COM language mappings to throw an error
// if the user attempts to create the object.
[ uuid(00D7BA3B-20FF-11D3-B8F7-0020781238D4),
  noncreatable, helpstring("OSBuffer Class") ]
coclass OSBuffer
{
    [default] interface IOSBuffer;
};
```

Step Five: Provide Access to the Non-Creatable Class

Non-creatable objects are eventually creatable, just not directly by the client. Other objects in the server are responsible for creating them indirectly for the client, through an interface method. Add another method to IDraw named **GetOSBuffer()** using the Add Method Wizard. Depending on the ordering of your IDL interface definitions, you may have to make a forward declaration to IOSBuffer. The IDL code will look like the following:

```
// Forward declaration (if IDraw is defined before IOSBuffer in the IDL file).
interface IOSBuffer;
[...]
interface IDraw : IUnknown
{
    HRESULT Draw();
    // Returns a reference to the non-creatable sub object.
    HRESULT GetOSBuffer([out, retval] IOSBuffer** pBuffer);
};
```

Notice that the new IDraw method returns an IOSBuffer pointer to the client. Next, we need to implement the GetOSBuffer() method for both CoLine and CoHexagon. We will be passing COSBuffer as a template parameter to CComObject<>. After that, we will call the static CreateInstance() method, and if successful, query for IID_IOSBuffer. Implement GetOSBuffer() as the following for each creatable class:

```
// Create the inner object for the client.
STDMETHODIMP CCoLine::GetOSBuffer(IOSBuffer **pBuffer)
{
    // Create a brand new COSBuffer for the client.
    HRESULT hr;
    CComObject<COSBuffer>* pBuf = NULL;
    hr = CComObject<COSBuffer>::CreateInstance(&pBuf);
    // Now ask for the [default] IOSBuffer interface.
    if(SUCCEEDED(hr))
    {
        // Technically we are using a local copy so we should
        // AddRef() and Release().
        pBuf->AddRef();
        hr = pBuf->QueryInterface(IID_IOSBuffer, (void**)pBuffer);
        pBuf->Release();
    }
```

```
        return hr;
}
```

Now, if a client has obtained a valid IDraw interface from either CoLine or CoHexagon, they may call GetOSBuffer() and manipulate the IOSBuffer interface indirectly returned by the topmost CoLine and CoHexagon coclasses.

Step Six: A Visual Basic Test Client

Open up Visual Basic and create a new Standard EXE workspace. Set a reference to your ATLShapes type library from the Project | References menu. Now, create a simple GUI to create CoLines and CoHexagons. Also provide a way to set a name for each shape. Here is an initial GUI (we are not trying to win any user interface awards here):

Figure 9-13:
Yet another VB
test client.

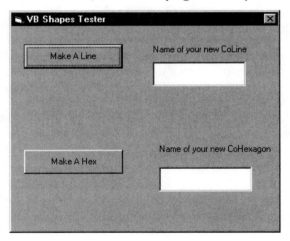

Add some private variables to your [General][Declarations] section to hold CoLine, CoHexagon, and IShapeID variables. When the user clicks on the Make *X* buttons, set the correct variable to a new instance and assign the name of the shape. For example:

```
' [General] [Declarations]
'
Private mHex As CoHexagon
Private mLine As CoLine
Private osb As OSBuffer              ' Next step...see below.
Private itfID As IShapeID
Private Sub btnGetHex_Click()        ' Create and name a hexagon.
    Set mHex = New CoHexagon
    mHex.Draw
    Set itfID = mLine
    itfID.ShapeName = txtHex.Text
    MsgBox itfID.ShapeName
End Sub
```

Now extend your GUI to include a way to access the OSBuffer object for a given shape (assume we have added two buttons to the main Form object). The code behind each Get *X*'s Buffer button will call the GetOSBuffer() method of the [default] shape interface (IDraw). Because we marked the IOSBuffer parameter as [out, retval], we can "receive" this interface pointer as a physical return value. Here is the VB code behind btnGetHexOSB:

```
' Call IDraw::GetOSBuffer and cache the IOSBuffer interface in the
' osb variable.
'
Private Sub btnGetHexOSB_Click()
    Set osb = mHex.GetOSBuffer
    osb.RenderToMemory
    Set osb = Nothing
    ''''''''''''''''' Dim WontWork as New OSBuffer
End Sub
```

To test the non-creatable nature of the OSBuffer object, uncomment the line of code above. That wraps up the VB test client.

Step Seven: Dynamically Obtain COM Categories

The final part of this lab will allow you to create some C++ clients that dynamically discover the ProgIDs of the objects belonging to your custom COM category. Begin by creating a new Win32 Console Application. For this step of the lab, you will need to copy over the correct MIDL-generated files (*_i.c and *.h) as well as the server's catids.h file.

When a COM client wishes to discover objects belonging to a COM category, the first step is to create an instance of a standard system-level COM object named the "component categories manager" that has the preassigned CLSID of CLSID_StdComponentCategoriesMgr. This object supports a standard COM interface named ICatInformation. With this interface, we can make requests of the manager, such as "look up all objects belonging to the Named Drawing Object category."

Begin by including <comcat.h>, and create an instance of the manager object.

The ICatInformation interface supplies the EnumClassesOfCategories() method, which allows you to obtain a standard COM enumerator interface, IEnumCLSID. From this interface, you may call Next() to fetch a batch of CLSIDs representing the objects belonging to some COM category. We will examine COM enumerators in gory detail in Chapter 11, so let's hold the details until then. Here is a main() function which requests the next 20 CLSIDs. Of course we only have two items belonging to this custom category, so we can test how many we <u>successfully</u> obtained using the final DWORD parameter of the Next() method:

```
// This C++ client is able to discover who is a Named Drawing Object.
int main(int argc, char* argv[])
{
    CoInitialize(NULL);
    ICatInformation *pCatInfo = NULL;
    HRESULT hr;
    // Create the categories manager.
    hr = CoCreateInstance(CLSID_StdComponentCategoriesMgr, 0,
        CLSCTX_SERVER, IID_ICatInformation, (void**)&pCatInfo);
    if(SUCCEEDED(hr))
    {
        IEnumCLSID *pCLSIDS = NULL;
        CATID catids[1];
        catids[0] = CATID_NamedShape;
        // I am looking for CATID_NamedShape...
```

```
        hr = pCatInfo->EnumClassesOfCategories(1, catids, -1, 0, &pCLSIDS);
        CLSID clsid[20];
        LPOLESTR progID;
        cout << "Here are the proud members of " << endl
             << "the Named Drawing Objects category" << endl << endl;
        do
        {       // Ask for the next 20 CLSIDs.
                DWORD numb = 0;
                hr = pCLSIDS->Next(20, clsid, &numb);
                if(SUCCEEDED(hr))
                {
                        // How many did I really get?
                        for(DWORD i = 0; i < numb; i++)
                        {
                                ProgIDFromCLSID(clsid[i], &progID);
                                char buff[30];
                                WideCharToMultiByte(CP_ACP, NULL, progID,
                                -1, buff, 30, NULL, NULL);
                                cout << buff << endl;
                        }
                }
        }while(hr == S_OK);
        pCLSIDS->Release();
    }
    pCatInfo->Release();
    CoUninitialize();
    return 0;
}
```

When you execute the code, you will see CoLine and CoHexagon have been identified as members of the Named Drawing Objects category:

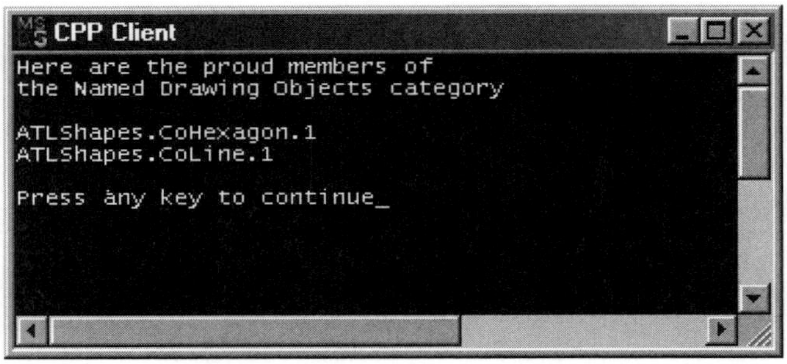

Figure 9-14: Interacting with the COM category manager.

Now, imagine if you were to create an MFC application that used similar code to place the ProgIDs of the Named Drawing Objects into a list box. You could allow the user to select a given shape, which you create dynamically based on the ProgID. This sort of functionality is the same as we see in VB when we pull up the Components dialog box to insert a new ActiveX control. This tool lists all objects belonging to the Control category, and creates the user-specified item.

Assume you have created a dialog-based MFC application using the MFC AppWizard. We could create a very simple GUI which contains a single list box to hold the ProgIDs of each member of the Named Drawing Objects category. We could allow the end user to select an item from this list to create an instance, as suggested by Figure 9-15:

Figure 9-15:
The Named
Drawing Objects
launcher utility.

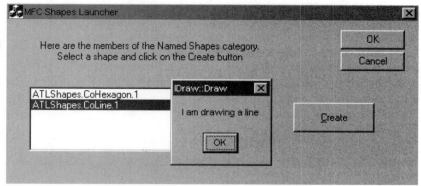

To load up all members of the CATID_NamedShape category, we could add the following code to OnInitDialog(). This is essentially the same code as we have seen in the Win32 Console client; however, we are now placing the ProgIDs into the list box, rather than the IO stream. Here are the relevant changes:

```
// After creating the category manager, place each ProgID into a list box.
do
{
    DWORD numb = 0;
    hr = pCLSIDS->Next(20, clsid, &numb);
    if(SUCCEEDED(hr))
    {
        for(DWORD i = 0; i < numb; i++)
        {
            ProgIDFromCLSID(clsid[i], &progID);
            char buff[30];
            WideCharToMultiByte(CP_ACP, NULL, progID, -1, buff,
                                30, NULL, NULL);
            // Add to the list box named IDC_SHAPELIST.
            CListBox *pList = (CListBox*)GetDlgItem(IDC_SHAPELIST);
            pList->AddString(buff);
        }
    }
}while(hr == S_OK);
```

The code behind the BN_CLICKED event handler is straight COM. Obtain the ProgID from the list box (based on the current selection) and call CoCreateInstance():

```
// Activate the correct object, based on the selection in the list box.
void CMFCClientDlg::OnMakeShape()
{
    // Figure out which item they clicked on.
    char progID[80];
    CListBox *pList = (CListBox*)GetDlgItem(IDC_SHAPELIST);
    pList->GetText(pList->GetCurSel(), progID);
    // Now make that object.
    CLSID clsid;
    wchar_t wide[80];
    mbstowcs(wide, progID, 80);
    CLSIDFromProgID(wide, &clsid);
    IDraw* pDraw = NULL;
```

```
if(SUCCEEDED(CoCreateInstance(clsid, NULL, CLSCTX_ALL, IID_IDraw,
        (void**)&pDraw)))
{
    pDraw->Draw();
    pDraw->Release();
}
else
    AfxMessageBox("Can't draw...Bad ProgID!");
}
```

If you would like to see the complete MFC test client, check out your CD-ROM. Better yet, create one of your own!

Chapter Summary

This chapter has taken you deep inside the support ATL offers for component housing. We began by reviewing the CComModule class. CComModule wraps up many details behind DLL and EXE COM servers. We then learned quite a bit about the ATL object map. We have seen that the object map is nothing more than an array of ATL_OBJMAP_ENTRY structures.

This structure has a number of fields, which point to coclass-specific functions. The information contained in an _ATL_OBJMAP_ENTRY structure centers around registration and creation details, as well as more advanced COM services such as component categories. Your server's object map may specify creatable (OBJECT_ENTRY) and non-creatable (OBJECT_ENTRY_NON_CREATEABLE) coclasses.

You have also seen how the fields of an _ATL_OBJMAP_ENTRY structure are always given a default implementation, and more often than not, these defaults give you the support you need. If you wish to override this behavior, ATL allows you to insert any number of macros and/or function prototypes in your coclass's header file.

Part 4

COM Patterns

Chapter 10

Scriptable Objects and ATL

Objectives:

- Come to understand the IDispatch interface and late binding.
- Learn how to implement a dispinterface with (and without) type information.
- Learn to create a dual interface, and why you might want to do so.
- Work with automation SAFEARRAYs.
- Access COM objects from MS Internet Explorer using VBScript.
- Understand ATL's support for IDispatch.

The vTable COM interface is a wonderful thing. As you have already seen, the popular languages of our time (VB, Java, C++) all have the ability to work with your COM objects and access their functionality using custom vTable interfaces. This was not always the case, however. Historically speaking, VB was unable to work with custom vTable interfaces, and the only way in which your object's functionality could be used was through a standard COM interface named IDispatch.

These days, the only COM-aware languages that must work with an object using IDispatch are scripting environments such as VBScript and JScript. In this light, we may call a COM object supporting IDispatch a *scriptable object*, although historically speaking IDispatch-based objects are termed *automation objects*. This chapter examines how to create scriptable COM objects and a number of late bound clients.

Smart Clients and the vTable Interface

Over the course of nine chapters, you have come to understand that the core element of COM is the interface. Each interface we have been building up to this point has been a vTable interface, which is expressed by the ATL Object Wizard as a "custom" interface. When creating COM objects that support custom vTable interfaces, the assumption is made that the clients using our coclasses have some manner in which to "include" our coclass-specific information. For example, a C++ client will typically make use of the preprocessor to include the following MIDL-generated files:

- **yourServer_i.c:** Contains the GUIDs defined in the IDL file. Allows clients to program against the associated constants (e.g., IID_IDraw, CLSID_CoDot, and so forth) to create your coclass and ask for various custom interfaces.

- **yourServer.h:** Contains the C and C++ interface definitions, allowing clients to declare interface variables for storage (e.g., IDraw*, IEngine*, IAmDrowning-InMacros*).

Using these files, C and C++ clients can compile the necessary externals into their own binary image and achieve what is known as *early (vTable) binding. Binding* is a term used to describe at what point the COM client "understands" the functionality of the COM objects it is using. As these MIDL-generated files are compiled directly into the C++ client binary image, we have "bound early" to the object.

An important corollary to early binding is that any syntactical errors in your client-side code can be resolved at compile time. If you have made a reference to some GUID not defined in the MIDL-generated files you are referencing, the compiler will let you know loud and clear that something is wrong. More likely than not, this is due to a simple typo (e.g., IDD_FooBar rather than IID_FooBar) in the client-side code.

The Visual Basic language also allows clients to work with early binding to access custom vTable interfaces using the MIDL-generated type library (the *.tlb file). As you have seen, by setting a reference to the server's type library, a VB client is able to also "understand" GUID and interface variables at compile time. You have also seen that the Visual Basic language is sophisticated enough to allow the VB developer to query for additional vTable interfaces beyond the [default] interface using the "Set =" syntax (as we first saw in Chapter 4). The type library is used for the same purpose in the Java/COM language mapping (COM wrappers) as well as the intrinsic Visual C++ COM support (remember the #import statement?).

Thus, Java, VB, and C++ clients can all "bind early" by making use of various MIDL-generated files. If our world was only composed of "vTable-able" languages, we would be able to end the discussion of binding right here. However, as you may have noticed, we have yet to use any of our COM objects from a web-enabled client. Here is a question: Could we use any of our CoCar projects from within an HTML page and VBScript? To answer this question, may I introduce "vTable-challenged" clients (lovingly referred to as *dumb* clients).

Dumb Clients: Life as a vTable-Challenged Language

Some COM-aware languages, such as VBScript, are not so lucky to have an upfront understanding of the objects they are using. Meaning, some COM-aware language mappings are not enlightened enough to allow direct access to custom vTable interfaces. Instead, the vTable-challenged client makes a shot in the dark when activating an object, hoping that "some object called X" has "some function called Y" which takes "some number of parameters of some type." This sort of object instancing is termed *late binding*, as it is at run time (not compile time) that the client understands the object it is attempting to use. Now, every language that is able to exercise early binding is also able to exercise late binding. As an example of late binding, here is a Visual Basic client calling into the Microsoft Excel EXE server, accessing the Application object and calling the CheckSpelling() method <u>without</u> setting a reference to a type library:

```
' This VB client has no type library reference selected.
' Rule: Object variable + CreateObject() = Late Binding (ergo IDispatch)
'
Private Sub btnLateBound_Click()
      Dim o As Object                              ' Holds IDispatch*
      ' I think there is an object called Application in a server called Excel.
      Set o = CreateObject("Excel.Application")    ' Query for IDispatch interface.
      Dim b As Boolean
      ' I think the method is called CheckSpelling() and I think it takes a String.
      b = o.CheckSpelling("Is COM Love?")
      If b Then
            MsgBox "It's in there!"
      Else
            MsgBox "Not a word..."
      End If
End Sub
```

Although you are aware VB can access your custom vTable interfaces, historically speaking VB was unable to obtain custom interfaces. In order to allow VB to get into the COM game, a very special standard interface was introduced named IDispatch. When a COM object exposes properties and methods via IDispatch, the dumb client is able to access the object's exposed functionality even if it is unable to work with custom interfaces. The intrinsic VB Object variable is used to hold the IDispatch interface which is retrieved with a call to the CreateObject() function. Note that we send in the ProgID of the coclass we are interested in, and allow the COM runtime to look up the correct CLSID from the system registry. Using the standard IDispatch interface, a client may exercise late binding. Contrast this idea to traditional vTable interfaces, in which a client obtains an initial interface (often IUnknown) and then widens the connection to that object using numerous calls to QueryInterface().

Again, late binding between a client and COM object happens at run time. It is at this point that the client is able to figure out if the object indeed exists, if the methods and properties exposed by the object's IDispatch implementation exist, and if the set of parameters (if any) sent into the method or property are of the correct type. As all this information is resolved as the client is executing, you might imagine that late binding is slower than early binding. You're right. Typically, late binding will be slower. As we will see in this chapter, when a COM client accesses an object via IDispatch, two invocations must be made to trigger the method request (there are ways to streamline this process however).

So Then, Who Needs IDispatch?

So, if early binding is faster (fewer round trips) and more type safe, and if Visual Basic, C++, and Java are able to work with early binding and custom vTable interfaces, why do we need to understand IDispatch in this day and age? In the current state of COM, any web-based client (such as Microsoft Internet Explorer) is unable to access a COM object's functionality in any other way but through IDispatch. This means if you are creating a web-based solution using VBScript or JScript, you cannot work with any objects created in this book thus far, as they do not support the IDispatch interface. Scripting languages are not compiled into binary executables, cannot access type information, and have no preprocessor! Therefore they have no way to access any of the MIDL-generated files. Rather,

VBScript and JScript code is embedded into the HTML file and interpreted on the fly at run time. Therefore your COM objects <u>must</u> support the IDispatch interface if you wish scripting clients to make use of them. Here is some VBScript code embedded within an HTML file that accesses the Excel spell checker using late binding:

```
' This block of scripting code dynamically activates the Application object of Excel.
'
<SCRIPT language = VBScript>
    dim o
    set o = CreateObject("Excel.Application")
    b = o.CheckSpelling("Is IDispatch Love?")
    If b Then
        MsgBox "It is in there!"
    Else
        MsgBox "Not a word..."
    End If
</SCRIPT>
```

The VBScript code above makes no use whatsoever of any custom interface. Using the CreateObject() method, the scripting engine loads up Excel and extracts the IDispatch interface from the Application object.

Sadly, there may be times when you as a C++ or VB developer are forced to access a COM object's functionality using IDispatch. Imagine you have a legacy COM server that was pre-engineered to only expose its functionality via IDispatch. This is not as uncommon as you may think. The typical ActiveX control exposes all of its custom functionality using IDispatch. Older versions of Microsoft Office expose their object model only using IDispatch. Thus, even though your client's language may support both early and late binding to a COM object, you might be forced to work with the IDispatch interface as the server does not supply custom vTable interfaces. As you will soon see, working with IDispatch can be a non-trivial endeavor in raw C++.

On the upside, most C++ frameworks provide some convenient wrapper classes which make working with the IDispatch interface much more palatable. MFC provides the COleDispatchDriver class, which will lovingly encapsulate you from low-level IDispatch calls <u>if</u> you have access to the server's type information. Nevertheless we will take the time to see how we can create servers that implement IDispatch, and how various clients may make used of this standard interface "in the raw."

The IDispatch Interface

The key to late binding is through the standard IDispatch interface. IDispatch is formally defined in IDL within <oaidl.idl> as the following:

```
// This standard COM interface is used for dynamic binding to a coclass.
[ object, uuid(00020400-0000-0000-C000-000000000046), pointer_default(unique) ]
interface IDispatch : IUnknown
{
    // Allows a client to see if the object can provide a type library.
    HRESULT GetTypeInfoCount( [out] UINT * pctinfo );
    // Get the type library.
    HRESULT GetTypeInfo(
```

```
        [in] UINT iTInfo,
        [in] LCID lcid,
        [out] ITypeInfo ** ppTInfo );
// Find the numerical ID of some method or property in the object.
HRESULT GetIDsOfNames(
        [in] REFIID riid,
        [in, size_is(cNames)] LPOLESTR * rgszNames,
        [in] UINT cNames,
        [in] LCID lcid,
        [out, size_is(cNames)] DISPID * rgDispId );
// Call that method or property!
HRESULT Invoke(
        [in] DISPID dispIdMember,
        [in] REFIID riid,
        [in] LCID lcid,
        [in] WORD wFlags,
        [in, out] DISPPARAMS * pDispParams,
        [out] VARIANT * pVarResult,
        [out] EXCEPINFO * pExcepInfo,
        [out] UINT * puArgErr );
};
```

As you can see, IDispatch derives from IUnknown like any COM compliant interface must do. Beyond the three inherited methods of IUnknown, IDispatch defines exactly four functions, and therefore a coclass implementing IDispatch must flesh out seven methods. The beauty of IDispatch is in its flexibility. Once a late bound client obtains a pointer to the object's IDispatch interface, it is possible for that client to invoke <u>any</u> property or <u>any</u> method exposed via IDispatch with <u>any</u> number of parameters of <u>any</u> type. This is no small feat. This proposition becomes even more interesting as you discover that a late bound client can perform this magic using exactly two of the four methods of IDispatch: GetIDsOfNames() and Invoke().

Accessing a coclass using IDispatch does come with some restrictions. First and foremost, each and every method parameter and property defined in your implementation of IDispatch must be variant compliant. If you recall from Chapter 4, I mentioned that IDL conceptually provides two sets of data types: the set C and C++ developers love, and a subset of these types that every COM language mapping can agree on. Keep in mind that the variant compliant set of data types has its roots in the Visual Basic Variant data type, and therefore your IDispatch implementations cannot have C++ centric data types as parameters.

As well, realize that when an object supports late binding, you should make use of the universal marshaler (a.k.a. type library marshaling), which was detailed in Chapter 5. This may not be a bad thing in most developer's minds, as this ensures out-of-process access to our COM interfaces without any additional work on our part.

The Methods of IDispatch

The following table shows a breakdown of each method of IDispatch:

Method of IDispatch	Meaning in Life
GetTypeInfoCount()	This method is used by clients wishing to know if the object's functionality is described in an associated type library. This method fills the [out] parameter to zero (0) if the object does not support type information or one (1) if it does.
GetTypeInfo()	Allows a client to access a component's type library programmatically. Typically this is done if the client needs to discover at run time the number of, and types of, parameters to send into a function.
GetIDsOfNames()	This method is a major player in late binding. A client calls this method to retrieve a numerical cookie (termed a DISPID) that identifies the number of the method or property it is attempting to call.
Invoke()	The real workhorse of IDispatch. This is the method that invokes the property or method on behalf of the client, based on the numerical cookie obtained from GetIDsOfNames().

One question that might cross your mind at this point is, how can a single interface allow a client to access any number of methods and properties contained in the coclass using only two methods? You know that once an interface is published, you cannot directly append items to the existing layout, or you will break polymorphism and crash clients (as detailed in Chapter 2). Objects implementing IDispatch do not append their own custom methods directly to the IDispatch interface, nor do they derive a new custom interface from IDispatch to expose additional functionality. Instead, each coclass implementing IDispatch maintains a dispinterface.

The Dispinterface and DISPIDs

A *dispinterface* is the term for a specific implementation of IDispatch by a given coclass. As a coclass exposes functionality using a single interface, it must identify each property and method with a numerical cookie called a *DISPID* (dispatch identifier). A DISPID is <u>not</u> a GUID, but a simple numerical index that specifies a given member of the dispinterface. The DISPID data type is defined in <oaidl.idl> as a LONG:

```
// DISPIDs are not GUIDs.
typedef LONG DISPID;
```

To obtain the associated DISPID for some property or method, the late bound client will send in the text name of the method or property it is hoping the object supports, by calling GetIDsOfNames(). Using this method, a late bound client is able to obtain the numerical value of a given property or method in the dispinterface. GetIDsOfNames() takes a total of five parameters:

```
// Breaking down GetIDsOfNames().
HRESULT GetIDsOfNames(
    [in] REFIID riid,            // Reserved, and will always be IID_NULL.
    [in] LPOLESTR * rgszNames,   // Text name of method/property.
    [in] UINT cNames,            // Number of names.
    [in] LCID lcid,              // The language ID.
    [out] DISPID * rgDispId );   // Place to hold the DISPIDs.
```

The first parameter is reserved for (possible) future use, and will always be IID_NULL. The second and third parameters represent the string name and the number of names requested.

Note: If a client calls GetIDsOfNames() with more than one name, the first name (rgszNames[0]) corresponds to the member name. Any additional names (e.g., rgszNames[1], (rgszNames[2])) correspond to the parameters for the method or property.

The fourth parameter is the locale requested (for example, U.S. English). The final parameter is a place to store the numerical value of the method or property (a.k.a. the DISPID). Here is a C++ client obtaining a pointer to an object's IDispatch interface, and calling GetIDsOfNames() to see if it supports a method named DrawASquiggle():

```
// Create an object using late binding, obtain an IDispatch pointer,
// and see if the object supports a method named 'DrawASquiggle'
int main(int argc, char* argv[])
{
    ...
    IDispatch* pDisp = NULL;
    CLSID clsid;
    DISPID dispid;
    // Obtain the CLSID (as we have no *_i.c file).
    CLSIDFromProgID(L"RawDisp.CoSquiggle", &clsid);
    // Create the CoSquiggle.
    CoCreateInstance(clsid, NULL, CLSCTX_SERVER, IID_IDispatch,
                    (void**)&pDisp);
    // See if the object supports a method named 'DrawASquiggle'
    LPOLESTR str = OLESTR("DrawASquiggle");
    pDisp->GetIDsOfNames(IID_NULL, &str, 1, GetUserDefaultLCID(), &dispid);
    ...
}
```

Note that the client-side code above obtains the language ID using the COM library function GetUserDefaultLCID(). The LOCALE_SYSTEM_DEFAULT constant can be used as well, to specify we are asking for the language ID used on the target machine (English, Latvian, Arabic, or whatnot). The scriptable objects we will be developing will all ignore the LCID parameter; however if you are interested in creating internationally aware COM objects, check out MSDN.

Once the client knows the DISPID that identifies the property or method, a call to Invoke() may be made to actually trigger the item in the dispinterface. As you may guess, one of the parameters to Invoke() is the DISPID. Here is a breakdown of each parameter of the Invoke() method:

```
// Breaking down the Invoke() method.
HRESULT Invoke(
[in] DISPID dispIdMember,          // DISPID of method or property.
[in] REFIID riid,                  // Reserved (also IID_NULL)
[in] LCID lcid,                    // Local ID (again).
[in] WORD wFlags,                  // Flag used to specify a property or method.
[in, out] DISPPARAMS * pDispParams, // An array of parameters for the method.
[out] VARIANT * pVarResult,        // A place to store the logical return value.
```

```
[out] EXCEPINFO * pExcepInfo,        // Error information (if any).
[out] UINT * puArgErr );             // Error information index (if any).
```

As you recall, a dispinterface can contain properties and/or methods. The value of the WORD parameter (wFlags) will specify if the client wishes to invoke a method (DISPATCH_METHOD), a "put" version of a property (DISPATCH_PROPERTYPUT), or a "get" version of the property (DISPATCH_PROPERTYGET). Recall that an interface property is identified by two methods in the object and marked in IDL with the [propput] or [propget] attributes. Using this flag, Invoke() can call the correct "get_" or "put_" method in the coclass.

The DISPPARAMS structure is an array of VARIANT compatible data types, which will contain the parameters for the invoked method (we will see the details of this structure in a moment). Finally, beyond the final two parameters (which are used for automation error handling) we have an [out] parameter of type VARIANT*. This will be used to hold the logical return value of the method (if any). To illustrate, here is our C++ client now calling the DrawASquiggle() method (using the obtained DISPID), which for the sake of simplicity takes no parameters and returns nothing:

```
// Call DrawASquiggle using IDispatch
int main(int argc, char* argv[])
{
    ...
    pDisp->GetIDsOfNames(IID_NULL, &str,1,
                    LOCALE_SYSTEM_DEFAULT, &dispid);
    // Package parameters and Invoke function number 'dispid'
    DISPPARAMS params = {0, 0, 0, 0};
    pDisp->Invoke(dispid, IID_NULL, LOCALE_SYSTEM_DEFAULT,
                DISPATCH_METHOD, &params, NULL, NULL, NULL);
    pDisp->Release();
    ...
}
```

Figure 10-1 illustrates a typical late bound client interaction. As you can see, activating some method in the object's dispinterface requires two round trips beyond the initial connection. As an optimization, the calling client may cache the DISPID of the method or property after the first round trip, and use it for subsequent calls to Invoke():

Figure 10-1:
Late binding
using IDispatch.

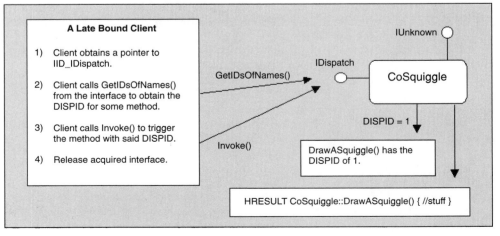

Of the four methods of IDispatch, GetIDsOfNames() and Invoke() are the members that make automation possible. GetTypeInfoCount() and GetTypeInfo() allow a client to ask the object if it supports any type information (i.e., a type library) and if so, retrieve it. The end result is the client is able to obtain an ITypeInfo interface. From this interface pointer, a client may dynamically thumb through the server's *.tlb file, and discover any documentation ([helpstrings]) held in the type information, create objects, extract IIDs, and so forth. More often than not, these methods will be of little use to you as a COM client, unless you are interested in building a type library browser utility such as the OLE/COM Object Viewer.

Approaches to Building a Raw Dispinterface in C++

Before we see how ATL is kind enough to create a complete implementation of IDispatch for you, we will begin by examining how we might create a dispinterface by hand using raw C++. Truth be told, you could implement a dispinterface using a number of possible techniques. One option is to go 100% C++ and avoid any type information. You might consider this "really late binding" as the COM client could not even open up an object browser to examine what the functionality of the coclass might be. Another option is to generate a type library for clients to examine in an object browsing utility, while still requiring all requests to funnel through your C++ implementation of IDispatch. This would give your COM client the luxury of examining the contents of your server at design time (for example, by using the VB Object Browser) while still forcing them to access your IDispatch implementation at run time.

Yet another approach is to make your type information work for you as you build the coclass. The COM library contains a set of functions that allow you to load up your type library at run time, and "peek" inside to see what the server contains. If you recall from Chapter 5, we made use of the COM library function LoadTypeLibEx() to automatically register our type information. When we develop "dual interface" objects later in this chapter, we will use a similar approach to provide an implementation of IDispatch for a coclass.

Implementing IDispatch in Raw C++

The first possible approach to take when developing a dispinterface is to do <u>everything</u> yourself. As with most programming endeavors, this gives you the biggest bang for the buck as far as flexibility is concerned, but requires much more coding. Assume you have a coclass named CoSquiggle that exposes its services exclusively through IDispatch. In other words, CoSquiggle will not derive from any custom interfaces such as IDraw, IShapeEdit, or whatnot. Clients must obtain an IDispatch pointer and call GetIDsOf-Names() and Invoke() to trigger the given method or property. The first step, then, is to create a class definition for CoSquiggle which derives from IDispatch, and prototypes the seven inherited methods (don't forget IUnknown!). Here is the header file for the CoSquiggle coclass:

```
// This coclass only supports IDispatch and thus late binding.
class CoSquiggle : public IDispatch
{
public:
    CoSquiggle();
    virtual ~CoSquiggle();
    // IUnknown methods.
    STDMETHODIMP_(DWORD)AddRef();
```

```
      STDMETHODIMP_(DWORD)Release();
      STDMETHODIMP QueryInterface(REFIID riid, void** ppv);
      // IDispatch methods.
      STDMETHODIMP GetTypeInfoCount(UINT *pctinfo);
      STDMETHODIMP GetTypeInfo(UINT iTInfo, LCID lcid,
            ITypeInfo **ppTInfo);
      STDMETHODIMP GetIDsOfNames(REFIID riid, LPOLESTR *rgszNames,
            UINT cNames, LCID lcid, DISPID *rgDispId);
      STDMETHODIMP Invoke(DISPID dispIdMember, REFIID riid, LCID lcid,
            WORD wFlags, DISPPARAMS *pDispParams, VARIANT *pVarResult,
            EXCEPINFO *pExcepInfo, UINT *puArgErr);
private:
      DWORD m_ref;
};
```

To fill out the details of CoSquiggle, we will begin with IUnknown. As an automation object is a true blue COM object, CoSquiggle will maintain a reference count, and thus AddRef() and Release() would be implemented in the standard and usual manner. QueryInterface() is also a "normal" implementation; however, this time we must be sure to return vPtrs for IID_IUnknown and IID_IDispatch exclusively:

```
// Bump the reference counter.
// (initialize m_ref to zero in the constructor of CoSquiggle)
STDMETHODIMP_(DWORD) CoSquiggle::AddRef()
{
      return ++m_ref;
}
// Standard Release() logic.
STDMETHODIMP_(DWORD)CoSquiggle::Release()
{
      --m_ref;
      if(m_ref == 0)
      {
            delete this;
            return 0;
      }
      return m_ref;
}
// A 100% dispinterface will always return two vPtrs to the COM client.
STDMETHODIMP CoSquiggle::QueryInterface(REFIID riid, void** ppv)
{
      // We do not support any custom interfaces here!
      if(riid == IID_IUnknown)
            *ppv = (IUnknown*)this;
      else if(riid == IID_IDispatch)
            *ppv = (IDispatch*)this;
      else
      {
            *ppv = NULL;
            return E_NOINTERFACE;
      }
      ((IUnknown*)(*ppv))->AddRef();
      return S_OK;
}
```

When it comes to the implementation of IDispatch::GetTypeInfoCount(), we have a no-brainer. Recall that a COM client can call this method to discover if the automation object supports an associated type library. If so, that client may make use of it at run time to examine the functionality of the server. This iteration of CoSquiggle does not support any type information, thus we can set the incoming UINT pointer to zero, informing the client we have no type information to return:

```
// GetTypeInfoCount() will set the UINT to zero if it does not support type
// information.
STDMETHODIMP CoSquiggle::GetTypeInfoCount( UINT *pctinfo)
{
    // We do not support type information in this object.
    *pctinfo = 0;
    return S_OK;
}
```

Implementing GetTypeInfo() is also easy in this case (and not much harder in other cases) as we don't have any type info to return! Assume for a moment that CoSquiggle did indeed support type information. If so, we would set the ITypeInfo* parameter to refer to our server's specific type library. Again, ITypeInfo provides a number of methods that a calling client can call to discover the interfaces, coclasses, helpstrings, and so forth defined in our IDL code. As mentioned, object browsers make heavy use of ITypeInfo (and related interfaces) to extract our type information. Here, we can simply set the ITypeInfo pointer to NULL, and return a strange little HRESULT, E_NOTIMPL, informing the client that we have no implementation of this method to speak of. While use of E_NOTIMPL is considered bad style, this should make sense to us in this context, as a COM client would have ideally called GetTypeInfoCount() to begin with and already discovered we have nothing by way of type information to offer:

```
// GetTypeInfo() returns a pointer to our type library's contents (if we have any).
STDMETHODIMP CoSquiggle::GetTypeInfo(UINT iTInfo, LCID lcid,
                                     ITypeInfo **ppTInfo)
{
    // Return NULL pointer as we do not support type info.
    *ppTInfo = NULL;
    return E_NOTIMPL;
}
```

So far so good, but now the work begins. Recall that clients using late binding must first make a call to GetIDsOfNames() to obtain the DISPID of the method they are looking to invoke. Assume CoSquiggle has three methods in its dispinterface, named DrawASquiggle(), FlipASquiggle(), and EraseASquiggle().

We may associate DISPIDs to each method with help of the preprocessor #define directive (or the C++ **const** keyword—take your pick). The client will send us a LPOLESTR, and if this is a string we recognize, we will set the rgDispId parameter to the correct DISPID:

```
// An implementation of GetIDsOfNames() allows a client to send in a string
// parameter for us to test against.
#define DISPID_DRAWSQUIG    1
#define DISPID_FLIPSQUIG    2
#define DISPID_ERASESQUIG   3
STDMETHODIMP CoSquiggle::GetIDsOfNames( REFIID riid,
```

```
          LPOLESTR *rgszNames, UINT cNames, LCID lcid, DISPID *rgDispId)
{
    // First off, we only support one name at a time.
    if(cNames > 1)
        return E_INVALIDARG;
    // Are they asking for the DISPID for DrawASquiggle?
    if(_wcsicmp(*rgszNames, L("DrawASquiggle") == 0)
    {
        *rgDispId = DISPID_DRAWSQUIG;
        return S_OK;
    }
    // Are they asking for the DISPID for FlipASquiggle?
    if(_wcsicmp(*rgszNames, L("FlipASquiggle") == 0)
    {
        *rgDispId = DISPID_FLIPSQUIG;
        return S_OK;
    }
    // Are they asking for the DISPID for EraseASquiggle?
    if(_wcsicmp(*rgszNames, L("EraseASquiggle") == 0)
    {
        *rgDispId = DISPID_ERASESQUIG;
        return S_OK;
    }
    else
        return DISP_E_UNKNOWNNAME;
}
```

Notice that this implementation of GetIDsOfNames() uses basic if/else logic to test the string against our known dispinterface members. By convention, return DISP_E_UN-KNOWNNAME when the late bound client asks for a DISPID you cannot account for.

The logic behind GetIDsOfNames() can grow quickly, as your automation objects support more and more functionality. For example, if CoSquiggle had a dispinterface defining 20 unique methods, this would entail testing between 20 possible strings and returning 20 unique DISPIDs. In raw C++ this is a bother; we will soon see how to make use of a server's type information and the COM library to resolve the implementation of GetIDsOfNames() to a few lines of code.

Finally, we have to provide an implementation of Invoke(). This is where the real action happens. Once the client has obtained the correct DISPID, it uses the acquired IDispatch pointer to call Invoke(), sending in the numerical cookie and any necessary parameters. The parameters sent into Invoke() are packaged up as an array of VARIANT data types, and held in the DISPPARAMS structure. It might be strange to think that one of the parameters to Invoke() is in turn a set of parameters. However, this is how a late bound client is able to send any number of parameters to an automation object. As luck would have it, the methods in our dispinterface (DrawASquiggle(), EraseASquiggle(), and FlipASquiggle()) do not take any parameters, and therefore we can ignore the processing of any client-supplied DISPPARAMS. Here, then, is an implementation of the Invoke() method for our late bound CoSquiggle:

```
// Now, based on the DISPID, call the correct helper function
STDMETHODIMP CoSquiggle::Invoke(
    DISPID dispIdMember,        // DISPID of dispinterface member.
    REFIID riid,                // Reserved.
    LCID lcid,                  // Locality.
```

```
    WORD wFlags,                // Are we calling a method or property?
    DISPPARAMS *pDispParams,    // Any arguments for the method.
    VARIANT *pVarResult,        // A place to hold the logical return value.
    EXCEPINFO *pExcepInfo,      // Any error information?
    UINT *puArgErr)             // Again, any error information?
{
    // We have no parameters for these functions, so we can just
    // ignore the DISPPARAMS.
    // Based on DISPID, call the correct member of the dispinterface.
    switch(dispIdMember)
    {
    case DISPID_DRAWSQUIG:
        DrawASquiggle();
        return S_OK;
    case DISPID_FLIPSQUIG:
        FlipASquiggle();
        return S_OK;
    case DISPID_ERASESQUIG:
        EraseASquiggle();
        return S_OK;
    default:
        return DISP_E_UNKNOWNINTERFACE;
    }
}
```

As you can see, Invoke() will examine the DISPID parameter and call internal helper functions accordingly. To keep things simple, assume that each helper function simply launches an appropriate MessageBox(). Now, as long as CoSquiggle has a class object to activate it and has been packaged up into a COM server (DLL or EXE), we can allow any COM-enabled language to make use of it, including the dumb clients of the world.

Client-Side Code and the VARIANT Data Type

When you are using the IDispatch interface from a C++ client, you will need to work with the VARIANT data type. The Invoke() method of IDispatch requires you to send in all parameters to the dispinterface member as an array of VARIANTs. While we already have a good idea what the possible values of a VARIANT can be, the VARIANT structure itself is realized in C++ as a union of all possible [oleautomation] compatible data types. Beyond specifying the union of all possible data types, the VARIANT structure also specifies a VARTYPE field. You use this field to specify what sort of thing the VARIANT represents (a BSTR, long, short, IUnknown pointer, and so forth). The definition of the VARIANT is expressed in IDL (<oaidl.idl>) as the following:

```
// The VARIANT structure may take on the value of any possible automation
// data type.
struct tagVARIANT {
  union {
    VARTYPE vt;                              // What is my current type?
    union {
      LONG       lVal;                       /* VT_I4 */
      BYTE       bVal;                       /* VT_UI1 */
      SHORT      iVal;                       /* VT_I2 */
      FLOAT      fltVal;                     /* VT_R4 */
```

```
    DOUBLE          dblVal;          /* VT_R8 */
    VARIANT_BOOL    boolVal;         /* VT_BOOL */
    _VARIANT_BOOL   bool;            /* (obsolete) */
    SCODE           scode;           /* VT_ERROR */
    CY              cyVal;           /* VT_CY */
    DATE            date;            /* VT_DATE */
    BSTR            bstrVal;         /* VT_BSTR */
    IUnknown      * punkVal;         /* VT_UNKNOWN */
    IDispatch     * pdispVal;        /* VT_DISPATCH */
    SAFEARRAY     * parray;          /* VT_ARRAY */
    BYTE          * pbVal;           /* VT_BYREF|VT_UI1 */
    SHORT         * piVal;           /* VT_BYREF|VT_I2 */
    LONG          * plVal;           /* VT_BYREF|VT_I4 */
    FLOAT         * pfltVal;         /* VT_BYREF|VT_R4 */
    DOUBLE        * pdblVal;         /* VT_BYREF|VT_R8 */
    VARIANT_BOOL  *pboolVal;         /* VT_BYREF|VT_BOOL */
    _VARIANT_BOOL *pbool;            /* (obsolete) */
    SCODE         * pscode;          /* VT_BYREF|VT_ERROR */
    CY            * pcyVal;          /* VT_BYREF|VT_CY */
    DATE          * pdate;           /* VT_BYREF|VT_DATE */
    BSTR          * pbstrVal;        /* VT_BYREF|VT_BSTR */
    IUnknown     ** ppunkVal;        /* VT_BYREF|VT_UNKNOWN */
    IDispatch    ** ppdispVal;       /* VT_BYREF|VT_DISPATCH */
    SAFEARRAY    ** pparray;         /* VT_BYREF|VT_ARRAY */
    VARIANT       * pvarVal;         /* VT_BYREF|VT_VARIANT */
    PVOID           byref;           /* Generic ByRef */
    CHAR            cVal;            /* VT_I1 */
    USHORT          uiVal;           /* VT_UI2 */
    ULONG           ulVal;           /* VT_UI4 */
    INT             intVal;          /* VT_INT */
    UINT            uintVal;         /* VT_UINT */
    DECIMAL       * pdecVal;         /* VT_BYREF|VT_DECIMAL */
    CHAR          * pcVal;           /* VT_BYREF|VT_I1 */
    USHORT        * puiVal;          /* VT_BYREF|VT_UI2 */
    ULONG         * pulVal;          /* VT_BYREF|VT_UI4 */
    INT           * pintVal;         /* VT_BYREF|VT_INT */
    UINT          * puintVal;        /* VT_BYREF|VT_UINT */
};
```

The comments that appear in the definition of the VARIANT type are the flags used to set the underlying type of VARIANT you are working with. In essence, the VARIANT structure allows you to express any automation-compatible data type, which can be used by all COM languages. The whole of these data types is expressed as a C union. To specify the sort of VARIANT you are defining, set the VARTYPE field of the structure using the correct VT_ flag.

Building a VARIANT

When you wish to create a VARIANT data type in the C++ programming language, you will make use of a handful of COM library functions, which shield you from the need to manage the memory associated to a given VARIANT. In many respects, working with the VARIANT is much like working with the BSTR data type, given that you manipulate it indirectly using API calls. To create a brand new VARIANT, you will begin by defining a VARIANT variable and initializing it using the VariantInit() COM library function:

```
// Create and initialize a VARIANT in C++
VARIANT myVar;
VariantInit(&myVar);
```

At this point, you have an empty (but safe) VARIANT structure. To establish what sort of data the variant is holding (BSTR, long, short, pointer to a BSTR, and so on), you set the VARTYPE field by specifying the correct VT_ flag. Let's say you want to create a VARIANT that starts out life as a short, which is to say VT_I2:

```
// Set VARIANT type
VARIANT myVar;
VariantInit(&myVar);
myVar.vt = VT_I2
```

Next, you will need to establish the value of this short by setting the correct member in the union with an appropriate value. As you can see from the definition of the VARIANT structure, a short is identified as the "iVal" member of the union:

```
// Each item in the VARIANT union has an associated VT flag and union member.
struct tagVARIANT {
  union {
    VARTYPE vt;
    union {
      LONG    lVal;      /* VT_I4 */
      BYTE    bVal;      /* VT_UI1 */
      SHORT   iVal;      /* VT_I2 */
...
}
```

Thus, to create a short with the value of 20 using the VARIANT data type:

```
// Create and initialize a VARIANT in C++
VARIANT myVar;
VariantInit(&myVar);
myVar.vt = VT_I2;
myVar.iVal = 20;
VariantClear(&myVar);
```

As another example, here is a VARIANT of type long, with the value of 5000:

```
// Another VARIANT.
VARIANT myOtherVar;
VariantInit(&myOtherVar);
myotherVar.vt = VT_I4;
myotherVar.lVal = 5000;
VariantClear(&myotherVar);
```

In addition to VariantInit() and VariantClear(), the COM library defines a set of additional functions that operate on the VARIANT data type. Some of the most common are shown below:

VARIANT Function	Meaning in Life
VariantInit()	Initializes a VARIANT structure.
VariantClear()	Frees up any memory consumed by the current VARIANT.

VARIANT Function	Meaning in Life
VariantCopy()	Copies the content of one VARIANT to another VARIANT. This method will also free any memory of the destination before performing the copy.
VariantChangeType()	Sets the underlying type of the VARIANT to another type.

CComVariant: An ATL Wrapper for the VARIANT Data Type

If you are going to be spending a good amount of time with this polymorphic data type, you will be happy to know that ATL provides a wrapper class to hide the raw library functions from your view. Much like CComBSTR, CComVariant provides a number of functions and overloaded operators which make working with the VARIANT structure much less painful. The member functions of this class make calls to the same VARIANT library functions that you would by hand, in a more OO-based manner.

> **Note:**   Recall that the Visual C++ compiler extensions supply the _variant_t type to help simplify VARIANT programming.

The DISPPARAMS Structure

Now that we can create a single VARIANT using the COM library, we are ready to look at the DISPPARAMS structure. Using IDispatch from a C++ client can be difficult. The trouble comes from the need to package up any necessary parameters to the method in the form of an array of VARIANTS, which is represented by the DISPPARAMS structure. DISPPARAMS is defined in <oaidl.idl> as the following:

```
// The DISPPARAMS structure allows you to send over all required parameters to
// a method using one data structure.
typedef struct tagDISPPARAMS {
  [size_is(cArgs)] VARIANTARG * rgvarg;              // Array of arguments.
  [size_is(cNamedArgs)] DISPID * rgdispidNamedArgs; // Array of named arguments.
  UINT cArgs;                                        // # of items in array.
  UINT cNamedArgs;                                   // # of named arguments.
} DISPPARAMS;
```

> **Note:**   The VARIANTARG constant seen above is a simple typedef to the VARIANT structure.

More often than not, you will only need to concern yourself with the first and third fields of the DISPPARAMS structure. As for the other fields, automation objects can support the idea of *named arguments*. The Visual Basic language allows you to pass parameters to a method in an arbitrary order. For example, the MsgBox() method of Visual Basic normally looks like the following:

```
' Here we have specified three of the five parameters in order.
'
MsgBox "This is the prompt", vbOKOnly, "Title in box"
```

Using named arguments, the VB developer may call MsgBox() as:

```
' How much flexibility does a programmer really need...
'
MsgBox Title:="Title in box", buttons:=vbOKOnly, prompt:="This is the prompt"
```

Why? Well, let's just say that VB tries to be as helpful as possible to the developers it services. Here's a rule to always keep firm in your mind: The more help VB provides VB programmers, the more miserable your life as a C++ programmer becomes. Given this bit of wisdom, you can now see that the second and fourth fields of the DISPPARAMS structure hold information about any named arguments which may be coming our way. CoSquiggle does not support any named arguments, so the values of these fields will be NULL. The other fields of the DISPPARAMS structure specify the upper bound of the array of VARIANT parameters, and the array itself. Given that none of the methods found in the dispinterface of CoSquiggle take parameters, a C++ client can assemble a DISPPARAMS structure quite easily:

```
// When you are calling a member of a dispinterface which does not require
// any arguments at all (named or otherwise) set up your DISPPARAMS as so:
DISPPARAMS params = {0, 0, 0, 0};
```

Most members of a dispinterface do take parameters, and thus we will be required to create some VARIANTS. For example, what if CoSquiggle defined a method that requires four longs, in order to draw the squiggle within some bounding rectangle:

```
// Here is a member of CoSquiggle's dispinterface which requires some parameters.
void DrawSquiggleInABox(long top, long left, long bottom, long right);
```

As a C++ client, you may set up your DISPPARAMS structure as so:

```
// Create an array of 4 VARIANTs.
VARIANT myVars[4];
VariantInit(&myVars [0]);      // Top
myVars [0].vt = VT_I4;
myVars [0].lVal = 20;
VariantInit(&myVars [1]);      // Left
myVars [1].vt = VT_I4;
myVars [1].lVal = 20;
VariantInit(&myVars [2]);      // Bottom
myVars [2].vt = VT_I4;
myVars [2].lVal = 90;
VariantInit(&myVars [3]);      // Right
myVars [3].vt = VT_I4;
myVars [3].lVal = 200;
// Package up the VARIANTS into DISPPARAMS
DISPPARAMS myParams = { myVars, 0, 4, 0};
// Call DrawSquiggleInABox() using Invoke().
pDisp->Invoke(dispid, IID_NULL, LOCALE_SYSTEM_DEFAULT,
              DISPATCH_METHOD, &myParams, NULL, NULL, NULL);
...
```

Again, as you can tell, working with IDispatch using straight C++ can become complex. Take heart, as chances are this will not be a very common task, especially as most coclasses implement a "dual interface" (which we examine soon). However, here again is how a C++ client can make use of CoSquiggle:

```cpp
// A late bound C++ client
int main(int argc, char* argv[])
{
    CoInitialize(NULL);
    IDispatch* pDisp = NULL;
    CLSID clsid;
    DISPID dispid;
    // Go look up the CLSID from the ProgID.
    CLSIDFromProgID(OLESTR("RawDisp.CoSquiggle"),&clsid);
    LPOLESTR str = OLESTR("DrawASquiggle");
    // Create the CoSquiggle.
    CoCreateInstance(clsid, NULL, CLSCTX_SERVER, IID_IDispatch,
                     (void**)&pDisp);
    // See if the object supports a method named 'DrawASquiggle'
    pDisp->GetIDsOfNames(IID_NULL, &str,1,
                         LOCALE_SYSTEM_DEFAULT, &dispid);
    // Call Invoke. We have no parameters, but must still
    // supply an DISPPARAMS structure.
    DISPPARAMS params = {0, 0, 0, 0};
    pDisp->Invoke(dispid, IID_NULL, LOCALE_SYSTEM_DEFAULT,
                  DISPATCH_METHOD, &params, NULL, NULL, NULL);
    // See ya!
    pDisp->Release();
    CoUninitialize();
    return 0;
}
```

So there you have it. IDispatch programming in C++: powerful, dynamic, and a real pain in the neck. Again, you will seldom need to access IDispatch from a C++ client, as most C++ clients will use early binding. Where IDispatch does make sense is from within the context of scripting clients. Again, here is some VBScript code that makes use of CoSquiggle from MS Internet Explorer:

```vbscript
' Some Web-enabled squiggling.
'
<HTML>
<BODY>
<SCRIPT language=VBScript>
dim o
set o = CreateObject("RawDisp.CoSquiggle")
o.DrawASquiggle
o.FlipASquiggle
o.EraseASquiggle
</SCRIPT>
</BODY>
</HTML>
```

To sum up our examination of IDispatch thus far, a given coclass that supports late binding must implement IDispatch. Of the four methods, GetIDsOfNames() and Invoke() are the core items that allow a client to dynamically call methods in the object's dispinterface. As we have also seen, implementing these methods by hand can be a bother if your coclass has an extensive dispinterface supporting numerous methods and properties.

The Automation Safe Array Data Type

No discussion of automation would be complete without an examination of the concept of a *safe array*. The safe array is an automation data type which allows you to send around a variable length array of variant compatible types. As you will see in Chapter 11, IDL allows you to send around traditional C style arrays as interface parameters, and your early bound clients are happy to work with these methods. Late bound clients are <u>not</u> happy to work with this type of array. Instead, late bound clients make use of a special self-describing data structure, the SAFEARRAY, defined in <oaidl.idl> as the following:

```
// Dual interfaces and raw dispinterfaces may send around variable length
// arrays of variant compliant data using the SAFEARRAY.
//
typedef struct tagSAFEARRAY {
      USHORT cDims;               // Number of dimensions in array.
      USHORT fFeatures;           // Used to deallocate memory in the array.
      ULONG cbElements;           // Size of each member in the array.
      ULONG cLocks;               // Number of locks on the array.
      PVOID pvData;               // The actual data in the array.
      // For each dimension in the array, the SAFEARRAYBOUND specifies the
      // number of elements in the array, and the value of the lower bound in the
      // array.
      SAFEARRAYBOUND rgsabound[];
} SAFEARRAY;
```

The SAFEARRAY structure contains another structure, SAFEARRAYBOUND, as one of its fields, which is defined as so:

```
// Holds information about each dimension in the array.
typedef struct tagSAFEARRAYBOUND {
  ULONG cElements;
  LONG lLbound;
} SAFEARRAYBOUND, * LPSAFEARRAYBOUND;
```

So, why in the world would a SAFEARRAY need to know the lower bound of the array? We all know arrays begin at index zero, right? Wrong, at least if you are a Visual Basic programmer. VB allows developers to do "cute" things such as create an array with a lower bound of 32 and an upper bound of 80. This might make the VB developer's life more satisfying, as he or she can loop over that array more intuitively (maybe not so for a tried and true C++ developer).

SAFEARRAY COM Library Functions

When you are working with the SAFEARRAY, you do have some help provided by the COM library. Rather than having to work with the raw structures yourself, you are provided with a set of API functions that allow you to create, access, and destroy the underlying structure. In this way, the SAFEARRAY is operated on in much the same way as the BSTR and VARIANT data type. Sadly, as of ATL 3.0, we do not have a comfy wrapper class to hide the grunge of working with this automation data type, so you will need to get familiar with the following core methods, as shown in the following table.

SAFEARRAY Library Function	Meaning in Life
SafeArrayCreate()	Creates a new SAFEARRAY structure.
SafeArrayGetDim()	Returns the number of dimensions of the array.
SafeArrayDestroy()	Destroys an existing SAFEARRAY structure, and deallocates all memory associated to the array.
SafeArrayGetElement()	Retrieves an item in the SAFEARRAY.
SafeArrayPutElement()	Inserts an item into the existing SAFEARRAY.
SafeArrayGetUBound()	Returns the value of the upper bound in the array.
SafeArrayGetLBound()	Returns the value of the lower bound in the array.
SafeArrayAccessData()	Locks the array and retrieves a pointer to the underlying data.
SafeArrayUnaccessData()	Unlocks the array and disposes of pointer obtained by SafeArrayAccessData().

Using SAFEARRAYS as Parameters

To illustrate using a SAFEARRAY, consider this overused and trivial example. Assume an ATL-based coclass contains a method taking a SAFEARRAY of longs and returns the sum. To begin coding the IDL, you will see that a SAFEARRAY can be defined as an array of VARIANTs. This should set well with you, as you are aware that a SAFEARRAY is by definition an array of variant compatible types. Here is some IDL code defining a dual interface named IAddArrays (more on dual interfaces soon):

```
// Add this array of VARIANTS.
[
    object, uuid(938EA4F3-5802-11D3-B926-0020781238D4),
    dual, helpstring("ICoATLSquiggle Interface"),
    pointer_default(unique)
]
interface IAddArrays : IDispatch
{
    [id(1), helpstring("Add this array because I am too lazy")]
    HRESULT AddThisArrayOfNumbers([in] VARIANT theArray,
                                  [out, retval] long* sum);
};
```

Assume this interface is implemented by the CHelloSafeArray object. Because we are expecting the COM client to pass us a safe array of longs (as opposed to an array of IDispatch pointers or BSTRs or whatnot) we will first want to check that we have the correct information in the array; otherwise we will return DISP_E_TYPEMISMATCH:

```
// Use the vt field of the VARIANT structure to determine what is
// inside this array.
STDMETHODIMP CHelloSafeArray::AddThisArrayOfNumbers(VARIANT theArray, long *sum)
{
    // We need to first ensure that we have received an array of longs.
    if((theArray.vt & VT_I4) && (theArray.vt & VT_ARRAY))
    {
        // Do stuff with the array...
        return S_OK;
```

```
        }
        return DISP_E_TYPEMISMATCH;
}
```

Once we are able to determine that we do indeed have an array of longs, we can determine the upper and lower bounds of the array, using the SafeArrayGetUBound() and SafeArray-GetLBound() API functions. To fetch out an item in the array, we may make use of SafeArrayGetElement(). Here is the complete code for the AddThisArrayOfNumbers() method:

```
// This method takes a batch of data and adds things up.
STDMETHODIMP CHelloSafeArray::AddThisArrayOfNumbers(VARIANT theArray, long *sum)
{
        // We need to first ensure that we have received an array of longs.
        if((theArray.vt & VT_I4) && (theArray.vt & VT_ARRAY))
        {
                // Fill a SAFEARRAY structure with the
                // values in the VARIANT array, using the 'parray' field.
                SAFEARRAY* pSA;
                pSA = theArray.parray;
                // Figure out how the array is packaged.
                long lBound;
                long uBound;
                SafeArrayGetUBound(pSA, 1, &uBound);
                SafeArrayGetLBound(pSA, 1, &lBound);
                // Loop over the members in the array and add them up.
                long ans = 0;
                long item = 0;
                for(long j = lBound; j <= uBound; j++)
                {
                        SafeArrayGetElement(pSA, &j, &item);
                        ans = ans + item;
                }
                // Set result.
                *sum = ans;
                SafeArrayDestroy(pSA);
                return S_OK;
        }
        return DISP_E_TYPEMISMATCH;
}
```

A Visual Basic client may use this method as so:

```
' A VB client creating a safe array, and sending it into the coclass
' for processing.
'
Private Sub Form_Load()
        ' Make an array with odd dimensions
        Dim VBArray(30 To 90) As Long
        ' Fill with some data
        Dim i As Integer
        For i = 30 To 90
                Randomize
                VBArray(i) = Rnd(i) * 30
        Next
        ' Send array in for addition.
        Dim o As New CHelloSafeArray
```

```
        MsgBox o.AddThisArrayOfNumbers(VBArray), , "The summation is..."
End Sub
```

A C++ client needs to do much more work. As mentioned, ATL does not offer a wrapper around the SAFEARRAY structure, and therefore we must write code making use of the various SAFEARRAY API calls. Here is a C++ client calling the AddThisArrayOf-Numbers() method. Take note of the use of SafeArrayCreate(), SafeArrayDestroy(), and SafeArrayPutElement():

```cpp
// C++ SAFEARRAY clients need to do more grunge.
int main(int argc, char* argv[])
{
        CoInitialize(NULL);
        HRESULT hr;
        IAddArrays* pInterface = NULL;
        hr = CoCreateInstance(CLSID_CHelloSafeArray, NULL, CLSCTX_SERVER,
                              IID_IAddArrays, (void**)&pInterface);
        // Make a safe array.
        SAFEARRAY* pSA = NULL;
        SAFEARRAYBOUND bound[1];
        bound[0].lLbound = 0;
        bound[0].cElements = 30;
        pSA = SafeArrayCreate(VT_I4, 1, bound);
        // Fill the array.
        for(long i = 0; i < 30; i++)
                SafeArrayPutElement(pSA, &i, &i);
        // Now pack up the array...
        VARIANT theArray;
        VariantInit(&theArray);
        theArray.vt = VT_ARRAY | VT_I4;
        theArray.parray = pSA;
        long ans = 0;
        pInterface->AddThisArrayOfNumbers(theArray, &ans);
        cout << "The summation of this array is: " << ans << endl;
        // Clean up.
        pInterface->Release();
        SafeArrayDestroy(pSA);
        CoUninitialize();
        return 0;
}
```

One problem with the safe array is that the use of such a construct entails that the client and coclass exchange a complete mass of data in one call. There is no manner to "pull" data from the object or work with that data in a more selective fashion. Often, a better approach is to create a COM collection, which we will do later in Chapter 11.

Lab 10-1: Developing a Scriptable Object in Raw C++

To help you understand how the IDispatch interface behaves, this lab will give you a chance to build a COM server in C++ that contains a single object supporting IDispatch. You will be developing a "dispinterface" for this object, which has been defined as a collection of properties and methods exposed via IDispatch. You will then create a series of late bound clients, including a web client using VBScript.

The solution for this lab can be found on your CD-ROM under:
Labs\Chapter 10\RawDisp
Labs\Chapter 10\RawDisp\CPP Client
Labs\Chapter 10\RawDisp\VB Client
Labs\Chapter 10\RawDisp\VBScript Client

Step One: Create the Initial Server and Coclass

Here we are again, avoiding the help of ATL and writing another raw COM server, so feel free to leverage your existing code (that which does not kill you will make you stronger!). Create a new Win32 DLL project workspace (an empty project). Insert a new C++ class named **CoSquiggle**. CoSquiggle is an automation object (a.k.a. scriptable object), which by definition supports only IDispatch. The dispinterface of CoSquiggle supports three methods, named DrawASquiggle(), FlipASquiggle(), and EraseASquiggle(). The header file of CoSquiggle begins life as so:

```
// This coclass only supports IDispatch and thus late binding.
#include <windows.h>
class CoSquiggle : public IDispatch
{
public:
    CoSquiggle();
    virtual ~CoSquiggle();
    STDMETHODIMP_(DWORD)AddRef();
    STDMETHODIMP_(DWORD)Release();
    STDMETHODIMP QueryInterface(REFIID riid, void** ppv);
    STDMETHODIMP GetTypeInfoCount( UINT *pctinfo);
    STDMETHODIMP GetTypeInfo( UINT iTInfo, LCID lcid, ITypeInfo **ppTInfo);
    STDMETHODIMP GetIDsOfNames( REFIID riid, LPOLESTR *rgszNames,
        UINT cNames, LCID lcid, DISPID *rgDispId);
    STDMETHODIMP Invoke( DISPID dispIdMember, REFIID riid, LCID lcid,
        WORD wFlags, DISPPARAMS *pDispParams, VARIANT *pVarResult,
        EXCEPINFO *pExcepInfo, UINT *puArgErr);
private:
    void DrawASquiggle();
    void FlipASquiggle();
    void EraseASquiggle();
    DWORD m_ref;            // Set to zero in constructor...
};
```

Now, provide a standard implementation for your IUnknown methods. AddRef() and Release() will be like any standard coclass implementation; however, be sure your QueryInterface() method only returns vPtrs for the IUnknown or IDispatch interfaces.

Now for the implementation of IDispatch. As our coclass has no type information to return to any interested clients, we may implement GetTypeInfoCount() and GetTypeInfo() quite easily:

```
// No type information here!
STDMETHODIMP CoSquiggle::GetTypeInfoCount( UINT *pctinfo)
{
    // We do not support type information in this object.
    *pctinfo = 0;
    return S_OK;
}
```

```
STDMETHODIMP CoSquiggle::GetTypeInfo(
  UINT iTInfo, LCID lcid, ITypeInfo **ppTInfo)
{
      // Return NULL pointer as we do not support type info.
      *ppTInfo = NULL;
      return E_NOTIMPL;
}
```

The GetIDsOfNames() method is responsible for returning a DISPID based on the incoming string. To represent the possible DISPIDs for your dispinterface, add some #define constants in your <cosquiggle.cpp> file and implement **GetIDsOfNames()** to return the correct DISPID to the client:

```
// The DISPID constants.
#define DISPID_DRAWSQUIG      1
#define DISPID_FLIPSQUIG      2
#define DISPID_ERASESQUIG     3
// Client gives us a string name, so do a lookup
// between the string and the cookie.
STDMETHODIMP CoSquiggle::GetIDsOfNames( REFIID riid,
      LPOLESTR *rgszNames, UINT cNames, LCID lcid, DISPID *rgDispId)
{
      // First off, we only support one name at a time.
      if(cNames > 1)
            return E_INVALIDARG;
      // Which member of the dispinterface do they want?
      if(_wcsicmp(*rgszNames, L"DrawASquiggle") == 0)
      {
            *rgDispId = DISPID_DRAWSQUIG;
            return S_OK;
      }
      if(_wcsicmp(*rgszNames, L"FlipASquiggle") == 0)
      {
            *rgDispId = DISPID_FLIPSQUIG;
            return S_OK;
      }
      if(_wcsicmp(*rgszNames, L"EraseASquiggle") == 0)
      {
            *rgDispId = DISPID_ERASESQUIG;
            return S_OK;
      }
      else
            return DISP_E_UNKNOWNNAME;
}
```

Next, implement **Invoke()** to call the correct private helper function of your dispinterface based on the DISPID:

```
// Now, based on the DISPID, call the correct helper function.
STDMETHODIMP CoSquiggle::Invoke( DISPID dispIdMember, REFIID riid,
            LCID lcid, WORD wFlags, DISPPARAMS *pDispParams,
            VARIANT *pVarResult, EXCEPINFO *pExcepInfo, UINT *puArgErr)
{
      // We have no parameters for these functions, so we can just
      // ignore the DISPPARAMS.
      // Call dispinterface member.
      switch(dispIdMember)
```

```
    {
    case DISPID_DRAWSQUIG:
        DrawASquiggle();
        return S_OK;
    case DISPID_FLIPSQUIG:
        FlipASquiggle();
        return S_OK;
    case DISPID_ERASESQUIG:
        EraseASquiggle();
        return S_OK;
    default:
        return DISP_E_UNKNOWNINTERFACE;
    }
}
```

Finally, provide an implementation for each private helper function, for example:

```
// Give some implementation for the dispinterface members.
void CoSquiggle::DrawASquiggle()
{
    // Drawing a squiggle...
    MessageBox(NULL, "Drawing a squiggle",
        "CoSquiggle Invoke", MB_OK | MB_SETFOREGROUND);
}
```

Go ahead and compile to ensure you have no typos.

Step Two: Provide a Class Factory and Component Housing

You know the drill here! Insert another new class that will work as the class factory for
CoSquiggle. Feel free to leverage an existing class factory, but be sure to modify
CreateInstance() to create a CoSquiggle:

```
// Create the squiggle.
STDMETHODIMP CoSquiggleClassFactory::CreateInstance(LPUNKNOWN pUnkOuter, REFIID riid,
                                                    void** ppv)
{
    // We do not support aggregation in this class object.
    if(pUnkOuter != NULL)
        return CLASS_E_NOAGGREGATION;
    CoSquiggle* pSquig = NULL;
    HRESULT hr;
    // Create the object.
    pSquig = new CoSquiggle;
    // Ask object for an interface.
    hr = pSquig -> QueryInterface(riid, ppv);
    // Problem? We must delete the memory we allocated.
    if (FAILED(hr))
        delete pSquig;
    return hr;
}
```

Next, insert a new CPP file to define the DLL component housing. As always, implement
DllGetClassObject() and **DllCanUnloadNow()** in the usual manner. Don't forget to
define global counters for locks and active objects, and increment and decrement accordingly (if you have worked through all the labs up until now, I can assume you know what
this would entail ... but feel free to look back on previous labs).

Also provide a DEF file for these exports, and a REG file to enter the ProgID and CLSID entries for your CoSquiggle, as shown below:

```
LIBRARY "RAWDISP"
EXPORTS
        DllGetClassObject       @1      PRIVATE
        DllCanUnloadNow         @2      PRIVATE


REGEDIT
; This is the ProgID
;
HKEY_CLASSES_ROOT\RawDisp.CoSquiggle\CLSID =
{F43C0966-577B-11d3-B926-0020781238D4}
; This is the CLSID
;
HKEY_CLASSES_ROOT\CLSID\{F43C0966-577B-11d3-B926-0020781238D4}
= RawDisp.CoSquiggle
HKEY_CLASSES_ROOT\CLSID\{F43C0966-577B-11d3-B926-0020781238D4}
\InprocServer32 = E:\ATL\Labs\Chapter 10\RawDisp\Debug\RawDisp.dll
```

Compile your DLL and be sure to merge your REG file. Now that we have a new coclass supporting IDispatch, we turn our attention to some client code.

Step Three: A C++ Client Using Late Binding

You have seen this code previously in this chapter. Create a Win32 Console Application. Create your CoSquiggle using CoCreateInstance() and ask for the IDispatch interface. From this interface, call GetIDsOfNames() and ask for access to some member of the CoSquiggle dispinterface; hold onto the DISPID. Now, using this DISPID, call Invoke() and send in an empty set of DISPPARAMS (as none of the methods in the dispinterface require parameters). As usual, release your acquired interfaces:

```
// A late bound C++ client.
int main(int argc, char* argv[])
{
    CoInitialize(NULL);
    IDispatch* pDisp = NULL;
    CLSID clsid;
    DISPID dispid;
    CLSIDFromProgID(L"RawDisp.CoSquiggle",&clsid);
    LPOLESTR str = OLESTR("FlipASquiggle");
    CoCreateInstance(clsid, NULL, CLSCTX_SERVER, IID_IDispatch,
                (void**)&pDisp);
    // Get DISPID.
    pDisp->GetIDsOfNames(IID_NULL, &str,1,
                        LOCALE_SYSTEM_DEFAULT, &dispid);
    // Trigger method.
    DISPPARAMS params = {0, 0, 0, 0};
    pDisp->Invoke(dispid, IID_NULL, LOCALE_SYSTEM_DEFAULT,
                DISPATCH_METHOD, &params, NULL, NULL, NULL);
    pDisp->Release();
    CoUninitialize();
    return 0;
}
```

Step Four: A Visual Basic Client Using Late Binding

When a VB client wishes to bind late to a COM object, the protocol is to declare an Object variable and set it to the return value of CreateObject(). This VB method takes the ProgID of the server object, which allows SCM to look up the related CLSID at run time. Create a new VB Standard EXE and create a functional GUI. The code behind the GUI is responsible for fetching the IDispatch pointer and calling the members of the dispinterface. You will notice that the VB IntelliSense is not functional. This should make sense, as you have not set a reference to any type information. Here is some possible VB client code. Note that I have added an incorrect call to InvertACircle(). Our CoSquiggle does not support this method, and therefore GetIDsOfNames() will return DISP_E_UNKNOWNNAME. As this is discovered at run time, the code compiles without error:

```
' This will hold the IDispatch pointer
'
' [General][Declarations]
Dim o As Object
Private Sub GetIDisp_Click()
    ' Go get IDispatch from the coclass
    Set o = CreateObject("RawDisp.CoSquiggle")
End Sub
Private Sub UseIDisp_Click()
    ' Call GetIDsOfNames and Invoke for each.
    o.DrawASquiggle
    o.FlipASquiggle
    o.EraseASquiggle
    o.InvertACircle ' This will trigger a runtime error!
End Sub
```

Step Five: A VB Scripting Client Using Late Binding

As C++, VB, and Java can all work with early binding, the need for IDispatch might seem illusive. But, as soon as you want to access your object from a web page, you will live by this COM interface. Using Notepad (yes, Notepad), type in the following HTML code, and save it as **vbscriptclient.htm** (be sure you substitute your ProgID if necessary):

```
' Some Web-enabled squiggling.
'
<HTML>
<HEAD>
<TITLE> Web Tester </TITLE>
</HEAD>
<BODY>
<SCRIPT language=VBScript>
    dim o
    set o = CreateObject("RawDisp.CoSquiggle")
    o.DrawASquiggle
    o.FlipASquiggle
    o.EraseASquiggle
</SCRIPT>
</BODY>
</HTML>
```

Note: All data types in VBScript are Variants.

Now, double-click on the HTML file. This will launch IE and load up your COM object!

You will see a warning box pop up as your page loads. This is because we have not specified that CoSquiggle is safe for scripting (we will fix this when we work with ATL later in this chapter). Here is CoSquiggle on the web:

Figure 10-2:
Late binding using MS Internet Explorer and VBScript.

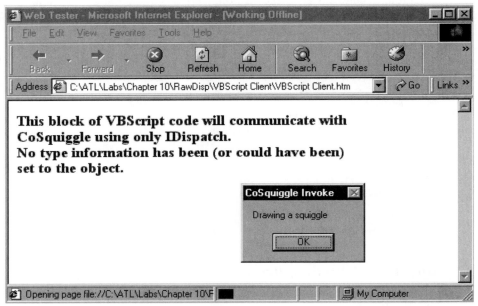

Now that you have seen how to create a very dynamic connection to an object using IDispatch as well as a very static connection to custom interfaces (and type information/MIDL-generated files), we can now turn our attention to a dual interface. But before we do, here is one final late bound client you may wish to try.

Step Six: Launch Your CoSquiggle from MS Visual Studio

Just for kicks, what if we were to create a new toolbar within the MS Visual Studio IDE that would launch your CoSquiggle? I am sure you can see the need to draw, erase, and flip a squiggle as you write real production software, so what the heck. Begin by accessing the **Tools | Macro** menu selection. This will launch a dialog box that allows you to automate your installation of Visual Studio using (of course) VBScript. Type in a name for your new macro, such as ExerciseTheSquiggle. The name you provide will end up being the name of the VBScript method invoked from the toolbar (see Figure 10-3).

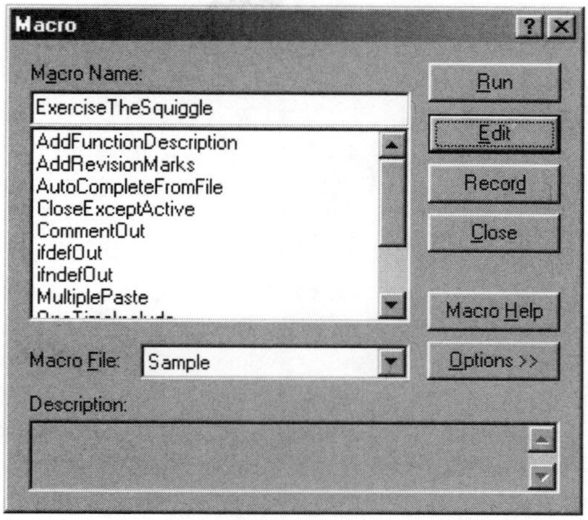

Figure 10-3:
Creating a new
Dev Studio
Macro.

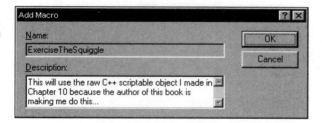

Once you have named your new macro, click on the Edit button to enter a description of this macro:

Figure 10-4:
Describing the
macro.

In the generated stub, write some VBScript code to do the job:

```
Sub ExerciseTheSquiggle()
'DESCRIPTION: This will use the raw C++ scriptable
'object I made in Chapter 10 because the author of
'this book is making me do this...
    dim o
    set o = CreateObject("rawdisp.cosquiggle")
    o.DrawASquiggle
    o.FlipASquiggle
    o.EraseASquiggle
End Sub
```

Now, save the <sample.dsm> file, and go back into the Tools | Macro dialog box. Select the **Options** button, and then the **Assign Macro to Toolbar** option. Find your macro in the list box, and drag and drop the macro text anywhere onto the IDE. Pick a toolbar button from the final dialog box and close everything down. Now click the new button to execute your macro, and get some real work done!

Understanding the Dual Interface

Now that you have discovered the dispinterface, you may wonder what the correct choice is for building a coclass. If you create a 100% automation object, you are ensured all COM language—including scripting clients—can make use of your object's functionality. As you can see, keeping a dispinterface up to date can be a bit of a bother. Writing C++ late binding code can also be a bit of a (huge) bother. On the other hand, you know and love vTable custom interfaces, and enjoy building coclasses that express themselves using QueryInterface(). However, doing so will keep scripting clients from using your COM objects. So what is the COM developer to do? Create objects that support dual interfaces.

Objects that support dual interfaces provide an IDispatch implementation as well as the set of custom vTable interfaces supported by the object. In this way, smart clients can simply access your custom interfaces (IDraw, IShapeEdit, ICreateCar, and so forth), while the dumb clients are still able to make use of your coclass using IDispatch. In this way, everyone is happy.

Building a dual interface object becomes even more easy to do if you make use of the COM library. For the most part, you write the IDL to describe the dual interface and use the associated COM library calls to fill in the details of GetTypeInfoCount(), GetTypeInfo(), GetIDsOfNames(), and Invoke(). This leaves writing your vTable methods as usual as your only task.

However, dual interfaces do have one very important restriction. If you build a dual interface object, every single parameter of every single method must be variant compliant. This includes the method parameters of your custom vTable interfaces as well. You are not allowed to "get sneaky" and attempt to write variant compliant dispinterface methods and non-compliant custom interface methods. Everyone must play by the same rules.

So then, in the world of COM today, we have three possible configurations between a coclass and the interfaces it supports, as shown in Figure 10-5. CoSquiggle is a pure automation object, which by definition supplies all functionality using IDispatch. CoFunnel supports a pure vTable interface, as it does not support IDispatch (and therefore is unusable from a scripting client). Finally, CoOval is a dual interface object, providing both early and late binding using IDispatch as well a custom interface.

Figure 10-5: Automation, vTable, and dual interface objects.

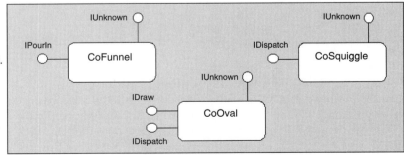

Developing Dual Interfaces in IDL and Raw C++

As most things in COM, writing a dual interface begins with the IDL code. Defining a dual interface in IDL looks like the following:

```
// A dual interface
[uuid(BDFD41A0-580A-11d3-B926-0020781238D4), object, dual]
interface ISquiggle : IDispatch
{
    [id(1)] HRESULT DrawASquiggle();
    [id(2)] HRESULT FlipASquiggle();
    [id(3)] HRESULT EraseASquiggle();
};
```

Like vTable interfaces, dual interfaces are themselves marked with the [uuid] and [object] attributes. Unlike a vTable interface, you must specify the [dual] attribute and derive your custom interface (in this case, ISquiggle) directly from IDispatch. Furthermore, each member in the dispinterface must be marked with a unique DISPID using the [id] attribute. This ensures that a coclass implementing this particular interface must contend with ten methods: three from IUnknown, four from IDispatch, and three methods of the custom ISquiggle.

Adding this interface to the library statement is exactly the same as working with a vTable object:

```
// A library statement for a server containing an object
// supporting a dual interface.
[uuid(BDFD41A1-580A-11d3-B926-0020781238D4), version(1.0)]
library DualObject
{
    importlib("stdole32.tlb");
    [uuid(BDFD41A2-580A-11d3-B926-0020781238D4)]
    coclass CoDualSquiggle
    {
        [default] interface ISquiggle;
    };
};
```

When you send this file into the MIDL compiler, you will receive the generated files you already know and love. Therefore, early bound clients can still include the *_i.c and *.h generated files (C and C++ clients) as well as your server's type library information (VB, Java, and C++ clients). However, as your object is now supporting the methods of IDispatch, you are also able to provide your functionality to the dumb (scripting) clients in the world.

Building a Dual Interface Coclass by Hand

To support a dual interface on a coclass, you need to ensure that external COM clients are able to query for the set of custom interfaces (ISquiggle) as well as the IUnknown and IDispatch interfaces. Furthermore, rather than deriving directly from IDispatch, the coclass will derive from the dual interface. If CoSquiggle were to be retrofitted to implement the dual ISquiggle interface, we would begin by modifying the class definition as so:

```
// An object supporting a dual interface inherits both IDispatch
// and the custom vTable interface.
class CoDualSquiggle : public ISquiggle
{
public:
    CoDualSquiggle();
    virtual ~CoDualSquiggle();
```

```
      // IUnknown prototypes...
      // IDispatch prototypes...
      // These must now be public (and use the correct COM macros)
      STDMETHODIMP DrawASquiggle();
      STDMETHODIMP FlipASquiggle();
      STDMETHODIMP EraseASquiggle();
private:
      ULONG m_ref;
};
```

Notice how the methods that were previously private helper functions in the raw dispinterface CoSquiggle (DrawASquiggle() and friends) have now been moved to the public sector. Think this one through. If a client queries for IID_ISquiggle, the client has access to each of the custom methods provided by ISquiggle, and the vTable of the coclass will direct the flow of logic to the correct function. On the other hand, if a client queries for IID_IDispatch, the coclass will assign a DISPID within GetIDsOfNames() and simply call these same functions from within the Invoke() implementation!

In effect, these same three methods will be called by both early and late bound clients—using two different mechanisms. We are still not finished retrofitting CoSquiggle to support this new dual interface. We now must make sure that clients can obtain a pointer to ISquiggle, and thus must update QueryInterface() as so:

```
// Be sure your QI returns vPtrs to both IDispatch and ISquiggle!
STDMETHODIMP CoDualSquiggle::QueryInterface(REFIID riid, void** ppv)
{
      // We do not support any custom interfaces here.
      // All object functionality is given via IDispatch
      if(riid == IID_IUnknown)
            *ppv = (IUnknown*)this;
      else if(riid == IID_IDispatch)      // <- This is for scripting clients!
            *ppv = (IDispatch*)this;
      else if(riid == IID_ISquiggle)      // <- For early clients!
            *ppv = (ISquiggle*)this;
      else
      {
            *ppv = NULL;
            return E_NOINTERFACE;
      }
      ((IUnknown*)(*ppv))->AddRef();
      return S_OK;
}
```

The implementation of DrawASquiggle(), FlipASquiggle(), and EraseASquiggle() will also need to be updated just a bit to use the correct COM macros. For example, here is DrawASquiggle(); the other methods would be updated in the same manner:

```
// Need to add the correct COM macros.
STDMETHODIMP CoDualSquiggle::DrawASquiggle()
{
      // Drawing a squiggle...
      MessageBox(NULL, "Drawing a squiggle",
                  "CoDualSquiggle", MB_OK | MB_SETFOREGROUND);
      return S_OK;
}
```

The previous implementation of IDispatch will not need to change one bit. GetIDsOf-Names() will still assign the correct DISPID. Invoke() will still call the correct function based on the DISPID. That's it! Now that you have seen how to build a dual interface object, the next lab will allow you to try it out for yourself and retrofit your previous CoSquiggle with the necessary changes.

As an added bonus, this lab will illustrate how to use MFC's COleDispatchDriver class to build an MFC application using a late bound connection. After that, we will look at using the type information from within the coclass, to provide a streamlined implementation of IDispatch.

Lab 10-2: Supporting Dual Interfaces

A dual interface is a hybrid of the dispinterface and a custom vTable interface. If you worked through the previous lab, you have seen that using a dispinterface as a C++ client can be a pain. However, if your object does not support IDispatch, you can't be web enabled. In this lab, you will extend your previous lab to support a single dual interface, thus allowing smart clients to acquire custom vTable interfaces, while still allowing dumb clients to use your object via IDispatch.

 The solution for this lab can be found on your CD-ROM under:
Labs\Chapter 10\DualObject
Labs\Chapter 10\DualObject\Dual VB Client
Labs\Chapter 10\DualObject\MFC Client

Step One: Add Type Information

Note: Although I am assuming that you will be making modifications to Lab 10-1, the CD solution works with an entirely new in-proc server (so you can have separate 100% dispinterface and dual solution sets).

Currently, CoSquiggle does not support any type information, and therefore your RawDisp project does not contain an IDL file. Open the RawDisp workspace from Lab 10-1 and insert a new IDL file named **dualobject.idl**. In this file, define a new dual interface named **ISquiggle**. Recall that the IDL definition of a dual requires the [uuid], [dual], and [object] attributes. Also recall that a dual interface derives from IDispatch, and therefore a coclass implementing a dual must support the four methods of IDispatch, the three methods of IUnknown, and any custom methods.

Add three methods to this dual interface (with a unique DISPID) named **DrawA-Squiggle()**, **FlipASquiggle()**, and **EraseASquiggle()**. Now, add a library statement which defines the CoSquiggle coclass supporting ISquiggle. Here is the complete IDL file (be sure to insert it into your project and turn off the MkTypLib compatible option):

```
// The IDL file for your dual CoSquiggle.
import "oaidl.idl";
// A dual interface.
[uuid(BDFD41A0-580A-11d3-B926-0020781238D4), object, dual]
interface ISquiggle : IDispatch
{
```

```
    [id(1)] HRESULT DrawASquiggle();
    [id(2)] HRESULT FlipASquiggle();
    [id(3)] HRESULT EraseASquiggle();
};

[uuid(BDFD41A1-580A-11d3-B926-0020781238D4), version(1.0)]
library DualObject
{
    importlib("stdole32.tlb");
    [uuid(BDFD41A2-580A-11d3-B926-0020781238D4)]
    coclass CoDualSquiggle
    {
        [default] interface ISquiggle;
    };
};
```

Compile your project, and ensure that your IDL code comes through clean. The MIDL compiler will still generate the same set of files you have grown accustomed to, so feel free to take a look.

Step Two: Update CoSquiggle

An object that supports a dual interface derives from that dual interface rather than directly from IDispatch. Modify CoSquiggle to derive from ISquiggle:

```
// This coclass supports IDispatch and the custom ISquiggle.
#include " dualobject.h"      // MIDL file defining ISquiggle.
class CoDualSquiggle : public ISquiggle
{
public:
...
};
```

In the previous lab, we defined three helper functions which were called from the Invoke() logic based on the incoming DISPID:

```
// Your previous lab had a number of private helper functions...
switch(dispIdMember)
{
case DISPID_DRAWSQUIG:
    DrawASquiggle();        // Private helper function.
    return S_OK;
case DISPID_FLIPSQUIG:
    FlipASquiggle();        // Private helper function.
    return S_OK;
case DISPID_ERASESQUIG:
    EraseASquiggle();       // Private helper function.
    return S_OK;
default:
    return DISP_E_UNKNOWNINTERFACE;
}
```

Late bound clients will still operate in exactly the same way. However, now that we also support a single custom vTable interface, early bound clients will call these same three helper functions <u>directly</u>.

```
// This coclass supports IDispatch and the custom ISquiggle.
#include " dualobject.h"
class CoDualSquiggle : public ISquiggle
{
public:
...
     // ISquiggle methods AND helper functions for Invoke()!
     STDMETHODIMP DrawASquiggle();
     STDMETHODIMP FlipASquiggle();
     STDMETHODIMP EraseASquiggle();
...
};
```

As you have used COM macros in your class definition, don't forget to update your implementation code to do the same. Finally, update CoSquiggle::QueryInterface() to return an ISquiggle vPtr. You may wish to add a diagnostic MessageBox() call to verify which interface was just handed out to the client, as shown below:

```
// CoSquiggle now offers services using ISquiggle and IDispatch.
#include " dualobject_i.c"                   // MIDL-generated file for IID_ISquiggle.
STDMETHODIMP CoDualSquiggle::QueryInterface(REFIID riid, void** ppv)
{
     if(riid == IID_IUnknown)
          *ppv = (IUnknown*)this;
     else if(riid == IID_IDispatch)          // <- This is for scripting clients!
     {
          *ppv = (IDispatch*)this;
          MessageBox(NULL, "Using IDispatch",
               "Late binding", MB_OK | MB_SETFOREGROUND);
     }
     else if(riid == IID_ISquiggle)          // <- For early clients!
     {
          *ppv = (ISquiggle*)this;
          MessageBox(NULL, "Using ISquiggle",
               "Early binding", MB_OK | MB_SETFOREGROUND);
     }
     else
     {
          *ppv = NULL;
          return E_NOINTERFACE;
     }
     ((IUnknown*)(*ppv))->AddRef();
     return S_OK;
}
```

All other methods of CoSquiggle will remain as is. Go ahead and recompile your server, because at this point you are finished! In the next step of this lab we will test each binding option using a Visual Basic client.

Step Three: A VB Client

If you would rather create a C++ client to test your new dual interface object, by all means, please do! Just query for ISquiggle or IDispatch and have your fun. Here we will take the quick and dirty option and create a VB client. This client allows the end user to specify the binding option before calling the methods of CoSquiggle. First off, set a

reference to the CoSquiggle type information (use the
Browse button to navigate to the debug folder), as we need
the information within for early binding. Next, add two
command buttons to your form, one for late binding and one
for early binding as shown in Figure 10-6:

Behind door number one, add some VB code to create a late
bound connection using IDispatch, as you have seen before:

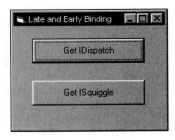

Figure 10-6: Keep it simple.

```
' Going late bound without any type information.
'
Private Sub btnLate_Click()
    Dim objLate As Object
    Set objLate = CreateObject("dualobject.codualsquiggle")
    objLate.DrawASquiggle
    objLate.EraseASquiggle
    objLate.FlipASquiggle
    Set objLate = Nothing
End Sub
```

Behind door number two, make an early connection, making use of the type information
provided by the CoSquiggle *.tlb file:

```
' Going early bound with type information.
'
Private Sub btnEarly_Click()
    Dim objEarly As DualObject.CoDualSquiggle
    Set objEarly = New CoDualSquiggle
    objEarly.DrawASquiggle
    objEarly.EraseASquiggle
    objEarly.FlipASquiggle
    Set objEarly = Nothing
End Sub
```

So then, as you can see, each type of binding will always ultimately call the same three
public methods of CoSquiggle; the only difference is how the client chooses to get there. If
the client has a pointer to IDispatch (i.e., the Object data type and CreateObject()) the
method to call is resolved using a DISPID. Early bound clients call directly into the correct
slot of the vTable, bypassing the dynamic lookup.

Step Four: An MFC Client

If you use MFC to build front ends for your COM servers, you will be happy to know that
you do have some framework support to help with IDispatch programming. To give this a
whirl, create a brand new EXE application using the MFC AppWizard (**File | New**). When
you are configuring your new project, be sure to add support for Automation in step 3 (Figure 10-7). This option adds a call to AfxOleInit() in your InitInstance() method, which
initializes the COM libraries (this also sets up your application to support a dispinterface of
its own, which we do not care about for this lab).

Figure 10-7:
Bootstrapping
the COM library
via MFC.

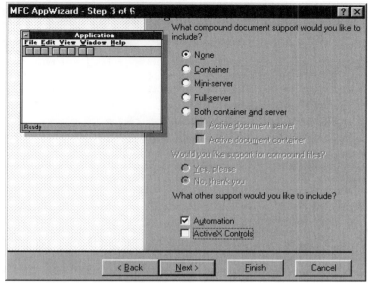

Once you have a new EXE, open up the MFC AppWizard (**Ctrl + W**) and insert a new
class **From a Type Library** using the **Add Class** button. From the resulting dialog box,
open your server's *.tlb file.

What you will see next is a dialog listing each IDispatch-based interface found in your
server's IDL file. As you can see, MFC is about to generate a new COleDispatchDriver
derived class, which is used to wrap up calls to Invoke() on your behalf:

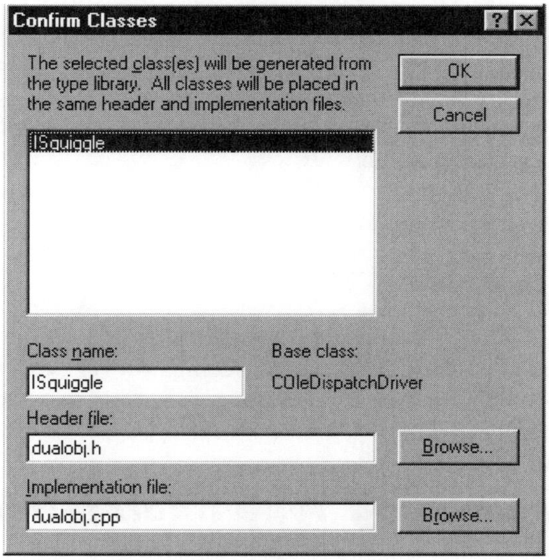

Figure 10-8:
Inserting a new
COleDispatch-
Driver class into
an MFC project.

If you examine the header file of this new class, you will see that each of the methods you
defined in your IDL have come through as public member functions:

```
// ISquiggle wrapper class
class ISquiggle : public COleDispatchDriver
{
public:
    ISquiggle() {}              // Calls COleDispatchDriver default constructor
    ISquiggle(LPDISPATCH pDispatch) : COleDispatchDriver(pDispatch) {}
    ISquiggle(const ISquiggle& dispatchSrc) : COleDispatchDriver(dispatchSrc) {}
// Attributes
public:
// Operations
public:
    void DrawASquiggle();
    void FlipASquiggle();
    void EraseASquiggle();
};
```

If you check out the implementation of each method, you will see a call to COleDispatch-Driver::InvokeHelper(). This handy method packs up your arguments into VARIANTS, places them into a DISPPARAMS structure, and calls Invoke(). For example, here is the code behind DrawASquiggle():

```
// Call Invoke(...[id(1)] ...)
void ISquiggle::DrawASquiggle()
{
    InvokeHelper(0x1, DISPATCH_METHOD, VT_EMPTY, NULL, NULL);
}
```

So then, what MFC has done is created an OO wrapper around the ISquiggle interface. To use this wrapper class, first create some GUI mechanism to trigger the calls to CoSquiggle (your lab solution uses a custom Toolbar button). In your squiggling activation code, use your new ISquiggle shim class by creating an instance, calling CreateDispatch(), and invoking each method of ISquiggle:

```
// CreateDispatch() does the work to grab your object's IDispatch interface.
void CMFCClientView::OnSquig()
{
    ISquiggle s;
    s.CreateDispatch("DualObject.CoDualSquiggle");
    s.DrawASquiggle();
    s.FlipASquiggle();
    s.EraseASquiggle();
}
```

That's it! MFC takes care of the grunt work.

To wrap up the story so far, when you support dual interfaces, you make your object as flexible as possible to the clients it serves. Now, before seeing how ATL can help, we will take a quick examination of using type information in the server code to make implementing the methods of IDispatch far less painful.

Building Your Dispinterface Using Type Information

So then, thus far we have examined how to create a raw dispinterface in C++, as well as defining and implementing a dual interface with the help of IDL. Before we examine what the ATL framework will do for us when working with IDispatch, we will examine one last way to build up an implementation for your dispinterface using the server's type information.

When you think about it, the MIDL-generated *.tlb file is a perfect snapshot that describes the entire exposed functionality within the COM housing. Using a type library, a client understands the coclasses, interfaces, and DISPIDs for each member in the dispinterface (using the [id] attribute). So, if a COM client can load our type information to make requests of the COM server, it only stands to reason that the COM server can also use its own type information if the need should arise.

When you are implementing a dual interface in raw C++, you have seen that updating the DISPIDs and Invoke() implementation can become tedious as you add more methods and properties to the coclass. When you add a new member to the dispinterface, this will typically entail updating your IDispatch logic to hand out the correct DISPID and trigger the correct function based on the DISPID. Rather than going through these steps by hand, what if we were provided a way to delegate the task of looking up a DISPID and triggering the correct method to the COM subsystem?

If we were to load up our type information from within the coclass, we could simply hold onto this type information during the lifetime of the coclass and, using some COM library methods, let COM worry about the dispinterface logic. By doing so, we only need to keep our IDL file up to date, and we can avoid having to write GetIDsOfNames() and Invoke() logic when we extend our dispinterface. The COM library does offer this very functionality, and as we will see, ATL uses this same approach when providing an implementation for your dual interfaces.

Assume we wish to modify CoSquiggle one last time. Here, we are going to make use of the coclass's own type information to implement the methods of IDispatch. We would begin by adding a new private member variable to CoSquiggle to hold onto the type information of the dual interface:

```
// This version of CoSquiggle will make use of its own type information to
// provide an IDispatch implementation.
class CoDualSquiggle : public ISquiggle
{
public:
    CoDualSquiggle();
    virtual ~CoDualSquiggle();
...
private:
    ULONG m_ref;
    ITypeInfo* m_ptypeInfo;       // To hold onto our type information.
};
```

The ITypeInfo interface is another standard interface provided by COM, which allows you to programmatically pull information from your type library at run time. For our current needs, we will only make use of a small subset of its overall functionality. To begin with, we need to load the object's type library using LoadRegTypeLib(). This function will retrieve an ITypeLib interface that represents the type library itself. From a valid ITypeLib pointer, we can access specific aspects of the type library. Here we are interested in obtaining the type information for CoSquiggle's dual interface (IID_ISquiggle). Here is the code:

```
// When this object comes to life, load up the type library and grab the
// type information for your dual interface.
CoDualSquiggle::CoDualSquiggle() : m_ref(0), m_ptypeInfo(NULL)
```

```
{
     ++g_objCount;
     // When our object is constructed, we are going to
     // load up the *.tlb file and store it in our ITypeInfo pointer.
     ITypeLib* pTypeLibrary = NULL;
     HRESULT hr;
     hr = LoadRegTypeLib(LIBID_DualObjectWithTypeInfo, 1, 0,
                         LANG_NEUTRAL, &pTypeLibrary);
     if(SUCCEEDED(hr))
     {
          pTypeLibrary->GetTypeInfoOfGuid(IID_ISquiggle, &m_ptypeInfo);
          pTypeLibrary->Release();
     }
}
```

> **Note:**   As constructors do not allow a return value, you have no way to test if
> the type information has been loaded correctly. An alternative approach would
> be to create a secondary creation method, and have your IClassFactory::Cre-
> ateInstance() implementation call the method in question before exiting. This is
> more "ATL-like," but for now, we will stick to using the C++ constructor to load
> our type info.

If the above code is successful (which it will be, as long as we have registered our type
information into the system registry) we now have programmatic control over the server's
type library. As the ITypeInfo interface has been AddRef-ed by GetTypeInfoOfGuid(), we
will need to release our reference to it when the object shuts down:

```
// Release the type information when our object dies.
CoDualSquiggle::~CoDualSquiggle()
{
     --g_objCount;
     m_ptypeInfo->Release();
}
```

Now for the real fun. Using this valid ITypeInfo pointer, we can update our existing
IDispatch implementation as follows. First, as we do provide real type information to any
interested COM client, we should update GetTypeInfoCount() to return "1" (we have it)
rather than "0" (we have nothing):

```
// This version of CoDualSquiggle has valid type information.
STDMETHODIMP CoDualSquiggle::GetTypeInfoCount( UINT *pctinfo)
{
     // We DO support type information in this object.
     *pctinfo = 1;
     return S_OK;
}
```

As we have informed the world we have type info, we better be sure we return our
ITypeInfo if we are asked. We would update GetTypeInfo() as such:

```
// Return our type information and be sure to AddRef() accordingly.
STDMETHODIMP CoDualSquiggle::GetTypeInfo(
  UINT iTInfo,
  LCID lcid,
```

```
  ITypeInfo **ppTInfo)
{
    // Return pointer as we DO support type info.
    *ppTInfo = m_ptypeInfo;
    m_ptypeInfo->AddRef();
    return S_OK;
}
```

Next in line, we can simplify GetIDsOfNames() a great deal. The COM library provides the DispGetIDsOfNames() function to perform an automatic lookup of a requested DISPID based off a string name. The magic happens with help from your type information. As long as your dual interface has made use of the [id] attribute to mark each member of your dispinterface, this COM helper function finds the correct DISPID on your behalf. The really great news is that your dispinterface can now grow over time without requiring you to update the implementation of GetIDsOfNames():

```
// Use the ITypeInfo pointer and DispGetIDsOfNames() to do the
// grunt work.
STDMETHODIMP CoDualSquiggle::GetIDsOfNames( REFIID riid,
              LPOLESTR *rgszNames, UINT cNames, LCID lcid,
              DISPID *rgDispId)
{
    // Now we just delegate the work of the lookup to our type library.
    return DispGetIDsOfNames(m_ptypeInfo, rgszNames, cNames, rgDispId);
}
```

Last but not least, we will use our type information to provide the implementation of Invoke(). Making use of the COM library function DispInvoke(), we shuttle in the client-supplied parameters and our ITypeInfo pointer. Again, the best news is that this allows us to forget about updating Invoke() each time we add new members to the dispinterface:

```
// Delegate all work to the COM library.
STDMETHODIMP CoDualSquiggle::Invoke( DISPID dispIdMember, REFIID riid,
              LCID lcid, WORD wFlags, DISPPARAMS *pDispParams,
              VARIANT *pVarResult, EXCEPINFO *pExcepInfo,
              UINT *puArgErr)
{
    // Again, delegate to the type info.
    return DispInvoke(this, m_ptypeInfo, dispIdMember, wFlags, pDispParams,
                 pVarResult, pExcepInfo, puArgErr);
}
```

Great! With this, we are now able to implement CoDualSquiggle's late binding behavior using the COM library and our server's type information. When our coclass is created, it loads up its type library, and gains access to ISquiggle's type information (and therefore the correct DISPIDs, function names, and parameters). If a client is making an early bound connection, this type information is never accessed, as the client is working directly with the ISquiggle vTable interface.

However, if the client has bound late using IDispatch, when (for example) DrawASquiggle() is called, GetIDsOfNames() looks up the DISPID from the loaded type information. Invoke() also makes use of this type information to ultimately call the same method (DrawASquiggle()) as an early bound client.

Lab 10-3: A Dual Object Implemented with Type Information

In this final raw C++ lab, we will make use of our own type information to help build a better dispinterface (read: less code to write). Here you will modify the implementation of CoSquiggle to make use of the COM library and your type information to fill out the details of Invoke() and GetIDsOfNames(). This approach is far easier than updating your dispinterface by hand as every new property and method comes along. Once you have come this far, understanding ATL's IDispatch implementation will be trivial, given that ATL follows the same approach as outlined in this lab.

The solution for this lab can be found on your CD-ROM under:
Labs\Chapter 10\DualWithTypeInfo
Labs\Chapter 10\DualWithTypeInfo\Dual VB Client

Step One: Load the Type Information

Note: Again, although I am assuming that you will be making modifications to Lab 10-2, this lab (and the solution) works with an entirely new in-proc server.

In this final iteration of the raw C++ CoSquiggle, we will modify our current implementation of IDispatch to make use of our type information. If you have not done so already, open up your previous version of CoSquiggle (Lab 10-2). This time around, CoSquiggle is going to make use of its own type information to implement its dispinterface. Begin by adding a private data member of type ITypeInfo* (beyond this, nothing else will need to change in your header file):

```
// This time with type info!
class CoDualSquiggle : public ISquiggleTI
{
...
private:
     ULONG m_ref;
     ITypeInfo* m_ptypeInfo;
};
```

Now, in your constructor, load your type information using the LoadRegTypeInfo() COM library function. Be sure to include your *_i.c MIDL-generated file to make use of the LIBID constant. If that call is successful, gain type information for your ISquiggle interface, and store it in your ITypeInfo pointer:

```
// Upon construction we load our type information.
#include "dualobjwithti_i.c" // MIDL-generated file...
CoDualSquiggle::CoDualSquiggle() : m_ref(0), m_ptypeInfo(NULL)
{
     ++g_objCount;
     // When our object is constructed, we are going to
     // load up the *.tlb file and store it in our ITypeInfo pointer.
     ITypeLib* pTypeLibrary = NULL;
     HRESULT hr;
     hr = LoadRegTypeLib(LIBID_DualObjectWithTypeInfo, 1, 0,
                         LANG_NEUTRAL, &pTypeLibrary);
     if(SUCCEEDED(hr))
```

```
    {
        pTypeLibrary->GetTypeInfoOfGuid(IID_ISquiggleTI, &m_ptypeInfo);
        pTypeLibrary->Release();
    }
}
```

In the destructor, be sure you release your type information:

```
// Unload our type info.
CoDualSquiggle::~CoDualSquiggle()
{
    --g_objCount;
    m_ptypeInfo->Release();
}
```

Step Two: Use that Type Information!

Next, we will need to reimplement all four methods of IDispatch to make use of your type information. Recall that the dispinterface is the summation of all properties and methods supported by a given coclass's IDispatch implementation. If you were to code GetIDsOfNames() and Invoke() in straight C++, this would entail adding a new string comparison condition in GetIDsOfNames() and a new case statement in Invoke(). Rather than updating everything by hand, the COM library provides methods that will route DISPIDs to methods in your coclass. The only trick to making this work is to ensure that the functions of your dispinterface (i.e., all the methods with the [id] attribute) have a method in the supporting coclass with the same signature. Begin by modifying GetTypeInfo() and GetTypeInfoCount() to inform the client that we do indeed have type information:

```
// Inform client we have some type info & return a pointer to that info.
STDMETHODIMP CoDualSquiggle::GetTypeInfoCount( UINT *pctinfo)
{
    // We DO support type information in this object.
    *pctinfo = 1;
    return S_OK;
}
// Don't forget to AddRef()! We have some other user!
STDMETHODIMP CoDualSquiggle::GetTypeInfo( UINT iTInfo, LCID lcid,
                                          ITypeInfo **ppTInfo)
{
    // Return pointer as we DO support type info.
    *ppTInfo = m_ptypeInfo;
    m_ptypeInfo->AddRef();
    return S_OK;
}
```

Now, reinvent your coding of GetIDsOfNames() to simply call the COM library function DispGetIDsOfNames(), sending in the client-supplied parameters:

```
// Client gives us a string name, so do a lookup
// between the string and the cookie.
STDMETHODIMP CoDualSquiggle::GetIDsOfNames( REFIID riid,
  LPOLESTR *rgszNames, UINT cNames, LCID lcid, DISPID *rgDispId)
{
    // We still only support one name at a time.
    if(cNames > 1)
```

```
return E_INVALIDARG;
        return DispGetIDsOfNames(m_ptypeInfo, rgszNames, cNames, rgDispId);
}
```

Do the same sort of update with your Invoke() method, this time calling DispInvoke():

```
// Now, based on the DISPID, call the correct helper function
// using type info.
STDMETHODIMP CoDualSquiggle::Invoke( DISPID dispIdMember, REFIID riid,
  LCID lcid, WORD wFlags, DISPPARAMS *pDispParams, VARIANT *pVarResult,
  EXCEPINFO *pExcepInfo, UINT *puArgErr)
{
    return DispInvoke(this, m_ptypeInfo, dispIdMember, wFlags, pDispParams,
                    pVarResult, pExcepInfo, puArgErr);
}
```

Go ahead and recompile your server! That is all we need to do in order to build a better dispinterface. To prove the point, go into your project's IDL file and add in another method (or property) to your dual interface. For example:

```
// Now when we update our dual interfaces, we will not need to update our IDispatch
// coding!
[uuid(99E314A7-58C2-11d3-B926-0020781238D4), object, dual]
interface ISquiggleTI : IDispatch
{
    [id(1)] HRESULT DrawASquiggle();
    [id(2)] HRESULT FlipASquiggle();
    [id(3)] HRESULT EraseASquiggle();
    [id(4)] HRESULT Explode();
};
```

Then, provide an implementation for your new method(s) (or properties):

```
// Again, early and late bound clients will each ultimately end up calling the
// same method.
STDMETHODIMP CoDualSquiggle::Explode()
{
    // Oh rats!
    MessageBox(NULL, "OH NO!", "CoDualSquiggle has EXPLODED",
            MB_OK | MB_SETFOREGROUND);
    return S_OK;
}
```

Finally, before testing our new dispinterface, we need to register the type information into the system. Add the following lines to your *.reg file (with your GUID and path, of course) and remerge:

```
; Need type information registered
;
HKEY_CLASSES_ROOT\TypeLib\{99E314A0-58C2-11d3-B926-0020781238D4}\1.0 = Dual With Type Info
Server Type Lib
HKEY_CLASSES_ROOT\TypeLib\{99E314A0-58C2-11d3-B926-0020781238D4}\ 1.0\0\Win32 =
E:\ATL\Labs\Chapter 10\DualWithTypeInfo\Debug\DualObjWithTI.tlb
```

Step Three: Use that Type Information Again!

Finally, we will update the previous VB client to call the new Explode() method (or whatever methods/properties you dreamed up). Simply add calls to both the early and late bound logic, and run the program.

So then, here is the summation of IDispatch programming thus far:

- You may build your dispinterface using straight C++. This can become a bother if you have a large dispinterface, as you need to continuously update your GetIDsOfNames() and Invoke() logic.

- You may build a dispinterface by leveraging your type information. In this case, you can simply update your IDL code and add methods to your coclass. The IDispatch logic now leverages your type information using the COM library.

For the next logical step, on to ATL!

Building your Dispinterface Using ATL

ATL provides such fantastic support for IDispatch that the work on your part becomes a non-issue. If you are creating a brand new coclass using the ATL Object Wizard, simply ensure you specify a dual interface from the Attributes tab:

Figure 10-9:
Specifying a dual interface with ATL.

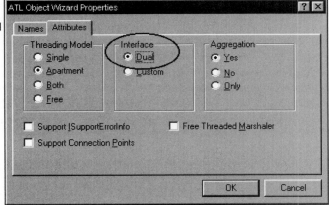

> **Note:** The ATL Object Wizard does not provide a way to support a pure dispinterface (i.e., IDispatch only).

When you specify a dual interface, you will see that your initial [default] interface has been configured with the correct IDL attributes to configure it as a dual. Assume we have created a new ATL DLL, and have inserted the CoATLSquiggle simple object. Our ICoATL-Squiggle interface definition would appear as such:

```
// The initial IDL definition for an ATL dual interface.
[
    object,
    uuid(938EA4F3-5802-11D3-B926-0020781238D4),
    dual,
    helpstring("ICoATLSquiggle Interface"),
    pointer_default(unique)
]
interface ICoATLSquiggle : IDispatch
{
```

```
     [id(1)] HRESULT DrawASquiggle();
     [id(2)] HRESULT FlipASquiggle();
     [id(3)] HRESULT EraseASquiggle();
};
```

As dual interface objects must be able to return an IDispatch pointer upon request, you will notice that your COM_MAP has been updated with a COM_INTERFACE_ENTRY listing to support late binding. Most importantly, your class will now derive from a new ATL template, IDispatchImpl<>:

```
// A dual interface ATL object will always derive from IDispatchImpl<>.
class ATL_NO_VTABLE CCoATLSquiggle :
     public CComObjectRootEx<CComSingleThreadModel>,
     public CComCoClass<CCoATLSquiggle, &CLSID_CoATLSquiggle>,
     public IDispatchImpl<ICoATLSquiggle, &IID_ICoATLSquiggle,
                          &LIBID_ATLDUALOBJECTLib>
{
...
BEGIN_COM_MAP(CCoATLSquiggle)
     COM_INTERFACE_ENTRY(ICoATLSquiggle)       // Smart clients.
     COM_INTERFACE_ENTRY(IDispatch)            // Dumb clients.
END_COM_MAP()
...
};
```

Beyond these slight changes, everything else is as you would expect. You can use all the same CASE tools to populate your interface and write the necessary implementations (e.g., Add Method Wizard, Add Property Wizard, Implement Interface Wizard). The logic of IDispatch is of no concern to you, as IDispatchImpl<> is doing the work of finding DISPIDs and calling Invoke() for any late bound client.

The IDispatchImpl<> Template

ATL provides a complete implementation of IDispatch using your server's type information. In fact, the code you examined in the previous section (CoSquiggle with type information) is just about the exact same code used by ATL! IDispatchImpl<> implements the four methods of IDispatch for your dual interface coclasses. The details of each method are fleshed out by use of an ATL helper class named CComTypeInfoHolder. This class is a wrapper around your type library and, as you might expect, is loading your server and extracting the type information for your dual interface, just as we did in the previous example. <atlcom.h> defines IDispatchImpl<> as so:

```
// IDispatchImpl<> provides a full implementation of IDispatch based off your
// server's type information.
template <class T, const IID* piid, const GUID* plibid = &CComModule::m_libid, WORD wMajor =
1, WORD wMinor = 0, class tihclass = CComTypeInfoHolder>
class ATL_NO_VTABLE IDispatchImpl : public T
{
public:
     // A typedef to CComTypeInfoHolder.
     typedef tihclass _tihclass;
     STDMETHOD(GetTypeInfoCount)(UINT* pctinfo)
     {
          *pctinfo = 1;
          return S_OK;
```

```
        }
        STDMETHOD(GetTypeInfo)(UINT itinfo, LCID lcid, ITypeInfo** pptinfo)
        {
                return _tih.GetTypeInfo(itinfo, lcid, pptinfo);
        }
        STDMETHOD(GetIDsOfNames)(REFIID riid, LPOLESTR* rgszNames,
                UINT cNames, LCID lcid, DISPID* rgdispid)
        {
                return _tih.GetIDsOfNames(riid, rgszNames, cNames, lcid, rgdispid);
        }
        STDMETHOD(Invoke)(DISPID dispidMember, REFIID riid,
                LCID lcid, WORD wFlags, DISPPARAMS* pdispparams,
                VARIANT* pvarResult, EXCEPINFO* pexcepinfo, UINT* puArgErr)
        {
                return _tih.Invoke((IDispatch*)this, dispidMember, riid, lcid,
                wFlags, pdispparams, pvarResult, pexcepinfo, puArgErr);
        }
protected:
        // An instance of CComTypeInfoHolder.
        static _tihclass _tih;
        static HRESULT GetTI(LCID lcid, ITypeInfo** ppInfo)
        {
                return _tih.GetTI(lcid, ppInfo);
        }
};
```

IDispatchImpl<> takes six parameters, four of which have default values. You must specify the GUID and name of the dual interface this template is wrapping using the first and second parameters. Beyond this, you may specify the major and minor version of your type library (which is defaulted to version 1.0), as well as your LIBID and the class that is holding onto your type information (which is by default the ATL CComTypeInfoHolder class).

   As you can see, the CComTypeInfoHolder class is held in the _tih member variable, which is used to provide the implementation of GetTypeInfoCount(), GetTypeInfo(), GetIDsOfNames(), and Invoke(). Finally, also notice that your coclass will inherit the GetTI() member function, which allows you to access the type information in your own coclass-specific coding.

The ATL Type Information Wrapper Class: CComTypeInfoHolder

This ATL helper class is responsible for holding onto your type information during the execution of your coclass. It is also defined in <atlcom.h>. The first point of interest is the public data members defined by the class. Note that your ITypeInfo interface, major and minor version number, LIBID, and so forth are all held by CComTypeInfoHolder:

```
// CComTypeInfoHolder maintains all relevant type information.
class CComTypeInfoHolder
{
public:
        const GUID* m_pguid;
        const GUID* m_plibid;
        WORD m_wMajor;
        WORD m_wMinor;
        ITypeInfo* m_pInfo;
```

...
};

Next we have the GetTI() member function, which does the work of loading the type library and holding onto the ITypeInfo interface. Here is a streamlined version, illustrating the relevant points under discussion:

```
// Load the type library and gain an ITypeInfo pointer to your dual interface.
inline HRESULT CComTypeInfoHolder::GetTI(LCID lcid)
{
    HRESULT hRes = E_FAIL;
    if (m_pInfo == NULL)
    {
        ITypeLib* pTypeLib;
        hRes = LoadRegTypeLib(*m_plibid, m_wMajor, m_wMinor, lcid, &pTypeLib);
        if (SUCCEEDED(hRes))
        {
            CComPtr<ITypeInfo> spTypeInfo;
            hRes = pTypeLib->GetTypeInfoOfGuid(*m_pguid, &spTypeInfo);
            if (SUCCEEDED(hRes))
            {
                CComPtr<ITypeInfo> spInfo(spTypeInfo);
                CComPtr<ITypeInfo2> spTypeInfo2;
                if (SUCCEEDED(
                    spTypeInfo->QueryInterface(&spTypeInfo2)))
                    spInfo = spTypeInfo2;
                LoadNameCache(spInfo);
                m_pInfo = spInfo.Detach();
            }
            pTypeLib->Release();
        }
    }
    return hRes;
}
```

Here, your type library is loaded with a call to LoadRegTypeLib(). GetTypeInfoOfGuid() is then called to obtain an ITypeInfo pointer to your dual interface (via some ATL smart pointer logic). This interface pointer is then held in the m_pInfo member variable.

With that aside (and given your current understanding of this approach to implementing IDispatch), the code of IDispatchImpl<> is quite straightforward. For each member of IDispatch, ATL simply leverages the CComTypeInfoHolder member variable. Again, here is the ATL implementation of GetIDsOfNames(), which in turn delegates all real work to your server's type library and the COM library:

```
// It can't get much easier than this.
STDMETHOD(GetIDsOfNames)(REFIID riid, LPOLESTR* rgszNames,
                         UINT cNames, LCID lcid, DISPID* rgdispid)
{
    return _tih.GetIDsOfNames(riid, rgszNames, cNames, lcid, rgdispid);
}
```

So then, ATL is using the same approach we used in our third version of CoSquiggle. Recall that we also loaded our type library, extracted type information for the dual interface, and delegated our IDispatch implementation to our ITypeInfo pointer. ATL makes late binding a non-issue. Just check the correct option in the ATL Object Wizard, and code some COM objects.

Regarding Multiple Dual Interfaces on a Single Coclass

As you build ATL COM objects that support a dual interface, you are bound to ask what to do when you wish to extend your object's functionality (i.e., add another interface). The Object Wizard provides options for custom and dual interfaces, and given what you know about the virtues of the dual interface, you may decide to extend CoSquiggle with another dual as so:

```
// IDL for another dual.
[ object, uuid(21D961E0-5F09-11d3-B928-0020781238D4), dual ]
interface IColor : IDispatch
{
    [id(1)] HRESULT SetTheColor([in] long colorID);
};
// A dual interface ATL object will always derive from IDispatchImpl<>.
class ATL_NO_VTABLE CCoATLSquiggle :
    public CComObjectRootEx<CComSingleThreadModel>,
    public CComCoClass<CCoATLSquiggle, &CLSID_CoATLSquiggle>,
    public IDispatchImpl<ICoATLSquiggle, &IID_ICoATLSquiggle,
                         &LIBID_ATLDUALOBJECTLib>,
    public IDispatchImpl<IColor, &IID_IColor,
                         &LIBID_ATLDUALOBJECTLib>
{
...
BEGIN_COM_MAP(CCoATLSquiggle)
    COM_INTERFACE_ENTRY(ICoATLSquiggle)
    COM_INTERFACE_ENTRY(IColor)
    COM_INTERFACE_ENTRY2(IDispatch, IColor)
END_COM_MAP()
...
};
```

Note that because we are using IDispatchImpl<> to provide coding details for the methods of IDispatch, we need to derive from this template twice (once for each dual interface). However, doing so will confuse the compiler, as we offer two possible ways to obtain the IDispatch interface. As you have already seen, ATL provides the COM_INTERFACE_ENTRY2() macro for this very ambiguity. However, this is not the problem.

The whole reason for supporting IDispatch is to allow dumb clients to access your server, given they provide no way for developers to directly call QueryInterface(). Now, if you have two (or more) dual interfaces on a single coclass, how are the dumb clients ever going to gain access to them? They can't! Dumb clients will only be able to access the dispinterface marked as the [default] interface. Period. A smart client will always choose to gain access to the custom vTable interfaces of your COM objects. Therefore, the whole idea of supporting multiple dual interfaces on a single coclass makes no sense.

Extending a coclass so that both smart and dumb clients are happy takes a bit of hoop jumping. One approach should be to define a single dual interface on the coclass, which is assumed to be used exclusively by dumb clients. Once you have added this dual interface, you safely version the object by adding additional custom vTable interfaces to the object. If you wish to allow the dumb clients to have access to the methods defined in a new vTable interface, simply extend the dispinterface of your existing dual.

For example, if CoSquiggle were to support the IColor interface, we could rewrite our IDL to define two <u>custom vTable interfaces</u>: IColor and ICoATLSquiggle (ICoATLSquiggle was originally a dual, which we have retrofitted to now be a pure vTable interface) and a new single dual for scripting clients:

```
// IDL for new vTable interface.
[ object, uuid(21D961E0-5F09-11d3-B928-0020781238D4), oleautomation ]
interface IColor : IUnknown
{
    HRESULT SetTheColor([in] long colorID);
};
// Retrofit our previous dual to be a vTable interface.
[ object, uuid(938EA4F3-5802-11D3-B926-0020781238D4) , oleautomation ]
interface ICoATLSquiggle : IUnknown
{
    HRESULT DrawASquiggle();
    HRESULT FlipASquiggle();
    HRESULT EraseASquiggle();
};
// This interface allows dumb clients to get at the functionality offered by the
// vTable interfaces.
[
    object,
    uuid(938EA4F3-5802-11D3-B926-0020781238D4),
    dual,
    helpstring("ICoATLSquiggle Interface"),
    pointer_default(unique)
]
interface ITheInterfaceForDumbClients : IDispatch
{
    [id(1)] HRESULT DrawASquiggle();
    [id(2)] HRESULT FlipASquiggle();
    [id(3)] HRESULT EraseASquiggle();
    [id(4)] HRESULT SetTheColor([in] long colorID);
};
```

In this way, we choose which methods of the sole [dual] will be accessible to late binding clients. This may or may not be the entire functionality supported by the set of vTable interfaces—that's a design choice. Notice as well that each vTable interface has been assigned the [oleautomation] attribute. This not only more clearly illustrates that these interfaces are VARIANT compatible, but has the added bonus of forcing ATL to register each interface under HKCR\Interface and mark each as using the universal marshaler.

And with this, we wrap up our formal discussion of scriptable COM objects. Here is a question: What if you wish to add late binding capabilities to a legacy ATL object that was not written to support IDispatch? Funny you should ask, as that is the topic of our next lab. Put CoCar on the web, and investigate the idea of a single dual interface on a coclass.

Lab 10-4: IDispatch Support in ATL

This lab will pull together all your knowledge of the IDispatch interface, and allow you to script your ATL CoCar from MS Internet Explorer. You will be modifying a previous coclass that was not configured to support IDispatch using the IDispatchImpl<> template.

Furthermore, you will contend with the reality that scripting clients can only access the [default] dual interface on an object—and see how to keep everyone happy.

 The solution for this lab can be found on your CD-ROM under:
Labs\Chapter 10\ScriptableCoCar
Labs\Chapter 10\ScriptableCoCar\Script Client

Step One: Adjust Your Existing IDL Code

Note: To keep things simple, I suggest you choose to retrofit your existing ATLCoCar project from Chapter 6.

Back in Chapter 6, you created an ATL-based server (ATLCarServer) containing a single coclass (ATLCoCar) with no support for scripting. At that time, CoCar supported a set of custom vTable interfaces:

```
// The original coclass has no support for IDispatch.
[ uuid(271CC4E1-0805-11D3-B8E5-0020781238D4)]
coclass ATLCoCar
{
    [default] interface ICreateCar;
    interface IStats;
    interface IEngine;
    interface IOwnerInfo;
};
```

To support IDispatch, you will need to edit your IDL code to support a single dual interface, which is intended to be used only by scripting clients. Define a new dual interface in IDL as the following:

```
// This interface is intended for scripting clients only.
[object, uuid(938EA507-5802-11D3-B926-0020781238D4), dual,
helpstring("If you are a smart client don't use me!"), pointer_default(unique) ]
interface IDualCoCar : IDispatch
{
};
```

Next, you need to decide which methods of your existing interfaces will be available to scripting clients. As you have seen, scripting clients are only able to access the [default] IDispatch interface, and therefore multiple dual interfaces are of little help. Update your dual interface to support the following dispinterface (just copy and paste the method prototypes from the existing vTable definitions):

```
// Your [default] dual will leverage the existing vTable methods.
interface IDualCoCar : IDispatch
{
    [id(1)] HRESULT SetPetName([in] BSTR petName);
    [id(2)] HRESULT SetMaxSpeed([in] int maxSp);
    [id(3)] HRESULT DisplayStats();
    [id(4)] HRESULT GetPetName([out, retval] BSTR* petName);
    [id(5)] HRESULT SpeedUp();
    [id(6)] HRESULT GetMaxSpeed([out, retval] int* maxSpeed);
    [id(7)] HRESULT GetCurSpeed([out, retval] int* curSpeed);
    [propget, id(8)] HRESULT Name([out, retval] BSTR *pVal);
```

```
    [propput, id(8)] HRESULT Name([in] BSTR newVal);
    [propget, id(9)] HRESULT Address([out, retval] BSTR *pVal);
    [propput, id(9)] HRESULT Address([in] BSTR newVal);
};
```

Finally, be sure that your dual interface is assigned as the [default], and mark each existing vTable interface with the [oleautomation] attribute:

```
// Mark the [default] as your new dual.
coclass DualCoCar
{
    [default] interface IDualCoCar;    // Script clients only get the [default] dual.
    interface IStats;
    interface IOwnerInfo;
    interface IEngine;
    interface ICreateCar;
};
```

Step Two: Update Your Coclass

To leverage ATL's support for dual interfaces, you must derive your coclass from IDispatchImpl< > and update your COM_MAP. As we support only a single dual (and rightfully so) we only need to tweak CATLCoCar as such:

```
// Update your coclass to implement IDispatch.
class ATL_NO_VTABLE CDualCoCar :
    public CComObjectRootEx<CComSingleThreadModel>,
    public CComCoClass<CDualCoCar, &CLSID_DualCoCar>,
    public IDispatchImpl<IDualCoCar, &IID_IDualCoCar,
                         &LIBID_SCRIPTABLECOCARLib>,
    public ICreateCar,
    public IStats,
    public IEngine,
    public IOwnerInfo
{
...

    BEGIN_COM_MAP(CDualCoCar)
        COM_INTERFACE_ENTRY(IDualCoCar)
        COM_INTERFACE_ENTRY(IDispatch)
        COM_INTERFACE_ENTRY(ICreateCar)
        COM_INTERFACE_ENTRY(IStats)
        COM_INTERFACE_ENTRY(IEngine)
        COM_INTERFACE_ENTRY(IOwnerInfo)
    END_COM_MAP()
...
};
```

We do not need to add any new code for the methods behind any of the existing interfaces, including our new dual. Recall that IDispatchImpl< > will use your type information to determine which method to call (in the coclass) for a given DISPID. As you have already written code for the custom vTable methods, these same methods will be called by late bound clients using IDispatch! The server is complete.

Step Three: Build a Web Client

Some of you might think I am being unfair, making you write VB, Java, and now HTML code in a book about ATL. Well, call me cruel (really though, COM is all about language independence). If you are not a webmaster, feel free to use the HTML test client included on your CD-ROM (be sure to update the ProgID). This page was built using MS Visual InterDev 6.0, and is straight HTML. The relevant parts of this page are listed below:

```
' For the most part, VBScript looks and feels like VB proper.
'
<SCRIPT language = VBScript>
dim o
Sub btnCreateCar_onClick
     set o = CreateObject("ScriptableCoCar.DualCoCar")
     o.SetPetName (petName.value)
     o.Address = ownerAddress.value
     o.SetMaxSpeed (maxSpeed.value)
     o.Name = ownerName.value
     txtSpeed.value = o.GetCurSpeed
End Sub
Sub btnSpeedUp_onClick
     if o.GetCurSpeed < o.GetMaxSpeed then
          o.SpeedUp
          txtSpeed.value = o.GetCurSpeed
     else
          msgbox o.GetPetName() & " is Destroyed!",,"Lead Foot!"
     end if
End Sub
Sub btnGetStats_onClick
     o.DisplayStats
     msgbox o.Name,,"Your name is:"
     msgbox o.Address ,,"You live here:"
End Sub
</SCRIPT>
```

When you run the script, IE will catch that your coclass is not marked as "safe for scripting" and will issue the following warning dialog:

Figure 10-10: Not safe for scripting! Need more GUIDs.

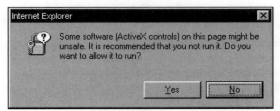

In Chapter 9, we spent some time discussing COM categories. As you recall, ATL allows you to add support for custom or standard CATIDs. If you wish to mark your new CoCar as web safe, add the following CATEGORY_MAP to your coclass and recompile:

```
// You must include the following header file to grab the correct GUIDs!
// #include <ObjSafe.h>
BEGIN_CATEGORY_MAP(CDualCoCar)
     IMPLEMENTED_CATEGORY(CATID_SafeForScripting)
     IMPLEMENTED_CATEGORY(CATID_SafeForInitializing)
END_CATEGORY_MAP()
```

When you do so, the ATL registrar will make additional entries under HKCR\CLSID\{guid} that informs IE your little automobile means no harm:

Figure 10-11:
Got the GUIDs;
safe for scripting
(and initializing).

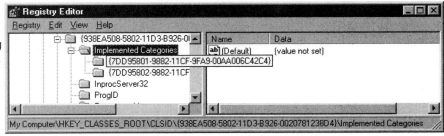

With that, here is your CoCar, in all its glory, from the mean streets of structured programming to the world of a web-enabled COM object.

Figure 10-12:
A web-based
CoCar client.

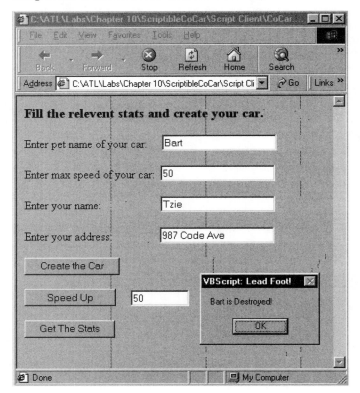

Chapter Summary

This chapter addressed the all-important idea of scriptable COM objects. As you have learned, not all COM languages are able to work with your custom vTable interfaces, and for them, we have IDispatch. This standard COM interface allows the dumb clients to access your server using a level of indirection provided by a dynamic lookup of numerical cookies and a resulting method invocation.

We examined a number of ways to build a dispinterface, and as you are sure to agree, ATL allows you to support IDispatch with no fuss. However, you did discover a very important issue in late binding: Dumb clients can only access the [default] dual interface of your coclass. We examined one approach to keep everyone happy, which was to establish a single [dual] coclass that allows your scripting clients to access the same functionality as vTable-able clients.

To safely extend your coclass with new behavior, add vTable interfaces to the object, and echo the changes in your default dual by adding additional DISPIDs. The ATL framework and IDispatchImpl< > ensure the correct methods will be called by both early and late bound clients.

Chapter 11

COM Enumerators and COM Collections

Objectives:

■ **Examine a number of techniques for returning complex data to COM clients.**

■ **Understand COM enumerators.**

■ **Examine ATL's support for COM enumeration.**

■ **Build a static and dynamic COM collection.**

■ **Understand ATL's support for COM collections.**

We have already seen how COM object "A" can contain a single COM object "B" (just have the outer object call CoCreateInstance() on the inner object). However, we have not examined how a given object can contain a collection of objects, which may be obtained by the client in a standard fashion. COM provides a mythical interface named IEnumXXXX that allows a client a fixed way to "pull" a batch of items from a coclass, rather than asking for an item one at a time. This pattern is termed *COM enumeration*, and in this chapter we will examine how to build such an object container.

We then investigate a *COM collection*, which is (in essence) a language-neutral variation on the COM enumeration pattern. We also examine some of the templates provided by the ATL framework to help build COM enumerators and collections, and see how COM clients can manipulate their contents.

Developing Complex Interface Parameters in IDL

The only way a COM client and COM object can communicate is through an interface. As we have seen, COM interface methods may take combinations of [in], [out], [in, out], and [out, retval] parameters. When using the [out, retval] attribute, however, you cannot create a COM interface that looks like the following:

```
// A given method can only have a single [out, retval].
// Even more restrictive, it must be the last parameter in the method.
```

```
[object, uuid(1626EA2F-5F3C-11D3-B928-0020781238D4), dual]
interface IFeebleAttempt : IDispatch
{
    [id(1)]
    HRESULT TakeThisThatAndTheOther ([out, retval] BSTR* msgOne,
                                     [out, retval] BSTR* msgTwo,
                                     [out, retval] BSTR* msgThree);
    [id(2)]
    HRESULT RetValInTheMiddle([in] int x, [out, retval] BSTR* msg, [in] int y);
};
```

By law, a given COM interface method can have exactly one [out, retval], which must be attributed to the final parameter in the function. Therefore, while [out, retval] is great for sending back a single value to the COM client, most COM applications have a need to send back what could be referred to as "bulk data transfer." One approach is to configure a given method that contains a number of [out] only parameters. In this way, a client is able to fetch a number of logical values in a single call. Be aware, however, that not all COM language mappings support [out] only parameters. Thus, to begin this chapter we will investigate some common bulk data transfer techniques before diving into COM enumerations and COM collections.

Defining IDL Arrays as Method Parameters

 Your companion CD includes the BulkServer ATL project (and a VB test client) that illustrate the techniques we are about to examine. Feel free to load it up and follow along.

The first trick a COM developer may employ to transfer bulk data between a client and coclass is to configure a method making use of an array of IDL base types. In this way, a COM client may send or retrieve a batch of items in a single round trip. Of course, the items in the array must be of the same type.

Assume you wish to define a method that takes a fixed array of BSTRs that may be received (and altered) by the coclass. A fixed size array may be specified in IDL using the [size_of()] attribute. Parameters that may be changed by the coclass are marked as [in, out]. If we have a standard vTable interface named IStringArray, the UseTheseStrings() method may be defined and implemented as so:

```
// This method takes some number of strings, which may be changed by the coclass.
[ object, uuid(1626EA2F-5F3C-11D3-B928-0020781238D4)]
interface IStringArray : IUnknown
{
    HRESULT UseTheseStrings([in] short size, [in, out, size_is(size)] BSTR names[]);
};
// First show the current strings in the array and then change them.
STDMETHODIMP CCoStringArray::UseTheseStrings(short size, BSTR names[])
{
    USES_CONVERSION;
    // Show each BSTR in a message box.
    for(int i = 0; i < size; i++)
    {
        MessageBox(NULL, W2A(names[i]), "Message from the client!",
                   MB_OK | MB_SETFOREGROUND);
        // Now change them.
        SysReAllocString(&(names[i]), L"This is different...");
    }
}
```

```
    return S_OK;
}
```

A Visual Basic client may exercise UseTheseStrings() as the following:

```
' Create some strings and send in for processing.
'
Private Sub btnStrings_Click()
     Dim o As New CoStringArray
     ' Initial string array.
     Dim strs(3) As String
     strs(0) = "Hello"
     strs(1) = "there"
     strs(2) = "from"
     strs(3) = "VB..."
     o.UseTheseStrings 4, strs(0)        ' Note calling syntax!
     ' See how they were changed.
     Dim i As Integer
     For i = 0 To 3
          MsgBox strs(i), , "New String from coclass"
     Next i
End Sub
```

This approach has a few drawbacks. First of all, this type of array is not variant compliant.
If we were to add the [oleautomation] attribute to the IStringArray IDL declaration and
recompile, we are saddened to see warning MIDL2039 : interface does not conform to
[oleautomation] attribute. One solution to this problem is to rework IStringArray to use a
variant compliant SAFEARRAY.

SAFEARRAYs as Method Parameters

To create an automation compatible array of types, you need to use the variant compliant
SAFEARRAY structure. As you recall from the previous chapter, a SAFEARRAY resolves
to an array of VARIANT types. Assume we have the following dual interface,
ICoSafeArray:

```
// This interface can return a SAFEARRAY as well as receive a SAFEARRAY.
[ object, uuid(E19D07B3-5FBF-11D3-B929-0020781238D4), dual ]
interface ICoSafeArray : IDispatch
{
     [id(1)]
     HRESULT UseThisSafeArrayOfStrings([in] VARIANT strings);
     [id(2)]
     HRESULT GiveMeASafeArrayOfStrings([out, retval] VARIANT* pStrings);
};
```

When implementing this interface, we might first turn our attention to the
UseThisSafeArrayOfStrings() method. Here, the client creates a SAFEARRAY of BSTRs
and sends them into the server for processing. As ATL 3.0 has no SAFEARRAY wrapper
class, we must drop down to low-level COM library calls.

   We implement UseThisSafeArrayOfStrings() by first verifying that the VARIANT
parameter coming our way is indeed an array of BSTRs by examining the vt field accordingly. Next, we will copy the contents of the array into a SAFEARRAY structure, and
iterate over the items using SafeArrayAccessData(). When we are all finished, we release
our control over the SAFEARRAY by calling SafeArrayUnaccessData():

```
// Client gives us a batch of strings packaged in a safe array, which we
// use as in our program.
STDMETHODIMP CCoSafeArray::UseThisSafeArrayOfStrings(VARIANT strings)
{
    USES_CONVERSION;
    // Be sure we have an array of strings.
    if((strings.vt & VT_ARRAY) && (strings.vt & VT_BSTR))
    {
        // Grab the array.
        SAFEARRAY *pSA = strings.parray;
        BSTR *bstrArray;
        // Lock it down.
        SafeArrayAccessData(pSA, (void**)&bstrArray);
        // Read each item.
        for(int i = 0; i < pSA->rgsabound->cElements; i++)
        {
            CComBSTR temp = bstrArray[i];
            MessageBox(NULL, W2A(temp.m_str), "String says...",
                    MB_OK | MB_SETFOREGROUND);
        }
        // Unlock it.
        SafeArrayUnaccessData(pSA);
        SafeArrayDestroy(pSA);
    }
    return S_OK;
}
```

Now we can begin to deal with returning a SAFEARRAY of BSTRs to the client. We will implement GiveMeASafeArrayOfStrings() by making use of the COM library function SafeArrayCreate() to create a SAFEARRAY of some bounds. Next, we will fill the array with BSTRs and finally send this back to the client for processing (and disposal):

```
// Create a set of strings and give them back to the clients.
STDMETHODIMP CCoSafeArray::GiveMeASafeArrayOfStrings(VARIANT *pStrings)
{
    // Init and set the type of variant.
    VariantInit(pStrings);
    pStrings->vt = VT_ARRAY | VT_BSTR;
    SAFEARRAY *pSA;
    SAFEARRAYBOUND bounds = {4, 0};
    // Create the array (client must free the array with SafeArrayDestroy()).
    pSA = SafeArrayCreate(VT_BSTR, 1, &bounds);
    // Fill the array with data.
    BSTR *theStrings;
    SafeArrayAccessData(pSA, (void**)&theStrings);
        theStrings[0] = SysAllocString(L"Hello");
        theStrings[1] = SysAllocString(L"from");
        theStrings[2] = SysAllocString(L"the");
        theStrings[3] = SysAllocString(L"coclass!");
    SafeArrayUnaccessData(pSA);
    // Set return value.
    pStrings->parray = pSA;
    return S_OK;
}
```

Now assume we have a VB client that creates the coclass and requests a batch of strings. To declare a SAFEARRAY in VB, create a Variant data type, which can hold the return value of GiveMeASafeArrayOfStrings(). We can determine the size of this array using the intrinsic UBound() function, and place each item in a list box (see Figure 11-1):

Figure 11-1: Working with a safe array of BSTRs.

```
' Get some SAFE strings from the coclass.
'
Private Sub btnGetASafeArray_Click()
    Dim o As New CoSafeArray
    Dim strs As Variant
    ' Grab a number of BSTRs from the coclass.
    strs = o.GiveMeASafeArrayOfStrings
    Dim upper As Long
    Dim i As Long
    upper = UBound(strs)
    For i = 0 To upper
        List1.AddItem strs(i)
    Next i
End Sub
```

When you are interested in sending variable length arrays of data between clients and servers, the SAFEARRAY can do wonders. You can create an array of any variant compliant type and provide a relatively simple way to work with bulk data.

The only down side, of course, is the items in the array must be the same type. If you wish to send around complex structures as parameters, you will need to roll your own UDTs.

Structures as Method Parameters

Another way to move bulk data between COM entities is to specify IDL structures as method parameters. This can be handy when you wish to group together related data under a specific name. Assume you have an interface method that allows a client to send in a structure as a parameter, which the coclass may reconfigure if necessary. We would begin by writing some IDL code to define the structure. To make things more interesting, let's define one of the fields of this structure to be from a custom enumeration. Here is the IPet interface, which has a single method taking a single complex parameter:

```
// A custom enumeration which specifies a type of pet.
typedef enum PET_TYPE
{
    petDog      = 0,
    petCat      = 1,
    petTick     = 2
} PET_TYPE;
// A structure describing the pet.
typedef struct MyPet
{
    short Age;
    BSTR Name;
```

```
        PET_TYPE Type;
}MyPet;
// An interface using the structure.
[ object, uuid(1626EA31-5F3C-11D3-B928-0020781238D4)]
interface IPet : IUnknown
{
        HRESULT WorkWithAPet([in, out] MyPet* p);
};
```

The implementation will take the incoming MyPet structure and dump out the current contents, then reassign the fields to some new values:

```
// Use this struct!
STDMETHODIMP CCoPet::WorkWithAPet(MyPet *p)
{
        USES_CONVERSION;
        // Show current Name of pet.
        MessageBox(NULL, W2A(p->Name), "Name of pet is", MB_OK);
        // Show current Age of pet.
        char buff[80] = {0};
        sprintf(buff, "%d", p->Age);
        MessageBox(NULL, buff, "Age of pet is", MB_OK);
        // Show current Type of pet.
        char* strType[3] = {"Dog", "Cat", "Tick"};
        MessageBox(NULL, strType[p->Type], "Type of pet is", MB_OK);
        // Now change everything.
        SysReAllocString(&(p->Name), L"Bubbles");
        p->Age = 200;
        p->Type = petTick;
        return S_OK;
}
```

Now before you rush out and try this at home, remember that the universal marshaler (oleaut32.dll) can only support the use of structure parameters using NT SP 4.0 (or Win98) and Visual Basic 6.0. If you do not have this configuration, you can still use structure parameters with C++ clients, provided that you build and register your own custom proxy/stub DLL. For this discussion, the world is a happy place and we all support the latest and greatest development workstations. Therefore, a VB client may work with this interface as so:

```
' Send in a structure for processing.
'
Private Sub btnStruct_Click()
        ' Make a pet.
        Dim pet As MyPet
        pet.Name = "Fred"
        pet.Age = 20
        pet.Type = petDog
        ' Send in for processing.
        Dim o As New CoPet
        o.WorkWithAPet pet
        ' See what happened after the call.
        MsgBox pet.Age, , "New Age of Pet"
        MsgBox pet.Name, , "New Name of Pet"
        ' Map enum to string.
        Dim t(2) As String
```

```
    t(0) = "Dog"
    t(1) = "Cat"
    t(2) = "Tick"
    MsgBox t(pet.Type), , "New Type of Pet"
End Sub
```

Developing structure parameters can be a step in the right direction. However, in COM the greatest level of power and flexibility comes to us when we configure methods which define interfaces themselves as parameter types. As we have seen, this approach allows us to (in effect) send objects as parameters. Unlike classic OOP, we never really hold a true object reference, but an interface pointer.

Returning COM Interfaces as Method Parameters

The final method of bulk transfer we will examine is to have a method return an interface pointer to some other COM object. As we examined in Chapter 9, this design allows the COM developer to expose some hierarchy of objects within a server. For example, assume we have a topmost and directly creatable COM object named CoBoat. This object supports a single IBoat interface. Assume the GetTheEngine() method of IBoat returns an IEngine interface to the calling client. This is the classic Has-A relationship (a boat "has a" engine).

To begin, assume you have inserted a new CoBoat Simple Object supporting a [default] IBoat interface. Now assume you have also inserted a CoEngine Simple Object with IEngine marked as the [default]. The [default] interface of CoBoat can be defined as the following:

```
// We gain access to the engine only if we have a boat.
[ object, uuid(E19D07B5-5FBF-11D3-B929-0020781238D4) ]
interface IBoat : IUnknown
{
    [helpstring("method GetTheEngine")]
    HRESULT GetTheEngine([out, retval] IEngine** pEngine);
};
```

An ATL implementation of GetTheEngine() could make use of CComObject<>, calling CreateInstance().

```
// This method creates an engine and returns an IEngine reference to
// the client.
STDMETHODIMP CCoBoat::GetTheEngine(IEngine **pEngine)
{
    // We need to create an inner object and give out IEngine.
    CComObject<CCoEngine> *pEng;
    CComObject<CCoEngine>::CreateInstance(&pEng);
    pEng->QueryInterface(IID_IEngine, (void**)pEngine);
    return S_OK;
}
```

To complete this test situation, let's say that IEngine has a single method named Rev().

```
To use CoBoat from a VB test client, we can write the following:
' Create a boat and grab the engine.
'
Private Sub btnRevMyBoat_Click()
    Dim i As CoEngine
```

```
      Dim myBoat As New CoBoat
      ' Get the inner object from the outer object.
      Set i = myBoat.GetTheEngine
      i.Rev
End Sub
```

> **Note:**   Recall that if you do not wish to allow COM clients to directly create
> subobjects (such as CoEngine) you will need to alter your OBJECT_MAP by
> specifying the OBJECT_ENTRY_NON_CREATEABLE macro, as well as add the
> [noncreatable] coclass attribute.

Understanding COM Enumeration

When you define interfaces that contain methods returning interfaces, you essentially allow the object user to fetch a single object at a time. However, what if you wished to develop a COM interface that allowed a client to request a <u>batch</u> of items during a single call? For example, assume we have a coclass that contains 100 instances of another object, say a CoCarLot object containing CoCars.

Internally, CoCarLot may maintain an array of ICreateCar interfaces to represent each CoCar object. Once a client is able to create an instance of CoCarLot, it may ask for a reference to some specific interface that provides access to the subobjects. Let's call this hypothetical interface IEnumerateCars. Now, in your opinion, what sort of methods would this interface contain? At minimum, we may wish to allow clients to request a batch of ICreateCar interfaces using one method. Another method may allow the client to skip over some elements in the collection, while another may allow the client to reset the cursor to the beginning of the collection.

Now assume we have another development effort under way. This time we have a CoEmployees coclass that maintains 600 CoEmployee objects. Again, we may define a custom interface called IEnumerateEmployees, which contains methods looking (and behaving) much like the previous IEnumerateCars interface. When you boil things down to their essence, the only thing truly different between IEnumerateCars and IEnumerateEmployees is what they provide access to (cars or employees). The general behavior of each interface will most likely be the same.

Rather than forcing each and every COM developer to create unique names for enumeration methods, we are given a standard to follow such that all COM enumeration interfaces have the same basic set of methods. This is a good thing of course, as a developer is able to feel more at home when working with enumeration interfaces developed by individual programmers.

This standard is provided by a fictitious COM interface: IEnumXXXX. The odd thing about this interface is that it really does not exist (even odder is that you will find an entry for IEnumXXXX in online help). This interface is simply a suggested form to follow when creating a COM enumeration object. Replace "XXXX" with the name of the subobjects you are providing access to (e.g., IEnumCars, IEnumEmployees, IEnumFrogs, or whatnot).

Standard Enumeration Interfaces

COM does provide a number of canned IEnumXXXX interfaces which provide a way to iterate over many standard COM data types. For example, IEnumConnectionPoints and IEnumConnections are used to allow a client to grab "outbound" interfaces and information about connected clients from a coclass (more on this later in Chapter 12). Here is a partial listing of some predesigned COM enumeration interfaces:

Standard Enumeration Interface	Meaning in Life
IEnumUnknown	Allows a client to iterate over a set of IUnknown interfaces. As you may expect, from a given IUnknown pointer the client can navigate to more interesting interfaces on the underlying object.
IEnumVARIANT	Allows a client to iterate over a collection of VARIANT data types.
IEnumString	Provides a way for a client to iterate over a collection of COM strings.
IEnumConnectionPoints	Allows a client to iterate over any "connection points" held in the container object. A connection point is a standard way for a coclass to send events to any interested clients.
IEnumConnections	Enumerates over the set of "interested clients" (i.e., connections) for a given connection point object.

Methods of COM Enumeration Interfaces

If this set of standard enumeration interfaces does not fit the bill for your current needs, you may create your own custom enumeration interface. However, regardless of which type of enumerator you are implementing (or using) each will have a similar set of methods. The names of each method will be the same (if you uphold the standard); however, the parameters to each method will more than likely be different, depending on what your container object is exposing (cars, employees, frogs, and so on). To qualify as a COM enumerator interface, you should support the following methods:

Enumeration Interface Method	Meaning in Life
Next()	Allows a client to request a batch of elements from the container (e.g., "Give me the next 10 frogs").
Skip()	Allows a client to skip over some number of items in the container (e.g., "Skip over 4 frogs").
Reset()	Moves the container's cursor back to the beginning of the collection (e.g., "Move to the beginning of the frog list").
Clone()	Allows a client to make a copy of the current enumeration (e.g., "Copy the current frog enumerator").

Given these four methods, you should now understand the form provided by the mythical IEnumXXXX interface:

```
// The IEnumXXXX interface does not exist in the real world, but provides
// a suggested form for all COM enumeration interfaces to follow.
interface IEnumXXXX : IUnknown
{
    HRESULT Next( [in] ULONG cElements,          // Number requested.
                  [out] XXX* rgIXXX,             // Array of XXX.
                  [out] ULONG* pFetched);        // How many were returned?
    HRESULT Skip( [in] ULONG cElements)          // Number to skip over.
    HRESULT Reset();                             // Move to beginning of list.
    HRESULT Clone( [out] IEnumXXXX**);           // Give out a copy.
};
```

Notice that a traditional COM enumeration does not provide a way to insert or remove items from the container's underlying set of objects. Given this, a COM enumerator object will typically maintain some set of items with some upper limit (a standard C-style array usually fits the bill quite nicely).

If these facts about the COM enumerator strike you as too limiting, hang in there. In just a bit we will discuss COM collections, which are a variation on the simple enumeration pattern and do provide a way to insert and remove items in an [oleautomation] compatible manner. To get the ball rolling, we will now develop a simple COM enumeration from the ground up in C++, and then see what ATL has to offer us by way of framework support.

Building a Custom COM Enumerator in C++

 Your companion CD-ROM contains the AgeEnum server (and C++ client), found under Labs\Chapter 11\AgeEnum. Again, feel free to load it up and follow along.

The COM enumeration pattern consists of three players. First we have the container class that is home to the entire set of subobjects under its management, for example, CoFrogHolder. Next, we have the subobjects themselves (CoFrog). The container object will maintain a set of these subitems and define a cursor variable representing the current item "pointed to" in the set (m_currFrog). Finally, we have the enumerator interface (IEnumFrogs), which allows the client to pull over some number of subobjects. It is the enumerator interface that allows the client to affect the position of the cursor.

Imagine a very simple container named CoAgeHolder, which maintains a set of unsigned longs representing some arbitrary ages of some item. A client may manipulate these ULONG types using the custom IEnumAge interface. If the client obtains the IEnumAge interface from the container, it now has a way to pull over batches of ULONGs using the Next(), Skip(), Reset(), and Clone() methods. Here is the IDL:

```
// The CoAgeHolder container will implement this enumeration interface.
[ object, uuid(B5F10D50-53F1-11d3-AB20-00A0C9312D57) ]
interface IEnumAge : IUnknown
{
    // Give me the next n number of ULONGs.
    HRESULT Next([in] ULONG celt,
                 [out, size_is(celt), length_is(*pCeltFetched)] ULONG* rgVar,
                 [out] ULONG * pCeltFetched);
    // Skip over n items.
```

```
    HRESULT Skip([in] ULONG celt);
    // Reset the internal cursor to the beginning.
    HRESULT Reset();
    // Give out a snapshot of the current enumerator.
    HRESULT Clone([out] IEnumAge ** ppEnum);
};
```

CoAgeHolder will derive from IEnumAge, and therefore must provide implementation for seven methods. We will ignore the code behind IUnknown, as I am quite sure you can envision these details by now. The coclass will specify a few points of private data, most notably a ULONG to represent the cursor and an array of ULONGs to hold the ages:

```
// This class is a container of ULONGs. Using the IEnumAge interface,
// a client can move the internal cursor around, and request a batch of ages.
const ULONG MAX = 10000;
class CoAgeHolder : public IEnumAge
{
public:
...
    // IEnumAge
    STDMETHODIMP Next(ULONG celt, ULONG* rgVar, ULONG * pCeltFetched);
    STDMETHODIMP Skip(ULONG celt);
    STDMETHODIMP Reset();
    STDMETHODIMP Clone(IEnumAge ** ppEnum);
    // Helper for Clone().
    SetIndex(ULONG pos);
private:
    ULONG m_currentAge;            // Internal cursor.
    ULONG m_theAges[MAX];          // Array of ages (ULONGs).
    ULONG m_refCount;
};
```

The constructor of CoAgeHolder will be responsible for filling the ULONG array with some test data.

```
// When the container is created, fill the array with some test data.
CoAgeHolder::CoAgeHolder()
{
    g_objCount++;
    m_currentAge = 0;       m_refCount = 0;
    // Fill the array with some arbitrary data.
    for(int i = 0; i < MAX; i++)
        m_theAges[i] = i * 10;
}
```

Now that the container has some valid data, we can examine the implementation details behind the IEnumAge interface, where the action really happens.

Implementing the IEnumAge Interface

Recall that once a client obtains a pointer to IEnumAge, it is able to call the set of methods that operates on the underlying array of ULONGs. Of these four methods, the easiest of all to contend with is Reset(), which will do just as you expect: relocate the cursor to the beginning of the array:

```
// Reset the internal cursor of the array.
STDMETHODIMP CoAgeHolder::Reset()
```

```
{
    m_currentAge = 0;
    return S_OK;
}
```

Of greater interest is the implementation of Next(). Clients will call this method when they wish to request a batch of items in a single round trip. Now, as we implement this method, we need to be aware that a client may ask for any number of items. Our CoAgeHolder contains exactly 10,000 ULONGs; if the client asks for 16,930 items, we need to be smart about this and check for overflow.

Furthermore, what if the internal cursor is currently at position 9,998 in the array and the client asks for 45 more items? Again, we need to check for possible overflow. Given these two issues, here is a possible implementation of the Next() method:

```
// Allow clients to grab a batch of ages...
STDMETHODIMP CoAgeHolder::Next(ULONG celt, ULONG* rgelt,
                                ULONG* pceltFetched)
{
    ULONG cFetched = 0;
    // While the number grabbed is less than the number requested
    // AND the cursor's position is still less (or equal to) than MAX.
    while(cFetched < celt && m_currentAge <= MAX)
    {
        rgelt[cFetched] = m_theAges[m_currentAge];
        m_currentAge++;
        cFetched++;
    }
    *pceltFetched = cFetched;      // How many could we hand out?
    return cFetched == celt ? S_OK : S_FALSE;
}
```

Here, the client tells us how many items it is interested in obtaining using the first ULONG parameter (celt), and provides a place to put the items (the second parameter) which happens to be an array of ULONGs. Finally, before exiting, we set the final parameter to the exact number we were able to give back (e.g., "You asked for 73 ages, I could only give you 51") and return an appropriate HRESULT (S_FALSE indicates overflow).

With Reset() and Next() accounted for, we will move onto the details of the Skip() method. Assume you are a client that has obtained an IEnumAge interface and reset the cursor to the beginning of the list. You then may wish to get the next five items, starting with the third item. Skip() may be called to move the internal cursor over some items, without returning any information to the client.

As with the Next() method, we will still need to check for possible overflow. By convention, we will return S_OK or S_FALSE based on whether or not we are able to skip all requested items:

```
// Move the cursor ahead some number, and check for wrap around.
STDMETHODIMP CoAgeHolder::Skip(ULONG celt)
{
    ULONG cSkipped = 0;      // How many we have skipped.
    while(cSkipped < celt && m_currentAge <= MAX)
    {
        m_currentAge++;
        cSkipped++;
    }
```

```
        if(cSkipped == celt)
            return S_OK;
        else
            return S_FALSE;
}
```

Last but not least, we have the Clone() method. When a client wishes to clone an existing enumerator, what it is asking for is a brand new copy of the enumerator interface (in this case IEnumAge) such that the underlying container (in this case CoAgeHolder) looks exactly like the current container. If you like, think of the Clone() method as the copy constructor for a COM enumerator.

Now, exactly what needs to take place in your Clone() method will be very specific to your own enumerator object. For CoAgeHolder, we only need to be sure that we "remember" the position of the cursor. More sophisticated enumerations may need to copy a good deal of internal state data.

If you recall, we held this value in a private data member we named m_currentAge.

To help with the implementation of Clone(), assume that CoAgeHolder defines a helper function which will set this data member to some value. Here, then, is all we need:

```
// Internal helper function for the Clone() method.
CoAgeHolder::SetIndex(ULONG pos)
{
    m_currentAge = pos;           // Set my index to your index.
}
// The client wants back a copy of the current container object.
//
STDMETHODIMP CoAgeHolder::Clone(IEnumAge** ppEnum)
{
    IEnumAge* pEnum;
    // Make new AgeHolder & set state.
    CoAgeHolder *pNew = new CoAgeHolder;
    pNew->SetIndex(m_currentAge);
    // Hand out IEnumAge (QI calls AddRef(), client will Release()).
    pNew->QueryInterface(IID_IEnumAge, (void**)&pEnum);
    *ppEnum = pEnum;
    return S_OK;
}
```

With this, we have a coclass implementing IEnumAge and each of the four methods expected in any given COM enumeration interface. Now that we have a COM coclass supporting a rather large number of age data, we can see how a C++ COM client can use IEnumAge to pull over a controlled batch of items.

Using a COM Enumerator Object

COM enumeration is a fancy way of saying, "Give me a bunch of items right now," with the added ability to skip over items and reset the internal cursor as well as make a copy of the current state of affairs. Consider the client output of Figure 11-2:

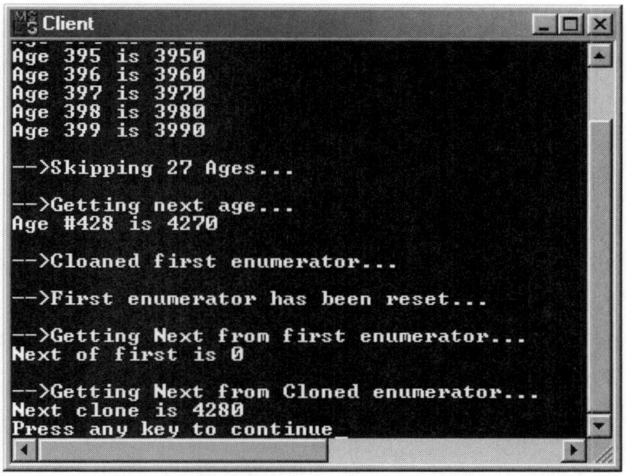

Figure 11-2:
A C++
enumeration
client.

First, the client asks for 400 ages directly, printing out each item. This would entail the use of the Next() method. In the following code, notice how the client is able to determine how many items were indeed fetched from the container using the final parameter of the Next() method (uElementsRead):

```
// Clients call the Next() method to grab n number of items.
void main()
{
...
    ULONG uElementsRead;
    ULONG pAges[1000];
    IEnumAge* pEAge;
    // Create the age holder and get the enumerator.
    CoCreateInstance(CLSID_CoRawAgeHolder, NULL,
                     CLSCTX_SERVER, IID_IEnumAge, (void**)&pEAge);
    // Go get 400 ages at once.
    pEAge->Next(400, pAges, &uElementsRead);
    // Show value for each of them.
    for(ULONG i = 0; i < uElementsRead; i++)
    {
        cout << "Age " << i << " is " << pAges[i] << endl;
    }
...
}
```

Given Figure 11-2, you can see that the Skip(), Clone(), and Reset() members were also called by the C++ client. Again, if you wish to explore this raw C++ enumerator in more detail, check out your companion CD-ROM.

Now that we have some theory behind us, let's see how ATL can help us build COM enumerators and create a more interesting enumerator that maintains a number of COM objects rather than simple ULONGs.

ATL's Support for COM Enumerations

Now that you have seen what a COM enumerator looks like in the raw, it is time to get some help using the ATL framework. As you have already seen, there is nothing terribly daunting about creating an enumerator yourself. In fact, you may very well choose to use the techniques you have just seen in an ATL project. Just write some IDL for your IEnumXXXX interface, and flesh out the implementation of Next(), Skip(), Clone(), and Reset(). If you would rather have some assistance with these details, ATL does provide a small set of classes on your behalf. In Figure 11-3, you can see the names of (and relationships between) the core ATL enumerator templates:

Figure 11-3: The core ATL enumerator templates.

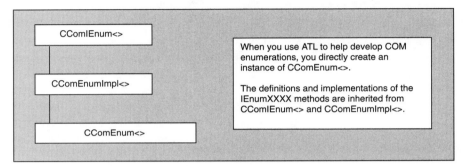

The most derived member in the ATL enumerator class hierarchy is CComEnum<>. This class will by used by your container object to provide an implementation of the Skip(), Next(), Clone(), and Reset() methods of your custom IEnumXXXX interface. The parameters to CComEnum<> can be a bit frightening to see all at once. So, before we create a full enumerator using ATL, we will ease into things by examining the hierarchy from the top down.

The CComIEnum<> Template

Recall that the general flavor of any COM enumerator interface has four methods; however, the type of thing enumerated will dictate the parameters to each method. ATL has abstracted these variations away using a C++ template. CComIEnum<> is that template, and is defined in <atlcom.h> as the following (note each method is pure virtual):

```
// CComIEnum provides the four methods for your COM enumerator.
template<class T>
class ATL_NO_VTABLE CComIEnum : public IUnknown
{
public:
    STDMETHOD(Next)(ULONG celt, T* rgelt, ULONG* pceltFetched) = 0;
    STDMETHOD(Skip)(ULONG celt) = 0;
```

> **Note:** ATL does provide an alternative set of templates which may be used to implement a COM enumeration: IEnumOnSTLImpl<> and CComEnum-OnSTL<>. As the name implies, these templates will only work with containers that represent the internal subobjects with an STL style container. Check out <atlcom.h> for formal definitions.

```
     STDMETHOD(Reset)(void) = 0;
     STDMETHOD(Clone)(CComIEnum<T>** ppEnum) = 0;
};
```

As you can see, the type "T" will serve as a placeholder for the type of thing you are enumerating. For example, if we were iterating over an array of frog objects, we can derive a class from CComIEnum<IFrog>. While you could inherit the pure virtual methods of your COM enumerator using CComIEnum<>, you really have not gained much. You would still need to write the IDL code for each member of the IEnumFrogs interface, as well as all the implementation code. CComIEnum<> is not meant to be a direct base class for your ATL coclass, but to serve as the base class for the next member in the chain, CComEnumImpl<>.

The CComEnumImpl<> Template

As the name suggests, this class provides the implementations for the methods of the CComIEnum<> abstract class. It is in here that the details of Skip(), Reset(), Clone(), and Next() are found. CComEnumImpl<> is also found in <atlcom.h> and is listed below (in a slightly condensed form):

```
// The members of CComIEnum<> are implemented here.
template <class Base, const IID* piid, class T, class Copy>
class ATL_NO_VTABLE CComEnumImpl : public Base
{
public:
...
     STDMETHOD(Next)(ULONG celt, T* rgelt, ULONG* pceltFetched);
     STDMETHOD(Skip)(ULONG celt);
     STDMETHOD(Reset)(void){m_iter = m_begin;return S_OK;}
     STDMETHOD(Clone)(Base** ppEnum);
     HRESULT Init(T* begin, T* end, IUnknown* pUnk,
          CComEnumFlags flags = AtlFlagNoCopy);
...
};
```

When ATL constructs an enumerator object, CComIEnum<> is passed in as the "Base" parameter to CComEnumImpl<>. The four inherited methods are implemented as you would expect: Next() will grab "celt" number of items and place them in the array. Clone() will return a new enumerator and so forth.

Notice, however, that CComEnumImpl<> also defines an Init() method. This member is used as a secondary creation method to provide the ATL enumerator object with a copy of (or instructions to share) the enumerated items. More on this in just a bit.

The CComEnum<> Template

At the end of the inheritance chain is CComEnum<>. This is the template you will be directly creating if you wish to build your COM enumerator using the ATL framework. As most of its functionality comes from the CComIEnum<> and CComEnumImpl<> templates, this class is quite simple.

CComEnum<> is in charge of supplying a COM_MAP to return your IEnumXXXX interface to interested clients, and that's it. Beyond deriving from the previously mentioned ATL templates, CComEnum<> also gains functionality from our good friend CComObjectRootEx<>. Here is the definition as found in <atlcom.h>:

```
// CComEnum<> is the end of the ATL inheritance chain. This is the class
// you will directly create when using ATL to build your COM enumerations.
template <class Base, const IID* piid, class T, class Copy,
                 class ThreadModel = CComObjectThreadModel>
class ATL_NO_VTABLE CComEnum :
     public CComEnumImpl<Base, piid, T, Copy>,
     public CComObjectRootEx< ThreadModel >
{
public:
     typedef CComEnum<Base, piid, T, Copy > _CComEnum;
     typedef CComEnumImpl<Base, piid, T, Copy > _CComEnumBase;
     BEGIN_COM_MAP(_CComEnum)
          COM_INTERFACE_ENTRY_IID(*piid, _CComEnumBase)
     END_COM_MAP()
};
```

CComEnum<> takes a number of parameters. Here is a breakdown of each required
parameter:

CComEnum<> Parameter	Meaning in Life
class Base	The name of the IEnumXXXX interface this ATL enumerator will be implementing (ex: IEnumPerson). This parameter will be passed over to CComIEnum<>.
const IID* piid	The GUID constant that identifies this custom IEnumXXXX interface (ex: IID_IEnumPerson).
class T	The type of items the enumerator will iterate over (ex: IPerson*).
class Copy	This one is new. This parameter defines the "copy semantics" used by the ATL enumerator object. You will specify a given _CopyXXX<> class here, which informs ATL how to copy your items (e.g., the Clone() method).

The ATL_Copy<> Templates

The fourth parameter of CComEnum<> is one of a handful of ATL-supplied "copy"
classes used by ATL enumerations and collections. As you already know, various COM
data types require different memory management details. COM text strings need to be
created and freed. COM interfaces need to be AddRef()-ed and Release()-ed. VARIANTs
need to be copied using VariantCopy(). Given that these data items typically end up in a
COM enumeration, ATL provides a set of classes that copy a given item with the correct
semantics. For example, ATL's implementation of Item() will make use of the
_CopyXXX<> class when filling the array of items for the interested client. Here is a rel-
evant subset of the ATL copy classes:

ATL Copy Template	Meaning in Life
_Copy<class T>	Used to copy simple data types. You may create an ATL enumeration of int, float, or long data types (or structures of these types). This class uses a simple memcpy() for its copy semantics.

ATL Copy Template	Meaning in Life
_CopyInterface<class T>	Used to maintain the correct reference count necessary for copying a COM interface. AddRef() and Release() are called automatically.
_Copy<VARIANT>	If your enumeration is maintaining a list of VARIANT structures, this class calls the correct variant system functions on your behalf.
_Copy<LPOLESTR>	Maintains the memory management details for COM strings.

Note: When you are building an ATL enumeration that maintains a set of COM objects you will always want to use the _CopyInterface<> template.

Building a CoPeopleHolder Enumerator Using ATL

To illustrate how to use ATL to build COM enumerators, let's create a CoPeopleHolder container class, which maintains an array of CoPerson subobjects, each supporting the IPerson interface. CoPeopleHolder provides controlled access to the CoPerson objects through the custom IEnumPerson interface:

```
// CoPeopleHolder implements this enumeration interface.
[ object, uuid(B5F10D50-53F1-11d3-AB20-00A0C9312D57) ]
interface IEnumPerson : IUnknown
{
    HRESULT Next([in] ULONG celt,
                 [out, size_is(celt), length_is(*pCeltFetched)] IPerson** rgVar,
                 [out] ULONG * pCeltFetched);
    HRESULT Skip([in] ULONG celt);
    HRESULT Reset();
    HRESULT Clone([out] IEnumPerson ** ppEnum);
};
```

Now, we need to insert a new ATL Simple Object to serve as the container class (CoPeopleHolder). Assume the default interface of CoPeopleHolder (IPeopleHolder) defines a single method named GetPersonEnum(). This method is responsible for returning the IEnumPerson interface to the interested client. Here is the IDL:

```
// Return a pointer to IEnumPerson.
[ object, uuid(FE41A722-53E5-11D3-AB20-00A0C9312D57) ]
interface IPeopleHolder : IUnknown
{
    [helpstring("method GetPersonEnum")]
    HRESULT GetPersonEnum([out] IEnumPerson** ppEnumPerson);
};
```

The next ATL Simple Object is named CoPerson. This coclass represents the internal subobjects that CoPeopleHolder is responsible for containing. The [default] interface of CoPerson defines two COM properties: Name and ID. CoPeopleHolder will still need to maintain an array of IPerson interfaces, which will be created during the FinalConstruct() call and freed from within FinalRelease():

```
// Create all the people when CoPeopleHolder comes to life.
HRESULT CoPeopleHolder::FinalConstruct()
{
    CComBSTR name[MAX] = {L"Fred", L"Alice", L"Joe", L"Mitch", L"Beth",
                          L"Mikey", L"Bart", L"Mary", L"Wally", L"Pete"};
    for(int i = 0; i < MAX; i++)
    {
        CComObject<CPerson>* pNewPerson = NULL;
        CComObject<CPerson>::CreateInstance(&pNewPerson);
        pNewPerson->put_ID(i);
        pNewPerson->put_Name(name[i].Copy());
        // Get IPerson from the new object and add to the array.
        IPerson* pPerson = NULL;
        pNewPerson->QueryInterface(IID_IPerson, (void**)&pPerson);
        m_theFolks[i] = pPerson;
    }
    return S_OK;
}
// Destroy all the subobjects.
void CoPeopleHolder::FinalRelease()
{
    for(int i = 0; i < MAX; i++)
    {
        m_theFolks[i]->Release();
    }
}
```

Now that we have an array of IPerson interfaces, we can make use of CComEnum<> to build the COM enumerator object. Before we see the final code block, we need to think through some steps. We will be creating a CComEnum<> object that takes four parameters:

■ The name of the IEnumXXXX interface it will be implementing.
■ The GUID of the custom enumerator interface.
■ The name of the interface the enumerator is handling.
■ The _Copy<> class, which will be used to take care of copy semantics.

Initially, we can envision the code as so:

```
// Sending in the necessary parameters to CComEnum<>.
CComEnum<IEnumPerson, &IID_IEnumPerson, IPerson*, _CopyInterface<IPerson> >
```

> **Note:** Be very careful here. You must have a space between the closing > > in the CComEnum<> definition. If you do not, the compiler will think you have typed a >> bit shift operator!

Now, as we are in ATL land we need to create our COM objects using CComObject<>, which is also a template! Thus, we need to drop in the previous line of code as the sole parameter to CComObject<>. In all its glory, here is the final line to create the ATL enumerator (held in a typedef to minimize further typing):

```
// We have three templates to worry about when creating an ATL enumerator.
typedef CComObject< CComEnum<IEnumPerson, &IID_IEnumPerson,
                IPerson*, _CopyInterface<IPerson> > > EnumPerson;
```

Once we have created the coclass, we need to call the Init() method of the ATL enumerator, informing it of the bounds of the IPerson* array and a flag which specifies how ATL should manage the array. Finally, we will give out the IEnumPerson* to the interested client. With this, we can now see all the code behind the GetPersonEnum() method:

```
// This method is in charge of returning the IEnumPerson interface to the client.
STDMETHODIMP CPeopleHolder::GetPersonEnum(IEnumPerson **ppEnumPerson)
{
    // Make the ATL enumeration object.
    typedef CComObject< CComEnum<IEnumPerson, &IID_IEnumPerson,
                        IPerson*, _CopyInterface<IPerson> > > EnumPerson;
    EnumPerson* pNewEnum = NULL;
    EnumPerson::CreateInstance(&pNewEnum);
    // Now fill the enumerator with all the IPerson objects.
    pNewEnum->Init(&m_theFolks[0], &m_theFolks[MAX], NULL, AtlFlagCopy);
    // Now return the enumerator.
    return pNewEnum->QueryInterface(IID_IEnumPerson, (void**)ppEnumPerson);
}
```

Enumeration Initialization Flags

The final parameter of the Init() method is used to specify how you wish your ATL enumerator object to handle the contents of the array. The set of permissible values is obtained from the following (C++!) enumeration, defined in < atlcom.h >:

```
// You may initialize your ATL enumeration with any of the following flags.
enum CComEnumFlags
{
    AtlFlagNoCopy        = 0,
    AtlFlagTakeOwnership = 2,
    AtlFlagCopy          = 3
};
```

Here is a breakdown of what each flag signifies:

Init() Flag	Meaning in Life
AtlFlagNoCopy	Signifies that the container object already has an existing array of items it is maintaining, and will share this set with the ATL enumerator object.
AtlFlagCopy	Signifies that although the container has an existing array of items, the ATL enumerator should maintain a separate copy of the data.
AtlFlagTakeOwnership	Informs the ATL enumerator that the container does not have a private copy of the data, and will fill the enumerator with data it will not be maintaining itself. In other words, the container does not have private state data representing the subobjects.

In our example, as CoPeopleHolder does have a private copy of IPerson interfaces, we can specify either AtlFlagNoCopy or AtlFlagCopy.

Client-Side Code

To see our tester in action, here is a C++ client making use of the Visual C++ native COM support:

```
// Using the ATL enumerator (assume we have #import-ed the *.tlb file).
int main(int argc, char* argv[])
{
    CoInitialize(NULL);
    HRESULT hr;
    ULONG uElementsRead;
    IPersonPtr pPerson[20];
    IPeopleHolderPtr pPeople(CLSID_PeopleHolder);
    IEnumPersonPtr pEnum;
    pPeople->GetPersonEnum(&pEnum);
    hr = pEnum->Next(90, (IPerson**)&pPerson, &uElementsRead);
    for(int i = 0; i < uElementsRead; i++)
    {
        _bstr_t name;
        name = pPerson[i]->GetName();
        cout << "Name is: " << name << endl;
        cout << "ID is: " << pPerson[i]->GetID() << endl;
        pPerson[i] = NULL;
    }
    pPeople = NULL;
    pEnum = NULL;
    CoUninitialize();
    return 0;
}
```

The next lab will allow you to build this enumerator for yourself. After that point, we will get to know COM collections, the language-neutral variation on the COM enumerator pattern. COM enumerations are very C++ centric.

Lab 11-1: Building an ATL Enumerator

In this lab you will build a COM enumerator with the assistance of ATL. You will define a custom variation on the IEnumXXXX interface, and use the ATL framework to help flesh out the details of Next(), Skip(), Reset(), and Clone(). Once you have developed the enumerator, you will build a C++ client to test the server.

The solution for this lab can be found on your CD-ROM under:
Labs\Chapter 11\ATLEnumServer
Labs\Chapter 11\ATLEnumServer\CPP Client

Step One: Establish the Container/Subobject Relationship

Begin by creating a new ATL DLL project named **ATLEnumServer**. Use the ATL Object Wizard to insert a new Simple Object named **PeopleHolder**. Be sure to select the Custom vTable option for your initial [default] interface (IPeopleHolder). This coclass will be used to hold onto a number of CPeople objects, and provide access to these items through a custom enumerator. Add a single method to IPeopleHolder named **GetPersonEnum()**. This method will take a single parameter of type IEnumPerson** (which we will define in the next step). Here is the IDL for IPeopleHolder:

```
// Clients can access our CPeople objects from this custom enumerator interface.
interface IPeopleHolder : IUnknown
{
     [helpstring("method GetPersonEnum")]
     HRESULT GetPersonEnum([out] IEnumPerson** ppEnumPerson);
};
```

Now, we need to insert another ATL Simple Object to represent the items held by the enumerator (people objects). Insert a new ATL Simple Object named **Person**. This coclass will have two properties in the [default] interface: Name and ID. Here is the IDL for IPerson:

```
// Each CPerson implements this [default] interface.
interface IPerson : IUnknown
{
     [propget] HRESULT Name([out, retval] BSTR *pVal);
     [propput] HRESULT Name([in] BSTR newVal);
     [propget] HRESULT ID([out, retval] short *pVal);
     [propput] HRESULT ID([in] short newVal);
};
```

Implement these properties in the CPerson coclass, using a CComBSTR to represent the Name property and a short to represent the ID:

```
// Implementing the person sub object.
STDMETHODIMP CPerson::get_Name(BSTR *pVal)
{
     *pVal = m_bstrName.Copy();
     return S_OK;
}
STDMETHODIMP CPerson::put_Name(BSTR newVal)
{
     m_bstrName = newVal;
     return S_OK;
}
STDMETHODIMP CPerson::get_ID(short *pVal)
{
     *pVal = m_ID;
     return S_OK;
}
STDMETHODIMP CPerson::put_ID(short newVal)
{
     m_ID = newVal;
     return S_OK;
}
```

Now we need to create a number of these CPerson objects when CPeopleHolder comes to life. Add a private array of type IPerson* in the private sector of CPeopleHolder, and populate this array inside FinalConstruct(). Assume the MAX constant has been set to 10, and fill each person with some initial data.

```
// Fill your IPerson* array with data when the CPeopleHolder is created.
// The class defines: IPerson* m_theFolks[MAX];
HRESULT FinalConstruct()
{
     // Some names for data.
     CComBSTR name[MAX] = {L"Fred", L"Alice", L"Joe", L"Mitch", L"Beth",
```

```
                            L"Mikey", L"Bart", L"Mary", L"Wally", L"Pete" };
    for(int i = 0; i < MAX; i++)
    {
        // Make a new person.
        CComObject<CPerson>* pNewPerson = NULL;
        CComObject<CPerson>::CreateInstance(&pNewPerson);
        pNewPerson->put_ID(i);
        pNewPerson->put_Name(name[i].Copy());
        // Get IPerson from the new object and place in array.
        IPerson* pPerson = NULL;
        pNewPerson->QueryInterface(IID_IPerson, (void**)&pPerson);
        m_theFolks[i] = pPerson;
    }
    return S_OK;
}
```

Because the CPeopleHolder class has created a number of CPerson objects, we need to
ensure that the objects are released during the FinalRelease():

```
// Free up each CPerson in the IPerson* array when CPeopleHolder is destroyed.
void FinalRelease()
{
    for(int i = 0; i < MAX; i++)
    {
        m_theFolks[i]->Release();
    }
}
```

Now that we have a container for the CPerson objects, our next step is to implement the
GetPersonEnum() method, which is currently empty. For that matter, we need to define
IEnumPerson!

Step Two: Define a Custom COM Enumeration Interface

The people holder object allows COM clients to access the subobject it is maintaining
using a custom enumerator interface. Write some IDL code to define the following
IEnumPerson interface (sorry, there is no wizard for this step):

```
// The custom enumerator interface that allows controlled access to all sub objects.
[ object, uuid(B5F10D50-53F1-11d3-AB20-00A0C9312D57) ]
interface IEnumPerson : IUnknown
{
    HRESULT Next([in] ULONG celt,
                 [out, size_is(celt), length_is(*pCeltFetched)] IPerson** rgVar,
                 [out] ULONG * pCeltFetched);
    HRESULT Skip([in] ULONG celt);
    HRESULT Reset();
    HRESULT Clone([out] IEnumPerson ** ppEnum);
};
```

Recall that the Next() method will allow a client to request some number of IPerson interfaces. Skip() allows the client to, well, skip over items in the IPerson* array. Reset()
moves the internal cursor to the beginning of the array, while Clone() allows the client to
maintain a snapshot of the current enumerator and obtain a new IEnumPerson enumeration. All of this logic will be supplied by the core set of ATL enumeration templates.

Step Three: Implement GetPersonEnum()

ATL does a great job of implementing the four methods for a custom enumerator interface, as long as you can follow the syntactic maze. In your implementation of GetPersonEnum(), use CComObject<> to create a new CComEnum<> object. When you initialize the CComEnum<> object, send in the upper and lower bounds of your IPerson* array. Finally, before you exit, set the client-supplied IEnumPerson** parameter to the IEnumPerson interface of your custom ATL enumerator object:

```
// This method is in charge of returning the IEnumPerson interface
// to the client.
STDMETHODIMP CPeopleHolder::GetPersonEnum(IEnumPerson **ppEnumPerson)
{
    // Create a new CComEnum<> of IPerson* interfaces.
    typedef CComObject< CComEnum<IEnumPerson, &IID_IEnumPerson,
        IPerson*, _CopyInterface<IPerson> > > EnumPerson;
    EnumPerson* pNewEnum = NULL;
    EnumPerson::CreateInstance(&pNewEnum);
    // Now fill the enumerator with copies of the IPerson objects.
    pNewEnum->Init(&m_theFolks[0], &m_theFolks[MAX], NULL, AtlFlagCopy);
    // Now return the enumerator (client will call Release()).
    return pNewEnum->QueryInterface(IID_IEnumPerson, (void**)ppEnumPerson);
}
```

Go ahead and compile the project to ensure there are no syntactical errors. In the final step, we will build a C++ client to work with this enumerator object (remember, COM enumerators are currently not directly usable from VB or late bound clients).

Step Four: A C++ Client

Create a new C++ Console Application. To help minimize the COM goo, we will make use of the #import statement, rather than raw COM library calls. We have already seen similar code in this chapter, but for completion, here is the full implementation of main():

```
// The C++ client.
#import "C:\ATL\Labs\Chapter 11\ATLEnumServer\ATLEnumServer.tlb"
no_namespace named_guids
int main(int argc, char* argv[])
{
    CoInitialize(NULL);
    IPeopleHolderPtr pPeople(CLSID_PeopleHolder);
    IEnumPersonPtr pEnum;
    pPeople->GetPersonEnum(&pEnum);
    HRESULT hr;
    ULONG uElementsRead;
    IPersonPtr pPerson[20];
    hr = pEnum->Next(90, (IPerson**)&pPerson, &uElementsRead);
    // I asked for 90 people, but the object returns how many were fetched.
    for(int i = 0; i < uElementsRead; i++)
    {
        _bstr_t name;
        name = pPerson[i]->GetName();
        cout << "Name is: " << name << endl;
        cout << "ID is: " << pPerson[i]->GetID() << endl;
        pPerson[i] = NULL;
    }
}
```

```
        pPeople = NULL;
        pEnum = NULL;
        CoUninitialize();
        return 0;
}
```

When you run your program, you will see the following output:

Figure 11-4:
Using a
collection of
COM objects.

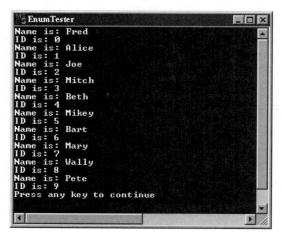

Not too bad. ATL has done most of the grunge work for you. When you are creating a COM enumeration with ATL, simply design the IEnumXXXX interface and the subobjects it is providing access to, and make use of the various framework templates.

As mentioned in this chapter, COM enumerators do not provide a standard way to insert additional items into the container. Furthermore, many COM language mappings do not have a way to work with custom enumeratations. The next logical step is to examine COM collections, which are more or less language-neutral enumerators.

An Overview of COM Collections

A *COM collection*, like a COM enumerator, is a coclass responsible for managing other related COM objects. Unlike a COM enumerator, COM collections expose their services using IDispatch, and therefore all COM clients are able to access the subobjects they contain.

A traditional COM collection provides methods that allow the object user to access an individual item by name, obtain the count of all items, and add and remove individual items. Contrary to what you may expect, there is no standard interface that represents a COM collection. As we have seen from our examination of enumerators, the items a given collection will hold depend on your specific development effort.

Each collection will support the same set of methods, with more or less the same signatures. When you develop your collection objects, you do have a good deal of flexibility; however, if you stick to the accepted format, users of your collection will already have a heads-up as to how to use it.

Standard Methods of a COM Collection

Although you have flexibility as to the methods of a collection object, most users will expect the following:

COM Collection Method	Meaning in Life
Item()	This allows a client to fetch a single named item from the collection. Items in a collection can be referred to by position (the tenth CoBoat) or some tag (the boat named "Viper").
_NewEnum	_NewEnum is a read-only property that allows your collection to be iterated over using the For...Each syntax of Visual Basic.
Add()	Allows a client to insert another COM object into the collection.
Remove()	Allows a client to remove an item from the collection.
Count()	This read-only property can be called by a client to obtain the current number of objects in the collection. As we will see, a collection can grow and shrink throughout its lifetime, and it is handy for the client to know how many items are currently being managed.

Although many COM collections do indeed support all five members, only Count(), Item(), and _NewEnum are mandatory. Therefore, let's begin to develop a collection that supports these first three methods, and tackle Add() and Remove() a bit later in the chapter.

Building a Simple COM Collection

If you would like to see the first iteration of the CoSquiggle collection for yourself, consult your companion CD-ROM (Squiggle Collection 1).

To illustrate building a COM collection, we will be creating a coclass that maintains ATL CoSquiggle objects. As you recall from Chapter 10, CoSquiggle was a wonderful (and production level) coclass that supported the dual interface, ICoSquiggle. In this incarnation of ICoSquiggle, we find the following layout:

```
// A CoSquiggle supports the following behavior.
[ object, uuid(9FB9E736-59BA-11D3-B926-0020781238D4), dual,
  helpstring("ICoSquiggle Interface"), pointer_default(unique) ]
interface ICoSquiggle : IDispatch
{
    [id(1), helpstring("method Draw")]
    HRESULT Draw();
    [propget, id(2), helpstring("property Name")]
    HRESULT Name([out, retval] BSTR *pVal);
    [propput, id(2), helpstring("property Name")]
    HRESULT Name([in] BSTR newVal);
};
```

The implementation of CoSquiggle allows each squiggle to be drawn (read: display a message box) as well as be assigned a pet name that is maintained in a private CComBSTR. To follow a popular convention used with collection objects, we will give the name

CoSquiggles to the collection that manages CoSquiggle objects. Typically, you will find COM collection objects taking the plural form of the object they are in charge of.

CoSquiggles maintains a fixed array of IDispatch pointers, which represent the set of CoSquiggle objects it will maintain. To begin implementing the collection, we set each index of the array to a new CoSquiggle during the FinalConstruct() invocation. As we are dealing with COM objects, FinalRelease() will be used to release the IDispatch references for each coclass:

```
// Create a set of CoSquiggles upon startup, and kill them when shutting down.
class ATL_NO_VTABLE CCoSquiggles:
     public CComObjectRootEx<CComSingleThreadModel>,
     public CComCoClass<CCoSquiggles, &CLSID_CoSquiggles>,
     public IDispatchImpl<ICoSquiggles, &IID_ICoSquiggles,
                     &LIBID_SQUIGGLECOLLECTIONLib>
{
public:
...
     HRESULT FinalConstruct()       // Create the squiggles!
     {
          for(int i = 0; i < MAX_SQUIGGLES; i++)
          {
               CComObject<CCoSquiggle> *pSquig = NULL;
               CComObject<CCoSquiggle>::CreateInstance(&pSquig);
               IDispatch* pDisp;
               pSquig->QueryInterface(IID_IDispatch, (void**)&pDisp);
               m_pArrayOfSquigs[i] = pDisp;
          }
          return S_OK;
     }
     void FinalRelease()            // Kill the squiggles!
     {
          for(int i = 0; i < 10; i++)
          {
               m_pArrayOfSquigs[i]->Release();
          }
     }
...
private:
     // Array of IDispatch pointers to represent the squiggles.
     IDispatch* m_pArrayOfSquigs[MAX_SQUIGGLES];
};
```

Notice that CoSquiggles is only smart enough to maintain a fixed array of CoSquiggle objects no greater than MAX_SQUIGGLES. At this stage of the game, this is permissible, as we will not yet allow clients to add or remove an item. Later on, we will rework this collection to make use of an STL vector to allow the number of CoSquiggle objects to grow and shrink on demand.

Now that we have set up some subobjects in the collection, we must provide a way in which the COM client can access them. Our collection supports a single dual interface, ICoSquiggles, which provides a minimal way for clients to work with the collection:

```
// Our collection supports the following members.
[ object, uuid(9FB9E734-59BA-11D3-B926-0020781238D4), dual,
  helpstring("ICoSquiggles Interface"), pointer_default(unique) ]
interface ICoSquiggles : IDispatch
```

```
{
    [id(DISPID_VALUE), helpstring("method Item")]
    HRESULT Item([in] VARIANT index, [out, retval] VARIANT* pItem);
    [propget, id(1), helpstring("property Count")]
    HRESULT Count([out, retval] long *pVal);
    [propget, restricted, id(DISPID_NEWENUM)]
    HRESULT _NewEnum([out, retval] LPUNKNOWN *pVal);
};
```

For the most part, this is a standard dual interface described in IDL. However, notice that we have specified some predefined DISPIDs for the Item() and _NewEnum members. This is not optional. Most COM language mappings will be on the lookout for the DISPID_VALUE and DISPID_NEWENUM constants when working with a collection object.

DISPID_VALUE is used to specify that this member of the dispinterface is the default method. Some COM language mappings (such as VB) recognize this DISPID, and thus specifying the item is optional, as it will be called automatically if no other method is present. By the same token, DISPID_NEWENUM is used to signal that this collection supports For...Next syntax. As _NewEnum is a hidden member of the dispinterface which is called secretly by Visual Basic, we have added the [restricted] attribute in its declaration. As far as Count() goes, any unique DISPID (greater than zero) will do.

Implementing Count()

This method of a collection simply returns the current number of items. As CoSquiggles will always have a fixed number, the implementation of Count() is trivial:

```
// Return the number of squiggles in the collection.
STDMETHODIMP CCoSquiggles::get_Count(long *pVal)
{
    *pVal = MAX_SQUIGGLES;
    return S_OK;
}
```

Implementing Item()

If you looked closely at the IDL definition of Item(), you will notice that we specified two VARIANTs:

```
// Give me a VARIANT and I will give you back a VARIANT.
HRESULT Item([in] VARIANT index, [out, retval] VARIANT* pItem);
```

Most developers who use collections want some degree of flexibility. A well-written Item() method should allow a client to specify a given member by name (for example, a text literal) or position. Nothing says parameter polymorphism like the VARIANT. Our implementation of Item() will require the user to specify a numerical index when referring to the CoSquiggle they are interested in obtaining. Once we find the correct item from our IDispatch* array, we set the [out, retval] to this particular IDispatch interface (e.g., the squiggle they asked for). Thus:

```
// Using the index, set the [out, retval] to the correct IDispatch pointer,
// thereby giving the client access to the correct CoSquiggle.
STDMETHODIMP CCoSquiggles::Item(VARIANT index, VARIANT *pItem)
{
    // Be sure we have a numerical index.
```

```
if(index.vt == VT_I2)
{
        // Be sure we are in range.
        if(index.lVal >=0 && index.lVal <= MAX_SQUIGGLES)
        {
                // Find the correct squiggle.
                IDispatch* pDisp = m_pArrayOfSquigs[index.lVal];
                // Add a ref!
                pDisp->AddRef();
                // Set the type of VARIANT and return
                pItem->vt = VT_DISPATCH;
                pItem->pdispVal = pDisp;
                return S_OK;
        }
}
return E_INVALIDARG;
}
```

There is not too much to say about this code block, as it is typical VARIANT programming. The only caution to be aware of is that we must be sure to AddRef() our new IDispatch reference, as we have another client making use of it.

Exercising Count() and Item() from within Visual Basic

Although we have not yet implemented _NewEnum, our collection object is ready to be taken out for an initial test drive. Assume we have a Standard EXE project, which has the following Click routine for a button named btnGetSquiggle3:

```
' Get access to the squiggle three and draw it.
'
Private Sub btnGetSquiggle3_Click()
    Dim squigColl As New CoSquiggles
    Dim o As CoSquiggle
    Set o = squigColl.Item(3)
    o.Draw
End Sub
```

Here, we create a brand new squiggle collection, and grab the third item in the collection. Once we have a reference to this CoSquiggle, we may access the Draw() method accordingly. As we have seen, the Item() method has been given a special predefined DISPID of DISPID_VALUE. This marks Item() as the default member in the dispinterface, and therefore we can shorten our VB code just a bit:

```
' DISPID_VALUE provides yet another way to save some keystrokes.
'
Private Sub btnGetSquiggle3_Click()
    Dim squigColl As New CoSquiggles
    Dim o As CoSquiggle
    Set o = squigColl(3)
    o.Draw
End Sub
```

If we really wanted some streamlined code, we could shorten things a bit more:

```
' Optimized access to the third item in the collection.
'
Private Sub btnGetSquiggle3_Click()
```

```
        Dim squigColl As New CoSquiggles
        squigColl(3).Draw
End Sub
```

Now, what if we wanted to iterate over all items in the collection, and grab each
CoSquiggle's name to place in a list box? First off,
assume that the collection object has set each
item's Name property to some value upon startup
(currently each CoSquiggle is unnamed). We could
make use of the Count property, and loop over
each member in the collection as so:

Figure 11-5: Using our initial collection.

```
' Loop over the items in the collection, and get
' each one's name.
'
Private Sub btnGetAllSquiggles_Click()
        Dim squigColl As New CoSquiggles
        Dim max As Long
        Dim i As Integer
        max = squigColl.Count
        For i = 1 To max
                List1.AddItem squigColl(i).Name
        Next i
End Sub
```

Implementing _NewEnum

We have a fine start for a custom collection object. However, we must also support the
_NewEnum property to be a compliant COM collection. Visual Basic developers are used
to iterating over a COM collection using a special bit of syntax. Using For...Each, a collection may be exercised as so:

```
' Looping through a collection using _NewEnum.
'
Private Sub btnGet_Click()
        Dim o as New CoSquiggles
        Dim s As CoSquiggle
        For Each s In o
                List1.AddItem s.Name
        Next
End Sub
```

What this code is basically saying is "for every CoSquiggle in the CoSquiggles collection,
call the get_Name() method." Note that we do not ever need to access the Count property
or Item() method. The For...Next syntax allows us to define a placeholder (in this case,
CoSquiggle) to morph itself among each item in the collection. However, if we were to try
this block of code, we would receive a runtime error. The offending line of code would be
"For Each s In squigColl." The reason? VB is asking our collection to Invoke the member
of our dispinterface that has been assigned the DISPID_NEWENUM value:

```
' VB calls _NewEnum whenever the For...Each syntax is used.
'
For Each s In squigColl          ' Calls Invoke() for DISPID_NEWENUM
        List1.AddItem s.Name
Next s
```

To implement _NewEnum, we must create a COM enumerator that supports the IEnumVARIANT interface (recall that COM does define some stock enumerator interfaces). The code behind get__NewEnum will look very much like the ATL code that provided access to our custom IEnumPeople interface. Here is the code behind get_NewEnum:

```
// This block of code allows VB-like iteration.
STDMETHODIMP CCoSquiggles::get__NewEnum(LPUNKNOWN *pVal)
{
      // Make a temp array of VARIANTS and fill with the current CoSquiggles.
      VARIANT* pVar = new VARIANT[MAX_SQUIGGLES];
      for(int i = 0; i < MAX_SQUIGGLES; i++)
      {
            pVar[i].vt = VT_DISPATCH;
            pVar[i].pdispVal = m_pArrayOfSquigs[i];
      }
      // Now make the enum with the monster template.
      typedef CComObject< CComEnum< IEnumVARIANT,
                        &IID_IEnumVARIANT, VARIANT,
                        _Copy< VARIANT > > > enumVar;
      enumVar* pEnumVar = new enumVar;
      pEnumVar->Init(&pVar[0], &pVar[MAX_SQUIGGLES], NULL, AtlFlagCopy);
      delete[] pVar;
      // Return the enum.
      return pEnumVar->QueryInterface(IID_IUnknown, (void**)pVal);
}
```

As we have an array of IDispatch pointers in our CoSquiggles collection, we need to convert these items to an array of VARIANTs before we can hand them over to CComEnum<>. Once we have done so, we can again make use of the ATL enumeration templates; however, this time we must specify the _Copy<VARIANT> template rather than _CopyInterface<T>. Furthermore, as IEnumVARIANT has already been defined (in <oaidl.idl>) we do not need to write any IDL code for this enumeration interface. We can just send on IEnumVARIANT and IID_EnumVARIANT as the first and second parameters to CComEnum<>, and return the IUnknown interface to VB. With this, our bare bones collection is complete.

Adding and Removing CoSquiggles

A COM collection must support the Count, _NewEnum, and Item() members. Add() and Remove() are optional, but most collections would like the ability to be a bit more dynamic than our current CoSquiggles collection. To allow the client to insert and remove members, we first need a way to allow CoSquiggles to store a varying number of IDispatch pointers, so clearly our fixed array won't do.

It is very commonplace to make use of the Standard Template Library (STL) when working with ATL projects. STL is a collection of generic C++ templates that provide a number of (non-COM) collections, dynamic arrays, string support, and so forth. We will be making use of the STL vector<> template, as this will allow us to work with any number of IDispatch pointers.

To begin, we will need to replace our static IDispatch array with a new STL vector. FinalConstruct() will fill the vector with three initial CoSquiggles using the push_back() member function. As always, FinalRelease() will call Release() on all interfaces. Here, we can make use of the size() method of the STL vector<> template to obtain the current number of CoSquiggles. Here are the changes thus far:

```
// This iteration of the squiggle collection maintains a vector of IDispatch interfaces.
class ATL_NO_VTABLE CSquiggleCollection2 :
...
{
public:
...
    HRESULT FinalConstruct()
    {
        for(int i = 0; i < 3; i++)
        {
            // First make a squiggle.
            CComObject< CCoSquiggle > *pSquig = NULL;
            CComObject< CCoSquiggle >::CreateInstance(&pSquig);
            // Fill squiggle with some data...
            // Get the IDispatch pointer and place in the STL vector.
            LPDISPATCH pDisp;
            if(SUCCEEDED(pSquig->QueryInterface(IID_IDispatch,
                                                (void**)&pDisp)))
            {
                m_vecSquiggles.push_back(pDisp);
            }
        }
        return S_OK;
    }
    void FinalRelease()
    {
        // Release all the squiggles from the vector.
        int size = m_vecSquiggles.size();
        for(int i = 0; i < size; i++)
        {
            LPDISPATCH pDisp;
            pDisp = m_vecSquiggles[i];
            pDisp -> Release();
        }
    }
...
private:
    std::vector< IDispatch* > m_vecSquiggles;
};
```

Before we get to Add() and Remove(), we should update our current implementation of Count, given that the size of the vector could be anything (get_NewEnum and Item() could be reworked in a similar manner, by making use of the vector's size() method):

```
// Grab the size of the vector.
STDMETHODIMP CSquiggleCollection2::get_Count(long *pVal)
{
    *pVal = m_vecSquiggles.size();
    return S_OK;
}
```

The Add() method is trivial; however, we do have some design issues to contend with. What parameters do we wish to have in our version of Add()? We have two choices. We can assume the client will create a CoSquiggle first, and send it into our collection. If this is the case, we may have an IDL definition as so:

```
// This Add() method takes a brand new CoSquiggle.
[id(2), helpstring("method Add")]
HRESULT Add([in] IDispatch *pnewSquiggle);
```

Alternatively, we may configure Add() to take state data, which we use to create a new CoSquiggle ourselves. This IDL might look like the following:

```
// This Add() method takes the name of a CoSquiggle, inferring that we create one
// ourselves in the coclass.
[id(2), helpstring("method Add")]
HRESULT Add([in] BSTR name);
```

We will assume the client will configure a new CoSquiggle and give it to us when it wishes to add it into our collection. Thus, all we have to do is place the new IDispatch* into the vector and call AddRef() on the incoming interface:

```
// Add in the new CoSquiggle.
STDMETHODIMP CSquiggleCollection2::Add(IDispatch *pnewSquiggle)
{
    // Here we are going to add a new squiggle the client gives us.
    m_vecSquiggles.push_back(pnewSquiggle);
    pnewSquiggle->AddRef();
    return S_OK;
}
```

Remove() is also very easy to implement, but again we have a design choice. How would we like to identify the item to remove? By numerical index? By an embedded key? Good question, but there is no hard and fast rule. If you wish to give your user maximum flexibility, you may define Remove() to take a VARIANT parameter, test for the type, and remove accordingly. For our purposes, let's assume the client identifies the number of the CoSquiggle to remove:

```
// Give me an index to remove...
STDMETHODIMP CSquiggleCollection2::Remove(long index)
{
    // Be sure we are in range.
    if(index >=0 && index <= m_vecSquiggles.size())
    {
        // Find the correct squiggle.
        IDispatch* pDisp = m_vecSquiggles[index];
        // Remove it.
        pDisp->Release();
        m_vecSquiggles.erase(m_vecSquiggles.begin() + index);
        return S_OK;
    }
    return E_FAIL;
}
```

After a quick check to ensure the client has sent us an index within range, we gain a reference to the squiggle and call Release(), thereby reducing its reference count by one. As well, we need to remove this item from the vector using the erase() method. With these minor modifications, we now have a language-neutral way to maintain a variable number of COM objects. To wrap it up, here is some VB code making use of these new items:

```
' Assume a CoSquiggles object named coll.
'
Private Sub btnAdd_Click()
     Dim o As New CoSquiggle
     o.Name = txtName
     coll.Add o
End Sub
Private Sub btnRemove3_Click()
     coll.Remove 3
End Sub
```

Lab 11-2: Building a Complete Custom Collection with ATL

This lab will allow you to create a custom collection with support for adding and removing coclasses, all of which are held in an STL vector. COM collections have the same general look and feel as COM enumerators, although a collection usually exports the underlying objects in an [oleautomation] friendly manner.

To illustrate this last point, your companion CD contains a VBScript client that grabs the current objects in the collection and exercises each one.

 The solution for this lab can be found on your CD-ROM under:
Labs\Chapter 11\Squiggle Collection 2
Labs\Chapter 11\Squiggle Collection 2\VB Client
Labs\Chapter 11\Squiggle Collection 2\VBScript Client

Step One: Create the Subobject

Begin by creating a new ATL DLL project named **ATLCollection**. Use the ATL Object Wizard to insert a new Simple Object named **CoSquiggle**. This simple coclass supports a single dual interface, which defines a property called Name and a method named Draw(). Populate your initial interface with these items, and implement them in your coclass. Be sure your Draw() logic informs the end user which item is being drawn. Here are the details behind each item:

```
// The Name property.
STDMETHODIMP CCoSquiggle::get_Name(BSTR *pVal)
{
     *pVal = m_bstrName.Copy();
     return S_OK;
}
STDMETHODIMP CCoSquiggle::put_Name(BSTR newVal)
{
     m_bstrName = newVal;
     return S_OK;
}
// The Draw() method.
STDMETHODIMP CCoSquiggle::Draw()
{
     USES_CONVERSION;
     CComBSTR temp;
     temp = "Drawing a squiggle named ";
     temp += m_bstrName;
     MessageBox(NULL, W2A(temp.m_str),
          "Information about this squiggle", MB_OK | MB_SETFOREGROUND);
```

```
        return S_OK;
}
```

Step Two: Create the COM Collection Interface

Now, insert another ATL Simple Object named **SquiggleCollection2**, and again be sure
that the [default] interface is configured as a dual. Begin by adding the expected items to
your ISquiggleCollection2 interface, allowing the client to work with the inner set of
CoSquiggle objects. Here is the IDL:

```
// The custom collection interface.
interface ISquiggleCollection2 : IDispatch
{
    [id(DISPID_VALUE), helpstring("method Item")]
    HRESULT Item([in] VARIANT index, [out, retval] VARIANT* pItem);
    [propget, id(1), helpstring("property Count")]
    HRESULT Count([out, retval] long *pVal);
    [id(2), helpstring("method Add")]
    HRESULT Add([in] IDispatch *pnewSquiggle);
    [id(3), helpstring("method Remove")]
    HRESULT Remove([in] long index);
    [propget, restricted, id(DISPID_NEWENUM)]
    HRESULT _NewEnum([out, retval] LPUNKNOWN *pVal);
};
```

Remember, the _NewEnum property must be assigned the default DISPID, DISPID_
NEWENUM, while Item() must be assigned DISPID_VALUE. Also notice that unlike the
previous ATL enumerator, we are working with IDispatch* interfaces rather than a custom
vTable interface. After all, that is the whole point of a COM collection: allow all
COM-enabled languages to access the objects.

Step Three: Implement the Initial Collection Object

Before we implement the methods of the ISquiggleCollection2 interface, we need to set up
some subobjects. Begin by overriding **FinalConstruct()** to fill up a vector of CoSquiggle
objects, named **m_vecSquiggles**. As the client can add and remove items to this collection, configure three initial items:

```
// This time we are making use of the STL to hold our IDispatch interfaces.
#include <vector>
#include "cosquiggle.h"
// Create three squiggles automatically.
// Class defines: std::vector< IDispatch* > m_vecSquiggles;
HRESULT FinalConstruct()
{
    for(int i = 0; i < 3; i++)
    {
        // First make a squiggle.
        CComObject< CCoSquiggle > *pSquig = NULL;
        CComObject< CCoSquiggle >::CreateInstance(&pSquig);
        // Give the new squiggle a name.
        CComBSTR temp[3] = {L"Mandy", L"Whoppie", L"Eric"};
        pSquig->put_Name(temp[i]);
        // Get the IDispatch pointer and place in the STL vector.
        LPDISPATCH pDisp;
        if(SUCCEEDED(pSquig->QueryInterface(IID_IDispatch, (void**)&pDisp)))
```

```
            {
                m_vecSquiggles.push_back(pDisp);
            }
        }
    }
    return S_OK;
}
```

Your collection will need to release all items in the vector when it is destroyed, so make a call to FinalRelease():

```
// Release all the squiggles from the vector.
void FinalRelease()
{
    int size = m_vecSquiggles.size();
    for(int i = 0; i < size; i++)
    {
        LPDISPATCH pDisp;
        pDisp = m_vecSquiggles[i];
        pDisp -> Release();
    }
}
```

Now that we have some default data, we can begin to implement each of the methods in the collection. The Count property is used by the client to obtain the current number of items held by the collection object. To implement this method, make a call to size() from your internal vector object:

```
// Return the current count.
STDMETHODIMP CSquiggleCollection2::get_Count(long *pVal)
{
    *pVal = m_vecSquiggles.size();
    return S_OK;
}
```

The Item() method allows a client to retrieve a given subobject from the collection. For our purposes, the Item() method will only allow the client to ask for a given squiggle by numerical index:

```
// Return the correct squiggle.
STDMETHODIMP CSquiggleCollection2::Item(VARIANT index, VARIANT *pItem)
{
    // Be sure we have a number.
    if(index.vt == VT_I2)
    {
        // Be sure we are in range.
        if(index.lVal >=0 && index.lVal <= m_vecSquiggles.size())
        {
            // Find the correct squiggle.
            IDispatch* pDisp = m_vecSquiggles[index.lVal];
            // Add the ref!
            pDisp->AddRef();
            // Set the type of VARIANT and return.
            pItem->vt = VT_DISPATCH;
            pItem->pdispVal = pDisp;
            return S_OK;
        }
    }
```

```
        }
        return E_INVALIDARG;
}
```

Finally, we will need to implement _NewEnum. This member will allow a VB client to iterate over our collection using an IEnumVARIANT enumerator:

```
// This block of code allows VB-like iteration.
STDMETHODIMP CSquiggleCollection2::get__NewEnum(LPUNKNOWN *pVal)
{
    // Make a temp array of VARIANTS and fill with the current CoSquiggles.
    int size = m_vecSquiggles.size();
    VARIANT* pVar = new VARIANT[size];
    for(int i = 0; i < size; i++)
    {
        pVar[i].vt = VT_DISPATCH;
        pVar[i].pdispVal = m_vecSquiggles[i];
    }
    // Now make the CComEnum object.
    typedef CComObject< CComEnum< IEnumVARIANT, &IID_IEnumVARIANT,
            VARIANT, _Copy< VARIANT > > > enumVar;
    enumVar* pEnumVar = new enumVar;
    pEnumVar->Init(&pVar[0], &pVar[size], NULL, AtlFlagCopy);
    delete[] pVar;
    // return the enum.
    return pEnumVar->QueryInterface(IID_IUnknown, (void**)pVal);
}
```

At this point, we have provided a way for a COM client to obtain any of our three CoSquiggle objects. To finish up this collection, we need to provide a way to add and remove items.

Step Four: Add and Remove Items

First, we will implement the Add() item. We have specified this member such that the client is responsible for creating a new CoSquiggle, setting the state, and sending it our direction. This comes to us as an IDispatch*, which we can insert into the vector:

```
// Here we are going to add a new squiggle the client gives us.
STDMETHODIMP CSquiggleCollection2::Add(IDispatch *pnewSquiggle)
{
    m_vecSquiggles.push_back(pnewSquiggle);
    pnewSquiggle->AddRef();
    return S_OK;
}
```

Removing an item is just about as easy:

```
// Remove the item from the vector, and release the reference.
STDMETHODIMP CSquiggleCollection2::Remove(long index)
{
    // Be sure we are in range.
    if(index >=0 && index <= m_vecSquiggles.size())
    {
        // Find the correct squiggle.
        IDispatch* pDisp = m_vecSquiggles[index];
        // Remove it.
        pDisp->Release();
```

```
            m_vecSquiggles.erase(m_vecSquiggles.begin() + index);
            return S_OK;
        }
        return E_FAIL;
    }
```

Now the collection is complete! To finish up this chapter, let's build a VB client.

Step Five: A Visual Basic Client

Open up VB and create a new Standard EXE project (don't forget to set a reference to your type library). Create a GUI that will display each CoSquiggle in a VB ListBox object. As well, we would like to have the client select a member from the list box and ask that item to draw itself. Figure 11-6 shows the initial design.

Figure 11-6: Grab the squiggles!

Here's the code behind this form:

```
' A helper function to refresh the list box.
'
Private Sub RefreshGUI()
    List1.Clear
    Dim s As CoSquiggle
    For Each s In coll
        List1.AddItem s.Name
    Next
End Sub
' Draw the selected squiggle (-1 indicates there is no item selected).
'
Private Sub btnDraw_Click()
    Dim i As Integer
    If List1.ListIndex <> -1 Then
        coll.Item(List1.ListIndex).Draw
    End If
End Sub
' Get all squiggles and put the name in the list box.
'
Private Sub btnGet_Click()
    RefreshGUI
End Sub
```

Next, we need to extend our GUI to allow the user to insert and remove items, as well as see the current count. See Figure 11-7 for an example.

The code behind the Add button will create a temporary CoSquiggle and send it into the collection object:

```
' Create a new CoSquiggle and place into the collection.
'
Private Sub btnAdd_Click()
    If txtName.Text <> "" Then
        Dim o As New CoSquiggle
        o.Name = txtName
        coll.Add o
        RefreshGUI
```

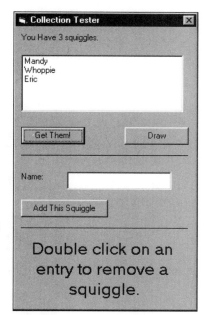

Figure 11-7: Squiggle driver.

```
        Else
                MsgBox "You did not enter a name for this squiggle..."
        End If
End Sub
```

When the user double-clicks on an item in the list box, we will ask the collection to remove this item from the vector and refresh the display:

```
' Remove the correct squiggle.
'
Private Sub List1_DblClick()
        coll.Remove List1.ListIndex
        RefreshGUI
End Sub
```

Finally, update RefreshGUI to set the label object with the current number of squiggles. That about wraps things up for this chapter. Don't forget that your collection is usable from the web (your lab solution contains a simple VBScript tester). In Chapter 12, we will examine the connectable object architecture, which (as fate would have) also makes use of enumerator interfaces.

Chapter Summary

COM interfaces can return simple data types, and often do just that. Many times it is desirable to allow the client to obtain a batch of data from the object it is working with. On the simple side of COM development, we have arrays, safe arrays, interface pointers, and custom UDTs. As we create interface methods using these items as parameters, we allow our COM clients to reduce round trips, and therefore speed up communications.

COM enumerators provide a pattern that allows a client to obtain batches of items in a manner appropriate to the client. Using Next(), the client may ask for a number of subobjects from the container. Reset() and Skip() allow the client to traverse the internal list, while Clone() allows the client to "remember" the current enumerator for future use.

While the enumeration pattern is great for C++ solutions, a raw IEnumXXXX interface will not work in the world of VB and/or VBScript. To expose a set of subobjects that all language mappings can get their hands on, you will need to develop COM collections. This pattern provides the Item(), Count(), Add(), Remove(), and _NewEnum members to allow clients to operate on a set of subobjects, as well as add and remove items at will.

As this chapter has shown you, ATL does provide some support for both COM enumerations as well as COM collections, and as long as you can stomach the maze of necessary templates, creating sophisticated object models can actually become a satisfying experience.

Chapter 12

Callback Interfaces and Connectable Objects

Objectives:

- **Understand the distinction between inbound and outbound interfaces.**
- **Learn how to implement callback interfaces.**
- **Build VB and C++ event sinks.**
- **Understand the architecture of connectable objects.**
- **Understand ATL's support for connectable objects.**
- **Get to know the IProvideClassInfo2 interface.**

COM objects can be viewed as the worker grunts of an application. Clients create them and bombard them with requests, until they have deemed they are no longer necessary. In this chapter we investigate a number of ways in which a COM object can be given a voice of its own, allowing it to communicate with the client(s) making use of it. In other words, this chapter is about enabling bidirectional communications.

We begin by examining a simple (but non-standard) approach of establishing bidirectional communication using callback interfaces. Along the way, we will see how Visual Basic and C++ clients may create "sink" objects to listen to what a coclass has to say. From here, we move into the standard COM protocol for bidirectional communications: connectable objects. After seeing what happens under the hood using straight C++, we then make use of the various tools offered by ATL.

The World of One-Way Communications

A standard coclass is composed of some number of interfaces that the client may acquire via calls to QueryInterface(). The set of interfaces implemented by a coclass and obtained by a client are termed *inbound interfaces*, in that the flow of communication comes from the client into the object. As you know, we may graphically represent each inbound interface with a distinct lollipop. In IDL, we mark the set of inbound interfaces for a coclass using the **interface** keyword. Thus, the following IDL definition may be represented by Figure 12-1:

```
// Some inbound interfaces on some coclass.
[uuid(9AB4976E-67E6-11D3-B929-0020781238D4)]
coclass CoObject
{
      [default] interface IOne;
      interface ITwo;
      interface IThree;
};
```

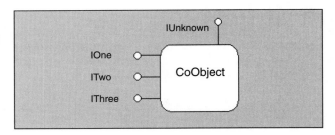

Figure 12-1: A coclass with four inbound interfaces.

While this is all well and good, we do not yet have a way for a coclass to communicate with the client. While we do have COM exception handling that allows the object to inform the client something has gone wrong, we have no way for our coclasses to report more general and object-specific information back to the client.

For example, what if we have a coclass wanting to inform the client that a worker thread has completed some background task? If we have built a GUI-based COM object, such as an ActiveX control, we might wish to tell the client when the coclass was clicked by the mouse. A financial package may have a COM object that needs to inform the client when a stock quote has been updated. How can we provide a way for a COM object to report information back to an interested client?

In reality, there are many ways to configure a two-way conversation. As we will see throughout this chapter, COM does define a standard protocol (connectable objects); however, a developer does have other options.

Polling an Object

The first (and worst) way a client can discover if something of interest has happened to a coclass is by polling the object. Here, a client obtains some inbound interface via QueryInterface() and continuously calls a method on that interface to see if some condition has been met. As an example, if an inbound interface named IMouseAction defines a method named WereYouClicked(), the client might call WereYouClicked() over and over again whenever it wishes to see if the coclass has indeed been clicked by the mouse.

The problem with this approach is that the client never really knows exactly when the coclass has been clicked, but rather asks the same question again and again, which can be a waste of round trips. Furthermore, the coclass may have been clicked some time ago (or at least since the last time it was asked), but must wait to inform anyone of the new state of affairs until WereYouClicked() is again called by the client. It is generally agreed upon that object polling is slow, inefficient, and not a great design pattern to lean on too heavily. The polling pattern is illustrated in Figure 12-2.

Figure 12-2:
Polling an object
is a waste of
time and energy.

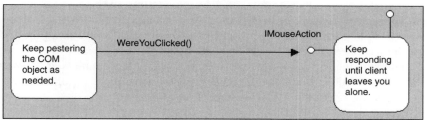

The Callback Mechanism

A better approach is to have the client provide a way for the object to inform it when the click event has occurred. Therefore, rather than asking the object the same question during idle clock cycles, the client simply tells the coclass "If this happens to you, tell me about it." In this case, the client implements an interface defined by the server in what is traditionally called a *sink object*. The client then passes a pointer to the sink interface into the coclass. The coclass holds onto this interface pointer, and calls methods <u>on the sink</u> when something interesting happens (e.g., "Hey! They clicked me!"). This is often called *firing* or *raising* an event.

Assume we have an outbound interface named IMouseEvents, which has a single method named IveBeenClicked(). The client will implement this interface in a sink and pass reference to the coclass. To allow the client to pass in the sink reference, the coclass might define an additional inbound interface (which we may call IIn) defining two methods named Advise() and Unadvise(). A client could call these methods when it wishes to be informed of events, and when it is no longer interested. This approach is typically called a *callback scenario*, as illustrated in Figure 12-3. Interfaces defined by the server and implemented by a client sink are termed *outbound interfaces* (sometimes known as *callback interfaces*).

Figure 12-3:
Bidirectional
communication
using a callback
interface.

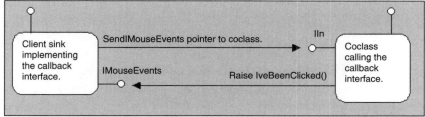

As you can see, we have flipped the roles here. The coclass (in some respects) is acting as a client, while the client's sink is acting (in some respects) as the server. So, before we begin to examine the ins and outs of COM's connectable object standard, we will first take a look at how to get two objects communicating using a callback interface.

Developing a Callback Mechanism in C++

To illustrate the callback technique, we will yet again extend the functionality of CoHexagon. Let's provide a way for CoHexagon to inform the client when it has completed its rendering task. To begin this coding example, we first need to define the callback interface. This interface will be implemented <u>by the client</u> and sent <u>to the coclass</u>. When something happens (e.g., we have finished drawing), the coclass will call methods back on the client sink using this interface pointer. To keep things simple, our callback interface (IShapeEvents) defines a single method with no parameters. Assume that we have added this interface definition to the CoHexagon's *.idl file:

```
// IShapeEvents is implemented by the client but
// defined in the server's type library.
[uuid(893D8210-688A-11d3-B929-0020781238D4), object]
interface IShapeEvents : IUnknown
{
     HRESULT FinishedDrawing();
};
```

Notice how IShapeEvents has not been set up as a raw dispinterface or even a dual interface. The reason is to reduce the coding of the client's sink object. If we were to define IShapeEvents as IDispatch savvy, the sink would need to contend with fleshing out the details of GetIDsOfNames(), Invoke(), GetTypeInfo(), and GetTypeInfoCount() as well as the methods of IUnknown, which for this example would be a bit of overkill.

To ensure that type library dependent languages can implement this interface, we must include it within the scope of CoHexagon's library statement. Take note, however, that we are not specifying IShapeEvents as an interface implemented by CoHexagon! This interface is only listed in the type information to allow clients to implement it in a sink object if they so choose:

```
// Clients need to reference this interface to implement it, so be sure it is visible.
[uuid(7005A5E0-688C-11d3-B929-0020781238D4), version(1.0)]
library HexCallBackServer
{
     importlib("stdole32.tlb");
     // Need to forward declare to get into type library.
     interface IShapeEvents;
     [uuid(881552B0-688C-11d3-B929-0020781238D4)]
     coclass CoHexagon
     {
          [default] interface IShapeEdit;
          interface IDraw;
     };
};
```

With the definition of callback interface out of the way, we now must provide some way to allow the client to send the coclass a pointer to the sink implementing the IShapeEvents interface. The coclass will hold onto this interface and use it to inform the client when it has indeed finished drawing. We will follow tradition and configure the coclass to support the Advise() and Unadvise() methods, which are defined within a custom interface named IEstablishCommunications. Keep in mind that the name of this interface and its methods are completely arbitrary. They could be called anything at all.

```
// IEstablishCommunications is implemented by the coclass to allow
// the client to send in the IShapeEvents* parameter.
[uuid(CB26A7F0-688B-11d3-B929-0020781238D4), object]
interface IEstablishCommunications : IUnknown
{
    // I want to hear when you are finished drawing.
    HRESULT Advise([in] IShapeEvents *pCallMe);
    // I am tired of listening to you.
    HRESULT Unadvise();
};
```

If we were to add the IEstablishCommunications interface to CoHexagon, we would of course need to derive from this interface, add a QueryInterface() provision, and list this new interface in our coclass type information. Notice that the Advise() method takes a single [in] parameter of type IShapeEvents*. The client will send in an IShapeEvents pointer that we hold onto during our lifetime, and thus we need a place to store it. Here are the relevant adjustments to the CoHexagon coclass:

```
// Provide a client a way to send in an IShapeEvents interface pointer.
class CoHexagon :
    public IDraw,
    public IShapeEdit,
    public IEstablishCommunications
{
public:
...
    // IEstablishCommunications
    STDMETHODIMP Advise(IShapeEvents *pCallMe);
    STDMETHODIMP Unadvise();
    // Used to talk back to client.
    IShapeEvents * m_ClientsImpl;
};
```

> **Note:** In this implementation of our callback, we are making the assumption that only a single client will be "listening" to our events. We will see how to configure a coclass to support multiple connections to outbound interfaces a bit later in this chapter.

Implementing Advise() is simple enough. Store the incoming interface pointer in our private IShapeEvents* member variable for later use. Unadvise() is just as easy. Set the private member variable to NULL:

```
// Client has sent me an interface to callback on.
STDMETHODIMP CoHexagon::Advise(IShapeEvents *pCallMe)
{
    m_ClientsImpl = pCallMe;
    m_ClientsImpl->AddRef();              // Add a reference to the client side sink.
    return S_OK;
}
// My cue to stop sending events to the client.
STDMETHODIMP CoHexagon::Unadvise()
{
    m_ClientsImpl->Release();             // Release hold on the client side sink.
    m_ClientsImpl = NULL;
```

```
        return S_OK;
}
```

The final task for the coclass is to call the FinishedDrawing() method where appropriate.

```
// As a coclass, we decide under what conditions to call the client-side interface.
STDMETHODIMP CoHexagonCallBack::Draw()
{
        // Perform any drawing code first and call client sink when finished.
        ...
        m_ClientsImpl->FinishedDrawing();
        return S_OK;
}
```

Using a Callback from Visual Basic

Any client that wishes to hear about CoHexagon's events is responsible for implementing the correct callback interface (IShapeEvents) in a sink object. If we were to build a Visual Basic client making use of our callback, the first step is to set a reference to the server's type information. Because we made sure to include the IShapeEvents interface within the scope of our library definition, this will be seen from the VB Object Browser.

Now that the VB workspace can reference IShapeEvents, we need a class to implement it. The Visual Basic language provides the **Implements** keyword for classes wishing to support COM interfaces. To keep things simple, we will let the form object implement IShapeEvents, although you most certainly could create a new Visual Basic class module to do the same.

When you wish to implement a sink object in Visual Basic, you simply list all interfaces within the [General][Declarations] scope using the **Implements** keyword. Once this has been done, VB allows you to fill in the details of each method from the code window. Simply select the interface from the right-hand drop-down list box, and each method from the left drop-down list box. Once you select each method, VB automatically generates stub code. Figure 12-4 illustrates these points:

Figure 12-4:
Implementing an interface in Visual Basic.

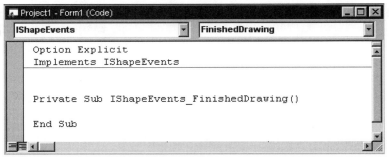

When the coclass detects it has completed its drawing cycle, it will call the client-side implementation of IShapeEvents::FinishedDrawing(). The client may then respond as it sees fit. Beyond implementing the outbound interface, all that is left to do is to inform the object we wish to be advised of the outgoing events via the IEstablishCommunications interface. Here is the complete code listing for the VB callback client:

```
' [General][Declarations]
' The client implements the callback interface.
'
Implements IShapeEvents
Private i As IEstablishCommunications
Private o As New CoHexagon
' This will eventually trigger the event.
'
Private Sub btnDraw_Click()
     o.Draw
End Sub
' The client creates the object and accesses IEstablishCommunication to
' call Advise(). The VB "Me" keyword is much like the "this" pointer.
' In this context, "Me" is the Form object implementing IShapeEvents.
'
Private Sub Form_Load()
     Set i = o
     i.Advise Me ' The form implements IShapeEvents.
End Sub
' The coclass will call this method using the callback.
'
Private Sub IShapeEvents_FinishedDrawing()
     MsgBox "Drawing is complete!", , "Event from CoHexagon"
     ' If you still are interested in listening, you may disconnect in Form_Unload()
     i.Unadvise
End Sub
```

Using a Callback from C++

Of course we can use our callback from a C++ client as well, using a bit more elbow grease. First, we also need to define a sink to implement the IShapeEvents interface. Assume we have such a class named CoSink, which will be available throughout the application as a variable in the global namespace. As CoSink is a global object, we can return fixed values from the implementation of AddRef() and Release(), as this object's lifetime is not based on external connections but is used throughout the application. The implementation of QueryInterface() will return a valid pointer to both IUnknown and IShapeEvents. The details of the sink's implementation of FinishedDrawing() are as you would expect by now:

```
// This class implements the outbound interface the coclass will be calling.
class CCoSink : public IShapeEvents
{
public:
...
     // The coclass will call this method when it is finished drawing.
     STDMETHODIMP FinishedDrawing()
     {
          MessageBox(NULL, "Drawing is complete!",
                    "Event from CoHexagon",
                    MB_OK | MB_SETFOREGROUND);
               return S_OK;
     }
};
```

With a sink in place, we may create the CoHexagon, and set an advisory relationship using IEstablishCommunications:

```
// A C++ client establishing communications with a coclass.
CCoSink g_sink;   // Will receive the events from the coclass.
int main(int argc, char* argv[])
{
...
    // Fetch IEstablishCommunications.
    IEstablishCommunications* pEC;
    CoCreateInstance(CLSID_CoHexagon, NULL,
        CLSCTX_SERVER, IID_IEstablishCommunications, (void**)&pEC);
    // Set up the advise.
    pEC->Advise((IShapeEvents*)&g_sink);
    // Trigger the event.
    IDraw* pDraw;
    pEC->QueryInterface(IID_IDraw, (void**)&pDraw);
    pDraw->Draw();
    // Disconnect from the event.
    pEC->Unadvise();
...
}
```

Lab 12-1: Building a Callback

In this lab you will extend the functionality of your raw C++ CoCar coclass to support the ability to send out events through a callback interface. As well, this lab will allow you to build a VB and C++ sink object, which will allow your clients to respond to what the CoCar has to say.

The solution for this lab can be found on your CD-ROM under:
Labs\Chapter 12\CarCallback
Labs\Chapter 12\CarCallback\CPP Client
Labs\Chapter 12\CarCallback\VB Client

Step One: Generate the IDL

To keep focused on the callback logic, this lab will extend the CoCar project you first created in Chapter 4, given that this lab already had you create the component housing, class factory, and initial IDL code. If you did not create that project, load up the CD solution and begin there.

Open your existing project (or make a copy) and define a callback interface named **IEngineEvents**, which will allow a client to hear when the automobile is about to explode (e.g., the current speed is 10 miles below the max) or has exploded (e.g., the current speed is at the max). Add the following interface to your existing IDL file:

```
// IEngineEvents is implemented by the client
// but defined by the server.
[uuid(893D8210-688A-11d3-B929-0020781238D4), object]
interface IEngineEvents : IUnknown
{
    HRESULT AboutToExplode();
    HRESULT Exploded();
};
```

Again, for ease of use, IEngineEvents is a custom IUnknown-derived interface rather than a dual. Next, we need to create an additional inbound interface, which the client may use to establish and terminate a connection to the engine events. Define a custom interface named IEstablishCommunications, which defines the Advise() and Unadvise() methods:

```
// IEstablishCommunications
// Used to allow a client to send us a valid sink.
[uuid(CB26A7F0-688B-11d3-B929-0020781238D4), object]
interface IEstablishCommunications : IUnknown
{
    HRESULT Advise([in]IEngineEvents *pCallMe);
    HRESULT Unadvise();
};
```

To finish up our IDL adjustments, we need to specify IEstablishCommunications as an additional inbound interface supported by CoCar, as well as forwardly declare IEngineEvents in our library statement (remember that a VB client has to see this interface in the type library to build the sink):

```
// Wrapping up the IDL.
[uuid(7005A5E0-688C-11d3-B929-0020781238D4), version(1.0),
helpstring("CarCallBack server")]
library CarCallBackServer
{
    importlib("stdole32.tlb");
    // Need to forward declare to get into typelib.
    // Not implemented by coclass!!!!
    interface IEngineEvents;
    [uuid(881552B0-688C-11d3-B929-0020781238D4)]
    coclass CoCarCallBack
    {
        [default] interface ICreateCar;
        interface IEstablishCommunications;
        interface IStats;
        interface IEngine;
    };
};
```

Step Two: Configure the CoCar

Now we need to update our CoCar to send out the events under the correct circumstances. First, add IEstablishCommunications to your class's inheritance chain and update your implementation of QueryInterface() to return an IEstablishCommunications pointer.

Now that we have support for this new inbound interface we need to code the Advise() and Unadvise() methods. To begin, add a private member variable of type IEngineEvents* (named **m_ClientsImpl**) to your private sector, and set it to NULL in the constructor. Your Advise() method will assign this member to the client-supplied sink object. Unadvise() will disconnect the client from the events services:

```
// IEstablishCommunications
STDMETHODIMP CoCarCallBack::Advise(IEngineEvents *pCallMe)
{
    // Store the client sink for future use.
    m_ClientsImpl = pCallMe;
    m_ClientsImpl->AddRef();
```

```
        return S_OK;
}
STDMETHODIMP CoCarCallBack::Unadvise()
{
        // Release reference and set to null.
        m_ClientsImpl->Release();
        m_ClientsImpl = NULL;
        return S_OK;
}
```

The final adjustment to make to your CoCar logic is to fire out each event when you see fit. For this lab, let's say that we fire the AboutToExplode() event when our car's current speed is 10 miles below the maximum speed. We will fire Exploded() when the car's current speed equals (or surpasses) the maximum speed. With this in mind, update your current implementation of SpeedUp(). Notice that we are only sending this event if we have a non-NULL IEngineEvents pointer:

```
// Only send events using a non-null pointer and if
// speed logic is just so.
STDMETHODIMP CoCarCallBack::SpeedUp()
{
        m_currSpeed += 10;
        if((m_maxSpeed - m_currSpeed) == 10 && (m_ClientsImpl != NULL))
        {
                // Fire the about to explode event!
                m_ClientsImpl->AboutToExplode();
        }
        if((m_currSpeed >= m_maxSpeed) && (m_ClientsImpl != NULL))
        {
                // Fire the exploded event!
                m_ClientsImpl->Exploded();
        }
        return S_OK;
}
```

With this, we have now equipped CoCar to send out two custom events using an outbound interface. The problem is, nobody is currently listening! To remedy this situation, the final steps in this lab will build up some clients and their respective sink objects.

Step Three: A Visual Basic Client

Building a sink in VB is extremely simple. Begin by creating a new Standard EXE workspace and set a reference to your updated type information. Open the VB Object Browser and locate the IEngineEvents interface. This is the interface you must now implement in a Visual Basic class module. Also note that you can see the additional inbound interface IEstablishCommunications:

Figure 12-5: The sink is responsible for implementing outbound interfaces.

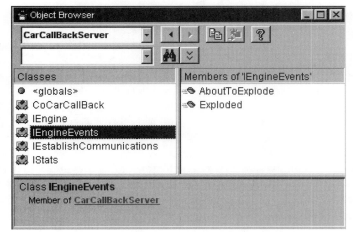

Build a simple GUI, which allows the end user to speed up the automobile. We will hardcode a pet name and maximum speed in the form's Load event, as well as set up the advisory connection. Now, using the **Implements** keyword, build a VB sink that responds to each event sent by the coclass. In your Form object's Unload event, terminate the connection. Here is the complete VB client code:

```
' [General][Declarations]
'
Option Explicit
' This client implements the callback interface
Implements IEngineEvents
Private i As IEstablishCommunications
Private o As New CoCarCallBack
' Increase the speed.
' This will eventually cause each event to be sent back to your sink.
Private Sub btnBurnRubber_Click()
     Dim e As IEngine
     Set e = o
     e.SpeedUp
     Label1.Caption = "Curr Speed: " & e.GetCurSpeed
End Sub
' The VB Sink!
Private Sub IEngineEvents_AboutToExplode()
     MsgBox "Prepare to meet thy doom..."
End Sub
Private Sub IEngineEvents_Exploded()
     MsgBox "Your car has exploded!"
End Sub
' Establish communications with the event set.
Private Sub Form_Load()
     o.SetMaxSpeed 80
     o.SetPetName "Brenner"
     Set i = o
     i.Advise Me
End Sub
Private Sub Form_Unload(Cancel As Integer)
```

```
      i.Unadvise
End Sub
```

If you now run your application, you will see each event captured in your client-side implementation.

In this step of the lab, we implemented IEngineEvents directly into the Form object. However, if you would rather have an independent VB class module responsible for implementing to the outbound interface, you can insert a new VB class module (**Project | Add Class Module**) and use the **Implements** keyword as before (use the VB Properties Window to set the name of this class).

Using this new VB class (which is included on your CD-ROM and is named CVBSink.cls) you may set up your advisory connection and allow the Form object to be a bit more independent. If you are up to the task, try to retrofit your current VB client to make use of CVBSink, rather than implementing IEngineEvents directly in the Form object. Or, forget all about it and start on the C++ client!

Step Four: A C++ Client

Create a new Win32 Console Application, and copy the necessary MIDL-generated files from your CoCar server (*_i.c and *.h). Insert a new C++ class to build your sink, and derive from IEngineEvents. Recall that this interface derives from IUnknown, which means your sink must implement a total of five methods. AddRef() and Release() can simply return some hard-coded number, as our sink is a global object whose lifetime is not dependent on outstanding references. QueryInterface() will return pointers to IUnknown and IEngineEvents. Beyond this COM goo, all we need to do is implement each method of the IEngineEvents interface:

```
// Our C++ sink object.
class CCoSink : public IEngineEvents
{
public:
    CCoSink();
    virtual ~CCoSink();
    // IUnknown as always...
    // IEngineEvents methods.
    STDMETHODIMP AboutToExplode()
    {
        MessageBox(NULL, "Prepare to meet thy doom...",
        "Event from coclass...", MB_OK | MB_SETFOREGROUND);
        return S_OK;
    }
    STDMETHODIMP Exploded()
    {
        MessageBox(NULL, "Your car is dead...", "Event from coclass...",
            MB_OK | MB_SETFOREGROUND);
        return S_OK;
    }
};
```

Your main() function will need to create a CoCar and establish communications using the global sink object:

```
// Create a global sink and go to town.
CCoSink g_sink;
```

```
void main(int argc, char* argv[])
{
    CoInitialize(NULL);
    HRESULT hr;
    IEstablishCommunications* pEC;
    hr = CoCreateInstance(CLSID_CoCarCallBack, NULL,
        CLSCTX_SERVER, IID_IEstablishCommunications, (void**)&pEC);
    // Set up the advise...
    pEC->Advise((IEngineEvents*)&g_sink);
    // Create the car.
    ICreateCar* pCC;
    pEC->QueryInterface(IID_ICreateCar, (void**)&pCC);
    pCC->SetMaxSpeed(50);
    // Grab the engine.
    IEngine* pE;
    pEC->QueryInterface(IID_IEngine, (void**)&pE);
    // Speed things up to get each event.
    for(int i = 0; i < 5; i++)
        pE->SpeedUp();
    pEC->Unadvise();
    pEC->Release();
    pE->Release();
    pCC->Release();
    CoUninitialize();
}
```

There you have it! Two clients making use of our car's callback functionality. What could be better? Next up, we will investigate COM's connectable object architecture.

COM's Connectable Object Architecture

The callback interface is a simple and efficient way to enable two COM objects to communicate with each other. The only problem with the callbacks we have just examined is that this approach does not provide a generic mechanism for bidirectional communication. The details of a callback interface are unique across projects, developers, and coclasses. For example, the methods used to set up and terminate the connection (such as Advise() and Unadvise()) may very well change among developers (such as Connect(), Disconnect(), ShutUp(), ad infinitum).

Given this, every object is different and we as COM developers have no way to treat COM objects with outbound interfaces in a polymorphic manner. Furthermore, late bound clients (such as IE) have no way to implement these ad hoc callbacks. Just as the mythical IEnumXXXX interface provides a way for COM collections to have a similar look and feel across the board, COM provides a number of standard interfaces that establish a standard protocol for bidirectional communication.

A *connectable object* refers to a COM class that contains any number of subobjects, each of which represent a possible and unique connection to an outbound interface. We will call each subobject a source of events (also called a *connection point* or *source object*). The general relationship between these key players can be seen in Figure 12-6:

Figure 12-6:
A generic example illustrating COM's generic connectable architecture.

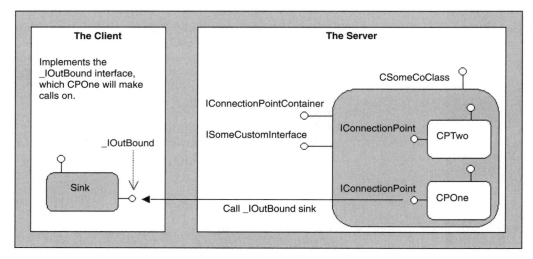

To begin analyzing this complexity, we begin with the coclass itself. CSomeCoClass is a COM object that implements the IConnectionPointContainer interface and most likely other domain-specific custom interfaces, such as ISomeCustomInterface.

IConnectionPointContainer allows the client to discover if the coclass has any source objects to establish an advisory relationship with. CSomeCoClass contains two source objects, CPOne and CPTwo. Each of these objects supports the standard IConnectionPoint interface. It is important to note that a given connection point object understands how to interact with a specific type of sink (e.g., the source object must be able to identify the GUID of the outbound interface the sink implements). In Figure 12-6, CPOne is able to call methods of the _IOutBound interface. Assume that CPTwo is able to communicate with sinks implementing another outbound interface (not shown here).

Understanding IConnectionPointContainer and IEnumConnectionPoints

The methods of IConnectionPointContainer allow the client to iterate over each source subobject or ask for a particular one by name. This level of indirection allows a coclass to support a number of outbound connections. Here is the formal definition of IConnection-PointContainer, as defined in <ocidl.idl>:

```
// This standard COM interface allows a client to examine all the connection point objects
// maintained by the coclass (a.k.a. connection point container).
[ object, uuid(B196B284-BAB4-101A-B69C-00AA00341D07) ]
interface IConnectionPointContainer : IUnknown
{
    // Give me an enumerator to look over all the connection point objects.
    HRESULT EnumConnectionPoints([out] IEnumConnectionPoints ** ppEnum);
    // Do you have a connection pointed named <guid>?
    HRESULT FindConnectionPoint([in] REFIID riid,
                                [out] IConnectionPoint ** ppCP);
};
```

Of the two methods of IConnectionPointContainer, FindConnectionPoint() is the most straightforward: A client is interested in a specific connection point identified by name. If the container supports that source object, the client receives an IConnectionPoint interface from that source object to establish communications.

EnumConnectionPoints() returns a standard COM enumerator (IEnumConnection-Points), which allows the client to iterate over all connection objects held in the container. If the client happens to find a source object it is interested in, it can make the appropriate connection using the fetched IConnectionPoint interface.

Like every IEnumXXXX interface, IEnumConnectionPoints defines the Next(), Skip(), Reset(), and Clone() methods. Given what you already know about COM enumerations, the use of this interface should be of little surprise. Here's the IDL:

```
// Using EnumConnectionPoints(), a client is able to receive an IEnumConnectionPoints
// interface.
[ object, uuid(B196B285-BAB4-101A-B69C-00AA00341D07) ]
interface IEnumConnectionPoints : IUnknown
{
        HRESULT Next([in] ULONG cConnections,
                     [out, size_is(cConnections), length_is(*pcFetched)]
                     LPCONNECTIONPOINT * ppCP,
                     [out] ULONG * pcFetched);
        HRESULT Skip([in] ULONG cConnections);
        HRESULT Reset();
        HRESULT Clone([out] IEnumConnectionPoints ** ppEnum);
};
```

To be honest, you will seldom (if ever) need to obtain a reference to IEnumConnection-Points, as the client will more than likely know the GUID of the outbound interfaces it is interested in listening to.

Furthermore, some COM language mappings (such as Visual Basic and VBScript) can only respond to events defined in the [default] source interface. Nevertheless, COM's connection point architecture is flexible enough to allow you to obtain an enumeration of connection points (provided that your language mapping can get you there).

Understanding IConnectionPoint and IEnumConnections

So then, once the client has obtained a pointer to IConnectionPointContainer, it will ultimately end up with an IConnectionPoint interface using FindConnectionPoint() or IEnumConnectionPoints(). With the acquired IConnectionPoint interface, the client may then call Advise() and Unadvise() to set up or destroy the connection (much like our previous callback example). Here is the IDL definition of IConnectionPoint, also defined in <ocidl.idl>:

```
// Each connectable object in the container implements this interface.
[ object, uuid(B196B286-BAB4-101A-B69C-00AA00341D07) ]
interface IConnectionPoint : IUnknown
{
        // Get the GUID of the source interface.
        HRESULT GetConnectionInterface( [out] IID * pIID);
        // Get the container maintaining the connection point.
        HRESULT GetConnectionPointContainer(
                    [out] IConnectionPointContainer ** ppCPC);
        // Hook me up!
        HRESULT Advise( [in] IUnknown * pUnkSink, [out] DWORD * pdwCookie);
        // Shut up already!
```

```
HRESULT Unadvise( [in] DWORD dwCookie);
// What other clients are listening to this connection?
HRESULT EnumConnections( [out] IEnumConnections ** ppEnum);
};
```

It was no odd twist of fate that our previous callback interface used methods named Advise() and Unadvise(). IConnectionPoint uses these methods for the very same reason as our ad hoc IEstablishCommunications: to establish and terminate a connection to a source object. The one small difference is that a connectable object returns a token ID to the client, which is used to determine which connection to terminate. It is very possible for multiple clients to be listening to the same connection, and therefore each client must be given a unique ID in order for the coclass to understand which client is disconnecting.

If a given client wants to know who else is listening to the events of a given source object, it may call EnumConnections(). This method of IConnectionPoint returns another standard COM enumerator, IEnumConnections, which returns information about the current active connections:

```
// Who else is out there?
[ object, uuid(B196B287-BAB4-101A-B69C-00AA00341D07)]
interface IEnumConnections : IUnknown
{
     typedef struct tagCONNECTDATA {
             IUnknown * pUnk;
             DWORD dwCookie;
       } CONNECTDATA;
     HRESULT Next([in] ULONG cConnections,
                 [out, size_is(cConnections), length_is(*pcFetched)]
                 LPCONNECTDATA rgcd,
                 [out] ULONG * pcFetched);
     HRESULT Skip([in] ULONG cConnections);
     HRESULT Reset();
     HRESULT Clone([out] IEnumConnections ** ppEnum);
};
```

Notice that what we are enumerating over is not a COM interface, but a structure named CONNECTDATA, which holds the IUnknown pointer of each client sink, as well as the assigned cookie ID:

```
// CONNECTDATA holds information for a client's sink and assigned cookie.
typedef struct tagCONNECTDATA
{
     IUnknown **pUnk;
     DWORD dwCookie;
}CONNECTDATA;
```

The final methods of IConnectionPoint allow you to obtain the GUID of the outbound interface (GetConnectionInterface()), as well as the interface of the container holding this connection point (GetConnectionPointContainer()). The later method is helpful as it allows you to navigate back to the original coclass from a source subobject. From here you can obtain additional inbound interfaces, as well as discover additional outbound interfaces (ponder that one for a moment).

So all in all, the standard connectable object protocol used by COM revolves around four standard interfaces. As you can see, this is far more complex than the callback pattern we created in the first part of this chapter. Fear not: ATL provides implementations for each of these standard interfaces. The following table summarizes the set of standard COM interfaces used to configure connections between two interested parties:

COM Connection Interface	Meaning in Life
IConnectionPoint	Used to allow a client to connect and disconnect to a source object, as well as discover any other clients that are listening to this source object.
IConnectionPointContainer	This interface allows a client to discover all the source objects the container object maintains. A single container may have numerous source objects under its management.
IEnumConnectionPoints	A standard COM enumerator interface which allows a client to iterate over all of the source objects held by the container.
IEnumConnections	Another standard COM enumerator interface which allows a client to iterate over the set of currently connected clients.

Building a Connectable Object in C++

To give a flavor of what these interfaces look like when implemented, let's examine what it would take to create the core pieces of a connectable object in C++ (to keep things simple, we will not be implementing the details of the enumerator interfaces).

 Your companion CD includes the RawConnObjServer example, which illustrates the key parts of a connection point container developed in raw C++.

To begin the journey, we need to define some source objects. As we will see, the underlying code for any connection point is very boilerplate. Given this, we will only focus on CPOne and the _IOutBound interface. CPOne supports IConnectionPoint, and like any COM object must implement the three methods of IUnknown. QueryInterface() will return pointers to IUnknown and IConnectionPoint, but nothing else. Keep in mind that when you use COM's standard connection protocol, you typically want each connectable object to have the flexibility to support any number of connected clients (rather than a single client, as in our callback example).

CPOne will maintain a list of all connected clients represented by an array (or STL vector) of IUnknown pointers. For our purposes, we will say no more than ten clients can be listening to any given connection point (recall that CPOne will receive these pointers via IConnectionPoint::Advise()). Here is the initial definition of CPOne:

```
// CPOne represents a connection to a single outbound interface.
class CPOne : public IConnectionPoint
{
public:
...
    // IUnknown as usual
    // IConnectionPoint
    STDMETHODIMP GetConnectionInterface(IID *pIID);
    STDMETHODIMP GetConnectionPointContainer(IConnectionPointContainer**ppCPC);
    STDMETHODIMP Advise(IUnknown *pUnkSink, DWORD *pdwCookie);
    STDMETHODIMP Unadvise(DWORD dwCookie);
```

```
        STDMETHODIMP EnumConnections(IEnumConnections**ppEnum);
private:
    ULONG m_ref;
    IUnknown* m_unkArray[MAX];    // MAX == 10.
    ULONG m_cookie;               // Client ID.
    int m_position;               // Index in the array.
};
```

Recall that a given connection point understands how to call methods for a particular outbound interface. For the current discussion, we will assume a very simple outbound interface named _IOutBound, which supports a single method named Test():

```
// This is implemented by the sink and called by the
// connectable object (CPOne).
[uuid(FA9D1721-6879-11d3-B929-0020781238D4), object]
interface _IOutBound : IUnknown
{
    HRESULT Test();
};
```

> **Note:**   A common practice used when developing outbound interfaces is to prefix an underscore to the interface name (e.g., _IOutBound). This is a cue to many high-level object-browsing tools to hide the interface from view.

Advising and Unadvising

Advise() is called by a client when it wishes to establish a connection with the source object. Again, to be as generic as possible, the client sends in the IUnknown pointer to the connection object. A connectable object will use this IUnknown interface to determine if the sink supports the correct outbound interface. Once this has been determined, the coclass adds the interface to its internal array (or vector) of interfaces and assigns a cookie (unique identifier) to the client:

```
// The client has implemented _IOutBound and wants to listen in...
// FYI, these new HRESULT values are defined in <olectl.h>.
STDMETHODIMP CPOne::Advise(IUnknown *pUnkSink, DWORD *pdwCookie)
{
    _IOutBound *pOutBound = NULL;
    // Do I have room for any more connections?
    if(m_position < MAX)
    {
        // Query the client for the _IOutBound interface
        // and store it for our use.
        if(SUCCEEDED(pUnkSink->QueryInterface(IID__IOutBound,
                            (void**)&pOutBound)))
        {
            m_unkArray[m_position] = pOutBound;
            m_cookie = m_position;
            // Give back a connection ID.
            *pdwCookie = m_cookie;
            m_position++;
            return S_OK;
        }
    }
```

```
        else
        {
            // Some client sent me a sink I can't use!
            return CONNECT_E_NOCONNECTION;
        }
    }
    return CONNECT_E_ADVISELIMIT;
}
```

Most Advise() methods will look about the same. First, if our array of IUnknown pointers is full (we have handed out our maximum number of connections) we return CONNECT_E_ADVISELIMIT immediately. Recall that a given connectable object is able to call methods (a.k.a. fire events) for a specific outbound interface. CPOne only knows how to talk to sink objects supporting _IOutBound, and thus the initial call to QueryInterface().

If this call is successful, we can store a pointer to this sink into our array, advance the position in the array by one, and assign the cookie. If this call was not successful, the client is attempting to communicate with a source object which does not "understand" the sink's outbound interface and should return CONNECT_E_NOCONNECTION.

Implementing Unadvise() is simply a matter of removing the specific sink pointer from the array based off the assigned cookie:

```
// A client named dwCookie wants to break a connection to the _IOutBound interface.
STDMETHODIMP CPOne::Unadvise(DWORD dwCookie)
{
    m_unkArray[dwCookie]->Release();
    m_unkArray[dwCookie] = NULL;
    return S_OK;
}
```

Finishing Up the Source Object

The next two methods every IConnectionPoint-enabled coclass must contend with are GetConnectionInterface() and EnumConnections(). The former is responsible for returning the interface identifier of the outbound interface this connection point is making calls to. As mentioned, EnumConnections() allows a client to obtain a COM enumerator to walk the list of connected clients. For our purpose, we will return E_NOTIMPL from within EnumConnections() to help ease the pain (we will wait for ATL to help us out with this one):

```
// Which sink interface can I talk to?
STDMETHODIMP CPOne::GetConnectionInterface(IID *pIID)
{
    *pIID = IID__IOutBound;
    return S_OK;
}
// I won't let you see my connections...
STDMETHODIMP CPOne::EnumConnections(IEnumConnections**ppEnum)
{
    return E_NOTIMPL;
}
```

The final method of IConnectionPoint allows a client to return to the container itself. As mentioned, this allows a client to return to the coclass from a connection point subobject.

The problem is, CPOne does not know who created it! To rectify this, let's give CPOne an overloaded constructor allowing the container to pass a pointer to itself. We can hold onto this pointer and use it within our implementation of GetConnectionPointContainer():

```
// The overloaded constructor.
CPOne::CPOne(IConnectionPointContainer* pCont)
{
    // Prep work...
    m_ref = 0;
    m_cookie = 0;
    m_position = 0;
    m_pCont = pCont;
    // Fill the array of IUnknown pointers with NULL.
    for(int i = 0; i < MAX; i++)
        m_unkArray[i] = NULL;
}
// Return pointer to the container.
STDMETHODIMP CPOne::GetConnectionPointContainer(IConnectionPointContainer**ppCPC)
{
    *ppCPC = m_pCont;
    (*ppCPC)->AddRef();    // Release() called when finished.
    return S_OK;
}
```

Firing the Event

The final bit of code relevant to this discussion is the actual call to the Test() method implemented by the client-side sink. Once a client has set up an advisory connection to CPOne, it is patiently waiting for us to call the Test() method at some point. To do so, here is a public helper function named Fire_Test(), which will be called by the container at some point. Here, we need to recall that any number of clients (up to ten) might be hooked into this event, and call each sink:

```
// Call the Test() method for each connected client.
HRESULT CPOne::Fire_Test()
{
    // For each active connection...
    for (int nConnectionIndex = 0; nConnectionIndex < MAX; nConnectionIndex++)
    {
        // Grab an IUnk from the array.
        IUnknown* pUnk = m_unkArray[nConnectionIndex];
        // Dynamically change it into a _IOutBound...
        _IOutBound* pOut = reinterpret_cast<_IOutBound*>(pUnk);
        if (pOut != NULL)
        {
            pOut->Test();    // Call client's implementation of Test().
        }
    }
    return S_OK;
}
```

If _IOutBound defined a number of events we would write similar Fire_ methods for each. In this way, a given source object is self sufficient, in that it has the ability to communicate with the sink.

Implementing a Connection Point Container in C++

So then, CPOne is complete (except for the enumerators). We now have to create the container for this connection point. CoSomeCoClass will need to add support for IConnectionPointContainer and define the details behind FindConnectionPoint() and EnumConnectionPoints(). To keep life sane, we will return E_NOTIMPL from the EnumConnectionPoints() method and focus on FindConnectionPoint():

```
// Our container will not support enumeration of our connection points.
STDMETHODIMP CoSomeObject::EnumConnectionPoints(IEnumConnectionPoints **ppEnum)
{
      // In reality the COM spec disallows returning E_NOTIMPL, but hey...
      return E_NOTIMPL;
}
```

FindConnectionPoint() allows a client to ask for a connection to a specific outbound interface. To begin, CoSomeObject must create any inner source objects, which it does in the constructor (which would be cleaned up in the destructor):

```
// Create a new CPOne object, and inform it of its parent.
CoSomeObject::CoSomeObject() : m_ref(0)
{
      // Send in parent pointer for use in GetConnectionPointContainer()
      m_pconnOne = new CPOne((IConnectionPointContainer*)this);
      m_pconnOne->AddRef();
      g_objCount++;
}
```

We can now implement FindConnectionPoint() quite easily; just test the incoming IID and fill the client's IConnectionPoint variable to our CPOne object. Do note that FindConnectionPoint() has a look and feel similar to QueryInterface(). The difference is the QueryInterface() hands out pointers to inbound interfaces, while FindConnectionPoint() hands out pointers to outbound interfaces:

```
// Hand out our connection.
STDMETHODIMP CoSomeObject::FindConnectionPoint(REFIID riid, IConnectionPoint **ppCP)
{
      // We only supply one CP right now...
      if(riid == IID__IOutBound)
            *ppCP = m_pconnOne;
      else
      {
            *ppCP = NULL;
            return CONNECT_E_NOCONNECTION;
      }
      (*ppCP)->AddRef();
      return S_OK;
}
```

Beyond adding a QueryInterface() provision for IID_IConnectionPointContainer, CoSomeObject() is just about complete. All we need to do is actually fire the Fire_Test() method back to the clients.

Assume our single inbound interface (ISomeInterface) defines the TriggerEvent() method, which simply turns around and calls the client-side sink:

```
// Fire at will!
STDMETHODIMP CoSomeObject::TriggerEvent()
{
    // Here we go! This will force CPOne to fire the test method to all
    // connected clients.
    m_pconnOne->Fire_Test();
    return S_OK;
}
```

IDL and Outbound Interfaces

Last but not least, we can now modify the project's IDL definition to indicate it has a coclass supporting an outbound interface. IDL provides the [source] attribute to mark outbound interfaces, and as mentioned many languages will only accept events from the [default] source interface. If you were to develop a coclass supporting a number of connectable objects, you would simply list multiple [source] interfaces, specifying one as the [default]:

```
// This coclass has two outbound interfaces, but only one is the default.
[uuid(FA9D1722-6879-11d3-B929-0020781238D4)]
coclass CoSomeObject
{
    [default]interface ISomeInterface;
    [default, source] interface _IOutBound;     // VB(Script) can get here.
    [source] interface _IAnotherOutBound;       // VB(Script) can't get here!
};
```

Using a Connectable Object from Visual Basic

Visual Basic makes the consumption of source objects completely painless. Unlike our previous callback example, we have no need to implement any interfaces on our end. Rather, we make use of the **WithEvents** keyword when declaring an instance of the coclass, and VB dynamically synthesizes a sink on our behalf. When you open the VB Object Browser,

Figure 12-7: Events of the [default, source].

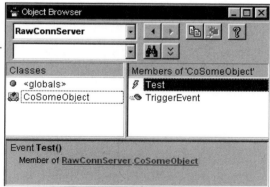

you will see that any event found in the [default, source] interface will be represented by a lightning bolt icon (Figure 12-7).

All we need to do is write the code executed as a result of the firing of the Test method. Once you have set a reference to the type library, you will create an instance of the coclass in the [General][Declarations] namespace using the **WithEvents** keyword. Here is the complete code:

Note: You cannot use the VB New operator when declaring a variable with events. You must first declare the variable, and create a new instance after the fact.

```
' [General][Declarations]
'
Private WithEvents rawObj As RawConnServer.CoSomeObject
Private Sub btnMakeObject_Click()
    ' Make the object.
    Set rawObj = New CoSomeObject
End Sub
Private Sub btnTrigger_Click()
    ' This will send the event.
    rawObj.TriggerEvent
End Sub
' Sink.
Private Sub rawObj_Test()
    MsgBox "The object just called me!", , "Test complete..."
End Sub
```

As you can guess, we have more work to do as a C++ client, but not that much.

Using a Connectable Object from C++

Now we need to examine how a C++ client can rig into our connection object. Much like the callback example, we need a sink object to implement _IOutBound. Here is the definition:

```
// The sink for _IOutBound.
#include "rawconnobjserver.h"       // MIDL-generated file.
class CCoSink : public _IOutBound
{
public:
    CCoSink();
    virtual ~CCoSink();
    // IUnknown
    STDMETHODIMP_(ULONG) AddRef();
    STDMETHODIMP_(ULONG) Release();
    STDMETHODIMP QueryInterface(REFIID riid, void** ppv);
    // _IOutBound
    STDMETHODIMP Test();            // Do something interesting here...
};
```

With this detail aside for the time being, here is the basic set of steps a C++ client will make to set up and tear down a connection:

```
// Here are the guts of a C++ connection (VB takes care of this internally).
CCoSink g_sink;
void main(int argc, char* argv[])
{
...
    // 1) Get IConnectionPointContainer.
    IConnectionPointContainer* pICPC = NULL;
    CoCreateInstance(CLSID_CoSomeObject, NULL, CLSCTX_SERVER,
                IID_IConnectionPointContainer, (void**)&pICPC);
    // 2) Find a connection point.
    IConnectionPoint* pCP = NULL;
    pICPC->FindConnectionPoint(IID__IOutBound, &pCP);
    // 3) Make a connection to this source object.
    ULONG cookie;
    pCP->Advise(&g_sink, &cookie);
```

```
// 4) Get the default inbound ISomeInterface.
ISomeInterface* pISomeIntf = NULL;
pICPC->QueryInterface(IID_ISomeInterface, (void**)&pISomeIntf);
// 5) Do something to trigger the event (this will call g_sink::Test())
pISomeIntf->TriggerEvent();
// 6) Release connection.
pCP->Unadvise(cookie);
...
}
```

So as you may agree, that is a heck of a lot of work to do just to get a connection between two COM objects (and that is without the enumerator interfaces!). If we had no other choice but straight C++ to build standard connectable objects, I'd bet we would find a lot of objects that were the "strong silent type." Of course, ATL makes this whole interaction nearly invisible using wizards, templates, and a few magical macros.

Building Connectable Objects with ATL

Having examined what it would take to get a connectable scenario up and running in straight C++, you have likely come to the following conclusions:

1. I will never write a connectable object in straight C++.
2. This is far too painful, and we did not even contend with the enumerators.
3. ATL better help out with this one.

Yes, connectable objects are a huge pain to get right without framework support, and the great news is that ATL does indeed make connection point development (just about) as easy as selecting the correct option in the Object Wizard. Using two core templates and a handful of helper classes, your ATL coclasses will be perfectly able to send out any number of events with minimal fuss and bother. Rest assured that the prefabricated ATL code is taking care of all the gory details we have just examined. To show you how easy things can be with a good framework on your side, let's re-create the previous example in ATL.

To begin, assume we have used the ATL COM AppWizard to create a new DLL workspace called ATLConnObjServer. We will now use the ATL Object Wizard to insert a new Simple Object named CoSomeObject which supports a [default] interface named ISomeInterface. Before you click that OK button, however, you will need to be sure that you select the option indicated in Figure 12-8.

Figure 12-8: Enabling your object to function as a connection point container.

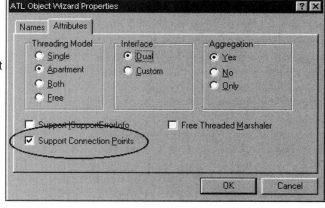

When you enable this option for an ATL coclass, you are saying that you wish this object to work as a connection point container, and thus support IConnectionPointContainer. As far as the generated code is concerned, you will first see that the coclass is derived from a further ATL template named

IConnectionPointContainerImpl< > together with a corresponding COM_MAP entry. As the name suggests, this ATL template provides a full implementation for FindConnection-Point() and EnumConnectionPoints().

In order for IConnectionPointContainerImpl< > to get its work done, it must be able to discover and identify each individual source object it maintains. The fact of the matter is, your coclass currently <u>does not</u> have any objects supporting IConnectionPoint (e.g., we don't have CPOne or CPTwo, but will insert these source objects in just a moment).

What you will find, however, is an empty ATL "connection point map" defined in your coclass. As you bring in more and more source objects into your container, this map will be populated with a number of CONNECTION_POINT_ENTRY macros. Here is the initial code:

```
// When you select the Support Connection Point option, your coclass
// is modified with the following.
// Therefore, if you forget to check this option, you will need to add the following
// by hand.
class ATL_NO_VTABLE CCoSomeObject :
     public CComObjectRootEx<CComSingleThreadModel>,
     public CComCoClass<CCoSomeObject, &CLSID_CoSomeObject>,
     public IConnectionPointContainerImpl<CCoSomeObject>,
     public IDispatchImpl<ISomeObject, &IID_ISomeObject,
                          &LIBID_ATLCONNOBJSERVERLib>
{
public:
     CCoSomeObject()
     {
     }
DECLARE_REGISTRY_RESOURCEID(IDR_COSOMEOBJECT)
DECLARE_PROTECT_FINAL_CONSTRUCT()
BEGIN_COM_MAP(CCoSomeObject)
     COM_INTERFACE_ENTRY(ISomeObject)
     COM_INTERFACE_ENTRY(IDispatch)
     COM_INTERFACE_ENTRY(IConnectionPointContainer)
END_COM_MAP()
// This map will hold all connection points (currently none).
BEGIN_CONNECTION_POINT_MAP(CCoSomeObject)
END_CONNECTION_POINT_MAP()
};
```

You will also see that the ATL Object Wizard has generated the first [default, source] interface in your IDL file's library statement. By default, ATL will name this initial outbound interface based on the initial inbound interface. Also note that ATL automatically creates a *raw dispinterface* to represent outbound interfaces. The reason? To enable communications with late bound clients. If you are not interested in supporting vTable-challenged clients, you can replace the definition to meet your design. Here is the initial IDL code:

```
// The Object Wizard will define a single outbound interface.
[ uuid(9788BFA3-6941-11D3-B929-0020781238D4), version(1.0),
helpstring("ATLConnObjServer 1.0 Type Library") ]
library ATLCONNOBJSERVERLib
{
     importlib("stdole32.tlb");
     importlib("stdole2.tlb");
     [ uuid(9788BFB1-6941-11D3-B929-0020781238D4),
```

```
        helpstring("_ISomeObjectEvents Interface") ]
    dispinterface _ISomeObjectEvents
    {
        properties:
        methods:
    };
    [ uuid(9788BFB0-6941-11D3-B929-0020781238D4),
      helpstring("CoSomeObject Class") ]
    coclass CoSomeObject
    {
        [default] interface ISomeObject;
        [default, source] dispinterface _ISomeObjectEvents;
    };
};
```

Now, you are free to compile the server as things now stand; however, you still have no subobjects implementing IConnectionPoint, and therefore have no events to fire. Before we build the source object, we first need to add methods into the outbound interface. As we are in ATL territory, we can populate our [source] interfaces using the Add Method Wizard just as we would with a standard inbound interface. Assume we have added an event named Test() to the [source] interface, which this time takes a single [in] BSTR parameter:

```
// The BSTR is [in] given that the coclass is calling the sink!
dispinterface _ISomeObjectEvents
{
    properties:
    methods:
        [id(1), helpstring("method Test")] HRESULT Test([in] BSTR bstrTest);
};
```

Bringing in the Connections: Another ATL Wizard

Once you have added some events to your [source] interface (and recompiled to refresh the type information) you are now ready to use the ATL Implement Connection Point Wizard. To activate this CASE tool, right-click on the coclass that you wish to hold the connection (in our case CoSomeObject) and select this option in the pop-up menu item. What you will see is a one-step tool which lists each and every unaccounted for [source] interface in your IDL file (see Figure 12-9).

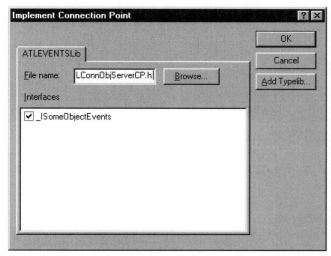

Figure 12-9: Generation of a complete implementation of a connection object à la ATL.

Notice that the tool will name the new file using a "CP" suffix. ATLConnObjServerCP.h is the name of our new header file that defines the connection class responsible for connecting interested clients to the

_ISomeObjectEvents interface. The ATL-generated class will be marked with a
"CProxy_" prefix before the name of the [source] interface (in this case
CProxy_ISomeObjectEvents). Here is a look into that generated proxy class:

```cpp
// The wizard generates similar code for each connection in your code.
template <class T>
class CProxy_ISomeObjectEvents : public IConnectionPointImpl<T,
                &DIID__ISomeObjectEvents, CComDynamicUnkArray>
{
public:
    HRESULT Fire_Test(BSTR bstrTest)
    {
        CComVariant varResult;
        T* pT = static_cast<T*>(this);
        int nConnectionIndex;
        CComVariant* pvars = new CComVariant[1];
        int nConnections = m_vec.GetSize();
        for (nConnectionIndex = 0; nConnectionIndex < nConnections;
            nConnectionIndex++)
        {
            pT->Lock();
            CComPtr<IUnknown> sp = m_vec.GetAt(nConnectionIndex);
            pT->Unlock();
            IDispatch* pDispatch = reinterpret_cast<IDispatch*>(sp.p);
            if (pDispatch != NULL)
            {
                VariantClear(&varResult);
                pvars[0] = bstrTest;
                DISPPARAMS disp = { pvars, NULL, 1, 0 };
                pDispatch->Invoke(0x1, IID_NULL,
                    LOCALE_USER_DEFAULT,
                    DISPATCH_METHOD, &disp, &varResult,
                    NULL, NULL);
            }
        }
        delete[] pvars;
        return varResult.scode;
    }
};
```

CProxy_ISomeObjectEvents is equivalent to the CPOne class we wrote by hand in the raw
C++ example. This class implements each method of IConnectionPoint, with help from
the IConnectionPointImpl<> template. More importantly, this proxy class has implemented a method called Fire_Test(). This is the name of the method we call from within
our CoSomeObject logic whenever we wish to send out the Test() event to all listening clients. As you can see, the generated code will iterate over the active connections, and call
the Test() method (via Invoke() with a DISPID of [id(1)]) on each client sink. Furthermore,
our BSTR parameter is packaged up into a VARIANT using the ATL CComVariant helper
class. Not bad for a mouse click!

Note: If you add, delete, or change any methods on your [source] interfaces,
you will need to rerun the Implement Connection Point Wizard to refresh the generated code.

Modifications in the CoSomeObject Coclass

Now that we have a real connection object for the container, we will see that the Implement Connection Point Wizard has made the following change back in the CoSomeObject coclass. First, the proxy object representing the connection has been added into our inheritance chain. Therefore, our class can call Fire_Test() whenever it wishes to send this event to connected clients. As well, you will most likely find that your connection map now has an (incorrect) entry. Yes, a bug. Here is what the code looks like before the fix (the erroneous line is in your connection map):

```
// The wizard has a bug!
class ATL_NO_VTABLE CCoSomeObject :
    public CComObjectRootEx<CComSingleThreadModel>,
    public CComCoClass<CCoSomeObject, &CLSID_CoSomeObject>,
    public IConnectionPointContainerImpl<CCoSomeObject>,
    public IDispatchImpl<ISomeObject, &IID_ISomeObject,
                    &LIBID_ATLCONNOBJSERVERLib>,
    public CProxy_ISomeObjectEvents< CCoSomeObject >
{
...
BEGIN_CONNECTION_POINT_MAP(CCoSomeObject)
    CONNECTION_POINT_ENTRY(IID__ISomeObjectEvents)
END_CONNECTION_POINT_MAP()
...
};
```

The MIDL compiler automatically creates a GUID constant marked with a "DIID_" prefix for all dispinterfaces. Note that the Implement Connection Point Wizard failed to take this into consideration, and listed our connection point entry with an "IID_" prefix (oops). This is annoying, but not a big deal to fix; add a "D" and move on:

```
// Fix the Wizard generated code by adding a 'D' to the connection entry.
BEGIN_CONNECTION_POINT_MAP(CCoSomeObject)
    CONNECTION_POINT_ENTRY(DIID__ISomeObjectEvents)
END_CONNECTION_POINT_MAP()
```

All you have to do at this point is call Fire_Test() from somewhere in your code and ATL will ensure each connected client gets your event. Assume our [default] interface has a method called TriggerTheEvent():

```
// As always, you will need to decide the conditions to fire your events.
STDMETHODIMP CCoSomeObject::TriggerTheEvent()
{
    // Do other stuff in this function...
    // Now fire the event.
    CComBSTR msg = "Take that!";
    Fire_Test(msg.Copy());
    return S_OK;
}
```

Digging Deeper into ATL's Support for Connection Points

Now that we have seen just how easy ATL makes connection points, we will take a deeper look into how the framework is doing its magic. As you know, a client can ask an object if it supports IConnectionPointContainer. If so, the object is in effect saying, "I have some number of subobjects which you can listen to." The client discovers these connection points by calling either EnumConnectionPoints() or FindConnectionPoint(). The IConnectionPointContainerImpl<> template of ATL takes care of all the grunge work. To get the job done, IConnectionPointContainerImpl<> must make use of the derived class's connection point map.

The BEGIN_CONNECTION_POINT_MAP() macro expands to define an array of _ATL_CONNMAP_ENTRY structures named "_entries." This same macro also defines a helper function named GetConnMap() to return the _ATL_CONNMAP_ENTRY array. Here is the definition in <atlcom.h>:

```
// This ATL map defines an array of _ATL_CONNMAP_ENTRY structures.
#define BEGIN_CONNECTION_POINT_MAP(x)\
    typedef x _atl_conn_classtype;\
    static const _ATL_CONNMAP_ENTRY* GetConnMap(int* pnEntries) {\
    static const _ATL_CONNMAP_ENTRY _entries[] = {
```

So then, what is _ATL_CONNMAP_ENTRY? I can assure you it is far simpler than the _ATL_INTMAP_ENTRY structure defined by the COM_MAP. _ATL_CONNMAP_ENTRY holds a single field, which contains the offset to a given connection point from the IConnectionPointContainer interface:

```
// The connection point map is an array of these guys.
struct _ATL_CONNMAP_ENTRY
{
    DWORD dwOffset;
};
```

To fill the array, we make use of the CONNECTION_POINT_ENTRY macro which computes the offset of the correct vPtr, using the offsetofclass() macro:

```
// CONNECTION_POINT_ENTRY computes the offset of the connection point to the
// IConnectionPointContainer interface.
#define CONNECTION_POINT_ENTRY(iid){offsetofclass(_ICPLocator<&iid>, \
    _atl_conn_classtype)-\
    offsetofclass(IConnectionPointContainerImpl<_atl_conn_classtype>, \
    _atl_conn_classtype)},
```

Finally, the END_CONNECTION_POINT_MAP() macro terminates the array:

```
// Terminate the array.
#define END_CONNECTION_POINT_MAP() {(DWORD)-1} };
```

Once we have a connection map in place, IConnectionPointContainerImpl<> can call GetConnMap() when it needs to find a given connection point for the client. <atlcom.h> defines IConnectionPointContainerImpl<>::FindConnectionPoint() as so:

```
// The client sends in a specific connection point IID, and we search the connection map
// for the correct entry.
STDMETHOD(FindConnectionPoint)(REFIID riid, IConnectionPoint** ppCP)
{
    if (ppCP == NULL)
        return E_POINTER;
    *ppCP = NULL;
    HRESULT hRes = CONNECT_E_NOCONNECTION;
    // Get the map of connections.
    const _ATL_CONNMAP_ENTRY* pEntry = T::GetConnMap(NULL);
    IID iid;
```

```
// Search the map until we reach the end.
while (pEntry->dwOffset != (DWORD)-1)
{
    // Get one of the entries.
    IConnectionPoint* pCP =
        (IConnectionPoint*)((int)this+pEntry->dwOffset);
    // Is it the same as what the client wants?
    if (SUCCEEDED(pCP->GetConnectionInterface(&iid)) &&
        InlineIsEqualGUID(riid, iid))
    {
        *ppCP = pCP;                 // Ah-ha! Found ya!
        pCP->AddRef();
        hRes = S_OK;
        break;
    }
    pEntry++;
}
return hRes;
}
```

EnumConnectionPoints() also makes use of the connection map to get its work done. However, it does not iterate over the map looking for a given entry, but to fill a COM enumerator for the client. The CComEnumConnectionPoints typedef defines the enumerator, and as you already have a good grasp of how ATL provides support for COM enumerators, I'd bet this does not look too offensive to your eyes at this point:

```
// This typedef is a COM enumerator for IConnectionPoint interfaces.
typedef CComEnum<IEnumConnectionPoints, &IID_IEnumConnectionPoints,
    IConnectionPoint*, _CopyInterface<IConnectionPoint> >
    CComEnumConnectionPoints;
// Return an enumerator of all the connections to the client.
// (error checking code removed for clarity)
STDMETHOD(EnumConnectionPoints)(IEnumConnectionPoints** ppEnum)
{
...
    // Make the connection point enumerator.
    CComEnumConnectionPoints* pEnum = NULL;
    ATLTRY(pEnum = new CComObject<CComEnumConnectionPoints>)
...
    // Get the connection map.
    int nCPCount;
    const _ATL_CONNMAP_ENTRY* pEntry = T::GetConnMap(&nCPCount);
    // Allocate and initialize a vector of connection point object pointers
    IConnectionPoint** ppCP =
        (IConnectionPoint**)alloca(sizeof(IConnectionPoint*)*nCPCount);
    int i = 0;
    while (pEntry->dwOffset != (DWORD)-1)
    {
        ppCP[i++] = (IConnectionPoint*)((int)this+pEntry->dwOffset);
        pEntry++;
    }
    // Copy the pointers: they will AddRef this object
    HRESULT hRes = pEnum->Init((IConnectionPoint**)&ppCP[0],
        (IConnectionPoint**)&ppCP[nCPCount],
        reinterpret_cast<IConnectionPointContainer*>(this), AtlFlagCopy);
...
```

```
        // Return the enumerator.
        hRes = pEnum->QueryInterface(IID_IEnumConnectionPoints, (void**)ppEnum);
        if (FAILED(hRes))
                delete pEnum;
        return hRes;
}
```

ATL's IConnectionPointImpl<> Template

Finally, we have the IConnectionPointImpl<> template, which is a base class for each
proxy class generated by the ATL Implement Connection Point Wizard. This template
maintains a dynamic array of IUnknown pointers, which represent the client-supplied
interfaces send in via IConnectionPoint::Advise() (the ATL utility class CComDynamic-
UnkArray represents this array). Here are the relevant parts of IConnectionPointImpl<>:

```
// IConnectionPointImpl<> provides framework support for the all important
// IConnectionPoint interface.
template <class T, const IID* piid, class CDV = CComDynamicUnkArray >
class ATL_NO_VTABLE IConnectionPointImpl : public _ICPLocator<piid>
{
        // Here is the typedef for IEnumConnections
        typedef CComEnum<IEnumConnections, &IID_IEnumConnections,
        CONNECTDATA, _Copy<CONNECTDATA> > CComEnumConnections;
        typedef CDV _CDV;
public:
        // Get the IID of this connection interface.
        STDMETHOD(GetConnectionInterface)(IID* piid2)
        {
                if (piid2 == NULL)
                        return E_POINTER;
                *piid2 = *piid;
                return S_OK;
        }
        // Get the connection point container.
        STDMETHOD(GetConnectionPointContainer)
                (IConnectionPointContainer** ppCPC)
        {
                T* pT = static_cast<T*>(this);
                // No need to check ppCPC for NULL since QI will do that for us
                return pT->QueryInterface(IID_IConnectionPointContainer,
                                        (void**)ppCPC);
        }
        // Not defined inline...
        STDMETHOD(Advise)(IUnknown* pUnkSink, DWORD* pdwCookie);
        STDMETHOD(Unadvise)(DWORD dwCookie);
        STDMETHOD(EnumConnections)(IEnumConnections** ppEnum);
        CDV m_vec;
};
```

Advise() will do as you expect. Increase the size of the dynamic array of IUnknown pointers and return a cookie to the connected client. To discover the IID for the outbound
interface this source proxy is able to communicate with, a call is first made to
GetConnectionInterface():

```
// Advise me.
template <class T, const IID* piid, class CDV>
STDMETHODIMP IConnectionPointImpl<T, piid, CDV>::Advise(IUnknown*
                                  pUnkSink, DWORD* pdwCookie)
{
    T* pT = static_cast<T*>(this);
    IUnknown* p;
    HRESULT hRes = S_OK;
...
    IID iid;
    GetConnectionInterface(&iid);
    // Get sink.
    hRes = pUnkSink->QueryInterface(iid, (void**)&p);
    if (SUCCEEDED(hRes))
    {
        pT->Lock();
        *pdwCookie = m_vec.Add(p);
        hRes = (*pdwCookie != NULL) ? S_OK:CONNECT_E_ADVISELIMIT;
        pT->Unlock();
        if (hRes != S_OK) p->Release();
    }
    else if (hRes == E_NOINTERFACE)
        hRes = CONNECT_E_CANNOTCONNECT;
    if (FAILED(hRes))
        *pdwCookie = 0;
    return hRes;
}
```

Unadvise() removes the client from the dynamic array based on the assigned cookie:

```
// Take me off the mailing list.
template <class T, const IID* piid, class CDV>
STDMETHODIMP IConnectionPointImpl<T, piid, CDV>::Unadvise(DWORD dwCookie)
{
    T* pT = static_cast<T*>(this);
    pT->Lock();
    // Get the correct unknown pointer from the CComDynamicUnkArray.
    IUnknown* p = _CDV::GetUnknown(dwCookie);
    // Remove it.
    HRESULT hRes = m_vec.Remove(dwCookie) ? S_OK :
                CONNECT_E_NOCONNECTION;
    pT->Unlock();
    if (hRes == S_OK && p != NULL)
        p->Release();
    return hRes;
}
```

To wrap up, ATL's support for connection points, EnumConnections(), creates a COM enumerator full of all the CONNECTDATA structures, based on the CComEnumConnections typedef. Also, be aware that the destructor of IConnectionPointImpl<> releases all remaining IUnknown references.

Easing a Client's Burden with IProvideClassInfo(2)

If you were keeping track of the interaction between a client, sink, and connection point, you should be a bit alarmed regarding the number of round trips to establish a connection. Think about this: The client first calls CoCreateInstance() to obtain IID_IConnection-PointContainer (#1). From this interface, the client obtains a connection point interface (#2). The client then calls Advise(), passing in the IUnknown of the sink implementing the outbound interface (#3). Then, the source object queries the <u>client</u> for the correct IID of the outbound interface (#4)! Four round trips later, we have established a two-way conversation. This is excessive, but keep in mind that COM's connection point architecture was deliberately designed to be extendable and as generic as possible. To help ease the client's burden, many connectable objects elect to support two additional standard interfaces: IProvideClassInfo and IProvideClassInfo2.

Using the methods of these interfaces, a client is able to receive a pointer to an ITypeInfo interface, and can discover the set of, and type of, interfaces the object supports. As well, a client is able to discover the IID [default, source] interface in one call. While some interactions will be unavoidable, IProvideClassInfo(2) can help some object consumers get the ball rolling with less fuss and bother. Each interface is defined in <ocidl.idl> as so:

```
// Allow a client to get the type information.
[object, uuid(B196B283-BAB4-101A-B69C-00AA00341D07), pointer_default(unique)]
interface IProvideClassInfo : IUnknown
{
    HRESULT GetClassInfo([out] ITypeInfo ** ppTI);
};
// Allow a client to get the IID of the [default, source] interface.
[object, uuid(A6BC3ACO-DBAA-11CE-9DE3-00AA004BB851), pointer_default(unique)]
interface IProvideClassInfo2 : IProvideClassInfo
{
    typedef enum tagGUIDKIND {
    GUIDKIND_DEFAULT_SOURCE_DISP_IID = 1
    } GUIDKIND;
    HRESULT GetGUID([in] DWORD dwGuidKind, [out] GUID * pGUID);
};
```

GetGUID() is configured to be extendable in that the first parameter specifies the type of GUID the client wants to obtain. Currently, the GUIDKIND structure only knows how to return the default source dispinterface of the coclass. In other words, IProvideClassInfo2 can only help you out if your [default, source] has been set up as a dispinterface, which as you recall, ATL does automatically.

To support these two interfaces on your coclass, ATL provides the IProvideClass-InfoImpl< > and IProvideClassInfoImpl2< > templates. Each is defined in <atlcom.h> if you want to check it out yourself; just keep in mind that IProvideClassInfoImpl2< > requires the CLSID of your coclass and the IID of the default source dispinterface.

As one interface derives from another, you will add the most derived template to your coclass's inheritance chain and add the appropriate COM_MAP entries. Typically you will want to grab the functionality of both interfaces, thus you may configure your ATL coclass as such:

```
// IProvideClassInfo(2) helps various COM language mappings obtain relevant
// information in a more timely fashion.
class ATL_NO_VTABLE CCoSomeObject:
    public CComObjectRootEx<CComSingleThreadModel>,
    public CComCoClass<CCoSomeObject, &CLSID_CoSomeObject>,
    public IConnectionPointContainerImpl<CCoSomeObject>,
    public IDispatchImpl<ISomeObject, &IID_ISomeObject, &LIBID_ATLCONNOBJSERVERLib>,
    public CProxy_ISomeObjectEvents<CCoSomeObject>,
    public CProxy_IAnotherOutbound<CCoSomeObject>,
    public IProvideClassInfo2Impl<&CLSID_CoSomeObject, &DIID__ISomeObjectEvents>
{
...
BEGIN_COM_MAP(CCoSomeObject)
    COM_INTERFACE_ENTRY(ISomeObject)
    COM_INTERFACE_ENTRY(IDispatch)
    COM_INTERFACE_ENTRY(IConnectionPointContainer)
    COM_INTERFACE_ENTRY_IMPL(IConnectionPointContainer)
    COM_INTERFACE_ENTRY(IProvideClassInfo)
    COM_INTERFACE_ENTRY(IProvideClassInfo2)
END_COM_MAP()
...
};
```

Note: If your coclass needs to send events to a web-based client, it must support IProvideClassInfo2.

Lab 12-2: Building a Connectable Object with ATL

This lab will give you the chance to build a connectable object using the ATL framework and the numerous CASE tools that are used in the process. For a change of pace, this lab will have nothing whatsoever to do with shapes or automobiles. As well, this lab will illustrate one possible technique for creating a C++ client sink using ATL.

The solution for this lab can be found on your CD-ROM under:
Labs\Chapter 12\ATLEvents
Labs\Chapter 12\ATLEvents\VB Client
Labs\Chapter 12\ATLEvents\CPPEventClient

Step One: Create the Initial Coclass

In this lab, you will be creating a small life simulation, modeling the growth of a person from childhood to old age. Begin by inserting a Simple Object into a new ATL EXE server named **CoChild**. Be sure you select **Support Connection Points** from the Attributes tab and a dual interface named **IChild**. In the default interface, add two properties and a single method, as so:

```
// AskChildQuestion() will be our cue to fire out a custom event.
interface IChild : IDispatch
{
    [propget, id(1)] HRESULT Name([out, retval] BSTR *pVal);
    [propput, id(1)] HRESULT Name([in] BSTR newVal);
```

```
[propget, id(2)] HRESULT Age([out, retval] short *pVal);
[propput, id(2)] HRESULT Age([in] short newVal);
[id(3)] HRESULT AskChildQuestion();
};
```

By way of a friendly reminder, if you configure your [default] interface as a custom vTable interface, be sure to add the [oleautomation] attribute to the IDL description. If you do not, the IChild interface cannot be marshaled between process boundaries. Recall that the [oleautomation] attribute forces registration of your interfaces and sets the ProxyStub-Clsid32 subkey to point to the universal marshaler.

Next, implement the **Age** and **Name** property for your CoChild class (we will get to AskChildQuestion() in just a bit).

Step Two: Add a Custom Event

Because you have specified support for connection points, the ATL Object Wizard has included a [default, source] interface in your IDL file. We will be adding a single event named **ChildSays()**, which will fire out a single BSTR parameter:

```
// Note that we specify the parameter as [in]!
dispinterface _IChildEvents
{
    properties:
    methods:
    [id(1), helpstring("method ChildSays")]
    HRESULT ChildSays([in] BSTR msg);
};
```

Before you run the Implement Connection Point Wizard, be sure you recompile your IDL file in order to refresh your type information. From the wizard, select your outbound interface. This tool will generate a connection point proxy class named CProxy_IChildEvents. If you examine this class, you will see Fire_ChildSays() will walk the list of currently connected clients, sending out the supplied BSTR to each.

If you examine your CoChild coclass, you will see your connection map has been updated (don't forget to check for the bug!), and the proxy class has been added to your inheritance chain. All we need to do now is fire our custom event.

Step Three: Fire the Custom Event

We will fire our custom event whenever a client calls the AskChildQuestion() method (as you may know, children always have something to say). Add a private CComBSTR to your coclass to represent the message and a helper function that will generate a random message based on the current age of the child. GetAMessage() will test the age member variable and send out a baby, toddler, teenager, or adult message:

```
// This helper function will grab a message based on the age of the child.
void CCoChild::GetAMessage()
{
    // Here are the possible messages.
    CComBSTR babyMsg[3] = {L"MommaDatta",
        L"Why sky is blue?", L"Poppa is yucks"};
    CComBSTR youngMsg[3] = {L"I love my parents",
        L"Can I have some candy please?", L"Read me a bedtime story"};
```

```
CComBSTR teenMsg[3] = {L"You don't know what it is like to be ME!",
        L"I want an eyebrow ring", L"My world is falling APART"};
CComBSTR adultMsg[3] = {L"I love COM",
        L"I want more COM", L"Life is COM. I love VARIANTS."};
// Must include <time.h> for these methods.
srand( (unsigned)clock() );
int item = rand() % 3;
// How old is the child?
if (m_Age >= 1 && m_Age <= 3)
        m_bstrMessage = babyMsg[item];
else if (m_Age >= 4 && m_Age <= 12)
        m_bstrMessage = youngMsg[item];
else if (m_Age >= 13 && m_Age <= 21)
        m_bstrMessage = teenMsg[item];
else if (m_Age >= 22)
        m_bstrMessage = adultMsg[item];
}
```

Now, we can fire our custom message to any interested client:

```
// When a client calls AskChildQuestion(), fill m_bstrMessage and fire our
// custom event.
STDMETHODIMP CCoChild::AskChildQuestion()
{
        // Go get a new message.
        GetAMessage();
        // Fire the message.
        Fire_ChildSays(m_bstrMessage);
        return S_OK;
}
```

Compile your server, and move onto the VB test client.

Step Four: A VB Test Client

Construct a VB EXE client that will allow the user to create a CoChild object, and set the Name and Age of this kid. Recall that the age of this child will be used to determine which array of BSTRs (baby, toddler, teenager, or adult) will be used to obtain a random message. Declare the CoChild in your [General][Declarations] section using the **WithEvents** keyword.

```
' Recall we cannot use the New keyword at the same time we create an object
' WithEvents.
'
Dim WithEvents kid As CoChild
```

Next, add a single VB Timer object to your form (note the stopwatch icon in Figure 12-10). Select this object, and using the VB Properties Window, configure your timer to have an interval of 500. Figure 12-10 shows the GUI under construction (assume the Make Kid button sets the CoChild to a new instance):

Figure 12-10:
Set your timer
object to an
interval of 500.

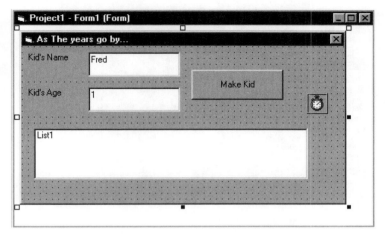

In the Timer event of your Timer object (which will now be called every ½ second), ask your child a question, and advance the Age property by 1, to ensure your child comes of age:

```
' The VB Timer object will call this function automatically. How often
' depends on the value of the Interval property.
'
Private Sub Timer1_Timer()
        ' Ask kid a question.
        kid.AskChildQuestion
        ' Raise the kid's age.
        kid.Age = kid.Age + 1
        txtAge = kid.Age
End Sub
```

Finally, in your CoChild event hander, take the incoming message and place it into the ListBox object:

```
' When the timer object asks your child a question, it will fire off the answer
' to this event sink.
'
Private Sub kid_ChildSays(ByVal msg As String)
        Dim s As String
        s = kid.Name & " is " & kid.Age & " and says: " & msg

        ' Add new string to top of list box.
        List1.AddItem s, 0
End Sub
```

Go ahead and run your project, and watch your child grow up:

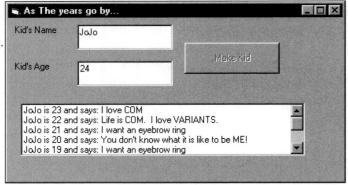

Figure 12-11:
The VB sink is
alive and kicking.

Next up, let's see how to achieve the same effect using C++.

Step Five: A C++/ATL Client

Setting up a VB sink is very simple. If we were to create a connection to the CoChild's [default, source] interface in raw C++, we would have quite a task ahead of us. Thankfully, ATL does provide a number of helper items (templates, sink maps, and global functions) to get a C++ event client up and running. Begin by creating a brand new Win32 Console Application (a Simple Project) named **CPPEventClient**.

First of all, our C++ client will need to make use of some ATL-specific code, and we must explicitly include <atlbase.h> and <atlcom.h>. Furthermore, as <atlcom.h> is looking for an instance of CComModule named _Module, we need to create a dummy object. Edit your existing cppeventclient.cpp file as so:

```
// We need to "fool" ATL into thinking we are creating a COM server.
//
#include <iostream.h>        // For cout.
#include "atlevents.h"       // MIDL-generated file.
#include "atlevents_i.c"     // MIDL-generated file.
#include <windows.h>
#include <atlbase.h>
CComModule _Module;
#include <atlcom.h>
int main(int argc, char* argv[])
{
     CoInitialize(NULL);
     CoUninitialize();
     return 0;
}
```

This will configure your C++ client to make use of the ATL event helpers.

As you recall, a client that wishes to be informed of events sent from a coclass needs to create a "sink" object which implements the [source] interface in question. CoChild defined the following dispinterface:

```
// The [default, source] interface.
dispinterface _IChildEvents
{
     properties:
```

```
methods:
[id(1), helpstring("method ChildSays")]
HRESULT ChildSays([in] BSTR msg);
};
```

Again, if we were to implement this interface in straight C++, we would need to contend with the implementation of the four methods of IDispatch (which is no fun at all). ATL provides a handy template that is used to implement the IDispatch interface for event sinks, named IDispEventSimpleImpl<>. Define the following class right before your main() loop (everything is inlined, so we don't need a separate header and *.cpp file for this sink class):

```
// Info for the events handler.
_ATL_FUNC_INFO OnLookAtKidInfo = {CC_STDCALL, VT_EMPTY, 1, {VT_BSTR}};
// The class implementing the sink.
class CKidSink : public IDispEventSimpleImpl<1, CKidSink, &DIID__IChildEvents>
{
public:
    CKidSink(IChild* pKid)
    {
        m_pKid = pKid;
        m_pKid->AddRef();
        // Attach to [default, source]
        DispEventAdvise((IUnknown*)m_pKid);
    }
    virtual ~CKidSink()
    {
        // Detach from source.
        m_pKid->Release();
        DispEventUnadvise((IUnknown*)m_pKid);
    }
    // Call this method when the kid talks.
    void __stdcall OnLookAtKid(BSTR msg)
    {
        USES_CONVERSION;
        cout << "Kid says: " << W2A(msg) << endl;
        SysFreeString(msg);
    }
    // IDispEventSimpleImpl<> needs a sink map.
    BEGIN_SINK_MAP(CKidSink)
        SINK_ENTRY_INFO(1, DIID__IChildEvents, 1, OnLookAtKid, &OnLookAtKidInfo)
    END_SINK_MAP()
private:
    IChild* m_pKid;
};
```

First off, we have created a sink object (CKidSink) deriving from IDispEventSimpleImpl<>. The first parameter is a simple numeric ID for the source object, and parameter two is the name of this sink class. The final parameter is the IID of the dispinterface defining the events.

In order for the IDispEventSimpleImpl<> template to do its magic, we need to provide an ATL sink map (using the BEGIN_SINK_MAP and END_SINK_MAP macros). This sink map is populated with the SINK_ENTRY_INFO macro (among others), which takes the following arguments:

```
// Arguments for the sink map.
BEGIN_SINK_MAP(CKidSink)
```

```
SINK_ENTRY_INFO(
        1,                      // ID of source.
        DIID__IChildEvents,     // IID of dispinterface.
        1,                      // DISPID in dispinterface.
        OnLookAtKid,            // Method to call for this event.
        &OnLookAtKidInfo)       // Info (parameters) from the event.
END_SINK_MAP()
```

The final parameter passed into the SINK_ENTRY_INFO macro is an _ATL_FUNC_INFO
structure, which specifies the parameters and return value for the given method of the
[source] interface. As AskChildQuestion() will send us a BSTR, we must specify the
_ATL_FUNC_INFO as so:

```
// Info for the events handler.
_ATL_FUNC_INFO OnLookAtKidInfo =
            {CC_STDCALL, VT_EMPTY, 1, {VT_BSTR}};
```

Notice that the sink object maintains a private IChild* member variable. The main() loop
will need to send us the IChild interface so we can call the ATL helper functions
DispEventAdvise() and DispEventUnadvise(). We do so in the overloaded constructor and
destructor of the sink:

```
// The sink object needs to Advise and Unadvise to the source:
CKidSink(IChild* pKid)
{
    m_pKid = pKid;
    m_pKid->AddRef();
    // Attach to [default, source]
    DispEventAdvise((IUnknown*)m_pKid);
}
virtual ~CKidSink()
{
    // Detach from source.
    m_pKid->Release();
    DispEventUnadvise((IUnknown*)m_pKid);
}
```

Finally, we need to implement the event handler itself. We will take the BSTR sent by
CoChild and pump it to the IO stream:

```
// Call this method when the kid talks.
void __stdcall OnLookAtKid(BSTR msg)
{
    USES_CONVERSION;
    cout << "Kid says: " << W2A(msg) << endl;
    SysFreeString(msg);
}
```

This completes the sink. The last step is to configure main to create the CoChild and set
up the sink object:

```
// Now we can get down to biz.
int main(int argc, char* argv[])
{
    CoInitialize(NULL);
    // Make the kid.
    IChild* pChild = NULL;
    CoCreateInstance(CLSID_CoChild, NULL, CLSCTX_SERVER, IID_IChild, (void**)&pChild);
```

```
// Make the sink.
CKidSink* kSink = new CKidSink(pChild);
// Play a game of 25 questions.
short age = 0;
for(int i = 0; i < 25; i++)
{
    pChild->get_Age(&age);
    cout << "Age is: " << age << " ";
    pChild->AskChildQuestion();
    // Watch the child grow.
    pChild->put_Age(age + 1);
    // Wait just a bit to allow a new random message to be generated.
    Sleep(500);
}
// Clean up.
delete kSink;
if(pChild)
    pChild->Release();
CoUninitialize();
return 0;
}
```

I would bet that this code is old hat by now. The only new logic to comment on is the creation of the sink object. When you run this new client you will see the following (possible) output:

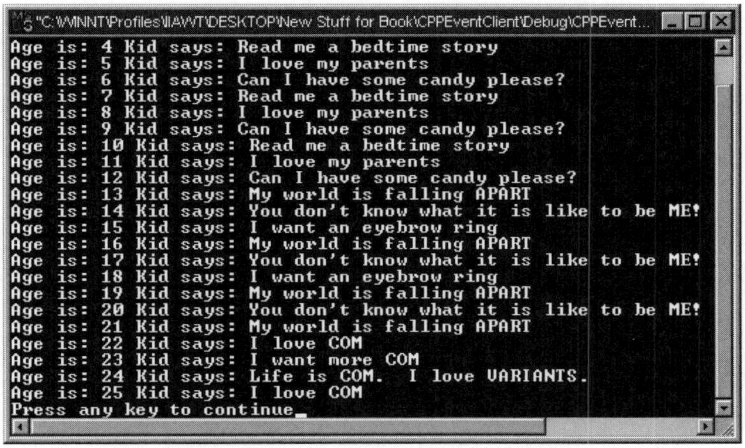

Figure 12-12:
The C++ sink
at work.

```
Age is: 4 Kid says: Read me a bedtime story
Age is: 5 Kid says: I love my parents
Age is: 6 Kid says: Can I have some candy please?
Age is: 7 Kid says: Read me a bedtime story
Age is: 8 Kid says: I love my parents
Age is: 9 Kid says: Can I have some candy please?
Age is: 10 Kid says: Read me a bedtime story
Age is: 11 Kid says: I love my parents
Age is: 12 Kid says: Can I have some candy please?
Age is: 13 Kid says: My world is falling APART
Age is: 14 Kid says: You don't know what it is like to be ME!
Age is: 15 Kid says: I want an eyebrow ring
Age is: 16 Kid says: My world is falling APART
Age is: 17 Kid says: You don't know what it is like to be ME!
Age is: 18 Kid says: I want an eyebrow ring
Age is: 19 Kid says: My world is falling APART
Age is: 20 Kid says: You don't know what it is like to be ME!
Age is: 21 Kid says: My world is falling APART
Age is: 22 Kid says: I love COM
Age is: 23 Kid says: I want more COM
Age is: 24 Kid says: Life is COM.  I love VARIANTS.
Age is: 25 Kid says: I love COM
Press any key to continue_
```

That wraps up our examination of how to configure two objects to talk with each other. The callback mechanism does entail fewer overheads (and less complexity) than the standard COM connection point protocol; however, custom callback interfaces are unusable among late bound clients (such as Internet Explorer). While a good deal of work needs to be done when building a connectable object by hand (raw C++), ATL makes it as simple as accessing the correct CASE tool. As we have also seen, ATL does provide some help establishing the client-side sink.

Chapter Summary

COM objects like to mingle with each other. Many times, a client will make requests of a coclass and require no further interaction. However, when you wish to allow your coclass to "talk back" to the client you have two basic approaches. First off, you can create a custom callback interface which is defined by the coclass and implemented by the client. Through the use of custom methods, a client may set up an advisory connection to the object, passing in a reference to the client-side sink. The only downfall to this strategy is that callback interfaces do not allow for a common standard.

COM provides a standard for bidirectional communications named connectable objects. Using IConnectionPointContainer, a client may discover the types of connection points held in the container. IConnectionPoint allows the client to Advise() and Unadvise() for a given connection. Building a connectable object by hand can be quite a chore, given that the object must maintain a list of each client currently connected to each connection point.

Luckily, ATL provides the Implement Connection Point Wizard, which automatically builds a connection point proxy based off your IDL code. The generated connectable object leverages code from IConnectionPointImpl< >, which maintains the list of connected clients and assigns numerical cookies to each.

Part 5

Windowing

Chapter 13

Using ATL as a Windowing framework

Objectives:

- Review the atoms of a Win32 Windows application.
- Understand the core set of ATL templates used to build a Windows application.
- Respond to system messages using the ATL message map.
- Build dialog boxes à la ATL to capture user input.
- Create an ATL main window manipulated by COM interfaces.

What would a developer's life be without the need to build a graphical user interface (GUI) once in a while? Most C++ developers who are in the business of building user interfaces tend to do so with the help of application frameworks such as MFC. Others opt for the RAD environment offered by Visual Basic. Yet another option is to use ATL as a windowing toolkit, which is the subject of this chapter.

Developing Windows applications with ATL places you somewhere in between the complexity of raw Win32 API programming and the safe and comfortable world of MFC (and very far removed from VB). We will begin this chapter with a quick review of the core parts of every Windows window: WinMain(), the WNDCLASSEX structure, and the almighty WndProc. We will then see how ATL can be used to wrap up much of this logic using a small handful of templates and a corresponding MSG_MAP.

And Now for Something Completely Different: ATL as a Windowing Toolkit

The Active Template Library is the preferred C++ framework for building COM components. Using integrated CASE tools, numerous maps, classes, and templates, a developer is able to live a relatively sane COM existence. Given that COM is the architecture behind all ActiveX-based technologies, it is no surprise that ATL shines as a framework for building ActiveX controls. These COM objects are unique in that they tend to move beyond the non-GUI business objects we have been examining thus far and provide an interactive user interface. Many ActiveX controls also provide a set of "property pages" that allow the consumers of these controls to configure the state of the object during design time. Because each of these COM technologies requires a user interface, it stands to reason that ATL provides some help constructing GUIs.

As a Win32 programmer, you have probably needed to develop a user interface at some time in your career. If you are a C++ snob, you may scoff at the idea of using Visual Basic as a tool for building your GUIs, and may opt to use the Microsoft Foundation Classes (MFC). Beyond providing a number of CASE tools (MFC AppWizard, ClassWizard, and so on) to help get the guts of a Windows application up and running, MFC provides a healthy dose of classes, which encapsulates you from the boilerplate details behind each and every window (e.g., WinMain(), the WndProc, and WNDCLASSEX, just to name a few such details).

Given that we already have the MFC framework to build full Win32 applications, why would ATL also provide help in this area? Again, the answer lies in the fact that not all COM objects are invisible logic crunchers. ATL's support for ActiveX controls and their associated property pages is provided in part by a set of window-based templates, as well as another ATL map to help process Windows messages. However, beyond using these windowing templates to create GUI-based COM objects, you are also able to build full-scale Win32 stand-alone EXEs using ATL.

As you will see, ATL provides a "just thick enough" wrapper around the Windows API. When you use ATL as a framework for building Win32 applications, you are <u>not</u> given as much support as you would find in MFC. For example, ATL does not provide support for the MFC ClassWizard utility, offers no support for Dialog Data Exchange and Validation (DDX/DDV) routines, and does not provide a document/view/frame/application paradigm. In general, when you are using ATL to build traditional Windows applications, you are back to working with raw Win32 primitives to get the job done (this is your cue to pull out that copy of Petzold's *Programming Windows* you thought you were finished with).

So then, in this chapter we will come to understand the set of ATL templates, structures, and CASE tools used to build main windows and dialog boxes. Once you have worked through this material you will be in a perfect position to build ActiveX controls using ATL (the subject of the next chapter), given that a full-featured control makes use of many of the following ATL windowing techniques.

The Atoms of a Windows Window

Developers who spend time building C++ Win32 applications are most likely to make use of a Windows framework, such as MFC. This is a smart choice, as a solid application framework can help bootstrap your efforts with numerous CASE tools, utility classes, and whatnot. That's the good news. The bad news is that a framework such as MFC can encapsulate the underlying details to such a degree that you might have little idea what is happening under the hood. So then, before we see what ATL will do to hide numerous details of a raw Win32 application, let's remember our roots and assemble a main window by hand. This is by <u>no means</u> a comprehensive review of Win32 development, but is intended to dust off any current cobwebs. If you wish to follow along, fire up Visual Studio and select a new Win32 Application (an empty project) named Win32Window.

You will find the Win32Window application on your companion CD under the Labs\Chapter 13\Win32Window subdirectory.

Every Win32 EXE has at minimum three major players: a WNDCLASSEX structure used to describe the characteristics of the window, WinMain() which serves as the application's entry point, and an associated windows procedure (a.k.a. WndProc) used to process incoming messages for a given window. Beyond driving the logic behind the application itself, the most significant task of WinMain() is to establish your application's message pump.

Constructing a Windows Message Pump

A message pump is responsible for grabbing incoming system (as well as user-defined) messages sent to a registered window and routing them to the corresponding WndProc function for processing. To begin coding our Win32 window, insert a new file (mainWnd.cpp) into your project and define a message loop as so:

```
// Our initial crack at WinMain() creates a message pump for this window.
#include <windows.h>                        // The keeper of all things Windows.
int WINAPI WinMain(HINSTANCE hInst, HINSTANCE hPrevInst,
                   PSTR szCommand, int iShow)
{
     // Create the windows message pump.
     MSG msg;
     while(GetMessage(&msg, NULL, 0, 0))
     {
          TranslateMessage(&msg);      // Process message...
          DispatchMessage(&msg);       // Send to WinProc...
     }
     return msg.wParam;
}
```

The GetMessage() API call is used to fill a MSG structure with information pertaining to the current message in the queue. TranslateMessage() and DispatchMessage() format and forward the current message to the registered WinProc for processing. Note that the GetMessage() call is under control of a while loop, which will fail only when a WM_QUIT message is plucked from the messages queue, at which time the window will be shut down. As we will see, WM_QUIT is posted using PostQuitMessage().

Building the WNDCLASSEX Structure

Now that we have a message pump on the lookout for incoming messages, we need to tell the operating system a bit about the window itself. Under Win32, a window is described within the context of a WNDCLASSEX structure. This structure contains fields that describe such things as the icons, cursor, and menu to use in conjunction with this window. More importantly, the WNDCLASSEX structure establishes the name of the WndProc function that will be receiving the messages sent from the message pump. Here is a peek at WNDCLASSEX, as defined in <winuser.h>:

```
// This Win32 structure is used to describe numerous aspects of the window you are
// busy constructing.
typedef struct tagWNDCLASSEX{
     UINT      cbSize;              // How big is this structure?
     UINT      style;              // Any number of CS_ flags.
```

```
WNDPROC     lpfnWndProc;        // Function to route messages to.
int         cbClsExtra;         // Any extra bytes to pack after this struct.
int         cbWndExtra;         // Any extra bytes to pack after the instance.
HINSTANCE   hInstance;          // Who owns this WNDCLASSEX?
HICON       hIcon;              // Large icon to use for this window.
HCURSOR     hCursor;            // Mouse cursor to use for this window.
HBRUSH      hbrBackground;      // Color of client area for this window.
LPCWSTR     lpszMenuName;       // Any menu to attach to this window?
LPCWSTR     lpszClassName;      // A string name for this type of window.
HICON       hIconSm;            // Small icon to use this window.
} WNDCLASSEX;
```

Every single Win32 window will need to fill this structure and register it with the system via the Win32 RegisterClassEx() function. As you can imagine, each field of the WNDCLASSEX structure can consist of a number of flags (or combination of flags), all of which are documented within online help.

To keep things simple, assume the window under construction does not have a menu, and will make use of system-defined large and small icon bitmaps. Furthermore, we will use a solid white background used to paint the window's client area and a standard system arrow icon as our mouse cursor. To set these options, we will need to make use of some further Win32 API calls such as LoadIcon() and LoadCursor(). Finally, we will assign the class name of this window to MyWin32Window. Here is our updated WinMain() implementation:

```
// Here we fill a WNDCLASSEX structure to define our window.
int WINAPI WinMain(HINSTANCE hInst, HINSTANCE hPrevInst,
                PSTR szCommand, int iShow)
{
    // We need to create a WNDCLASSEX structure to describe this window.
    WNDCLASSEX myWindow;
    myWindow.cbClsExtra = 0;
    myWindow.cbSize = sizeof(myWindow);
    myWindow.cbWndExtra = 0;
    myWindow.hbrBackground = (HBRUSH)GetStockObject(WHITE_BRUSH);
    myWindow.hCursor = LoadCursor(NULL, IDC_ARROW);
    myWindow.hIcon = LoadIcon(NULL, IDI_APPLICATION);
    myWindow.hIconSm = LoadIcon(NULL, IDI_APPLICATION);
    myWindow.hInstance = hInst;
    myWindow.lpfnWndProc = MyWindowProc;            // We'll get to this...
    myWindow.lpszClassName = "MyWin32Window";
    myWindow.lpszMenuName = NULL;
    myWindow.style = CS_HREDRAW | CS_VREDRAW;
    // Register the class.
    RegisterClassEx(&myWindow);
    MSG msg;
    while(GetMessage(&msg, NULL, 0, 0))
    {
        TranslateMessage(&msg);
        DispatchMessage(&msg);
    }
    return msg.wParam;
}
```

Showing the Window

Notice that once we have filled a WNDCLASSEX structure with all the relevant information (and registered this window using RegisterClassEx()) all we need to do to finish up WinMain() is to literally create and show the window. This is done with three additional API calls.

First, CreateWindow() is used to load our window into memory and establish the rectangular dimensions of the window. Take note that CreateWindow() returns an almighty HWND variable, which we must store for use throughout our program. The HWND data type is a handle to the window we have just registered with the system, and is the first parameter to numerous other Win32 API functions.

Once the window is created in memory, we follow up with a call to ShowWindow() (which tells the window how to display itself) and UpdateWindow() (which forces a WM_PAINT message into the message queue). As you can see below, some of the parameters of CreateWindow() are the same parameters received by WinMain() itself. This final bit of logic can be sandwiched right between the class registration and message loop logic:

```
// Create and show the window.
HWND hwnd;
hwnd = CreateWindow("MyWin32Window",          // Class name (again).
                    "My Raw Window",           // Caption of this window.
                    WS_OVERLAPPEDWINDOW,       // Style flags.
                    10, 10, 200, 200,          // Size of window.
                    NULL,                      // Parent handle.
                    NULL,                      // Menu handle.
                    hInst,                     // First parameter of WinMain()
                    NULL);                     // Any additional creation parameters.
ShowWindow(hwnd, iShow);                       // Our HWND and the 3rd parameter of WinMain()
UpdateWindow(hwnd);
```

Processing the Messages: Building a Windows Procedure

WinMain() is now complete, and as you can see we are again knee-deep with standard boilerplate code. Before we see how ATL provides a complete implementation of this logic on our behalf, we need to investigate the next major player in a Windows EXE, the WndProc function. When you establish your WNDCLASSEX structure for a given window, the lpfnWndProc ("long-pointer-to-a-function") field must be set to the name of the function that is ready to process the events being spit out from the message pump. For the current window under construction, we specified lpfnWndProc as:

```
// Call this function when you have a message for me...
myWindow.lpfnWndProc = MyWindowProc;
```

So, somewhere in our program we need to have a function indeed called MyWindowProc. The name of a window's WndProc function can be anything within the syntactical constraints of C++ (WndProc, MyRadWndProc, XXXX, or what have you). The parameters and return type, however, must always be the same. Here is the prototype of our window's procedure function:

```
// The callback function must have this signature, but may take any valid name.
LRESULT CALLBACK MyWindowProc(HWND, UINT, WPARAM, LPARAM);
```

Again, this function will be called whenever your window has been sent a message from the system (all those "WM_" messages) as well as any user-defined messages, notification messages, and so forth. As a Win32 developer, it is up to you to decide which of the hundreds of messages you care to process. For example, if you want to paint some text into the client area, your WndProc function needs to respond to WM_PAINT. If you want to do some special processing when the left mouse button has been clicked in your client area, you need to contend with WM_LBUTTONDOWN. The entire set of system-defined messages can be discovered within <windows.h> and friends. Learning about all the messages you can respond to is largely a matter of time spent as a Windows developer.

Note: MFC developers intercept messages indirectly by using the ClassWizard CASE tool. Even though this tool is unavailable in ATL development, we do have a slimmed-down variation which we can make use of (as we will see in a bit).

So then, if your particular WndProc function responds to a tiny set of possible Windows messages, what about all the others which you may well receive that you do not care about? Luckily, the DefWindowProc() API function can be used as your back door. If your WndProc responds to WM_PAINT, WM_CREATE, and WM_DESTROY messages (and nothing else), the remaining messages will be sent into the default windows procedure for processing. We can now finish up our Win32 EXE project by providing the following implementation of MyWindowProc():

```
// Pick out the messages you want to respond to, and send all others
// to the default windows procedure.
LRESULT CALLBACK MyWindowProc(HWND hwnd, UINT msg,
                              WPARAM wParam, LPARAM lParam)
{
    // Variables for painting.
    HDC hDC;
    PAINTSTRUCT ps;
    RECT clientRect;
    // Which message have we been given?
    switch(msg)
    {
    // We are coming to life.
    case WM_CREATE:
        MessageBox(NULL, "Your window is about to be created",
        "Message from WM_CREATE", MB_OK | MB_SETFOREGROUND);
    return 0;
    // We need to be rendered.
    case WM_PAINT:
        hDC = BeginPaint(hwnd, &ps);
        GetClientRect(hwnd, &clientRect);
        DrawText(hDC, "The Raw Win32 Window", -1,
                &clientRect,
                DT_CENTER | DT_VCENTER | DT_SINGLELINE);
        EndPaint(hwnd, &ps);
    return 0;
    // We are going down, must place a WM_QUIT into the queue
    // to terminate the message pump.
    case WM_DESTROY:
        PostQuitMessage(0);
    return 0;
```

```
}
// Let system handle everything else.
return DefWindowProc(hwnd, msg, wParam, lParam);
}
```

With this final piece of the puzzle in place, we can now compile our program and run the application. You will see a message box pop up in response to WM_CREATE, just before the main window comes to life, as seen in Figure 13-1:

Although the above code is by no means mind numbing, Win32 programming (not unlike COM) requires a good deal of boilerplate code. If you are an MFC veteran, you may have never been exposed to the details of WinMain() and related items (which may or may not be a good thing). As you already know the evils of linking into the MFC libraries from within an ATL project, we will spend the rest of this chapter learning about some of the support ATL provides for building stand-alone Windows applications.

Figure 13-1: A simple Win32 window.

The ATL Windowing Framework

ATL does provide a handful of templates and utility classes which can ease your Win32 EXE development burden. Many of these templates are not intended for direct use in your application, but exist simply to provide base class functionality to other templates. The core ATL windowing templates are shown below in Figure 13-2, all of which are defined in <atlwin.h>.

Figure 13-2: The ATL windowing hierarchy.

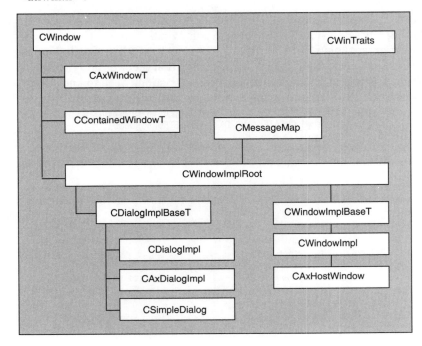

> **Note:** If you do not explicitly include <atlwin.h> into your ATL projects, you will not bring in the definitions of the templates seen in Figure 13-2.

Typically, you only need to be concerned with a small set of the ATL windowing classes, specifically CWindow, CWinTraits<>, CDialogImpl<>, CSimpleDialog<> and CWindowImpl<>. Using this subset, you are given just enough support to build both stand-alone EXEs and interactive dialog boxes.

As you can see, many of the ATL windowing templates have an "-Ax-" infix (for example, CAxHostWindow). Beyond providing the guts of a basic window, these "-Ax-" classes provide additional support for responding to ActiveX control events as well as code to host and site the control within the client area of the window.

ATL also provides the CMessageMap class. This class provides a helper function, which allows for a table-driven WndProc for use by the main window. As you may suspect, ATL has another map (the MSG_MAP) that is used in conjunction with the functionality provided by the CMessageMap base class. Now, before you begin to think "code bloat," rest assured that the ATL MSG_MAP table is <u>extremely lightweight</u> in comparison to MFC's MESSAGE_MAP structure.

The various "-T<>" helper templates (e.g., CWindowImplBaseT<>) provide core functionality to many of the core ATL templates, and for the most part can be safely ignored. Finally, CWinTraits<> allows the ATL developer to store all window styles in a convenient C++ template. To begin learning our way around this new hierarchy, we begin at the top, with CWindow.

Understanding CWindow

CWindow defines an underlying HWND data type and numerous wrappers to Win32 API windowing functions. Recall from our previous Win32 example that each window is identified by a corresponding HWND, which is obtained by a call to CreateWindow(). Also recall that just about every Win32 API windowing function requires an HWND as the first parameter (which should make some sense, as these functions need to know what window they are manipulating!). CWindow maintains a public HWND data member: m_hWnd. This member variable begins life by being set to NULL in the constructor of CWindow (as seen in <atlwin.h>):

```
// CWindow wraps your HWND.
class CWindow
{
public:
    static RECT rcDefault;        // A default rectangle for the window's size.
    HWND m_hWnd;
    CWindow(HWND hWnd = NULL)
    {
        m_hWnd = hWnd;
    }
    // Tons of methods which wrap API calls and make use of m_hWnd.
...
};
```

The methods of CWindow are far too many to enumerate here and would prove to be redundant, as they are all listed within online help. The code behind these methods do not require much commentary, as they simply call the Win32 API function they are responsible for wrapping, using m_hWnd as the initial parameter.

To get a flavor of some of these member functions, here are a few well-known API calls wrapped by CWindow:

```
// A sampling of CWindow methods (all defined inline).
BOOL Invalidate(BOOL bErase = TRUE)
{
    ATLASSERT(::IsWindow(m_hWnd));
    return ::InvalidateRect(m_hWnd, NULL, bErase);
}
BOOL InvalidateRect(LPCRECT lpRect, BOOL bErase = TRUE)
{
    ATLASSERT(::IsWindow(m_hWnd));
    return ::InvalidateRect(m_hWnd, lpRect, bErase);
}
HDC BeginPaint(LPPAINTSTRUCT lpPaint)
{
    ATLASSERT(::IsWindow(m_hWnd));
    return ::BeginPaint(m_hWnd, lpPaint);
}
void EndPaint(LPPAINTSTRUCT lpPaint)
{
    ATLASSERT(::IsWindow(m_hWnd));
    ::EndPaint(m_hWnd, lpPaint);
}
```

I think you get the general idea. Now, as most of the remaining ATL windowing classes take CWindow as a template parameter, you are able to make use of CWindow's functionality as you build your windows and dialog boxes with ATL. In addition to wrapping dozens of global Win32 API calls, CWindow does provide an interesting HWND operator which can prove to be quite helpful:

```
// CWindow provides an HWND operator.
operator HWND() const { return m_hWnd; }
```

While this looks rather bland, the net result is that you can use a valid CWindow object in place of any Win32 function that requires an HWND parameter. The final point of interest is the Create() method. This method takes a number of parameters (most of which are optional) to indirectly call CreateWindowEx() on your behalf. If this call is successful, the underlying m_hWnd is then set to the newly created window:

```
// CWindow::Create() wraps the creation of your window.
HWND Create(LPCTSTR lpstrWndClass, HWND hWndParent,
        LPRECT lpRect = NULL, LPCTSTR szWindowName = NULL,
        DWORD dwStyle = 0, DWORD dwExStyle = 0,
        HMENU hMenu = NULL, LPVOID lpCreateParam = NULL)
{
    if(lpRect == NULL)
    lpRect = &rcDefault;
    m_hWnd = ::CreateWindowEx(dwExStyle, lpstrWndClass, szWindowName,
                dwStyle, lpRect->left, lpRect->top, lpRect->right - lpRect->left,
                lpRect->bottom - lpRect->top, hWndParent, hMenu,
```

```
                           _Module.GetModuleInstance(), lpCreateParam);
        return m_hWnd;
}
```

> **Note:** In addition to wrapping the Win32 API, CWindow also contains a set of
> helper methods for common windowing tasks (e.g., CenterWindow()). See
> online help for complete details.

Typically you will not need to directly create a CWindow object. In reality, this class is not extremely useful on its own, but is very useful as a parameter to the remaining ATL windowing templates.

Building a Better Window with ATL

To illustrate the usefulness of ATL's windowing library, let's re-create the previous raw Win32 window example in ATL. After we get this window up and running, we will take a deeper look inside the provided functionality. Keep in mind that whenever you are using any of the ATL windowing templates you must explicitly make a preprocessor include to <atlwin.h>. The best place to do so is within your precompiled header file:

```
// <stdafx.h> must include <atlwin.h>
extern CExeModule _Module;
#include <atlwin.h>
#include <atlcom.h>
```

Creating a main window in ATL begins by deriving a custom C++ class from CWindowImpl<>, which takes three template parameters. The first parameter is the name of the class itself, which we will call CMainWindow. CWindow is the default second parameter, which gives CWindowImpl<> most of its functionality. The final default parameter is a CWinTraits<> template, which we will get to in just a moment. Bottom line, here is how we can begin to create a new C++ class which leverages the ATL framework:

```
// To create an ATL window, begin by deriving from CWindowImpl<>.
class CMainWindow : public CWindowImpl<CMainWindow, CWindow,
        CWinTraits<WS_CAPTION | WS_POPUPWINDOW | WS_VISIBLE, 0 > >
{
public:
        CMainWindow();
        virtual ~CMainWindow();
};
```

Using CWinTraits<>

CWindowImpl<> takes a CWinTraits<> template as its final parameter. This handy ATL utility class wraps up all the window styles (e.g., WS_xxx) and extended window styles (e.g., WS_EX_xxx) in a nice clean package. CWinTraits<> takes two parameters: an OR-ing together of basic styles and an OR-ing together of extended styles. Because many window types (such as CMainWindow) have a similar set of styles, ATL does provide a set of typedefs to help streamline this final parameter passed into CWindowImpl<>:

```
// ATL predefines four CWinTraits<> typedefs.
typedef CWinTraits<WS_CHILD | WS_VISIBLE | WS_CLIPCHILDREN | WS_CLIPSIBLINGS, 0>
        CControlWinTraits;
```

```
typedef CWinTraits<WS_OVERLAPPEDWINDOW | WS_CLIPCHILDREN |
WS_CLIPSIBLINGS, WS_EX_APPWINDOW | WS_EX_WINDOWEDGE>
    CFrameWinTraits;
typedef CWinTraits<WS_OVERLAPPEDWINDOW | WS_CHILD | WS_VISIBLE | WS_CLIPCHILDREN |
WS_CLIPSIBLINGS, WS_EX_MDICHILD>
    CMDIChildWinTraits;
typedef CWinTraits<0, 0>
    CNullTraits;
```

Note: A related class, CWinTraitsOR<>, allows you to leverage these existing ATL typedefs by OR-ing in additional custom traits. Again, see online help for more details.

If we make use of CFrameWinTraits, our definition of CMainWindow cleans up quite a bit:

```
// Slim things down with a CWinTraits<> typedef.
class CMainWindow : public CWindowImpl<CMainWindow, CWindow,
                                       CFrameWinTraits>
{
public:
    ...
};
```

The final point of interest concerning CWinTraits<> is that this template defines two public member functions which allow you to extract a DWORD representing the current set of basic styles (GetWndStyle()) as well as the set of extended styles (GetWndExStyle()):

```
// You may fetch out the set of styles using CWinTraits<> helper functions.
template <DWORD t_dwStyle = 0, DWORD t_dwExStyle = 0>
class CWinTraits
{
public:
    static DWORD GetWndStyle(DWORD dwStyle)
    {
        return dwStyle == 0 ? t_dwStyle : dwStyle;
    }
    static DWORD GetWndExStyle(DWORD dwExStyle)
    {
        return dwExStyle == 0 ? t_dwExStyle : dwExStyle;
    }
};
```

Creating and Destroying the ATL Window

As for the implementation of the constructor of CMainWindow, we will keep things well encapsulated by making a call to CWindowImpl<>::Create(), specifying the size of this window (making use of the default static rectangle defined by CWindow) as well as a caption for the title bar:

```
// Create and destroy this window.
CMainWindow::CMainWindow()
{
    // Create my window.
    Create(NULL, CWindow::rcDefault, "My ATL Window");
```

```
        ShowWindow(SW_SHOWNORMAL);
}
```

The destructor can make a quick check to ensure the m_hWnd variable is valid (just to be safe) and call the DestroyWindow() method to clean things up:

```
// Destroy the underlying m_hWnd when our object is going down.
CMainWindow::~CMainWindow()
{
    if(m_hWnd)
        DestroyWindow();
}
```

Responding to Windows Messages in ATL

CWindowImpl<> has sheltered us from having to create and register this window by hand, but we are currently unable to receive any messages such as WM_PAINT, WM_DESTROY, or WM_CREATE. As CWindowImpl<> inherits some of its functionality from CMessageMap, we must ensure that our derived class has a valid "message map" defined within it. The ATL MSG_MAP provides a lightweight way to route a given Windows' message to a specific member function in your class. Unlike a traditional Win32 API program, we will not have to construct a WndProc function by hand and test the incoming message with a gigantic switch statement. Rather, we will populate our MSG_MAP with a number of macros to do the grunt work of responding for a given message. You can define an empty MSG_MAP as so:

```
// In order to create our CMainWindow, we must supply a message map.
class CMainWindow : public CWindowImpl<CMainWindow, CWindow,
    CWinTraits<WS_CAPTION | WS_POPUPWINDOW | WS_VISIBLE, 0 > > >
{
public:
    CMainWindow();
    virtual ~CMainWindow();
    // Enable a table driven WndProc.
    BEGIN_MSG_MAP(CMainWindow)
    END_MSG_MAP()
};
```

We will take a closer look at these macros and CMessageMap later. For the time being, just understand that this map provides the ATL equivalent of the raw WndProc we wrote by hand in the previous Win32 example.

The Add Windows Message Handler Wizard

Once you have defined an empty MSG_MAP in an ATL-based window you are now ready to populate the map using the Add Windows Message Handler CASE tool. To activate this tool, right-click on your MSG_MAP savvy class from ClassView. You will be presented with the following dialog box:

Figure 13-3:
The ATL Add
Windows
Message
Handler Wizard.

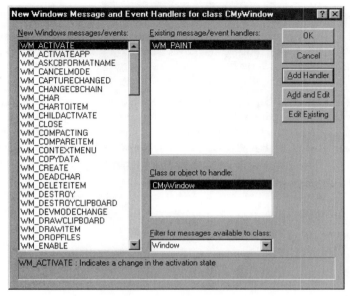

Like all CASE tools, this new ATL wizard simply saves you some typing. You are always free to edit your MSG_MAP by hand, and in some cases you may need to. In many ways, this tool can be seen as a no-frills version of MFC's ClassWizard utility (in fact, you may have bumped into this same tool when using the Visual C++ dialog editor).

The process of routing a message to an ATL window class is simple: Select the class to handle from the appropriate list box (in this case CMainWindow), then select the message(s) you wish to respond to by double-clicking on the message name (or select one and click Add Handler). For this example, go ahead and select WM_PAINT and close the tool.

If you examine the header file of your CMainFrame class, you will see your MSG_MAP has been updated with a new MESSAGE_HANDLER macro, as well as stub code for an inlined function named OnPaint. Following the lead of MFC, all standard windows message handlers are named by dropping the "WM_" prefix in place of "On-" followed by the name of the message in lowercase (for example: WM_PAINT == OnPaint, WM_CREATE == OnCreate, WM_DESTROY == OnDestroy, and so forth):

```
// The Add Windows Message Handler Wizard populates your MSG_MAP.
class CMainWindow : public CWindowImpl<CMainWindow, CWindow, CFrameWinTraits>
{
public:
    CMainWindow();
    virtual ~CMainWindow();
    // The WM_PAINT message will now be routed to OnPaint().
    BEGIN_MSG_MAP(CMainWindow)
        MESSAGE_HANDLER(WM_PAINT, OnPaint)
    END_MSG_MAP()
    LRESULT OnPaint(UINT uMsg, WPARAM wParam, LPARAM lParam, BOOL& bHandled)
    {
        return 0;
    }
};
```

> **Note:** Like all ATL CASE tools, there is no corresponding option to remove code entered with this tool. To do so by hand, delete the MESSAGE_HANDLER macro from your message map as well as the generated stub code.

We will see exactly what MESSAGE_HANDLER resolves to in a bit; however, its purpose should be clear. When a given message is routed to your window (e.g., WM_PAINT) the framework will call a given function (e.g., OnPaint()). The signature used for each function handled using the MESSAGE_HANDLER macro will always have the same signature as seen here. All that is left to do is write the code to execute in response to this message:

```
// Paint some centered text into the client area.
LRESULT OnPaint(UINT uMsg, WPARAM wParam, LPARAM lParam, BOOL& bHandled)
{
    // This example makes use of a number of Win32 API calls.
    // See online help (if necessary).
    PAINTSTRUCT ps;
    BeginPaint(&ps);
    HDC hDC = GetDC();
    RECT r;
    GetClientRect(&r);
    DrawText(hDC, "My ATL Window", -1, &r, DT_SINGLELINE |
            DT_VCENTER | DT_CENTER);
    EndPaint(&ps);
    ReleaseDC(hDC);
    return 0;
}
```

If we were now to create an instance of our CMainWindow class, we would see a full-fledged window come to life (Figure 13-4). The following code snippet will do nicely:

```
// Create the ATL window.
CMainWindow theWind;
```

The companion CD contains the SimpleATLWindow project which illustrates the development and use of CMainWindow.

Figure 13-4: An ATL-based window.

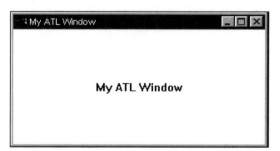

Our simple ATL window handles only a single message, which is not making use of any of the parameters sent into the message handler function (WPARAM, LPARAM, and so on). If you are a Win32 developer, you are aware that each Windows message uses the information contained in the WPARAM and LPARAM parameters in its own unique way. For example, if you are handling a WM_MOUSEMOVE message, you can "crack" out information contained in these parameters to discover relevant mouse-related details (the [x, y] coordinates of the cursor, the state of the keyboard, and so on) from the LPARAM parameter. ATL provides little help with the cracking of message-specific information, and you will need to fall back on your understanding of the Win32 API to fully work within the realm of ATL windows development. This topic is beyond the scope of this book, so find that copy of Petzold!

Understanding CWindowImpl<>

Now that we have created a main window with ATL, we can begin to dig into some of the nasty details. CWindowImpl<> wraps up the grunge of creating a WNDCLASSEX structure using the DECLARE_WND_CLASS macro. CWindowImpl<>'s Create() method then registers the resulting WNDCLASSEX. Here is the formal definition of CWindowImpl<>:

```
// CWindowImpl<> wraps up the details of creating and registering your window.
template <class T, class TBase = CWindow, class TWinTraits = CControlWinTraits>
class ATL_NO_VTABLE CWindowImpl : public CWindowImplBaseT< TBase, TWinTraits >
{
public:
    // Create a WNDCLASSEX structure.
    DECLARE_WND_CLASS(NULL)
    HWND Create(HWND hWndParent, RECT& rcPos,
            LPCTSTR szWindowName = NULL,
            DWORD dwStyle = 0, DWORD dwExStyle = 0,
            UINT nID = 0, LPVOID lpCreateParam = NULL)
    {
        // Register the WNDCLASSEX structure.
        ...
    }
};
```

Now truth be told, ATL takes a couple of twists and turns to define your window's WNDCLASSEX structure (imagine that, huh?). In reality, this Win32 structure is hidden away as a field in another structure: _ATL_WNDCLASSINFO. So, to follow the winding path, the DECLARE_WND_CLASS macro first expands to define a variable of type CWndClassInfo, which can be retrieved using the GetWndClassInfo() method, also inserted as a result of the DECLARE_WND_CLASS macro:

```
// ATL provides a window class structure indirectly using the CWndClassInfo
// helper structure. The fields of this structure are filled in the following...
#define DECLARE_WND_CLASS(WndClassName) \
static CWndClassInfo& GetWndClassInfo() \
{ \
    static CWndClassInfo wc = \
    { \
        { sizeof(WNDCLASSEX), CS_HREDRAW | CS_VREDRAW | \
        CS_DBLCLKS, StartWindowProc, \
        0, 0, NULL, NULL, NULL, (HBRUSH)(COLOR_WINDOW + 1), \
```

```
                NULL, WndClassName, NULL }, \
                NULL, NULL, IDC_ARROW, TRUE, 0, _T("") \
        }; \
        return wc; \
}
```

The definition of CWndClassInfo ends up defining _ATL_WNDCLASSINFO, where your WNDCLASSEX structure is hidden deep from view:

```
// The WNDCLASSEX we all know and love.
struct _ATL_WNDCLASSINFOA
{
        WNDCLASSEXA m_wc;        // Your window class structure.
        LPCSTR m_lpszOrigName;
        WNDPROC pWndProc;
        LPCSTR m_lpszCursorID;
        BOOL m_bSystemCursor;
        ATOM m_atom;
        CHAR m_szAutoName[13];
        ATOM Register(WNDPROC* p)
        {
                return AtlModuleRegisterWndClassInfoA(&_Module, this, p);
        }
};
```

> **Note:** Remember, the Windows API defines Unicode (W) and ANSI (A) versions for all windowing primitives. Based on preprocessor definitions, the correct version is obtained. Thus, _ATL_WNDCLASSINFO results in either _ATL_WNDCLASSINFOA or _ATL_WNDCLASSINFOW.

Modifying the Default WNDCLASSEX Settings

ATL does a fine job of creating and filling a WNDCLASSEX structure on your behalf; however, if you should ever wish to change the default settings, you can obtain a reference to the m_wc data member in your derived class using GetWndClassInfo(). From this member, you can tweak the WNDCLASSEX fields to your own liking. If we were to extend the constructor of CMainWindow with the following code, we would see a window much like Figure 13-5.

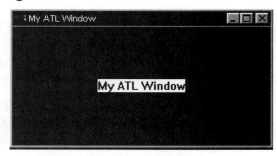

Figure 13-5: Tweaking WNDCLASSEX in ATL.

```
// Change the hbrBackground field of WNDCLASSEX to a black background.
CWndClassInfo &winInfo = GetWndClassInfo();
winInfo.m_wc.hbrBackground = (HBRUSH)GetStockObject(BLACK_BRUSH);
```

Uncovering ATL's WndProc Implementation

As we have seen, the DECLARE_WND_CLASS macro is used to populate the CWndClassInfo structure, which ultimately sets up the fields of WNDCLASSEX. If you looked carefully, you may have noticed an entry named StartWindowProc. If you did not look carefully, here is the DECLARE_WND_CLASS macro expansion one more time:

```
// ATL provides a window class structure indirectly using the CWndClassInfo
// helper class.
#define DECLARE_WND_CLASS(WndClassName) \
static CWndClassInfo& GetWndClassInfo() \
{ \
    static CWndClassInfo wc = \
    { \
        { sizeof(WNDCLASSEX), CS_HREDRAW | CS_VREDRAW | \
        CS_DBLCLKS, StartWindowProc, \
        0, 0, NULL, NULL, NULL, (HBRUSH)(COLOR_WINDOW + 1), \
        NULL, WndClassName, NULL }, \
        NULL, NULL, IDC_ARROW, TRUE, 0, _T("") \
    }; \
    return wc; \
}
```

This name is used to fill the lpfnWndProc field of the WNDCLASSEX structure. Given the requirements of a Win32 Windows application, you can assume that ATL has some method named StartWindowProc(). This method is defined in CWindowImplBaseT<>, the templatized base class to CWindowImpl<>:

```
// StartWindowProc() configures a WndProc for your ATL window.
template <class TBase, class TWinTraits>
LRESULT CALLBACK CWindowImplBaseT< TBase, TWinTraits >
::StartWindowProc(HWND hWnd, UINT uMsg, WPARAM wParam, LPARAM lParam)
{
    // Figure out who this window is.
    CWindowImplBaseT< TBase, TWinTraits >* pThis =
        (CWindowImplBaseT< TBase, TWinTraits >*)
            _Module.ExtractCreateWndData();
...
    pThis->m_hWnd = hWnd;
    // Configure the WNDPROC.
    WNDPROC pProc = (WNDPROC)&(pThis->m_thunk.thunk);
...
}
```

This method associates the ATL-defined WndProc (pProc) to your custom ATL window. Once this association has been made, the ATL MSG_MAP structure will be consulted to determine what to do with the incoming messages.

CMessageMap and ProcessWindowMessage()

Every ATL window (including dialog boxes) inherits a single pure virtual function named ProcessWindowMessage(), which is defined in CMessageMap as the following:

```
// All CWindowImpl<> derived classes inherit this pure virtual function.
// Therefore, every ATL window (or dialog) must implement this method.
class ATL_NO_VTABLE CMessageMap
```

```
{
public:
    virtual BOOL ProcessWindowMessage(HWND hWnd, UINT uMsg,
                    WPARAM wParam, LPARAM lParam,
                    LRESULT& lResult, DWORD dwMsgMapID) = 0;
};
```

When a window's MSG structure has been packaged up, it will be sent into your class's implementation of ProcessWindowMessage(). If the given message is not handled by your class, CWindowImplBaseT< >::WindowProc() will forward the message to DefWindowProc():

```
// In essence, CWindowImplBaseT<> forwards all messages to your class's
// implementation of ProcessWindowMessage().
// If your class does not handle the current message, it is passed to the
// DefWindowProc().
template <class TBase, class TWinTraits>
LRESULT CALLBACK CWindowImplBaseT< TBase, TWinTraits >
::WindowProc(HWND hWnd, UINT uMsg, WPARAM wParam, LPARAM lParam)
{
    ...
    MSG msg = { pThis->m_hWnd, uMsg, wParam, lParam, 0, { 0, 0 } };
    ...
    BOOL bRet = pThis->ProcessWindowMessage(pThis->m_hWnd, uMsg,
                                wParam, lParam, lRes, 0);

    ...
    // Do the default processing if message was not handled.
    if(!bRet)
    {
        if(uMsg != WM_NCDESTROY)
            lRes = pThis->DefWindowProc(uMsg, wParam, lParam);
        else
        {
            ...
        }
    }
    return lRes;
}
```

So, to make a long story short, ATL forwards all Windows messages to the ProcessWindowMessage() function defined by your CWindowImpl< > derived class. If your class does not handle the current message, it will be eaten by DefWindowProc(). Given that ProcessWindowMessage() is a pure virtual function, your custom window must implement this method or else be deemed an abstract base class. The next logical question is where is ProcessWindowMessage() hiding within your CWindowImpl< > derived class?

The ATL Message Map

Every ATL class must supply a MSG map, using the BEGIN_MSG_MAP and END_MSG_MAP macros. Together, these macros define an implementation of ProcessWindowMessage() for your class:

```
// ProcessWindowMessage() is placed in your class using the BEGIN_MSG_MAP macro.
#define BEGIN_MSG_MAP(theClass) \
```

```
public: \
     BOOL ProcessWindowMessage(HWND hWnd, UINT uMsg, \
     WPARAM wParam, LPARAM lParam, LRESULT& lResult, \
     DWORD dwMsgMapID = 0) \
     { \
          BOOL bHandled = TRUE; \
          hWnd; \
          uMsg; \
          wParam; \
          lParam; \
          lResult; \
          bHandled; \
          switch(dwMsgMapID) \
          { \
          case 0:
// END_MSG_MAP closes the initial definition of ProcessWindowMessage().
#define END_MSG_MAP() \
          break; \
          default: \
          ATLTRACE2(atlTraceWindowing, 0, \
          _T("Invalid message map ID (%i)\n"), dwMsgMapID); \
          ATLASSERT(FALSE); \
          break; \
     } \
     return FALSE; \
}
```

Now, if you pull these two macros together, what do you have? A gigantic switch statement! Yes indeed, ProcessWindowMessage() is doing the same thing we did by hand in the previous Win32 example. As you can see, dwMsgMapID is the test point of the switch. Case 0 is a catchall for any and all standard Windows messages (WM_CREATE, WM_PAINT, and so forth). All of these "WM_" messages end up under the case 0 condition, and are tested using a simple if...else syntax. While you could implement this logic by hand, ATL provides a number of macros to do so on your behalf.

Populating your MSG_MAP

The MSG_MAP of CMainWindow has a single entry for WM_PAINT, which was placed there using the MESSAGE_HANDLER macro. The two parameters of this macro are the message we are handling (WM_PAINT) and the function to call in response (OnPaint). When expanded, MESSAGE_HANDLER makes the call to the correct member function, and returns a BOOL (bHandled) indicating if the message should be sent into the DefWindowProc(). This BOOL is declared by the BEGIN_MSG_MAP macro. Here is the expansion of MESSAGE_HANDLER:

```
// This macro is used to fill up all the "case 0" conditions (i.e., windows messages)
#define MESSAGE_HANDLER(msg, func) \
     if(uMsg == msg) \
     { \
          bHandled = TRUE; \
          lResult = func(uMsg, wParam, lParam, bHandled); \
          if(bHandled) \
               return TRUE; \
}
```

Notice that bHandled will be sent in by reference to the message handler function. This gives you the chance to change the value of this parameter before exiting the handler, to determine if the current message should be sent into DefWindowProc(). A value of TRUE indicates the message has been fully handled, and does not need to enter the default windows procedure, whereas FALSE says DefWindowProc() needs to be called.

Also note that END_MSG_MAP always returns FALSE, signifying that your message map did not handle the message, which allows CWindowImplBaseT<>::WindowProc() to call DefWindowProc() on your behalf.

If you handle a message, but still wish to pass it into the DefWindowProc(), you can set the bHandled parameter yourself in a given message handler:

```
// Set the handled flag to inform WindowProc() if it should send this to the
// DefWindowProc()
LRESULT OnPaint(UINT uMsg, WPARAM wParam,
                LPARAM lParam, BOOL& bHandled)
{
    ...
    // I did some work, but still send this into the default window's proc.
    bHandled = FALSE;
    return 0;
}
```

Alternative Message Map Macros

The MESSAGE_HANDLER macro is not the only valid macro that may appear in an ATL message map. Like most ATL maps, your message map may be populated with any number of macros. MESSAGE_HANDLER is the most common of all your options, and is used to handle all standard windows message. Some of the more useful macros are listed in the following table:

ATL MSG_MAP Macro	Meaning in Life
CHAIN_MSG_MAP	Allows your class to "inherit" the messages found in the MSG_MAP of a base class.
MESSAGE_ RANGE_HANDLER	Routes a contiguous numerical range of messages to a single function.
COMMAND_ID_HANDLER	Maps a WM_COMMAND message to some function, using the ID of the control (or menu item).
COMMAND_HANDLER COMMAND_ RANGE_HANDLER	Like COMMAND_ID_HANDLER, but takes the ID as well as the notification code of the control (or menu item).
NOTIFY_HANDLER NOTIFY_RANGE_HANDLER NOTIFY_ID_HANDLER	Like the set of _COMMAND_ macros, but for a WM_NOTIFY event rather than a WM_COMMAND event.

Each of these alternative MSG_MAP entries will tweak the code behind ProcessWindow-Message(). Many of these macros will be automatically inserted based off your selections of the Add Windows Message Handler Wizard. We will see examples of some of these alternatives when we discuss ATL's support for building interactive dialog boxes, as well as ActiveX controls in Chapter 14.

ATL's Support for Dialog Box Development

With your current understanding of how ATL "does windows," you will find the process of building a dialog box is relatively trivial. ATL supplies a total of three dialog-based templates, each of which provides a different level of boilerplate functionality. Here is a high-level overview of each dialog template:

ATL Dialog Box Template	Meaning in Life
CSimpleDialog<>	This is the perfect choice for creating a modal dialog box that requires no user interaction beyond the standard OK and Cancel buttons.
CDialogImpl<>	Used to display a modal or modeless dialog box with no support for ActiveX control containment.
CAxDialogImpl<>	Used to display a modal or modeless dialog box with support for ActiveX control containment.

Working with CSimpleDialog<>

There are times when you need to display a dialog box with more flair than a simple call to MessageBox(), but less flair than a full-blown dialog used to gather user input. The classic example is an About box. You might need to fashion such a dialog, complete with your company logo, a few blocks of static text (tech support, URL, 800 number, and so on) but not much else. By this, I mean no user input is required beyond closing the dialog.

For these simple dialogs, ATL provides the aptly named CSimpleDialog<> template. The only required parameter for this template is the resource ID of the dialog template you have constructed using the Visual Studio resource editors. A second default parameter determines if the dialog should be centered on the screen. Once you create an instance of this class, you make a single call to DoModal(), and your dialog magically appears centered on the desktop.

Assume we have some function which is responsible for showing an About box for your ATL application, which we will call AboutBox(). To grab a dialog resource template, you simply go under the Insert | Resource menu selection and choose the type of dialog box you wish to insert into your project.

In Figure 13-6, we will insert a simple Dialog resource type to bring in a vanilla flavored box, with a default OK

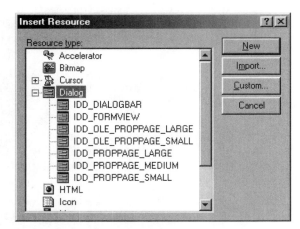

Figure 13-6: Inserting a new Dialog resource.

and Cancel button. Once you select New, you will be provided with a dialog template to which you may add whatever images or text you desire using the Visual Studio editing tools. Let's say you have built your About box, and assigned it the identifier IDD_ABOUTBOX. To launch this dialog using CSimpleDialog<>, just send it the dialog ID as your template parameter:

```
// Simple dialogs require no user input beyond dismissing the box.
// Don't forget to include your project's resource file to get the definition
// of IDD_ABOUTBOX.
#include "resource.h"
void CMyWindow::AboutBox()
{
    CSimpleDialog< IDD_ABOUTBOX> dlg;
    dlg.DoModal();
}
```

Examining CSimpleDialog<>

The definition of CSimpleDialog<> makes a call to the API DialogBox() function within its implementation of DoModal(). Beyond this, a message map entry has been made for WM_INITDIALOG. This Windows message is sent just before the dialog is made visible to the end user. The default implementation simply centers the dialog on the screen. The final method of note is OnCloseCmd(), which closes the dialog using EndDialog(). This is a shared function called when a WM_COMMAND message is sent in response to the OK or Cancel button being clicked (with some help from COMMAND_RANGE_HANDLER):

```
// The definition of CSimpleDialog<>.
template <WORD t_wDlgTemplateID, BOOL t_bCenter = TRUE>
class CSimpleDialog : public CDialogImplBase
{
public:
    int DoModal(HWND hWndParent = ::GetActiveWindow())
    {
        ...
        int nRet = ::DialogBox(_Module.GetResourceInstance(),
                MAKEINTRESOURCE(t_wDlgTemplateID), hWndParent,
                (DLGPROC)StartDialogProc);
        m_hWnd = NULL;
        return nRet;
    }
    BEGIN_MSG_MAP(thisClass)
        MESSAGE_HANDLER(WM_INITDIALOG, OnInitDialog)
        COMMAND_RANGE_HANDLER(IDOK, IDNO, OnCloseCmd)
    END_MSG_MAP()
    LRESULT OnInitDialog(UINT /*uMsg*/, WPARAM /*wParam*/,
                        LPARAM /*lParam*/, BOOL& /*bHandled*/)
    {
        if(t_bCenter)
            CenterWindow(GetParent());
        return TRUE;
    }
    LRESULT OnCloseCmd(WORD /*wNotifyCode*/, WORD wID,
                        HWND /*hWndCtl*/, BOOL& /*bHandled*/)
    {
        ::EndDialog(m_hWnd, wID);
```

```
            return 0;
        }
};
```

Now that we can display a dialog box with no user interaction, we are ready to examine how to create a more elaborate dialog box using CDialogImpl<>.

Building an Interactive Dialog with ATL

When you need to create a dialog that must respond to user input, CSimpleDialog<> won't cut the mustard. To develop a more interactive box, you will need to create a new C++ class that derives from either CDialogImpl<> or CAxDialogImpl<>. Recall that the difference between these two templates is in their support (or lack thereof) for hosting ActiveX controls. Unlike the process of building a Win32 window with ATL, interactive dialog boxes are inserted into your ATL projects using the ATL Object Wizard, as seen in Figure 13-7:

Figure 13-7: Inserting a dialog box using the ATL Object Wizard.

This selection from the Miscellaneous category inserts a new dialog into your current ATL project. By default, this class is derived from the full-blown CAxDialogImpl<> template. Therefore, you (by default) have a dialog that is able to host ActiveX controls. This template gathers most of its functionality from CDialogImpl<> and its immediate base class CDialogImplBase<>.

When you use the ATL Object Wizard to insert a new dialog box, you will be given a dialog box resource template to design your GUI as well as a new C++ class derived from CAxDialogImpl<>. Here is a look at the initial header file:

```
// Your new CAxDialogImpl<> derived class, courtesy of the ATL Object Wizard.
class CTestDialog : public CAxDialogImpl<CTestDialog>
{
public:
    CTestDialog() {}
    ~CTestDialog() {}
    enum { IDD = IDD_TESTDIALOG };
BEGIN_MSG_MAP(CTestDialog)
    MESSAGE_HANDLER(WM_INITDIALOG, OnInitDialog)
```

```
        COMMAND_ID_HANDLER(IDOK, OnOK)
        COMMAND_ID_HANDLER(IDCANCEL, OnCancel)
END_MSG_MAP()
    LRESULT OnInitDialog(UINT uMsg, WPARAM wParam, LPARAM lParam,
                         BOOL& bHandled)
    {
        return 1; // Let the system set the focus
    }
    LRESULT OnOK(WORD wNotifyCode, WORD wID, HWND hWndCtl,
             BOOL& bHandled)
    {
        EndDialog(wID);
        return 0;
    }
    LRESULT OnCancel(WORD wNotifyCode, WORD wID, HWND hWndCtl,
                 BOOL& bHandled)
    {
        EndDialog(wID);
        return 0;
    }
};
```

Adding a Custom Handler

The wizard has generated an initial message map, with entries for WM_INITDIALOG, as well as WM_COMMAND handlers for the dialog's initial OK and Cancel buttons via the COMMAND_ID_HANDLER macro. This alternative message map entry is used to route commands from a specific widget to some method in your class. This is much like the MESSAGE_HANDLER macro; however, rather than responding to standard Windows messages (e.g., WM_CREATE), COMMAND_ID_HANDLER responds exclusively to WM_COMMAND messages, given the ID of the widget:

```
// This MSG_MAP macro is used to respond to WM_COMMAND messages,
// using a control's resource ID as a base line.
#define COMMAND_ID_HANDLER(id, func) \
    if(uMsg == WM_COMMAND && id == LOWORD(wParam)) \
    { \
        bHandled = TRUE; \
        lResult = func(HIWORD(wParam), LOWORD(wParam), \
                    (HWND)lParam, bHandled); \
        if(bHandled) \
            return TRUE; \
    }
```

Because your new dialog class supports an ATL message map, you are able to use the same Add Windows Message Handler Wizard as before. The upside of this story is that as you build the GUI front end of your dialog box, you may respond to numerous control-specific messages, in the same vein as the MFC ClassWizard. To illustrate this, assume we have assembled the following GUI for a new dialog template:

Figure 13-8:
Designing an
interactive
dialog.

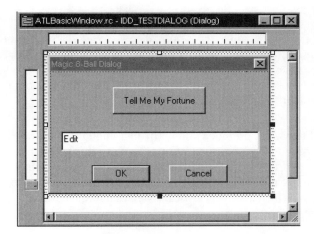

The goal of this dialog box is to generate a string message in response to the clicking of our custom button (IDC_GETMESSAGE). This message will be placed into the dialog's edit control (IDC_MSG).

Using the Windows Message Handler CASE tool, we may select the IDs of the individual controls, and elect to respond to given notifications. If we want to respond to the BN_CLICKED event for IDC_GETMESSAGE, we make the selection in the wizard and type in a method name to handle the event, as shown in Figure 13-9.

Figure 13-9:
Responding to
BN_CLICKED.

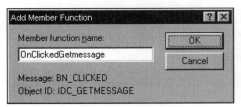

If we examine the changes made in our dialog class, we will see an additional entry in our message map, as well as stub code for the command handler. Here is a simple implementation of the OnClickedGetmessage() method, which makes use of the CWindow::SetDlgItemText(). Figure 13-10 shows a test run.

```
// When the custom button is clicked, send a string to the edit box.
LRESULT OnClickedGetmessage(WORD wNotifyCode, WORD wID, HWND hWndCtl, BOOL& bHandled)
{
    // Place a message into IDC_MSG
    SetDlgItemText(IDC_MSG, "You will never program CORBA");
    return 0;
}
```

Figure 13-10:
The 8-Ball never
lies.

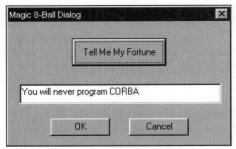

On a related note, the SetDlgItemText() method of CWindow has a counterpart named GetDlgItemText(), which is used to extract the current text within an edit field based off the resource ID. In fact, CWindow provides a large number of "control-specific" helper functions that allow you to perform basic manipulation of radio buttons, combo boxes, and other basic controls. Keep in mind that you will still be expected to dive headlong into Win32 API function calls to execute more elaborate code.

> **Note:** There is an unsupported set of ATL control wrapper classes that can be used when developing ATL Windows applications. <atlcontrols.h> is included as part of the Atlcon sample program included with MSDN. These C++ classes look and feel much like their MFC equivalents, and are worth checking out if you plan to do any hardcore Windows-based ATL development.

That covers the basics of how ATL provides you with "just enough" framework support to allow you to create lightweight Windows applications. To close this chapter, the following lab will give you a chance to create a full Windows window as well as a simple dialog box using ATL. Even if you do not plan to use ATL to build traditional Windows applications, the information presented in this chapter is critical when building GUI-based COM objects, such as ActiveX controls.

Lab 13-1: ATL Windowing

Here, you will build a main window with the ATL framework, complete with a working menu and a custom About box. However, rather than building a simple stand-alone window, the ATL window developed in this lab will expose its services to the outside world from a standard COM interface. In this way, you allow COM clients to create, manipulate, and kill a standard Windows window.

The solution for this lab can be found on your CD-ROM under:
Labs\Chapter 13\ATL Window
Labs\Chapter 13\ATL Window\Client

Step One: Create the Initial Project

In this lab you will be creating an ATL window that can be manipulated with a custom COM interface. Begin by creating a new EXE workspace using the ATL COM AppWizard. As we are going to make use of a number of ATL windowing-specific templates, you must specifically include <atlwin.h>. As mentioned, the best place to do so is in your project's precompiled header file. Be sure you add this line after the definition of CExeModule:

```
// Preparing the project to use the ATL windowing templates.
class CExeModule : public CComModule
{
public:
    LONG Unlock();
    DWORD dwThreadID;
    HANDLE hEventShutdown;
    void MonitorShutdown();
    bool StartMonitor();
    bool bActivity;
};
extern CExeModule _Module;
// Must add <atlwin.h> after the declaration of CExeModule!
#include <atlwin.h>
```

Step Two: Create Custom Resources

Begin by inserting a new Icon resource into your project using the **Insert | Resource** menu selection. As this icon will be used to represent your window, render some interesting image and assign this image an ID of IDI_MAINICON. See Figure 13-11 for an example.

Figure 13-11:
Our custom icon.

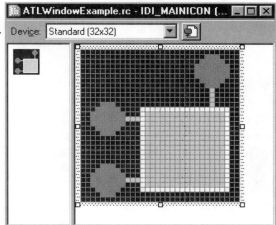

Now insert a custom menu (**Insert | Resource**). We don't need any massive functionality here; a topmost menu item with a single selectable submenu will do just fine. Later we will associate this menu item to a command handler used to show a custom About box. Assign the ID of the menu resource itself to **IDR_MAINMENU**, and the subitem to **IDM_ABOUT**. See Figure 13-12.

Figure 13-12:
A simple test menu.

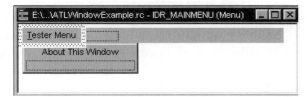

The final custom resource we need for this lab is a new dialog template. This will be hosted in a later step by the CSimpleDialog<> template, and will serve as a simple About box. Assign a resource ID of IDD_ABOUTBOX.

Figure 13-13:
A simple About box.

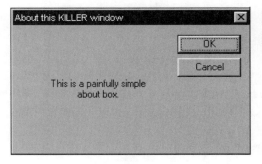

Now that we have some resources, we can move onto the more interesting world of code.

Step Three: Create a CWindowImpl<> Derived Class

The next step is to create a C++ class derived from CWindowImpl<>. There is no "Insert New Window" Wizard as of ATL 3.0, so we need to create this class by hand. Name this class CMyWindow, and define an empty message map:

```
// Be sure to include the extra spaces between your template parameters!
class CMyWindow : public CWindowImpl<CMyWindow, CWindow,
    CWinTraits<WS_CAPTION | WS_POPUPWINDOW | WS_VISIBLE, 0> >
{
```

```
public:
    CMyWindow();
    virtual ~CMyWindow();
    BEGIN_MSG_MAP(CMyWindow)
    END_MSG_MAP()
};
```

This window will allow a COM client to paint some text onto the client area and draw a circle of some size and color. All of this behavior can be captured by the following member functions, which you should add to CMyWindow's public sector:

```
// These are public methods of your new window.
void ChangeText(BSTR newString);
void DrawACircle(int x, int y, int width, int height);
void ChangeTheColor(OLE_COLOR newColor);
```

To fill out the implementation of each function, we will need to also create some private data members. Add a CComBSTR to represent the text to be drawn, an OLE_COLOR variable to represent the color used to paint the circle, and a RECT to hold the bounding box of the circle itself. Finally, add a COLORREF data member:

```
// Private data members.
private:
    RECT m_Rect;                // Size of circle.
    CComBSTR m_Text;            // Text to paint.
    OLE_COLOR m_clrFillColor;   // OLE color of circle.
    COLORREF m_colFore;         // GDI color of circle.
```

COLORREF is a Win32 data type that stores the red-green-blue value of some color. The OLE_COLOR data type is an OLE data type used to express color. Given that your client will hand you an OLE_COLOR type, we will need to translate this into a COLORREF for use with the Win32 GDI functions.

Let's begin by implementing ChangeTheColor(), which simply assigns the internal OLE_COLOR and invalidates the client area to redraw the client area:

```
// Set the OLE_COLOR.
void CMyWindow::ChangeTheColor(OLE_COLOR newColor)
{
    m_clrFillColor = newColor;
    Invalidate();
}
```

ChangeTheText() performs the same sort of operation on the CComBSTR:

```
// Set the text.
void CMyWindow::ChangeText(BSTR newString)
{
    m_Text = newString;
    Invalidate();
}
```

The DrawACircle() method takes four integers which build up the bounding rectangle used to draw our circle. Fill the private m_Rect data member with each value, and call Invalidate() to refresh the image:

```
// Set the bounding rectangle of this circle.
void CMyWindow::DrawACircle(int top, int left, int bottom, int right)
{
```

```
    m_Rect.left      = left;
    m_Rect.right     = right;
    m_Rect.top       = top;
    m_Rect.bottom    = bottom;
    Invalidate();
}
```

Now that we have some initial behavior, we are ready to add some code to construct the window. Call the Create() method of CWindowImpl< >, passing in an initial size as well as our custom menu item and icon. Notice that the menu is attached using a default parameter of Create(), whereas our icon is set by tweaking the WNDCLASSEX structure. Finally, our constructor should assign all state data to some initial values. Here is the lineup:

```
// Prep our state.
CMyWindow::CMyWindow()
{
    // Set the BSTR.
    m_Text = "Default String";
    // Set color.
    m_colFore = RGB(0, 255, 0);
    // Set bounding rectangle of the circle.
    m_Rect.left      = 10;
    m_Rect.right     = 70;
    m_Rect.top       = 10;
    m_Rect.bottom    = 70;
    // Set the custom icon.
    HICON hCustomIcon = LoadIcon(_Module.GetResourceInstance(),
                    MAKEINTRESOURCE(IDI_MAINICON));
    GetWndClassInfo().m_wc.hIcon = hCustomIcon;
    // Load the custom menu.
    HMENU hMenu = LoadMenu(_Module.GetResourceInstance(),
                MAKEINTRESOURCE(IDR_MAINMENU));
    // Call the inherited Create() method to get window going.
    RECT r = {200, 200, 500, 500};
    Create(NULL, r, "My ATL Window", 0, 0, (UINT)hMenu);
}
```

Your destructor should clean things up by calling DestroyWindow():

```
// Kill this window.
CMyWindow::~CMyWindow()
{
    if(m_hWnd)
        DestroyWindow();
}
```

The next order of business is to add a WM_PAINT message handler. Access the Add Windows Message Handler CASE tool from ClassView, and route this message to your custom CMyWindow class. This will populate your message map with a new MESSAGE_HANDLER entry as well as stub code for a method named OnPaint(). In this method, we will need to render the current text, and paint a circle with the correct color and within the correct bounding rectangle. To do so will require that we translate the client-supplied OLE_COLOR into a valid COLORREF using OleTranslateColor(). The remaining code is straight Win32 GDI logic:

```
// Render the text and circle.
LRESULT CMyWindow::OnPaint(UINT msg, WPARAM wparam, LPARAM lparam, BOOL& handled)
{
    PAINTSTRUCT ps;
    HDC hdc = GetDC();
    HBRUSH hOldBrush, hBrush;
    BeginPaint(&ps);
    // Draw text.
    USES_CONVERSION;
    TextOut(hdc, 70, 70, OLE2A(m_Text.m_str), m_Text.Length());
    // Make a filled circle.
    OleTranslateColor(m_clrFillColor, NULL, &m_colFore);
    hBrush = CreateSolidBrush(m_colFore);
    hOldBrush = (HBRUSH)SelectObject(hdc, hBrush);
    Ellipse(hdc,m_Rect.left,m_Rect.top,m_Rect.right,m_Rect.bottom);
    // Clean up.
    SelectObject(hdc, hOldBrush);
    DeleteObject(hBrush);
    EndPaint(&ps);
    ReleaseDC(hdc);
    return 0;
}
```

The final step is to rig up the selection of your custom menu item to a command handler function. In this case, the ATL CASE tools will not give us too much assistance, so we need to edit our message map by hand. Add in a COMMAND_HANDLER macro, which handles the selection of your submenu:

```
// Update your message map to handle the selection of your custom menu item.
BEGIN_MSG_MAP(CMyWindow)
    MESSAGE_HANDLER(WM_PAINT, OnPaint)
    COMMAND_HANDLER(IDM_ABOUT, 0, OnAbout)
END_MSG_MAP()
```

Every COMMAND_HANDLER has the exact same signature. In your implementation of OnAbout(), use CSimpleDialog<> to launch your About box:

```
// Don't forget to include <resource.h>.
LRESULT OnAbout(WORD wNotifyCode, WORD wID, HWND hWndCtl, BOOL& bHandled)
{
    CSimpleDialog<IDD_ABOUTBOX> d;
    d.DoModal();
    return 0;
}
```

At this point we have a full (but trivial) main window written using the ATL framework. The next step is to allow the outside world to access it.

Step Four: Create the COM Object

Now that we have a custom window object, we will need to expose its functionality to the outside world from a COM coclass. Using the ATL Object Wizard, insert a Simple Object named **CoWindow** (keeping all defaults).

We will now need to populate our [default] interface with a set of methods, all of which issue commands to an inner CMyWindow object. First, add a private member variable to

CoWindow of type CMyWindow, named **m_theWnd**. Next, add the following methods to the ICoWindow interface:

```
// This single interface of the coclass allows the outside world to manipulate our
// CWindowImpl<> derived object.
interface ICoWindow : IDispatch
{
    [id(1), helpstring("Creates the CMyWindow object")]
    HRESULT CreateMyWindow();
    [id(2), helpstring("Kills the CMyWindow object")]
    HRESULT KillMyWindow();
    [id(3), helpstring("Draws the circle")]
    HRESULT DrawCircle([in] int top, [in] int left, [in] int bottom, [in] int right);
    [id(4), helpstring("Changes the color")]
    HRESULT ChangeTheColor([in] OLE_COLOR newColor);
    [id(5), helpstring("Changes the text")]
    HRESULT ChangeWindowText([in] BSTR newText);
};
```

The CreateMyWindow() and KillMyWindow() methods allocate and deallocate the private CMyWindow data member maintained by CoWindow:

```
// User wants a new window.
STDMETHODIMP CCoWindow::CreateMyWindow()
{
    m_theWnd = new CMyWindow;
    m_theWnd->CenterWindow();
    return S_OK;
}
// User is tired of the window.
STDMETHODIMP CCoWindow::KillMyWindow()
{
    if(m_theWnd)
        delete m_theWnd;
    return S_OK;
}
```

The remaining methods can be implemented by simple delegation. For example, ChangeWindowText() takes the incoming BSTR and sends it into the ChangeText() method of CMyWindow(). As you recall, we set up this method to assign a new BSTR and refresh the window:

```
// Allow user to change the text.
STDMETHODIMP CCoWindow::ChangeWindowText(BSTR newText)
{
    // Change the text.
    if(m_theWnd)
        m_theWnd ->ChangeText(newText);
    else
        return E_FAIL;
    return S_OK;
}
```

For completion, here are the remaining methods of ICoWindow:

```
// Draw!
STDMETHODIMP CCoWindow::DrawCircle(int top, int left, int bottom, int right)
{
```

```
        if(m_theWnd)
            m_theWnd -> DrawACircle(top, left, bottom, right);
        else
            return E_FAIL;
        return S_OK;
}
// Change the color.
STDMETHODIMP CCoWindow::ChangeTheColor(OLE_COLOR newColor)
{
        if(m_theWnd)
            m_theWnd -> ChangeTheColor(newColor);
        else
            return E_FAIL;
        return S_OK;
}
```

And now for the final task—a client to drive the window.

Step Five: A Visual Basic Test Client

For ease of implementation, let's build a VB client. Once you have created a new Standard
EXE workspace, set a reference to your new ATL server. Design a GUI which allows the
end user to create and kill the window, change the text, and set the dimensions (and color)
of the circle. Here is one possible GUI configuration:

Figure 13-14:
A VB tester
application.

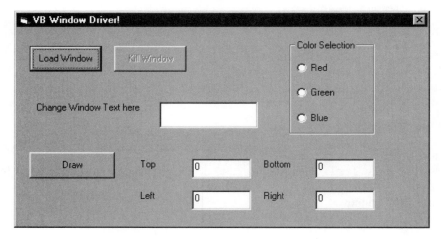

The code behind this form is straightforward. Declare a CoWindow variable in your [General][Declarations] section, and use the front end to call each member of the [default]
interface. Here is the complete VB code listing:

```
' [General][Declarations]
'
Option Explicit
Private w As ATLWINDOWEXAMPLELib.CoWindow
Private Sub btnDraw_Click()
     w.DrawCircle CInt(txtTop), CInt(txtLeft), CInt(txtBottom), CInt(txtRight)
End Sub
Private Sub btnKill_Click()
```

```
        w.KillMyWindow
        btnLoad.Enabled = True
        btnKill.Enabled = False
End Sub
Private Sub btnLoad_Click()
        w.CreateMyWindow
        btnLoad.Enabled = False
        btnKill.Enabled = True
End Sub
Private Sub Form_Load()
        Set w = New CoWindow
        btnLoad.Enabled = True
        btnKill.Enabled = False
End Sub
Private Sub OptionBlue_Click()
        Dim c As Long
        c = RGB(0, 0, 255)
        w.ChangeTheColor c
End Sub
Private Sub OptionGreen_Click()
        Dim c As Long
        c = RGB(0, 255, 0)
        w.ChangeTheColor c
End Sub
Private Sub OptionRed_Click()
        Dim c As Long
        c = RGB(255, 0, 0)
        w.ChangeTheColor c
End Sub
Private Sub Text1_Change()
        w.ChangeWindowText Text1.Text
End Sub
```

When you run your test client, you are now able to create the window, assign text, and color and size the rendered circle. Here is a test run:

Figure 13-15: CMyWindow in action.

When you select your custom menu item, you will see your dialog box pop up, and as you can see, your custom icon is placed in the upper left-hand corner of the window.

As mentioned earlier in this chapter, the windowing support provided by ATL is a nice middle of the road solution between the raw Win32 API and a full framework such as MFC. This lab illustrated the use of ATL to create a main window. Even if you do not intend to use ATL as a Windows framework, you will find many of these same templates show up when building an ActiveX control.

Chapter Summary

The ATL framework provides a number of helpful templates that can be used to create main windows as well as interactive dialog boxes. The core class is CWindow, which wraps an underlying HWND and defines a large number of methods used to call API functions on your behalf. As it turns out, most of the remaining ATL windowing templates use CWindow as a parameter and therefore can leverage its functionality.

CWindowImpl< > and the MSG_MAP structure are used to hide the details of creating and registering your windows class, and assemble your WndProc. As we have seen, BEGIN_MSG_MAP expands to implement ProcessWindowMessage() which is (in essence) the gigantic switch statement Win32 developers know and love. A message map is populated using a variety of additional macros, with MESSAGE_HANDLER being the most common for a typical main window.

CSimpleDialog< >, CDialogImpl< >, and CAxDialogImpl< > each provide a different level of support for a Window's dialog box. CSimpleDialog< > displays a modal dialog with no support for user input. CDialogImpl< > derived classes provide user interaction, but offer no support for ActiveX controls. Finally, CAxDialogImpl< > gives you some additional support needed to build a dialog box hosting an ActiveX control.

Chapter 14

Developing ActiveX Controls with ATL

Objectives:

- Understand ActiveX controls and property page objects.
- Get to know the core interfaces required by an ActiveX control.
- Understand stock, custom, and ambient properties.
- Build a Full Control with the ATL framework.
- Learn about COM's client-driven persistence model.
- Build property pages using the ATL framework.
- Build a Licensed Class Factory with IClassFactory2.

An ActiveX control is a high powered coclass, quite different from the previous COM objects built thus far, in that they typically offer a visual aspect. However, most ActiveX controls make use of each of the core COM services we have already examined. In this chapter, you will extend your current COM knowledge and learn about a number of new standard interfaces that deal specifically with GUI-based tasks such as rendering, sizing, activation, and property persistence. As well, you will see how ATL provides a stock implementation for each of these new interfaces. By the end of this chapter, you will be well equipped to build full ActiveX controls and any associated property page objects you may wish to support. In addition, this chapter introduces you to a number of control-centric details such as font manipulation, GDI routines, bitmap rendering, basic animation, and a web-based client.

Understanding the ActiveX Control

As far as COM-based technologies go, the ActiveX control is at the top of the mountain. An *ActiveX control* is a graphical building block, used in the context of another application. A perfect example of this sort of binary GUI-based reuse is found within the Visual Basic IDE. When you begin building a new VB application, you typically assemble a user interface using items from the VB Toolbox (Figure 14-1). All of these items are ActiveX controls.

Figure 14-1:
A palette of
ActiveX controls.

Any development environment worth its salt has the ability to include additional ActiveX controls into the IDE, and therefore as part of your current project. Again using VB as an example, if you select the Project | Components menu item, you are presented with the dialog box shown in Figure 14-2, which allows you to select any registered controls into your current project workspace.

Figure 14-2:
Inserting
additional
ActiveX controls
in VB.

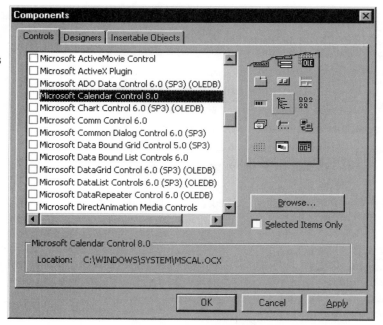

When you select additional controls using the Components dialog, new icons appear in the VB toolbox, and you are then able to work with these graphical COM objects just like the intrinsic VB controls. For example, if we were to place an MS Calendar control onto a VB Form object (Figure 14-3), we would find that all of the available properties appear in the VB Property Window (if the control is selected). Additionally, if we open up the code window and select the Calendar object, we are able to write event handlers for the set of events sent by this control. ActiveX controls integrate so completely into the IDE you are using that you seldom even regard these items as COM objects supporting a set of standard and custom interfaces.

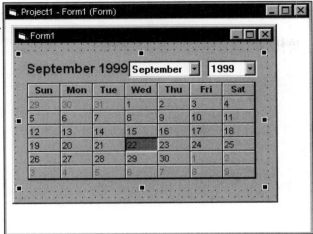

Figure 14-3:
The MS Calendar Control.

Understanding Property Pages

Many ActiveX controls also have associated *property pages*, which are hosted within a tabbed dialog box. It is important to note that property pages are COM objects, and expose standard COM interfaces (typically IPropertyPage) that allow the control and the dialog host to interact with them. These pages allow the user of the control to set the properties provided by the control at design time from a friendly tabbed dialog box. Although most environments provide alternative ways to set a control's state at design time, property pages provide a standard way to do so (after all, not all COM savvy environments have the equivalent of a VB Property Window). Figure 14-4 shows the set of property pages used by the MS Calendar control:

Figure 14-4:
Property pages for the MS Calendar control.

As you can see, three pages are provided for this particular ActiveX object. The General tab is a custom property page, which allows us to set properties unique to the Calendar coclass. The Font and Color tabs provide access to standard pages, which are commonly used by many ActiveX controls. A given control may have any number of custom and standard property pages, which will vary based on the complexity of your object's property set.

Invisible at Runtime Controls

So, as we have just seen, the ActiveX control is a GUI-based COM object, which may have a set of associated property pages. To put one wrinkle in our current understanding, it is important to note that some controls are "invisible at runtime." These controls are also graphical building blocks <u>at design time</u>.

At run time, the visible interface of the control is hidden from view, while the services it provides churn away in the background. The VB Timer control is an example of such an item (the Timer control is used to capture WM_TIMER messages). At design time, the VB developer sees a visible timer icon on the form, which disappears during execution:

Figure 14-5:
An invisible at runtime control.

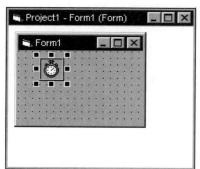

Now that we have a better grasp of the purpose of an ActiveX control, we will spend the rest of this chapter learning how to create one of our own using the ATL framework. Even though these coclasses are very complex given the functionality they provide, the good news is a typical ActiveX control will make use of just about everything you have learned about COM up to this point. As for the new topics necessary to build a full control, the ATL framework is here to pick up the slack. However, before we begin coding the example control used in this chapter, we need to spend a bit of time getting comfortable with the basic services and additional interfaces used in a typical ActiveX control.

The Makeup of a Typical ActiveX Control

ActiveX controls tend to have a common set of requirements. In a nutshell, a full-blown control will need to provide the following basic behaviors, all of which are exposed using standard COM interfaces:

- A set of custom properties and methods exposed via IDispatch. This is what makes your control a unique entity. Although an ActiveX control does not <u>have</u> to provide its services using IDispatch, most will, to allow web-based scripting languages to access their functionality.

- A set of events exposed through a [default, source] dispinterface. Beyond providing support for IConnectionPointContainer many ActiveX controls support a connection proxy for a related interface: IPropertyNotifySink.

- The ability to be rendered as needed by the control container. This ability is provided by additional COM interfaces such as IViewObject, IViewObject2, and IViewObjectEx.

- The ability to be *persisted* by the container. In other words, a control should be able to save and load its state when asked to do so. This behavior is provided when a control implements a number of COM persistence interfaces such as IPersistPropertyBag, IPersist, IPersistStorage, and IPersistStreamInit.

- The ability to handle standard windowing messages, given that most controls respond to some type of user input. In ATL, this is provided by the MSG_MAP structure as well as various windowing templates we examined in Chapter 13.

- Some set of property pages to allow the user to set properties at design time. Each property page supports the standard IPropertyPage interface (and possibly IPropertyPage2). As well, the coclass needs to support ISpecifyPropertyPages to expose these pages to the container.

- The ability to run "in-place active" as an embedded object. This allows containers such as MS Word and Excel to make use of your controls using IOleInPlaceObject (among others). Support for these OLE-centric interfaces is optional; however, without them your control cannot run as an OLE object.

- Most controls support COM exception handling, using ISupportErrorInfo.

As you can see, you already know a good deal about what a control is capable of, given your understanding of various standard COM interfaces. The remaining aspects of an ActiveX control (such as rendering and persistence) are provided by additional COM interfaces. To serve as a road map for the remainder of this chapter, the following table outlines the core interfaces required to build a full-blown ActiveX control, with a brief description of the acquired functionality.

COM Interfaces	Meaning in Life
IConnectionPointContainer IConnectionPoint IPropertyNotifySink	Used to establish connections with the ActiveX control.
ISpecifyPropertyPages IPropertyPage(2)	ISpecifyPropertyPages is used to determine which property pages are used by the control. IPropertyPage(2) is implemented by the individual property page objects.
IOleInPlaceActiveObject IViewObject(2) IViewObjectEx IOleInPlaceObject IOleInPlaceObjectWindowless	Used to allow the control host to render the ActiveX control. Hit testing, sizing, and generic drawing abilities are provided by this set of interfaces.
IOleControl IOleObject IOleWindow IDataObject	Core ActiveX control support. Used to establish communication between the container and the control, enable in-place activation, and transmit data between the two parties.
IQuickActivate	Allows a container to grab a batch of interfaces from a single interface.
IPersist IPersistStorage IPersistStreamInit IPersistPropertyBag	Allows the control host to save and load the control's properties, in a variety of client-specified formats.
IProvideClassInfo(2)	Allows container to grab type information from the control and quickly discover the default [source] dispinterface.

Some controls may choose not to implement all of the listed interfaces. At minimum (according to the official word from Microsoft), the only interface an ActiveX control really must support is our good friend IUnknown, and dwell a self-registering DLL (exporting DllRegisterServer() and DllUnregisterServer()). However, most people who are willing to spend money on a control expect to do more than obtain a pointer to IID_IUnknown all day long. Therefore, most production controls do implement the listed interfaces, in addition to the domain-specific logic that makes your control unique.

ATL Object Wizard Options

When you develop your controls in ATL, you'll be happy to find that default implementations of these standard COM interfaces are provided for your consumption. Writing a full ActiveX control by hand would be a significant undertaking, and unlike the first 13 chapters of this book, we will not be beginning with a raw C++ example to illustrate building an ActiveX control (thank me later). Rather, we will leverage what you already know about COM and ATL, and jump right into the ATL templates and CASE tools used when building ActiveX objects. On a related note, we will not be examining the details of each and every method of each and every standard COM interface used for an ActiveX control. If you need to see more details than this chapter provides, I will assume you know how to check things out on your own accord. That being said, let's begin seeing how ATL can get the ball rolling and reexamine the options provided by the ATL Object Wizard (Figure 14-6):

Figure 14-6: Available control selections as of ATL 3.0.

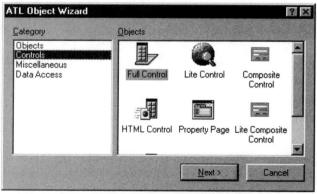

In Chapter 6, we took a look at the various types of COM objects you can insert into an ATL workspace using the ATL Object Wizard. In this chapter we will be building a Full Control; however, the available options are:

Object Wizard Control	Meaning in Life
Full Control	This ActiveX control supports all necessary COM interfaces to be used by any ActiveX container.
Lite Control	Supports a subset of the required interfaces necessary to host the control in MS Internet Explorer (and VB).

Object Wizard Control	Meaning in Life
Composite Control	A control that is able to host other controls as part of its composition. You are provided a dialog template to assemble the GUI of the control.
Lite Composite Control	A composite control supporting only the interfaces necessary for MS Internet Explorer (and VB).
HTML Control	This control is a full control, with the additional ability to display DHTML web pages within its window frame.
Lite HTML Control	You guessed it; this control supports the necessary interfaces for MS IE (and VB), and the ability to support DHTML web pages.
Property Page	Used to represent a single custom property page for use by the control. You are provided with a dialog template to assemble your GUI.

Configuring a Full Control with the ATL Object Wizard

First and foremost, be aware that ActiveX controls are always hosted in-process. This of course means that your initial ATL project workspace must be configured as a DLL. If you have previous experience developing and using controls in other frameworks, you may be used to seeing the *.ocx (OLE control extension) file type. This is just another way to identify in-proc servers, and the fact that ATL picked *.dll over *.ocx is irrelevant. Let's build a DLL server named AXShapesServer.

 AXShapesServer is included on your supplemental CD, under the Labs\Chapter 14 subdirectory.

Once you have established your component housing using the ATL COM AppWizard, you are now able to select which type of ActiveX control you wish to place into the DLL. Keep in mind that it is possible for a single DLL to contain any number of ActiveX controls, in the same way that a given DLL can contain any number of Simple Objects (after all, an ActiveX control is just a COM object). This may help ease your distribution issues, given that all controls are contained in a single DLL. On the other hand, this will increase the size of your binary (which may or may not be problematic).

Figure 14-7: Setting the names for ShapesControl.

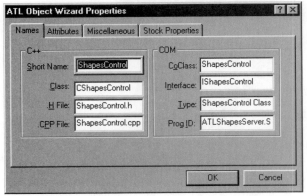

We will insert a single Full Control using the ATL Object Wizard. This new control will be named ShapesControl (Figure 14-7).

As you can see, Full Controls have two additional configuration tabs above and beyond Names and Attributes. From the Attributes tab (Figure 14-8), be sure to select support for connection points to enable our control to fire events to the container. This example does not need to support COM exceptions;

however, if you need to do so, you may enable this support and use the techniques described in Chapter 7. Also note that two of your threading options have been disabled: You cannot enter into the process-wide MTA. This is not a flaw in the wizard, but a requirement of how ActiveX controls operate (they require thread affinity).

Figure 14-8:
Enabling
connection
points for
ShapesControl.

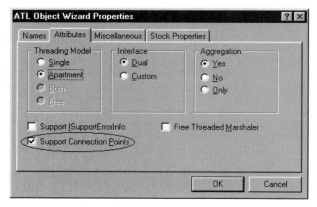

Options Provided by the Miscellaneous Tab

The Miscellaneous tab allows you to specify a number of odds and ends about how your ActiveX control should behave. As all of these features help establish the visible capabilities of your control, it should be clear why a Simple Object did not provide this configuration option. The only additional option to check for the ShapesControl is the Insertable selection as seen in Figure 14-9. This allows your control to be accessed by the Insert Object dialog box found in numerous products, such as MS Word.

Figure 14-9:
ActiveX controls
have additional
settings above
and beyond a
simple coclass.

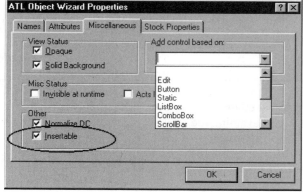

Again, the options available from the Miscellaneous tab help configure how your control is to behave when rendered by (and used by) a container. As many of these options are not very self-descriptive, here is a rundown of each option.

Miscellaneous Option	Meaning in Life
Opaque	Enable this option if your control is rendered into a full rectangle, as it informs the host it has no need to render a background beneath the object. Other controls render an irregular foreground, and require the host to render a background behind the control.
Solid Background	Opaque controls can select this option to be provided with a default solid background.
Invisible at Runtime	This configures your control to have a visible presence only at design time (like the VB Timer control).
Acts Like a Button	When a host has numerous controls composing its GUI, selecting this option will make your control the "default" item.
Acts Like a Label	This option allows the control to receive focus from the Tab key.
Normalize DC (device context)	Establishes the drawing coordinates used for your control to be (0, 0) based. When this option is deselected, you will need to bypass the OnDraw() function used by default, and override the OnAdvancedDraw() method provided by the framework to establish your own scaling options.
Insertable	This option allows your control to appear as a valid entry from the standard Insert Object dialog box used by containers such as MS Office.
Windowed Only	Determines who is responsible for creating a window to host the control. If selected, the control takes care of things; if not, the container is expected to. Be aware that not all hosts have this capability!
Add Control Based On	ATL provides a way to build your control based on existing window types. For example, you may wish to build a stylized button control which adds additional functionality beyond "being pressed."

Later in the chapter, we will see how some of these selections translate into real code, but for now let's press on and examine the final tab related to ATL ActiveX controls and learn about stock properties in the process.

The Stock Properties Tab

The final configuration option that needs to be made is which (if any) stock properties will be supported by our control. A *stock property* is simply a standard, well-known property, common across most controls. For example, many controls wish to provide a way to set the background color of the control's view area. Controls that display text may wish to support the Font property. Rather than having each developer create unique properties that do more or less the same thing, COM defines a predefined set of stock properties. ShapesControl will make use of the Font, Background Color, and Caption stock properties (Figure 14-10).

Figure 14-10:
Stock
properties of
ShapesControl.

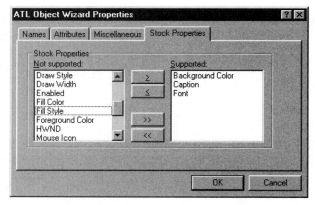

Each stock property has a preassigned DISPID, all of which are defined in <olectl.idl>. As well, each stock property operates on a specific type of data. Given this, an ActiveX control container "understands" what these properties are used for, and can integrate them into the development environment, call them at run time, and so forth.

The constant used to refer to a specific stock property can be determined by prefixing "DISPID_" to the capitalized name of the property (for example, DISPID_FONT, DISPID_BACKCOLOR, DISPID_CAPTION, and so on). The following table describes the meaning of each stock property and the underlying data type:

Stock Property	Data Type	Meaning in Life
Appearance	short	Determines how the control is painted (flat or 3D).
AutoSize	Bit flag	Enables or disables sizing capabilities.
BackColor ForeColor	OLE_COLOR	Configures the background and foreground color for the control.
BackStyle	long	Configures the transparent or opaque status of the control.
BorderColor BorderStyle BorderVisible BorderWidth	OLE_COLOR long long long	Used to establish the attributes of the control's border.
Caption Text	BSTR	The caption (and text) used for the control.
DrawMode	long	Configures the GDI drawing mode for the control.
DrawStyle DrawWidth	long long	Configures the style of the pen used to draw lines for this control.
Enabled	BOOL	Enables and disables the control.
FillColor FillStyle	OLE_COLOR long	Configures the color and pattern of the control's brush.
Font	IFontDisp*	Sets and retrieves the font used to render text in the control.
HWND	HWND	Allows access to the control's underlying window handle.
MouseIcon MousePointer	IPictureDisp* long	Configures the icon to use when the mouse is over this control.

Stock Property	Data Type	Meaning in Life
Picture	IPictureDisp*	Allows your control to handle icons, bitmaps, and metafiles using a standard property.
TabStop	BOOL	Enables and disables the tab stop support for this control.

Examining the Initial Full Control: The IDL Code

Examining your new project files may give you a serious headache. The header file for your new control has an elaborate inheritance chain and a hefty COM map. Before we get to these details, we will take a high-level overview, beginning with your project's IDL file. As always, you have been provided with a [default] dual interface, library statement, and coclass definition. Because we supported the connection point protocol, we also have an empty [source] dispinterface. The major changes are due to the fact that we specified support for some stock properties, all of which are listed as [propput] and [propget] methods:

```
// Like any property, stock properties are documented in your IDL definition.
[ object, uuid(03FBA31F-71D1-11D3-B92D-0020781238D4), dual,
helpstring("IShapesControl Interface"), pointer_default(unique) ]
interface IShapesControl : IDispatch
{
      [propput, id(DISPID_BACKCOLOR)]
      HRESULT BackColor([in]OLE_COLOR clr);
      [propget, id(DISPID_BACKCOLOR)]
      HRESULT BackColor([out,retval]OLE_COLOR* pclr);
      [propputref, id(DISPID_FONT)]
      HRESULT Font([in]IFontDisp* pFont);
      [propput, id(DISPID_FONT)]
      HRESULT Font([in]IFontDisp* pFont);
      [propget, id(DISPID_FONT)]
      HRESULT Font([out, retval]IFontDisp** ppFont);
      [propput, id(DISPID_CAPTION)]
      HRESULT Caption([in]BSTR strCaption);
      [propget, id(DISPID_CAPTION)]
      HRESULT Caption([out,retval]BSTR* pstrCaption);
};
```

As you can see, each stock property has been listed with the correct preassigned DISPID which has been assigned to the correct underlying data type. All [propget] functions are configured to support [out, retval] parameters, allowing integration among various COM language mappings.

The Updated Registry Script (RGS) File

Like any COM object, ActiveX controls need to be registered with the system before they are ready for use. However, unlike a simple coclass, ActiveX controls have a number of additional values to be registered. If your COM object is indeed a control, the Control subkey should be added. As controls have a bitmap that is used for the toolbar icon, a ToolboxBitmap32 key should be added to provide the path to the valid BMP file. The set of additions can be seen under HKCR\CLSID\{ <guid> }:

Figure 14-11:
Additional
registration
details for an
ActiveX control.

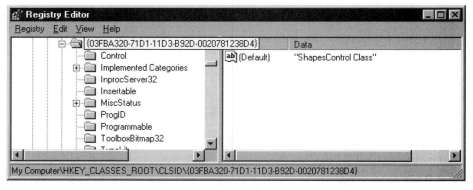

Of course, your RGS file has been modified to insert these necessary entries:

```
HKCR
{
    AXShapesServer.ShapesControl.1 = s 'ShapesControl Class'
    {
        CLSID = s '{03FBA320-71D1-11D3-B92D-0020781238D4}'
        'Insertable'
    }
    AXShapesServer.ShapesControl = s 'ShapesControl Class'
    {
        CLSID = s '{03FBA320-71D1-11D3-B92D-0020781238D4}'
        CurVer = s 'AXShapesServer.ShapesControl.1'
    }
    NoRemove CLSID
    {
        ForceRemove {03FBA320-71D1-11D3-B92D-0020781238D4} = s
        'ShapesControl Class'
        {
            ProgID = s 'AXShapesServer.ShapesControl.1'
            VersionIndependentProgID = s 'AXShapesServer.ShapesControl'
            ForceRemove 'Programmable'
            InprocServer32 = s '%MODULE%'
            {
                val ThreadingModel = s 'Apartment'
            }
            ForceRemove 'Control'
            ForceRemove 'Insertable'
            ForceRemove 'ToolboxBitmap32' = s '%MODULE%, 101'
            'MiscStatus' = s '0'
            {
             '1' = s '131473'
            }
            'TypeLib' = s '{03FBA313-71D1-11D3-B92D-0020781238D4}'
            'Version' = s '1.0'
        }
    }
}
```

As you can see, you are given the standard ProgID entries, and a number of new settings
under HKCR\CLSID. As we specified that ShapesControl is usable from OLE containers,

we have an entry for the Insertable subkey. MiscStatus represents the combination of bits based on your selections in the Miscellaneous tab. The most interesting addition to your RGS file is the ToolboxBitmap32 entry.

The ATL Object Wizard has provided you with a new custom bitmap resource which can be found on the ResourceView tab and is shown in Figure 14-12. The location of this bitmap image will be set to the value of the ToolbarBitmap32 subkey.

Figure 14-12:
The initial
toolbox image.

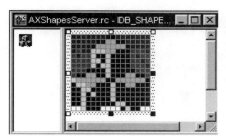

To really take ownership of your controls, you should edit this image with the Visual Studio resource tools to represent the essence of your control. ShapesControl has such an updated image, which will be seen whenever you include your control into some IDE for use (Figure 14-13):

Figure 14-13:
Our updated
toolbar bitmap
image.

Dissecting the Inheritance Chain of a Full Control

Most of the interesting code generation has taken place within the header file of CShapesControl. Although the list of inherited functionality looks intimidating, you have already seen a few of these ATL templates over the course of this book. For example, IConnectionPointContainerImpl< > is present given that your control supports connectable objects. Because a Full Control is just a fancy COM object, CComObjectRootEx< > still provides the hooks for IUnknown. CComCoClass< > is still used to provide a default class factory. IProvideClassInfo2Impl< > is also present in a Full Control (recall that IProvideClassInfo2 is used to discover the [default, source] dispinterface of your class). We will get to know the additional templates later in this chapter, but here is an initial (and commented) look at each base class template:

```
// The inheritance chain for a Full Control.
class ATL_NO_VTABLE CShapesControl :
    // Support for IUnknown.
    public CComObjectRootEx<CComSingleThreadModel>,
    // Support for stock properties (and marks the [default] interface).
    public CStockPropImpl<CShapesControl, IShapesControl, &IID_IShapesControl,
                          &LIBID_AXSHAPESSERVERLib>,
    // Establishes communication with container & provides windowing support.
    public CComControl<CShapesControl>,
    // Persistence support.
    public IPersistStreamInitImpl<CShapesControl>,
    // Support for ambient notifications.
    public IOleControlImpl<CShapesControl>,
    // Provides linking & embedding services.
```

```
      public IOleObjectImpl<CShapesControl>,
      // More linking & embedding services.
      public IOleInPlaceActiveObjectImpl<CShapesControl>,
      // Support for IViewObject(2)[Ex]
      public IViewObjectExImpl<CShapesControl>,
      // Behavior for a windowless control (drag & drop & windows messages)
      public IOleInPlaceObjectWindowlessImpl<CShapesControl>,
      // Connection point protocol.
      public IConnectionPointContainerImpl<CShapesControl>,
      // Support to persist properties into a storage.
      public IPersistStorageImpl<CShapesControl>,
      // Allows client to obtains CLSIDs for the set of pages used with this control.
      public ISpecifyPropertyPagesImpl<CShapesControl>,
      // Support for fast activation of object.
      public IQuickActivateImpl<CShapesControl>,
      // Uniform data transfer.
      public IDataObjectImpl<CShapesControl>,
      // Obtain [default, source] and type information.
      public IProvideClassInfo2Impl<&CLSID_ShapesControl,
              &DIID__IShapesControlEvents, &LIBID_AXSHAPESSERVERLib>,
      // Informs container a [bindable] property has changed.
      public IPropertyNotifySinkCP<CShapesControl>,
      // Class factory.
      public CComCoClass<CShapesControl, &CLSID_ShapesControl>
{
...
};
```

After we complete the ShapesControl, we will take a more detailed look at many of these ATL classes and the services they provide. For the time being, let's examine the rest of the generated code.

Wizard-Generated Maps

If you examine your control's COM map, you will see that each interface brought into the CShapesControl coclass has been given an interface entry. Remember that when your coclass supports a COM interface that does not derive directly from IUnknown, a separate provision must be made for each base interface. For example IViewObject, IViewObject2, and IViewObjectEx are all present in your COM map, although IViewObjectExImpl<> provides implementation of each interface:

```
// As mentioned, ActiveX controls express themselves with a number of
// COM interfaces!
BEGIN_COM_MAP(CShapesControl)
    COM_INTERFACE_ENTRY(IShapesControl)          // Your [default] interface.
    COM_INTERFACE_ENTRY(IDispatch)
    COM_INTERFACE_ENTRY(IViewObjectEx)
    COM_INTERFACE_ENTRY(IViewObject2)
    COM_INTERFACE_ENTRY(IViewObject)
    COM_INTERFACE_ENTRY(IOleInPlaceObjectWindowless)
    COM_INTERFACE_ENTRY(IOleInPlaceObject)
    COM_INTERFACE_ENTRY2(IOleWindow, IOleInPlaceObjectWindowless)
    COM_INTERFACE_ENTRY(IOleInPlaceActiveObject)
    COM_INTERFACE_ENTRY(IOleControl)
    COM_INTERFACE_ENTRY(IOleObject)
```

```
    COM_INTERFACE_ENTRY(IPersistStreamInit)
    COM_INTERFACE_ENTRY2(IPersist, IPersistStreamInit)
    COM_INTERFACE_ENTRY(IConnectionPointContainer)
    COM_INTERFACE_ENTRY(ISpecifyPropertyPages)
    COM_INTERFACE_ENTRY(IQuickActivate)
    COM_INTERFACE_ENTRY(IPersistStorage)
    COM_INTERFACE_ENTRY(IDataObject)
    COM_INTERFACE_ENTRY(IProvideClassInfo)
    COM_INTERFACE_ENTRY(IProvideClassInfo2)
END_COM_MAP()
```

Also notice that you are provided with a default message map, allowing this control to respond to various Windows messages. Like a traditional window, your ActiveX control may populate the message map using any of the messaging macros detailed in Chapter 13. Here is the initial listing:

```
// Your initial message map.
BEGIN_MSG_MAP(CShapesControl)
    CHAIN_MSG_MAP(CComControl<CShapesControl>)
    DEFAULT_REFLECTION_HANDLER()
END_MSG_MAP()
```

Your control's message map "inherits" the map defined by the CComControl<> base class template. If you examine the MSG map for CComControl<>, you will see your derived ActiveX object already responds to the following windows messages:

```
// Messages provided to your control from CComControl<>.
// <atlctl.h>
BEGIN_MSG_MAP(thisClass)
    MESSAGE_HANDLER(WM_PAINT, CComControlBase::OnPaint)
    MESSAGE_HANDLER(WM_SETFOCUS, CComControlBase::OnSetFocus)
    MESSAGE_HANDLER(WM_KILLFOCUS, CComControlBase::OnKillFocus)
    MESSAGE_HANDLER(WM_MOUSEACTIVATE, CComControlBase::OnMouseActivate)
END_MSG_MAP()
```

As we specified the ShapesControl to support the connection point mechanism, we have a connection point map in place, with a default listing for the IPropertyNotifySink interface (we will have more to say about its role later on). Your [default, source] interface is not yet a part of this map, as we have not run the Implement Connection Point Wizard:

```
// Your initial connection point map.
BEGIN_CONNECTION_POINT_MAP(CShapesControl)
    CONNECTION_POINT_ENTRY(IID_IPropertyNotifySink)
END_CONNECTION_POINT_MAP()
```

The final map of your ATL control is the *property map*. This map is used to persist the values of your custom properties, using a client-specified persistence protocol. This same map is used to specify any property pages used by this control. We will discuss this map, and persistence in general, later in the chapter. Here is the initial listing:

```
// The ATL property map is used to specify property pages for this control
// as well as providing support for property persistence.
BEGIN_PROP_MAP(CShapesControl)
    PROP_DATA_ENTRY("_cx", m_sizeExtent.cx, VT_UI4)
    PROP_DATA_ENTRY("_cy", m_sizeExtent.cy, VT_UI4)
    PROP_ENTRY("BackColor", DISPID_BACKCOLOR, CLSID_StockColorPage)
    PROP_ENTRY("Caption", DISPID_CAPTION, CLSID_NULL)
```

```
        PROP_ENTRY("Font", DISPID_FONT, CLSID_StockFontPage)
        // Example entries
        // PROP_ENTRY("Property Description", dispid, clsid)
        // PROP_PAGE(CLSID_StockColorPage)
END_PROP_MAP()
```

Extending Our Full Control with COM Categories

One map that is not automatically included by the Object Wizard is the category map. Most ActiveX controls will want to implement the "safe for initialization" and "safe for scripting" categories to play well with a web-based host. If we do not add support for these categories, MS IE will display security warnings when attempting to work with this control. To mark our control as safe, add a category map to the initial generated code (don't forget the CATID constants are defined in <objsafe.h>):

```
// If we want to support COM categories, we must manually add
// the ATL category map by hand.
BEGIN_CATEGORY_MAP(CShapesControl)
    IMPLEMENTED_CATEGORY(CATID_SafeForScripting)
    IMPLEMENTED_CATEGORY(CATID_SafeForInitializing)
END_CATEGORY_MAP()
```

If you open up the OLE/COM viewer utility and look under the Controls category, you will find ShapesControl is now supporting these COM categories:

Figure 14-14: Hunting down our control from the OLE/COM Object Viewer.

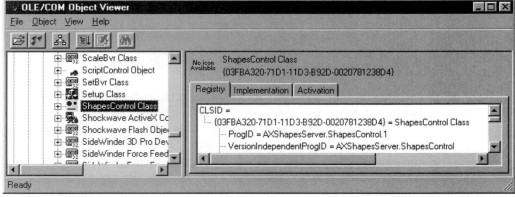

Adding a Custom Property to CShapesControl

The initial files generated by the ATL Object Wizard do indeed constitute a Full Control. You can compile the project and make use of the current functionality. However, your control does not have any unique support beyond a new Toolbox bitmap and a few COM categories. To build a custom coclass, we must extend the boilerplate code.

CShapesControl will allow the user to pick from a variety of graphical objects, which will be rendered on the control's view area. We will call this property ShapeType. Assume that ShapeType can only accept a small range of valid shapes, which would be best expressed by a custom enumeration. To begin defining the ShapeType property, add the following enumeration to your IDL file:

```
// A custom enumeration used with our custom property.
[uuid(6019BEB1-7307-11d3-B92D-0020781238D4), v1_enum]
typedef enum CURRENTSHAPE
{
    [helpstring("The Circle")] shapeCIRCLE      = 0,
    [helpstring("The Square")] shapeSQUARE      = 1,
    [helpstring("The Rect")]   shapeRECTANGLE   = 2
} CURRENTSHAPE;
```

Like any ATL COM object, we may add our new custom property using the Add Property Wizard (Figure 14-15). As for the type of property, specify CURRENTSHAPE (this is not available from the drop-down combo box, so manually enter the correct data type):

Figure 14-15: Adding the initial custom ShapeType property.

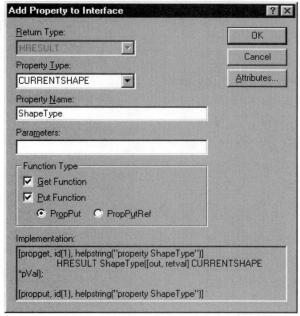

Now, add a member variable named m_shapeType (of type CURRENTSHAPE) to CShapesControl, and set the default type to shapeCIRCLE in the constructor. The get_ShapeType() method simply returns the current value of the m_shapeType value:

```
// Set default shape.
CShapesControl()
{
    m_bWindowOnly = TRUE;
    m_shapeType = shapeCIRCLE;
}
// Return the current type of shape.
STDMETHODIMP CShapesControl::get_ShapeType(CURRENTSHAPE *pVal)
{
    // Return the current value to container.
    *pVal = m_shapeType;
    return S_OK;
}
```

put_ShapeType() will set the value of m_shapeType (provided it is within bounds) and make a call to FireViewChange() to redraw the control:

```
// Set the value (if in range), and redraw the image.
STDMETHODIMP CShapesControl::put_ShapeType(SHAPETYPE newVal)
{
    // Check bounds.
    if(newVal >= shapeCIRCLE && newVal <= shapeRECTANGLE){
        m_shapeType = newVal;
        FireViewChange();
        return S_OK;
    }
    return E_FAIL;
}
```

FireViewChange() is defined by CComControl< >, and may be called whenever you need to inform the container it is time to be redrawn. ActiveX controls can be drawn under two circumstances: within a window or as a metafile (if you are an embedded object). The implementation of FireViewChange() tests for each possibility and places a WM_PAINT message into the queue, which is handled by OnDraw():

```
// As found in <atlctl.h>.
inline HRESULT CComControlBase::FireViewChange()
{
    if (m_bInPlaceActive)
    {
        // Active
        if (m_hWndCD != NULL)
            ::InvalidateRect(m_hWndCD, NULL, TRUE);          // Window based
        else if (m_spInPlaceSite != NULL)
            m_spInPlaceSite->InvalidateRect(NULL, TRUE);     // Windowless
    }
    else // Inactive
        SendOnViewChange(DVASPECT_CONTENT);
    return S_OK;
}
```

Rendering Your Control with OnDraw()

The default implementation of OnDraw() paints a simple string within the boundaries of the control. Of course you will typically delete much of this code as you paint the visual appearance of your custom object. Here is the initial logic behind OnDraw():

```
// OnDraw() is used when rendering the visual aspect of your control.
HRESULT OnDraw(ATL_DRAWINFO& di)
{
    RECT& rc = *(RECT*)di.prcBounds;
    Rectangle(di.hdcDraw, rc.left, rc.top, rc.right, rc.bottom);
    SetTextAlign(di.hdcDraw, TA_CENTER|TA_BASELINE);
    LPCTSTR pszText = _T("ATL 3.0 : ShapesControl");
    TextOut(di.hdcDraw,
        (rc.left + rc.right)/2,
        (rc.top + rc.bottom)/2,
        pszText,
        lstrlen(pszText));
```

```
    return S_OK;
}
```

OnDraw() takes a single parameter of type ATL_DRAWINFO. This structure is filled and formatted by the ATL framework, and contains a number of fields that prove very useful as you render your control. For example, you may obtain a valid device context by accessing the hdcDraw field. The dimensions of your current bounding rectangle are held within the prcBounds field. Under most circumstances, these two fields provide just enough information required to render your control. Just make use of the Win32 GDI functions and "paint the picture."

Many of the remaining fields of ATL_DRAWINFO are useful only if your control is being rendered into a Windows metafile, rather than directly into a window. This last statement illustrates a very important point: ActiveX controls can be rendered under two circumstances. First, the control may be asked to render itself directly into a window. In this case, the ATL framework will set NULL values for the fields relating to metafile rendering, and draws the image using a standard WM_PAINT message (as seen in the implementation of FireViewChange()).

Metafile rendering, on the other hand, takes place when your control is being rendered at <u>design time</u>, such as when you are building a VB solution, as well as when your control is hosted as an embedded object. A *metafile* is a visual snapshot of your control's visible appearance. When an ActiveX host container requires such a snapshot, it sends in a metafile HDC, a bounding rectangle, and a *drawing aspect*, which specifies the format the control should draw itself (icon, print preview format, thumbnail) as specified by the DVASPECT enumeration.

In either case, the code you add to the OnDraw() method will be used to render the image. If you ever wish to perform different blocks of drawing logic based on the type of rendering taking place (windowed or metafile), you can perform a simple test using GetDeviceCaps(), and test for a value of DT_METAFILE. The ATL_DRAWINFO structure is defined in <atlctl.h> as the following, with some comments for the more useful fields:

```
// This structure is formatted by the framework, and sent into OnDraw().
struct ATL_DRAWINFO
{
    UINT cbSize;                // Holds the size of this structure.
    DWORD dwDrawAspect;         // DVASPECT flag.
    LONG lindex;                // Amount to render (ignore).
    DVTARGETDEVICE* ptd;        // Information about the target device.
    HDC hicTargetDev;           // Metafile HDC.
    HDC hdcDraw;                // A valid HDC to use during rendering.
    LPCRECTL prcBounds;         // Rectangle in which to draw
    LPCRECTL prcWBounds;        // Metafile rectangle.
    BOOL bOptimize;             // Are we optimized?
    BOOL bZoomed;
    BOOL bRectInHimetric;       // Size in HIMETRIC coordinates.
    SIZEL ZoomNum;
    SIZEL ZoomDen;
};
```

Customizing OnDraw()

Our ShapesControl needs to render a shape within the view, based off the current value of m_shapeType. To begin refitting OnDraw() to suit our needs, we will test against the current shape, and render the image using a thick blue pen. This task requires that we drop down to the Win32 GDI function level. To create the pen, we need to make a call to CreatePen() and specify the pen style, width, and color (represented by the RGB macro). Once the pen is constructed, we select it into the device context (which we can obtain from ATL_DRAWINFO) and render the correct shape. When we are all finished with this drawing cycle, we restore the old pen (and thus restore the device context) with a second call to SelectObject(). Here is the relevant code:

```
// Using Win32 GDI calls, draw a circle, square, or rectangle based on
// the value of the ShapeType property.
HRESULT CShapesControl::OnDraw(ATL_DRAWINFO& di)
{
    // Let's get the HDC right away and use throughout this code.
    HDC hdc = di.hdcDraw;
    // Get the size of this view.
    RECT& rc = *(RECT*)di.prcBounds;
    Rectangle(hdc, rc.left, rc.top, rc.right, rc.bottom);
    // Configure a big blue pen.
    HPEN oldPen, newPen;
    newPen = CreatePen(PS_SOLID, 10, RGB(0, 0, 255));
    oldPen = (HPEN) SelectObject(hdc, newPen);
    // Which shape?
    switch(m_shapeType)
    {
    case shapeCIRCLE:
        Ellipse(hdc, rc.left, rc.top, rc.right, rc.bottom);
        break;
    case shapeSQUARE:
        Rectangle(hdc, rc.left, rc.top, rc.right, rc.bottom);
        break;
    case shapeRECTANGLE:
        Rectangle(hdc, rc.left + 20, rc.top + 30, rc.right - 20, rc.bottom - 30);
        break;
    }
    SelectObject(hdc, oldPen);
...
    return S_OK;
}
```

So far so good! We have a custom property that can control the shape rendered in the control's view. If you wish to run a simple test at this point, launch VB and insert your component using the Components dialog box. Place an instance of your control onto the VB form, select it, and examine the property window. As you can see, the ShapeType property has integrated into the VB IDE (Figure 14-16).

Figure 14-16: Our custom ShapeType property.

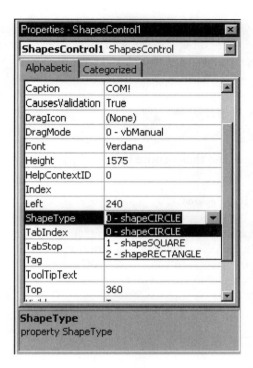

Go ahead and change the value a few times. You should see the image rendered in your control update when you commit the changes.

Rigging Up the Caption and Font Stock Properties

When we began this project, we specified support for the stock Caption property. The Object Wizard responded by adding CStockPropImpl<> into our inheritance chain and by placing a CComBSTR member variable (m_bstrCaption) into our class. Because ATL is taking care of the [propput] and [propget] implementation for us, all we need to do is use m_bstrCaption when we see fit. For this control, we will center the caption into the control's view area. Here are the changes we need to make to our current OnDraw() implementation:

```
// Render the value in the Caption stock property.
// Don't forget to define USES_CONVERSION; within scope of OnDraw().
SetTextAlign(di.hdcDraw, TA_CENTER|TA_BASELINE);
TextOut(di.hdcDraw,
    (rc.left + rc.right)/2,
    (rc.top + rc.bottom)/2,
    W2A(m_bstrCaption),
    m_bstrCaption.Length());
```

With this additional change to OnDraw(), we can now modify the Caption property (at design or run time) and have the view render the correct string. To fully finish up our control's text manipulation logic, we should account for the stock Font property. To represent the current Font selection, we have been provided an IFontDisp data member, wrapped up within an ATL smart pointer. The IFontDisp interface is implemented by a COM font object, which also supports the more general IFont interface. From an IFont interface, we can obtain the underlying HFONT data member and use it to set our device context. Thus, to make use of the Font stock property will require us to query the m_pFont smart pointer for IID_IFont, and from there, grab the HFONT itself. Add the following code (before your call to TextOut()) to OnDraw():

```
// Draw the Caption stock property with the correct font.
HFONT oldFont, newFont;
CComQIPtr<IFont, &IID_IFont> pFont(m_pFont);
if (pFont != NULL)
{
    pFont->get_hFont(&newFont);
    pFont->AddRefHfont(newFont);
    oldFont = (HFONT) SelectObject(hdc, newFont);
}
```

The other font-related detail is to configure an initial font for our ActiveX control to use when first placed into a container. In the constructor of your control, you will need to configure a FONTDESC (font description) structure and create a COM font object using OleCreateFontIndirect(). Here is the updated constructor:

```
// Set a start-up font.
CShapesControl()
{
    m_bWindowOnly = TRUE;
    m_shapeType = shapeCIRCLE;
    m_bstrCaption = "Yo!";
    m_clrBackColor = RGB(255, 255, 0);
    // Create a default font to use with this control.
    static FONTDESC _fontDesc =
    { sizeof(FONTDESC), OLESTR("Times New Roman"),
    FONTSIZE(12), FW_BOLD, ANSI_CHARSET, FALSE, FALSE, FALSE };
    OleCreateFontIndirect( &_fontDesc, IID_IFontDisp, (void **)&m_pFont);
}
```

Setting the BackColor

To finish accessing our stock properties, we need to make use of the member variable representing our current BackColor (m_clrBackColor of type OLE_COLOR). This [automation] compliant data type is the standard COM way to represent a combination of red, green, and blue values (the RGB macro can be used to specify the range of each as seen in the constructor code of CShapesControl). As the Win32 GDI functions work with the window's COLORREF type, we must make a call to OleTranslateColor() before calling the GDI functions to render the color of the controls background. Here is the final and complete implementation of OnDraw() given this final adjustment:

```
// The completed OnDraw().
HRESULT CShapesControl::OnDraw(ATL_DRAWINFO& di)
{
    USES_CONVERSION;
    COLORREF colBack;
    HBRUSH oldBrush, newBrush;
    HPEN oldPen, newPen;
    HFONT oldFont, newFont;
```

```
// Let's get the HDC right away and use throughout this code.
HDC hdc = di.hdcDraw;
// Get the size of this view.
RECT& rc = *(RECT*)di.prcBounds;
Rectangle(hdc, rc.left, rc.top, rc.right, rc.bottom);
// Fill the background using the BackColor stock property.
OleTranslateColor(m_clrBackColor, NULL, &colBack);
newBrush = (HBRUSH) CreateSolidBrush(colBack);
oldBrush = (HBRUSH) SelectObject(hdc, newBrush);
FillRect(hdc, &rc, newBrush);
// Draw the correct shape with a big blue pen.
newPen = CreatePen(PS_SOLID, 10, RGB(0, 0, 255));
oldPen = (HPEN) SelectObject(hdc, newPen);
switch(m_shapeType)
{
case shapeCIRCLE:
     Ellipse(hdc, rc.left, rc.top, rc.right, rc.bottom);
     break;
case shapeSQUARE:
     Rectangle(hdc, rc.left, rc.top, rc.right, rc.bottom);
     break;
case shapeRECTANGLE:
     Rectangle(hdc, rc.left + 20, rc.top + 30, rc.right - 20, rc.bottom - 30);
     break;
}
// Draw the Caption stock property with the correct font.
CComQIPtr<IFont, &IID_IFont> pFont(m_pFont);
if (pFont != NULL)
{
     pFont->get_hFont(&newFont);
     pFont->AddRefHfont(newFont);          // Lock font for use.
     oldFont = (HFONT) SelectObject(hdc, newFont);
}
SetTextAlign(hdc, TA_CENTER|TA_BASELINE);
SetBkMode(hdc, TRANSPARENT);
TextOut(hdc, (rc.left + rc.right)/2, (rc.top + rc.bottom)/2,
          W2A(m_bstrCaption), m_bstrCaption.Length());
// Reset DC & clean up.
SelectObject(hdc, oldPen);
SelectObject(hdc, oldBrush);
SelectObject(hdc, oldFont);
pFont->ReleaseHfont(newFont);              // Free font.
return S_OK;
}
```

Again, as you can see, building a control with ATL does demand that you gain (or already have) comfort with the Win32 API. Unlike MFC ActiveX control development, you are not provided with numerous utility classes (such as CPen, CBrush, CDC, and so on) that wrap raw handles.

If we load up ShapesControl into VB, we are now able to manipulate the Caption, BackColor, and Font stock properties using the VB property window. Here is one such configuration:

Figure 14-17: Exercising our properties.

Firing a Custom Event

Like any COM object, ActiveX controls may send events to any interested client. In fact, ActiveX controls typically send a number of events, many in response to some user interaction. Adding an event to an ATL control is exactly the same as adding an event to any other coclass. For our purpose, we will keep things simple and fire out a COM event whenever the mouse has clicked ShapesControl. Add the following method to your [default, source] dispinterface:

```
// We will send out the (x, y) of where we were clicked.
dispinterface _IShapesControlEvents
{
    properties:
    methods:
    [id(1), helpstring("method ClickedControl")]
    HRESULT ClickedControl([in] short X, [in] short Y);
};
```

Next, compile your project, and using the Implement Connection Point Wizard, bring in support for the connection proxy. When you go back to examine the code changes, you will see that you are now derived from CProxy_IShapesControlEvents<>, and your connection map has been updated (probably incorrectly) with a new CONNECTION_POINT_ENTRY macro. Be sure your entry uses the correct "DIID_" prefix.

As CProxy_IShapesControlEvents<> has defined the Fire_ControlClicked() method, we now need to raise this event when our control receives a WM_LBUTTONDOWN event. Use the Add Windows Message Handler Wizard (as detailed in Chapter 13) to intercept this event. As you know, this will result in an additional MESSAGE_HANDLER macro entry used to route the flow of execution to the function handling this message. In the wizard-supplied stub code, call Fire_ControlClicked(), passing to the container the (x, y) location of the mouse cursor (here is an example of the need to "crack" out some information from the LPARAM parameter):

```
// Tell the container we have been clicked at location (x, y)
LRESULT OnLButtonDown(UINT uMsg, WPARAM wParam, LPARAM lParam,
BOOL& bHandled)
{
    // Figure out (x, y) and fire event.
    short xPos = LOWORD(lParam);
    short yPos = HIWORD(lParam);
    Fire_ClickedControl(xPos, yPos);
    return 0;
}
```

To extend the VB tester to capture our event, add two Label objects onto the main form. In the handler for the ClickedControl event, add the following (output in Figure 14-18):

```
' Your event has integrated into the VB IDE, just
' like an intrinsic control.
'
Private Sub ShapesControl1_ClickedControl(ByVal X
As Integer, ByVal Y As Integer)
    LabelX.Caption = "X Position: " & X
```

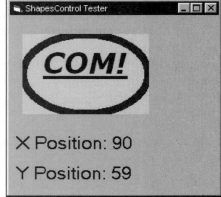

Figure 14-18: Responding to the custom event.

```
        LabelY.Caption = "Y Position: " & Y
End Sub
```

Configuring Property Persistence

If you have been fooling around with our VB test client, you may have noticed a strange pattern. When you set the various properties of your control at design time things seem fine. Your ShapeType setting holds, and you can see the effects of selecting various settings from the VB property window. However, when you run the program, you are always placed back at the default shapeCIRCLE value defined in the constructor of ShapesControl. Even stranger, the BackColor, Caption, and Font properties all seem to be "remembered" at run time.

As pointed out earlier in this chapter, the ATL Object Wizard has added a new item called a *property map*, which is in charge of saving and loading the values of your custom properties via the COM persistence model. ATL always ensures that any stock property is saved and loaded correctly when asked to do so by a container; however, the job of persisting your custom properties is up to you. We will hold off on the details behind COM persistence and the property map for now; however, adding the correct support to save your custom properties is painless. Simply add a new PROP_ENTRY macro for each custom property. The first parameter is the name of the property you are persisting, followed by the DISPID used to identify it:

```
// Persisting our custom ShapeType property.
BEGIN_PROP_MAP(CShapesControl)
    PROP_DATA_ENTRY("_cx", m_sizeExtent.cx, VT_UI4)
    PROP_DATA_ENTRY("_cy", m_sizeExtent.cy, VT_UI4)
    PROP_ENTRY("BackColor", DISPID_BACKCOLOR, CLSID_StockColorPage)
    PROP_ENTRY("Caption", DISPID_CAPTION, CLSID_NULL)
    PROP_ENTRY("Font", DISPID_FONT, CLSID_StockFontPage)
    // Example entries
    // PROP_ENTRY("Property Description", dispid, clsid)
    // PROP_PAGE(CLSID_StockColorPage)
    PROP_ENTRY("ShapeType", 1, CLSID_NULL)
END_PROP_MAP()
```

Because we do not yet have a property page used to edit the ShapeType property, we can enter CLSID_NULL as the final parameter to the PROP_ENTRY macro. If you now go back and test your control from within VB, you will see that the values you set at design time are correctly held over into run time, as well as between sessions.

Adding a Custom AboutBox to ShapesControl

I am sure you are proud of your new ActiveX control. Most people who write controls with ATL are exceptionally proud of their work, and it is only fitting that we create a standard About box to show off just a bit. As it turns out, COM defines a (very) small number of stock methods that all ActiveX containers understand. Unlike stock properties, ATL does not provide a default implementation of stock methods. On the other hand, COM always assumes the following DISPIDs for each stock method:

Stock Method	DISPID	Meaning in Life
AboutBox	DISPID_ABOUTBOX	Shows a standard About box.
Refresh	DISPID_REFRESH	Redraws the control.
DoClick	DISPID_DOCLICK	Simulates a mouse click.

To add support for DISPID_ABOUTBOX, begin by adding a new method to your [default] interface, and change the DISPID of the member to DISPID_ABOUTBOX. The name of the method called in response to DISPID_ABOUTBOX is irrelevant, but it makes sense to name our method AboutBox():

```
// Add the following to your [default] interface.
[id(DISPID_ABOUTBOX), helpstring("method AboutBox")]
HRESULT AboutBox();
```

Recall from the last chapter that ATL provides the CSimpleDialog<> template when you need to show a dialog with minimal fuss and bother. About boxes usually have little user interaction, so we will make use of CSimpleDialog<> in the implementation of our AboutBox() method. First, however, we need to insert a new dialog resource. Feel free to be creative when designing your About box, and assign a relevant resource ID. As for the code behind AboutBox(), this is all you need:

```
// Implementing the stock AboutBox() method.
STDMETHODIMP CShapesControl::AboutBox()
{
    // Show the about box.
    CSimpleDialog<IDD_ABOUT> dlg;
    dlg.DoModal();
    return S_OK;
}
```

Now, how you access this dialog will vary among IDEs. In Visual Basic, you will find that the properties window has a special property named About located at the top of the property list. When you select this option, you will trigger the code above:

Figure 14-19: The custom About box for ShapesControl.

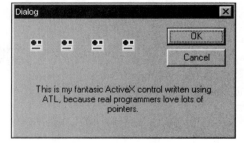

Completing the VB Test Client

The ShapesControl now has enough functionality to build a full test client (we will add support for property pages later in the chapter). Place a group of radio buttons onto the main form to allow the user to select the desired shape at run time. To keep each radio button mutually exclusive, VB demands that you draw the frame object <u>first</u> and then draw each radio button directly into the frame:

Figure 14-20:
The VB client.

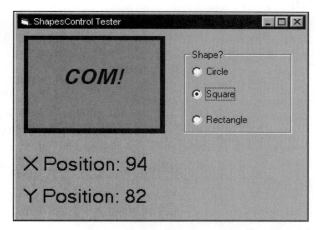

I am sure you can gather what the code behind this GUI looks like. Set the ShapeType property to the correct value based on which radio button was clicked, for example:

```
' Setting our property at runtime.
'
Private Sub OptionSquare_Click()
    ShapesControl1.ShapeType = shapeSQUARE
End Sub
```

That wraps up the major code behind the ATL ShapesControl project. Before we move on to take a deeper look as to how all this ATL code works under the hood, the following lab will give you a chance to build another (more interesting) ActiveX control. This new project not only reinforces all the topics presented so far, but also supplies additional logic for bitmap rendering, as well as illustrating some simple animation techniques.

Debugging ActiveX Controls

Before you begin, let me point out that the process of debugging an ActiveX control is very much like debugging a simple coclass. You may select an EXE to host your control during a debug session (using the Project | Setting selection). As well, Visual Studio supports a helpful tool called the ActiveX Control Test Container, which you can run from your Tools menu (you can also select this tool as the debugging host). When you launch this utility you are able to insert your control and change properties and methods, capture events, and so forth. This tool has a number of bells and whistles, which can help track down bugs and test the intended behavior of your object. Feel free to use this tool throughout the labs if you wish. Our initial test client will be VB; however, we will also host our control in a web page later in this chapter. Now, onto the lab!

Lab 14-1: Building a Full ActiveX Control with ATL

This lab will allow you to build a non-trivial ActiveX control with the ATL framework. You will be pulling together all of the materials presented thus far to build a control with support for connection points, COM properties and methods, windowing features (an About box), and so on. As well, this lab will introduce you to basic animation techniques, as our control will have the ability to cycle through a number of bitmap images based on the internal state of the object. This lab will also serve as the basis for the next lab in this chapter, where we extend its functionality with "bindable" properties, persistence, and a custom property page.

The solution for this lab can be found on your CD-ROM under:
Labs\Chapter 14\AXCarServer
Labs\Chapter 14\AXCarServer\VB Client

Step One: Prepare the Project Workspace and Resources

Create a new in-process server named **AxCarServer** with the ATL COM AppWizard, using the remaining defaults. Next, insert a Full Control using the ATL Object Wizard. From the Names tab, enter **AxCar** into the short name field, and leave all other names as is. From the Attributes tab, add support for connection points. This lab does not use COM's exception handling support, so you can leave that option unselected. Now, from the Miscellaneous tab, the only extra selections you need to make are to check the Insertable and Windowed Only features (Figure 14-21). These options set up our control to supply its own window, and be "insertable" into OLE document containers. We do not need any stock properties for this project, as the bitmap images will fill the entire space of the control. When you have made your selections, close the Object Wizard.

Figure 14-21:
Our control is in charge of supplying the window, and may be inserted as an embedded object.

This control will illustrate simple animation by displaying a number of bitmaps based on the internal state of the automobile. For example, if the car is safely below the maximum speed, we will cycle through three bitmaps that show our car driving down the road. If the current speed is approaching the maximum speed, we will cycle through four images, with the fourth showing the car beginning to break down. Finally, if we have cracked the engine block (i.e., hit the max speed), we cycle over five images, with the final image showing a fatal explosion. Given these design requirements, your next task is to create five new bitmaps for display.

Using the Visual Studio resource editor, insert five new bitmaps (**Insert | Resource**) and show off your artistic abilities. You may be a great graphic artist, but I would not apply that title to myself. My images express my feelings about my first automobile (a lemon).

Be sure to assign meaningful resource IDs to each bitmap. To do so, right-click on the bitmap resource from your Bitmap folder in ResourceView and select **Properties**.

The images used in this lab are shown in Figures 14-22 through 14-26. Notice that the clouds move towards the left as the images advance. Also notice the exhaust coming out of the automobile is a bit different on each frame to help further the animation. As well, the fourth image (IDB_ALMOSTBLOWNUP) shows some red smoke rising from the car, while the final image (IDB_BLOWNUP) displays a doomed automobile.

Figure 14-22:
IDB_LEMON1

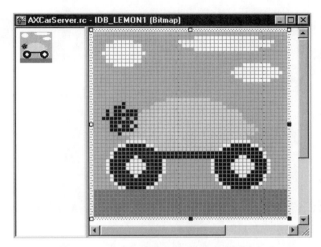

Figure 14-23:
IDB_LEMON2

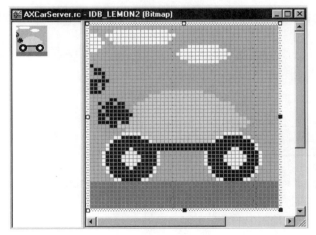

Figure 14-24:
IDB_LEMON3

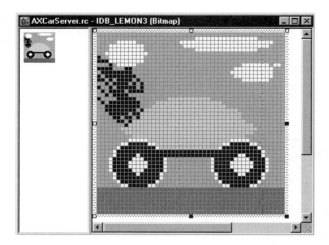

Figure 14-25:
IDB_ALMOST-
BLOWNUP

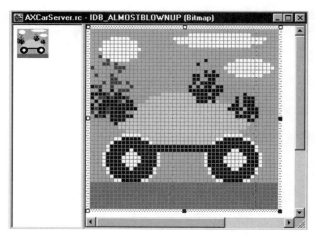

Figure 14-26:
IDB_BLOWNUP

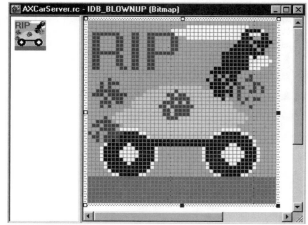

To finish up our resource editing, you may wish to change the default toolbar bitmap to personalize your control. Recall that IDEs will used this image to represent your control in the toolbox at design time. Once you have created your new bitmaps we are ready to get to the next step and populate our [default] interface.

Step Two: Design Our Custom Interface

Given that ActiveX controls can be used from "dispinterface only" clients, you know that your control should export all of its functionality from the single [default] interface (as dumb clients have no way to query for others). We will be adding the following methods to IAxCar: SpeedUp(), CreateCar(), and AboutBox() as well as the following properties: Animate, Speed, MaxSpeed, and PetName. The DISPIDs for the custom items can be left to their defaults; however, be sure to assign the predefined value DISPID_ABOUTBOX to AboutBox(). To integrate more fully into the container at design time, the Animate property will make use of a custom enumeration. Here is the IDL (feel free to use the ATL CASE tools, where appropriate, to populate the interface):

```
// A custom enum used to set the animation.
[uuid(8FB31CF0-7490-11d3-B92E-0020781238D4), v1_enum]
typedef enum AnimVal
{
    [helpstring("Animate")]            Yes  = 1,
    [helpstring("Don't Animate")]      No   = 0
} AnimVal;
// Our default dual interface.
[object, uuid(65A0EEBF-745F-11D3-B92E-0020781238D4), dual,
helpstring("IAxCar Interface"),pointer_default(unique) ]
interface IAxCar : IDispatch
{
    [id(1), helpstring("Add 10 to current speed")]
    HRESULT SpeedUp();
    [id(2), helpstring("Set the name and max speed of the car")]
    HRESULT CreateCar([in] BSTR petName, [in] short maxSp);
    [propget, id(3), helpstring("Should I animate?")]
    HRESULT Animate([out, retval] AnimVal *newVal);
    [propput, id(3), helpstring("Should I animate?")]
    HRESULT Animate([in] AnimVal newVal);
    [propget, id(4), helpstring("The max speed")]
    HRESULT MaxSpeed([out, retval] short *pVal);
    [propput, id(4), helpstring("The max speed")]
    HRESULT MaxSpeed([in] short newVal);
    [propget, id(5), helpstring("Car's pet name")]
    HRESULT PetName([out, retval] BSTR *pVal);
    [propput, id(5), helpstring("Car's pet name")]
    HRESULT PetName([in] BSTR newVal);
    [propget, id(6), helpstring("Current speed")]
    HRESULT Speed([out, retval] short *pVal);
    [propput, id(6), helpstring("Current speed")]
    HRESULT Speed([in] short newVal);
    [id(DISPID_ABOUTBOX), helpstring("About AxCars")]
    HRESULT AboutBox();
};
```

Step Three: Implement the Custom Properties

CAxCar will need to make use of the following member variables to implement your custom properties. Add them to your private sector, and assign default values in your constructor:

```
// CAxCar's initial private data.
short m_maxSpeed;                    // Holds the car's max speed.
CComBSTR m_bstrPetName;              // Holds the car's pet name.
AnimVal m_bAnimate;                  // Holds animation flag (Yes or No)
short m_currSpeed;                   // Holds the car's current speed.
// Constructor.
CAxCar()
{
    m_bWindowOnly = TRUE;            // Must ensure a valid handle.
    m_maxSpeed = 0;
    m_bstrPetName = L"";
    m_currSpeed = 0;
    m_bAnimate = No;
}
```

Implementing Animate, Speed, MaxSpeed, and PetName should be old hat to you by now. The [propput] method makes a new assignment to the correct data member, and the [propget] returns the correct value. Flesh out the details of each property, and move on to step 4.

Step Four: Implement the CreateCar() and AboutBox() Methods

The CreateCar() method should also pose no problems. Simply assign the private state variables to the incoming parameters. Even though we expose each data point as a custom property, this method allows the activating client to save a round trip when creating the control:

```
// Set state data.
STDMETHODIMP CAxCar::CreateCar(BSTR petName, short maxSp)
{
    m_maxSpeed = maxSp;
    m_bstrPetName = petName;
    return S_OK;
}
```

Now as for the AboutBox() method, we first need to create a new dialog resource. Go ahead and do so now. We will be making use of the CSimpleDialog<> template we examined in Chapter 13 to show our dialog. Recall that the only required parameter to this ATL template is the resource ID of the dialog. Figure 14-27 gives an example, which uses a Picture Holder widget to show the IDB_BLOWNUP image.

Figure 14-27:
IDD_ABOUTBOX

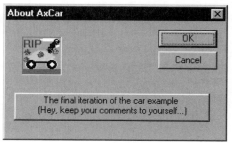

Now that we have a dialog resource, implementing AboutBox() is a no-brainer:

```
// Show who made this lovely control.
// (be sure to include resource.h!)
STDMETHODIMP CAxCar::AboutBox()
{
    CSimpleDialog<IDD_ABOUTBOX> d;
    d.DoModal();
    return S_OK;
}
```

Because we have assigned this method to the well-known DISPID_ABOUTBOX, the end user can trigger the code in our AboutBox() method from the IDE. In Visual Basic, this is available from the (About) property found in the Property Window, as seen in Figure 14-28:

Figure 14-28:
This will trigger
the code in your
AboutBox()
method.

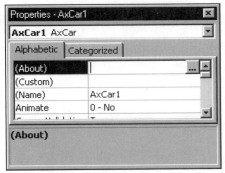

Step Five: Build Our [default, source] Interface

The CAxCar coclass is capable of firing two events to the container. The first event will be sent when the car is about to explode (10 miles below the maximum speed). The second event will be sent when the car does explode. Add the following methods to your [default, source] dispinterface:

```
// Feel free to use the Add Method CASE tool.
[uuid(65A0EEC1-745F-11D3-B92E-0020781238D4),
helpstring("_IAxCarEvents Interface")]
dispinterface _IAxCarEvents
{
    properties:
    methods:
    [id(1), helpstring("method BlewUp")] HRESULT BlewUp();
    [id(2), helpstring("method AboutToBlow")] HRESULT AboutToBlow();
};
```

Now, build the connection point proxy class using the Implement Connection Point Wizard, after you have recompiled your IDL file. As we have seen in Chapter 12, this tool will add a new proxy class to your inheritance chain which defines the Fire_XXX() methods for use in your class. We will send these events in a moment. Also recall from Chapter 12 that this CASE tool tends to add the incorrect entry to your connection map. Be sure your map specifies the "DIID_" prefix for your event interface:

```
// Fix the bug...
BEGIN_CONNECTION_POINT_MAP(CAxCar)
```

```
        CONNECTION_POINT_ENTRY(IID_IPropertyNotifySink)
        CONNECTION_POINT_ENTRY(DIID__IAxCarEvents)
END_CONNECTION_POINT_MAP()
```

Step Six: Add the Animation Logic Variables

Now that we have built the basic infrastructure of CAxCar, we can focus on the logic responsible for rendering the bitmaps in an animation cycle. To begin this process, we need to add a few more data members to our private sector. First, we will define an array of HBITMAPs to hold the five bitmap images we designed in step one. As well, we need a variable to identify the current frame in the animation. Recall that we will be showing from three to five bitmaps during the animation loop. If the car is safely below the maximum limit, we render the first three. If we are about to blow up, we render the first four. If we did blow up, we render all five. To help avoid "magic numbers," we will also define some constants to hold the current maximum frames. Add the following constants to the header file of CAxCar:

```
// Some constants to refer to what the images are used for.
const int MAX_IMAGES      = 5;  // Total number of images.
const int MAX_NORMAL      = 3;  // Upper frame limit for safe speed.
const int ABOUT_TO_BLOW   = 4;  // Upper frame limit for about to die.
const int BLOWN_UP        = 5;  // Upper frame limit for destroyed car.
```

As well, here is the complete set of private data for CAxCar:

```
// Need more data!
short m_maxSpeed;                  // Holds the car's max speed.
CComBSTR m_bstrPetName;            // Holds the car's pet name.
short m_currSpeed;                 // Holds the car's current speed.
HBITMAP m_carImage[MAX_IMAGES];    // An array of bitmaps to render.
AnimVal m_bAnimate;                // Holds animation flag (Yes or No)
short m_currImage;                 // Holds the current image in the array.
short m_currMaxFrames;             // Holds the number of frames to cycle over.
```

Now, let's fill up our HBITMAP array with the bitmap resource IDs. For this animation cycle to work correctly, it is very important that the numerical values of your bitmap IDs are <u>in order</u>. If you added images sequentially, this should already be the case. To be sure, however, open up your <resource.h> file (**File | Open**) and be sure your IDs are arranged correctly:

```
// Your <resource.h> file should have an (n+1) numbering scheme.
#define IDB_LEMON1          201
#define IDB_LEMON2          202
#define IDB_LEMON3          203
#define IDB_ALMOSTBLOWNUP   204
#define IDB_BLOWNUP         205
```

Override FinalConstruct() in your CAxCar class, and load up your images using the LoadBitmap() API call. The first parameter to this function is the HINSTANCE of your control, which can be obtained from the project-wide CComModule global variable. Notice that we are using IDB_LEMON1 (the resource ID of the first bitmap) as a baseline:

```
// Load up all bitmaps.
HRESULT FinalConstruct()
{
    for(int i = 0; i < MAX_IMAGES; i++)
```

```
        {
            m_carImage[i] =
            LoadBitmap(_Module.m_hInst,
                MAKEINTRESOURCE(IDB_LEMON1 + i));
        }
        return S_OK;
}
```

Next, override FinalRelease() to free up the bitmap handles using DeleteObject():

```
// Free up the resources.
void FinalRelease()
{
    for(int i = 0; i < MAX_IMAGES; i++)
        DeleteObject(m_carImage[i]);
}
```

The remaining new data members (m_currMaxFrames and m_currImage) can be assigned in the constructor as so:

```
// Set all new state data.
CAxCar()
{
    m_bWindowOnly = TRUE;   // Must ensure a valid handle.
    m_maxSpeed = 0;
    m_bstrPetName = L"";
    m_currSpeed = 0;
    m_bAnimate = No;
    m_currImage = 0;
    m_currMaxFrames = MAX_NORMAL;
}
```

Step Seven: Configure the Timer

To cycle among the bitmap images, we will need some way to advance the current frame. For this lab, we will advance the current frame from within a WM_TIMER handler. Use the Add Windows Message Handler Wizard to route a WM_TIMER message to your CAxCar class. This will update your message map and add stub code for a method named OnTimer(). The implementation of this method needs to increment the current frame, and test against the current maximum frame (which could be from three to five, based on the speed of the car). When you have advanced the frame, force a redraw of the control via FireViewChange():

```
// Increase the frame and test for upper bounds.
// Redraw when finished.
LRESULT CAxCar::OnTimer(UINT uMsg, WPARAM wParam, LPARAM lParam, BOOL& bHandled)
{
    // If we are at the max, reset to the first frame.
    m_currImage = m_currImage + 1;
    if(m_currImage >= m_currMaxFrames)
        m_currImage = 0;
    FireViewChange();
    return 0;
}
```

Now that OnTimer() is ready to advance our frame, we need to enable a window timer. Go to your current implementation of the Animate property, and edit it to call SetTimer() or

KillTimer() based on the AnimVal parameter. This will allow your end user to start and stop the animation cycle through a COM property:

```
// Create or terminate the timer.
STDMETHODIMP CAxCar::put_Animate(AnimVal newVal)
{
    // Set the animation property.
    m_bAnimate = newVal;
    // Test for a valid window before calling these CWindow methods.
    if(::IsWindow(m_hWnd) && (m_bAnimate == Yes))
        SetTimer(1, 250);
    else if(::IsWindow(m_hWnd))
        KillTimer(1);
    return S_OK;
}
```

The last step we need to do before actually rendering the bitmaps in OnDraw() is to advance the current max frame variable. We will do this in the SpeedUp() method. After advancing m_currMaxFrames, send out each of your custom events:

```
// Set the current upper limit of frames and send out our custom events.
STDMETHODIMP CAxCar::SpeedUp()
{
    // Speed up and check for problems...
    m_currSpeed += 10;
    // About to explode?
    if((m_maxSpeed - m_currSpeed) <= 10)
    {
        Fire_AboutToBlow();
        m_currMaxFrames = ABOUT_TO_BLOW;
    }
    // Maxed out?
    if(m_currSpeed >= m_maxSpeed)
    {
        m_currSpeed = m_maxSpeed;
        Fire_BlewUp();
        m_currMaxFrames = BLOWN_UP;
    }
    return S_OK;
}
```

Step Eight: Draw the Images

Everything is now in place! The last detail is to render the correct bitmap within our implementation of OnDraw(). The code behind OnDraw() is not too nasty, but ATL does force you to drop to the Win32 API. Here is the full implementation:

```
// Draw our bitmaps.
HRESULT CAxCar::OnDraw(ATL_DRAWINFO& di)
{
    RECT& rc = *(RECT*)di.prcBounds;
    Rectangle(di.hdcDraw, rc.left, rc.top, rc.right, rc.bottom);
    BITMAP bmInfo;
    HBITMAP oldBitmap;
    HBITMAP newBitmap;
    HDC memDC;
    SIZE size;
```

```
    // Get the stats on the current image.
    GetObject(m_carImage[m_currImage], sizeof(bmInfo), &bmInfo);
    size.cx = bmInfo.bmWidth;
    size.cy = bmInfo.bmHeight;
    // Grab the current image.
    newBitmap = m_carImage[m_currImage];
    // Create offscreen DC and select object into it.
    memDC = CreateCompatibleDC(di.hdcDraw);
    oldBitmap = (HBITMAP)SelectObject(memDC, newBitmap);
    // Now transfer to screen.
    StretchBlt(di.hdcDraw, rc.left, rc.top, rc.right, rc.bottom,
            memDC, 0, 0, size.cx, size.cy, SRCCOPY);
    // Clean up.
    SelectObject(di.hdcDraw, oldBitmap);
    DeleteDC(memDC);
    return S_OK;
}
```

So to recap what we have accomplished, here is the basic flow of animation logic: The Animate property is used to start and stop the animation. Internally this will create or kill a timer resource. The WM_TIMER method handler is responsible for increasing the current frame, while checking m_currMaxFrames for overflow. The value of m_currMaxFrames represents the upper limit of frames, which is adjusted by the SpeedUp() logic.

Step Nine: A Visual Basic Container

For ease of use, we will use VB as our test container. Begin by creating a new Standard EXE workspace, and insert your control using the **Project | Components** menu selection:

Figure 14-29:
Inserting our
control.

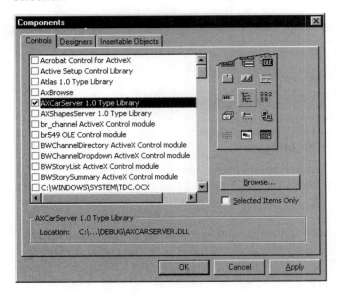

When you close this dialog box, you should see your control's toolbar bitmap pop up in the VB Toolbox. Create a GUI which allows the user to enter a pet name and maximum speed for the CAxCar object, as well as buttons to speed up and create the car. Finally, place a Label control on your form to print out diagnostic messages based on the control's incoming events, and another to hold the current speed. Here is one possible design (Figure 14-30) and the code behind it:

Figure 14-30: The VB test client.

```
' Event sinks.
'
Private Sub AxCar1_AboutToBlow()
    lblEventMsg.Caption = "Your car is about to blow up, careful!"
End Sub
Private Sub AxCar1_BlewUp()
    lblEventMsg.Caption = "Your car has EXPLODED!"
End Sub
' Create the car and start animation.
'
Private Sub btnMakeCar_Click()
    AxCar1.CreateCar txtPetName, txtMaxSpeed
    AxCar1.Animate = Yes
End Sub
' Speed up. This will adjust the images you see
' based on the current max frame.
'
Private Sub btnSpeedUp_Click()
    AxCar1.SpeedUp
    lblCurrSpeed.Caption = "Current Speed: " & AxCar1.Speed
End Sub
' Show control defaults in edit boxes when starting
'
Private Sub Form_Load()
    txtPetName = AxCar1.petName
    txtMaxSpeed = AxCar1.MaxSpeed
End Sub
```

Go ahead and run your project. You should see your car animate down the road, getting progressively more worn down based on your current speed.

Figure 14-31: Approaching critical speed!

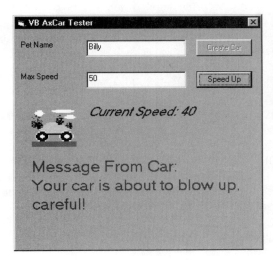

That wraps up the first iteration of our ActiveX CoCar control. As you have seen, developing a control can take a bit of work, even with this simple tester coclass. Now that you have built a control with ATL, it is time to look deeper into the framework and begin to examine these new ATL templates.

Framework Support: CComControl<> and IPropertyNotifySinkCP<>

ATL controls inherit a majority of their functionality from the CComControl<> template and its base classes, CComControlBase<> and CWindowImpl<>:

```
// CComControl is a core base class to any full control.
template <class T, class WinBase = CWindowImpl< T > >
class ATL_NO_VTABLE CComControl : public CComControlBase, public WinBase
{
public:
...
};
```

The functionality provided by CComControl<> itself is not too elaborate. Beyond providing a default message map which is chained together in your derived class (as we saw earlier in the chapter), CComControl<> provides implementations for the methods of the COM interface IPropertyNotifySink. The definition of this interface is found in <ocidl.idl>:

```
// If a control implements this interface, it is able to inform the container
// when a given property has changed, or is about to change.
[ object, uuid(9BFBBC02-EFF1-101A-84ED-00AA00341D07)]
interface IPropertyNotifySink : IUnknown
{
    // Item DISPID has changed.
    HRESULT OnChanged( [in] DISPID dispID );
    // Item DISPID is about to change, OK with you?
    HRESULT OnRequestEdit( [in] DISPID dispID);
};
```

This interface is used to establish another type of connection between the control and client beyond a typical IConnectionPointContainer interaction used to handle your custom events. IPropertyNotifySink is used to inform a client when a given property in the [default] interface has changed or is about to change, giving the client a chance to react. Like a standard connectable object, the host container will create a sink to receive events from the IPropertyNotifySink interface, and your class will call the methods of the IPropertyNotifySink proxy to notify the container when necessary. CComControl<> provides an implementation of each method for you using FireOnChanged() and FireOnRequestEdit().

If you examine your inheritance chain for CShapesControl, you will see that one of your base classes is named IPropertyNotifySinkCP<>. This ATL template is used to bring in the signatures for the two methods of IPropertyNotifySink, via a typedef to another ATL class, _ATL_PROP_NOTIFY_EVENT_CLASS. The levels of indirection are common in ATL source code, and while it may seem like a bit of a maze, it does allow you to extend the framework where you see fit. Here are the relevant players used to support the IPropertyNotifySink interface:

```
// IPropertyNotifySinkCP is one of your base classes, which indirectly brings
// in support for IPropertyNotifySink.
template <class T, class CDV = CComDynamicUnkArray >
class ATL_NO_VTABLE IPropertyNotifySinkCP :
    public IConnectionPointImpl<T, &IID_IPropertyNotifySink, CDV>
{
public:
    typedef CFirePropNotifyEvent _ATL_PROP_NOTIFY_EVENT_CLASS;
};
// CFakeFirePropNotifyEvent sets the stub code for the methods of IPropertyNotifySink,
// but CComControl<> implements them.
class CFakeFirePropNotifyEvent
{
public:
    static HRESULT FireOnRequestEdit(IUnknown* /*pUnk*/, DISPID /*dispID*/)
    {
        return S_OK;
    }
    static HRESULT FireOnChanged(IUnknown* /*pUnk*/, DISPID /*dispID*/)
    {
        return S_OK;
    }
};
typedef CFakeFirePropNotifyEvent _ATL_PROP_NOTIFY_EVENT_CLASS;
```

Supporting [bindable] and [requestedit] Properties

So now that you have support for IPropertyNotifySink, when might we indeed call FireOnRequestEdit() and FireOnChanged()? First off, you should not call these methods unless the properties you are providing notifications for have been marked with the IDL [requestedit] and [bindable] attributes. Those properties marked with [requestedit] should call FireOnRequestEdit() within any [propput] implementation <u>before</u> changing the value. This will in effect say to the container, "Hey, I want to change this property, got a problem with this?" The container might very well say, "Yes I have a problem with that; don't change the value just yet or you will mess things up on my end" and return a failed

HRESULT to you. If you wish to give your container the chance to vote on your property assignments, first add the [requestedit] attribute to the correct property in your IDL file. Next, in your [propput] implementation code, call FireOnRequestEdit() and test the returned HRESULT.

As for FireOnChanged(), this is a method that should only be called for a property marked with the [bindable] attribute. If you have properties marked with the [bindable] attribute, your client expects to be informed when a change has occurred, and thus you should call FireOnChanged() <u>after</u> you have assigned a new value within a [propput] implementation. Here are the relevant changes we would need to make in ShapesControl's ShapeType property to tell when a property is about to change and when it has changed:

```
// Making ShapeType bindable and giving a container the chance to say 'NO'.
interface IShapesControl : IDispatch
{
...
    [propget, id(1), helpstring("property ShapeType"), bindable, requestedit]
    HRESULT ShapeType([out, retval] CURRENTSHAPE *pVal);
    [propput, id(1), helpstring("property ShapeType"), bindable, requestedit]
    HRESULT ShapeType([in] CURRENTSHAPE newVal);
};
STDMETHODIMP CShapesControl::put_ShapeType(CURRENTSHAPE newVal)
{
    // Is this change OK with the container?
    if(FAILED(FireOnRequestEdit(1)))        // [id(1)] = ShapeType
        return S_FALSE;
    // Check bounds.
    if(newVal >= shapeCIRCLE && newVal <= shapeRECTANGLE)
        m_shapeType = newVal;
    // Redraw the view (i.e., call OnDraw())
    FireViewChange();
    // Tell container we have changed the value.
    FireOnChanged(1);                       // [id(1)] = ShapeType
    return S_OK;
}
```

Framework Support: CComControlBase

CComControlBase is one of the base classes to CComControl<>, the other being CWindowImpl<>, which we examined in the previous chapter. CComControlBase provides quite a bit of functionality to an ActiveX control, and can be broken down into the following categories:

■ CComControlBase maintains all the pointers necessary to communicate with the container. Typically you can leave well enough alone; however, each member is reachable from your derived class, and is listed in online help.

■ CComControlBase defines all of the stock property data members for use by CStockPropImpl<>.

■ CComControlBase defines a number of methods to grab "ambient properties" from your container.

■ CComControlBase intercepts the client's request to render the control, normalizes the device context, fills the _ATL_DRAWINFO structure, and calls OnDraw().

- CComControlBase defines the SetDirty() and GetDirty() methods to flag a property that should be saved (or determine if it needs to be saved).

Let's begin with the SetDirty() method. When you change the value of a custom property, you need to somehow inform the control that the new value should be saved when a container is asking to do so. CComControlBase defines a BOOL data member (m_bRequires-Save) to hold the current "dirty value." The way to tell your container a property is now different (and should be saved) is to call SetDirty() within the implementation of each and every [propput] method. GetDirty() returns the state of the dirty flag. The implementation of each method is trivial:

```
// Mark the control "dirty" so the container will save it
void SetDirty(BOOL bDirty)
{
    m_bRequiresSave = bDirty;
}
// Obtain the dirty state for the control
BOOL GetDirty()
{
    return m_bRequiresSave ? TRUE : FALSE;
}
```

Here is how the ShapeType property could make use of this new functionality:

```
// This iteration of ShapeType now sets the dirty flag to tell the container
// it should be saved.
STDMETHODIMP CShapesControl::put_ShapeType(CURRENTSHAPE newVal)
{
    // Is this change OK with the container?
    if(FAILED(FireOnRequestEdit(1)))   // [id(1)] = ShapeType
        return S_FALSE;
    // Check bounds.
    if(newVal >= shapeCIRCLE && newVal <= shapeRECTANGLE)
        m_shapeType = newVal;
    // Set dirty flag.
    SetDirty(TRUE);
    // Redraw the view (i.e., call OnDraw())
    FireViewChange();
    // Tell container we have changed the value.
    FireOnChanged(1); // [id(1)] = ShapeType
    return S_OK;
}
```

Framework Support: Ambient Properties

Now onto the other relevant feature provided by CComControlBase: the support for ambient properties. Here is the scoop. An ActiveX control container will have a GUI style all its own. For example, it might have a green background and use an 18-point, bold italic MS Sans Serif font. Currently, the ShapesControl begins life with a 12-point, Times New Roman font. Figure 14-32 illustrates the initial problem:

Figure 14-32:
Two competing
fonts.

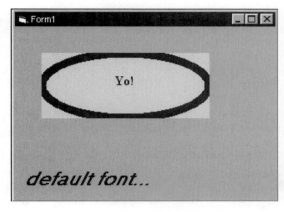

If we, as the control designer, want to ensure that our control "looks and feels" like the container it is living in, we need to ask the container what its current look and feel is via ambient properties. *Ambient properties* are properties on the container that we might make use of in the logic of the control. By doing so, we allow our control to have the correct look and feel of its host. Not only is this a great way to avoid any ugly GUI clashes, but it also saves the user of your controls the bother of setting the properties by hand. The complete set of ambient methods defined by CComControlBase is defined in online help, but here are some of the more interesting ambient methods:

CComControlBase Ambient Method	Meaning in Life
GetAmbientAppearance()	Gets the container's APPEARANCE property.
GetAmbientBackColor()	Gets the container's BACKCOLOR property.
GetAmbientDisplayName()	Gets the container's DISPLAYNAME property.
GetAmbientFont()	Gets the container's FONT properties.
GetAmbientForeColor()	Gets the container's FORECOLOR property.
GetAmbientTextAlign()	Gets the container's TEXTALIGN property.
GetAmbientUserMode()	Gets the container's USERMODE property.

To illustrate the use of ambient methods, assume we want to ensure that the font used by ShapesControl was the same font as used by the container which is using it. We would need to change our current implementation of OnDraw() to obtain the container's HFONT via GetAmbientFont(), rather than our default font assembled in our constructor. Here is the updated OnDraw():

```
// Drawing our text with the container's current font.
HRESULT CShapesControl::OnDraw(ATL_DRAWINFO& di)
{
...
    // Draw the Caption stock property with the AMBIENT font.
    // CComQIPtr<IFont, &IID_IFont> pFont(m_pFont);
    // if (pFont != NULL)
    // {
    IFont* pFont;
    GetAmbientFont(&pFont);
    pFont->get_hFont(&newFont);
    pFont->AddRefHfont(newFont);
    oldFont = (HFONT) SelectObject(hdc, newFont);
    // ...
    SetTextAlign(hdc, TA_CENTER|TA_BASELINE);
    SetBkMode(hdc, TRANSPARENT);
```

```
TextOut(hdc, (rc.left + rc.right)/2, (rc.top + rc.bottom)/2,
        W2A(m_bstrCaption), m_bstrCaption.Length());
// Reset DC & clean up.
SelectObject(hdc, oldPen);
SelectObject(hdc, oldBrush);
SelectObject(hdc, oldFont);
pFont->ReleaseHfont(newFont);
pFont->Release();
return S_OK;
}
```

With this code change, we can now rest assured that when someone uses our control, our font is the same as the container's. Now, just because you can use ambient properties does not mean you have to. You may wish to have your control maintain a unique look and feel, and force the users of your control to set individual properties. However, when you do use ambient properties, you typically can save yourself and the control user a bit of work. Figure 14-33 shows the results of the above code changes.

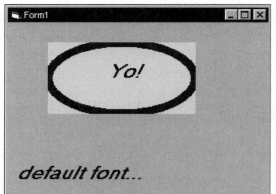

Figure 14-33:
One unified font.

Responding to Ambient Changes

The final note on using ambient properties is to realize that the values of a given ambient may change at any time. Just because the background color of a container may be purple today does not guarantee it will be tomorrow. To ensure that your control is informed when the container changes the value of a given ambient, your control may override the OnAmbientPropertyChange() method defined by IOleControlImpl<>. The default implementation of this method simply returns S_OK; however, you may test the incoming DISPID of the ambient property, and program accordingly. The DISPID constants for each ambient property are listed within <olectl.h>, and all have the "_AMBIENT_" infix. As an example, here is how we can discover that a container just changed the background color:

```
// Overriding OnAmbientPropertyChange() to respond to a change in the
// ambient properties.
STDMETHOD(OnAmbientPropertyChange)(DISPID dispid)
{
    if(dispid == DISPID_AMBIENT_BACKCOLOR)
    {
        ATLTRACE("The client changed the background color again...\n");
        // Redraw, or whatever you need to do...
    }
    return S_OK;
}
```

Framework Support: Stock Properties and CStockPropImpl<>

Just like a custom property you might add to a COM interface, a stock property has a get_ and put_ function to allow the container to obtain and alter the value represented by the property itself. ATL provides a default implementation for each stock property using the CStockPropertyImpl<> template. As soon as you add support for a stock property using the ATL Object Wizard, this template is added to your class derivation:

```
// If you select any stock properties from the ATL Object Wizard, you will be
// derived from CStockPropImpl<>.
class ATL_NO_VTABLE CShapesControl :
    public CComObjectRootEx<CComSingleThreadModel>,
    public CStockPropImpl<CShapesControl, IShapesControl,
            &IID_IShapesControl,&LIBID_AXSHAPESSERVERLib>,
...
{...};
```

CStockPropImpl<> provides accessor and mutator methods for each stock property. The parameters to this template should be obvious by now. What may not be obvious is that CStockPropImpl<> expects the [default] interface to be IDispatch savvy in order to work correctly. Therefore, be sure your primary default interface has been declared as a [dual].

CStockPropImpl<> implements a given stock property by providing boilerplate code which notifies the container a property has been changed (for every put_ method) or returns the current value of the property (for each get_ method). To define the member variables used for each stock property, CComControlBase establishes a union of all stock property member variables:

```
// These member variables of CComControlBase are used by CStockPropImpl<>'s
// implementation of the [propput] and [propget] methods.
union
{
    IPictureDisp* m_pMouseIcon;
    IPictureDisp* m_pPicture;
    IFontDisp* m_pFont;
    OLE_COLOR m_clrBackColor;
    OLE_COLOR m_clrBorderColor;
    OLE_COLOR m_clrFillColor;
    OLE_COLOR m_clrForeColor;
    BSTR m_bstrText;
    BSTR m_bstrCaption;
    BOOL m_bValid;
    BOOL m_bTabStop;
    BOOL m_bBorderVisible;
    BOOL m_bEnabled;
    LONG m_nBackStyle;
    LONG m_nBorderStyle;
    LONG m_nBorderWidth;
    LONG m_nDrawMode;
    LONG m_nDrawStyle;
    LONG m_nDrawWidth;
    LONG m_nFillStyle;
    SHORT m_nAppearance;
    LONG m_nMousePointer;
```

```
    LONG m_nReadyState;
};
```

Given the name of each variable, I think you can gather which stock property each one represents. Your derived class needs to provide the actual storage for the stock properties you have selected from the ATL Object Wizard. If you examine the header file for CShapesControl, you will see the wizard has inserted the correct data members into your class:

```
// Your class will contain member variables for the stock properties you selected.
OLE_COLOR m_clrBackColor;
CComBSTR m_bstrCaption;
CComPtr<IFontDisp> m_pFont;
```

When you wish to set or get the property, you will call the CStockPropImpl<> method (e.g., put_BackColor(), get_BackColor()). Exactly how CStockPropImpl<> actually implements these [propget] and [propput] functions depends on the underlying data type.

ATL's Stock Property Macros

For complex data types (meaning any COM interface, such as IFontDisp), CStock-PropImpl<> implements the accessor and mutator using some more elaborate COM code, taking care of interface reference counting and necessary memory management. For the remaining simple data types, CStockPropImpl<> makes use of three ATL macros. While you will most likely never need to directly use (or pay mind to) these macros, here is a brief description of each:

ATL Stock Property Macro	Meaning in Life
IMPLEMENT_STOCKPROP	Defines a [propput] and [propget] method for any stock property that is not a BSTR, BOOL, or COM interface. The implementation code informs the container of the new change.
IMPLEMENT_BOOL_STOCKPROP	A special case of the previous macro, which provides [propput] and [propget] methods for BOOLs.
IMPLEMENT_BSTR_STOCKPROP	Another special case to handle the manipulation of a BSTR property.

To get a feeling as to what these macros do, consider ATL's implementation of the BackColor stock property:

```
// CStockPropImpl<> code.
IMPLEMENT_STOCKPROP(OLE_COLOR, BackColor, clrBackColor, DISPID_BACKCOLOR)
```

The parameters to this macro are the name of the data type of the property, the friendly name of the property, the member variable defined by CComControlBase (without the "m_" prefix), and the DISPID. When this macro expands, we are provided with the actual code that sets or retrieves the value. Note that the "dirty flag" is automatically set. Also note that FireOnEditRequest() and FireOnChanged() are called when the template expands.

```
// Defining accessors and mutators for a basic stock property.
#define IMPLEMENT_STOCKPROP(type, fname, pname, dispid) \
    HRESULT STDMETHODCALLTYPE put_##fname(type pname) \
    { \
        ATLTRACE2(atlTraceControls,2,_T("CStockPropImpl::put_%s\n"), #fname); \
        T* pT = (T*) this; \
        if (pT->FireOnRequestEdit(dispid) == S_FALSE) \
            return S_FALSE; \
        pT->m_##pname = pname; \
        pT->m_bRequiresSave = TRUE; \
        pT->FireOnChanged(dispid); \
        pT->FireViewChange(); \
        pT->SendOnDataChange(NULL); \
        return S_OK; \
    } \
    HRESULT STDMETHODCALLTYPE get_##fname(type* p##pname) \
    { \
        ATLTRACE2(atlTraceControls,2,_T("CStockPropImpl::get_%s\n"), \
                  #fname); \
        T* pT = (T*) this; \
        *p##pname = pT->m_##pname; \
        return S_OK; \
    }
```

The basic functionality of the [propget] method is to simply return to the container the value of the data member representing the stock property. The [propput] method sets the new value and informs the container of the changes. The remaining stock property macros build similar implementation, with the net result being that ATL has established all the code required, allowing your ActiveX control to support stock properties—without requiring you to write the code.

Framework Support: IViewObjectExImpl<>

When you configure your control based on options from the Miscellaneous tab, you are indirectly configuring which items from the VIEWSTATUS enumeration will be present in your control. Recall that one of the standard COM interfaces required by an ActiveX control is IViewObjectEx, which defines a single method named GetViewStatus(). The purpose of this interface is to report to the control container if the control is opaque, and if so, if it has a solid background. VIEWSTATUS is defined in <ocidl.idl> as so:

```
// Members of the VIEWSTATUS enumeration are used by
// IViewObjectEx::GetViewStatus().
typedef /* [v1_enum] */
enum tagVIEWSTATUS
{
    VIEWSTATUS_OPAQUE          = 1,
    VIEWSTATUS_SOLIDBKGND      = 2,
```

```
     VIEWSTATUS_DVASPECTOPAQUE           = 4,
     VIEWSTATUS_DVASPECTTRANSPARENT      = 8,
     VIEWSTATUS_SURFACE                  = 16,
     VIEWSTATUS_3DSURFACE                = 32
}  VIEWSTATUS;
```

The IViewObjectEx interface is in fact derived from IViewObject2, which is in turn derived from IViewObject. This set of interfaces works towards the common goal of rendering your object on the container. Each interface is fully defined in online help; however, to give you a feeling of the behaviors provided by these three interfaces, here is a list of methods for each:

```
// IViewObject is used to provide core rendering support to a coclass.
// <oleidl.idl>
[ object, uuid(0000010d-0000-0000-C000-000000000046) ]
interface IViewObject : IUnknown
{
     HRESULT Draw( ...);
     HRESULT GetColorSet (...);
     HRESULT Freeze (...);
     HRESULT Unfreeze(...);
     HRESULT SetAdvise (...);
     HRESULT GetAdvise ( ...);
};
// Extends IViewObject by providing a way to obtain the size of the object.
// <oleidl.idl>
[ object, uuid(00000127-0000-0000-C000-000000000046) ]
interface IViewObject2 : IViewObject
{
     HRESULT GetExtent(...);
};
// Extends IViewObject2 by providing support for flicker-free drawing, non-rectangular
// regions and hit testing of these objects.
// <ocidl.idl>
[ object, uuid(3AF24292-0C96-11CE-A0CF-00AA00600AB8) ]
interface IViewObjectEx : IViewObject2
{
     HRESULT GetRect(...);
     HRESULT GetViewStatus(...);
     HRESULT QueryHitPoint(...);
     HRESULT QueryHitRect(...);
     HRESULT GetNaturalExtent (...);
};
```

ATL provides a default implementation of IViewObjectEx (and therefore IViewObject2 and IViewObject) using the IViewObjectExImpl<> template. While we will not discuss the details of each method here, one insight is that IViewObject::Draw() ultimately calls CComControlBase::OnDraw(), giving you the chance to use any GDI logic necessary to render your control. The full definition of IViewObjectExImpl<> is in <atlctl.h>.

Framework Support: COM Persistence

COM objects tend to maintain a stateful existence, especially as far as ActiveX controls are concerned. As we have seen earlier in the chapter, ATL provides a property map, which is used to save and load the values of your custom properties at a container's request. COM's persistence model is unique in that different containers have unique ways to save the state of an object. Some containers wish to save an object's state out as a stream of bytes. Others may wish to save stateful information using OLE structured storage, while still others might wish to save state information using a name-value association called a *property bag*. Typically, a COM object does not know who is using it and what sort of persistence they wish to employ. As a COM object, the best we can do is provide support for <u>each</u> type of persistence and let the container use whichever persistence model it so desires.

COM provides a number of standard interfaces to support each type of client-specified persistence, the core of which is IPersist. From this base interface, a number of other standard COM interfaces are derived, each adding a number of methods to support storage into a stream, storage, or property bag. ATL provides a set of templates that takes care of the implementation behind each variety of COM persistence: IPersistStreamInitImpl<>, IPersistStorageImpl<>, and IPersistPropertyBagImpl<>. If you examine your control's inheritance chain, you can see the Object Wizard has already added support for IPersist-StreamInitImpl<> and IPersistStorageImpl<>. However, if you wish to have your control save its state into a property bag, you will have to derive from IPersistProperty-BagImpl<> (and update your COM map) yourself. This is something you should most always do, as Internet Explorer is <u>only</u> able to persist a control's state in using a property bag:

```
// To round out your control's persistence support, manually add support for
// IPersistPropertyBag<>.
class ATL_NO_VTABLE CShapesControl :
...
    public IPersistStreamInitImpl<CShapesControl>,
...
    public IPersistStorageImpl<CShapesControl>,
...
    public IPersistPropertyBagImpl< CShapesControl >
...
{
...
BEGIN_COM_MAP(CShapesControl)
...
    COM_INTERFACE_ENTRY(IPersistPropertyBag)
END_COM_MAP()
...
};
```

The nice thing about ATL's persistence support (beyond the various implementation templates) is that the property map works with all three varieties. ATL always provides a property map for full controls, which we have previously updated to support the persistence of our custom ShapeType property:

```
// Our property map.
BEGIN_PROP_MAP(CShapesControl)
    PROP_DATA_ENTRY("_cx", m_sizeExtent.cx, VT_UI4)
    PROP_DATA_ENTRY("_cy", m_sizeExtent.cy, VT_UI4)
    PROP_ENTRY("BackColor", DISPID_BACKCOLOR, CLSID_StockColorPage)
    PROP_ENTRY("Caption", DISPID_CAPTION, CLSID_NULL)
    PROP_ENTRY("Font", DISPID_FONT, CLSID_StockFontPage)
```

```
    PROP_ENTRY("ShapeType", 1, CLSID_NULL)
END_PROP_MAP()
```

The ATL Property Map Macros

The BEGIN_PROP_MAP macro expands to define an array of ATL_PROPMAP_ENTRY structures, which can be obtained by the resulting GetPropMap() method. As with other ATL maps, END_PROP_MAP terminates the array:

```
// Property map macros are defined in <atlcom.h>
#define BEGIN_PROP_MAP(theClass) \
...
    static ATL_PROPMAP_ENTRY* GetPropertyMap()\
    {\
        static ATL_PROPMAP_ENTRY pPropMap[] = \
        {
#define END_PROP_MAP() \
            {NULL, 0, NULL, &IID_NULL, 0, 0, 0} \
        }; \
        return pPropMap; \
    }
```

Each ATL_PROPMAP_ENTRY structure holds all relevant information of each of COM's persistence models. Here is the definition:

```
// The ATL property map is an array of these...
struct ATL_PROPMAP_ENTRY
{
    LPCOLESTR szDesc;           // String name for property bags.
    DISPID dispid;              // DISPID of item being saved.
    const CLSID* pclsidPropPage; // CLSID of the property page.
    const IID* piidDispatch;    // Interface which supports this property.
    DWORD dwOffsetData;         // Offset to data.
    DWORD dwSizeData;           // Size of item in bytes.
    VARTYPE vt;                 // What kind of variable is this?
};
```

Rather than filling the array of ATL_PROPMAP_ENTRY structures by hand, we are provided with a small set of property macros. PROP_ENTRY is used for properties that are supported by your [default] interface. If you have properties contained in another dispinterface supported on your coclass, you can specify the name of this alternative interface using PROP_ENTRY_EX. PROP_DATA_ENTRY is used to save out data in your control which cannot be obtained by a COM interface. Here is the expansion of each macro, all of which can be found in <atlcom.h>:

```
// These macros populate the fields of the ATL_PROPMAP_ENTRY structure.
#define PROP_ENTRY(szDesc, dispid, clsid) \
        {OLESTR(szDesc), dispid, &clsid, &IID_IDispatch, 0, 0, 0},
#define PROP_ENTRY_EX(szDesc, dispid, clsid, iidDispatch) \
        {OLESTR(szDesc), dispid, &clsid, &iidDispatch, 0, 0, 0},
#define PROP_DATA_ENTRY(szDesc, member, vt) \
        {OLESTR(szDesc), 0, &CLSID_NULL, NULL,\
        offsetof(_PropMapClass, member), \
        sizeof(((_PropMapClass*)0)->member), vt},
```

The property map is also used to specify which property pages are used to represent design time access to specific properties. As of yet, we do not have any custom pages in AXShapesServer.dll, and therefore we specified CLSID_NULL when listing the property map entry for ShapeType. Notice, however, that our stock BackColor and Font entries <u>do</u> specify particular CLSIDs which identify two stock pages:

```
// The property page map is also used to associate properties to pages.
BEGIN_PROP_MAP(CShapesControl)
    PROP_DATA_ENTRY("_cx", m_sizeExtent.cx, VT_UI4)
    PROP_DATA_ENTRY("_cy", m_sizeExtent.cy, VT_UI4)
    PROP_ENTRY("BackColor", DISPID_BACKCOLOR, CLSID_StockColorPage)
    PROP_ENTRY("Caption", DISPID_CAPTION, CLSID_NULL)
    PROP_ENTRY("Font", DISPID_FONT, CLSID_StockFontPage)
    PROP_ENTRY("ShapeType", 1, CLSID_NULL)
END_PROP_MAP()
```

Even though Caption is a stock property, there is not a stock page that can be used to manipulate the underlying value. Given this, it is time to learn how to build property pages using ATL.

ActiveX Controls, Property Pages, and the Container

We have already seen two ways to tweak the properties of the ShapesControl: at design time (using the VB properties window) or run time (by writing code to call the members of the [default] interface). A production level control typically provides a third way to allow the users of the control to modify its state: property pages. As you recall, a property page is a COM object supporting IPropertyPage, and optionally IPropertyPage2. Like any COM object, property pages have CLSIDs that are used to identify them. To allow your container to grab the list of CLSIDs which represent the pages used by your control, the control must implement the ISpecifyPropertyPages interface. This standard COM interface has a single method called GetPages(), which returns an array of CAUUID structures:

```
// Return the set of CLSIDs for the control's pages.
[object, uuid(B196B28B-BAB4-101A-B69C-00AA00341D07)]
interface ISpecifyPropertyPages : IUnknown
{
    typedef struct tagCAUUID {
        ULONG cElems;
        [size_is(cElems)] GUID * pElems;
    } CAUUID;
    HRESULT GetPages( [out] CAUUID * pPages );
};
```

ATL provides a default implementation of this interface from its ISpecifyProperty-PagesImpl<> template, which can be seen from your control's inheritance list:

```
// ISpecifyPropertyPages is used by a client to grab the CLSIDs of your control's
// property page objects.
class ATL_NO_VTABLE CShapesControl :
...
    public ISpecifyPropertyPagesImpl<CShapesControl>,
...
{};
```

The actual implementation of GetPages() is delegated to a helper function called (appropriately enough) GetPagesHelper(). This method iterates over your class's property map, reading the pclsidPropPage field of each ATL_PROPMAP_ENTRY structure. If a non-NULL entry is discovered, it will fill the given index of the CAUUID structure with the correct CLSID. Here is the essence of this function:

```
// Fill up the CAUUID array with the GUIDS of our control's pages.
HRESULT GetPagesHelper(CAUUID* pPages, ATL_PROPMAP_ENTRY* pMap)
{
...
    // Does this property have a page? CLSID_NULL means it does not.
    if (!InlineIsEqualGUID(*pMap[i].pclsidPropPage, CLSID_NULL))
    {
        BOOL bFound = FALSE;
        // Search through array we are building up to see if it is already in there.
        for (int j=0; j<nCnt; j++)
        {
        if (InlineIsEqualGUID(*(pMap[i].pclsidPropPage), pPages->pElems[j]))
        {
            // It's already there, so no need to add it again
            bFound = TRUE;
            break;
        }
        }
    }
    // If we didn't find it in there, then add it.
    if (!bFound)
        pPages->pElems[nCnt++] = *pMap[i].pclsidPropPage;
...
}
```

When the end user opens up your control's property sheet, a dialog box is created to host each page (representing a tabbed dialog). This dialog maintains an individual *page site* (an object implementing IPropertyPageSite) for each page used by the control. When the container obtains the list of CLSIDs from the control, it will pass the CAUUID structure into the dialog, allowing it to call CoCreateInstance() for each one, and ask each page for its IPropertyPage interface. Here is the definition for IPropertyPage:

```
// Each property page implements this interface, which is used by the property page
// to communicate with the site:
[object,uuid(B196B28D-BAB4-101A-B69C-00AA00341D07)]
interface IPropertyPage : IUnknown
{
    typedef struct tagPROPPAGEINFO {
        ULONG cb;
        LPOLESTR pszTitle;
        SIZE size;
        LPOLESTR pszDocString;
        LPOLESTR pszHelpFile;
        DWORD dwHelpContext;
    } PROPPAGEINFO;
    HRESULT SetPageSite([in] IPropertyPageSite * pPageSite);
    HRESULT Activate([in] HWND hWndParent, [in] LPCRECT pRect,
                     [in] BOOL bModal);
    HRESULT Deactivate();
    HRESULT GetPageInfo([out] PROPPAGEINFO * pPageInfo);
```

```
    HRESULT SetObjects([in] ULONG cObjects,
                       [in, size_is(cObjects)] IUnknown ** ppUnk);
    HRESULT Show([in] UINT nCmdShow);
    HRESULT Move([in] LPCRECT pRect);
    HRESULT IsPageDirty();
    HRESULT Apply();
    HRESULT Help();
    HRESULT TranslateAccelerator( [in] MSG * pMsg);
};
```

As you can see, IPropertyPage defines a handy structure (PROPPAGEINFO) which identifies all the necessary information for a given page (e.g., the tab's caption, online help information). Among the numerous methods of IPropertyPage, the ones to keep focused on are Apply() and Show().

The Apply() method is called in response to the end user selecting the dialog box's Apply button. This signals to the dialog box that it is time to update the associated control with new values contained in the page's GUI widgets (i.e., call the correct [propput] methods of the control's [default] interface).

Show() is called when a given page object is about to be made visible to the user. This method is important because this is our chance to make sure the data placed in the dialog box widgets is up to date (i.e., call the correct [propget] functions in the control's [default] interface). For example, if we have an edit box used to set a control's Age property, the correct value should be placed into the box when it comes to life.

So to summarize the interaction of the key players, the container obtains a list of CLSIDs from the control using ISpecifyPropertyPages, to understand which pages work with the given control. The pages are hosted in a tabbed dialog box that sets up a page site (which is a COM object implementing IPropertyPageSite) for each page. So, what exactly is your responsibility as an ATL developer? Create the individual pages using the ATL Object Wizard. The framework takes care of the communications between each player.

Building Property Pages with ATL

Building a set of property pages for your ActiveX control is relatively painless. To begin the process, you access the ATL Object Wizard. Choose Controls from the Category section, and insert a new Property Page object as seen in Figure 14-34:

Figure 14-34: Inserting a new property page à la ATL.

When you insert a new page, you will be presented with a unique configuration dialog. The Names and Attributes tabs are the same as always. The only difference is that you will not be adding any custom interfaces to a property page object, and thus the Interface edit field is disabled (typically, the only interface a property page will implement is the standard IPropertyPage). The Strings tab (Figure 14-35) allows you to set the text that will be used to identify the caption of this page in the tabbed dialog box, as well as any context-sensitive help paths:

Figure 14-35: The text in the Title selection will be the string used on the tab for your custom page.

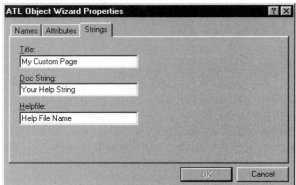

When you finish inserting your new page using the ATL Object Wizard, you will be given a dialog resource to assemble your GUI and a new class representing the page. For this example, we will construct a user interface which allows the user to enter text for our stock Caption property, as well as select the current shape:

Figure 14-36: The GUI of our custom property page.

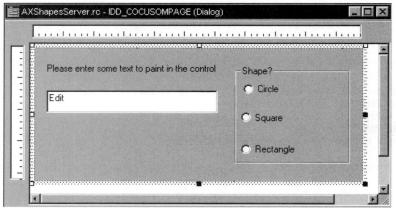

Now that we have a visual front end, we can examine how to move the values into our control's properties. As you can guess, we need to suck out the text in the edit box and send it into put_Caption(). Likewise, we need to discover the current shape and send that value into put_ShapeType(). The code behind this process will take place in the Apply() method of your new C++ class wrapping this dialog resource template.

We will also need to configure the page in such a way that the current values of the control's properties are shoved into our GUI widgets before the page is made visible. To make these code adjustments, let's get to know IPropertyPageImpl<>.

Framework Support: IPropertyPageImpl<>

When you insert a new property page, you will be given a C++ class deriving from a few ATL base classes. First, you inherit basic IUnknown support from CComObject-RootEx<>. Your class factory is provided via CComCoClass<>. As well, you gather in the core windowing and dialog support provided by ATL, as you are also derived from CDialogImpl<>. Most importantly, every ATL property page will derive from IPropertyPageImpl<>, which provides the implementation details of IPropertyPage.

Note: As a property page is a valid COM object, you will see a new coclass statement within your project's IDL file.

Here is the initial class definition:

```
// Initial code for an ATL property page.
class ATL_NO_VTABLE CCoCustomPage :
    public CComObjectRootEx<CComSingleThreadModel>,
    public CComCoClass<CCoCustomPage, &CLSID_CoCustomPage>,
    public IPropertyPageImpl<CCoCustomPage>,
    public CDialogImpl<CCoCustomPage>
{
public:
    CCoCustomPage()
    {
        m_dwTitleID = IDS_TITLECoCustomPage;
        m_dwHelpFileID = IDS_HELPFILECoCustomPage;
        m_dwDocStringID = IDS_DOCSTRINGCoCustomPage;
    }
    enum {IDD = IDD_COCUSTOMPAGE};
DECLARE_REGISTRY_RESOURCEID(IDR_COCUSTOMPAGE)
DECLARE_PROTECT_FINAL_CONSTRUCT()
BEGIN_COM_MAP(CCoCustomPage)
    COM_INTERFACE_ENTRY(IPropertyPage)
END_COM_MAP()
BEGIN_MSG_MAP(CCoCustomPage)
    CHAIN_MSG_MAP(IPropertyPageImpl<CCoCustomPage>)
END_MSG_MAP()
    STDMETHOD(Apply)(void)
    {
        ATLTRACE(_T("CCoCustomPage::Apply\n"));
        for (UINT i = 0; i < m_nObjects; i++)
        {
            // Do something interesting here
            // ICircCtl* pCirc;
            // m_ppUnk[i]->QueryInterface(IID_ICircCtl, (void**)&pCirc);
            // pCirc->put_Caption(CComBSTR("something special"));
            // pCirc->Release();
        }
        m_bDirty = FALSE;
```

```
            return S_OK;
      }
};
```

IPropertyPageImpl<> defines three DWORD data members which are used to hold the resource IDs for the custom strings used for this page, based on your selections from the String tab. We have an initial COM map supporting IPropertyPage, and a message map which gathers default messages from IPropertyPageImpl<>. The only other item of note is the Apply() method which has been defined in your class (with some suggested comments to boot). Recall that this method of IPropertyPage will be called when the user wishes to commit the given modifications. Your job is to send the new data to the control.

Programming the Apply() Method

The logic behind the Apply method will always have the same general flavor: Obtain the [default] interface of the control and call the correct [propput] methods to assign the new values gathered from the GUI widgets. In many IDEs, it is possible to use a property page to apply changes to any number of selected objects. For example, this VB form has four ShapesControls selected (Figure 14-37); any new values that were specified in the property page should apply to each of them. IPropertyPageImpl<> maintains an array of IUnknown pointers, which represent each control currently selected by the end user at design time.

Figure 14-37: The effects of clicking the Apply button should affect all selected controls.

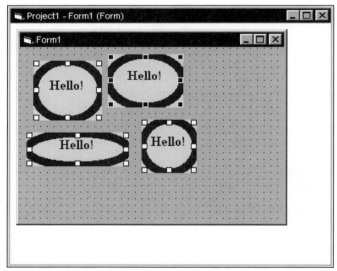

You will also need to add code to your IPropertyPageImpl<> derived class to enable or disable the Apply button maintained by the host dialog. For example, we need to enable the Apply button whenever a radio button has been selected or when any new text has been entered into the edit box. IPropertyPageImpl<> provides the SetDirty() method, which sets the value of an underlying BOOL (m_bDirty). Based on the truth or falsity of this data item, the framework will enable or disable the button accordingly. With this in mind, we need to handle an EN_CHANGE message for the edit box, and BN_CLICKED messages for each radio button. Each of these handlers will call SetDirty(TRUE) to enable the Apply button. Beyond this, each of the BN_CLICKED handlers will set the current value of the shape (assume our property page class maintains a private CURRENTSHAPE data member).

To ensure the end user's changes affect each selected control, the Apply() logic should iterate over each of the IUnknown pointers (the m_ppUnk array maintained by IProperty-PageImpl<>) and call put_Caption() and put_ShapeType() using the new values. Here, then, are all the necessary changes to program our custom property page Apply() method (with the correct command handlers):

```
// CCoCustomPage
#include "shapescontrol.h"
class ATL_NO_VTABLE CCoCustomPage :
...
{
...
// Inserted with the Add Message Handler Wizard.
BEGIN_MSG_MAP(CCoCustomPage)
    CHAIN_MSG_MAP(IPropertyPageImpl<CCoCustomPage>)
    COMMAND_HANDLER(IDC_RADIOCIRCLE, BN_CLICKED,
                    OnClickedRadioCircle)
    COMMAND_HANDLER(IDC_RADIORECT, BN_CLICKED,
                    OnClickedRadioRect)
    COMMAND_HANDLER(IDC_RADIOSQUARE, BN_CLICKED,
                    OnClickedRadioSquare)
    COMMAND_HANDLER(IDC_EDITCAPTION, EN_CHANGE,
                    OnChangeEditCaption)
END_MSG_MAP()
    STDMETHOD(Apply)(void)
    {
        // Loop over each selected control.
        for (UINT i = 0; i < m_nObjects; i++)
        {
            // First set the caption.
            IShapesControl* pSC = NULL;
            CComBSTR temp;
            GetDlgItemText( IDC_EDITCAPTION, temp.m_str);
            m_ppUnk[i]->QueryInterface(IID_IShapesControl,
                                        (void**)&pSC);
            pSC->put_Caption(temp);
            // Now set the shape.
            pSC->put_ShapeType(m_currShape);
            pSC->Release();
        }
        m_bDirty = FALSE;       // Changes are made; set dirty flag to false.
        return S_OK;
    }
    LRESULT OnClickedRadioCircle(WORD wNotifyCode, WORD wID,
                                HWND hWndCtl, BOOL& bHandled)
    {
        m_currShape = shapeCIRCLE;
        SetDirty(TRUE);
        return 0;
    }
    LRESULT OnClickedRadioRect(WORD wNotifyCode, WORD wID, HWND
```

```
                                hWndCtl, BOOL& bHandled)
    {
        m_currShape = shapeRECTANGLE;
        SetDirty(TRUE);
        return 0;
    }
    LRESULT OnClickedRadioSquare(WORD wNotifyCode, WORD wID, HWND
                                hWndCtl, BOOL& bHandled)
    {
        m_currShape = shapeSQUARE;
        SetDirty(TRUE);
        return 0;
    }
    LRESULT OnChangeEditCaption(WORD wNotifyCode, WORD wID, HWND
                                hWndCtl, BOOL& bHandled)
    {
        SetDirty(TRUE);
        return 0;
    }
private:
    CURRENTSHAPE m_currShape;
};
```

We now must go back into the control's property map, and associate the ShapeType and Caption property to this page. The ATL Object Wizard has already defined a CLSID constant for this purpose, which is listed at the beginning of your property page's header file. Here are the changes:

```
// Rigging our properties to the correct page.
BEGIN_PROP_MAP(CShapesControl)
    PROP_DATA_ENTRY("_cx", m_sizeExtent.cx, VT_UI4)
    PROP_DATA_ENTRY("_cy", m_sizeExtent.cy, VT_UI4)
    PROP_ENTRY("BackColor", DISPID_BACKCOLOR, CLSID_StockColorPage)
    PROP_ENTRY("Caption", DISPID_CAPTION, CLSID_CoCustomPage)
    PROP_ENTRY("Font", DISPID_FONT, CLSID_StockFontPage)
    PROP_ENTRY("ShapeType", 1, CLSID_CoCustomPage)
END_PROP_MAP()
```

With this, we can now load up our pages using the VB (Custom) selection from the property window (Figure 14-38), and use the page to alter the appearance of the selected controls.

Figure 14-38: The custom page in action.

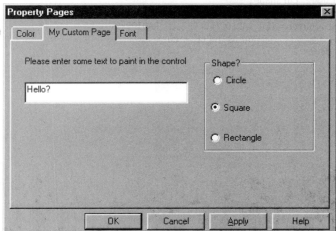

Going the Other Direction: Prepping the GUI Widgets

The Apply() method is used to call the methods of your control's [default] interface using the new values container in the GUI widgets. In other words, the flow of communication is from the page site to the control. When your page is about to be displayed, it would be nice if the edit box really did contain the correct string, and if the correct radio box was indeed focused. Currently, when we pull up our custom page, the text is empty and no radio button is selected. What we need is a way to reverse the flow of communication from the object to the page sink. To do so requires overriding the Show() method maintained by IPropertyPageImpl< >, or alternatively handling a WM_INITDIALOG message in the C++ page wrapper class.

Given that the end user may have selected any number of controls before launching your property pages, you will still be making use of the held array of IUnknown pointers. However, under this context, you will need to decide which of the selected controls will be used to fill the values of the property page. IPropertyPageImpl< > holds the current count within the m_ppUnk array using the m_nObjects data point. I have chosen to use the first object selected to fill the values of the GUI items, but you may choose otherwise. Add a handler for WM_INITDIALOG, and add the following code:

```
// Fill the values of the edit box and radio selection using the
// IShapesControl interface of the first selected control.
LRESULT OnInitDialog(UINT uMsg, WPARAM wParam, LPARAM lParam,
                     BOOL& bHandled)
{
    USES_CONVERSION;
    // Show the values from the first selected item.
    if (m_nObjects > 0)
    {
        // Get the first item selected.
        IShapesControl* pSC = NULL;
        CComBSTR temp;
        m_ppUnk[0]->QueryInterface(IID_IShapesControl, (void**)&pSC);
        // Set the caption.
        pSC->get_Caption(&temp.m_str);
        SetDlgItemText(IDC_EDITCAPTION, W2A(temp.m_str));
        // Now set focus to the correct radio item.
        CURRENTSHAPE curShape;
        pSC->get_ShapeType(&curShape);
        CheckRadioButton(IDC_RADIOCIRCLE, IDC_RADIORECT,
                         IDC_RADIOCIRCLE + curShape);
        // All done!
        pSC->Release();
        SetDirty(FALSE);
    }
    return 0;
}
```

ShapesControl now has a custom property page which can be used to edit the properties of the [default] interface. This wraps up the complete implementation of our ShapesControl tester. In the next (and final) lab of this book, you will add a custom page to the AXCar control developed in the previous lab. Before we get there, let's see what it would take to get ShapesControl (or any ActiveX control) up on a web page.

Using an ActiveX Control from a Web Page

As you can see, creating a full control with ATL demands quite a bit of knowledge. You need to be very comfortable with not only COM itself, but the ATL framework and the Win32 API as well. The reason ATL is popular, despite its complexity, is the end result is a very lightweight binary, just the right thing for low bandwidth downloading over the Internet. When you insert a control with the ATL Object Wizard, one of the generated files is a simple HTML file that loads your control into the current browser on your development machine. This file, which is located in your project's subfolder, simply uses the <OBJECT> tag to specify the CLSID of the control you wish to load, as well as give it an ID to refer to during the scope of the page:

```
<HTML>
<HEAD>
<TITLE>ATL 3.0 test page for object ShapesControl</TITLE>
</HEAD>
<BODY>
<OBJECT ID="ShapesControl"
        CLASSID="CLSID:03FBA320-71D1-11D3-B92D-0020781238D4">
</OBJECT>
</BODY>
</HTML>
```

If you open this file in Visual Studio, you may right-click anywhere on the file and select the Preview option to see how your control will appear on a web page (see Figure 14-39).

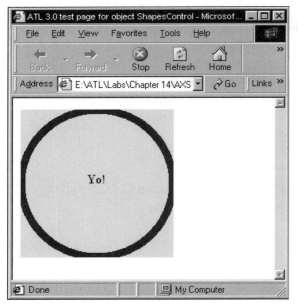

Figure 14-39: Hosting ShapesControl in IE.

While it is inspiring to see our control hosted in a web page, we have no code to respond to our [default, source] interface, or allow the end user to manipulate our properties. The act of manipulating our [default] interface is straightforward; create a VBScript block which makes use of them. To respond to our custom event requires an additional bit of script.

Manipulating ShapesControl on the Web

During the course of developing ShapesControl, one addition we made to the default generated code was to add support for property bag persistence. Web browsers make exclusive use of this approach, which may be manipulated with the <PARAM> tag. Let's initialize our control with a shape of SQUARE (i.e., 1) and the text "We Love COM":

```
<HTML>
<HEAD>
<TITLE>ATL 3.0 test page for object ShapesControl</TITLE>
</HEAD>
<BODY>
<OBJECT ID="ShapesControl" CLASSID="CLSID:03FBA320-71D1-11D3-B92D-0020781238D4">
    <PARAM NAME = "ShapeType" VALUE ="1">
    <PARAM NAME = "Caption" VALUE = "We Love COM">
</OBJECT>
</BODY>
</HTML>
```

Figure 14-40:
Using our property bag support.

Next, we should provide a way to capture our custom ClickedControl() event. In VBScript, we define an event sink as so:

```
<HTML>
<HEAD>
<TITLE>ATL 3.0 test page for object ShapesControl</TITLE>
</HEAD>
<BODY>
<OBJECT ID="ShapesControl" CLASSID="CLSID:03FBA320-71D1-11D3-B92D-0020781238D4">
    <PARAM NAME = "ShapeType" VALUE ="1">
    <PARAM NAME = "Caption" VALUE = "We Love COM">
</OBJECT>
<script LANGUAGE = "VBScript" FOR = "ShapesControl"
        EVENT = "ClickedControl(xPos, yPos)">
        MsgBox "X= " & xPos & " Y= " & yPos
</script>
```

```
</BODY>
</HTML>
```

The VBScript FOR EVENT syntax allows you to write event sinks for any methods

Figure 14-41:
Capturing our
event in
VBScript.

defined in the [default, source] interface of your control. Because VBScript is very loosely typed, we do not specify the type of parameter being received in the ClickedControl() event (everything is assumed to be a Variant) and simply pass them into the MsgBox method for a simple display (Figure 14-41).

A Licensed Class Factory and IClassFactory2

The final issue we will address is the ability to build a licensed control. Recall that the IClassFactory2 interface is a COM interface that derives from IClassFactory and adds support to test for a valid LIC file before loading your control:

```
// IClassFactory2 ensures the end user of your control has a valid *.LIC file
// before creating the object.
[object,uuid(B196B28F-BAB4-101A-B69C-00AA00341D07),pointer_default(unique)]
interface IClassFactory2 : IClassFactory
{
     typedef struct tagLICINFO {
          LONG cbLicInfo;
          BOOL fRuntimeKeyAvail;
          BOOL fLicVerified;
     } LICINFO;
     HRESULT GetLicInfo([out] LICINFO * pLicInfo);
     HRESULT RequestLicKey([in] DWORD dwReserved, [out] BSTR * pBstrKey);
     HRESULT CreateInstanceLic([in] IUnknown * pUnkOuter,
                               [in] IUnknown * pUnkReserved,
                               [in] REFIID riid,
                               [in] BSTR bstrKey,
                               [out, iid_is(riid)] PVOID * ppvObj);
};
```

ATL provides a stock implementation of this interface with the CComClassFactory2<> template. Also recall that when you want to override the default class factory provided by

CComCoClass, you simply insert the following alternative class factory macro in your class definition:

```
// We now support a licensed class object.
class ATL_NO_VTABLE CShapesControl :
...
{
...
// IClassFactory2
DECLARE_CLASSFACTORY2(CTheLicense)
...
};
```

Once you have specified support for IClassFactory2, you will need to write a helper class, which ATL expects to implement the following functions:

- VerifyLicenseKey(): Tests the incoming BSTR against the known value.
- GetLicenseKey(): Returns the *.LIC file.
- IsLicenseValid(): Returns TRUE if the machine using this control contains a valid license.

If you are serious about licensing your ActiveX controls, you will need to download the (free) License Package Authoring Tool from the MS Site Builder Network web page. This tool can be used to create license files that are packaged into a binary format to prevent tampering from web-based clients. Furthermore, you would obviously want to create some encryption algorithm when creating the key itself. To keep things simple, here is a simple licensing class named CTheLicense, which implements the methods required by CComClassFactory2<>:

```
// This helper class implements the necessary methods required by
// CComClassFactory2<>
class CTheLicense
{
public:
    CTheLicense();
    virtual ~CTheLicense();
    static BOOL VerifyLicenseKey(BSTR bstr)
    {
        return wcscmp(bstr, L"YouGottaHaveThis") == 0;
    }
    static BOOL GetLicenseKey(DWORD reserved, BSTR* pBSTR)
    {
        *pBSTR = SysAllocString(OLESTR("YouGottaHaveThis"));
        return TRUE;
    }
    static BOOL IsLicenseValid()
    {
        DWORD result;
        result = GetFileAttributes("C:\\ Test.lic") == (DWORD)-1;
        if(!result)
        {
            MessageBox(NULL, "All systems go", "Creating object",
                    MB_OK | MB_SETFOREGROUND);
            return TRUE;
        }
        else
```

```
        {
                MessageBox(NULL, "Uh oh", "Can't make object",
                        MB_OK | MB_SETFOREGROUND);
                return FALSE;
        }
    }
};
```

To complete this test, you need to create a file indeed named Test.lic which resides in your C drive (the path used for the sample solution is E:\ATL\Labs\Chapter 14\AXShapesServer\Test.lic). When a user attempts to use your control, IClassFactory2 is obtained by the client, and if a valid license key is not where it should be, the creation process is terminated. For example, if we delete (or rename) Test.lic and attempt to use ShapesServer from VB, we are shown the following error (Figure 14-42). If you replace the deleted Test.lic file, your control will be created as usual.

Figure 14-42:
The result of <u>not</u> having a valid *.lic file.

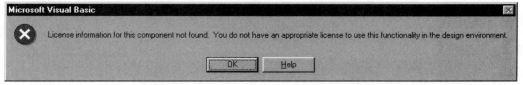

Lab 14-2: Adding Property Pages and Property Persistence

This lab extends the CAxCar control you built in the previous lab. First, we will retrofit your custom methods to support the [bindable] and [requestedit] attributes and update our [propput] methods accordingly. We also update our control to handle persistence using a COM property bag. Finally, we create a custom property page to allow the end user to configure our control, and update our property map to associate the Animate, Speed, and PetName properties to this new page.

The solution for this lab can be found on your CD-ROM under:
Labs\Chapter 14\AXCarServer
Labs\Chapter 14\AXCarServer\VBClient

Step One: Enhance Our Custom Properties

As you have learned, COM provides a unique interface named IPropertyNotifySink, which allows a container to approve or disapprove of a property reassignment, as well as be informed when a property has changed. In IDL, we mark our properties as [requestedit] and/or [bindable] to enable this behavior. Let's retrofit our properties to do this very thing. Begin by adding the correct IDL attributes to each property in your [default] IAxCar interface. For example:

```
// Binding our properties to the client's property sink.
[object, uuid(65A0EEBF-745F-11D3-B92E-0020781238D4), dual,
helpstring("IAxCar Interface"),pointer_default(unique) ]
interface IAxCar : IDispatch
{
...

    [propget, id(3), helpstring("Should I animate?"), bindable, requestedit]
```

```
    HRESULT Animate([out, retval] AnimVal *newVal);
    [propput, id(3), helpstring("Should I animate?"), bindable, requestedit]
    HRESULT Animate([in] AnimVal newVal);
...
};
```

Once you have updated each property in this way, you now must go and reengineer your [propput] methods to make use of the FireOnEditRequest() and FireOnChanged() methods. Here is the updated implementation for the Animate property (Speed, MaxSpeed, and PetName would have similar tweaks):

```
// Request and notify.
STDMETHODIMP CAxCar::put_Animate(AnimVal newVal)
{
    // Is it OK to update the Animate property?
    if(FAILED(FireOnRequestEdit(3)))            // [id(3)] = Animate
        return S_FALSE;
    // Set the animation property.
    m_bAnimate = newVal;
    if(::IsWindow(m_hWnd) && (m_bAnimate == Yes))
        SetTimer(1, 250);
    else if(::IsWindow(m_hWnd))
        KillTimer(1);
    // Tell container we have changed the value.
    FireOnChanged(3);                           // [id(3)] = Animate
    return S_OK;
}
```

When you are making use of [bindable] and/or [requestedit] properties, you may wish to define your own DISPID constants to reference in your source code, rather than the magic numbers seen above.

In any case, realize that the parameter sent into the FireOnRequestEdit() and FireOnChanged() methods is the DISPID of your custom property (i.e., the [id] attribute in your IDL definition).

Step Two: Support Property Persistence

Our previous lab did not incorporate property persistence in order to keep things focused on the animation logic. Here we will need to make some adjustments so a container can remember the values behind our custom properties between sessions. ATL provides automatic support for persistence into a stream or storage using the IPersistStorageImpl<> and IPersistStreamInitImpl<> templates (and the required COM map entries). We currently have no support for IPersistPropertyBag.

A property bag is just what its name implies: a name/value pair that can be used by clients such as MS Internet Explorer to persist your control's state. By default, the ATL Object Wizard does not add the necessary support, so we need to update the generated code. To do so is simple: Extend your class's inheritance chain with an entry for IPersistPropertyBagImpl< > and add a COM map entry for IPersistPropertyBag.

Now that our control has full support for all types of COM persistence, we should edit our [propput] methods with one final addition. When you make a new assignment to the underlying variable of a COM property, call **SetDirty()** to mark that this property has changed. In this way, the client "understands" which items need to be persisted. Here is the final iteration of put_Animate(). Update the logic for put_PetName(), put_MaxSpeed(), and put_Speed() in the same way:

```
// Mark this property as dirty when we assign a new value.
STDMETHODIMP CAxCar::put_Animate(AnimVal newVal)
{
    if(FAILED(FireOnRequestEdit(3)))   // [id(3)] = Animate
        return S_FALSE;
    // Set the animation property.
    m_bAnimate = newVal;
    if(::IsWindow(m_hWnd) && (m_bAnimate == Yes))
        SetTimer(1, 250);
    else if(::IsWindow(m_hWnd))
        KillTimer(1);
    // Set dirty flag.
    SetDirty(TRUE);
    // Tell container we have changed the value.
    FireOnChanged(3);                    // [id(3)] = Animate
    return S_OK;
}
```

Now that we provide the ability to save and load our information, we must edit our property map. As of ATL 3.0, there is no "Edit Property Map Wizard," so we need to do this by hand (which is not a big deal). Open up your class's header file, find the property map, and update accordingly:

```
// Persisting our properties.
BEGIN_PROP_MAP(CAxCar)
    PROP_DATA_ENTRY("_cx", m_sizeExtent.cx, VT_UI4)
    PROP_DATA_ENTRY("_cy", m_sizeExtent.cy, VT_UI4)
    PROP_ENTRY("Animate", 3, CLSID_NULL)
    PROP_ENTRY("Speed", 4, CLSID_NULL)
    PROP_ENTRY("PetName", 5, CLSID_NULL)
    PROP_ENTRY("MaxSpeed", 6, CLSID_NULL)
END_PROP_MAP()
```

Step Three: Create a Custom Property Page

Our control has custom properties, and to be as user friendly as possible, we should create a custom property page to allow the end user to edit them at design time. First we need to decide which properties to make available. Let's allow the user to access the Animate, MaxSpeed, and PetName property from our custom page (but not the current speed). When you are building a page with ATL, the first step is to access the ATL Object Wizard and insert a new PropertyPage object from the Controls category. Using this tool, add a new page using **ConfigureCar** as the short name. From the String tab, edit the Title string to your liking. Recall that this string is used as the caption for the tab itself, and will be placed in your project's string table should you ever wish to change it. Close down the wizard when you are done. Next, we need to build a GUI front end using the new dialog template. We have three custom properties to provide access to. Given their functionality, it makes sense to add two edit boxes and a single check box. Here is a possible design:

Figure 14-43:
A custom
property page.

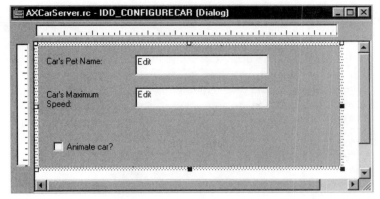

To associate these widgets to the correct properties of IAxCar, begin by routing an EN_CHANGE notification for each edit box, as well as a BN_CLICKED notification to the check box, using the Add Windows Message Handler CASE tool. In the implementation of each handler, enable the Apply button by calling **SetDirty()**:

```
// This SetDirty() method enables or disables the Apply button of the dialog box
// hosting your page.
LRESULT OnClickedCheckanim(WORD wNotifyCode, WORD wID, HWND hWndCtl,
BOOL& bHandled)
{
    SetDirty(TRUE);
    return 0;
}
```

As for the logic behind the Apply() method, we need to fetch the values contained in each GUI widget, and send them into the correct property of the selected controls. Recall that IProperyPageImpl<> is maintaining an array of IUnknown pointers (m_ppUnk), which represents each control selected within the container. Use this array to update each object. The count of currently selected controls is maintained in the m_nObjects data member. Here is the necessary logic:

```
// Transfer the information in the widgets back to each control.
STDMETHOD(Apply)(void)
{
    // Loop over all objects.
    for (UINT i = 0; i < m_nObjects; i++)
    {
        // First set the pet name.
        IAxCar* pCar = NULL;
        CComBSTR temp;
        GetDlgItemText( IDC_EDITNAME, temp.m_str);
        m_ppUnk[i]->QueryInterface(IID_IAxCar, (void**)&pCar);
        pCar->put_PetName(temp);
        // Now set the animate prop.
        pCar->put_Animate(
            (AnimVal)IsDlgButtonChecked(IDC_CHECKANIM));
        // And the max speed.
        pCar->put_MaxSpeed(GetDlgItemInt(IDC_EDITSPEED));
        pCar->Release();
    }
```

```
        m_bDirty = FALSE;
        return S_OK;
}
```

Next, we need to "move data the other direction." When the user pulls up your property page, it would be nice it the current values in the control are placed in the correct widget. For example, the PetName should be plopped into the IDC_EDITNAME edit box, the Animate check box should reflect the current value, and so on. A common place to update these widgets is within the handler for a WM_INITDIALOG message, which is sent just before the dialog is made visible. Add a **WM_INITDIALOG** entry to your message map, and the following code:

```
// Set the widgets to the current values of the first selected control.
LRESULT OnInitDialog(UINT uMsg, WPARAM wParam, LPARAM lParam, BOOL& bHandled)
{
        USES_CONVERSION;
        // Show the values from the first selected item.
        if (m_nObjects > 0)
        {
                IAxCar* pCar = NULL;
                short tempSP;
                CComBSTR temp;
                // Get the first item selected.
                m_ppUnk[0]->QueryInterface(IID_IAxCar, (void**)&pCar);
                // Set the max Speed.
                pCar->get_MaxSpeed(&tempSP);
                SetDlgItemInt(IDC_EDITSPEED, tempSP);
                // Now check Animate selection.
                AnimVal curAnim;
                pCar->get_Animate(&curAnim);
                CheckDlgButton(IDC_CHECKANIM, (BOOL)curAnim);
                // Finally, set the Pet Name.
                pCar->get_PetName(&temp.m_str);
                SetDlgItemText(IDC_EDITNAME, W2A(temp.m_str));
                // All done!
                pCar->Release();
                SetDirty(FALSE);
        }
        return 0;
}
```

For the final step, we need to once again go back to our property map and edit each exposed property to use our custom page, rather than CLSID_NULL (no page). The ATL Object Wizard has generated a CLSID for this page, which can be found at the top of the class's header file. Using this constant, update your control's property map as so:

```
// Rigging our properties to the correct page.
BEGIN_PROP_MAP(CAxCar)
        PROP_DATA_ENTRY("_cx", m_sizeExtent.cx, VT_UI4)
        PROP_DATA_ENTRY("_cy", m_sizeExtent.cy, VT_UI4)
        PROP_ENTRY("Animate", 3, CLSID_ConfigureCar)
        PROP_ENTRY("Speed", 4, CLSID_NULL)
        PROP_ENTRY("PetName", 5, CLSID_ConfigureCar)
        PROP_ENTRY("MaxSpeed", 6, CLSID_ConfigureCar)
END_PROP_MAP()
```

Finally, we can test our new page. Place an instance of your updated (and recompiled) control into a VB project, and locate the (Custom) property from the VB Property Window (Figure 14-44):

Figure 14-44: Launching our page.

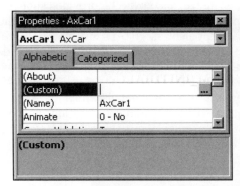

With this, the chapter comes to a close. If you want to extend the functionality of your ATL control, you may wish to put together a web-based test client, or use MFC, Delphi, or even MS Word to test your control (recall we did set the Insertable option). To insert your controls into a MS Office product, access the **Insert | Object** menu item and find your control (Figure 14-45). You can then create a VBA macro to exercise your CAxCar.

Figure 14-45: Inserting our CAxCar into MS Word.

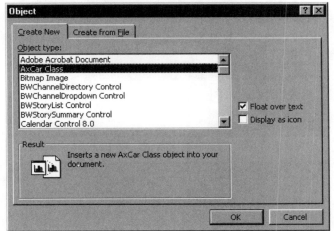

If you like, you may want to create a licensed class factory for your AXCar control (feel free to steal the initial code from the ShapesServer project found on your CD-ROM). As well, you may wish to add a category map and build a web-based tester.

Hopefully this chapter pulled together all the information you have gained throughout this book. You have seen how the ActiveX control requires a deep understanding of core COM, and how ATL can make your life easier.

Chapter Summary

This chapter rounded out your understanding of COM by introducing you to the fine art of building an ActiveX control with ATL. As you have seen, ActiveX controls are used as graphical building blocks in larger applications. To supply the additional services above and beyond a simple coclass, controls implement a number of standard COM interfaces to allow support rendering, persistence, and property page objects. Building a full control in

ATL begins with the ATL Object Wizard. The framework provides stock implementations for each of the necessary COM interfaces, as well as all the previous templates and maps examined throughout this book.

We examined the use of COM persistence, and how ATL provides support for each of the client-specified persistence techniques using a handful of templates and the property map. This map serves double duty, in that it also associates a given property to the correct property page. A property page is yet another COM class supporting the standard IPropertyPage interface. The container discovers the set of pages that works with your coclass by querying for ISpecifyPropertyPages.

We discovered a number of minor (but important) details which make for a polished control: component categories, About boxes, and custom enumerations used with bound properties. Finally, we have seen how to make use of our object from a web page, as well as Microsoft Visual Basic, and how to create a licensed class factory.

Index

INTERTECH-INC.COM

The leader in hands-on workshops for Enterprise Web Developers.

Andrew Troelsen is an instructor and partner at Intertech. Intertech delivers 3- to 5-day hands-on workshops for Enterprise Web Developers.

Intertech is a Microsoft Certified Solution Provider and Sun Authorized Java Center, and offers a complete COM line-up.

Free Stuff from
Intertech
www.Intertech-Inc.com/Wordware

WWW.INTERTECH-INC.COM

The Companion CD-ROM

The companion CD-ROM contains complete solutions for all of the lab work in this book. To install these files onto your hard drive, double-click on the Labs.exe self-extracting archive. This will move all files onto your hard drive under C:\COM ATL\Labs. Also note that each project will need to be recompiled before you can test the solutions!

Beginning with Chapter 3, every "raw C++" lab makes use of a custom *.reg file which must be merged into your system registry. If you forget to do so, the client solutions will not work! Be aware that the *.reg files make use of hard-coded path names, which may not be the same as where you have chosen to install the sample code. Thus, you will need to edit the path to your specific path. For example, the CarInProcServer lab in Chapter 3 has the following *.reg file listing. Modify the section in **bold** to the correct path:

```
HKEY_CLASSES_ROOT\CLSID\{7AD2D539-EE35-11d2-B8DE-0020781238D4}\InprocServer32 =
C:\ATL\Labs\Chapter 03\CarInProcServer\Debug\CarInProcServer.dll
```

Also realize that the ATL solutions must be registered on your machine before the clients can make use of them. ATL servers do not make use of *.reg files, but enter the correct information programmatically. To register the ATL sample solutions, simply rebuild the project. This will automatically register the COM server.

The CD also contains COM and DCOM specifications.

Warning: Opening the CD package makes this book non-returnable.